The Collingridge Guide to
Collectors' Alpines

The author of *Collectors' Alpines*, Royton Heath, has been growing these plants as a hobby for more than 50 years and in his book he lists 1850 plants, giving details of their cultivation and individual requirements. He writes from personal experience, giving botanical descriptions of the plants so that the book serves as a source of identification as well as a guide to culture.

There are chapters on propagation, general management, pests and diseases, and exhibiting. The section on alpine house and frame construction is amply supplemented with some excellent line drawings, and another chapter describes potting and seed composts, made up according to Mr Heath's own recipes, since he feels that the John Innes composts are too rich for alpines.

Mr Heath has won hundreds of awards at horticultural shows. He has broadcast on the B.B.C. and lectures to horticultural and specialist societies. Somehow he has found time to collect and study alpines in their natural habitat. Many of the photographs in the book were taken by him.

Also by Royton E. Heath

ALPINES UNDER GLASS

SHRUBS FOR THE ROCK GARDEN
AND ALPINE HOUSE

ROCK PLANTS FOR SMALL GARDENS

MINIATURE SHRUBS

The Collingridge Guide to

Collectors' Alpines

Their cultivation in frames
and alpine houses

Royton E. Heath
FLS FRIH(NZ)

COLLINGRIDGE BOOKS

Published in 1981 by Collingridge Books
an imprint of The Hamlyn Publishing Group Limited
Bridge House, 69 London Road,
Twickenham, Middlesex, England TW1 3SB

First published 1964 under the title "Collectors' Alpines"
by W. H. and L. Collingridge Limited
Second edition 1981
Fourth impression 1987
ISBN 0 600 36784 3

Set in 11pt Bembo

Printed in Great Britain
by
Butler and Tanner, Ltd.,
Frome, Somerset

CONTENTS

Part 1: Cultivation

Introduction   *page* 13

1. Introduction. The Site. Water Tank. The Alpine House. Staging. Painting. Heating. Shading   19

2. Alpine Frame. Plunge Beds. Frames. Propagating Frames. Heated Propagating Frame. Potting Shed   39

3. Tools. Pans. Drainage Materials. Labels   54

4. Loam. Leaf-mould. Peat. Chippings. Composts. Sterilisation   62

5. Seed. Seed Composts. Division. Cuttings. Types of Cuttings. Cutting Frames   71

6. Watering. Ventilation. Shading. Cleanliness. Routine Work. Care of House. Repotting. Feeding   99

7. Pests and Diseases. Spraying Equipment. Insecticides and Fungicides. Pests. Diseases   125

8. Exhibiting. Schedules. Treatment of the Plants. Staging   143

Part 2: The Plants

9. Introduction. Nomenclature. Botanical Terms   153

10. Dwarf Conifers   161

11. General List   183

Appendices   520

Index   537

ILLUSTRATIONS

Colour Photographs

(Photographers as credited)

Androsace alpina (H. Esslemont)	*facing page*	48
Androsace ciliata (H. Esslemont)		48
Androsace sarmentosa var. *watkinsii* (S. Mitchell)		49
Androsace wulfeniana (Dr. D. M. McArthur)		49
Calceolaria darwinii (W. Cairns)		64
Chrysanthemum alpinum (H. Esslemont)		64
Crocus chrysanthus (S. Mitchell)		65
Crocus scardicus (J. and J. Archibald)		65
Cyclamen orbiculatum var. *coum* (S. Mitchell)		144
Cyclamen europaeum (H. Esslemont)		144
Daphne petraea (W. Cairns)		145
Daphne striata and *Gentiana acaulis* (James Aitken)		145
Dianthus neglectus (Royton E. Heath)		160
Diapensia lapponica (J. Grant Roger)		160
Dionysia aretioides 'Paul Furse' (H. Esslemont)		161
Dionysia bryoides (R. J. Mitchell)		161
Dionysia michauxii (H. Esslemont)		224
Erigeron aureus (B. H. Barritt)		224
Eritrichium nanum (H. Esslemont)		225
Fritillaria michailovskyi (H. Esslemont)		225
Gentiana ornata (L. Beer)		240
Geum reptans (H. Esslemont)		240
Haberlea rhodopensis (A. Evans)		241
Iris winogradowii (H. Esslemont)		241
Kalmiopsis leachiana 'M. le Piniec' (J. D. Crosland)		320
Kelseya uniflora (H. Esslemont)		320
Paraquilegia anemonoides (J. Main)		321
Phyllodoce caerulea (S. Mitchell)		321
Pleione forrestii (H. Esslemont)		336
Pleione pogonioides (J. D. Crosland)		336
Potentilla nitida (S. Mitchell)		337
Primula allionii (H. Esslemont)		337
Primula rubra (H. Esslemont)		400
Primula pubescens 'The General' (D. M. Morison)		400
Primula bracteosa (Royton E. Heath)		401
Pulsatilla occidentalis (B. H. Barritt)		401
Pulsatilla vernalis (Betty W. Ritchie)		416
Pulsatilla vulgaris 'Rubra' (S. Mitchell)		416
Ranunculus parnassifolius (H. Taylor)		417
Rhododendron myrtilloides (R. J. Mitchell)		417

9

Rhododendron forrestii (Scottish Rock Garden Club)   496
Rhododendron forrestii var. *repens* (H. Esslemont)   496
Rhododendron nakaharai (Dr. I. Simson Hall)   497
Sempervivum arachnoideum (Royton E. Heath)   497
Soldanella pusilla (S. Mitchell)   512
Tulipa kaufmanniana (S. Mitchell)   512
Viola cenisia (S. Mitchell)   513
Viola dubyana (H. Esslemont)   513

Black and White Photographs

(All taken by Author)

Andromeda polifolia compacta   *between pages*   72–73
Androsace hirtella
Androsace imbricata
A selection of alpine house plants
Andryala agardhii
Aquilegia bertolonii
Arabis bryoides
Arenaria tetraquetra
Asperula suberosa   *between pages*   120–121
Boykinia jamesii
Calceolaria tenella
Campanula barbata var. *alba*
Campanula pilosa
Campanula pilosa var. *dasyantha*
Celmisia argentea
Celmisia du-rietzii
Celmisia hookeri
Chrysanthemum hosmariense   *between pages*   184–185
Crocus candidus 'Subflavus'
Crocus fleischeri
Crocus kotschyanus
Cypripedium speciosum
Dianthus 'Bombardier'
Draba mollissima
Dryas octopetala var. *minor*
Edraianthus pumilio   *between pages*   248–249
Erigeron leiomerus
Fritillaria pyrenaica
Gentiana verna
Geranium dalmaticum
Globularia stygia
Gypsophila aretioides
Hebe macrantha
Helichrysum coralloides   *between pages*   312–313

Helichrysum frigidum
Helichrysum virgineum
Heloniopsis orientalis var. *yakusimensis*
Jasminum parkeri
Lewisia pygmaea
Linum elegans
Myosotis rupicola
Narcissus bulbocodium var. *romieuxii*   *between pages*   376–377
Narcissus triandrus 'Albus'
Nomocharis mairei
Oxalis enneaphylla
Paeonia cambessedesii
Phlox nana var. *ensifolia*
Phyteuma comosum
Primula marginata 'Caerulea'
Primula marginata var. 'Linda Pope'
Primula 'Pandora'   *between pages*   440-441
Ranunculus calandrinioides
Raoulia eximia
Raoulia grandiflora
Rhododendron leucaspis
Rhodohypoxis 'Ruth'
Sanguinaria canadensis 'Flora Plena'
Saixfraga florulenta
Saxifraga 'Petraschii'
Trachelium asperuloides   *between pages*   488–489
Tulipa aucheriana
Tulipa pulchella
Tulipa tarda
Chamaecyparis obtusa 'Minima'
Chamaecyparis obtusa 'Minima' (ten-year-old plant raised from a
   cutting)
Juniperus communis 'Echiniformis'
Microcachrys tetragona

Line Drawings

1. Layout plan of site   *page*   22
2. Water storage tank   24
3. The alpine house: external view   26
4. The alpine house: internal view   27
5. Plan and layout of the alpine house   29
6. Internal shading to alpine house   35
7. Shading to roof of alpine house   36
8. Shade racks to lower panels of alpine house
    roof   37
9. Shade rack at south end of alpine house   37
10. The alpine frame   40

10a. Lights for the alpine frame   *page* 42

11. Range of frames   46

12. Propagating frames E and F   48

13. Heated propagating frame   50

14. The potting shed   52

15. Wood dibber   55

16. Square pans from cement   58

17. Compost firmer   76

18. Dicotyledons, monocotyledons   79

Types of Cuttings:

    Green; Half-ripened; Hardwood; Root; Leaf   83–86

19. Gravity-fed watering to cutting frame   92

20. Wire-netting frame for doorway of alpine house   106

21. Repotting plants in compost 'D'   121

22. Facsimile of card index   122

Pests:

    Ants; Aphids; Caterpillars, Capsid bugs; Mealy bugs;
    Millipedes; Red spider mite; Scale insects; Slugs and snails;
    Springtails; Thrips; Vine weevil grubs; Woodlice   133–140

23. Fish-netting on roof ventilators of the alpine house   141

24. Types of foliage   156

25. Arrangement of flowers   157

26. Layering cedars and pines   168

INTRODUCTION

Over a decade has passed since the appearance of my first book on alpines which was but a personal record of specimens grown under glass in the alpine house and dealt with just over five hundred species and varieties which I was cultivating at that time. This book has long been out of print and as I have received so many letters asking if it is still obtainable I decided to write a new book, very much enlarged so as to include a really comprehensive collection of plants which I have successfully grown during the last twenty-five years.

There have been many new species or varieties collected, introduced or re-introduced over the past fifty years. A large number were difficult to cultivate, either because of climatic conditions or owing to ignorance of their needs after they had arrived here as seeds, cuttings or plants. The coming of the jet age has done untold good in allowing specimens of plants in first-class condition to be carried from one hemisphere to another in a matter of days whereas hitherto weeks were required in transit by land and sea. This often meant a dehydrating effect on plants, which had to pass through the tropics, and large numbers arrived dead or too far gone for any reasonable chance of establishment in this country.

Many plants which a few years ago were considered difficult, sometimes even impossible, to cultivate are today easy and even commonplace. This is the result of research, as material became available for this work, so that today there are a much larger number of plants from which to choose in building up a really comprehensive collection.

That the cultivation of rock plants today is on the increase there can be no doubt. Two specialist societies, the Alpine Garden Society and the Scottish Rock Garden Club, number over eleven thousand enthusiasts alone, to say nothing of the Royal Horticultural Society's huge membership, of which a good proportion are probably interested in growing alpines. At all the national shows, it is the rock garden displays which seem to attract a large number of the public, who never seem to tire in their admiration of the dwarf exhibits.

Today after two crippling world-wars the large gardens have for the most part disappeared, those remaining, with few exceptions, being taken over by the National Trust or, in conjunction with the Royal Horticultural Society, kept in order for public display. That the big botanical gardens like Kew, Edinburgh, Oxford and Cambridge to mention the more important ones, do exceedingly good work in cultivating alpines there is no doubt. It is, however, in that great preponderance of small gardens cultivated by a growing army of amateur gardeners that the love of alpines is more personal, producing really fine healthy specimens, that delight the eye. Here is where the alpine house or even a couple of frames come into their own, for in a mere few square yards, provided there is a reasonable amount of light, a large collection can be safely housed and cultivated.

Small in stature but not in beauty there is nothing to compare with these examples of Nature's handiwork, and one may have edelweiss from the Swiss Alps sitting shoulder to shoulder with dwarf rhododendrons from the Himalayas, winter flowering narcissus species of the Atlas Mountains, cassiopes from Japan, *Campanula piperi* of North America and the autumn-flowering Asiatic gentians. This list could be extended almost indefinitely with floral representatives from every mountain of the world, requiring but common sense and the willingness to devote a little time to achieving success in their cultivation.

There are a number of reasons for growing alpines in either an alpine house or in frames, apart from the primary question of space. First of all some plants require individual attention if there is to be any reasonable chance of their successful cultivation; this cannot always be given if they are grown outdoors amongst the more vigorous plants. Secondly a number of the high alpine plants require protection from our winter weather, not necessarily from cold although this too can do harm if extra severe (temperature will be dealt with later), but from alternating spells of cold with mild rainy weather which cause an excess of atmospheric moisture.

Nature has provided the foliage of a large number of high alpines with a covering of fine hairs, in many cases woolly, this being a protection against loss of moisture in their natural home, where, owing to the ever moving air and hot sun in the rarefied atmosphere, with their dehydrating effect on the tissues of the plant, atmospheric humidity is at a premium during the growing period. Humans too suffer from this, developing an extraordinary thirst at high altitudes as any alpine rambler will tell you. These plants are also naturally protected during the winter months by snow which keeps them dry and in a state of suspended animation. When taken from their alpine reaches to the lowlands the high atmospheric moisture content, such as is nearly always experienced in winter in this country, is too readily absorbed by the foliage to the detriment of the plants which often die from rotting set up by this excess. Although nothing can be done about the atmospheric moisture outside, under glass it is possible by adequate ventilation plus slight artificial heat to minimise this problem.

The protection of plants which are just on the borderline of hardiness has also to be considered. It may be objected from the alpine purist's point of view that such plants have no place in a collection, but what a loss if such plants as *Cyclamen libanoticum, persicum* and *rohlfsianum*, some of the hypericums, Asiatic primulas, calochortus and many others were excluded. Here there would be a real loss to the cultivator who wants to grow a fully comprehensive collection.

What is hardy has always been a bone of contention between gardeners from different parts of the country. Many plants are considered hardy on the cold eastern side owing to the new growth being retarded through a more or less constant cool period in the early months of the year. These same plants in the inland gardens are liable to be cut by frosts, which have a habit of forming after moist muggy periods in early spring when growth has already commenced. On the western seaboard too, many plants elsewhere considered tender thrive quite safely without protection. The only answer seems to be, grow what plants you will, provided the plant can stand a temperature down to near freezing without harm. It is surprising what a few sheets of newspaper loosely placed over the pans will do to minimise a severe fall in temperature, but this can only be a temporary measure. Should there be a period of prolonged frost when the thermometer stays below freezing point, some other means of retaining heat will be required. All this will be fully dealt with later.

The third and possibly the most important reason for giving glass protection to alpines is that a number of alpines are early flowering, in fact some will start to flower in December. Protection is absolutely essential to save them from being spoiled by wind, rain, snow and fog which would be experienced in the open garden at this period. *Asphodelus acaulis, Narcissus bulbocodium* var. *romieuxii, Ranunculus calandrinioides*, many of the Kabschia and Engleria saxifragas, and Asiatic and European primulas such as *P. edgeworthii* and *P. allionii* are good examples of subjects needing this treatment.

Today there are shows for alpines practically all over the country and the number of exhibitors is ever increasing. Both the Alpine Garden Society and the Scottish Rock Garden Club have extensive shows throughout the year. There are also really active local groups, attached to both the parent societies, which hold meetings and lectures on all aspects of growing alpines, a fair amount of these dealing with the cultivation of plants in pans.

On a number of occasions these local groups also hold shows of their own where there is generally a good selection of pan plants on view, and many useful tips can be picked up. To do justice to the plants for showing purposes it is, with very few exceptions, almost essential to have an alpine house or at least frame protection of some sort so that the plants can be properly groomed and sheltered from inclement weather outdoors.

From the foregoing it should be quite clear that a case has been made for alpine house or frame culture and that a really comprehensive work on this form of culture is needed. Far be it from me to say that I am best qualified to do this work, but lack of entries from others plus the measure of success gained over a long period of time, not forgetting personal experience (often lacking in gardening books) has resulted in my writing what must be the most complete work on the subject to date.

Introduction to the Second Edition

Not surprisingly, considering how much they have to offer, the interest in alpine plants increases year by year. This is reflected in the membership of both The Alpine Society and The Scottish Rock Garden Club, some 7,000 and 4,000 respectively, and my own observations when lecturing around the country.

It is, therefore, an especial pleasure to introduce this new edition of a book which is written for the true enthusiast and which, in its first edition, attracted many kind comments. I have added, in the Appendices, descriptions of recently introduced plants and others of special note as well as references to the numerous name changes which have occurred since 1964.

I would thank, too, the photographers whose photographs are reproduced on the colour pages (the black and white photographs were all taken by myself) and The Scottish Rock Garden Club who have so generously allowed me the use of their colour blocks. This is very much appreciated.

I am especially appreciative of the outstanding line drawings which the late Mr F. V. W. Sedgeley prepared for this book from my indifferent sketches—truly a major contribution.

I would also like to thank The British Agrochemicals Association for their advice on bringing the pest and disease chapter completely up to date.

1981   Royton E. Heath

PART ONE

Cultivation

1. Introduction. The Site. Water Tank. The Alpine House. Staging. Painting. Heating. Shading

2. Alpine Frame. Plunge Beds. Frames. Propagating Frames. Heated Propagating Frame. Potting Shed

3. Tools. Pans. Drainage Materials. Labels

4. Loam. Leaf-mould. Peat. Chippings. Composts. p 69 Sterilisation

5. Seed. Seed Composts. p.73 Division. Cuttings. Types of Cuttings. Cutting Frames

6. Watering. Ventilation. Shading. Cleanliness. Routine Work. Care of House. Repotting. Feeding

7. Pests and Diseases. Spraying Equipment. Insecticides and Fungicides. Pests. Diseases

8. Exhibiting. Schedules. Treatment of the Plants. Staging

CHAPTER ONE

Introduction. The Site. Water Tank. The Alpine House.
Staging. Painting. Heating. Shading.

Introduction

Great importance is often attached to the position of the alpine house and
the majority of experts believe that a site in full sunshine is essential. This
may be the ultimate aim but on how many plots of ground is this practicable? After all the average gardener has to adapt his own site to suit his
circumstances. From any angle an alpine house is not a thing of beauty
to which all other features of the garden are relegated to a minor role. A
point which is often overlooked is that most cultivators are away from
home most of the day. Unless there is someone who can attend to the
shading at the time when the sun is at its zenith, intense damage can be
done to a collection of plants in the space of a few hours. That this can be
adjusted before leaving is quite true but this preparation defeats its own
ends if what promised to be a fine day turns to dull cloudy conditions, a
far from unusual occurrence during our summers.

A more suitable siting according to my experience is one in which the
sun is filtered by adjacent trees which throw their shadows on the south
side of the house, this doing much to minimise any ill effects from strong
sunshine. These remarks apply primarily to the midland and southern
counties of the British Isles. In the northern counties and Scotland a more
exposed position can be safely given, for in those latitudes the actinic
rays of the sun are not so powerful.

That this ideal is not attainable in a large number of small gardens,
which are attached to the modern suburban houses, is soon apparent.
But even here good alpines can be successfully grown, as can be seen at
many of the large alpine shows, the exhibitors often taking premier
awards for plants grown under such conditions. Even a lean-to erected
against the wall of a house will grow its quota of good alpines, but in all
instances where the ideal is unobtainable through one cause or another,
extra care will be needed in keeping the glass of the house spotlessly clean.

19

There are many good cleansers with a soap base, or detergents can be used, which give good results with very little physical effort.

Alpine houses and frames can be purchased ready to be erected on the site and there are a number of firms manufacturing them today, these ranging in prices to suit most pockets. A great deal depends on whether the house is constructed from wood, which to my mind is still the most satisfactory material. There is no problem of drip from the roof or eaves, which sometimes occurs in houses of galvanised iron, aluminium or concrete, especially should the evening temperature show a sudden drop after a warm sunny day. This can often happen in late autumn or early spring, both critical periods. Any wetting of the foliage, caused by condensation, can easily set up decay through rotting, resulting in death in the case of the most susceptible plants, or else in the symmetrical cushions being spoilt through the necessary removal of the decaying rosettes.

Although there is no doubt that a large number of houses in use today constructed of galvanised iron, aluminium or concrete are giving satisfaction, this timely warning of acute condensation is necessary for the plants most likely to suffer are those which are difficult and expensive to replace. The section on artificial heating will, however, tell how this difficulty can be overcome quite easily, so if the preference is for an alpine house constructed of material other than wood it can be bought with confidence.

Whatever the material used in the construction of the house it is essential that ventilators are fitted along both sides and eaves. This is a most important point for at all times good ventilation, without draught, is necessary for the well-being of its occupants. The house should, for preference, be on a cement base, where this is possible, as a dry footing precludes any reasonable chance of damp conditions rising from the bare earth beneath, especially after a very wet period. It is an added advantage if the sides of the house are constructed of brickwork. This gives a more equable temperature, the bricks absorbing heat slowly and releasing it gradually after the sun has set.

Most reputable firms will quote for an alpine house to be erected on a concrete foundation with brick sides. Bear in mind, however, that size and width of house ordered should conform with the standard pattern of the manufacturers' houses, otherwise costs will rise alarmingly, for it means that the firm concerned will have to make a new pattern instead of utilising those which are used for their normal sizes. Whatever the size chosen it must not be smaller than 8 feet by 6 feet for there are very serious limitations in trying to cultivate alpines in a small house. The temperature rise and fall alone can be as much as 50°F(25°C) in the space of a few hours to the detriment of the occupants.

I think it will be useful to give a more comprehensive detailed study of the construction of a layout which I adopted with success and which can be considered a more or less ideal arrangement of the alpine house and its frames as both are really complementary to each other. If an alpine house is not available, possibly through shortage of space, it does not preclude the use of this plan for, with certain alterations and adaptations to suit one's own ideas, it can be modified quite simply. A number of constructional aids are given. In this age of 'do it yourself' anyone who wishes to go ahead can easily obtain costs from brick, timber and other merchants and the erection should not be outside the abilities of keen amateurs. Even if the work carried out simply consists of laying the foundations, the brick sides of the house, and pillars for the frames, a great saving is made in the total expense. Alternatively these plans if shown to a suitable contractor will enable him to carry out the work to his client's wishes; here again I must emphasise the need to keep to standard sizes as far as possible so that there will be a great saving in the ultimate cost.

The Site

I have taken as an example a site which I laid out twenty years ago and have modified it, leaving in only those parts which have shown good results during the test of time and have incorporated fresh ideas, which have proved their worth over a number of years. Fig. 1 shows the layout of the alpine house, plunge beds, frames and propagating frames. The house and frames are built in close proximity to each other. This makes it easy to move plants from house to frame or *vice versa*, either to replace specimens which have finished flowering with those just starting, or to remove plants which have to spend the summer outside in the plunge beds. It is also a great saver of labour, for plants in their pots, especially the larger sizes, are no light weight to move around.

The whole site was marked out. This measured 40 by 20 feet, and was levelled with the aid of a spirit level, driving in small pieces of wood at different places to obtain this level. After this an inch of hard core, broken bricks or concrete, any of which are suitable, was placed on top of the levelled base and the whole concreted to a depth of 3 inches. This mixture consisted of four pails of shingle to one of cement, mixed dry. Water was added until it could be worked without showing an excess of moisture, or allowing it to become runny.

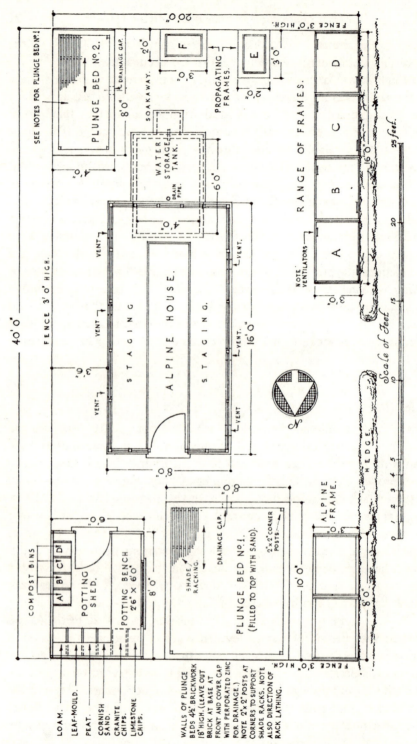

1. Layout plan of site

The Water Tank

Before the foundations were laid a hole in the south end of the site (Fig. 1), was dug and a concrete tank constructed, 4 by 6 by 3 feet, so arranged that 4 by 4½ feet of it was under the foundation outside, the other 4 by 1½ feet inside the house. Wood shuttering in the form of a box was used to contain the cement mixture until set (Fig. 2), this measured 4 by 6 by 3 feet. The size of the hole when completed was 4½ by 6½ by 3 feet 3 inches deep, thus allowing a space of 3 inches all round. After laying a base at the bottom of the hole 3 inches deep the wooden shuttering was then laid on the base, centralised and a concrete mixture as above was then shovelled round. All sides were well rammed down as work progressed thus eliminating air holes.

After a period of nine days, during which the hole was kept moist and shaded from drying wind and sunshine, the box was removed and with a mixture of equal parts fine sand and cement, a ½ inch rendering was applied to the rough cement sides and base thus forming a water-tight box. When completed the top of the box was level with the surrounding soil. Before the foundations for the alpine house and frames were laid a piece of galvanised corrugated sheet iron resting on light angle-iron, 7 feet by 4 feet 6 inches was laid across the south end of the concrete tank, to form a rigid base for the 3 inches of concrete above on which the south end of the alpine house was built. Before the rendering was applied a drainage pipe was cemented in, to take off any surplus water after the tank was filled, this leading to a small soak-away.

The tank is fed by the guttering on both sides, the down pipes leading into the tank ensuring a good supply of rain water throughout the whole of the year, as it will hold approximately 675 gallons of rain water. Another advantage of this method is that water can be taken from the tank inside the house, a boon when watering the plants, saving a great deal of labour in carrying water to the house from an outside source. This is not the only point. There is also the fact that in many districts, the water supply originating from chalkbeds is often hard. In my own case is extremely hard, and this would prove fatal to those plants such as the larger majority of that great *Ericaceae* family which embraces all the rhododendrons, cassiopes, ericas etc. which require an acid medium in which to grow. Mains water today has also a certain amount of chlorination and if used for pan plants over a long period will most certainly build up a large degree of harmful chemical deposits. I wonder how many choice plants have been lost by this means? It would cause me no surprise to find that the casualty figure was high. The temperature of the water in the tank is warmer than that in an outside source, being akin to that in the alpine house.

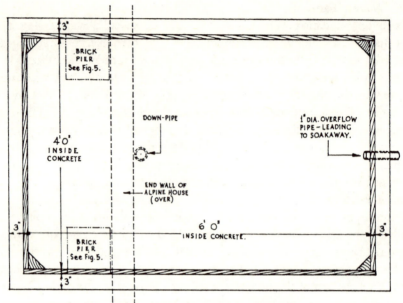

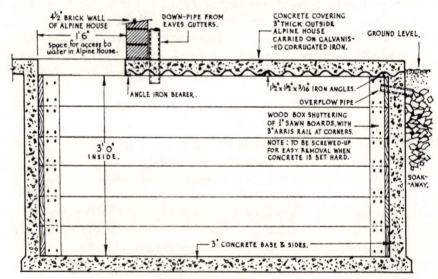

2. *Water storage tank*

After the foundations of the site have been laid it should be covered with sacks and kept moist. Allowing at least nine days for the concrete to set, then all will be ready to go ahead with the construction of the brick sides for the house, and pillars for the frames.

The Alpine House

The site of the house is next marked out on the foundations and the brick sides are built to the required size. The house on the plan (Fig. 1), is 16 by 8 feet. This is a standard size, so the wooden framework of the house from the sides to the ridge is easily obtained from firms dealing in the manufacture of glass houses and alpine houses. As can be seen the house runs north to south, with the entrance at the north end. This is ideal, as it is possible to shade the south end during the summer months, an almost impossible task if the door is at this end. The house being placed in this position obtains the maximum of light which is of great importance during the winter months when daylight is at a premium. The sun following an even course over the house from east to west helps the plants to retain their dwarf stature.

The sides are constructed of bricks laid on their broad face and built up to a height of 3 feet 3 inches, which works out to thirteen courses of 9 by $4\frac{1}{2}$ inch brickwork. The first row starts with full bricks laid longways while the second row is commenced with the first brick laid longways only over the first half of the brick on the first row and carried on until the required height is reached. The diagram (Fig. 3) will give a clear idea of this, thus throughout the whole of the brick sides, no one joint is over another.

When laying the fifth row, three air bricks should be inserted on each of the long sides, but not facing each other (Fig. 3). This will allow a current of air to circulate without causing a draught, thus keeping the atmosphere in the house buoyant at all times, even when it is necessary to close down all top and side ventilators during heavy rain or snow. It is also a great advantage during a spell of foggy weather, when these will give just a gentle circulation of air, thus preventing the foggy particles of moist dust and grime settling on the hairy and cushion-like plants, which quickly show their resentment of a dirty, stagnant, heavy moisture-laden atmosphere.

The number of bricks required for this operation is easily worked out as each brick measures 9 by $4\frac{1}{2}$ by 3 inches and the thirteen courses of brick will require approximately 900. Old stock bricks are best if readily obtainable and there are a number of builder's merchant's yards from which they can be purchased. The reason for using old stock bricks is that they are impervious to frost, consequently no flaking and subsequent disintegration takes place. Should a softer brick have to be used, it may be necessary to render the completed sides with a cement to stop gradual deterioration of the bricks, especially in exposed cold gardens. The cement rendering should consist of two parts soft sand to one part cement, water is added

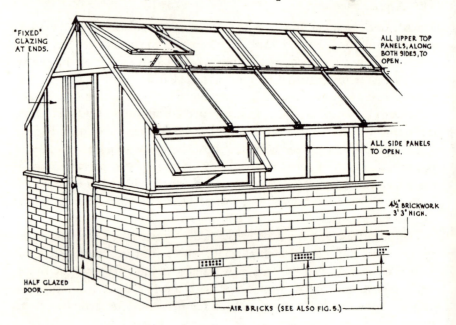

3. *The alpine house: external view*

cautiously to give a stiff but workable mixture which is then applied evenly over the whole surface with a smoothing trowel.

When the sides are completed the next stage is to obtain the framework of the house itself. No detailed plan is given for this part, as it is best purchased from a firm specialising in the making of this type of house, or a local contractor will be only too pleased to quote for this work. I can give a general idea of what is suitable by quoting the figures of my own house; these can be amended to suit the owner's own whims or fancies.

From the top of the sides to the eaves the distance is 18 inches, consisting of independent windows in each side of the house thus allowing for full ventilation. These windows cover the whole length of the sides of the house, each being separated from its neighbour by 2-inch wooden uprights. The eaves to the ridge gradually rise to a height of 7 feet. Along both sides, half-way between the eaves and ridge, ventilators are fitted, six on each side. As with the sides these work independently of one another and are fitted with the usual casement stays and pegs. Two pegs should be fitted on each ventilator frame, which will obviate the possibility of banging one's head against the casement stays with painful results when the ventilators are closed. The side ventilators too, should be fitted with two pegs making a great saving of plant space on the staging, which would have to be left clear if only one was fitted (Fig. 4).

Glass

A number of amateurs are under the impression that any kind of glass will be suitable for the alpine house and frames. This is far from true. It is

4. *The alpine house: internal view*

essential that good quality glass be used, free from all blemishes, such as bubbles, which can do damage by acting as a magnifying lens, causing burns and scorching. The grade known as twenty-four ounce, the weight per square foot, is the best for the purpose. Naturally if you are buying a house from a manufacturer of greenhouses, the glass is already supplied and cut to shape. However, it is always worthwhile to inspect it, for the plants depend a great deal on the amount of light which is passed by the glass.

Recently there has been a great deal of high pressure salesmanship of plastic substitutes for glass, but these claims have unfortunately not been proved in use. Alpines growing under glass depend for their well-being on getting the available light and this is to a great extent lacking where plastic materials are used. Those which are bonded together with a wire frame lose a tremendous amount, the wire net acting as a shade. The life of such material is short, and in a matter of three years the whole starts to corrode and break away. Plastic sheeting tends to colour with age and scratches easily, picking up and retaining dirt which is almost impossible to eradicate. There is no doubt that at present glass is unique, no substitute having been found to replace it although it is second best to growing under natural conditions.

The Staging

The staging of the house is a matter of importance as the usual wooden slatted staging supplied with a greenhouse is not suitable. This allows too great a current of air to pass round and under the porous pots, causing them to dry out rapidly, which can prove extremely dangerous to their occupants, if a constant watch is not maintained. Another point is that they are not really strong enough unless reinforced extensively.

I have approached the matter in a different way, by providing a staging of great durability, thus saving time in constant watering. The reason for needing a staging of great strength will be readily understood as all plants are plunged to their rims in equal parts gravel and coarse sand, the total weight being considerable.

Brick pillars were constructed to support the staging to a height of 2 feet 9 inches, eleven courses of brickwork, two bricks to each course, so the supports are 9 inches by 9 inches when completed. Fourteen such pillars were built and placed in position (Fig. 5). The two pillars at the middle of the south end of the house were built from the base of the water tank, making a height of 5 feet 9 inches or approximately twenty-two courses of bricks laid on their faces so that the total number of pillars constructed to support the staging was sixteen.

When completed the sixteen pillars were rendered with a cement mixture consisting of two parts soft sand to one of cement, giving a smooth surface so that all cracks and crannies in the brickwork which could provide homes for pests were eliminated. The height of these supports allows 6 inches from the base of the staging to the edge of the side ventilators. When the pans are placed on the base of the staging the rims are, with the exception of plants in extra large pans, just below the bottom of the side ventilators. Thus a current of air flows over the tops of the pans, not round the sides, where it could cause excessive drying out with harmful effect on the occupants.

The actual stages consist of $\frac{1}{16}$th inch thick corrugated, galvanised iron sheeting, 2 feet 3 inches wide. This is the size of the old wartime Anderson

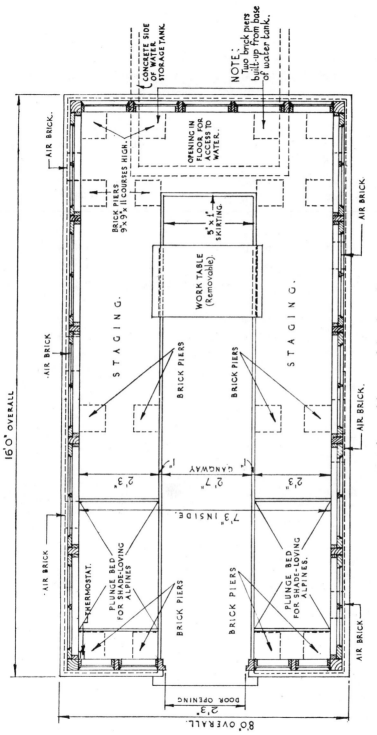

5. *Plan and layout of the alpine house*

air-raid shelter uprights which have proved highly successful in the past. However, these are now likely to be unobtainable and a suitable substitute for the iron sheets is the new proprietary material Uni-cem, which is being manufactured as a replacement for asbestos – now no longer recommended for garden or, indeed, for any other use. This new material is also corrugated and, like the iron sheets, can be adequately supported by longitudinal bearers of 4 by 2 inch timber. When the staging is in position the front is then boarded up, using lengths of wood 5 inches by 1 inch thick to retain the mixture of gravel and sand.

I have found over a long period that by using this method of staging and filling to the top with gravel and sand mixture, then plunging the pots, the excessive evaporation from the sides of the porous pans is reduced during hot summer months. This not only maintains the plants under more normal conditions with the consequent higher health standard, but it is also a great labour saver as it reduces the time that has to be spent on watering.

In the winter the soil in the plunged pans is maintained in a greater state of equilibrium both as regards moisture content and temperature. Any water required during this season can be given by keeping the surrounding mixture of gravel and sand just moist. The only drawback to this method is that the plants will tend to root in the plunging mixture.

This rooting can be avoided to a great extent if the plants are lifted occasionally and, where practicable, any stray roots carefully returned inside the pan.

After the completion of the staging there will be a 2 foot 7 inch pathway down the centre of the house. This is a sufficient width for normal working purposes, allowing plenty of room to move pans from one side to the other.

A small square of wood to serve as a table can be constructed, to carry out minor work, such as the removal of dead flowers, foliage or for top-dressing the plants with fresh chippings etc. This table should be 1 inch thick, 2 feet 11 inches by 2 feet 6 inches, with two battens fixed underneath running the whole length, 2 inches in, so that it slides along the top of the wooden supports of the staging without it being possible to accidentally fall to the floor of the house (Fig. 5). It is surprising how useful this gadget is and, if used in conjunction with a stool, it makes a comfortable working bench. Under the staging, one on each side, wooden frames are constructed of 1 inch timber, 6 feet by 2 feet by 6 inches deep. These are filled with peat and here can be grown a selection of plants which require shade for their well-being (Fig. 5).

Painting

The normal procedure is to paint the woodwork of the house with two coats of white paint containing lead, after a recommended undercoat has been applied. This is suitable provided maintenance is carried out every three years with an added coat of paint to preserve the woodwork from decay, but there is a more permanent method which will eliminate the need for either the initial painting or periodical repainting.

All woodwork both inside and out of the house should be given three coats of Cuprinol green. This is a stain which is not injurious to plants when dry, it preserves the wood and the first application is the last. It is less unsightly than paint, being of a restful shade of green. The appearance of the wood is also enhanced as the stain brings out the grain. If it is decided to use cedar for the upper part of the alpine house the initial cost will be higher, but the wood will last almost indefinitely provided it is oiled occasionally with linseed oil; about once every three or four years will be found satisfactory.

Heating

It has been maintained over more years than I care to remember that heat of any kind is taboo in the alpine house. Why, I cannot imagine. I lost many plants through ignorance on my part when first starting to grow alpines but the severe winter of 1947 really convinced me that something had to be done to curtail these losses. All the alpine purists are against heat but I noticed after that disastrous winter when garden periodicals were asking for short articles on what plants had been killed or badly cut back, there were many tales of woe from a number of the purists, especially where shrubs were concerned.

That this could have been avoided is only too true and since I installed heat in 1948 not one plant has been lost through frost, to say nothing of the many plants which would have surely died but for the drying up of atmospheric moisture, by using artificial heat, at a time when this moisture would have been absolutely fatal to many high alpines. All leaves have some form of breathing organs known as stomata. These are pores through which the plants not only breathe but also transpire moisture. In a damp atmosphere such as is often encountered, especially in winter in this country, the stomata of many high alpine plants, which are generally adapted with a fringe of fine hairs to catch and retain all available moisture in their exposed naturally dry habitats, become clogged up with excessive moisture which often results in the death of the plant through suffocation.

It is impossible to imitate nature to any great degree when growing these plants. After all, plants from most mountain ranges of the world are bunched together in one house, how is it possible to give each and all the natural environment it requires? A compromise has to be found and I find that a small amount of heat, especially during prolonged cold spells is the key to success.

First and foremost it is essential to keep the soil and roots of the plants in pans from freezing during extensive cold spells, when the temperature drops below freezing. No doubt the plunge material, owing to its bulk, will help in postponing the time when this will occur, but it will eventually freeze should the cold spell be prolonged. In their native habitat on the vast mountain ranges from which the majority of the plants come, they are normally covered with snow six months of the year. It falls before (and this is the crux of the matter) the soil is frozen to any appreciable depth, certainly before the frost can reach the root-hairs of the plants. Thus at no time are these roots subjected to freezing temperature.

It has been found that the difference in temperature between the air surface of snow and that at a depth of one foot is as much as 20°F (10°C). What then will be the difference when snow lies not one but many feet deep? It has been discovered that plants actually grow while covered with a blanket of snow. For example in the Alps in early spring, *Soldanella alpina* will push bursting buds through this protective covering and break into flower. Even those extremely saxatile plants which inhabit the fissures on exposed rock formations in nature, where no protective layer of snow can rest, are guarded to a great extent by forming a root system which delves deep down in cracks and crevices in the rocks, the tips being protected from frost by the great rock depth which surrounds them.

How different the conditions in cultivation where the plants and root systems are contained in small pans rarely more than 5 inches deep. Throughout the winter months when they should be resting they have to contend with alternate periods of thaw and frost, tending to cause fresh growth in the milder spells which suffers disaster at the next period of prolonged icy weather.

During long cold periods when the temperature remains below freezing point, both day and night, the occupants of the pans and the soil will surely freeze. This causes the tiny fibrous roots to fracture. At best it will result in the weakening of the plants, although more often in total loss, particularly in the case of evergreens. The cause here is drought, as the frozen roots are unable to replace the moisture lost by transpiration. Evergreens exude moisture from their leaves in all temperatures down to freezing point. During the long cold spells when the soil and roots in the pan are frozen, the temperature in the alpine house has only to rise above freezing for a short period for transpiration to occur. Exceedingly frosty spells often have clear skies during the day which bring about a fairly rapid rise in temperature, a state of affairs which is disastrous for the plants, for the frozen roots cannot replace the moisture thus lost. The sun falling on an evergreen plant whose roots and soil are frozen will cause the foliage to wilt, followed by shrivelling and browning, in other words the leaves wither and die through desiccation as they have no means of replacing moisture lost through evaporation.

Another reason for the use of heaters is that they set up currents of air and keep the atmosphere buoyant in spells of moist, stagnant weather which occur frequently throughout an English winter. These can be harmful to alpine plants, especially those normally covered with snow or whose foliage is thick and woolly, these being constructed to catch and retain all available moisture in their forever-dry windy habitats. In cultivation these act as sponges, absorbing an ever-increasing amount, until saturation point is reached, this excess being detrimental if not fatal to high alpines in winter. Many too, come into flower very early in the year, long before the risk of frost is past and during these periods, especially after clear sunny days, the temperature will rapidly drop below freezing often spoiling these early blooms.

With reasonable care and foresight the installation, maintenance and running costs of supplying heat to the alpine house can be very low. Heat is not required after all for growing purposes, only to exclude frost. A thermostat which can be set to operate at 34°F (1°C) and work within 2° on either side of this temperature should be installed, in a position where it cannot be affected by sunlight first thing in the morning. A site in the coldest part of the house is best, otherwise there is a danger of the plants freezing around this area. I found after experimenting that the most suitable place was just inside the door, fitted on the left side of the bottom window, protected from the east by the framework (Fig. 5). Here no sunshine reaches it until all frost has normally disappeared.

The heating equipment consists of two tubular 9 feet long electric heaters totally enclosed, both being shock and waterproof. These have a loading of 60 watts per foot making 1,080 watts total, or a fraction over one kilowatt, so the total running cost per hour is really rather small where electricity is obtained on a flat rate. This works out to be extremely low as the normal climatic conditions in this country rarely provide constant frost over long periods. Winters of 1947 and 1962 were the exceptions which proved the rule, but for a complete winter season the cost is not prohibitive, in fact many weeks will go by without use of power at all.

Fitting is not carried out as with ordinary greenhouse heaters, but the heaters are installed just below the eaves, where they maintain a reasonably dry atmosphere if used during damp or foggy weather. Naturally these remarks can only apply to those who have electricity installed in the alpine house at the time of building. It is almost essential for the serious grower of alpines, for it allows work to be carried out at all times of the year even in the depths of winter, when daylight is at a premium. Cost of installation should not be too high, but it is not possible to give figures, for a great deal depends on how far the alpine house is from a source of supply. The installation should only be carried out by a competent electrician, who is able to install the necessary fuses to protect the source of supply, for this work has to be passed by the local Electricity Board.

Another cheap and economical method of keeping the pans and their occupants from completely freezing is by the installation of a low wattage resistance cable, the actual wattage being 120 on a 50-foot length, giving eight hours of heat for a unit. It is easy to install, all that is necessary is to lay the cable on the base of the staging following the maker's instructions and if used in conjunction with a thermostat it can be left indefinitely without any maintenance. The actual cable is tough, rot-, acid- and water-proof and almost indestructable.

Should it not be possible to install electricity, one of the many oil lamps on the market can be used. These lamps are practically foolproof but have the one initial drawback, that once alight they will keep burning all night, even if the temperature rises, for they cannot be automatically controlled. There are other means of heating such as by hard fuel, oil such as used for central heating, or gas, but these are not recommended as the amount of heat required in an alpine house is so small that it does not warrant the cost of installation of these types of equipment.

Shading

There is one more point to be dealt with before we leave the alpine house, and this is the shading. During the late spring and summer months, shading in one form or another will be found necessary to break the strong sunlight and provide cool conditions in which the alpines delight. Normally this will be from the end of April to the end of September in the southern counties, the northern counties and Scotland a week later, removing the shading a week earlier in September.

In connection with shading in the house the question arises as to whether it is intended to keep the plants in the house throughout the year, or whether the housing of the plants is to be of a more temporary nature, only bringing them in for flowering, grooming for exhibition or protection of those plants which will not successfully withstand our winters outside in frames. If for the latter temporary purpose it will only be necessary to run a couple of wires inside the whole length of each side of the house, just below the ridge ventilators and the eaves. Green muslin, tiffany or scrim blinds cut to size and fitted top and bottom with rings are threaded onto the wires (Fig. 6). This arrangement will give satisfactory shading while the plants are housed in the early summer period. They can be drawn when the sun strikes that side of the house and then on the opposite side when it moves across, pulling back the original shading when the sun moves away.

SCRIM OR MUSLIN WITH BRASS
CURTAIN RINGS SEWN TO TOP AND
BOTTOM EDGES, RUNNING ON
EXTENSIBLE CURTAIN WIRES.

6. *Internal shading to alpine house*

This method has a drawback: although breaking the direct rays of the sun it does nothing to cool the house, which even with all ventilators and the door open to their fullest extent is liable to reach a high temperature on hot days, through the sun's rays striking the glass.

There are washes on the market which can be applied to the glass. The colour of the best known is a light green, although some people like to use a mixture of whitening and water. Whatever kind is employed it should be used on the inside of the house, not the outside as is often advocated. The green proprietary washes are supposed to be waterproof under normal conditions. This may be true, but if a hot summer day is experienced, and the heat should be broken by heavy thunder storms and torrential rain, this will certainly remove a large amount of the wash. A succeeding sunny spell will require further applications of the wash, not an easy task unless the remains of the old wash have been completely removed. Should the wash consist of whitening and water then it is imperative that it goes inside, for the first shower of rain will remove the best part of it, if on the outside.

Whatever type of colour wash is applied the problem is that once on, should the summer prove to be dull and cloudy, a not unusual occurrence in this country, the plants will suffer, becoming drawn up and out of character, owing to the poor diffused light. This may not be too serious for ordinary occupants of a greenhouse, but for alpines it is disastrous, for once drawn up and out of character they never regain it, to say nothing of

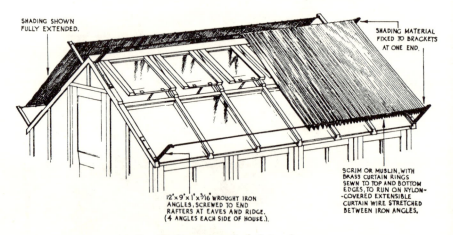

SHADING SHOWN
FULLY EXTENDED.

SHADING MATERIAL
FIXED TO BRACKETS
AT ONE END.

12"x 9"x 1"x ³⁄₁₆" WROUGHT IRON
ANGLES, SCREWED TO END
RAFTERS AT EAVES AND RIDGE.
(4 ANGLES EACH SIDE OF HOUSE.)

SCRIM OR MUSLIN, WITH
BRASS CURTAIN RINGS
SEWN TO TOP AND BOTTOM
EDGES, TO RUN ON NYLON-
-COVERED EXTENSIBLE
CURTAIN WIRE STRETCHED
BETWEEN IRON ANGLES.

7. *Shading to roof of alpine house*

the plant tissues becoming soft, making them a much easier prey to pests and diseases.

If the house is to be used all the year round either of the following methods can be adopted. One is to fit scrim or muslin blinds outside the house, and run these on nylon-covered wires, drawn taut from brackets attached to the corners of the eaves and ridge (Fig. 7). The brackets should be 12 by 9 inches in length, made of mild steel. The short side should protrude 9 inches away from the glass, which allows the top ventilators to be opened and also provides a gap for the passage of air between the glass and the scrim, thus helping to keep the alpine house cool.

Nylon-covered spring wire, as used for curtains, is then stretched between the iron supports and on these are threaded the scrim or muslin which has brass rings sown on top and bottom at 3 inch intervals along their length. A hook is fixed on the iron supports at both ends, so that once the curtains have been drawn they can be fixed into position. Before attaching the blinds to the wires they are best dipped in Cuprinol. This not only helps to preserve the material but also imparts a light, restful green.

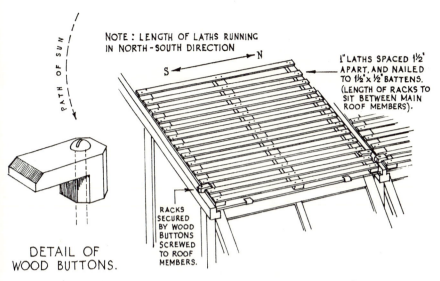

PATH OF SUN

NOTE : LENGTH OF LATHS RUNNING
IN NORTH-SOUTH DIRECTION

N

S

1" LATHS SPACED 1½"
APART, AND NAILED
TO 1½" x ½" BATTENS.
(LENGTH OF RACKS TO
SIT BETWEEN MAIN
ROOF MEMBERS).

RACKS
SECURED
BY WOOD
BUTTONS
SCREWED
TO ROOF
MEMBERS.

DETAIL OF
WOOD BUTTONS.

8. *Shade racks to lower panels of alpine house roof*

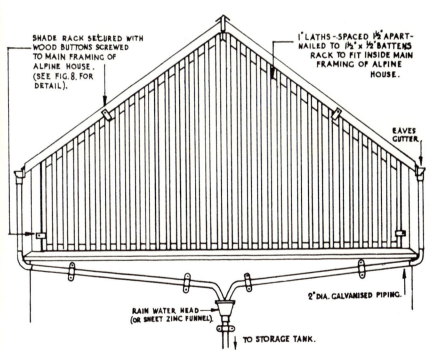

SHADE RACK SECURED WITH
WOOD BUTTONS SCREWED
TO MAIN FRAMING OF
ALPINE HOUSE.
(SEE FIG. 8. FOR
DETAIL).

1" LATHS -SPACED 1½" APART-
NAILED TO 1½" x ½" BATTENS
RACK TO FIT INSIDE MAIN
FRAMING OF ALPINE
HOUSE.

EAVES
GUTTER.

2" DIA. GALVANISED PIPING.

RAIN WATER HEAD
(OR SHEET ZINC FUNNEL).

TO STORAGE TANK.

9. *Shade rack at south end of alpine house*

A method I have used with success is wooden shade racks and I propose to give constructional details of these racks for a house 16 feet long; six shade racks will be required on each side, the frames being constructed with $1\frac{1}{2}$ inch by $\frac{1}{2}$ inch battens of timber. All timber should be treated with Cuprinol to preserve it. Building-plaster laths 1 inch wide are cut to size and nailed, spaced $1\frac{1}{4}$ inch apart horizontally, so that when fixed into position with wooden buttons on the outside of the house they cast an ever moving shadow as the sun passes over the house from east to west (Fig. 8). If possible the racks on the east side should be placed in position while the sun is rising. After it has passed its zenith, the racks on the west side can be put in place and those on the east removed. Naturally if the weather is cloudy it will not be necessary to use the racks during this period.

These shade racks are quite inexpensive to make and will last for a long time. When in position, a circulation of air can pass between the shade racks and the windows of the house, keeping the glass cool. It will be necessary to use some form of colour-wash for the top ventilators, either green or white, as these cannot be fitted with this type of shade rack successfully. Whatever method of shading is adopted, the window at the south end of the house must also be shaded. Here a rack made to size (Fig. 9) can be fitted with the laths running vertically instead of horizontally.

CHAPTER TWO

Alpine Frame. Plunge Beds. Frames.
Propagating Frames. Heated Propagating Frame.
Potting Shed.

Frames are a necessary adjunct to an alpine house, for here should be housed plants which resent being kept under glass during hot summer months. There are also a large number of plants which have nothing to commend them once their flowering season is over. These are best plunged outside in the frames to make way for new plants to take their place in the alpine house. Conifers too need to be kept in a half shady frame for the greater part of the year, being taken into the house for only short periods, otherwise they tend to become drawn up out of character, losing the compact shapes for which these delightful miniatures are noted. There is also less chance of their being disfigured by scale and pests, which can so easily cause trouble unless a careful watch is maintained.

Few members of the families *Ericaceae* and *Gesneriaceae*, and none of the Asiatic primulas, will tolerate the dry conditions which are natural in the alpine house during summer. They are best plunged in a shady frame outside, then in late autumn, before the likelihood of major frosts, can be brought into the house for the winter, plunging them in the bed under the staging. Another important point is that even the avid sun-lovers including the genera Sedum and Sempervivum tend to be happier if given a spell in a sunny frame after flowering and while making fresh growth. The foliage and growth will be much firmer and the difference in texture of the leaves can be clearly seen.

Bulbous plants and corms such as tulips, crocuses, narcissi, fritillarias, many of the cyclamens etc., have to be kept in the frame during the season while they are forming roots and growing, then fetched into the alpine house when the buds are showing colour. After flowering and when the foliage has died down they are returned to the frame. The lights are put on and the water supply restricted so that the dormant bulbs and corms receive the ripening so essential to their continued good health.

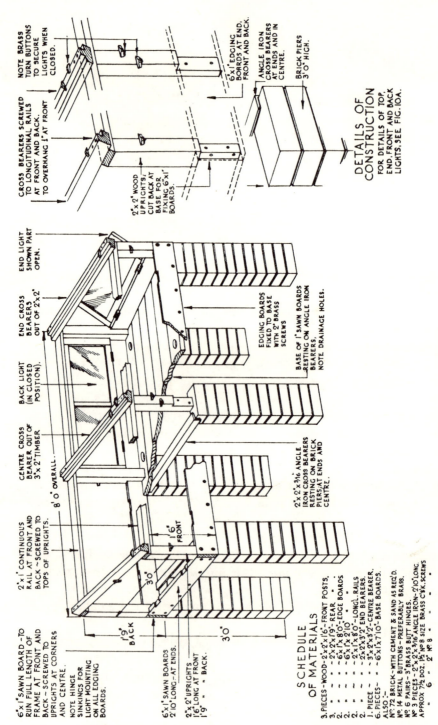

NOTE BRASS TURN BUTTONS TO SECURE LIGHTS WHEN CLOSED.

CROSS BEARERS SCREWED TO LONGITUDINAL RAILS AT FRONT AND BACK. TO OVERHANG 1" AT FRONT

2"x 2" WOOD UPRIGHTS. CUT BACK AT BASE FOR FIXING 6"x1" BOARDS.

6"x1"EDGING BOARDS AT END, FRONT AND BACK.

ANGLE IRON CROSS BEARERS AT ENDS AND IN CORNERS

BRICK PIERS 3'0" HIGH.

DETAILS OF CONSTRUCTION

FOR DETAILS OF TOP, END, FRONT AND BACK LIGHTS, SEE FIG. IOA.

END LIGHT SHOWN PART OPEN.

END CROSS BEARERS OUT OF 2"x2"

BACK LIGHT (IN CLOSED POSITION).

CENTRE CROSS BEARER OUT OF 3"x2" TIMBER

8'0" OVERALL.

2"x1" CONTINUOUS RAIL AT FRONT AND BACK ~ SCREWED TO TOPS OF UPRIGHTS.

6"x1"SAWN BOARD ~TO RUN FULL LENGTH OF FRAME AT FRONT AND BACK ~ SCREWED TO UPRIGHTS AT CORNERS AND CENTRE.

NOTE HINGE SINKINGS FOR LIGHT MOUNTING ON ALL EDGING BOARDS.

EDGING BOARDS OF 1" SAWN BOARDS FIXED TO BASE WITH 2" BRASS SCREWS.

BASE OF 1" SAWN BOARDS RESTING ON ANGLE IRON BEARERS. NOTE DRAINAGE HOLES.

2" x 2" x 3/16" ANGLE IRON CROSS BEARERS RESTING ON BRICK PIERS, AT ENDS AND CENTRE.

6"x1" SAWN BOARDS 2'10" LONG~AT ENDS.

2"x2" UPRIGHTS 1'6" LONG AT FRONT 1'9" " BACK.

1'9" BACK

1'6" FRONT

3'0"

3'0"

SCHEDULE OF MATERIALS

3. PIECES – WOOD – 2"x 2"x 1'6" – FRONT POSTS.
3. " – " – 2"x 2"x 1'9" – REAR "
2. " – " – 6"x 1"x 8'0" – EDGE BOARDS.
2. " – " – 6"x 1"x 2'10" "
2. " – " – 2"x 1"x 8'0" – LONGL. RAILS
2. " – " – 2"x 2"x 3'2" – END BEARERS.
1. PIECE – " – 3"x 2"x 3'2" – CENTRE BEARER.
6. PIECES – " – 6"x 1"x 7'10" – BASE BOARDS.

ALSO :–
No 72 BRICK – WITH CEMENT & SAND AS REQ'D.
No 14 METAL BUTTONS – PREFERABLY BRASS.
No 6 PAIRS – 3" BRASS BUTT HINGES.
No 3 PIECES – 2" x 2" x 3/16" ANGLE IRON – 2'10" LONG.
APPROX 7½ DOZ. 1½ No 8 SIZE BRASS C'SK. SCREWS
" 6 " 2" No 8 " " " "

10. The alpine frame

Alpine Frame

As the object of this work is to deal with the growing of alpines in pans, either in an alpine house, or in frames if the grower has only space for these, it will be necessary to give a few constructional details of suitable frames for the plants as a permanent home to be occupied during their flowering season, or grooming period if they are being grown for exhibition purposes. The alpine frame will to all intents and purposes be a house in miniature and there are a number of suitable ready-made articles which will meet the purpose. They need to be placed on supports approximately 3 feet from the ground so that all work can be carried out at a comfortable level. Nothing can be more tiring than having to stoop to lift pans if the frame is at ground level not to mention how much easier it is to do odd jobs such as removing dead foliage, flowers, and deceased parts, and keeping a watch for pests, if the frame is raised.

A few figures will be helpful and Fig. 10 gives a general idea of size, measurements and materials required to build this miniature alpine house. The overall size is 8 by 3 feet, laid on brick pillars built 3 feet high of single bricks, placed on their broad face, so that the completed pillars are 9 inches long by $4\frac{1}{2}$ inches wide and 3 feet tall, six pillars in all are required to take the weight of the completed frame.

The base of the frame is contructed from six pieces of timber, 7 feet 10 inches long, 6 inches wide by 1 inch thick. The thickness given is the minimum needed to hold the weight of the pans with 3 inches of plunging material, this being sand or a mixture of pea gravel and sand. Thicker wood can be used if available. There are a number of firms who deal in reclaimed timber from old houses etc., which if obtainable would be ideal for the purpose as well as being cheaper than new wood. Reinforcement to the base is by three angle iron strips, 2 feet 10 inches long, 2 by 2 inches wide and $\frac{3}{16}$ths inch thick. These are placed as shown in the diagram with $\frac{1}{2}$ inch screws, into the base of the frame, after they have been painted with two coats of bituminous paint to preserve them from the moisture which will accumulate at the base.

All wood used in the construction of this frame must be given two coats of Cuprinol to render it rotproof and this is applied before, not after, the frame is put together. This is important, for unless it is done it will mean that at the joints, no preservative will be present and rotting will take place in a short period. Six drainage holes, one at each corner and two in a central position should be cut, to allow surplus water to drain away.

Fixing is by using either $1\frac{1}{2}$ or 2 inch brass screws, to prevent rusting and deterioration, and for joining the base boards to the sides these should be 2 inches long. The sides of the frame are constructed from four pieces

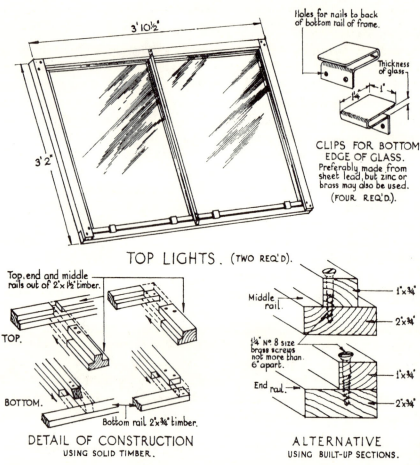

Holes for nails to back of bottom rail of frame.

Thickness of glass

1"

1¼"

CLIPS FOR BOTTOM EDGE OF GLASS.
Preferably made from sheet lead, but zinc or brass may also be used.
(FOUR REQ'D).

3' 10½"

3' 2"

TOP LIGHTS. (TWO REQ'D).

Top, end and middle rails out of 2"x 1½" timber.

TOP.

BOTTOM.

Bottom rail 2"x ¾" timber.

DETAIL OF CONSTRUCTION
USING SOLID TIMBER.

Middle rail.

1"x¾"

2"x¾"

1¼" No. 8 size brass screws not more than 6" apart.

End rail.

1"x¾"

2"x¾"

ALTERNATIVE
USING BUILT-UP SECTIONS.

NOTE:

In addition to the Top Lights shown above, lights are required for the front, back and ends of the Alpine Frame. These are shown in outline below. Corner joints may be made as shown in detail of construction, but using 1½" x 1" timber (solid), or 1½"x½" (built-up).

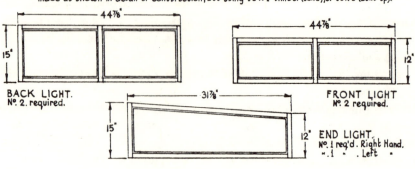

44⅞"

15"

BACK LIGHT.
No. 2 required.

44⅞"

12"

FRONT LIGHT
No. 2 required.

31⅞"

15"

12"

END LIGHT.
No. 1 req'd. Right Hand.
" 1 " . Left "

10a. *Lights for the alpine frame*

of timber. The front and back are 8 feet long by 6 inches wide and 1 inch thick. The two sides, 2 feet 10 inches by 6 inches and 1 inch thick, and the four are joined by brass screws 1½ inch in length.

The six uprights to hold the top and side lights are from 2 inch squared wood, the three front pieces being 1 foot 6 inches and the three rear 1 foot 9 inches high, so that when the top lights are fitted this will give the necessary slope to drain off rain water.

The two front lights are constructed from 1½ inch sash bars with a middle glazing bar of the same size, this being necessary to divide what would be too large an area of glass if left in one piece. The overall measurements for these lights are 3 feet 8⅞ inches by 1 foot. The two rear lights only differ in being 1 foot 3 inches tall instead of 1 foot as in the front. The two side lights are approximately 2 feet 7⅞ inches at the base, the front side 1 foot and the rear 1 foot 3 inches. The glass is cut to shape in one piece for each side (Fig. 10a). All these lights are attached to the side of the frame by brass hinges, 3 inches long, two to each light, buttons are placed in the centres and buttons for holding the lights when closed are fixed at the top of each end of the upright supports, to hold them in position.

On the six uprights the tops should be lightly tapered to allow for the 3 inch drop from rear to front, two pieces of timber 8 by 2 by 1 inches are joined lengthwise in the front and rear across the pillars. The 1 inch gap at either side when these are fitted will allow a current of air at all times above the plants, even when the frame is completely closed. On top of these supports are screwed, one at each end, two guide strips 3 feet 2 inches by 2 inch square and a centre bearer 3 by 2 inches by 3 feet 2 inches. The overlap of 2 inches will allow the two top lights to keep off driving rain from the closed frame.

The two top removable lights which have outside measurements of 3 feet 10½ inches by 3 feet 2 inches are the standard type of lights and can be constructed quite easily. The wood should be 2 inches wide by 1½ inch deep for the rear and sides and the front rail only ¾ inch deep and a glazing bar fitted down the centre. Buttons are fitted on the guide strips so that when the two lights are in position they can be secured. Throughout the summer months the lights can be completely removed except during rainy spells and in their place shade racks fitted made to the same size as the lights. The racks are constructed from 1½ by 1 inch battens. Builders' laths are nailed on them leaving a gap of 1½ inch between each lath.

There is a right and a wrong way of placing the laths on the framework of the battens, depending on the siting of the frame. If the frame faces north or south the laths are placed vertically while if the situation is east or west then the laths should be horizontal. The reason for this is that the sun travelling as it does across the sky from east to west must be broken by the laths sited across its path.

Plunge Beds

Fig. 1 shows two plunge beds on the site, one 10 feet by 8 feet facing south and the other 8 feet by 4 feet facing west. Both these beds are constructed of brick, that is single bricks laid on their broad face to a height of 18 inches. Provision is made for drainage by omitting one half brick at the front base of the beds and a piece of perforated zinc cemented in. At the same time four pieces of 2 inches by 2 inches timber are cemented in at each corner, these being 3 feet tall at the rear of the beds and 2 feet 6 inches at the front. The purpose of these is to hold the shade racks which are needed during the hot months. They are constructed on the same principle as for the alpine frame and in the case of bed No. 1 the shade laths run back to front and in No. 2 side to side.

After making allowance for the drainage by putting in a few broken crocks the beds are filled with sand and the whole is then watered with a strong solution of permanganate of potash to kill off fungus spores. It also irritates the skins of any worms present in the sand, and brings them to the surface, when they can easily be removed. The plants can then be plunged into the sand up to the rims of the pans. There is no overhead protection fitted to the beds with the exception of the shade racks, so that the plants plunged here are generally the more robust types of shrubs and dwarf ericaceous plants. The main object of these beds is that after flowering in the alpine house, plants can be placed here for the summer months. They may also be used as temporary beds to house a collection of plants which have been repotted and need the shade provided by the racks to help them in becoming re-established.

Frames

Frames A, B, C and D on the plan of the site (Fig. 1) are used to house collections of plants which normally need protection from inclement weather even during the summer months, but are not housed in the alpine house permanently. There are many uses for this type of frame. One can be used to ripen off bulbous plants when water has to be withheld during that period, another for a collection of cyclamens which do better in a frame than in the alpine house during their off-flowering period, or for Asiatic primulas which must be in a cool frame in summer yet protected from overhead rain during that season.

The frames themselves (Fig. 11) are the normal 4 by 3 feet construction, the minimum depth being 1 foot in the front rising to 18 inches at the rear, made with timber which with a little alteration can be bought ready for erection or made at home. The type required must have the lights attached to the body of the frame by hinges with stays and buttons so that air can be admitted when necessary. All must have bases as they are to be placed on 4½ inch thick brick walls, 3 feet high. Five brickwork cross walls will be needed to support the frames, these being of the single brick type laid on its broad edge.

The first wall is placed at the beginning of the first frame, the second started 4 feet, the third 8 feet 1 inch, fourth 12 feet 2 inches and the fifth at 16 feet 2 inches. Four pieces of 2 inch square timber are required to make a frame base 16 feet 3 inches long by 3 feet wide. This, when constructed, is screwed flush to the bottom of the batch of frames providing a rigid support for these as well as a base for carrying the floor of the frames. The floor is made of 1 inch thick timber cut into 3 feet lengths. The width should be according to available material, but not less than 4 inch sections. These are secured by screws onto the top of the frame base. After fixing, drainage holes are cut into the floor of the frames, two for each is sufficient, one in front and the other at the rear. As with all timber used this must be given at least two coats of Cuprinol to preserve it before fixing to the base of the frames.

It will be necessary to provide a certain amount of ventilation which can be brought into action during periods of wet or stormy weather when the lights have to be closed. This is provided by obtaining eight small bakelite sliding ventilators—a size roughly 6 by 4 inches will be ample. Sections are cut away in the front and rear of each frame, not opposite each other, but staggered so that there is an infiltration of air rather than a draught (Fig. 11). During very gusty weather the ventilators on the windward side can be kept closed, the others will still allow a circulation of air.

Shade racks will also have to be provided for these frames and this can be arranged quite simply. Wooden supports made of 1½ by 1 inch timber are used, ten in all. Five are at the front, these being 3 feet tall of which 1 foot is used for fixing to the frame leaving a clearance between the top of the frame and the shade rack of 2 feet. At the rear of the frames the height of the wooden supports is 3 feet 6 inches of which 1½ foot are used for fixing to the frame and the other 2 feet extends beyond to hold the shade racks.

The two front edges of the lights are cut diagonally with a saw to allow free passage of the lights past the shade rack supports. Four racks are constructed, each being 4 feet long by 3 feet 1 inch wide, the racks resting on the supports. A ¼-inch hole is drilled at each corner of the shade racks

SHADE RACK ~ 4'x 3' 1", SECURED TO SUPPORT FRAMEWORK WITH 4 BOLTS & WING NUTS.

4'x 6' SLIDING VENTILATORS TO BACK AND FRONT BOARDS (NOTE STAGGERED POSITIONS).

BASE OF 1" SAWN BOARDS, 3'O" LONG-LAID CROSS-WISE, RESTING ON 2'x 2" BASE FRAME. (NOTE DRAINAGE HOLES).

HINGED TOP LIGHTS, 4'O"x 3'2" (SEE FIG.10A FOR CONSTRUCTION). Note: Front corners cut back to clear shade rack vertical supports.

CASEMENT STAY.

SHADE RACK OF PLASTERER'S LATHS BRADDED TO 1½"x ½" BATTENS.

SHADE RACKS SECURED EACH WITH FOUR 3/16" DIA. BOLTS, WING-NUTS AND WASHERS.

END RACK BEARERS OF 1½"x ½" BATTENS.

1½"x 1" VERTICAL SUPPORTS FOR SHADE RACKS. FRONT 3'O" LONG. BACK 3'6". SCREWED TO FRONT AND BACK BOARDS AT ENDS AND AT DIVISIONS.

FRONT, BACK AND END BOARDS SCREWED TO BASE FRAME AT ABOUT 6" C.C.

2'x 2" BASE FRAME-TO REST ON BRICKWORK.

DETAIL OF GENERAL CONSTRUCTION.

DETAIL OF MOUNTING FOR INTERMEDIATE SHADE RACKS.

HOLES FOR 3/16" BOLTS.

3"x ½" BATTEN AT INTERMEDIATE POSITIONS - TO ALL FOR FIXING ADJACENT SHADE RACKS.

2'x 2" BASE FRAME.

DETAIL OF BASE FIXING

BASE BOARDS 1" THICK x 3'O" LONG SCREWED DOWN TO BASE FRAME.

FRONT AND BACK BOARD - ALSO ENDS AND DIVISIONS OF 1" THICK SAWN BOARDS.

4½" BRICK-WORK CROSS WALLS, 3'O" LONG LAID IN CEMENT MORTAR.

16'5" OVERALL

4'O" INSIDE
3'O" INSIDE
2'O"
1'6" BACK
3'O"
1'O" FRONT.

11. Ranoe of frames

and these are fixed to the supports by wing nuts which hold them quite securely (Fig. 11). The method of construction of the racks themselves is the same as noted for the alpine frame.

The sizes given for the frames are what are known as standard sizes in the trade thus making them easy to obtain. However there is nothing to prevent anyone who is constructing all the frames and lights himself from changing them to suit his own site. It is also possible to obtain all these frames in either metal or a metal alloy and these will fulfil the same purpose. A word of warning here, however, a sharp lookout for condensation with its accompanying drip must be kept, as all metal frames are prone to this defect, which can be dangerous to any woolly or cushion plants housed in these frames.

Propagating Frames

The two propagating frames E and F on the plan of the site (Fig. 1) are constructed of brick, the outside measurements being 3 feet by 2 feet for each frame. Brick is much more suitable than wood or metal for this type of frame. It maintains a more equable temperature, retaining the heat from the sun much longer and releasing it slowly after the sun has set. Moisture, so essential to the rooting of cuttings, is more constant and the need for watering is much less during the time that the cuttings are making roots. Frame E is used for the ordinary type of cuttings which root quickly in a warm atmosphere, as facing west this frame receives plenty of sunshine during the day. Frame F is sited facing north and is ideal for rooting cuttings which require a cooler atmosphere, for in this situation there is not a great deal of direct sunlight falling on the frame.

The plan (Fig. 12) will give a general idea of the construction of these two frames. The bricks are laid on their broad side and built to a height of 1 foot 6 inches all round, making in all a box 3 feet by 2 feet by 1 foot 6 inches deep; these are outside measurements. A small gap is left in the front right-hand corner for drainage into which a piece of perforated galvanised iron or zinc sheet is cemented to facilitate drainage and at the same time to stop ingress of pests into the rooting compound.

When completed a wooden frame is made to hold the light, this being two pieces, one for the rear and the other for the front. The sizes are 2 feet 5¼ inches by 3 inches by 1 inch and 2 feet 5¼ inches by 2 inches by 1 inch. The difference between the width of the rear and front is to allow for the drop to take off all surplus moisture. The two side pieces are cut from timber 1 foot 3¼ inches long, 3 inches deep at the rear tapering to 2 inches at the front and 1 inch thick. When joining the two side pieces these are fitted flush to the corners with the ends inside the front and rear sections.

Galvanised 1 inch nails are then driven into the bottom inch all round on both sides of the wooden frame. After painting with three coats of Cuprinol the frame is sited carefully on top of the brick base.

Fixing to the base is by making a mixture of two parts sand to one part cement into a firm mix with water and applying it to the top of the brick base to a depth of 2 inches, after making sure that the bricks have been

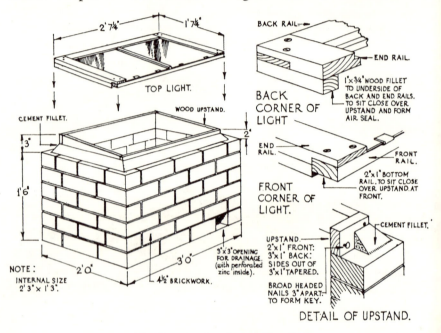

12. *Propagating frames E and F*

well damped down. While still moist press the wooden frame into the cement mix until it touches the brick base, then with a trowel smooth off the cement to a depth of 1½ inch on both sides of the frame and allow to set. The galvanised nails will hold the frame in position quite securely. The light is made from 2 inches by 1 inch thick wood and is cut to size, for the front and back of the frames, so that it fits completely over the wooden frame making a tight joint, very necessary when a close atmosphere is required for striking cuttings. A central glazing bar is used so that when glazed the glass can be secured by putty and clips.

After a period of nine days the completed frame should be given a good wash down inside with a strong solution of permanganate of potash, a half ounce to two gallons of boiling water, applied with a stiff brush and working it well in. The frame is now ready for the cutting compost and the procedure is as follows.

Above: *Androsace alpina* (see page 193)

Below: *Androsace ciliata* (see page 194)

Above: *Androsace sarmentosa* var. *watkinsii* (see page 520)

Below: *Androsace wulfeniana* (see page 198)

Broken crocks or bricks are placed in the base of the frame to a depth of 6 inches, graduating these as far as possible by using large pieces first and gradually filling in with the smaller material. Whatever size is used, none must be smaller than a pea, otherwise there will be a danger of blocking the drainage. Following this, a good sprinkling of HCH powder is put over the drainage material, to keep most pests at bay for a long period. Over the top of this is laid a thin layer of roughage, half rotted leaf-mould, or the residue of peat after sieving through a $\frac{1}{16}$th inch sieve will be found suitable. All that is needed is enough to completely cover the drainage material, so that there is no possible danger of the cutting compost being washed down, thus completely stopping the drainage. For ease of reference the types of cutting compost for these and the heated frame will be dealt with under the chapter headed propagation.

Heated Propagating Frame

The majority of alpine plants can be easily propagated by vegetative means, that is by cuttings from either green or ripened wood but there are a number which are difficult or even impossible to increase by these orthodox methods in a cold frame. A classic example is the scarce *Phlox nana ensifolia*, the scarcity being due not to any difficulty in cultivation but until recently the only known method of increase was by root cuttings, a task not lightly undertaken in disturbing a specimen plant for that purpose. This is where the heated frame comes into its own, for many plants can be propagated quite successfully by using heat, when it is not possible by any other means. I have struck cuttings of *Phlox nana ensifolia* in six weeks in such a frame.

For a heated frame there are two methods of applying constant heat over a long period and for both electricity is used. The first is by burying low voltage resistance wire in the cutting medium, just on top of the roughage material of either leaf-mould or peat over the drainage. This is a commercial proposition requiring a stepdown transformer from the mains, to reduce the voltage to a safe level and it is both efficient and safe provided the maker's instructions are carried out. There is no possibility of any danger from shock should the cable be shorted in any way or handled accidentally because of its low voltage.

The amount of current consumed depends on the size and situation of the heated frame. Naturally if used outdoors the cost of maintaining a reasonable degree of heat will be much higher than if installed in the alpine house. It has one disadvantage. In a small frame a thermostat would have to be installed for the heat will rise rapidly. It can also be costly over a long period, for once the current is switched on it must be maintained until the cuttings have rooted.

4

The other method of applying bottom heat which I propose to describe in detail, is much more economical in use and both the frame and heating appliances can be satisfactorily constructed by a handyman at very little cost, in a couple of hours (Fig. 13). It is primarily for use on the staging of the alpine house but there is no reason why it cannot be put in position

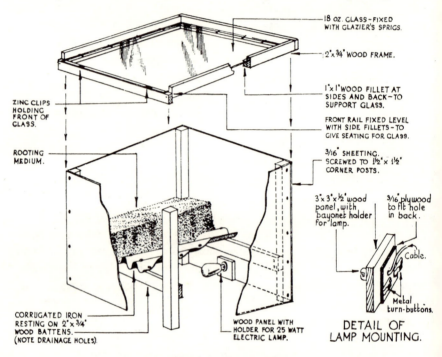

18 OZ. GLASS – FIXED WITH GLAZIER'S SPRIGS.

2'×¾" WOOD FRAME.

1"×1" WOOD FILLET AT SIDES AND BACK – TO SUPPORT GLASS.

ZINC CLIPS HOLDING FRONT OF GLASS.

FRONT RAIL FIXED LEVEL WITH SIDE FILLETS – TO GIVE SEATING FOR GLASS.

ROOTING MEDIUM.

3/16" SHEETING, SCREWED TO 1½"×1½" CORNER POSTS.

3"×3"×½" wood panel, with bayonet holder for lamp.

3/16" plywood to fit hole in back.

Cable.

Metal turn-buttons.

CORRUGATED IRON RESTING ON 2'×¾" WOOD BATTENS. (NOTE DRAINAGE HOLES).

WOOD PANEL WITH HOLDER FOR 25 WATT ELECTRIC LAMP.

DETAIL OF LAMP MOUNTING.

13. *Heated propagating frame*

where there is a reasonable amount of light, such as near a window in the potting shed, or even in a cold frame, where it will function satisfactorily. The overall size of the frame is 2 by 1½ by 1½ feet at the back, falling to 15 inches at the front. The two sides, front and rear pieces are made from insulating material $\frac{3}{16}$th inch thick, which is easy to work and drill, only needing an old hand saw for cutting. This can be obtained from any builder's yard and is quite reasonable in price.

The four sides are fixed on to 1½ inch square battens. These should be preferably of some durable hard wood, such as oak or teak etc., or cedar can be used, which ensures a long life to the frame which will have to withstand a very humid atmosphere. If a soft wood is used it must be treated with a wood preservative, Cuprinol, to maintain a useful life, but on no account must creosote or any other wood preservative with a tar base be used, for these are injurious to plant life. Two pieces of wood battens, 15 inches long for the front of the frame and two pieces 18 inches long for the rear are required. All fixing is done with $\frac{1}{2}$ inch brass screws; the holes for these are easily made in the material with a metal bit. Five inches from the base at the front of the frame a batten, 2 feet by 2 inches by $\frac{3}{4}$ inch thick is screwed on to insulating sheeting and at the rear a similar piece is also fixed, in this case 6 inches from the bottom of the frame. A piece of galvanised iron is cut to size so that when fitted on the batten there is a drop of an inch from the back to the front of the frame. Drainage holes are drilled in the iron to allow all excess water to seep away.

The frame light is made of 2 inches by $\frac{3}{4}$ inch wood, the front and rear pieces being 2 feet long and the two side pieces $18\frac{1}{2}$ inches in length. The frame is constructed as shown in the diagram. The front rail is fixed half an inch down to form a seating for the glass which is held in position by 1 inch square batten fitted at sides and rear, also two zinc clips to hold the glass at the front of the light.

The heating is provided by an electric bulb and for this size of frame, a 25-watt bulb will suffice. It will be found that the wattage will raise the temperature inside the heated frame by at least 20°F (10°C) above that of the outside. The cost of such heating is easily computed for a unit of electricity (1 kilowatt or 1,000 watts) will take forty hours to use if a 25-watt bulb is installed. You will find this a small price to pay for the benefit of rooting difficult plants successfully.

Fig. 13 shows a method of fixing a lamp holder to the frame. The holder must be of the all-weather type which can be obtained easily from any electrical stores. If used inside the alpine house or potting shed, the electric cable known as 'cab type' is suitable, but if installed outside in a cold frame, it will be necessary to use lead-covered cable suitably earthed and protected by fuses, for the lead from the mains to the frame.

Potting Shed

Although not a necessity, a potting shed will do much to ease the work carried out in growing a collection, especially if the number of plants in cultivation is large. It will allow storage space for materials such as pots, pans, labels, tools and the different ingredients for composts under a single roof. Whatever type of work is carried out, such as preparing cuttings, repotting, sowing seed, mixing compost etc., everything is to hand.

The size of the shed need not be large, one 8 feet by 6 feet as shown in Fig. 1 will be quite suitable and this type of shed is obtainable from timber merchants in sections ready to assemble, only needing a dry base to erect it with a minimum of labour. The cost is reasonable if ordinary wood and a regular size is used; naturally if required in precast concrete or hardwood, such as teak or oak, the cost will be proportionately higher. The life of the shed will be extended however if the dearer woods are used, and a shed constructed of concrete would be both indestructable and vermin proof.

14. *The potting shed*

The bench should be a firm fixture and a close-grained hardwood, for example oak or teak, will give the best service. A good deal of work will be carried out here, such as repotting, mixing of materials for composts, label writing and plant surgery amongst other things. The need for a firm hard wood will soon be apparent, for the continual rubbing of its surface with abrasive materials, such as sand, chippings etc., would soon render a soft wood bench useless. It should, in a shed of the suggested size, be about 6 feet long by 2 feet 6 inches wide, which will give a large working surface, sufficient for all the necessary chores. It must be fitted on the light side of the building, that is where the windows are. In the plan it is shown as sited on the left, the reason being that there is a 3 feet party fence on the other side. Naturally it can be placed to suit one's own circumstances.

At the far end of the shed, the last 2 by 6 feet is divided into six bins to hold the compost materials and on the side facing the bench, bins one foot square hold the different prepared soil mixtures. Above these bins bench shelves can be fitted to run along both sides and the rear end, to hold insecticides, tools, spraying machines etc. The space under the bench can be utilised for the storage of pans and pots.

A small wooden box should be kept handy so that after repotting, top-dressing or general work on the plants the residue of old soil, leaves etc. can be swept straight into this container and removed. On no account should a mixture of rubbish, old compost and new soils be used as a makeshift, otherwise there would be a likelihood of infection, either from pests or diseases, these being thus transmitted from plant to plant. Fig. 14 gives a pictorial view of the interior and layout of the potting shed.

CHAPTER THREE

Tools. Pans. Drainage Materials. Labels.

As in all branches of gardening a certain number of tools are necessary for cultivating alpines in pans, but these should be kept to a minimum, as an excess only leads to confusion and untidiness, to say nothing of their getting mislaid, so only the bare essentials will be mentioned here and cultivators can extend to suit their own special requirements.

Tools

One-gallon watering-can with coarse rose. Necessary for damping down under the staging during long spells of hot dry weather.

Two-quart can, Haws. This is bought with two roses and an extension pipe. The roses will give a fine and medium flow and cover all the watering needs in the house for which a sprinkler is required. The extension pipe gives a small controlled flow, allowing for watering plants which resent over head watering, or for watering during winter months, as it allows the water to be placed around the sides of the pan and not over the plants.

Sprayer with three nozzles. A useful tool for applying a fine, medium or coarse mist, also for spraying insecticides if a heavy infestation of pests occur.

Quart spraying machine for insecticide. This is hand pumped, putting the insecticide mixture under heavy pressure and allowing the spray to be directed to a small given area with one hand, so that the other can be used to lift up the foliage of the plant being sprayed. It is invariably on the underside of the leaves that the insects tend to congregate.

Stainless steel dibber. A small tool which should not be more than 4 inches long is ideal and it is surprising the number of uses that can be found for this article, such as stirring up the surface of the soil in the pans, putting cuttings into propagating frames, making holes in the compost for inserting small seedlings etc.

Small wooden dibber. It should be made of good, hard, solid wood, oak or teak for preference, shaped to a point at one end like a wedge and notched at the other, the size being approximately 6 inches in length (Fig. 15).

It is useful for the removal of seedlings from the seed pans to the work bench for potting on, without damaging or bruising the delicate plants. With a little practice it is surprising how quickly one can gain proficiency in the use of this little tool. In spite of the care taken in trying to use the fingers for carrying out this operation, a great number of failures can be traced to damage of the seedlings at this stage.

Pot brush. This is for cleaning out the pans. Pot brushes can be obtained in different sizes, but a small one is best for it can be used for any size of pan, even the small ones, reaching down to the base, a well-known breeding

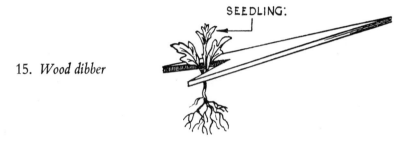

SEEDLING:

15. *Wood dibber*

spot for pests and diseases. If a large size is used it will be impossible to carry this out efficiently.

Pair of forceps. It will pay to purchase a good strong pair, about 4 inches in length with a good grip. Useful for extracting dead leaves and rosettes from the small rosette forming plants, such as androsaces, saxifragas, dionysias etc.

Pair of sharp scissors. Needed for cutting away dead or diseased portions of plants. These should never be allowed to remain, for if not quickly noted and removed, loss of the complete plant is more than a probability. They will also be found useful for cutting back plants after flowering or for any shaping required on dwarf shrubs.

Good lens. Of great assistance in searching for the minute pests, especially red spider which is hardly discernible by the naked eye.

Fine camel hair brush. In the open rock garden fertilisation is carried out generally by bees, other insects or the wind, whereas under the protection of the alpine house the wind is non-existent and the visits from pollinating insects are often a rare occurrence. To ensure a worthwhile crop of seed therefore hand pollination must be carried out. Although they may be self-fertile, in many flowers the stigma is not receptive at the same time as the pollen grains are ripe, so it is often necessary to pollinate by carrying ripe pollen with the camel hair brush to stigmas which are ready for fertilisation. These may be on different flowers on the same plant, or on other plants. A rough and ready guide as to whether the stigma is receptive, is that at this period it is quite sticky and the pollen grains adhere readily.

Two Sieves. These are needed to rub through the leaf-mould and peat, also for sifting Cornish sand. The best size is ¼ inch for peat and leaf-mould, the other a ⅛ inch for use with Cornish sand. These sieves can be bought as two complete units, or with a single wooden or metal side and interchangeable mesh.

Two Thermometers. Two will prove sufficient and both should be what is known as the minimum-maximum type, thus it is possible to record the fluctuation in temperature over the twenty-four hours. These differ from the orthodox types in having a U-shaped tube, the mercury extending up part of both sides of the shaped tube; this allows of two graduated scales reading in opposite directions. There are two small metal rods inside each upright of the tube, which are pushed up as the temperature rises or falls, the one on the left reading the minimum and that on the right the maximum, the reading being taken from the base of the rods. These rods remain stationary after being pushed by the mercury to show both the minimum and maximum temperature and can only be set by the use of a small magnet provided, which allows them to be drawn back to the top of the mercury. By resetting once every twenty-four hours, at the same time keeping a written record, it will be possible to obtain a general idea of fluctuations of temperature inside the house or frame. This allows the cultivator to adjust shading, ventilation, watering etc., so that there is a more equable reading over the period. Violent fluctuations which are harmful to the plants must be avoided as far as possible. The thermometers should be fixed in positions where the direct rays of the sun do not strike them, as only shade temperatures are required.

Small wooden cabinet. It is advisable to have on hand all the above tools so time is saved in not having to go backwards and forwards to fetch them as required. Money is well spent in obtaining a small cabinet which can be kept under the staging in the house, to hold tools, insecticides, labels, very necessary to have on hand, for often a new plant arrives, or is given by a fellow gardener and it is of the utmost importance to label this at once. In a large collection it is surprising how one's memory fails if this is neglected. The size of the cabinet is best left to the cultivator's own needs, but it is preferable to have one constructed from a hard wood for maximum life.

Water tank

This will be found extremely useful, especially during periods when overhead watering is taboo. The pans containing the plants can be placed in the tank in which there is 2 inches of water and allowed to soak it up.

The tank can be of any size to suit the cultivator's requirements, from a small enamel bath to a galvanised tank made to his own specifications. For a large collection of plants I would suggest a galvanised tank, 4 feet long by 2 feet 3 inches wide and 6 inches deep. This will fit underneath the staging quite easily and be large enough to water a good number of plants at the same time.

One last but very important point is that all tools after use should be thoroughly cleaned, especially if used in cutting away diseased material, or after having been in contact with pests which are notorious carriers of diseases. If of stainless steel, all that is needed is a damp rag which has been moistened in a weak solution of permanganate of potash, but other kinds should be wiped with an oily rag kept specially for that purpose after being treated with disinfectant.

Pans

A good supply of pans will be required for a really representative collection of alpines. I have always used half pots, not the so-called alpine pans, which in my opinion are too shallow for the cultivation of alpines. This is a personal preference but I have found that alpines, being naturally long rooting plants, require a deeper root run than is generally supposed. They also need good drainage, at least an inch of which has to be used, thus very little room is left for the growing compost if shallow pans are used.

A number of the following sizes will meet most requirements, depending on the extent of the collection, but allowance should be made for plants that are naturally fast growing. Nothing is more annoying than to find that pans are not available when plants need repotting. This sometimes leads to putting off what is an important job, the health of the plants suffering in consequence. It is not only cheaper to purchase complete casts of the different sizes of pans, but also all pans in each individual cast will be of the same size, quite a labour saver when plunging plants.

Sizes	Diameter at top in inches	Sizes	Diameter at top in inches
Thimbles	2	Twenty-fours	$8\frac{1}{2}$
Sixties	3	Sixteens	$9\frac{1}{2}$
Fifty-fours	4	Twelves	$11\frac{1}{2}$
Fourty-eights	$4\frac{1}{2}$	Eights	12
Thirty-twos	6		

The measurements are taken $\frac{1}{2}$ inch down inside the rim. A number of square pans are useful and take up less room on the staging, besides being easier for packing if exhibiting, but the cost is much greater than that of the orthodox round pans. These square pans can be constructed at home quite cheaply, all that is required is a wooden former or formers, the size or sizes depending entirely on the purpose for which they will be needed. The small wooden bung is cut from a broom shank and is needed for the drainage hole. Fig. 16 gives a good idea of the method and used in conjunction with these notes it will be possible to produce first class containers.

A sheet of brown paper larger than the required size of the pan is laid on a flat surface and the wooden former is placed in the centre. A mix is

SHORT PIECE OF
BROOM HANDLE TO
FORM DRAINAGE
HOLE.

TOP EDGE
SLIGHTLY
ROUNDED.

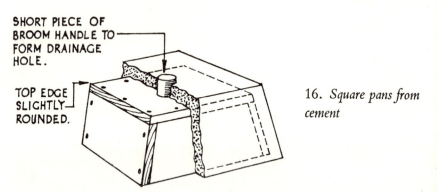

16. *Square pans from cement*

made consisting of one part cement, one part peat to two parts sharp sand, all ingredients should be well mixed dry first and then a little water added until the whole is just moist. This is important for the cement is applied to the former by hand, about $\frac{1}{2}$ inch thick and just smoothed out with a trowel, if too wet the mix will not retain its shape. Cover with a damp sack or rags and leave for at least nine days, when the complete pan can be gently eased out of the former, which can be used over and over again. Naturally if a selection of formers are made up, it is possible to build up a good collection of pans over a period of time. Another advantage is that knowing the size of the available space on the alpine house staging it will be possible to build the square pans to size so that the maximum number of plants can be accommodated.

Another type of pan that is often used for growing the rarer high alpine plants, especially those with a long rooting system, is called the 'Long Tom'. This is at least twice the depth of the normal pans thus allowing the room needed for extra drainage material, required for this type of plant.

Most gardeners will want to raise plants from seed as this method is very often the only way of obtaining plants from abroad. To do this seed pans will also be required. Shallow pans are quite suitable, approximately 3 inches in depth, irrespective of the size of pan. Pans are generally preferable to the old shallow wooden seed boxes which are used for raising annual bedding plants each year, which are not only perishable, lasting but a year or two, but also provide a congenial home for woodlice and other pests. A number of small pots used for cacti, 1½ inch in diameter for the first potting up of seedlings will also be found useful. No new pan must be used before having been soaked for at least twenty-four hours in water. It is surprising the amount they will absorb during this period, the reason being that every trace of moisture has been extracted during the oven firing process. Failure to do this will have disastrous results, for any moisture in the compost when used for potting up will be absorbed by the dry pan, not the plant. (See note on plastic pots, Appendix 3, p. 535.)

Cleanliness is essential when dealing with pans. Far too many cultivators who normally take rigid precautions in their alpine houses to keep them clear of pests and diseases will use a dirty pan for repotting. It is the dirt adhering to the pan, especially at the base where the drainage goes, that the very thing they wish to avoid is only awaiting the opportunity to infest what is otherwise clean compost. Here is the breeding home of nematodes, woodlice, slugs etc. All pans should be scrubbed after use and before using for new plants in a small bath which will hold up to twenty. Warm water is best, adding a soap powder or one of the many detergents on the market today. Special care should be taken that all dirt is removed from the base of the pan. A rinsing in clean, cold water to which has been added a few crystals of potassium permanganate will complete the job.

Drainage

Much has been written on the suitablity of different materials for drainage and possibly plenty more will be, for all writers seem to have their own choice of what is suitable. I often wonder however how much is based on actual experience? There is no doubt that drainage is important and the health of the plants will depend a great deal on its efficiency, so this point should be given first consideration when growing a collection of alpine plants.

I have experimented over a number of years with various materials, ranging from broken crocks through crushed bricks to chippings. The conclusion I have drawn is that the most efficacious is a sharp silver sand, which goes under the trade name of Cornish silver sand. This consists of particles from the size of a small pea to a pin's head and is definitely silicious in nature, the larger pieces resembling a hard quartz.

For the crock required to cover the hole at the base of the pan there are two materials which are normally used. One, through constant use over an untold length of time by gardeners of the old school, is a small piece of crock roughly broken to fit over the hole completely, placed so that it is convex in relation to the base of the pan. This allows the drainage material to settle without blockage to the drainage vent. I think that all this material has to commend it is, 'What was good enough for my father and his father is good enough for me'. In more leisurely days before the first world war, when labour costs were less than they are today, a boy could be put to work on a rainy day chipping these crocks. This is out of the question however in this jet age, where time is money. No doubt crocks were efficient enough as a drainage medium, but they also provided a first class residence for slugs, woodlice and other kindred pests.

The other material is far superior. This consists of small pieces of perforated zinc, which can be purchased in two sizes or cut from a piece of the perforated metal. The purchased pieces are better, being circular in shape. The outer edge is flat while the centres are convex, thus the pieces when placed on the base of the pan allow an air space but no ingress to pests.

For the drainage itself, the Cornish sand is first of all put through the $\frac{1}{4}$ inch sieve. The residue, consisting of the large particles, is used for the drainage, and placed to a depth of $\frac{1}{2}$ inch or more according to the amount required. The first layer allows rapid passage of surplus water. At the same time there are a number of air spaces left between the particles, which are beneficial to the roots as well as keeping the whole moist but not stagnant. The remainder of the sand is then put through a $\frac{1}{16}$-inch sieve and here again the residue is used, just enough on the surface of the larger particles to cover and fill up any surface crevices. Lastly a thin layer of roughage is placed over the sand to prevent the compost filtering down and blocking up the drainage. The roughage can be from flaked leaf-mould or the residue of peat after sieving.

This method has one very great advantage over the use of other materials such as broken crocks or bricks. When repotting and after the plant is carefully removed, it will be observed that all the sand used for the drainage falls gently away leaving the long feeding roots hanging free, ready for repotting and the working in of fresh compost round the roots. On the other hand when broken crocks or bricks are used, normally the roots will be found adhering to them making it a difficult task to free them without fracturing a large number, and causing a check to the plant.

Labels

In no other form of gardening are labels so important, for in a collection of any size it will be a long time before a cultivator can remember all the names of the plants. Not only are there specific and varietal but also generic names which have to be memorised. Unlike many other forms of gardening which can make use of common names, botanical names must be used in a collection of alpines, which is primarily a botanical collection of plants, in the truest sense of the word. The large majority originate either as imported living material or seed from nature's vast expanse of mountain ranges.

There are many types of labels on the market and a choice can be made to suit one's inclination and purse. There are aluminium strips, and white or green celluloid labels, both of which are written on with a waterproof ink. Those with a plastic base are useful and have much to commend them.

Naturally their usefulness is limited to the length of time they remain legible. Here a snag arises, in that the human element being what it is, the chore of rewriting a number of labels is often put off for what appears at the time more important tasks. Then it is often too late and more time is wasted in research trying to identify plants. This invariably happens when they are out of flower, making the task more difficult. Where cost has to be considered there is no doubt that the foregoing are cheap and good, provided their limitations are borne in mind.

I do not think that there is anything to compare with the soft leadstrip label. The initial cost of the machine is fairly high but once obtained labels can be run off *ad lib*. These are obtainable in at least two sizes and the names of the plants are impressed on them in a very short time with the machine. When completed they are indestructible. A special paint, made in a few colours can be bought with the set and this is rubbed into the recesses made by the machine, the surplus afterwards being rubbed off with a piece of rag leaving a very legibile name.

Another advantage is that lead labels already printed with the name of the plant can be purchased for a few pence each. This cuts out the cost of the printing machine but it will turn out to be a false economy if a large number of labels are required. Once printed the labels can be bent to any shape to suit one's own purpose as they are made of a lead alloy that can be bent as many times as required without fear of breakage.

Labels will also be needed in the seed and cutting pans. These may be of wood, cut 2 or 3 inches in length. They are dipped in Cuprinol to preserve them and then given a coat of white paint and marked with an indelible pencil. It will be found that they remain legible long enough for the purpose required, this being from two to three years.

CHAPTER FOUR

Loam. Leaf-mould. Peat. Chippings. Composts. Sterilisation.

When taking into consideration the many and varied types of plants which are cultivated in a collection of alpines it will soon be apparent that they will not grow in a standard compost. In a fully typical collection there will be plants from most mountain ranges of the world. Asiatic and occidental cheek by jowl, primulas from the Himalayas and the Bernese Oberland, aquilegias from Japan and the Americas, androsaces from the Swiss Alps, 'Vegetable Sheep', *Raoulia eximia*, from the South Island mountain ranges of New Zealand, 'Blue Buttercups' from the Burmese Alps and so on. In fact this list could be extended almost *ad infinitum*.

It is therefore obvious that composts which suit the high saxatile plants like the Aretian androsaces, drabas etc., which have fine, hairy rosettes to catch all available moisture of their natural habitat, demanding a poor soil and faultless drainage in dry atmospheric conditions, will not do for the woodland plants from the foothills such as the shortias, pyrolas etc., with their specially adapted smooth foliage allowing all surplus moisture to be easily shed; inhabiting as they do humus-laden soil in their native haunts and having a humid atmosphere. To grow them in cultivation side by side in a similar atmosphere, it is only by the use of shade and modification of soil that much success is achieved. Surprisingly enough, many plants which a few years ago were considered almost impossible to grow in this country, have now settled down and become, if not easy at least amenable to careful cultivation.

My opinion, though this must be a personal one and I must leave the reader to judge whether my own record will bear it out, is that in the past, far too much attention has been paid to the necessity of having numerous ingredients for making composts. Many experiments have been made and a great deal of research carried out over a good number of years by both amateur and professional growers. They often have good results, each claiming that this or that is essential to the well-being of the plants. This means that a large number of gardeners new to the growing of alpines in pans become bewildered. They are presumed to require an unwieldy stock of materials to satisfy their needs and are often discouraged from the beginning. This is only one aspect of the matter. Space too is required to store the different materials and in small gardens it is lacking, so once again a barrier is often raised between the would-be growers and their ultimate aim.

I too suffered from frustration when first starting to cultivate these plants. Lack of space was my greatest enemy, as I had but little to spare for storage. It became necessary therefore to experiment as to what was essential, eliminating this and that until I came down to the bare essentials. These have stood me in good stead over thirty-five years of growing alpines. After all, practical experience plus the record of achievement can be the only answer.

What I have tried to do in these last few lines is to save many keen growers both space and money, particularly those lingering on the threshold, needing but a little push one way or the other. Both are precious and the time saved is without doubt far better spent in caring for plants. The old saying that one can only learn by experience need not be true in our jet age; it is far better that one should profit by other people's experience thus curtailing one's apprenticeship.

Loam

This is the basis, with a single exception, of all the composts and must be considered the most important as it is from this that the plant derives eighty per cent of its nourishment. Like other ingredients, loam varies from one district to another and ranges from a light to a really heavy medium. Other things being equal, a medium heavy loam is to be preferred for by using this it can easily be lightened by the addition of sand, whereas if a light loam is chosen it cannot be strengthened. Another essential point is that the loam must be from a neutral source. That coming from a chalky district should be avoided, for a large number of alpine plants are calcifuge and a limy loam in the confines of a pan would be lethal. Lime can always be added, but I have not found this necessary, even for the most avid lime lovers. For these a top-dressing of limestone chippings will, through watering, release enough free lime to satisfy their needs.

The loam should be greasy in texture and full of well-rotted fibre, this being the residue of the grass roots from the stacking of pasture land from which it is made. Once a good source is found, it is best to obtain it always from this source.

Leaf-mould

It should be made from leaves of either oak or beech trees as there is no doubt that they provide the best source of supply. Care is needed if beech is used, for the tree is indigenous to limestone or chalky stations. There will be a certain percentage of free lime in the rotted leaves which could prove extremely harmful if used in composts for lime-hating plants. In the open garden this would not matter so much, as distributed over a wide area the acidity or alkalinity of the soil would be affected little. Contained however in the confines of a small pan and being possibly one-quarter of the whole bulk, results could be disastrous.

A test of leaf-mould is that it should be dark, moist and when rubbed between the palms of the hands it should flake easily.

Peat

There are many kinds of peat, some which are much too acid such as rhododendron peats containing bracken roots and sand or many of the dark blacky greasy types highly impregnated with sand which when drying out become dusty. If small quantities only are required the best type is that which is sold in bales or loose under various names such as moss, sedge or granulated peat. It should be granular in texture and not dusty when broken down. Peat is sterile, provides humus, opens the compost, retains moisture and, being slow to decompose, makes an ideal component for all composts.

Sand

This is often a source of trouble to amateurs. Many think that any will do, whereas the soft builders' sand, will bind the compost together. This has the opposite effect from that which is needed—a mechanical means to open the texture of the composts. There are a number of suitable sands, such as Bedfordshire silver or any coarse potting sand sold by good horticultural sundriesmen. After experimenting however over a good number of years the one which has stood the test of time is that known as Cornish silver sand.

This sand is used for all the composts noted here and also for drainage purposes as well, details of which are noted under the heading 'Drainage' (page 59). When sieved through different meshes it provides the open medium for seed, cuttings and all potting composts.

Chippings

A quantity of both limestone and granite chippings will be required for top-dressing the plants. The limestone is for plants which are naturally

Above: *Calceolaria darwinii* (see page 224)

Below: *Chrysanthemum alpinum* (see page 242)

Above: *Crocus chrysanthus* (see page 250)

Below: *Crocus scardicus* (see page 523)

lime-lovers and the granite for lime-haters. Both kinds of chippings should be bought free of dust, otherwise there will be a tendency to pack when used. It is far from easy to wash chippings that contain a good percentage of dust or small particles, to say nothing of loss when this has been washed away. These five materials will supply all that is needed for making the different composts and top-dressings for the plants in this book. The four mixtures will, if used intelligently, grow the vast majority of plants.

Composts

If all the different composts that have been advocated for the cultivation of both easy and difficult alpines were to be recorded here, a book many times the size of this volume would have to be compiled to hold them. There is no doubt that soil mixtures can be varied almost *ad infinitum* and good results obtained. After all a large number of plants will grow in almost any soil, even if only for a short period. It is therefore a mistake to be dogmatic over composts.

A number of cultivators seem to think that it is necessary to study these plants in their natural habitats and to give them similar soil to that in which they grow. This would be a good policy provided it were possible to imitate all conditions under which they grow. This includes not only a similar compost but also similar atmospheric conditions, temperature and, what must be the most important point of all, their long winter's rest generally under snow, conditions that are impossible to imitate in cultivation.

As I mentioned before, the majority of alpines are, like humans, very adaptable. They will grow in almost any well-balanced compost provided it is an open medium, which quickly allows all surplus water to drain away. Their will to live is great but bad drainage is a sure way to early departure.

To digress for a moment I have been asked many times both in letters and by questions at lectures, whether the John Innes composts can be adapted for growing alpine plants. I have tried both the seed and potting compost and found that they provide too rich a medium. You will certainly achieve a good-sized plant in a shorter period. Under these conditions, however, the plants tend to lose their dwarf, compact form, becoming much too lax on this rich diet. Another question often asked is cannot these composts be lightened and made poorer with the addition of sand and chippings. Unfortunately the John Innes composts are balanced mixtures evolved after a long period of experimentation and any addition of other materials to their formula upsets the balance.

In my first book on this subject I gave eight different types of composts, which did not include a special one for the difficult high alpines which require a really sparse soil to have any hopes of successful cultivation. Now, after further experimenting over the last ten years, I have reduced this number to four, including the high alpine plant mixture. These four have grown a large and varied selection of plants ranging from sun to shade lovers, also easy and difficult plants with success.

Preparing the Composts

When prepared the composts should have three general characteristics which are essential to good growth and flower. These are first the possession of a good physical condition that is granular in texture with the ability to admit air, a very essential need, and also the ability to absorb water at the same time allowing free drainage of the excess. Second is the need for a balanced diet. The compost should contain essential food substances to maintain life and good health—the heavy loam advised will provide this. Lastly a clean medium that is free from all harmful fungi, weed seed and pests. Partial sterilisation properly carried out will ensure this which is dealt with more fully later in this chapter.

As just mentioned it is essential that the ingredients used for making the composts should, as far as practicable, be clean from weed seed, fungus spores, pests, harmful bacteria, earthworms, eelworms and larvae of many kinds which attack the roots of plants. A great deal of harm can be done if infected composts are used, as some of the plants listed here will have to remain for a long period without repotting. The little extra care taken in assuring that they are started in a clean medium will be well repaid. Nothing is more disappointing than to have a rare plant suddenly collapse and die because a dirty soil infected, for example, with the larvae of the vine weevil, has been used. An impossible case you may say, but I can assure you that it is not so. I know of at least two cases where, owing to infected soil being introduced for potting up a collection of primulas, the whole lot were completely destroyed by this pest. It necessitated an expensive sterilisation of the rest of the alpine collection to eradicate the larvae.

It will only be necessary to sterilise the loam and leaf-mould. Both the sand and peat are normally weed-free and should not give any trouble provided the materials are stored under cover where no weed seeds can blow into them.

Chemical Sterilisation

There are two methods by which the materials can be sterilised, chemical and applied heat. Dealing with the chemical method first, it is a means by which a partial sterilisation can be obtained, comparable to soil that is heated to 140°F (60°C). There is not, therefore, a complete destruction of pests and diseases which requires an approximate temperature of 180°F (82°C). No check can be kept as with heat sterilisation, which is another drawback and also great care has to be taken to make sure that no fumes remain in the materials after sterilisation.

There are several chemicals available for this purpose but the one most commonly met with is commercial formaldehyde (formalin). The strength is generally about 40%. This should be further diluted to a 2% solution, approximately one part formalin to forty-nine parts water. At least 2 gallons of this mixture are required for each bushel of soil. All large pieces of soil must be broken down. The leaf-mould should be sieved to remove roughage and it is necessary for the ingredients to be well moistened. The material is then thoroughly saturated with the solution using a coarse-rosed watering can.

The soil and leaf-mould should be covered for two days with a heavy layer of sacks to retain the gas, which is highly volatile. After this treatment the sterilised material is spread out thinly to dry if possible in a cool, windy spot for approximately four weeks. If any smell of the fumes which are fatal to plant life remains after this time, the mixture should be left until such time as the smell has disappeared. Care is necessary when carrying out the sterilisation process for the gas is injurious to health in a concentrated form.

Heat Sterilisation

There are a number of reliable commercial heat sterilising units on the market, ranging from small sets suitable for the average amateur, to large appliances for the commercial grower. All these carry the maker's guarantee and, provided their instructions are followed, the results will mean a good weed and pest free product. In recent years a number of amateurs have, owing no doubt to the gardening press advocating clean compost, attempted to sterilise their own materials with varied results. In many instances this has resulted in the ingredients being either over- or under-sterilised, both with unsatisfactory results and a consequent disappointment, often resulting in a doubt as to whether there is anything in this sterilising business, or whether it is just another fad or sales talk.

Unless efficient means to sterilise the materials are at hand it is far better either to purchase them already sterilised or leave them alone. The word sterilise is a misconception when used in this sense. Complete sterilisation, which is what is obtained when the temperature is raised to 260°F (126°C), destroys all soil life. This is useless, for the resultant medium is one which cannot under any circumstances hold and maintain life. On the other hand a temperature below 120°F (49°C) will do little to rid the materials of harmful pests and weed seeds. Loam and leaf-mould should be heated to temperatures between 120°F and 180°F (49°C and 82°C), which alters the structure of the materials physically, chemically and biologically.

The alteration to the physical structure is due to partial decomposition of the humus content of the material thus rendering it in a condition more suitable for the beneficial bacteria to work upon. The heating also causes changes in its colloidal state, so when watered the whole saturates much more easily and the particles are more retentive of the moisture. There is a great chemical alteration in the soil as partial sterilisation not only releases but increases the available nitrogenous, phosphatic potassium compounds. This applies especially to the nitrogenous compounds. To maintain this state the heating treatment should be quick and the maximum temperature reached in the shortest time, followed by rapid cooling. The best method to achieve this cooling is to spread the material thinly in a cool spot.

Biologically the soil is altered when sterilised by heat. Depending on the optimum temperature being attained, pests, fungi and weed seeds are eliminated without any harmful results. Earthworms are killed at 130°F (54°C), fungi, pests and weed seeds at 170°F (76°C). If treated for about fifteen minutes at these temperatures there will be little chance of any injurious bacteria or other pests remaining alive. As noted above heat rapidly increases the nitrogenous compounds and an excess of the free ammonia produced can be detrimental to a compost, upsetting the chemical balance. From 180°F (82°C) to 212°F (100°C) the increase of the ammonia is particularly rapid; so for the amateur the optimum, when best results are obtained, is around 180°F (82°C).

For those who do not wish to go to the expense of either buying a sterilising unit or materials already sterilised, the following information will be useful provided a domestic electric cooker is available. I can recommend this method having used it with success over a long period. An average sized oven can accommodate up to a gallon in bulk of the material, either leaf-mould or loam, to be sterilised. On no account must these be sterilised together. They should be uniformly moist, but not wet. Large pieces of soil should be broken down, for if allowed to remain it will be difficult, if not impossible, for the heat to penetrate in the given time. If leaf-mould is being treated it should be rubbed down to remove any large, undecomposed matter.

The material must be placed loosely on a piece of dry sacking which is tied at the four corners with string and suspended from a grill placed high in the oven. After closing the door the current is switched on and the thermostat set to 350°F (171°C) or warm position and allowed to remain on for twenty minutes. The power is then turned off and the material removed. Should a gas cooker be used in place of the electric it is set to a lower temperature, No. 1 on the regulator. This gives an approximate reading of 290°F (143°C), for when gas is used the required temperature is reached more quickly. Cooling after sterilisation as noted before should be rapid and is best achieved by opening the sacking out in a cool windy spot and spreading the soil or leaf-mould out in a thin layer. After a few hours it will be ready for use. Only the amount that is needed at the time should be prepared. I have found that the useful life of unused compost prepared from sterilised materials is short. Naturally no soil or leaf-mould will remain free from infection for any appreciable period after sterilisation.

Composts for Plants in Pans

The loam and leaf-mould used for making the different composts should on no account be sieved but rubbed down between the fingers. Gloves of course can be worn if care of the hands is important. All the fibre found in the loam, rotted grass roots etc., should be retained and pulled out, cut into small pieces and mixed with the compost.

All plants like an open medium and this is more important in the confines of a small pan. Unlike conditions in the open ground where the balance is not so easily upset, the artificial growing medium is more sensitive and liable to detrimental changes. Oxygen is an essential part of the compost and is just as necessary to the plant roots as it is to human beings. This is the major reason why plants in pans thrive in a soil that is granular in texture. The coarse texture leaves minute air spaces where oxygen can be absorbed, holding it in store for the fibrous roots which will take it in all the year round. It is also a means of keeping the compost sweet owing to the air being constantly replaced after watering, by the rapid draining of these interstices which quickly refill with air.

Compost A

Equal parts of loam, leaf-mould and coarse sand. An ideal mixture for plants in pans which require a light, open, porous medium with good drainage. This is a good soil for all easy plants, sun loving bulbs and dwarf conifers.

Compost B

Equal parts of loam, leaf-mould, peat and coarse sand. A compost with a good body, more retentive of water but still drains well. Will grow all shade loving plants, bulbs and conifers satisfactorily.

Compost C

Leaf-mould, four parts; loam and coarse sand, one part each. This mixture has proved its worth for me over a number of years, after many experiments, for all dwarf rhododendrons and other choice ericaceous plants. It provides the humus so beloved by these plants, an even greater necessity when these are grown in what are often arid pans.

Compost D

Cornish silver sand, three parts; flaked leaf-mould, one part. A compost which will grow the difficult and rare high altitude alpines. A word of warning will not be out of place here. This compost must have the Cornish silver sand in the mixture, as no other sand will take its place successfully. There may be some hesitation on the part of a number of cultivators in growing plants in such a sparse medium. I can only point to my own success but I do not lay claim to having green fingers. To my mind there is no such thing, just 75% common sense and 25% good luck!

I do not advocate the transfer of large growing specimens to this mixture, especially those which are intolerant of root disturbance once established. All trace of the old compost must be removed without fail before planting in a compost of this nature, so it will be necessary to start with small specimens. More detailed instructions will be given in the chapter on repotting.

CHAPTER FIVE

Seed. Seed Composts. Division. Cuttings. Types of Cuttings. Cutting Frames.

In no other sphere of gardening is the study of propagation more essential than in that of the cultivation of alpines. Many are rare and difficult, as a number are not easily obtained in commerce, making it necessary to increase one's own stock to keep plants in cultivation. A good number of plants and seeds are introduced annually from botanical expeditions. These are normally paid for by private subscriptions or sponsored by the leading botanical gardens, with the result that it is many years before they become obtainable commercially. There are a number of reasons why such a scarcity of plants exist. A collection of alpines after all contains a selection from all parts of the world. It only shows the adaptability of plant life that the majority settle down in this country at all.

First of all the plant may not set viable seed here; if it does there is often a great possibility of it not breeding true. Aquilegias are notorious for this interbreeding but how can they be increased except by this means? Secondly some do not strike easily from cuttings, which is the normal method used by amateurs. More plants are increased by this means than any other, for this includes root and leaf cuttings, as well as the orthodox method of stem cuttings. A number of these small plants have a habit of almost flowering themselves to death, making it extremely difficult to obtain unflowered material for cuttings. Lastly all rock plants are small in stature when compared with other occupants of the garden, so that the amount of available cuttings is less.

There are five well-known methods of increasing the stock of a collection: by seed; cuttings which include leaf, stem and root; division; layering and grafting. Only the first four are of interest to the ordinary amateur, for grafting is to be avoided at all costs. The reason why grafting is often used commercially is that it produces a larger, faster growing plant in a shorter time. If applied to rock plants, those which are increased by this method will invariably, in a short space of time, lose all their

71

natural characteristics and become but a travesty of their normal beauty. There is one well-known exception to the rule and that is the extremely slow growing daphne, *D. petraea* and its variety *grandiflora*. Although these will strike from cuttings they will take many years to become flowering plants, whereas if grafted onto the taller growing *D. mezereum* they still retain their dwarf stature, but a flowering specimen can be obtained in two or three years.

As with all the practical hints put forward in connection with propagation, times and methods given can only be approximate, for plants vary from plant to plant, district to district and no two similar periods of the year are alike. Therefore common sense and experience must be applied when dealing with all branches of stock increase.

Seed

Seed is nature's normal method of plant reproduction and in a large proportion breeds true. If obtainable it should certainly be used, for every new seedling is a separate entity with all the vigour of its race. Unlike a cutting it is less liable to disease such as virus infections and inherent faults. Unfortunately, however, some genera, such as Aquilegia, Lewisia, Penstemon etc., cannot be relied upon to breed true from seed for they will cross only too readily with all and sundry kindred species. This is more prevalent in the confines of the alpine house where other species of the same genera grow in close proximity.

One consolation is that it is often possible for an outstanding new hybrid to appear or even a new colour break which is always a point to look for in a crop of seedlings. The raising of plants from seed can be profitable as well as a method of obtaining fresh blood. There is no doubt that plants grown from seed ripened on the parent in this country are much more reliable, as well as hardier than those from introduced seed. They also take more kindly to cultivation.

A number of genera produce seed with poor viability, needing immediate sowing if any degree of success is required. For example genera such as Anemone, Pulsatilla and Primula are notoriously bad germinators unless the seed is sown immediately. The Petiolaris section of the Asiatic primulas must be sown green, to have any chance of germination. Failure to do this generally leads to total loss.

Delay in sowing fresh seed will often lead to slow germination—up to three years is not an unduly long period. This is something to be avoided if space and time are lacking for the seed pans will have to be stacked in a cool spot and kept watered. Inspection at frequent intervals is also needed so that any covering may be removed, in case germination takes place.

Above: *Andromeda polifolia* var. *compacta* (see page 191)

Below: *Androsace hirtella* (see page 196)

Above: *Andosace imbricata* (see page 196)

Below: A selection of alpine house plants: back row, *Rhododendron pemakoense*, *Narcissus minor* and *Saxifraga* seedling, Engleria section; centre row, *Draba mollissima*, *Cassiope lycopodioides* and *Saxifraga* 'Petraschii'; front row, *Primula* 'Pandora', *Saxifraga* 'Boydii' and *Primula bracteosa*

Above: *Andryala agardhii* (see page 199)

Below: *Aquilegia bertolonii* (see page 204)

Above: *Arabis bryoides* (see page 208)

Below: *Arenaria tetraquetra* (see page 210)

Gentians are notoriously slow germinators if the seed is not sown when ripe, often not germinating at all the same year, if sown in the spring following their harvesting. The great difficulty if the seed is sown when ripe, probably late July and August, is to keep the seedlings growing throughout the winter. This is where an alpine house which is heated to exclude frost will help, by keeping them growing during this difficult period. No seed pans should be emptied for at least three years after the seed is sown, but they must be exposed to all available frost and snow which often has the effect of hastening germination.

The life of the seed is generally in relation to its size, the smaller the seed the less time it will remain viable. Normally the depth to sow should not be more than the size of the seed. With very small seed all that is necessary is to broadcast it thinly on the surface and, at most, cover with a very fine sprinkling of sand. The ordinary type of rock plant seed is best sown at the end of February or early March. This gives the seedlings a good six months growth during spring and summer, resulting in really fine healthy young plants already potted up for flowering the following spring.

Seed Composts

I am giving three types of composts which will be numbered 1, 2 and 3 so that they will not be confused with the potting mixtures. The number of the compost will be noted under the heading of propagation in the list of plants. These are not offered as the only types in which seedlings may be grown, but they have proved their worth over many years. As it will only be on rare occasions that a bushel of compost of any one of the seed mixtures will be required I will give the size of box which can be constructed easily to hold a quarter of a bushel, an amount more in keeping with the average amateur's need. The inside measurements of the box which is best made of wood are 10 by 10 by $5\frac{1}{2}$ inches deep. By doubling the depth a half bushel measure is available.

Compost 1

A mixture that has been found suitable for all the ordinary and easy types of alpine seed is the John Innes seed compost. It will be noted in the previous chapter on compost suitable for growing alpine plants that the John Innes mixtures were not found suitable. This applies however to mature plants, not for a mixture in which the seed of easy alpines are sown. It can be obtained ready for use from any suitable nursery or garden sundriesman. It must be correctly made up to the formula with the necessary ingredients and the loam must be sterilised as advised by the John

Innes Institute. Failure in this respect will certainly do a great deal of harm. Unsterilised soil will contain not only fungi and disease spores but also a good crop of weed which will readily germinate to the detriment of the alpine seed.

It can of course be mixed at home as required. Only the amount needed at the time should be made for its lasting qualities are strictly limited. All the following ingredients are mixed by bulk, not weight, and are best used dry after mixing, storing the compost for a day or two before use. Take two parts of medium-heavy sterilised loam from a reliable source, full of rotted grass roots. The soil should be rubbed down between the hands into a light granular texture. All fibrous material must be retained and if large should be cut into small pieces with scissors and mixed into the loam. On no account should the loam be sieved. This will spoil the texture of the finished compost and cause it to pack readily, a state of affairs to be avoided, for it is essential that the soil be open and granular in texture. Add one part of sieved peat, one part of Cornish sand and well mix the whole together dry. Afterwards to this is added $1\frac{1}{2}$ ounce of superphosphate of lime and $\frac{3}{4}$ ounce of chalk to each bushel of compost. If this mixture is to be used for plants which are lime haters the chalk should be omitted.

Compost 2

The more difficult and rare plants need a light, open soil in which to germinate and the following has been tried and found suitable. Equal parts by bulk of medium heavy fibrous loam and leaf-mould. Both the loam and leaf-mould should be sterilised and then rubbed down to a fine granular texture. The particles are better if small but should not be sieved. To this is added two parts of Cornish sand, after sieving through a $\frac{1}{16}$-inch sieve as the larger particles are not needed.

Compost 3

Shade-loving dwarf rhododendrons and other ericaceous and woodland plants like a more spongy yet still open medium. This consists of equal parts leaf-mould, peat and Cornish sand. The leaf-mould must be sterilised and rubbed down fine, the peat and sand should be sieved through a $\frac{1}{16}$-inch sieve, and the whole well mixed together.

Both composts 2 and 3 need a very fine sprinkling of superphosphate of lime, just under $\frac{1}{2}$ ounce for a quarter of a bushel of mixture or to be more precise $\frac{3}{8}$ of an ounce. The superphosphate is needed by the seedlings in their early growth. In fact it is essential as a plant food as soon as the seed starts to germinate, so it must be mixed with the composts, not applied afterwards. As an experiment sow some seed in a small pan containing a compost to which the fertiliser has been omitted and another with it, then note the difference in growth after germination has taken place.

Seed Pans

Pans are used in preference to the wooden flats for raising alpine plants from seed and there are three reasons for their use. First of all pans are rot proof, especially as it may be necessary to retain the pans over a period of years. If through any reason boxes have to be used they should be well soaked in a wood preservative like Cuprinol to retard rot. Secondly pans are less liable to attack from woodlice which are attracted to damp wood in which to make a home. They like nothing better than a supply of young seedlings for a meal. Lastly my own opinion is, a more uniform temperature and moisture content of the seed compost so necessary for good germination is obtainable by using the porous pan for the raising of alpine plants from seed.

All pans must be scrupulously clean for seed raising and these and all crocking materials are best washed in hot soapy water or water containing one of the many detergents in commerce today. Give these a good scrubbing with a pot brush to remove all dirt and stains. After this treatment a plunge into a strong solution of permanganate of potash, to act as a partial steriliser and a deterrent to formation of fungi, lichens etc. The pans should then be placed on one side to dry, but do not allow them to become too dry, otherwise they will extract all the moisture from the seed compost. Wet pans must not be used for they will cause the soil to adhere to the sides. Thus when attempting to remove the seedlings it will be found that both the soil and roots of the seedlings have become attached to the pans and a subsequent loss of seedlings is likely to occur. New pans must not be used as received from the makers, for they will have been kiln fired and need soaking for at least twenty-four hours before use. These also must be partly dried.

The preparation of the pans for raising plants from seed is simple. At the same time it is necessary to take care, for there is a possibility that they will have to remain in use for a long period. First of all a piece of perforated zinc should be placed over the vent of the pan. This is preferable to crocks which are often used, for the zinc will prevent the entry of undesirable pests such as woodlice, slugs, worms etc., from making a home in the drainage, to say nothing of the damage these will do to the young seedlings. After the piece of zinc, an inch of drainage material is put in. This can consist of broken brick, chippings or the residue of Cornish sand after being riddled through a $\frac{1}{16}$-inch sieve. On top of this a thin covering of peat roughage or flaked leaf-mould should be placed, just enough to prevent the seed compost from filtering down and blocking up the drainage. Lastly the compost suited to the seed is used and the pan filled to within half an inch of the top and made firm. It is essential that the soil around the sides of the pan be also firmed, otherwise there will be poor germination in this area.

It is a good practice to have a number of small wooden discs of different sizes or metal lids, of which three should be sufficient (Fig. 17), the sizes being 2, 4 and 6 inches in diameter. A small block of wood fixed

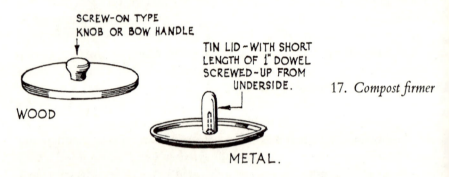

SCREW-ON TYPE
KNOB OR BOW HANDLE

TIN LID – WITH SHORT
LENGTH OF 1" DOWEL
SCREWED – UP FROM
UNDERSIDE.

WOOD

METAL.

17. *Compost firmer*

to each will allow them to be used in making firm the seed compost. It will be found that these three sizes will be enough for all types of seed pans. After completion the seed pans should be placed in a container holding 2 inches of water and left there until the surface of the compost darkens, then the pans should be removed and all surplus water allowed to drain away.

Seed Sowing

The seeds of alpine plants are bound to vary in size and shape, thus they will be found ranging in size from a pin's head down to dust. This means that different methods of sowing must be used in relation to size. All very fine and minute seed is best sown by mixing with four parts of coarse sand. A fine grade is needed here although if a $\frac{1}{32}$-inch sieve is available a sieving of Cornish sand through this will give the right medium to use. This mixture of seed and sand is sprinkled thinly over the compost in the seed pan and no further treatment or action is needed.

There are several ways by which the mixture can be sown evenly and thinly. Horticultural sundriesmen sell mechanical seed sowers; large sugar sifters, or one of the many cardboard canisters in which curry powder, pepper etc., are packed are ideal for the purpose. Whatever method is pressed into service it cannot be too strongly emphasised that the sand used must be dry. This can mean the difference between success and failure, as it will be found impossible to get damp sand and seed to mix uniformly. With larger seed a good maxim to follow is to sow to a depth that is equal to the width of the seed. Naturally it can only be applied to seed sufficiently large enough to handle this way. Intermediate seed between this size and the very small is best mixed with two parts coarse sand, sown thinly and given a very fine sprinkling of sieved sand over the mixture. The emphasis is on the word fine, just a bare coverage is all that is needed. Where practicable seeds large enough to handle are best sown individually, not too thinly, but leaving enough space between the seeds. Thus the seedlings can develop naturally after germinating, which results in sturdy young plants that can be potted on quite easily without too much root disturbance.

Although the majority of experts stress sowing seed thinly, the germination results do not always bear out the efficaciousness of this method. It has been found that especially with fine seed, a thicker sowing often brings better results. No satisfactory scientific explanation has to my knowledge ever been put forward as to why this should be so, but I have often wondered whether the fine seed which is produced in quantity is only partially fertile? Anybody trying this method of sowing should treat the word thicker with caution for only experience will give the correct answer, but a general idea is to use double the quantity of seed that would normally be sown.

Seed of dwarf orchids, rhododendrons, most other ericaceous and many woodland plants can be raised successfully by being sown direct on to a thin layer of sphagnum moss which has been laid on top of the appropriate sowing medium and well firmed down. No other covering is given but on no account must the surface be allowed to dry out.

There is another method of raising plants from seed, especially the rare kinds in vogue today. This is by sowing in the appropriate compost in transparent plastic containers. These are obtainable as small square or oblong cases about 3 inches deep and range in sizes of 4, 5 and 6 inches square and oblongs 4, 5 and 6 inches by 3 inches wide. Their original use was for the storage of food in refrigerators and all have a close fitting lid.

About $1\frac{1}{2}$ inch of compost is placed in the container over a little rough drainage after which a good watering is given, then all surplus is drained away and the compost well firmed. The seed is sown on top in the orthodox manner, then the lid is replaced and not removed until germination has taken place. No watering is needed at all after the initial application, but once the seedlings appear the lid must be removed, to allow air. The young plants should be pricked off as soon as possible. There is no doubt that this method has much to commend it to amateurs who have only a limited amount of time to spare, for after the seed is sown the boxes can be stacked away in a cool dark corner, needing only a daily glance to watch for germination.

Treatment after Sowing

When all the sowing has been completed, the pans should be placed in a frame facing north if this is practicable. If space is limited however the pans can be stacked one upon the other, these being covered with asbestos sheeting or pieces of slate. It is at this point that the amateur should carefully consider the position as to the amount of seed raising to be carried out. It must be remembered that when the seed has germinated it will have to be pricked out into individual pans and space will have to be found for these as they certainly cannot be stacked one upon the other.

I have found it a good idea for several keen amateurs to get together and each raise a pan or two of different seed, thus spreading the load, at the same time these limited collections will certainly benefit from the better attention that can be given to them. The pans must be kept moist, but should only need an occasional watering for provided the pans are plunged in a cool frame or stacked in a corner, protected from winds, the covering of asbestos or slate will do much to contain the moisture content of the compost.

Any watering required must be carried out by partial immersion. On no account should overhead watering be applied for not only will this possibly mean disturbance of the seed, often washing it to the side of the pan, but the water itself from the watering-can may be contaminated with spores of lichen, liverwort etc. The surface of the compost becomes a first class breeding ground for disease. In districts where liverwort is rife an infestation will quickly spread over the surface of the pan destroying the seedlings or even stopping germination. A daily inspection should be carried out after a week has passed, especially if the seed is sown while the weather is still warm, for germination can take place any time after this period. Some experts advise the turning of the coverings daily but this will not be necessary. The mere lifting of them will allow any condensation which has formed on the covers to run off. Naturally as soon as there is any sign of germination, the covers must be removed completely.

Potting On

With very few exceptions, all seedlings when they have formed their first true leaves must be removed from the seed pan and potted on, the exceptions being noted under propagation in the list of plants. Although germination may be spasmodic it is essential to do this, otherwise there will be a grave danger of the seedlings becoming elongated and weak. There is also the greater difficulty of removing them without damage to their root system, which can cause a severe check, if not total loss, of the young plants.

For the benefit of gardeners who are attempting their first raising of plants from seed, the first pair of leaves to appear in the seed pans are either dicotyledons (Fig. 18), these being invariably spoon-shaped and

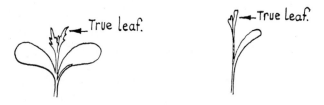

18. *Dicotyledons, monocotyledons*

are borne by the majority of shrubs and herbaceous perennials, or mono-cotyledons (Fig. 18) such as are produced by corms, bulbs, tubers and grasses which start life with a single lance-shaped leaf. The true leaves are those which are similar to that borne by the adult plant and appear shortly after the cotyledons are formed. The majority of monocotyledons should not be disturbed during their first year of life but left in the seed pan until the following year, then when growth commences they can be potted on. This can mean the difference between success and failure, a classic example being the genus Nomocharis which at one time was considered difficult or even impossible to raise from seed, owing to the seedlings being pricked off on their first year of growth and after dying down failing to appear the following season. If left in their seed pan until the following season they can be moved quite safely.

When removing the young seedlings from the seed pan it is essential to do this operation with great care. It is possible that more plants are lost during this period than at any other time of their lives. Any damage to the root system will invariably show in the adult plant if it survives to reach that stage. Most probably it will not, especially if the seedlings are those which normally form a tap root, the result being, at the best only a weak, deformed plant. The compost in the pan should be thoroughly moistened by immersion in a tank, taking care that the top surface is damp but not sodden. It will be found that provided the young seedlings have only just formed their first true leaves, they will come away cleanly, complete with roots ready to be potted on. The tool as noted in the chapter on tools and shown in Fig. 15 should be used for this purpose. It is surprising how quickly a number of seedlings can be removed from the seed pan and potted on without damage. If the seed pan has been well moistened it will be very simple to lift the delicate young seedlings from the soil without damaging or bruising them. The cotyledons form a collar which resting in the notch of the tool enables the seedlings to be held upright without touching them by hand and all ready to be placed in their new pans.

Overpotting at this stage of the young plant's life is not recommended as this often results in poor weakly plants. On the market there are small pans which are used extensively for cacti in their juvenile state. These are approximately $1\frac{1}{2}$ inch in diameter and 2 inches deep, making first class utensils for the seedlings first move. The depth is sufficient for crocking, drainage and compost, also a little top-dressing of small chippings round the collar of the plant.

The compost for the first potting-on should be light, but at the same time it will be necessary to have a certain amount of food to keep the seedlings growing, a very essential measure. Any check at this stage will mean a weak plant liable to fall an easy prey to disease. Compost B as noted in Chapter Four will provide the necessary food, at the same time its humus content will retain enough moisture without excess.

After placing a piece of crock or perforated zinc over the vent, followed by a little drainage material, top up with a small amount of roughage to prevent the compost from seeping down and blocking up the drainage. A half inch of compost should then be placed in the pot. The young seedling which is suspended in the tool (Fig. 15) is held in the centre of the pot and the compost should be worked very carefully around the small fibrous roots, taking care not to damage them. The soil is gently firmed in, leaving a small part of the neck of the plant free, where the stem joins the root. The space between this and the stem should be filled with Cornish sand sieved through a $\frac{1}{16}$-inch sieve to remove the dust. This top-dressing serves a twofold purpose. First it protects the most vulnerable part of the plant, the neck, from collar rot and secondly it keeps the surface of the compost from caking and drying.

The final stage is to place all newly potted seedlings in a north facing cold frame, and keep it closed for a few days until the seedlings have recovered from the check of transplanting. This will become apparent by the young plants showing fresh signs of growth. From then on air in increasing quantities must be given over a period of a week, by which time the seedlings should have become re-established. Once the plants have begun to grow strongly the light can be removed unless there is any likelihood of frost or very heavy rain. From this first potting they can be moved as required using the appropriate compost as the plants fill the pans with roots. On no account must they be allowed to become pot bound, for strongly growing healthy plants in their early stage of life should be the main object.

Under normal circumstances, a number, especially the vigorous types, will have filled their first pot in a month. Therefore a routine inspection should be carried out after the lapse of that period by taking the most strongly growing plant, removing the top-dressing and gently knocking the plant from the pot. This will give the grower an indication of the state of affairs at a glance. If the roots are showing on the outside of the ball of soil it will indicate that a repot is necessary. Once again it cannot be emphasised too strongly, that it is in the juvenile stage that all plants must be kept growing without check if a fine healthy adult specimen is the ultimate aim.

Division

It is possible to increase a large number of alpine plants by division, especially the easy growing species and varieties. In fact all herbaceous plants, with the exception of those forming a tap root, can be propagated by this method. It is not recommended generally that plants be divided, more so if they are well grown specimens as they will certainly be spoilt for a number of years. But it is suitable for small plants and those which have either become too large and unwieldy, or specimens which are showing signs of decay.

The most favourable time for carrying out division is in early spring when growth has commenced and the sap is rising. Early April until the end of May is the most suitable period, according to the district in which the plants are growing. In the cooler north and drier east the later date is more suitable, whereas in the warmer southern districts the early to middle dates will be ideal. These dates can be extended a week or two either way if the spring is late or advanced.

The division of the plant is carried out by removing the top-dressing of chippings and turning the pan upside down, then giving a gentle tap on the rim. The plant should come away quite easily. Care must be taken not to disturb the ball of soil at this stage, for if this occurs there is a likelihood of damaging the root system. The specimen should be placed in a bowl containing clean water and all the soil washed away from the roots, by using the fingers and gently probing the roots until the soil has come

away. It should be possible to divide the plant quite simply, making sure
that each section has a number of roots attached.

The divided pieces of plant are then placed on a sheet of brown paper
and dry sharp sand poured over the roots. This will facilitate the handling
of the divisions, for the sand allows the roots to be spread out when
repotting. If the roots are left without using sand it will be found that
they adhere together, making repotting a difficult task. A light compost
of equal parts leaf-mould, loam and sand should be used for the first
potting, after which the plant is placed in a cool shady frame, this being
kept closed until re-establishment has taken place. Air is then admitted
in increasing quantity until the plant is hardened off ready for its permanent quarters. It is possible to tell when the plant becomes established,
for it will be noted that at first the divided piece has a flaccid look as if
suffering from lack of moisture. Then when the roots have taken hold,
the foliage becomes crisper and attains a healthy sheen once more. All
flower buds must be removed from divided plants as all the energy has
to be diverted to root formation, vitally necessary for their re-establishment. Difficult, rare or delicate plants which normally only have a very
small root system, consisting of a few wiry pieces and which do not
root easily from cuttings in the normal manner should be carefully
divided, making sure that each division has a few roots attached. These
are treated as cuttings and placed in the cutting frame until re-established.

Cuttings

It would be safe to say that over 80% of stock increase carried out by
professional and amateur gardeners is by vegetative means, usually by
cuttings. Often it is the only means of increase, for a large number of
alpine plants do not set viable seed in cultivation. There is also no other
way to reproduce hybrids, sports and certain colour forms where these
will not breed true from seed. Grafting is often carried out to increase
shrubs or conifers, thus providing a larger saleable specimen in a shorter
space of time. This is especially true where stock grown on its own roots
is slow in coming to maturity.

This method of propagation is to be avoided at all costs where it is
desired to increase dwarf plants for the alpine house. The grafted specimen
will invariably be more vigorous and quicker growing than a similar
one rooted from a cutting. As the ultimate aim is to produce natural slow
growing plants, any departure from the normal procedure should be
avoided if the scenic balance is not to be overthrown and the true individual characteristics of the plant destroyed. There is one exception to
the rule here as mentioned earlier, and that is the delightful *Daphne*

petraea and its variety *grandiflora*. These, as cuttings, must be the classic example of the slowest growers on earth, whereas when grafted they will still be extremely slow. Flowering plants are obtained however in two to three years and the natural characteristics of the plant retained.

One of the greatest advantages of reproduction of plants by cuttings, is that, unlike seed in which there is a limited period every year to raise plants, they can be propagated by this method at almost any time by taking cuttings of either green, half-ripened or hardwood. With the aid of a little bottom heat to induce rooting, even the winter need not be an out of season period.

No matter what type of material is to be used for cuttings, it must always be borne in mind that on no account must they be taken from flowering shoots. These will not strike, or if they do will rarely grow into first class plants. This is easily understood, for their natural aim is reproduction of the species and as nature's normal method in this matter is the production of seed all the available strength is diverted to the buds with this aim in view.

There are five different kinds of cuttings from which new plants can be raised and these I propose to deal with in some detail. They are green, half-ripened, hardwood, root and leaf cuttings. The small line drawings adjacent to the notes on each type of cutting will help in giving a picture of the type of cutting under review. Details are given on how the particular cutting is prepared for insertion and this should be put into practice when cuttings are taken.

Green Cuttings

A large number of alpine plants can propagated by this method but a gentle hand is needed in preparing this type of cutting, for as the name implies they are taken from the green growing tips of the plants to be propagated. These are soft and delicate and care is needed when preparing them. The lower leaves are best removed by a slight upward pull, not downward, which will certainly bring away the outer covering of the stem, thus retarding rooting if not stopping it altogether. A razor blade is used and a cut made

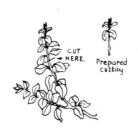

just below a node on the stem. This is the part where the leaves are joined to the stem at the base of which new shoots are borne. Roots will form more quickly here than at any other part of the shoot, although there are exceptions to the rule. The genera Atragene and Clematis are notable examples, rooting better from inter-nodal cuttings. The cut should be cleanly made, making sure that no bruising occurs, afterwards removing all foliage to one-third of its length. Only a small batch of cuttings should be prepared at any time, for green cuttings quickly flag. This must be avoided as much as possible, so only enough material should be prepared as can be dealt with at once.

These are best rooted in a closed sunny frame if at all possible, but a great deal of watering will be necessary for on no account must the compost be allowed to dry out. Many will root in a matter of days in a frame of this type. If rooted in a half shady frame, which requires less watering, from one to two weeks will suffice. Naturally everything depends on the season and type of weather experienced at the time the cuttings are taken, but in normal weather conditions May and early June are the best times. If spring is early, the date can be advanced a week or two, or retarded if spring is late or cold. All dates quoted are for the south of the country, in the Midlands an extra week's growth will be necessary and in the north and Scotland up to two weeks.

Half-ripened Cuttings

These are removed from the plant to be propagated, when the base of the cutting, where it joins the main stem, is mature. The growing tip,

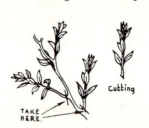

although still green, is firm but not hard. The ability to know just when the cutting is ready and firm enough to remove from the parent plant can only be gained with experience. It is recommended that this type of cutting be taken over a period, inserting them in the propagating frame with the date attached to each batch. The time taken for some or all of them to root will give the propagator a general idea of what to look for and he will be able to distinguish between a good or bad cutting. The cutting is ready if when bent it cracks or breaks readily. Most evergreen plants including dwarf shrubs and conifers can be increased by this type of cutting and the use of bottom heat will be beneficial in a number of cases. Not only will this speed up the time taken for the cutting to root, but also it is often the only way in which certain types of plants will root at all. June and July, and possibly the first two weeks in August are the normal times in which to take cuttings of this nature.

Hardwood Cuttings

The majority of cuttings which are struck from hardwood or well-ripened wood are from deciduous plants, the growth being mature and firm along the whole length of the stem from which the cutting is to be taken. These are generally taken from the parent plant at the end of October, but this period is only approximate, for it is possible to take this type of cutting right up to the end of the year with good results. The stem to be propagated should be given a quick sharp downward pull so that it comes away with a heel of the old wood attached. The heel is neatly trimmed, taking care not to cut into the core of the old wood. Should there be any foliage still remaining, this must be removed.

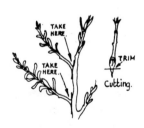

The prepared cuttings are then put into the cutting frame, close but not touching each other. Here they remain throughout the winter until the following spring, when rooting will commence.

Root Cuttings

This method is only another form of vegetative reproduction and is normally used where other means have failed, as when there is an inability to set viable seed, or to strike from cuttings in the orthodox way.

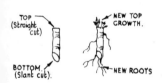

In some instances even where seed is set, the form or variety does not breed true. It is not a method which is to be advised if other means are available, for the specimen to be used for propagation is certainly spoilt for two or three years. Examples of plants which can be increased by root cuttings are *Morisia monantha*, lewisias and *Phlox nana ensifolia*.

The plant is carefully removed from its pan and after taking away all drainage material, the roots are gently washed free of soil and the thong-like roots, not less than the thickness of a pencil, are chosen for propagation. Only one or two can be taken if the plant is not to suffer unduly and these are cut into pieces ¾ to 1 inch in length. Smaller sections should be avoided, as they will not root. The base of the cutting should be cut slightly on the slant so that the propagator knows which is the base and which is the top when inserting the cuttings. Reversing the cuttings will almost certainly result in failure. They are not likely to strike unless placed in the rooting medium in the correct position, although I have heard of exceptions which prove the rule.

The pieces of root are best inserted in pans, the mixture being equal parts of leaf-mould and sharp sand. The top of the root cutting should be just above the surface of the compost. Another inch of Cornish sand is placed over this and the compost is well watered. The pan is then plunged in a closed frame where fresh growth will soon take place. They should be allowed to grow on steadily for six weeks to two months keeping the soil just moist. The cuttings can then be treated as rooted cuttings and potted on in the appropriate mixture. April and May are the ideal months for taking this kind of cutting.

Leaf Cuttings

There are a number of alpine plants which can be increased by taking leaf cuttings, and this generally applies to plants which form rosettes from a central rootstock. The family *Gesneriaceae* contains a number

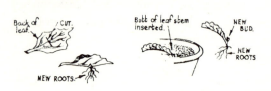

of genera which produce species that are capable of being increased readily by this method, examples being haberleas, ramondas, jankaeas etc. The varied species and forms of lewisias can also be relied upon to provide material for leaf cuttings. In fact as a number of this genus hopelessly hybridise among themselves, leaf cuttings can ensure reproduction of the species, hybrid or a good colour form. Provided care is taken when removing the leaf from the parent plant, there is no reason why 100% success cannot be achieved.

All chipppings and loose soil should be removed from around the collar of the plant to be propagated. The leaf must then be held firmly, as near the base as possible, and given a sharp downward tug so that the whole leaf, complete with its short basal stalk, is removed. It is very important that the base of the stalk is intact for it is at the point where the base was joined to the main stem of the parent plant that the embryo plant is contained.

Although not strictly leaf cuttings, a plant which makes a thick fleshy main stem, such as some of the European primulas, *P. marginata* and its varieties for instance, sometimes begin to rot at the apex of the stem, owing to water having lodged there. If the top is completely cut away back to clean healthy stock, then all foliage removed, it will be found that at the junction where the foliage joined the stem small fresh rosettes will appear. After a few weeks, but still while small, they can be removed and dibbled into rooting compost, where they will soon make sturdy young plants.

For leaf cuttings a pan should be filled with equal parts of finely sifted leaf-mould and Cornish sand. The sand should be sifted through a

$\frac{1}{16}$-inch sieve, well mixed with the leaf-mould and thoroughly moistened, and the whole made firm. The leaf cuttings are laid horizontally on the surface of the compost and the short basal stalk pressed into the mixture, making this firm so that the leaf cannot move, for firmness is essential for rooting. This can be accomplished by using a piece of bent wire or, what I consider preferable, a small stone placed over the base of the leaf. Not only does the stone protect the base but also this vital part is kept moist and cool. The pan is then placed in the cutting frame which must be kept closed. Rooting actually takes place quickly, but new rosettes are generally slow to form. A careful watch must be maintained for as soon as these are discernible the stone must be removed. After approximately four to six weeks the young plantlets will be ready to pot on in the suitable compost.

General Methods of Rooting Cuttings

As already noted there are a number of methods of rooting cuttings and those of root and leaf have been dealt with in detail. Now follows the way in which the normal cuttings are rooted, whether green, half or fully ripened wood. There are a number of different methods by which cuttings can be rooted, but only three will be dealt with here. These are in general use by both professional growers and the large majority of amateurs, and it will be found that the largest number of plants can be successfully propagated vegetatively by using any one of these methods.

North Facing Frame

This frame will be found most suitable for the majority of growers, who owing to business commitments have to be away from home the best part of the day. A frame of this description needs very little attention once the cuttings are inserted. In fact unless the weather is extremely hot, it will only be necessary to visit it once every few days, to make sure that the rooting compost is moist and to remove any dead vegetation. Another advantage of this type of frame is that the propagator is not restricted in the choice of plants to be increased, as would be the case of a frame in full sun. The sunny frame will be of no use in propagating dwarf rhododendrons or other ericaceous plants including woodlanders, which demand a certain amount of shade if success is to be achieved.

To sum up, if only one type of propagating frame can be employed, owing to space restriction, lack of time or money, then the north facing frame will be the most suitable. Irrespective of whether the plants to be increased are sun or shade lovers, this frame will give satisfactory results, the only disadvantage being that they take longer to root. The chapter on frames and Fig. 12 give all the necessary details for constructing a frame of this type, or a similar ready made one can be used. It is as well to emphasise here that a brick frame is better than any made of wood, metal or other material, for both the moisture and temperature are not subject to any great fluctuation over the twenty-four hours in a brick built frame.

Extremes of temperature are not conducive to the rooting of cuttings and the less fluctuation there is, the greater degree of success will be achieved. The high humidity content of a brick frame means that watering is cut to a minimum. The brick sides, being porous, absorb and hold a great deal of moisture, giving this off as the temperature rises during the day. Another advantage is that there is less likelihood of pests making a home in the base, which is rot proof, whereas it is at this juncture that the decay takes place in wooden constructions thus attracting pests such as woodlice etc.

Preparation of Frame

When completed and sited in a suitable position the frame must undergo preparatory treatment before use. This is essential for as with all gardening operations good hygiene should be practised if satisfactory results are required. All too often a batch of cuttings is ruined, either by pests or diseases owing to neglect at the beginning. Nothing is more disappointing or disheartening than to lose material for cuttings, which is often hard to come by, when in the first instance a few simple rules of cleanliness carried out would have prevented the loss. My own opinion is that the use of insecticides in the cutting frames should be avoided, for in the close atmosphere they can become extremely toxic. The cuttings which are already devoting all available energy in attempting to form roots will find great difficulty in combating this new handicap. I have no scientific basis for this theory only personal experience. Possibly the clogging up of the pores of the leaves by the spreader agent used may have a bearing on this but it would be interesting to have the opinions of insecticide manufacturers or research workers carried out with controls, to prove or disprove this opinion.

First of all the frame must be well washed down inside with a strong solution of permanganate of potash, about half an ounce of the crystals to two gallons of boiling water. This solution should be well worked in with a stiff brush. A small piece of cloth placed in the vent at the base will function as a stopper, so the mixture can be well swilled round. The next step is to allow the solution to drain away and then with a hose thoroughly wash down with clean water.

There are two schools of thought on rooting cuttings in frames today. One is quite modern and to date experiments show that it has much to commend it, especially for the amateur whose time is limited, for watering is cut down to almost nil during the time the cuttings are being rooted. This method is to place the cuttings in small pots and to cover these with polythene bags to exclude air and loss of moisture. A large number of alpines can be rooted successfully by this method. There are, however, exceptions to the rule and it will be found that a number of the soft herbaceous and evergreen herbs, with a covering of hairs on the foliage, have a tendency to rot under the prevailing extremely moist conditions. This does not mean that trials should be abandonded in attempting to root this kind of material by this method, for I do not think sufficient experiments have yet been carried out to condemn the polythene bag for rooting all and sundry material.

The other and older method is to use the bed of the frame for rooting the cuttings in. It has stood the test of time and the only disadvantage that can be found is that once a batch of cuttings has commenced to root it will be necessary to admit air, whether the other occupants have rooted or not. This can be overcome to a certain extent by removing all cuttings as they root, either to another prepared frame or potting them on in small thumb pots. There is no need to rush this work for even if the cuttings begin to root, a few extra days in a closed propagating frame will do them no harm. It will be best to deal with both these methods in some detail, then the propagators can chose the method best suited to their purpose.

First for rooting cuttings in pots enclosed in polythene, the frame should be filled to within 6 inches of the top with coarse river sand. Before placing this sand in the frame a liberal sprinkling of HCH powder should be spread over the base and sides of the frame. If the brickwork is damp, a condition which it should be in, the powder will adhere to the bricks. This forms a formidable barrier against a large variety of pests, for whatever the source of the sand, it is always possible that a certain amount of infection can be picked up before use. After firming the sand it should be well watered with a strong solution of permanganate of potash, dissolved in boiling water and applied when hot. Two teaspoonfuls of the crystals to each gallon of water is the strength required.

A uniform size of pot should be chosen. Those known as thimbles, that is 2 inches across the top of the pot will be found quite suitable, unless a large number of plants are to be propagated, for each pot must contain cuttings of only one species, hybrid or variety. It is better that the pots used are from the same cast so that they are uniform in size. It is preferable to keep these pots for this purpose only, then after use they can be sterilised before re-use. Once the holes are made in the sand and the pots inserted to their rims it will not be necessary to remake the holes when inserting a fresh batch of pots filled with cuttings.

They should be crocked in the usual manner. Over a little drainage a covering of leaf roughage is placed followed by the rooting compost. This should consist of two parts Cornish sand, which has been riddled through a $\frac{1}{16}$-inch sieve to remove the large particles, to one part of horticultural peat, which has also been sieved to remove lumps. Both these ingredients should be well mixed together dry and then pots filled to within $\frac{1}{2}$ inch of the rim and made firm. To ensure that the compost is firm, especially round the sides of the pots, not normally an easy matter with round containers, a small tool can be used. This will do the job quickly, uniformly and efficiently and can easily be constructed from a small disc of wood, a hardwood like teak or oak for preference, of $\frac{1}{2}$ inch thickness. The diameter of the disc should be the same as that of the pot just over half an inch below the rim. Attached to the disc is a small wooden knob for holding (Fig. 17). With this it will take only a few minutes to make the compost firm in a complete set of pots for the cutting frame, especially if the pots are all the same size as suggested earlier.

Before placing in the cutting frame the pots must be well watered. The water should contain enough permanganate of potash crystals to colour it a deep pink. This is best carried out by immersion in a tank containing enough to reach the sides of the pot just below the compost level. Overhead watering is not recommended at this stage. Not only will it disturb the surface of the compost which has been firmed, but it will also fail to moisten it completely should the peat content have been used dry. The containers can be left in the tank until the surface of the compost darkens with moisture. They are then removed and allowed to drain.

The second and more orthodox method of using a frame for propagation of plants by cuttings will now be dealt with. The empty brick frame is washed down as recommended above and then a small piece of perforated zinc is placed against the drainage hole at the front of the frame. Next, a liberal sprinkling of HCH powder is dusted over the base and sides of the brickwork, the bricks being previously damped down so that the powder adheres to the surface. The frame is filled to one-third of its depth with broken brick or rubble. This too should be moistened and sprinkled with HCH powder. Over the drainage material a layer of peat roughage (the residue after sieving) should be placed, using just enough to form a thin layer without leaving any of the drainage crocks showing. Leaf-mould roughage is not recommended, for unless sterilised it is rarely disease and pest free. This layer is to prevent the rooting compost from seeping down after constant watering amongst the drainage, eventually blocking it up.

The remainder of the frame is then filled to within 6 inches of the top with compost, consisting of two parts coarse sand to one part peat. After placing in the frame it must be well firmed down. The best method is to use a plank of wood large enough to stand on, then starting in each corner making sure that the wood is placed close to the brickwork, it should be firmed by treading.

Before use the compost in the frame should be well watered with a strong solution of permanganate of potash, two teaspoonfuls of the crystals to a gallon of boiling water and applied hot. Allow to stand for one day. Then give a good watering with clean water, rain water for preference if available. After this close the frame for twenty-four hours to obtain an even temperature throughout the rooting compost. The surface of the compost should be covered with a thin layer of Cornish sand which has been passed through a $\frac{1}{16}$-inch sieve, thus removing the large particles which are not required. The propagating frame is then ready to receive the cuttings.

The South Frame

This is a method widely used by commercial growers for rooting soft cuttings, which will root in a few days. It is a more economical proposition for the professional, to whom time is money. It is also useful for cultivators who are either retired or able to spend a great deal of time in the garden. They are then able to keep the necessary watch on this type of frame during any hot spells which may occur, for this has to be kept well watered at all times.

The frame is similar to the brick one just described but is sited in full sun. After using a little drainage in the base, impregnated with HCH powder followed by a thin layer of peat roughage, the rest of the frame is filled to within 4 inches of the top with pure coarse river sand for preference and made firm. Another product that can be used is vermiculite. This has the amazing property of absorbing up to 200 times its own volume of water, thus requiring less attention. It is necessary to obtain the grade specified for horticultural purposes, as there are different grades used for many commercial purposes, such as insulating against heat and cold. The vermiculite has to be soaked in water for twenty-four hours before use, thus absorbing the necessary amount of moisture that is required. Adding water to the dry material in the frame is both useless and a waste of time for under these conditions the product cannot absorb it.

A constant watch is necessary if this type of frame is used for rooting cuttings, for they must not be allowed to flag. The sand or vermiculite must be maintained in a moist condition at all times. There is a method which can be adopted by the general handyman, so that not only is watering cut to a minimum but there is less likelihood of disturbance of

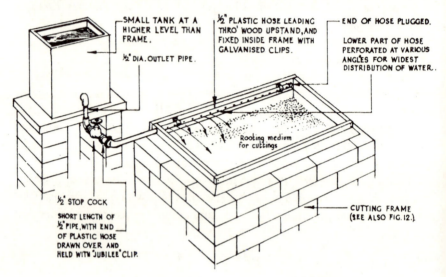

19. *Gravity-fed watering to cutting frame*

the cuttings. When constructing the frame a small piece of plastic $\frac{1}{2}$-inch hose, in which a series of small needle holes are made after sealing off one end, is fixed with galvanised clips on to the rear wall of the frame (Fig. 19). The plastic hose is joined to a union attached to a small tank. Any size will do, but one containing approximately two gallons of water will be ideal. Being gravity fed, all that is necessary is to fill it with water. This will spray into the frame of its own accord, without opening the frame.

Whatever method is used it is essential to keep the cuttings from flagging. On no account must the rooting compost be allowed to dry out, for this could wipe them out completely in a matter of hours. The frame-light should be given a light coating of whitewash, to restrict the sun's rays during late spring and summer. These could cause burning should there be any globules of water on the cuttings. As soon as rooting takes place, in a matter of a few days, the cuttings must be removed immediately. They should be potted up in a very light mixture, using equal parts of leaf-mould, loam and sand, for both the sand and vermiculite are devoid of plant food. The potted up cuttings are best placed in a closed shady frame until they have become re-established.

Frame with Bottom Heat

Chapter Two deals with the type and construction of a simple propagating frame. In this frame electricity is used as a means of supplying bottom heat, to assist in rooting cuttings which are difficult, or even impossible, by other means.

The frame, after being placed in position, should be prepared for use in the following manner. First small pieces of perforated zinc must be placed over the drainage holes. An inch of drainage material, old crocks, broken bricks or the residue of Cornish sand after being riddled through a ⅛-inch sieve, is then placed on the corrugated iron. Over this a thin layer of peat roughage is spread evenly, followed by the rooting compost. This should consist of one part finely sieved peat and two parts of Cornish sand, the sand having been sieved through a ¹⁄₁₆-inch sieve. These ingredients must be well mixed together dry and then watered after mixing again to ensure that the peat is really damp. The frame is filled to within 4 inches of the top, which is the measurement from the front of the frame, so there will be 7 inches of clearance at the rear. The compost is well firmed down by pressing with a flat board, making sure that the corners are well firmed too. A good soaking with a solution of permanganate of potash, followed by clean water as advised for the other frames is then carried out.

After allowing sufficient time for the water to drain away, the frame light should be placed in position and the heat turned on. The frame should be left for twenty-four hours, by which time the compost will have reached its maximum temperature. A small minimum and maximum thermometer is useful when using this type of frame, as it records both the lowest and highest temperatures over any given period of time. It is as well to take a daily reading, at a stated time each day, then reset for the following twenty-four hours. A small note pad left adjacent to the frame can be used for recording the temperatures, for any great fluctuations must be avoided as far as possible. It is essential to maintain a steady temperature while rooting cuttings.

The non-conductivity of the insulating sheeting used in the making of the frame will do much to minimise heat loss. This also helps to stabilise temperature changes inside the frame when the temperature outside is fluctuating. Should there be a prolonged frosty or cold spell and the temperature falls below 60°F (15°C) a lamp of greater wattage can be installed during this period. An ideal range of temperature for the striking of cuttings by bottom heat is 60°F (15°C) during the night, rising to 70°F (21°C) by day for spring, summer and autumn. This figure however can be safely reduced in winter to 50°F (10°C).

The fitting of a small thermostat in the circuit is a greater refinement. This is attached to the body of the frame, as near as possible to the soil, for it is soil temperature that is required. Under these circumstances it will be necessary to fit a 100-watt lamp. This will cover all outside changes of temperature and by setting the thermostat at 65°F (18°C) a steady, constant heat will be maintained both day and night.

Management of Cutting Frames

The earlier part of this chapter gives details of the different types of cutting materials which can be used, which vary according to the time of the season when they are taken. The small line drawings are self-explanatory and give the method by which the cuttings are prepared.

There are on the market today several types of rooting compounds, these being obtainable in either liquid or powder form. If used with care, according to the maker's instructions, they have proved very useful in helping to root cuttings which are difficult to root by orthodox methods. Possibly those in powder form are best for the amateur. Unlike the liquid, in which the cuttings have to be immersed for varying periods of time, it is only necessary to dip the end of the cutting which has been previously moistened, in the powder. All surplus is then shaken off by giving the prepared cutting a sharp tap with the finger. The cutting is then ready for insertion. The powder is made in three grades A for soft, B for half-ripened, and C for mature cuttings.

Care is needed for all types of cuttings to root them successfully. As with all other aspects of alpine gardening, attention to detail will certainly pay. The majority of alpine plants, especially those being grown in pans under glass, normally have very little available material for cuttings. In a number of cases every shoot is a flowering one, thus it is essential that what is available must be treated with care if a season's work is not to be lost. 'Green fingers' is a much abused phrase, and it is often offered as an excuse when things go wrong by saying, 'Oh! he (or she) has green fingers'. This is a fallacy and a little searching will reveal that not enough attention was paid, possibly to what seemed a minor point. To my mind 'green fingers' is only a synonym for care and common sense, for combined these will produce good results.

A hole large enough to take the cuttings, so that the base rests on the bottom is made in the rooting compost with a small wooden dibber.

The depth of the hole depends on the size of the cutting. It should be such that if the plants to be propagated are evergreens, the foliage is just above the surface of the compost when the base is touching the bottom of the hole. The cutting is then firmed by inserting the blunt end of the dibber in the compost round the cutting, and with an inward movement pressing the dibber towards the cutting. The cuttings should be put in rows close to each other but not actually touching. When all the shoots have been inserted and firmed, they should be well watered in, using a watering-can with a fine rose attached to settle the compost round the cuttings.

If the method to be employed is by using small pots enclosed in polythene bags, the cuttings are inserted round the sides of the pots in holes made with the dibber. They should be put in together in a single operation and should be close but not touching each other. With the blunt end of the dibber they can be firmed by pressing the soil against the cuttings from the centre of the pot towards the sides. Each pot should be well watered. After placing the polythene bag over the rim and fixing this with a rubber band, they are plunged into the propagating frame. It should not be necessary to water these again until rooting takes place, unless the weather is exceptionally dry, then all that is necessary is to plunge the pot into a tank containing a couple of inches of water for a few minutes. Water near to the temperature of the frame is best, for cold water from the mains will possibly retard rooting by lowering the temperature of the cutting frame.

When dealing with some of the small cushion plants, or those whose foliage is covered with hairs or felt, it is advisable to surface the rooting compost with $\frac{1}{4}$ inch of really sharp silver sand. This is best put on dry, just before inserting the cuttings. Thus when a hole is made with the dibber a trickle of sand falls to the bottom of the hole, which helps to protect the base and the neck of the cuttings from rot. It is at these vulnerable points that it invariably takes place. Irrespective of what type of cuttings are being used, either green, semi-hard or ripened wood, no more than those which can be dealt with in one season should be taken. They can with advantage be placed in water before and after preparation until they are dibbled in.

Labelling is very important and the labels should be prepared before the cuttings are placed in the frame. Nothing is worse than finding after placing a batch of cuttings in the propagating frame when a period of a few weeks has elapsed and rooting has commenced, that no name is available. At the time they were taken the propagator may think that it will be easy to remember the names of the plants. After a week or two, however, the memory can play some funny tricks, especially if there are several species or varieties involved.

There are a number of different labels on the market today which are suitable, including the old type of a wood strip, given a coat of white paint and the name and date written on with a garden pencil. Another form which is very popular is the small aluminium tag which can be impressed with a blunt pencil or marked with a waterproof ink. Whatever type is used, the name of the plant and date when the cuttings were taken should be written clearly, then placed in front of each batch of cuttings.

The following is the method I have used with success over a number of years. It has the advantage of providing a concise record from the time the cuttings are taken until they root or rot. Thus over a period of years it is possible to get a general idea of the best type of cuttings for different genera, species and varieties, also the time when they are likely to give the most successful percentage of strikes.

No. on label	Plant	Type of cutting	Date taken	Date rooted	Remarks
1	Aethionema kotschyi	Green	26/6/53	8/7/53	Sunny frame
3	Androsace spinulifera	Green	26/6/53	11/7/53	Sunny frame
6	Andromeda polifolia	Green	26/6/53	5/8/53	Shady
	Andromeda minima	Green	26/6/53	5/8/53	Shady
7	Cassiope fastigiata	Green	30/6/53	7/8/53	Shady
12	Pentstemon caespitosus	Green	30/6/53	21/7/53	Sunny
13	Crassula sediformis	Green	30/6/53	14/7/53	Sunny
15	Phlox nana var. ensifolia	Green	30/6/53	—	Did not root
16	Phlox bryoides	Green	30/6/53	3/8/53	Sunny
18	Sempervivum ciliosum	Rosettes	30/6/53	14/7/53	Sunny

A hundred small aluminium strips are obtained. Size is immaterial so long as it is possible to mark them in rotation from 1 to 100 leaving enough to go into the compost. As these are to be used again it is far better to use a good waterproof ink, so that they will remain legible for a long period. Next an exercise book is ruled up with the headings as shown in the specimen page and all the relevant details are entered as each batch of cuttings is inserted into the cutting-frame. A label corresponding with the entry in the book is then placed in front of each different type of cutting and remains in that position until the cuttings have rooted. It can then be removed and placed on one side until next required. It is far better to use the labels in strict rotation from 1 to 100. This should more than suffice for the average amateur's requirements in a single season, and the following year a fresh start can be made. Should there be a large number of plants to propagate, it will be found far better to number up to 200 or more than to duplicate the numbers which would be likely to cause confusion.

Both the heated and unheated frames must be kept closed until rooting has taken place. It will be necessary to keep an eye on the frames during the late spring and summer to see that no drying out takes place. This could prove fatal to the cuttings and when water is given it must be at the same temperature as that of the frame. Every two weeks a teaspoonful of permanganate of potash should be added to every two gallons of water and substituted for the plain water. This will keep in check any growth of liverwort, moss or lichen, as the spores of these seem to be ever present. The overhead watering which has to be carried out in frames containing cuttings is a ready means of introducing diseases. It is also beneficial, in that it is a weak fertiliser and can be of use to the cuttings once they have rooted. A careful watch should be kept for any sign of decaying vegetation on cuttings. This must be removed at once before it can set up general decay amongst the other occupants of the frame.

Watering of the heated frame when carried out during the winter months is best done with water at approximately the same temperature as the frame. The unheated frame, however, should only be kept moist and all surplus moisture which accumulates on the lights should be wiped off daily. A little air is beneficial when the weather permits and is best given before noon. The frames should be closed down to trap all available sunshine, which supplies a certain amount of heat during that time. In spells of damp, foggy or frosty weather it is better to withhold water until these conditions have passed.

As soon as the cuttings have rooted, which is generally indicated by new growth, carefully lift one from the cutting bed to see if the roots have formed. They must be potted on, for in the cutting frame there is little or no nourishment. If the cuttings are allowed to stand for a period after rooting it will be found that they produce long roots far in excess of the normal size in a good medium. Consequently when potted up part of the root system becomes surplus and rots away. This can set up complete rotting of the roots before they have a chance to become established.

The compost for potting up should consist of equal parts of loam and leaf-mould to two parts of coarse sand. For this mixture both the leaf-mould and loam should be sieved through a ⅛-inch sieve and the ingredients well mixed. The general idea is to provide a close grained medium which will enable the rooted cutting to build up a strong root system. When potting has been completed, the cuttings are placed in a shady frame which is kept closed until they are established and new growth has commenced. Air can then be given in increasing quantities until the plants are hardened off, after which the frame lights can be removed completely.

CHAPTER SIX

*Watering. Ventilation. Shading. Cleanliness. Routine Work.
Care of House. Repotting. Feeding.*

Growing plants in pans, either in the alpine house or frames is, after all, an artificial means to an end. It is surprising the number of growers who are under a false impression that the protection afforded by these is beneficial. There can be nothing further from the truth. Without exception no plant is as happy here as in its natural environment. Nature after all intended plants to grow outdoors, not in a house under glass. Their very structure demands access to direct sunlight in varying quantities. Whereas in the house or frames they are inevitably deprived of a certain amount of essential light, either through obstruction by the actual building, or the glass which is rarely clean. There is invariably a film of dust or condensation on it which will reduce the available light to a certain extent.

It is a matter of great importance that all available natural light reaches the foliage of the plants. It is here that chemical action takes place resulting in clean healthy tissue. The efficiency of this is measured by the amount of chlorophyll present, this in its turn depends on the amount and intensity of light which reaches the leaves. It is one of the reasons why all plants without exception benefit from a spell in an open frame during part of the late spring or summer. Not only is natural light essential, but no amount of artificial watering can replace rain and its attendant atmospheric conditions, a thing impossible to simulate under glass. Unfortunately for a number of reasons given earlier in this book, many alpines will not give of their best if allowed to remain outdoors the whole year. They have to be grown in the alpine house or frames, but provided sensible cultivation is undertaken there is no reason why good plants cannot be grown under these conditions.

Watering

There are three important points concerning the management of an alpine house or frame, namely watering, fresh air and cleanliness. All are

99

under the control of the cultivator and fresh air and cleanliness should present no great difficulty. The mastering of the art of watering is, however, not only the most difficult to acquire, but also the most important single factor in the art of cultivating alpine plants successfully. There is no doubt that a larger number succumb to over-watering than to any other cause. Even if the death of plants is attributed to some other cause, it is often the fact that the original weakening is due to errors in watering, thus leaving them easy prey to pests and diseases. A rough idea can be given with regard to watering in that evergreens need more water than the deciduous plants. Bulbs and corms require drier conditions once their foliage has died down. Large leaved plants require more than small, thick leaved less than thin leaved, and green leaf plants more than grey or silver, descending in ratio from dark green to silver grey.

October to April Watering

When in doubt, Don't. During this period, overwatering kills whereas lack of water is soon noticed and can easily be rectified.

Spring-Summer Watering

Provided the drainage is ample and working correctly a liberal supply of water can be given during the whole of the growing season. This is normally from the beginning of April until the end of July, but there are exceptions to the rule for a number of plants, such as *Narcissus bulbocodium romieuxii, Ranunculus calandrinioides, Primula allionii* etc., are early flowering. There are also a number of late flowering alpines including the autumn cyclamen, galanthus etc.

These must be kept moving once the buds are forming and during flowering. Any dryness at this period will certainly affect the plant adversely, often causing the buds to drop. Common sense must be applied when watering, for it must be borne in mind that plants from all parts of the world are being cultivated in one small area and their specific watering needs have to be catered for. Fortunately the majority of plants are easy and good tempered, as for the others, time and experience will be needed to successfully gauge the amount required.

I can only point out the few general basic principles and it is surprising how quickly one learns to tell whether plants need water by looking at them. A plant in good health and with plenty of moisture in the compost shows its well-being in the appearance of the foliage. Unless the soil is absolutely dry, under which conditions the plant will wilt and the leaves droop to relieve excessive transpiration the general appearance is of firm foliage with a clean bright look. Provided they are not directly in the rays of the sun the plant will be cool to the touch. It is not easy to put this down on paper, but as said before, the cultivator soon becomes an expert in knowing if his plants are in need of water. There is no doubt that plunging the pans in a mixture of gravel and sand on the staging reduces the amount of water needed. Plants standing on an open staging quickly lose moisture through the sides of the porous pans, owing to the amount of drying air circulating through the alpine house.

Good supplies of water during the spring and summer also help to wash the carbon dioxide out of the soil which accumulates there in the winter months. This has a deleterious effect on the plants and should be removed as soon as possible in the early part of the year. Whenever water is given, it must be given in quantity. It is of no use just to wet the chippings and the first $\frac{1}{2}$ inch or so of the compost. This will do more harm than good, often resulting in the bottom half of the pan and its contents becoming bone dry.

It is not easy to counteract this under-watering before the damage is done. The only way to make sure, if it is suspected that the soil is dry at the base of the pan, is to immerse the pan in water to within $\frac{1}{2}$ inch of its rim. Allow it to soak for at least half an hour, making sure that the water has penetrated the whole ball of soil, which if dry is, especially when full of roots, extremely water resistant. When watering the method is to water until the water comes out of the drainage hole at the base of the pan. During the month of August watering must be carried out carefully. At this time of the year the majority of plants are ripening their new growth in readiness for the next year's floral display. All watering should be reduced to a minimum. Remember the compost should be just moist, neither wet nor arid. I think, and this is only a personal opinion, that more plants are lost at this time than at any other. When I say lost I do not mean that they die at once. Excessive water in August will, however, result in a continued flow of sap with a resultant check in ripening, thus the growth remains in at best what is only a semi-ripe condition. At the onset of winter this growth soon becomes an easy prey to disease. Alternating spells of cold and muggy periods, such as are sometimes experienced in this country, often result in the total collapse of the plants.

Without exception all plants will benefit from an overhead spray of cool, clear water especially during hot weather. The best time to apply this is during the evening, after the sun has passed off the alpine house. Spraying while the sun is on the house will cause considerable disfigurement of the plants. This is due to the burning action of the sun's rays on flowers and foliage, caused by the water droplets acting as magnifying glasses. A fairly fine spray is best and the use of the hand spray with the finest nozzle will enable the operator to give the plants good coverage. The spray should be used in good weather from late April until the end of August, but is best confined to really warm days during August.

As with all gardening operations it is useless to be dogmatic and the times given here must be used with common sense. In the cooler northern counties, it may be necessary to withhold the spray until the end of May and then discontinue it at the end of July. August can be a really wet period, especially in Scotland. All these hints on watering also apply to the alpine frame and to plants in the plunge beds which, during the growing and flowering periods, require much water.

If the weather is excessively hot the floor and staging of the house should if this is possible be well watered several times a day. Cold mains water is ideal, for the purpose is to reduce the temperature of the house, and at the same time create a buoyant and cool atmosphere. A good plan is to lay a hose inside the house, on the floor and allow a steady trickle of water to cover the base of the house. This will certainly reduce the temperature by several degrees and at the same time create a certain amount of humidity, so beneficial to plants during a hot dry spell.

Even the keenest of gardeners must sometimes have a holiday. If taken in August, all that is necessary is to give the plants a good soaking and they should be fairly safe for two weeks. Should the holiday be an extended one, it may be necessary to call in outside help to overcome this problem. Naturally if someone who grows alpine plants is available so much the better, for they will at least have the right approach to the job. Alpine plant growers are as a rule friendly folk and it is normally possible to arrange for an exchange during each other's annual vacation. If, however, nobody is available, the following will do much to minimise any harmful effects to the plants.

Remove all plants from the alpine house and plunge them into frames, according to their preference for sun or shade. If the available room is not sufficient to accommodate all the plants ultilise old bricks to make up a plunge bed. Fill this with sand or gravel, or even dig a hole in the soil about 6 inches deep and after filling with sand, plunge the pans into this. As these makeshift plunge beds will be open to the weather, only the really hardy plants, hardy in health, not frost hardy, and with the ability to withstand our changeable weather, should be put into them. For example all dwarf conifers, flowering shrubs, phlox, campanulas etc., will be quite happy under these conditions.

The evening before, or better still the morning of departure if there is time, the whole collection should be thoroughly watered, that is until the water percolates through the vent at the base of the pans. This applies to all plants under glass in frames. Should the weather be wet, however, a not unusual occurrence in an English summer, those in open plunge beds may not need watering at all. This is where common sense must be applied, for as remarked earlier too much water in August can be harmful. Those frames and plunge beds fitted with shade racks should have these placed in position, for even if the weather during the holidays is dull, the plants will come to less harm than if the racks were omitted and a heat wave experienced.

A number of alpine growers often take their vacation in June, going abroad to the mountains of Europe to study and collect plants growing in their natural habitat. This raises an awkward situation, for the plants left behind will be either flowering or making new growth. It will be at this period that they need a sufficient supply of water to keep them growing during the period of absence. I am going to suggest two methods which can be adopted.

Firstly, if it is possible to enlist the services of a fellow alpine enthusiast all will be well. Before leaving on the journey a good watering should be given to the plants. It will then only be necessary for the stand-in to visit the house and frames every three to four days, to give the plants a further supply. Naturally no hard and fast rule can be laid down, for should the weather be wet or cool it may be only necessary to water once a week or possibly not even so much. This, however, can safely be left to the discretion of the gardener who is attending them.

The other method, which unfortunately is not so satisfactory as the first, may become 'Hobson's choice' if there is nobody available to carry out any watering during the holidays. This is as advocated for those taking their vacation in August, that is to remove all plants, whether flowering or not from the alpine house. The only exception to the rule is that bulbous plants that have finished flowering or those which are in bloom, can be given a good soaking and should come to no harm for a period of roughly two weeks. These by the way should have all flowers and buds removed unless seed is required. All plants are best plunged in a shady sheltered spot or shade racks provided, for the main purpose is to limit both sun and wind to a minimum. This reduces the possibility of the compost in the pans drying out. Irrespective of the weather on the morning of departure, all plants and plunge materials must be given a thorough soaking and the plants left without overhead cover except for sun racks during the whole period. Over-watering will certainly be less harmful than under-watering at this time of the year.

Autumn and Winter Watering

As the days shorten and the nights lengthen, so the need for water becomes less. The short days of autumn are often still, bringing in their wake a cold foggy atmosphere, densely laden with moisture. The large majority of alpine plants are already covered with a protective blanket of snow in their natural surroundings, which keeps them dry until spring returns. A compromise has to be reached in cultivation and water must be given sparingly, but on no account must they be allowed to get bone dry. Unlike their brethren under snow whose roots can reach down to available moisture to replace what little is given off by the transpiration in an almost static temperature and atmospheric conditions, plants in the alpine house in this country have to go through alternating periods of cold, muggy, wet and dry spells. Thus it is necessary to maintain a minimum of available moisture to counterbalance these varying conditions.

There is no doubt that plunging the pans to their rims in a gravel and sand mixture relieves the cultivator of a great deal of watering, for the large bulk employed will certainly do much to maintain an even moisture content and stable temperature during the autumn and winter. All evergreens should be watched carefully and kept just on the moist side, for they require a certain amount of moisture at all times. The hairy cushion plants should not require any further supply of water after October, if the plunging material is kept moist. If it is noticed, however, that the cushions are beginning to look lax or are starting to open, then it will be necessary to remove the pan from the plunge material and dip it in a tank containing approximately 2 inches of water for a period of ten to fifteen minutes. This allows enough water to percolate through the drainage into the potting compost but not enough to wet the collar of the plant.

It is a good maxim never to water on days when the temperature is lower than average for the time of year. Never water on dull, windless or foggy days. If required always water in the morning so that all available use of the sun and moving air will dry up the surplus. Should the weather suddenly deteriorate after watering, such as when a quick drop in temperature occurs, or mist and fog appear, it will be necessary to switch on a little heat. This helps to maintain a buoyant atmosphere as well as drying up excess moisture.

The above remarks also apply to those plants which are grown outside in the alpine frames or plunge beds during the winter. Naturally greater care is needed here. Without full protection including heat as afforded by the alpine house, the pans will be less liable to dry out during the winter months. The need for watering will thus be cut down to a minimum.

Ventilation

During the hot summer months or even in May and early June, the sun's rays are generally strong enough to raise the temperature to astronomical heights in a greenhouse which is poorly ventilated. This is a state of affairs which must be avoided at all costs where the growing of alpines is concerned. There is one type of atmosphere during spring and summer which all alpines abhor, a state where the house is both hot and clammy. It is absolutely essential to ensure a coolish environment with plenty of fresh air if the plants are to give of their best.

A correctly constructed alpine house has a complete range of ventilators, on sides and roof, running the whole length of the house on both sides. These are generally three to four in number in each side and roof. There are also either air bricks or shutters in the base, laid so that they do not face each other across the bottom of the house, under the staging. These allow a current of air to circulate without causing draughts, such as would happen if they were directly opposite each other. All these ventilators serve a double purpose, primarily to maintain a buoyant atmosphere so beloved by alpine plants and also at the same time to maintain a temperature compatible with their needs.

Ventilation, Spring and Summer

Unless the weather is wet with driving rain or there is an excessive amount of wind during the spring and summer months, all the ventilators should be fully opened, including any fitted under the staging. This ensures that the air is constantly changed, entering through the air bricks, door and side ventilators. As it is heated, it rises at the same time absorbing all excess moisture and leaves via the roof. This maintains a constant flow of cool air over and around the plants.

This is as near as it is possible to imitate the condition of plants growing in their natural habitat, for in the high alpine meadows and screes there is an ever flowing current of air. Photographers of alpine plants often have to spend an abnormal amount of time waiting patiently for a lull to photograph what seems to be a constantly moving object. If the weather becomes squally then the ventilators on the side facing the wind should be closed. The same applies should there be an excessive amount of rain, especially during heavy thunderstorms. The door is best left open as well, when the weather is hot, but some protection will be needed from birds and cats which can easily gain entrance and damage the plants. A framework of 2 by $\frac{1}{2}$ inch battens, the same size as the door and covered with $\frac{1}{2}$-inch mesh chicken wire net, can be constructed to overcome this problem. The frame is attached to the doorway by wooden buttons

(Fig. 20). This diagram will give a general idea of the framework and its attachments.

If all the plants are plunged, it is possible to admit a greater amount of constantly moving fresh air, this flowing over and through the foliage without actually drying out the pans. Complete ventilation will have to

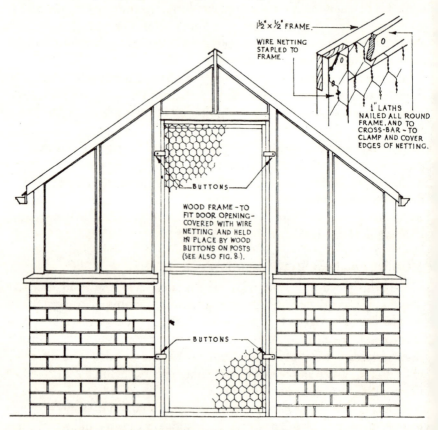

20. *Wire-netting frame for doorway of alpine house*

be watched very carefully if the pans are not plunged but left on the staging. The rapid movement of air round the sides would soon rob them of moisture, thus they would need a great deal more watering than those plunged. Plunging the pans is not only beneficial for the plants but is also a boon for the cultivator who has to be away from the home the best part of the day, or even three or four days. The plants can be left with confidence, knowing that they will not lack water during this period. These remarks also apply to the alpine frame, where in spring and summer complete ventilation is essential.

Ventilation, Autumn and Winter

During autumn, winter and early spring, air should be admitted on all possible occasions, to the alpine frames as well as to the house. The object here is to keep the atmosphere buoyant by changing the air when conditions permit without causing draughts. On dull, muggy days with little or no wind, all ventilators can be opened. If the atmospheric moisture content is high causing a certain amount of condensation to form as the day progresses it may be necessary to apply a little heat, just to rid the house of this excess. Should no heat be available it may be necessary to leave the roof ventilator open on one side and see that the air brick under the staging is free on the other.

Naturally the ventilators on the side away from the direction of the wind are opened, or if there is a calm, the regional weather bulletins will give possible wind directions for the area that are likely to arise during the next twelve hours. It is worth while to study these weather bulletins, especially during the late autumn and winter months. By intelligent interpretation of the forecasts they can prove of great value in deciding which course to take with regard to ventilation during the night.

When there are periods of rain and sleet the top ventilators should be closed on the side from which the wind is blowing. During snowy weather however it is better to shut all roof ventilators, for snow will creep into the house irrespective of direction of fall. If no heating is installed and there is a likelihood of frost, which normally occurs after bright days with any wind dropping as night approaches, the house should be closed down in the early afternoon. This retains all available heat for as long as possible. Should a night of keen frost be followed by bright early sunshine the house is best opened fully to prevent a too rapid rise in temperature as this can be harmful to the plants. A covering of newspaper will certainly help if placed over the plants should frost threaten, and may be left in position for a few days if the temperature remains low, without damage to the plants.

Fogs are much more dangerous than cold. They not only encourage the growth of fungi, but being moisture and dirt laden, more so near cities where the atmosphere has a high chemical content of a harmful nature, they can do a great deal of damage to alpine plants. Under these conditions since the air is stagnant and moisture laden, water soon settles on the foliage of the plants, especially those of a hairy or woolly nature. This covering is nature's protection against the ever moving drying atmosphere in their native habitat. The hairs or wool act as a shield against transpiration from the leaves and gives them the ability to trap every drop of available moisture.

When the great majority of these woolly plants are dry under snow our dirt laden fogs reverse the trend of nature by maintaining excessive moisture combined with harmful chemicals. These soon clog the stomata on the leaves often causing collapse and death. This is where the old theory that the alpine house should be closed on foggy days is discredited. The main purpose should be to maintain a buoyant atmosphere at these times, by opening some of the roof ventilators and those beneath the stages. The electric heater can prove of immense value by setting up convection currents, keeping the air moving which in its turn helps to dry and reduce atmospheric moisture. A small electric fan placed high in the house can also be used with advantage during foggy weather. The current of air set up will not only keep it from depositing moisture and harmful chemicals on the foliage but will also have a drying effect, so essential at this critical time.

It is not so easy in the alpine frame. Here overall conditions are much moister but by opening alternate side ventilators it will induce a slight current of air thus avoiding complete stagnation. All moisture which has a tendency to collect on the inside of the frame lights should be wiped off daily, to help reduce humidity.

None of these hints in themselves provides a complete answer, but they will do much to avoid casualties during foggy weather.

Shading

Shade in some form or other must be given to the plants from late spring until the beginning of autumn. Even avid sun lovers like the sempervivums and sedums resent being baked in the heat rays of the sun which seem to be intensified after passing through glass in the alpine house and frames. In their natural habitat many of the plants are exposed to sun without any form of protection from its rays; even the atmosphere is more rarefied at high altitudes. However, these are tempered with a cool, almost cold ever-present current of air. When these plants are brought down to lower altitudes and grown in an alpine house and in frames, the calm atmosphere coupled with the burning rays of the sun through glass will prove harmful to a collection unless some method of shading is adopted.

As explained in Chapter One there are a number of ways in which shading can be applied and constructional details have been given for making wooden shade racks for this purpose. I propose, however, to go briefly over several other methods that can be adopted. On the market there is a powder which is dissolved in hot water and applied to the glass with a brush. According to the dilution the colour ranges from pale to mid green. It supplies a light restful filtered light but has two disadvantages. Once applied it has to remain until the autumn whatever the weather, so that a cool, cloudy summer will induce a certain amount of drawing-up of the plants. The other is that it does little to reduce the temperature of the house for the sun's rays striking the glass cause heating to take place. Unless the house is large there may be extremes of temperature in sunny weather with this shading.

Scrim or muslin which has been treated with a preservative can be used satisfactorily. There are two methods of shading with this. First that of blinds fitted outside the house on galvanised spring wire (Fig. 7). This method has four advantages, it is cheap to buy and lasts for a number of years without replenishment. The shading can be adjusted to suit the weather conditions, during cool cloudy days the curtains can be drawn back. In the morning the curtains on the east side of the house are drawn across while the west side being in the shade is left clear. As the sun makes its way across the house the curtains on the west side are then pulled and those on the east side drawn back. This will give the maximum amount of light without exposing the plants to the harmful rays of a hot summer day. Last but by no means least, the shading standing away from the glass, allows a current of air to circulate between it and the glass reducing heat to a minimum. Some amateurs fix the scrim or muslin inside the house on runners but this really has nothing to commend it over being fixed outside, unless the house is only used for housing the plants in the winter and during their flowering period in spring and early summer (Fig. 6).

The last method is outside the scope of the ordinary amateur, although they have been constructed at home by people who are adept with tools. They are the professionally-made roller blinds, which are worked by pulleys and consist of slatted laths on cords or ribbons which are attached to rollers, these being pulled up and down on guide rails as required. The initial outlay is high but with care they will last a long time.

The above have been dealt with so that a choice can be made to suit one's own idea of what is required, taking into consideration the cost, all these can be amended or adapted for the prevailing local conditions. Whatever form of shading is used the side ventilators will have to be shade washed, either with a mixture of whitening and water or a coloured shade wash. Although shade material could be fitted it is not a practicable proposition. The south end too will need either a shade rack as described on page 38 or a colour wash, for here the sun will be on the glass for most of the day.

The remarks apply to the frames outside too. Here, where possible, the lights should be removed during the summer months and shade racks as described in Chapter Two fitted. If the alpine frame is being used in place of an alpine house it may be necessary to retain the lights. This keeps excessive rainfall from reaching the woolly cushion plants and also prevents damage of the flowers by wind as well as rain. A similar kind of shade rack as already described on page 43 can be employed or curtains could be made on the same principle as for the house. These cannot be used, however, if the lights are removed for they will cause drip during wet weather with disastrous results.

No hard and fast rule can be given as to when the method used for shading, whether it be colour wash, wood slats, scrim, or roller blinds, be brought into use. A great deal will depend on season and position of alpine house and frame. In the southern counties late April to the end of September is about right in a normal year, the northern counties and Scotland two weeks later in the spring and one week earlier in September, and on the mild western seaboard two weeks later in spring until the end of September. These are average times under average conditions, but how often do they apply in our erratic weather? All periods must be adapted, not only to local conditions, but also to meet the vagaries of our weather. Unfortunately a hot dry spell in April can often be followed by a cold wet May, so amateurs using a colour wash as shading may find themselves at a disadvantage if it has to be applied early.

Cleanliness

Cleanliness of the house and alpine frames is of the utmost importance, for neglect of this will do a great deal in helping to provide the ideal breeding ground for both pests and diseases. Although bound up closely with these it should be made a part of the routine work to be carried out as with other aspects of care and maintenance.

During the early part of autumn and before the majority of the plants are placed in their winter quarters, the alpine house and frames should be given a thorough cleansing. This ensures that they are as far as possible disease and pest free. A period should be chosen when the weather forecast is set fair for a couple of days. There is often such a time in early autumn, but not when frost is forecast, so that the work can be carried out in dry conditions. All pans should be removed from the alpine house and placed outside. It will not be necessary to plunge them so they can be left adjacent to the house, saving labour in moving them any distance. The whole house is then thoroughly cleaned, starting with the roof timbers or metal framework and using a hot soapy solution, containing a disinfectant. The woodwork or ironwork should be well scrubbed to remove all dirt, fungi and pests which may be lurking there. Before leaving the roof a hand syringe can be used, spraying all cracks and crevices where there are joins, as these are ideal breeding grounds for pests.

Next, using a hot solution of water and liquid soap, or one of the many detergents, the whole area of glass from the ridge to the eaves should be given a good wash, removing all traces of dirt and grime. After rinsing wipe dry with a clean cloth. The side ventilators and rear of the house are then cleaned in the same manner not forgetting the syringe for the cracks and crevices and also the glass. This is a good time to go over all hinges and ventilator stays with the oilcan. It is surprising how often this small important point is neglected, until the day arrives when a hinge breaks through being completely rusted up.

During these operations, if the staging of the house is made up as a plunge bed, it must be covered with old sheets of paper so that there is no contamination with disinfectant while cleaning the upper part of the house. Although in a diluted state, there is always a remote possibility of a build-up of harmful fumes should a warm spell occur, and any appreciable amount would be absorbed by the plunging materials.

All old rubbish such as soil, chippings, leaves etc., which has a habit of collecting on the floor and under the staging should be swept up and removed. The same programme of cleansing should be carried out on the walls and floor of the alpine house paying special attention to where the staging rests on the supports, for this is another ideal breeding ground for pests. If a plunge material is used, a good watering with boiling water to which has been added enough permanganate of potash crystals to colour it deep purple should be given. At the same time give the sand and gravel mixture a good mixing with a trowel, a mechanical way of helping to destroy worms, lichen and liverwort, which may have obtained a foothold. Leave all ventilators and also the door open for the following day, by which time the fumes will have dispersed.

The next day while the inside is having an airing the outside of the house should be cleaned down. The glass will need a good washing with a strong solution of soap or detergent, taking care that all dirt and colourwash is removed thoroughly. It is essential to obtain the maximum amount of available light during the coming winter months. After the wash down clean warm water is used to wash away traces of the cleansing materials.

A point which is often overlooked when this task is carried out, is that the operator often forgets to stop up the gutter down-pipes. The result is that the rainwater supply becomes contaminated and, if used, could prove harmful to the plants. It will be necessary to pack some cloth into the pipe where it joins the gutter and after washing down, remove the surplus in the gutters by sweeping out with a brush and wiping dry, afterwards removing the cloth. Attention should be paid to air bricks if fitted, making sure that these are clear and free from pests. With a powder blower then puff into the holes a liberal amount of HCH powder. This will retain its efficiency over the winter months and bar ingress to most pests.

Unless the shading material is of the fixed roller type, it should be removed, inspected and put on one side if necessary for repair, a task which can be carried out during the winter months. Do not leave it until the following spring when time is at a premium. If the shading is made of wood slats, these can be stored away neatly in the potting shed, garage or any dry place. Should scrim or muslin be the material used, it must be dismantled from the house and if possible washed, folded and put away, ready for next summer. It is surprising how much dirt is collected over the course of a season. If allowed to remain it can easily destroy the fabric. The same procedure should be adopted for the alpine frame and plunge beds thus ensuring a clean start for the winter.

When the pans are returned to the alpine house or frames, the sides and bottoms should be brushed over with a stiff hand brush to remove dirt and scum which may have formed. At the same time a careful search should be made in the drainage hole of the pans for any pests lurking there. Any decayed foliage and wood should be removed: this is an operation that must be attended to at all times of the year. It is doubly important during autumn and winter for mildew will quickly spread amongst vegetation, subsequently attacking healthy material if not attended to at once.

A weekly routine job should be to go over the pans with an old kitchen fork stirring up the top-dressing and lightly aerating the soil, which has a tendency to pack after constant overhead watering. It will also help to keep weeds and moss in check, stopping them from gaining a firm roothold with harmful results, owing to disturbance of the plant's roots if allowed to root deeply. Dying rosettes of cushion plants are best removed with forceps, afterwards filling up by working extra chippings from the side of the pan towards the centre. No attempt should be made to place compost in the vacant hole left by the removal of the rosette, for this invariably sets up rotting where it comes into contact with the minute leaves.

Old flowering heads and stems should be removed as soon as the flowers die off. Naturally if required for seed they must be retained and only a small proportion allowed to develop seed. Many rare plants, growing as they do under extreme artificial conditions, will attempt to the best of their ability to achieve nature's object, the propagation of the species by using all available energy in producing seed, very often to the detriment of the specimen. So it is far better to allow only sufficient to be set that can be usefully employed. Retaining seed pods on cushion plants can be dangerous too. Many a fine specimen of Androsace has been lost through neglecting to remove old flowering stems, a tedious job but far better than the death of a plant four or more inches across. Here I speak from experience, for it is these dying flower stems that attract the many mildew and other fungus spores which quickly attack the living healthy material. Working, as they invariably do, out of sight beneath the rosettes, it is not until the wilting of the adjacent rosettes is noticed that the damage becomes apparent.

A small sliding wooden tray is a useful gadget to fit on the upright wooden supports of the staging. This should have two check bars to prevent the tray from falling to the ground (Fig. 5). By sliding this along to the different plants which require attention, much labour is saved and first aid repairs can be carried out. There are many uses for this, amongst which the following can be suggested: top-dressing; plant inspection for diseases and pests; removing old wood; dead flowers, foliage etc. It also helps to maintain tidiness, for the temptation to throw the dead flowers and foliage on the floor of the alpine house is resisted.

Feeding and Repotting

I propose to deal with the question of repotting of plants as part of this chapter on Care and Maintenance. Although, strictly speaking, this operation should be carried out in the potting shed there are a large number, if not the majority, of cultivators who do not possess this refinement, so what is written here about the repotting of plants applies to alpine house and/or potting shed. The feeding of plants is also closely linked with repotting so is best dealt with here. The question of when to repot is a vexed one. This does not mean what time of the year, but how long between repotting. There are at least two schools of thought on this subject: those who advocate repotting often and those who say only repot when necessary. I am not going to be dragged into a battle between these schools, for as with watering, no hard and fast rules can be laid down and common sense and experience must be applied. My own view on the subject has always been to keep the plant growing. This means food, in some shape or form. The amount available in a pan is strictly limited and once used must be replaced, or there will be a gradual decline in the health of the plant. This can only be achieved in two ways: one by artificial feeding, which properly carried out gives ideal results and the other is by renewing the compost at frequent intervals.

When plants are young the majority (there are exceptions to the rule which are dealt with in the List of Plants), need to be kept growing, making a root system capable of supporting the plants over a good number of years. This is a state of affairs best achieved by repotting as soon as the roots have thrust their way through the ball of compost at the side of the pan. The roots, after finding their way barred, should not be allowed to go inwards again forming a knotted mass which will quickly become impervious to air or water with dire results.

By carrying out this system of repotting until the plant is housed in the largest pan practicable for its type, a good specimen is obtained which will be both healthy and disease resistant. Once the limit is reached, then the skill of the cultivator is tested to its utmost. It is from this point forward that a system of feeding to maintain health and floral beauty is necessary. A lesson can be taken from the Japanese, past masters of growing normal sized trees as dwarfs, for although the object is not the same, they induce dwarfness by judicious root and stem pruning. Health and vitality are maintained by feeding systematically throughout the life of the plant, which can be hundreds of years old.

A similar system of feeding can be applied to alpine plants. Let us admit after all, how many so-called dwarf conifers would remain dwarf if removed from the confines of a pan and grown outdoors? Yet it is possible to see large collections of these plants in good health which have reached the limit of practicable pan size. This is all due to careful top-dressing, with new compost worked in around the surface roots or a weekly dose of a mild, balanced fertiliser during the growing season. On the other hand I have seen conifers which are but a travesty of their natural selves. These are often bare in the stems and if opened, a great deal of dead wood and foliage is observed. When I have asked, 'How often are they repotted or fed', a look of horror spreads across the faces of their owners. In a voice of amazement the answer is, 'What, feed an alpine'? as though I have suggested something criminal.

Where, oh! where does this fallacy come from that to grow good alpine plants in pans one must starve them? That there are exceptions to this rule there is no doubt but these are in the minority. When I first started growing many years ago it was one of the first sayings one heard. 'Poor, poor, poorest of soil for alpines'. This is utter rot and I would like to kill it once and for all. Let the members of the Alpine Garden Society look at some of the early pictures of plants in their bulletins which not only won first prizes at the Society's National Shows but also the premier award such as the Farrer Memorial Medal, then ask themselves how far they would get today? For there is no doubt that when I first took up alpine growing in pans, to mention fertilisers was heresy, yet in Takedo's book on Japanese alpine plants common sense prevails with his hints on feeding of plants to ensure success in cultivation.

Even today how many books on alpine plants advocate the feeding of the plants? Are they afraid of the words fertiliser or manure? Yet they advise top-dressing. What is that but a feeding plan without which the plants will eventually die either by starvation, or by pests and diseases owing to their weakened state? Another fallacy that has been passed down is that alpine plants in their natural habitat are in lean, hungry soils, so in cultivation similar conditions must prevail. So be it, but ask yourself the reason why the majority of alpine plants have long rambling roots, especially in the barren screes and moraines. The root system for example of *Thlaspi rotundifolium* is almost impossible to collect in its entirety, the roots having become so long in their quest for food. It is not plain water the roots are rambling for, but a mixture of water and the necessary chemical constituents that can be absorbed by the roots to support life, otherwise we could grow plants suspended in plain water. No plant will make a larger root than that required to provide sustenance for the stems, foliage, flowers and fruit, and the reason that the majority of alpines have such a large root system is solely to search for food to support the plant. If this were available locally there is no doubt that the roots would soon adjust themselves to the available supply. How much room is there in a small pan for food to supply this demand? When freshly planted in a balanced compost the specimen thrives because food is available. By judicious watering sufficient nourishment to support life is at hand. After it has been used up however the roots will certainly begin to elongate in search of food and will continue to do so until checked by the sides of the pan.

One of the reasons why plants which are plunged will have to be watched is that the roots are attracted by the damp plunging material. No matter how sterile it was when first used, it will have accumulated a small percentage of available food washed out from the pans after constant watering. As an experiment leave a plant of *Helichrysum virgineum*, a gross feeder, in a plunge bed for a year and then try to remove it complete with the roots. It will be found that the amount of roots outside of the pan are at least five times that inside. It should now be apparent why plants in their young state must be kept moving by potting on as necessary into new compost. Once the ultimate size of pan is reached, life is sustained by careful feeding with a balanced fertiliser.

All the foregoing may seem dogmatic, but it is supported by facts. After all results speak for themselves and my percentage of prize winning over a number of years leaves me in no doubt as to what makes a plant grow and thrive. I am afraid far too many writers of gardening books are plagiarists handing down one fallacy after another and I would like to see personal experience play a much larger part in published works.

To summarise, as mentioned before, young growing plants which are to be repotted at suitable intervals should require no additional nutriment. Old, established plants however will need feeding. This should be a balanced liquid fertiliser diluted as directed for pot plants and should be given every other week during the growing season and weekly after the flower buds begin to form and until they open. As with watering operations enough fertiliser should be used so that it completely moistens the whole of the compost in the pan. After the growing and flowering season has finished, no more fertiliser should be applied. It will be necessary to allow the plant to ripen wood or seed for the next season. Failure to do this will, under the warm moist conditions of the alpine house and frames, keep the plants growing and producing new green stems and foliage. These are sure to be focal points for attack by pests and diseases and the seeds will fail to ripen in time to produce next year's flowers.

Repotting

Repotting plants is carried out according to the season in which they flower. Those flowering in early spring and summer are repotted after flowering, late summer and autumn flowering plants in April or May when the plants begin their new growth. This is a general rule for repotting, but nothing hard and fast can be laid down. If seed is required repotting has to be delayed until it ripens, otherwise there is a possibility of the seed being useless. There is also a chance that the plant will be weakened after its struggle to re-establish itself from the check of repotting as well as producing seed.

Some families, of which *Compositae* can be cited, make a tremendous amount of root formation in a short time. A number are gross feeders and so have to be repotted at frequent intervals. This can be safely done at any period of the year with the exception of mid winter or in frosty spells. All plants which have a tendency to outgrow their pans are far better repotted than allowed to become pot bound often with sad results. When the plants are eventually repotted the congested mass of roots will become matted together, making it extremely difficult to disentangle them for repotting without causing injury.

Many amateurs are inclined to overpot their plants. That is to say they use a pan larger than is necessary, thinking no doubt that this will save labour by repotting at less frequent intervals. Unfortunately it is not true and will lead to trouble. Irrespective of the amount of root made by the plant the whole of the compost has to be watered and unless utilised will quickly sour. There is a limit to the amount of moisture a plant can assimilate through its roots. A sour soil means an unhealthy plant and must be remedied without fail.

After a plant has been potted on for a period of approximately three weeks and does not appear to be in good health it should be turned out of its pan and inspected. By now the roots should have commenced to grow into the new compost. If they have not it is best to remove the new soil and place the plant into a smaller pan, just large enough to accommodate it and a small amount of fresh compost worked gently in. The plant should be placed in a frame and syringed daily, but not watered until there is a return to health.

Another danger of overpotting is that it may cause weak lax growth, cushion plants are prone to this fault which not only spoils their appearance but makes the entry of pests and diseases easier. Good living too may make plants produce an abundance of growth and foliage but very few flowers, a state which must be avoided. Certain plants like the Kabschia saxifrages will actually flower more freely if they are slightly pot bound.

When purchasing new plants, which should be young well grown plants, take note whether the roots are coming out of the vent at the base of the pan. Reject these in favour of a smaller plant which, although healthy, has a root system that as far as possible is comfortably contained in the pan. No plants which are obtained from an outside source should be introduced to the general collection before they have been repotted. There are two reasons. First, although they may be perfectly pest and disease free, it always pays to be sure. I have found root aphis on plants that looked perfectly normal until the old compost was removed from the roots and the white woolly substance shielding the pests was brought to light. An introduction like this into the alpine house could quickly affect a large part of the collection, the genera Primula, Androsace and Dionysia being extremely susceptible. Once a hold is obtained great damage is done before it is apparent, to say nothing of the difficulty of eradicating it when discovered. The second reason is that plants generally as bought from nurserymen are growing in a compost which is fairly rich. These people after all have to make a saleable plant in as short a time as possible, especially these days when labour charges are high. Bearing these two reasons in mind all plants should as far as possible have all the old compost removed and repotted in the type of soil in which it is intended to grow them. Naturally the time of year the plants are obtained will have a bearing on this, for it would be foolhardy to take such drastic measures in late autumn or winter. Spring is the best time to obtain new specimens, for they are beginning to make new growth, the roots are active, and they will move with the minimum of check.

All rare plants which are grown in compost D, Chapter Four, must be treated with care. It is important when growing them in this special compost that only small specimens are used. The shock of removing all the old compost from the plants should not be attempted with plants more than a year old.

Dealing with the repotting of new plants first, choose the type of pan required and put in a piece of perforated zinc. This should be followed by broken crocks or drainage consisting of the residue of Cornish sand after having been passed through a $\frac{1}{8}$-inch sieve, $\frac{1}{4}$ inch is sufficient, followed by another $\frac{1}{4}$ inch of the already sifted sand which is now passed through a $\frac{1}{16}$-inch sieve and here again the residue is used. Naturally it is better to prepare a fair amount of sand and the two sizes should be kept ready in separate boxes. Over the two grades of drainage is now placed a thin layer of peat or leaf roughage, just enough to prevent the compost from washing down and blocking it up. According to the type of plant being repotted a small amount of the appropriate soil as noted against the plant in the list, is placed over the roughage.

Remove all surface chippings from the plant and place the fingers of the right hand under the foliage so that there is a gentle but firm hold on the plant. Should the stems and foliage extend over the edge of the pan these must be gently squeezed towards the centre while removing the pan so that no damage is done to the plant. Holding the plant thus, the plant and pan is turned upside down and the rim is given a sharp tap on the edge of the potting shed bench, side of the alpine house staging, or with the wooden handle of a trowel. This should be sufficient to part the soil and plant from its container which is then lifted free.

Sometimes the roots adhere firmly to the side of the pan. This often happens if, when the plant is freshly potted up, a pan which is still wet is used. It may be necessary under these circumstances to break the container, so that as little damage as possible is done to the root system. Naturally care must be used, a few gentle taps with a hammer will break the pan sufficiently to allow removal of the plant. Although this is a drastic measure it is much better than forcing the plant out, minus a large proportion of its roots.

Another method which sometimes helps is to use a small rounded piece of wood. This should be just thick enough to go through the drainage hole, a thin piece would do more damage than good. Place the wood in the hole, turn the pan upwards and tap the wood gently on the bench, to release the plant. Care must be used, however, to make sure that the wood does not penetrate the ball of soil, destroying roots en route.

Once the plant is freed from its pan the drainage crocks should be gently eased away. If not pot bound the soil is removed, using a small wooden dibber to release the crocks from the roots. On no account must this be attempted if they are matted into a root-bound ball, for more harm than good will be done. Under these circumstances the plant is best immersed up to its neck in a bowl filled with water and the compost gently washed away leaving the roots free. The plant is then laid on its side and a generous sprinkling of dry sharp sand placed over the roots keeping them from becoming matted together.

The plant is now ready for its new pan. Holding it gently but firmly in the left hand it is suspended over the already prepared pan, the compost worked in with the right hand, spreading the roots as this operation is carried out and firming each layer of soil up to within 1 inch of the rim of the pan. If correctly positioned the neck of the plant will be approximately $\frac{1}{4}$ inch below the rim allowing up to $\frac{3}{4}$ inch for chippings.

The soil is best used in a dry state, not dust dry so the loam content would require a great deal of soaking to absorb moisture, but dry enough for the compost to run freely. This is fairly important, for if a damp soil is used not only would it be difficult to work in amongst the roots but would certainly pack when firmed. This could be a harmful state of affairs, for all plants depend to a great extent for their health on an open friable mixture which allows a rapid circulation of both air and water. When completed to about 1 inch from the rim, a light tap of the pan on the bench should settle the soil.

The pan is then stood in a tank containing water and as soon as the surface of the soil darkens it is removed and top-dressed with the suitable chippings, working these in gently. If the plant is a cushion, it is necessary to see that the cushion is both compact and firm. All plants without exception after this treatment must spend at least a week in a close frame and should be given a daily overhead spray if the weather is hot and dry. Special care is needed should the plants be potted up in compost D. On no account must this soil be allowed to dry out, but it is surprising how quickly the rarer plants respond to this treatment, provided as noted before they are small well-rooted specimens.

The repotting of plants already growing in suitable composts present no great difficulty, although those growing in compost D require a different technique and will be dealt with later. All that is necessary is to remove the plant from its pan and if the drainage is as advocated in Chapter Three it will fall away quite easily, leaving the delicate roots hanging loose without breaking. With a small pointed dibber, carefully loosen the soil on the side of the ball exposing a few roots in this area for it will help them to spread quickly into the fresh compost. Next a pan just larger than the size from which the plant has been taken is prepared with drainage and a thin layer of roughage, over which a little of the type of compost to be used is sprinkled. Hold the plant gently but firmly by its neck and lower into the new pan. Using a wooden dibber work the compost in between the hanging roots, spreading these out evenly, not bunched together in a mass. The old ball of soil containing the plant should then rest on the base of the compost. Holding it in a central position fresh soil is carefully worked down the side of the pan, firming each layer lightly before inserting more soil. A gentle tap on the bench when this has been completed to within 1 inch of the top of the pan will settle the compost and plant. It is then immersed in a tank of water until the soil darkens on the surface after which it should be removed and top-dressed with granite or limestone chippings, according to its needs.

For the rare and difficult plants which are growing in compost D, repotting is carried out with no disturbance at all of the root system. Naturally it is necessary to know the best time to carry out this operation. Although no hard and fast rules can be laid down, it will be found that this period is when the roots appear through the vent of the pan. A pan is chosen that will comfortably take the old one with its occupant, so that resting on the base of the new pan the rim of the old one is approximately 1 inch below that of the new. A little drainage is placed in the new pan over which a film of roughage and then a small amount of compost D is placed. Next remove all chippings round the plant in its old pan and, with a pair of pliers, carefully break away enough of the rim of the pan to bring it within the top of the old compost. The pan and plant are then put into the new pan. Fresh compost is worked down the sides and made firm up around the base of the collar of the plant. It is finally top-dressed with the appropriate chippings. Fig. 21 will give a clear picture of what is required. No doubt many queries will be made as to how often a plant can be repotted using this method. The answer as far as it has affected me is only twice. This will generally cover the life span of these rare plants, which are not generally long lived.

All freshly repotted plants are best placed in a shady spot for a few days to recover from their move. Should the weather be hot and dry an overhead spraying will be beneficial in the evenings. Irrespective of what type of plant is being repotted they should have a good watering a day or two before being repotted. Any attempt to repot a dry plant will lead to difficulties if not failure, as it is almost impossible, except with many

Above: *Asperula suberosa* (see page 213)

Below: *Boykinia jamesii* (see page 220)

Above left: *Calceolaria tenella* (see page 225)   Above centre: *Campanula barbata* var. *alba* (see page 230)

Below: *Campanula pilosa* (see page 233)

Above: *Campanula pilosa* var. *dasyantha* (see page 234)

Below: *Celmisia argentea* (see page 239)

Above: *Celmisia du-rietzii* (see page 521)

Below: *Celmisia hookeri* (see page 522)

hours of soaking to get water to penetrate to the centre of the old ball of soil. Once repotted the water will quickly percolate through the new compost leaving the old dry and this will soon be apparent, by the plants dying off in parts if not totally.

It will save a great deal of time and labour if a systematic approach is made to the task of repotting. As far as possible all plants requiring the

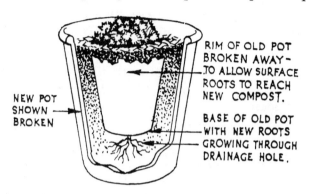

21. *Repotting plants in compost 'D'*

same compost are best repotted at one time, thus obviating the necessity of preparing several different composts at any one period.

Repotting Bulbs

Whatever type of bulbous plant is being repotted, and this includes corms and tubers, it will be necessary to place the freshly potted plants in a frame and cover them with a layer of peat or bulb fibre for a few weeks until they are re-established and have formed fresh roots. Once growth has commenced the plants should be brought into the light and all peat or fibre removed.

A general rule is that when potting up bulbs or corms, they should be planted twice their height deep. As a precaution against rot, a little sharp sand should be placed in the hole in which the base of the bulb will rest.

Top-dressing

As mentioned earlier in this chapter there comes a time when it is not possible to carry out any further repotting. Artificial feeding has to be resorted to, for the specimen to remain in good health. A number of plants can have this feeding supplemented by top-dressing and all plants which have a tendency to make a number of roots near the surface will benefit from this treatment. It includes most conifers, rhododendrons,

ericaceous and other woodland plants, all which will be noted individually
in the List of Plants, so that it is only necessary to give the method here.

Water the plant well the day before and then remove all moss or
chippings, with a pointed dibber. Carefully loosen up the surface of the
compost occasionally, turning the pan on its side to remove the loose soil.
Do not break or disturb the surface roots more than can be helped and

BOYKINIA JAMESII.   SAXIFRAGACEAE

COMPOST ·A. NEUTRAL.   N.W.AMERICA(PIKES PEAK)

POSITION SUNNY.

COLOUR   CHERRY RED.

REMARKS.
MUST BE PLANTED FIRMLY. WATER WITH DILUTE LIQUID
FERTILISER EVERY SECOND WEEK FROM APRIL TILL JUNE.

PROPAGATION
SEED COMPOST 2. FEB. DIVISION AFTER FLOWERING.

FRONT.

FLOWERING   REPOTTED.
9 ·MAY 1947.   18 4· 1946.
15. APRIL 1948.   25. 5. 1947.
19 "   1949.   29 5. 1948.
9   "   1950.   25 5. 1949.
                                   20 5. 1950.

AWARDS. 1ST A.G.S. LONDON MAY 1948.
        1ST   "   "   "   1949.
        1ST   "   "   1952.
        1ST   "   "   APRIL.1953.
        ROYAL HORTICULTURAL SOCIETY'S CULTURAL
                        28 APRIL 1953. COMMENDATION.

OBTAINED. APRIL 1945   DEATH AND REASON IF KNOWN.
ORCHARD NEVILLE
    NURSERIES.
                        BACK

22. *Facsimile of card index*

it is not advisable to go deeper than a maximum of $\frac{1}{2}$ inch. A mixture of the
type of compost suited to the plant is then carefully worked in amongst
the roots and firmed, afterwards well watered in and the chippings replaced.

If only to warn the unwary, a method which one sometimes finds
advocated for plants which have reached their ultimate size in pans is
mentioned here. This is an operation however which calls for great skill
and is not to be recommended with plants which are both rare and valuable,

unless one is willing to take the risk involved. This is to remove the specimen from its pan and then ease away very carefully a part of the old compost afterwards returning it to the same pan and filling in with fresh soil. This may seem simple reading it in print, but not only is it extremely difficult to work in fresh compost at all, it is just as hard trying to fit the old plant back into the same container, unless more compost has been removed than is good for it.

Record Pad

In every alpine house there should be attached, in some convenient position, a pad on which can be recorded everything of importance concerning the collection. The main items are dates of flowering, which assist in judging the approximate time that the plants come into flower, very useful for exhibition purposes; date of repotting and type of compost used, a temporary recording during the actual operation which is afterwards recorded on a card; a record of spraying operation, thus obviating the necessity of remembering what type of spray, generator bomb or aerosol was last used. Memory can play tricks, especially during a busy season. Although at the time most people think that they can remember, after a week I guarantee the number who can, and do, would be a fraction of the whole. There are a host of other little chores which are worth recording. Very often a picture can be built up in one's mind at a minute's notice of any particular plant in the collection, as to its habit, flowering, susceptibility to pests and diseases etc.

Card Index

I have found the above of utmost value in growing a collection of plants. It is a permanent recording of a plant's life history, from the moment it comes into one's possession, either as a gift, bought from a nursery, a rooted cutting or from seed. It is not only of extreme value when growing rare and difficult plants, where it often provides the clue to success or failure, but it also records the life of the plant from the time it is acquired until it either dies or is passed on, marking milestones in its history such as repotting, type of compost used, date of flowering, exhibiting, prizes won etc. The card index, a facsimile of which is shown in Fig. 22, may be thought to entail unnecessary clerical work. With the aid of the record pad, however, kept in the house on which all relevant details have been recorded as they occur, the index can be brought up to date at a period when time can be spared. I find that it is an ideal pastime during the winter months, when it can be done in comfort in front of the fire. At the same time one can relive again the pleasure given by the plants during the past season, tinged often with regret at the passing of an aged monarch, possibly only a few inches in height or across, or one of the many intractable children, wildling of the hills of whom it can be truly said, here today, gone tomorrow.

CHAPTER SEVEN

Pests and Diseases. Spraying Equipment. Insecticides and Fungicides.
Pests. Diseases.

Pests and Diseases

All alpine plants grown under glass are more susceptible to pests and diseases than those cultivated outdoors. No matter how light and airy the structure is, it is still an unnatural means and plants raised under these conditions cannot be as healthy and strong as those in their natural surroundings. Pests find the warm humid conditions greatly to their liking and, protected as they are, multiply rapidly. Their natural enemies, such as birds and other predatory insects who normally help to keep an infestation within reasonable limits, are absent; thus unchecked there is a great possibility of epidemic. A point which is often overlooked is that although the plants in a collection of alpines are small in relation to the majority of ordinary plants grown, pests are not scaled down in proportion. Consequently an attack can have far worse results to these miniatures, unless quickly checked, often killing them outright.

It will be necessary to keep a constant watch for an outbreak and immediate action taken if any signs appear. A bi-weekly check should be part of the routine especially during the growing season. March to October are the months in which pests are active and breeding is almost continual. It must not be thought however that they are inactive during other months of the year, even in winter a mild spell will almost certainly help to increase their numbers. Good cultivation of really healthy, virile plants should be the objective, as these are extremely resistant to both pests and diseases. It would appear as if Nature in her main object, the perpetuation of the species, has no time for weaklings and there is no doubt that they are the first to succumb to any infection. Fresh air, not draughts, obtained by good ventilation will help plants to resist infection.

Alpine plants which form tight rosettes must be regarded as suspect. They provide an ideal breeding ground, deep in the heart of the plant, rarely discernible to the naked eye and requiring a search with forceps and

125

magnifying lens to discover their whereabouts. A good maxim is to assume that the alpine house is never free from pests and on this basis a routine should be planned to combat what, if ignored, could mean disaster.

As a preventive, a weekly spraying during the growing season with HCH should be alternated with an application of a systemic insecticide. These can be bought ready for use, only needing dilution to the required strength. Alternatively, one can use pyrethrum-based insecticides which have the real advantage of being free of toxicity problems and readily available in several forms, including aerosols.

I would stress the importance of following the manufacturer's instructions implicitly when using any garden chemical. Under-strength applications are likely to be ineffective, or less effective than they should be, while over-strength applications could be damaging or even fatal to the plants being treated.

Which leads to the question: when is it best to spray? This is best done on light, airy days, preferably early in the morning before the sun is high to ensure that no scorching takes place. The ideal conditions for carrying out this task—unfortunately rarely encountered—is when the sun is obscured and a light breeze is blowing. A period of two hours should be allowed to elapse after spraying, and then a further spray of clear water should be applied to help rid the foliage of the residue of the spreader base as this tends to clog up the stomata of the leaves if left.

Where only one or two pans are infested it will pay to remove all top-dressing and turn the plant on its side so that the insecticide runs off the plant to the ground and not on to the soil in the pan. Make sure when spraying the insecticide that the underside of the foliage receives as much attention as the top, as it is generally here that insects congregate to feed and breed. With this method of spraying a primary object is to keep the soil in the pans free from insecticides which can be toxic in too large a dose.

Infestation by different pests depends to a certain extent on the geographical location. There is no doubt that in the warmer, drier southern counties the likelihood of an epidemic is much greater than in the cooler atmosphere of the north of the country. The north does not, however, have it all its own way, for there is a greater risk of fungus diseases in such climatic conditions to balance things up. One of the greatest problems in the south is the mite commonly known as the red spider mite, which thrives under the dry conditions prevailing there. It is difficult to eradicate successfully, unless prompt action is taken when an infestation is noticed. As it is not discernible to the naked eye, a great deal of damage can be caused by this pest before the leaves show the characteristic mottling, as if etched with a fine needle. The families *Campanulaceae* and *Primulaceae* (and within the latter, especially the Asiatic primulas and androsaces) are very susceptible to attack by this mite and once it has obtained a good hold it will be found extremely hard to control.

Fungus diseases should not give rise to any great trouble with a collection of plants grown in an alpine house, for the airy conditions required are not conducive to the well-being of this type of disease. Those likely to be met with are rust and forms of mildew, the latter being more prevalent if the summer has been wet and muggy. Rust is often found amongst the silver saxifrages and can cause disfigurement. The alpine frames and propagating boxes are more susceptible to other fungus diseases, the atmosphere having a larger moisture content, providing the ideal situation in which the spores of fungi can readily germinate. A constant watch must be kept and swift action taken at the slightest signs of an outbreak. Cleanliness will do much to avoid an attack, and on no account must any dead wood, rotting foliage, flowers etc., be allowed to remain, for these provide the ideal breeding grounds for such troubles.

Spraying Utensils, Insecticides, Fungicides

Before providing a summary of the pests and diseases most likely to be encountered in growing a collection of alpines under glass, details are given of necessary materials which should be kept in stock, to deal with any outbreak which may arise. These may seem formidable and will possibly bring misgivings into the ordinary cultivator's heart. Although you may never see half of the pests and diseases listed, it is necessary to give a comprehensive list of these as well as the most up to date remedial measures so that a personal choice can be made to suit the occasion, should this become necessary. To be forewarned is to be forearmed.

Let us have a look at some of the different types of spray available. First, the aerosol, which consists of a container filled with a solution of the required insecticide or fungicide—even, if needed, a combined insecticide/fungicide—which is delivered under pressure when a small plunger is activated (a plunger similar to those found on some paint sprayers). When this is done a cloud of vapourised chemical is emitted to give blanket coverage of the pest or disease which is causing trouble. Always choose a dull day for application and make sure that the ventilators and the doors (or door) of the alpine house are fully closed. Start at the rear of the house with the canister pointing slightly towards the roof, then walk slowly backwards pressing the plunger at the same time. The spray mist will then settle on the foliage of the plants.

The drawback to this method of pest and disease control is that the vapour is discharged into the air and not directly at the plant itself, for the very important reason that the propelling agent in the aerosol can cause damage—through freezing action—to tender flowers and foliage. Thus, the most vulnerable part of the plant, the underside of the leaves, where pests in particular tend to congregate, are unlikely to receive adequate attention. I doubt, therefore, if a hand-held aerosol spray is as effective as a spray which makes direct contact with the plant.

A piece of electrically-operated equipment which I have relied on to keep my alpine house pest and disease free for many years is a thermostatically controlled vapouriser. One can alternate the chemicals used and for ease of operation and reliability there is nothing to compare with it.

Applications of direct sprays can be made with efficiency these days, either with a small pressurised sprayer which is primed by pumping action before use, or, as is more often used, a sprayer activated by working continuously a trigger grip below the outlet nozzle. Both of these hand-held sprayers are easy to use, allowing complete flexibility of operation and, consequently, the ability to reach those parts of the plant (especially under the leaves) where trouble is likely to lurk. It is also, of course, possible to make use of a larger sprayer if this is desired.

Smoke generators offer another effective method of control for a range of pests and diseases—HCH being used, for example, in the case of pests, tecnazene in the case of diseases. When these are used, however, it is extremely important to make sure that all the ventilators and the doors (or door) of the alpine house are tightly closed, and there should be no attempt to enter the house again until the smoke released has completely dispersed. This may take several hours. The size of smoke generator needed will depend on the size of the house and advice on the capacity of the generator in question will be given on the label by the manufacturer, together, of course, with instructions on correct application.

The cubic capacity of your alpine house is calculated in the following way. Add the height of one side of the house to the eaves, to the distance from ground level to ridge and divide by two to obtain the average height. The resultant figure is then multiplied by the length and width (in feet) and this gives the cubic capacity of the structure. For example, if the height of the eaves is 5 feet, from the ground to the ridge is 10 feet, the length of the house is 16 feet and the width is 8 feet, the cubic capacity will be $5+10=15 \div 2=7\frac{1}{2} \times 16 \times 8 = 960$ cubic feet. When calculating the amount of fumigant needed the operator should work to the nearest 1,000 cubic feet. Given a cubic capacity of 960 cubic feet, a fumigant with 1,000 cubic feet capacity should be used, and if, for example, the figure is 2,100 cubic feet, a fumigant recommended for 2,000 cubic feet is adequate.

The systemic—as opposed to contact—sprays which are now freely available have added a new dimension to pest and disease control for these are readily absorbed by the leaves and roots and circulate in the sap of the plant in a highly toxic form. In the case of sap-sucking insects, the odds against them surviving are greatly lengthened for not only is the chemical more persistent than surface contact sprays but the insects do not even have to be present on the plants at the time of spraying for them to fall victim to it.

With both insecticides and fungicides a clear distinction must be made between chemicals which are protective and those which are curative. The importance of this distinction is that with protective sprays it is necessary to think well ahead and be fully alive to the troubles which are likely to affect particular plants. I am also particularly keen on alternating the use of chemicals, both insecticides and fungicides, whenever this is possible. This helps to prevent the build-up of resistant strains. Garden chemicals should always be carefully stored and preferably locked away in a container so that children and pets cannot gain access to them. If the label on a container becomes illegible, or if for any other reason it is no longer possible to follow the manufacturer's instructions precisely, do not use the chemical but dispose of it immediately.

To summarise, there is no doubt that for a large collection of plants a continuous thermostitically controlled vapouriser is best. However, where price is a consideration, smoke generators used at intervals will prove a good second, followed in order of merit by hand aerosols and sprayers.

It will be found useful to have ready the means to combat any outbreak that may occur, and although it is not necessary to have all the following, a choice is given so that cultivators can choose the utensils best suited to their purpose. All spraying machines must be kept clean and the pump mechanism oiled. The washers should not be allowed to dry out otherwise they will soon become brittle and useless, requiring constant renewal. After use sprayers should be washed clean with hot water and detergent, then rinsed with clean water. If this is neglected, residue of old insecticides or fungicides will soon gum up working parts and the very fine nozzles, since the spreader which is used (to allow the chemical to form a film over the foliage of the plants) becomes tacky when dry.

It seems to me to be very much to the good that so much trouble is taken nowadays to make garden chemicals as safe as possible and to eliminate from amateur use some of the specifics, like pure nicotine and neat metaldehyde (both still available in different form), which were so relied upon in the past.

For some years now there has been available an invaluable little booklet, regularly updated and entitled "Directory of Garden Chemicals", which is a guide to the wide range of chemicals available, their chemical and trade names and the names of the suppliers, as well as advice on their safe and effective use. This booklet is published by the British Agrochemicals Association and, at the time of writing, it is in its fifth edition. It can be obtained from the Association's address, Alembic House, 93 Albert Embankment, London, SE1 7TU for a modest price.

Quart Pneumatic Pump Sprayer

This type of sprayer operates by filling it to three-quarters of its capacity with material suitably diluted. The pump is used to obtain a good working pressure and is operated by depressing a lever which releases a valve. The gardener is thus able to use the other hand to turn over the leaves of the plants so that the spray reaches all parts.

There are several models of this sprayer on the market and it is best to obtain one which has not only an adjustable nozzle but is also capable of taking extension tubes to get the spray into awkward corners of the staging without undue disturbance of the plants.

Small Hand Sprayer

Many models of small hand sprayer are available with adjustable nozzles which can be set from a really coarse to a very fine spray. In addition to its use as a delivery system for garden chemicals, such a sprayer is also ideal, when filled with clear water, for removing dead insects from foliage after fumigation has been carried out or liquid insecticides have been used. It is also useful for damping down before the use of smoke generators.

Small Duster

An appliance which works on the principle of a pair of bellows and is used for distributing insecticides or fungicides in powder form. The action causes the very fine powder containing the insecticide or fungicide to float in the atmosphere and settle over a wide area. The one great advantage of this method is that the material has a greater persistency than a liquid spray.

Smoke Generators

The size required will be governed by the cubic capacity of the house (see page 128 for advice on determining this factor).

A Select List of Insecticides and Other Pesticides

Borax

A liquid insecticide, which ants take up readily as food for the nests, with the result that all the occupants, including the queens, are speedily destroyed.

Carbaryl

Now used instead of DDT (long banned for amateur use), Carbaryl has a useful life of up to two weeks from application. It is, among other things, effective against woodlice, caterpillars, weevils and leatherjackets.

Derris

An especially safe insecticide for use against many pests, including aphids, caterpillars and red spider mite.

Dimethoate

A systemic insecticide which also has a contact action, available as a spray for the control of aphids and red spider in particular.

HCH

Formerly known as BHC, HCH is available as gamma-HCH or lindane, in dust and liquid form.

Malathion

Very effective against a large number of pests and normally applied as a spray although also available as an aerosol and a dust. Must not be used on plants belonging to the *Crassulaceae*, which includes the genera *Sedum* and *Sempervivum*, as these would be damaged by such contact.

Nicotine

As mentioned earlier in this chapter, pure nicotine is no longer available to amateur gardeners. Nicotine shreds have been replaced by liquid formulations of nicotine. Such formulations are particularly effective in controlling sap-sucking insects like aphids and thrips.

Metaldehyde

Slugs and snails should not be found in a well-kept alpine house, but they do occasionally appear, perhaps brought in with plants from an outside source. There is always the possibility that they will infest frames. Neat metaldehyde is no longer available, but mixtures of bran and metaldehyde are, as well as pelleted and liquid formulations.

Methiocarb

A very effective slug and snail killer. It is not affected by the weather in the same way as metaldehyde.

Permethrin

This insecticide is an excellent control for white fly and all kinds of caterpillars, including the egg stages. It gives up to 21 days' protection.

Pirimicarb

This quick-acting specific aphicide is harmless to bees, ladybirds and lacewings.

Pirimiphos-methyl

This insecticide has numerous uses. It can be used as a dust against ants and woodlice; in liquid form (but not as an aerosol) against red spider mite, scale insects and other pests; and as a dust or liquid drench against such soil pests as springtails, wine weevil grubs and wireworms.

Resmethrin

This insecticide is effective as a control of the white fly, in the context of the alpine house.

A Select List of Fungicides

Benomyl

This systemic fungicide is a useful chemical with which to combat mildews of various kinds.

Copper Compound

A copper compound in liquid form used for the prevention of damping-off of seedlings. Any sign of this disease should be treated at once, using the mixture diluted at the correct rate, and watering the seed pans well.

Sulphur

Both green and yellow sulphur are available in puffer application packs, for use against mildew.

Tecnazene

This fumigant is used in both smoke pellet and smoke cone forms against grey mould.

Thiophanate-methyl

A systemic fungicide which is effective against mildew, grey mould and numerous other diseases.

Thiram

This broad-spectrum fungicide gives good control of grey mould, mildews and rust, with repeat applications. It is protective rather than curative, re-spraying being necessary at 10–14-day intervals.

PESTS

The following list of pests, damage caused and remedial action to be taken, are those most likely to be found in alpine houses and frames. It is possible that only a few will be encountered, but a more or less comprehensive list is given, including line drawings of the pests (not to scale) so that they can be identified with a fair degree of certainty. Where pests are concerned their rapid rate of increase can soon turn a minor attack into an epidemic, causing possible loss of valuable plants.

Ants

Ants are not normally found in pans of alpine plants but they can gain ingress to both house and frames from their nests outside, carrying both aphids (greenfly) and mealy bugs to plants for feeding.

CONTROL. A few drops of an ant killer placed on a piece of glass where the ants can be seen entering the alpine house or frames will not only remove the odd ant but any returning to their nests will carry the insecticide with them to the detriment of the whole colony. An insecticide containing HCH or pirimiphos-methyl in powder form can be used to deter them. Should a pan become infested, then the chemicals mentioned will control them quickly.

Aphids

Under this heading are included all the many different species of blackfly and greenfly (which are more numerous than any other type of pest) liable to infect plants under glass. These can cause great damage with the resultant weakening of the plants if they survive at all, for aphids take only a few days to reach maturity after which they reproduce rapidly over a considerable period. They are also noted carriers of the different forms of virus diseases which are impossible to eradicate in the plant once it is affected.

SYMPTOMS. Being sap suckers they cause distortion of growth and foliage, especially the growing tips, crippling new growth if not checked. Plants often look flaccid and have the general appearance of ill health.

CONTROL. Dimethoate, pirimiphos-methyl or HCH applied as sprays, or the last-mentioned as a smoke. Dimethoate is a systemic insecticide best applied in spring and early summer when the sap is rising as, being absorbed into the sap, it is highly toxic to all forms of aphids. This is an all the year round pest and a watch during mild spells in winter will often lead to a discovery of infestation. Indeed, constant vigilance is necessary if this pest is to be kept under control. As noted above, the symptoms are easily spotted. I would suggest varying your control chemicals as much as possible also.

There is one species of aphid which can be highly destructive in a collection where members of the family *Primulaceae* are grown. It is known as primula root aphid and if introduced into the house or frame will quickly infest all genera, species, hybrids and varieties of that family. The symptoms are that attacked plants appear unhealthy and leaves show yellowing and wilting. All pan plants of *Primulaceae* brought in from an outside source should be thoroughly inspected before allowing them into the alpine house or frames where if they have primula root aphid they will quickly create an epidemic. There are two likely spots on the plant where the pests tend to congregate, these are at the collar and the roots. With this aphid, as with others, be constantly watching for signs of attack, especially in spring and summer.

The plant should be carefully removed from its pan or pot and if the roots are covered with a white, woolly, sticky substance there is no doubt that aphids are present. It is the waxy, woolly covering which protects the pest from normal spraying with insecticide that should now receive attention, separating it from the roots—so far as this is possible, for only those which are exposed can be attended to—before applying the spray.

Doing this will facilitate the absorption of the systemic insecticides and so give a more rapid control of the pest.

Fortunately, we now have systemic insecticides to help us with this battle and the aphids feeding on the sap of the plants is vulnerable to this method of attack from the inside, as it were, of its protective covering of wool. The application of the recommended systemics in early spring by spraying the surface of the soil is a sure preventive, but should an infected plant be introduced, it should be sprayed immediately, irrespective of season.

Caterpillars

These pests can do a great deal of damage in a very short space of time and often adapt their colour to their surroundings so that they are difficult to detect. There are many kinds amongst which the larvae of the angle-shades and tortrix moth can be quoted as examples.

SYMPTOMS. Leaves and the soft succulent stems of plants are eaten away. Leaves gummed together to form a cocoon will certainly contain a caterpillar. Generally found from May to October.

CONTROL. Derris, HCH and carbaryl dusts; pirimiphos-methyl or permethrin sprays. Also combined insecticide containing resmethrin, trichlorphon and malathion applied as spray. Remove and destroy leaves gummed together.

Capsid Bugs

Although not a common pest where alpines are grown, they are occasionally found and it is necessary to take immediate action if noticed.

SYMPTOMS. Any puckering of the foliage should be investigated, for these pests cause a great deal of damage by sucking the sap and also attacking the growing tips. Many members of the family *Compositae* are liable to attack by this pest and they are generally found to be most active from June to October.

CONTROL. Nicotine, HCH, malathion or dimethoate applied as a spray to plants in alpine house or frame.

Mealy Bugs

This is another sap sucking pest which can do a great deal of damage in a short period. They seem to have a liking for succulents and a watch on plants from the family *Crassulaceae*, such as the genera Sempervivum and Sedum, should be kept. White patches of a woolly substance on the stems and foliage are almost sure to be the protective covering of these insects. SYMPTOMS. Distortion of foliage in succulents. This is noticed as an irregular growing leaf or stem, due to sap restriction through removal by these pests and the presence of the white wool will help in identification.

CONTROL. A systemic insecticide gives the best method of control, both in the house and frames and should be applied in late spring or early summer; this will do much to prevent an attack. Malathion can be used on all plants with the exception of those belonging to the family *Crassulaceae* or if there is a bad infestation, a smoke generator containing HCH will give good control in the alpine house.

Millipedes

These should not be present in the soil if good hygiene is practised and the soil sterilised before use, but as often happens a stray may be introduced accidentally or bought in a pan which contains infected compost.

SYMPTOMS. A total collapse of the plant, and on examination it is found that the stem at soil or just below soil level is eaten away and there are pests present.

CONTROL. Prevention by using clean compost is really the only answer, for generally there is no cure as the plant is normally damaged beyond recovery. If there is a suspicion that these pests are present a good dusting of HCH powder will help.

Red Spider Mite

A dangerous pest having no relation to spiders, the name being descriptive, for it looks like a minute edition of that family. As it thrives in a warm dry atmosphere the alpine house, and to a lesser degree the frames, make ideal breeding grounds and naturally it is more prevalent in the drier, warmer southern counties than in the cooler, moister north. There are two families which are very susceptible to this pest and these act as host plants if allowed to become infested. The two in question are *Campanulaceae* and *Primulaceae*. Of the latter the Asiatic primulas and the genus Androsace are extremely vulnerable to attack.

SYMPTOMS. All foliage which turns yellow prematurely or mottled and on examination is found to be covered with thin lines, as if etched with a needle, is suspect and should be examined with a good lens, for this pest is not usually discernible with the naked eye. The insect is pale and whitish in its juvenile state becoming reddish brown when adult, with four pairs of legs.

CONTROL. Red spider mite is one of the most difficult pests to control under alpine house conditions, where the atmosphere is generally drier than in the open garden. It is much more persistent in the south than in the northern and western parts of Britain. Red spider mite is a sap-sucking insect which has several distinct stages in its life cycle and no one insecticide will give complete control. It is, therefore, necessary to use insecticides based on the following four chemicals, in succession, during all periods of the year: these chemicals are malathion and dimethoate—the latter being systemic—derris and pirimiphos-methyl. These chemicals should be applied as a spray. This is another pest against which constant vigilance is necessary.

Scale Insects

These are more often found on the branches and stems of hardwood plants, such as trees or shrubs and can become a serious menace unless checked.

SYMPTOMS. Black markings on the foliage. Any plants showing these symptoms should be examined with a lens for any brownish-grey shell-like humps on the branches and stems, for these are the protective coverings of these pests.

CONTROL. Being sap suckers they can be kept in check both in the alpine house or frames by using a systemic insecticide in early spring covering the whole plant and soil. Malathion or pirimiphos-methyl will also do much to control this pest.

Slugs and Snails

They should not be present in a collection of pan plants grown in the alpine house although sometimes found in the plunge material outside. Slugs have a liking for the vent of the pans and a watch should be kept when bringing plants into the alpine house from the frames and plunge beds.

SYMPTOMS. Both are nocturnal feeders and will devour new green shoots and foliage at an alarming rate, leaving behind a clue, in the form of slime trails.

CONTROL. Metaldehyde, crushed and mixed with bran, proprietary metaldehyde-based pellets, methiocarb pellets, or liquid metaldehyde formulations placed on small pieces of slate near the affected plant will trap these pests.

Springtails

Most likely to be found where conditions are to their liking, a moist and damp atmosphere. Seed pans are a favourite haunt and the cutting frames are sometimes infested. They are small, greyish, wingless with pronounced antennae and jump when disturbed.

SYMPTOMS. Leaves eaten from small plants and seedlings collapse due to the stem being gnawed at soil level.

CONTROL. Soil sterilisation will help to keep this pest in check. HCH or pirimiphos-methyl can be applied as a soil dust both in house and frames; alternatively, apply a spray of HCH or malathion over the soil in the pan, or a smoke generator containing gamma-HCH is useful in the alpine house.

Thrips

These are very small active insects, only about $\frac{1}{20}$ inch in length and when disturbed are quick moving and difficult to see.

SYMPTOMS. Sap sucking pests which cause distortion of foliage and flowers and can be traced by the appearance of a silvery-white streaking over the surface of the leaves.

CONTROL. Systemic insecticides applied to plants and compost in late spring in frames and alpine house will do much to prevent an attack. Apply dimethoate, or use malathion as a contact spray.

Vine Weevil Grubs

The grubs of this pernicious pest are more deadly than the adult weevil which is an insect about $\frac{1}{3}$ inch in length, the body being black in colour with yellow speckling. The grubs vary in size from $\frac{1}{4}$ to $\frac{1}{3}$ inch and are a dirty white with brown heads. They can do a tremendous amount of damage, even killing plants completely. As they multiply rapidly, a collection of alpine plants can be crippled in a short space of time. They have a special liking for members of the family *Primulaceae*, especially the genera Primula and Cyclamen.

SYMPTOMS. Plants look unhealthy and yellow or collapse totally owing to severance of roots at base of the neck. The adult lives by eating away the edges of the leaves.

CONTROL. For control of the grubs, the surface of the compost should be dusted with HCH in September; alternatively, treat the compost with pirimiphos-methyl applied as a liquid, making sure that it completely wets the whole of the compost in the pans. The adult is best controlled by a HCH smoke generator in August.

White Fly

This pest is sometimes met with in the alpine house although books on rock plants grown under greenhouse conditions do not classify this as a pest of this type of plant. Given a hot dry summer they can be a real nuisance, as infestation is built up in a matter of days, generally unnoticed owing to their small size. They do not normally attack plants in the frames, for they cannot thrive except in a high temperature.

SYMPTOMS. Leaves show signs of mottling where the sap has been sucked and there are black sooty deposits. They are not generally active until the weather begins to warm up in late spring, then increase rapidly throughout the summer months.

CONTROL. A HCH smoke generator is a suitable form of control. This should be used at high temperatures for best results, a hot evening where the heat of the house is likely to be maintained at 70°F (21°C) for four hours. A spray containing malathion, HCH, dimethoate, resmethrin or permethrin is helpful for controlling high infestations; use when the temperature is high, but not during direct sunshine.

Wireworms

If the loam has been properly sterilised there should not be any trouble from this pest, but if old or new plants have been introduced from un-known sources in dirty soil, there is a possibility of infestation and unknown to the cultivator, many a rare bulb or tuber has provided a meal for wireworms.

SYMPTOMS. Bad or weakened growth of plants, especially of thick rooted bulbs and tubers, may be due to this pest which works underground and any plant which shows this characteristic, after making sure that the trouble is not caused by the vine weevil grub eating at the base of the plant, is likely to have been attacked by wireworms.

CONTROL. Soil sterilisation is the best method but a soil insecticide containing gamma-HCH can be tried.

Woodlice

In an alpine house where strict hygiene is practised woodlice should not present much of a problem, for they are pests which feed primarily on decaying organic matter and breed in dark damp corners. This is one of the reasons why seed pans are preferred to wooden flats, for wood, especially damp wood, is a great attraction. In the alpine house,

plunge beds and cutting frames, a dusting of HCH or carbaryl when preparing the plunge material will prevent any great infestation.

SYMPTOMS. They attack plants, especially young specimens, by gnawing the small tender roots and stems which results in the collapse of the plants in extreme cases, or retarding of growth.

CONTROL. In the alpine house a HCH smoke generator can be used—early autumn is a good time; while outside, all the frames can be given a liberal dusting of carbaryl powder over the surface of the plunge material to assist in keeping them at bay. Or spray with pirimiphos-methyl.

Earthworms

There are two others which can be classified as pests where plants are grown in pans. Beneficial in the open ground earthworms are harmful when contained in pans, for they cause root disturbance with their tunnelling and subsequent blockage of drainage. Under normal circumstances the plant is best taken carefully from its pan and the worm removed with a pair of forceps. For old-established specimens and plants which resent disturbance a solution of potassium permanganate, a deep purple in colour, should be poured over the surface of the compost, then the worms will come to the surface and can be removed.

Birds

The other danger is from birds. If they gain entry into a house they can do irreparable damage in a short space of time, for they will for no accountable reason pull a plant to pieces, especially cushions, in a few minutes. It is generally the finest specimens of the rare and difficult plants which are the first objects of their attentions. The wire netting door as shown in Fig. 20 will keep them from gaining ingress at this entrance but if they are at all troublesome it may be necessary to tack small mesh fish-netting over the edges of the ventilators, so that when these are open to their fullest extent, the netting provides a barrier (Fig. 23). I have found blackbirds the most troublesome, they are not timid or easily frightened and seem completely indifferent to bird scarers which are sometimes used as a deterrent inside the house. Frames too should be similarly protected if the birds are a nuisance, but for some unknown reason they do not seem to cause so much trouble in the open.

DISEASES

Fortunately in a well run alpine house diseases are not common, for the adequate ventilation which prevails plus good cultivation does not provide the ideal breeding ground. Even in summers which are damp and warm when fungi can easily spread into epidemic proportions in the garden, a well ventilated house with its drier atmosphere is less liable to attack, especially from grey moulds. The alpine frames and plunge beds on the other hand are more susceptible, for here the atmosphere has a greater moisture content, so there is a larger risk of contamination, especially with mould, and a close watch is essential during the early autumn months for mildew, a very prevalent disease at this period.

There are three types of diseases most likely to be met with in which control can be successfully accomplished (there are many more including

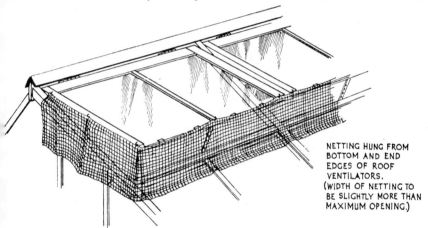

NETTING HUNG FROM BOTTOM AND END EDGES OF ROOF VENTILATORS. (WIDTH OF NETTING TO BE SLIGHTLY MORE THAN MAXIMUM OPENING.)

23. *Fish-netting on roof ventilators of the alpine house*

the virus diseases but these are outside the scope of this chapter, requiring elaborate apparatus to diagnose them correctly); these are the various root and basal stem rot diseases which attack young plants and seedlings; mildews, moulds and rusts.

Damping-off Disease

There is no cure for plants and seedlings once they have been attacked and these are best removed and destroyed before affecting others in the near vicinity. Good hygiene will eliminate 90% of the trouble and periodical sterilisation of the loam and leaf-mould is always beneficial as it destroys the harmful fungi.

Overhead watering with a liquid copper compound used according to the maker's instructions will prevent an attack or control one already started. A drawback is that these chemicals should not be used more than once on the same plant or seedling, for they have a tendency to harden the outside tissue, thus restricting their natural growth.

Mildews

There are many forms of mildew and for our purpose grey mould can be included. The main difference is that mould will only spread badly in a humid atmosphere, whereas the mildews, depending on which type they are, will spread in a humid or dry atmosphere. Dusting with sulphur helps in checking these diseases and spraying with benomyl or the systemic thiophanate-methyl is effective. Thiram is another alternative.

Rusts

Not so prevalent as mildews or moulds, rust can sometimes be seen on plants kept under glass and the silver saxifrages are prone to this disease. A liquid copper fungicide or mancozeb, used according to the maker's instructions will effectively stop the spread of this disease.

CHAPTER EIGHT

*Exhibiting. Schedules. Treatment of the Plants.
Staging.*

Exhibiting

One of the reasons why the rapidly growing number of amateurs are cultivating plants in an alpine house is for exhibition purposes. There is no doubt that nothing creates greater enthusiasm than that of showing a selection of plants, for it is only by open competition with other growers that the real test of skill in cultivation is brought to its ultimate peak. There is a problem however. Far too many amateurs are diffident about testing their skill against others, stating that they have but a poor chance of emulating the success of the experts, forgetting that the experts of today were the novices of yesterday. Very often it is the plant which is left at home, through this cause, that should be on show.

It would appear that once plantsmen can be induced to take the plunge, they soon become hardened exhibitors gaining knowledge, showmanship and what is most important of all, the friendship of fellow exhibitors to whom one can impart and from whom one can receive a great deal of useful hints on growing the more difficult species. Some people are natural pot-hunters. It is part of their make-up and there is no known cure. Others get the competition bug and human nature being what it is, the urge to beat one's fellow men provides the stimulus to produce better plants. All this makes for good clean healthy competition. Those who seek however to cultivate this show mania to the exclusion of all else, often lose the joy and pleasure of growing good plants for their form and beauty alone. Above all else they lose that tranquillity of mind which the tending of these delightful miniatures brings, a far from common thing in this bustling world of ours today.

Naturally all Show Secretaries will disagree with me on this, for their business is to fill the benches with entries. This is a good thing in a way for the Shows are the shop windows of the Societies, in which is displayed the gem to entice the less expert members to further effort. Everything in moderation should be the ultimate goal and so I will conclude thus, 'You have been warned'.

There are a good number of shows for alpines held every year in different parts of the British Isles. The Alpine Garden Society holds nine, three in London, and one each at Birmingham, Taunton, Harrogate, Southport, Belfast and Nottingham, the shows covering a period from March to September. The Scottish Rock Garden Club too stages shows for alpines in different parts of Scotland, there being nine in all. These are held at each of the following places: Edinburgh, Glasgow, Penicuik, Dumfries, Dundee, Aberdeen, Dumfermline, Perth and North Berwick. Both of these Societies are ever on the watch to extend the shows, where there can be shown that there is a need, and also what is more important, the necessary support forthcoming from the local members. They are always willing to give a sympathetic consideration, provided the members rally round to make the show a success, by exhibiting. This in its turn then encourages the trade to put up displays which increase the overall general effect.

A number of local Horticultural Societies are now including open classes in their Spring Shows for rock plants, and these can be a good testing ground for cultivators living in the district to obtain their first insight into the art of exhibiting. A word of warning should be given here. Unlike the National Shows, in which for example a well-grown difficult plant with a few flowers would normally take precedence over a well-flowered easy specimen, on the local Societies' show bench it could be the well-flowered specimen that is more likely to catch the judge's eye. Some cultivators may say 'Why exhibit at the local shows', if this is the case, but the main idea is to get the growers who have never exhibited before 'blooded' locally. The enthusiasm which is then aroused soon provides this impetus to carry them on to the bigger stakes.

Schedules

Schedules for the shows should be studied closely and entries for the numerous classes made accordingly. At the local shows these will consist of only a few open classes—generally about three, although at the larger provincial shows this number may be increased and very likely will include a class for a rock garden to be built on a site. This gives an exhibitor a chance to display his or her artistic talent, for it is only on rare occasions that these miniature rock gardens are planted correctly with alpines normally found in association with one another in their habitat. This is when the Show Schedule should be studied carefully, for if the class states a rock garden planted for effect then natural associations are of

Above: *Cyclamen orbiculatum* var. *coum* (see page 258)

Below: *Cyclamen europaeum* (see page 256)

Above: *Daphne petraea* (see page 266)

Below: *Daphne striata* and *Gentiana acaulis* (see pages 267 and 297)

secondary importance, although an effective natural planting will stand a greater chance.

In the National Shows held by the Alpine Garden Society and the Scottish Rock Garden Club, the sections are mainly confined to alpines. A noticeable feature is that schedules are so arranged that the exhibitor who is just beginning to show will receive the greatest encouragement. By this method it does not put the exhibitor who is showing for the first time in unfair competition with the specialist, although there is nothing to prevent the novice from entering that field in competition with the expert. What is more, it will certainly not be the first time that a major prize has been literally snatched from under the noses of these specialists by a beginner.

As a general rule the sections are divided into classes for families, but there will also be classes for six pans of different genera. It will be useful to know that all things being equal the exhibitor whose plants cover a wider range of families, genera and true species or natural hybrids against garden hybrids will certainly take preference when judged. This also applies to three pan classes, which will also state that they must be of distinct genera and generally a single pan class, plants which are not eligible for the other classes. There may be classes for what is known as everyday plants. These are the easy plants which will only be judged for their floral display, not for rarity, if entered. Examples are Aubrieta, *Phlox subulata*, some of the campanulas such as *garganica, pulla, cochlearifolia, Draba aizoides, D. imbricata, Erinus alpinus*, many penstemons, *Primula auricula, P. denticulata, P. rosea* and a host of others. Normally the plants would not be grown in pans at all, but lifted from the open ground and potted up for the show. They are mentioned here because a number of beginners will try their skill with these first of all and from this start, progress to the more difficult plants.

The word distinct often raises queries but it normally means distinct varieties, so that for example two colour forms of *Primula allionii* would be correct. It is always worth while to raise this point with the Show Secretary before judging commences. Naturally in some of the classes it will say distinct genera and this is self explanatory. It means three plants from different genera, for example one Androsace, one Draba and one Calceolaria. These should, other things being equal, stand a better chance of the prize than say one Androsace, one Primula and one Cyclamen, for the former are from the families *Primulaceae, Cruciferae* and *Scrophulariaceae*, whereas the latter are all from *Primulaceae*.

There are several things that the judges will be looking for. A plant should be in character, that is similar to its counterpart in nature. Flowers should be perfect and in quantity, where this is called for in the schedule.

All cushion plants must be compact and firm, any looseness will certainly lose points. Both conifers and shrubs grown on their own roots will gain more favour than grafted specimens and where colour foliage is called for, the leaves should be well marked. Plants carrying fruit will normally gain as many points as those in flower. Aromatic plants should be those in which the stems and foliage are scented. There should not be more than one species, variety of a species or a hybrid in a single pan. The only exception to this rule is if there is a class for a collected type of soil with plants showing natural plant association or a specified pan of different plants, grown for effect. There can of course be more than a single specimen in a pan, after all one single dwarf narcissus or tulip would not look very well, but other things being equal, there is no doubt that for example a well-grown single plant of saxifrage would certainly take a prize against several small pieces in the same pan.

As the majority of plants will be classified according to their families I am appending a list which will save a lot of searching when deciding to exhibit. A great deal of disappointment will thus be avoided if this list is used to check entries before sending them in to the Show Secretary or by referring to individual plants in the List of Plants, pp. 170 to 519.

Boraginaceae. Eritrichium, Lithospermum, Mertensia, Myosotis, Omphalodes etc.

Campanulaceae. Adenophora, Campanula, Codonopsis, Cyananthus, Trachelium, Edraianthus, Phyteuma, Wahlenbergia etc.

Caryophyllaceae. Arenaria, Dianthus, Gypsophila, Lychnis, Melandrium, Sagina, Saponaria, Silene etc.

Compositae. Anacyclus, Aster, Chrysanthemum, Crepis, Erigeron, Helichrysum, Inula etc.

Coniferae. Abies, Cedrus, Cupressus, Juniperus, Pinus, Taxus, Tsuga, Thuja etc.

Crassulaceae. Cotyledon, Crassula, Sedum, Sempervivum etc.

Cruciferae. Aethionema, Alyssum, Arabis, Aubrieta, Cardamine, Draba, Iberis, Morisia, Petrocallis, Thlaspi etc.

Diapensiaceae. Diapensia, Galax, Schizocodon, Shortia etc.

Ericaceae including *Vacciniaceae* and *Pyrolaceae.* Andromeda, Calluna, Cassiope, Erica, Gaultheria, Loiseleuria, Pernettya, Phyllodoce, Pyrola, Rhododendron, Rhodothamnus etc.

Gesneraceae. Didissandra, Haberlea, Jankaea, Ramonda etc.

Labiatae. Nepeta, Origanum, Teucrium, Thymus etc.

Leguminosae. Anthyllis, Astragalus, Cytisus, Genista, Lupinus, Ononis etc.

Orchidaceae. Cyripedium, Ophrys, Orchis etc.

Primulaceae. Anagallis, Androsace, Cyclamen, Dionysia, Dodecatheon, Primula, Soldanella etc.

Ranunculaceae. Anemone, Aquilegia, Callianthemum, Caltha, Eranthis, Isopyrum, Ranunculus, Thalictrum etc.

Rubiaceae. Coprosma, Houstonia, Mitchella, Nertera etc.

Saxifragaceae. Boykinia, Deinanthe, Saxifraga, Tiarella etc.

Scrophulariaceae. Calceolaria, Penstemon, Verbascum, Veronica etc.

Preparation for Exhibiting

The plants selected for exhibition should be taken into the alpine house at least a week before the show, so that they may be prepared. It will be advantageous to have at least two plants, not necessarily identical, but eligible for the classes concerned, so that when the day of the show arrives, the better of the two can be chosen for entering. It is better to choose specimens which are full of buds that are just commencing to open, especially so if the weather is at all mild or warm, for by the time the move to the show is over, the buds will have opened. There is no doubt that plants sent to the show before the buds are opened are a better prospect than if they are in full flower. By the time judging commences, the warm atmosphere of the hall will have had the effect of the flower buds breaking into a display of fresh floral beauty. If there are a number of plants which, owing possibly to a warm spell, show signs of opening their flowers before the day of the show, they should be removed from the house and placed in a cool spot, either a north facing frame, or if this is not available a shady corner of the garden where a light should be placed over them to prevent damage to blooms. Sometimes a plant that is specially required for the show seems to lag behind, the buds refusing to open. If a greenhouse which has heat is available, removal to this and a spraying with water at not less than the temperature of the house will do much to bring the plant forward. Even a night in a warm living room in the house will work wonders, but common sense must prevail and care be taken that the plants do not become drawn and out of character. This is where experience counts, but that cannot unfortunately be bought with money. It can only be learned the hard way but once mastered the eye will invariably inform you as to the correct method to adopt. I have often been asked what plants to choose out of a good selection, by people who today are classified as experts. We all have to learn and I can assure you that advice is given ungrudgingly by all keen growers of which a majority are only concerned with the exhibition of well-grown plants, discounting their own entries.

Pots and pans must be thoroughly cleaned on the outside and the rim where there is a great tendency for algae to collect. Pumice stone will remove stains on the outside of the pans quite easily. This should be used moistened with water and rubbed on the pan with a gentle circular movement afterwards wiping clean with a damp cloth. The next procedure is to match up the pans if there are entries for more than one plant in a class. Nothing detracts from what would otherwise be a well-matched entry than for example, in a three-pan class, two of the plants in 9-inch pans and the third in a 5- or 6-inch.

This can be overcome by inserting the 5- or 6-inch pan inside an empty 9-inch, disguising it by making sure the larger pan is deeper than the smaller. When it is placed inside, the rim will rest below the edge of the larger. The space between the two pans is then filled to the top with the appropriate chippings, so that it appears as if the plant is growing in the larger pan. Sometimes shallow pans have to be used with larger pots, larger in depth, not size, and here it is perfectly legal to place the shallow pan on top of another which has been turned upside down, thus ensuring a certain amount of uniformity on the show bench.

Grooming of the plants should take place the day before the actual show unless there are a large number of entries, and then it will pay the exhibitor to start a few days ahead, commencing with those plants which are normally tidy and whose flowers are lasting, leaving those with fleeting blooms until the last day. All dead foliage, rosettes and, in the case of shrubs, old wood must be removed. Rosettes of cushion plants after removal leave a small gap in the plant and on no account must sand or a piece of rock be inserted to hide this as I have sometimes seen. Any judge worthy of the name will notice this artifice immediately to the detriment of the exhibitor. All that is necessary is to work in more chippings around the outside of the plant, so the gap where the rosette has been removed is eliminated, by this outside pressure.

Shrubs which have grown out of shape can sometimes be improved by the complete removal of a branch to obtain a symmetrical specimen. Care must be taken here, for no general pruning or pinching back should be attempted, or this will certainly lose marks on the show bench. Nothing looks worse than a plant which bears traces of last year's foliage, often brown and wrinkled. All this dead material must be removed, a tedious job, but worth while for the finished specimen will be much improved. This is where experience counts. It is possible after a period of time to get a general idea of what will be ready in time for a given show and the intervening period will be well spent, if a beginning is made on the overall grooming of the plants some weeks before the occasion. I know that the ideal situation is that there should not be any dead or rotting foliage at any time, but this state of perfection is rarely obtainable in a large collection, especially in busy springtime, although it is very desirable.

The last stage in grooming is the renewal of all the top-dressing of chippings. Where there are entries in classes calling for more than a single specimen and both lime-loving and lime-hating plants are shown together, it will be advantageous to top-dress with a neutral medium, such as granite chippings, to provide the uniformity so necessary in a well groomed display. All plants must be clearly labelled and the general rule is that there should only be the botanical name of the plant, and country of origin. It is important that the plant be correctly named. Any doubt as to this should be verified with either the Show Secretary or one of the experts, who are normally in attendance at the shows. Although wrong names will not disqualify unless the correct name of the plant makes it invalid for the class in which it is entered, it will certainly mean loss of points when being judged.

A last point on choosing plants for a show: with the exception of a class specified for everyday rock garden plants it should be borne in mind that a well flowered easy plant will not gain as many points as a well cultivated difficult or rare specimen, showing few flowers but a great deal of preparatory work.

Before dispatching the plants all should be well watered, for two days on the show benches in a hall full of people can soon dehydrate plants. It is surprising how dry the atmosphere becomes in a crowded exhibition hall. Packing calls for great care and there is really nothing better than the use of newspaper, rolled into irregular shapes, placed down beside the pans as a cushion. This is a cheap but reliable method and to my mind is even superior to boxes of peat in which the pans are plunged, a messy and far from easy idea to put into operation, to say nothing of the peat adhering to the sides of the pans when lifted out at the show. There are two schools of thought as to whether the plants should be staged over-night or on the day of the show. My own preference is for the overnight staging of the plants, for they can be placed on the benches and time taken to remake any damage done through travel; the following morning can be used to advantage in staging the exhibits, without the rush that occurs when the exhibits are brought on the morning of the show. This is important, for it is surprising how much grooming is needed after the plants have travelled any distance.

Just before judging commences, all the exhibits should be sprayed with a fine nozzle spray, one which gives a spray as fine as an atomiser is best; this will work wonders on the exhibits, giving them a fresh dewy morning look.

There are two last points I would like to mention before closing this chapter. Never question the judge's decision; it must be final and should never be reversed. Any judge worthy of his salt will certainly give his reasons, if asked, why a preference was made for one exhibit against another. There are generally three judges and the majority counts. Secondly if in doubt, ask the Show Secretary, that overworked, underpraised individual, who takes all the kicks but is ever ready to help all and sundry.

PART TWO

The Plants

9. Introduction. Nomenclature. Botanical Terms
10. Dwarf Conifers. Introduction. Nomenclature. Cultivation. Pruning. Propagation. The Register. Cuttings. Air-Layering. Suitable Species and Forms. List of Dwarf Conifers
11. General List

CHAPTER NINE

Introduction.   Nomenclature.   Botanical Terms.

Introduction

In this work I have tried to include all worthwhile plants in cultivation today suitable for the alpine house. It is not possible to say that it is a complete dossier on all available material, for a number are nothing more than botanical curiosities, fit only for mounting as dried specimens in some herbarium, thus recording their existence on earth. Quite probably a few noted here would qualify for that distinction according to the likes and dislikes of different cultivators but to please everybody is an impossible task, after all 'beauty is in the eyes of the beholder'. Some of the species included can on no account be strictly classified as alpines in the true sense of the word. In fact a number have never even seen snow in their natural habitat. The tendency today is, however, to include all plants as suitable that are generally small in stature, good from the floral effect, slow in growth like the dwarf conifers, and also rare and difficult plants are admitted.

What is the definition of an alpine? I am not going to be drawn into this age-old argument for like all things in nature there can be no hard-and-fast dividing line separating the types which can be placed and classified; although the generally accepted distinction is: all plants growing above the tree line in nature. This too is an impossible situation, for above the tree line in different parts of the globe can range from sea level in the barren wastes of the Arctic to 15,000 feet or more in the tropics. I presume that a correctly sited alpine is a plant growing in the Alps and when first used the description meant the mountains of Europe. The extention of the term alpine to the vast Asiatic and American ranges came after the word had passed into popular usage. There is no doubt that an alpine purist would exclude from a collection a large range of worthwhile plants, some being difficult or even impossible to grow outdoors. Their omission would leave us much poorer in both floral beauty and knowledge of the world's plant life. Many woodlanders included in the families *Ericaceae, Diapensiaceae, Gesneriaceae* etc., cannot even in the remotest sense of the word be classified as alpines, although a few dwarf

153

rhododendrons take the place of heather at high altitudes in the Himalayas. These too would have to be excluded if only true alpines, i.e. plants growing above the tree line in nature, were allowed in the collection. How much poorer we would be, if abandoned by the alpine grower as a non-alpine and shunned by the ordinary gardener as being too small in stature these neglected plants were to disappear from cultivation.

It is far better to use the word alpine to describe the type of house or frame in which the plants are grown and choose to suit one's own taste from the vast wealth of nature's flora. The only criterion is that those chosen are reasonably small in stature, have some decorative value, either beauty of form, floral or fruit display and are hardy enough to stand an average English winter. Where possible natural species or first crosses should be chosen in preference to distorted man-made monstrosities in which all the delicacy and beauty of form has been bred out, producing specimens fit only for the compost heap. Many alpine specialists will be amazed at some of the plants listed here, these being in their eyes unsuitable for pan culture owing to the ease with which they can be cultivated outdoors. I make no apology, for the easy species and varieties are but the stepping stones to the more difficult and it is surprising how soon the specialist forgets he was once a novice standing on the threshold of his hobby.

For ease of reference and as the majority of dwarf conifers require similar culture conditions it has been decided to list them in a section of their own following this introduction. There is no doubt that these dwarf coniferous trees have today a large number of followers. This has created a demand which is difficult to supply, for the majority are slow growing, taking many years to reach 2 feet when cultivated in pans. This has led to a number of undesirable plants being used that are far from dwarf. It is difficult to say how this can be overcome, for there are few experts on these miniatures in this country and even less reliable written material to which the grower can turn for guidance. It is to be hoped that the section on these plants will help to sort the wheat from the chaff.

Nomenclature

In no other section of gardening is the naming of plants so important as in that of a collection of alpines from all the mountain ranges of the world. These are with but few exceptions natural wildlings, growing in nature unassisted by man and have been named according to the International Code of Botanical Nomenclature by reputable botanists, and a description published in a language which is in itself international. Latin is used, for in earlier times botanical works were written in Latin or Greek, these being the languages of the learned of those days. Latin, being a dead language, is used universally today for all the natural sciences.

It is not impossible to attach common names to these plants which could be easily remembered, but these would not mean the same to gardeners in different districts, for they vary from one locality to another and country to country. A well-known example which is often quoted is the bluebell of Scotland. In Scotland it is a campanula, whereas in England it is the wild hyacinth. By the use of the correct Latin names which are respectively *Campanula rotundifolia* and *Endymion non-scriptus* there can be no doubt in the mind of the gardener which plants are meant. Another example is the Houseleek which is the common name for the genus Sempervivum. There must be well over 200 species in this genus to say nothing of the varieties and hybrids, so how can one know which plant is being talked about? How different it is if a correct name is used such as *Sempervivum arachnoideum*, this being the species which is covered with fine hairs like a cobweb and often referred to as the Cobweb Houseleek. I have chosen this example because the answer would be 'Ah! the Cobweb Houseleek, well, we know that, so why use such a name as *Sempervivum arachnoideum*'? The answer is that the name Cobweb Houseleek would mean nothing to a gardener in Japan, Italy, Germany or Hong Kong, whereas the botanical name is constant and any gardener irrespective of his nationality can easily trace the plant by referring to a library which contains botanical and gardening books, and then find it with a valid description either in Latin or in the language of the country concerned.

It should be apparent that some uniformity is necessary and the answer is as adopted, a universal language such as Latin which is acceptable to all countries in the world, this being translated into the appropriate language for the non-technical. It is surprising how easy it is to master the names. Once this has been accomplished it becomes an open sesame to gardeners of all nations, helping to overcome language barriers and linking them together in a common bond. Another point to remember is that unless commemorative the specific name describes some aspect of form, or the locality where the plant grows in nature. For example *Salix reticulata* means netted, which applies to the leaves with their heavy network of veins, or *Moltkia petraea*, growing on rocky ground. There is no doubt that the small amount of time spent in learning these Latin names is well repaid. They lead to a more comprehensive knowledge of the plants being grown than would otherwise be possible.

As a guide to correct nomenclature I initially relied on The Royal Horticultural Society's *Dictionary of Gardening*. Since then the five-volume *Flora Europaea* and *The Flora of Japan* have been published and these are the important sources for name changes incorporated in this edition. All such changes are listed in Appendix 2. A number of well-known plants have been moved from family to family, genus to genus and new families, genera and species have even been created, to conform with the International Code of Botanical Nomenclature. These changes mostly reflect late discoveries of earlier descriptions and names which, under the rules, must take priority. Where these changes apply cross references are given or the old name retained as a synonym.

A number of nurserymen who, after all, grow plants to sell for a living are loth to use these amended names which are unknown to a large number of customers. When ordering plants which are not listed under their new names the catalogue should be searched to see if they are retained under the old. Another change has also been made. Normally the families to which certain genera belong used to be known as natural orders, but now it is correct to use the word family or families to denote them. It will be found that there are plants described here which are not

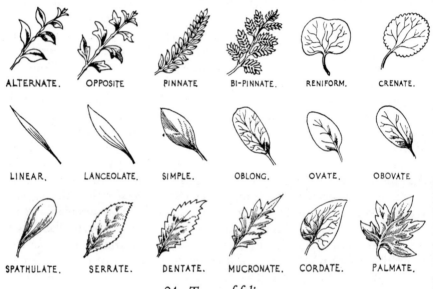

ALTERNATE.   OPPOSITE.   PINNATE.   BI-PINNATE.   RENIFORM.   CRENATE.

LINEAR.   LANCEOLATE.   SIMPLE.   OBLONG.   OVATE.   OBOVATE

SPATHULATE.   SERRATE.   DENTATE.   MUCRONATE.   CORDATE.   PALMATE.

24. *Types of foliage*

to be found in the *Dictionary of Gardening*. This is due either to the fact that since publication of that work there have been a number of new plants introduced to cultivation, or not listed for one reason or another. The science of botany and the craft of gardening are not static, and revision from time to time is always necessary.

All Latin specific names whatsoever their derivation are printed with lower case initials and both generic and specific names are in italics, thus conforming with the International Code of Botanical Nomenclature and carried into practice by all botanical institutions such as Kew, Edinburgh, Oxford, Cambridge etc. The method of printing the names of the plants as universally adopted is: first the generic name, followed by the specific and where applicable any varietal name. Varieties found growing in the wild have been given a name in Latin form, but prefixed by var. Garden forms generally have ordinary non Latin names, are distinguished by capital initial letters and are enclosed within single quotation marks. In introducing the genus immediately after the generic name is given the family to which this genus belongs. This will help cultivators who wish to exhibit and are not sure to which family the plants belong. All synonyms of species which are shown abbreviated to syn. are listed where required after the recognised name in use. Any changes in generic status are marked by a cross reference, such as for example, *Anemone vernalis* see *Pulsatilla vernalis*. This is but one instance where a generic name which has been in use for a long time embracing a number of well-known plants has now been altered. Four other abbreviations are used, these being E, denoting the plant is evergreen; D meaning the plant is deciduous (it loses its foliage

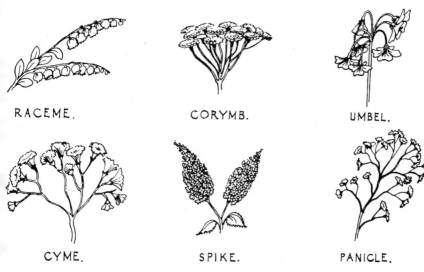

RACEME. CORYMB. UMBEL.

CYME. SPIKE. PANICLE.

25. *Arrangements of flowers*

during the winter); H a herbaceous perennial, dying back to a growth bud in winter, and B for a bulb or corm.

It is not possible to write a book of this kind without reference to, or the use of a number of botanical terms, otherwise descriptions would be too long and unwieldy. These however have been kept to a minimum and the following list used in conjunction with the diagrams of foliage and flower arrangements will help to record in the cultivator's mind some idea of the plant being described (Figs. 24 and 25).

Botanical Terms

Acuminate,	long pointed, generally applied to the extension of the midrib past the apex of the leaves.
Adventitious,	generally applied to plants whose stems root where they come in contact with the soil.
Anther,	the end of the stamen bearing the pollen.
Apex,	the tip as applied to leaf, flower and stem.
Apical,	end of an organ, terminal point.

Apiculate,	having a point, leaves, petals.
Appressed,	lying close to or flat for its whole length.
Axil,	the angle formed by the junction of the leaf stalk and stem.
Berry,	a fruit in which the seed is enclosed in a soft succulent mass.
Bifid,	twice cleft divided into two.
Binate,	divided in two.
Biserrate,	double toothed, each tooth divided again.
Biternate,	in two clusters of three, generally leaves.
Bracteate,	provided with bracts.
Bracts,	modified leaves at the base of the flower.
Calyx,	outer covering of the flower, outside the petals.
Campanulate,	bell-shaped.
Capitate,	flowers growing in a head.
Cartilaginous,	gristly, tough.
Ciliate,	margined with hairs.
Cleistogamous,	flowers which fertilise themselves without opening.
Concave,	hollowed out, saucer-like.
Convex,	domed with rounded surface, like an over-turned saucer.
Coriaceous,	thick, leathery.
Corolla,	the inner envelope of the flower, the petals.
Corona,	an appendage between the petals and stamens, for example the cup of the daffodil.
Corymbose,	arranged in flattish heads, flowers.
Crenulate,	notched with rounded teeth.
Cuneate,	wedge shaped, narrow to base.
Decurved,	turned down.
Denticulate,	minutely toothed.
Dioecious,	having male and female flowers on different plants.
Drupe,	a fruit in which the seed is covered by a stone which in turn has an outer covering of a succulent nature.
Elliptic,	shaped like an ellipse.
Ensiform,	sword-like, generally applied to leaves.
Fastigiate,	with parallel erect branches.
Glabrous,	hairless, smooth.
Glandular,	covered with hairs having glands at their tips.
Glaucous,	covered with a white or greyish bloom.
Hirsute,	rough, hairy.
Imbricated,	covered with overlapping scales, like tiles on a roof.
Imparipinnate,	feathered, but having the terminal section unequally so generally of leaves.
Indumentum,	the hairy substance which sometimes cover parts of the plant.

Involucre,	a ring of bracts surrounding several flowers.
Labellum,	lip, here specifically applied to the structure of one of the floral lobes of orchids.
Lamellae,	in thin plates or scales.
Leguminose,	resembling the pea family.
Linear,	narrow with sides almost parallel.
Lingulate,	with small tongues or tongue-like membranes.
Median,	central, having a middle channel, line etc.
Membraneous,	having the texture of membranes.
Monocarpic,	dies after fruiting once.
Monoecious,	having male and female flowers separate on the same plant.
Monotypic,	a genus with only one species.
Mucronulate,	with a diminutive sharp point.
Obconic,	of conical form and attached at the point.
Obcordate,	reversed heart-shaped.
Obovoid,	inversely solid egg-shaped.
Obtuse,	blunt.
Partite,	cleft but not quite to base.
Pectinate,	comb-shaped.
Pedicel,	the stalk supporting a solitary flower.
Pendulous,	hanging down.
Perfoliate,	having the stem as it were passing through a leaf.
Perianth,	the floral envelope consisting of sepals, petals or both.
Petiolate,	having a leaf stalk.
Petiole,	the leaf stalk.
Pilose,	covered with long soft hairs.
Pinnate,	feathered, generally applied to leaves.
Pinnatisect,	pinnately divided.
Plicate,	folded.
Puberulous,	somewhat downy.
Pubescent,	covered with soft hair or down.
Radical,	rising from the root at or below soil level.
Recurved,	bent down.
Reticulate,	in the shape of a net, generally applied to the leaf veins.
Revolute,	rolled back from margin or apex, generally of leaf.
Rhomboid,	diamond shape, an equilateral oblique figure.
Rugose,	wrinkled.
Scapes,	the flowering stem bearing one or more flowers.
Serrulate,	toothed, with minute teeth.
Sessile,	without stalk or stem.
Stellate,	minutely star-shaped.
Stipules,	small appendages to the base of the leaf stalk.
Stoloniferous,	having suckers or runners.

Striated,	marked with vertical grooves, generally of a distinctive colour.
Ternate,	divided into threes.
Ternatisect,	ternately divided.
Tomentum,	dense covering of short soft hairs.
Tortuous,	twisted and entangled.
Triangularis,	three-angled or sided.
Tridentate,	thrice toothed or pronged.
Trifid,	with three parts, the division at least half way.
Triternate,	divided into threes.
Truncate,	ending abruptly, as if cut off.
Whorl,	flowers or foliage arranged in a circle round the stalk or branches.

Above: *Dianthus neglectus* (see page 270)

Below: *Diapensia lapponica* (see page 270)

Above: *Dionysia aretioides* 'Paul Furse' (see page 524)

Below: *Dionysia bryoides* (see page 272)

CHAPTER TEN

DWARF CONIFERS

Introduction. Nomenclature. Cultivation. Pruning. Propagation.
The Register. Cuttings. Air-Layering. Suitable Species and Forms.
List of Dwarf Conifers.

Introduction

As a backbone to a collection of alpines growing in pans, nothing is more
suitable and delightful than a number of well grown dwarf conifers. In
the alpine house they add a touch of colour with their many shades of
foliage. This ranges from silver through greys to grey-green, light green
to yellow and on through the darker hues, not forgetting the red-brown
and purple coloration taken on by a number during the winter months,
thus providing beauty in this normally colourless period. There is no
doubt that from an aesthetic viewpoint they help to break up the otherwise flat row after row of pans containing as a rule, low growing cushion and
other similar types of plants. Thus suitably placed at different vantage points
these conifers will help to give and maintain a scenic balance at all times
of the year, particularly during the winter months when flowers are scarce.

Today they are becoming increasingly popular and even the smallest
collection contains a few, but unfortunately this state of affairs is bringing
in its trail a number of difficulties. Demand exceeds the supply; this,
coupled with the slowness of growth of the true dwarf conifer, makes
prices high. This state of affairs has led to the appearance on the market of
plants which cannot by any stretch of the imagination be classified as
dwarf plants. On the other hand a number are cuttings taken from dwarf
conifers and grafted on to a more vigorous rootstock, thus producing a
larger specimen in a shorter period of time. These will in the course of a
few years produce a plant growing out of all proportion and generally
useless for inclusion in a collection, unless frequently renewed as they
become too large; a costly business.

To a certain extent the general public must take a share of the blame for
this state of affairs for when buying dwarf conifers they expect a large
specimen for a few shillings. They are amazed, disappointed and often
annoyed when they receive a plant often less than an inch across. The poor
nurseryman who has possibly spent up to three or four years growing on
these extremely slow-growing conifers is often unjustly accused of
supplying nothing more than rooted cuttings. This is a state of affairs that

can lead to one of two things. Either the nurseryman has to give up growing these plants with the resulting greater shortage of supply, or he has to
resort to grafting. This method has its repercussions. After a few years
these grafted specimens grow into large plants or revert to the arborescent
type from which they originated, either as dwarf seedlings or 'witches'
brooms'. The nurseryman who is blamed for selling forest trees as dwarf
conifers often decides to give up propagating these plants, thus the supply
position becomes even more acute.

To digress for a moment on how these seedlings and 'witches' brooms'
occur and are perpetuated will not come amiss to those who are just
beginning to grow a collection of dwarf conifers. To date no satisfactory
explanation has yet been given as to why normal arborescent trees capable
of growing up to 120 feet in height can produce seed from which dwarf
trees will grow that will be less than 2 feet in height when twenty to
thirty years old. It is only on rare occasions that the dwarf characteristics
are fixed for the next generation of seedlings. If seed is produced at all it
will normally revert once again to forest trees. The only other method by
which dwarf conifers are obtained is from witches' brooms. These are
abnormal shoots from the end of the branches of arborescent trees
resembling bird's nests with a congested mass of dwarf branchlets. There
have been several theories put forward as to why they appear. The best
known are: some abnormal constriction of the sap; deformity set up by
infection from insect attack; or bud mutation or fungus infection. Whatever the cause it will be found that they invariably come true if propagated
by cuttings and to a lesser degree by grafts, although with the latter they
often tend to bear abnormal shoots similar to the type of tree from which
they originated. It is always worthwhile to study stands of arborescent
conifers in the chance of discovering whether there are any witches'
brooms present.

One often sees advertisements in some of the gardening periodical
listing dwarf conifers 6 to 9 inches in height at a cost of anything from fifty pence to £1 per plant. Whether this is done through
ignorance or not is open to question, but these offers must be looked upon
with suspicion, for a true dwarf conifer of this size on its own roots would
without exaggeration be in many cases in the region of fifty years old. For
example the illustration of the ten-year-old cutting of *Chamaecyparis*
obtusa 'Minima' growing on its own roots will give an idea of the actual
slow growth of a miniature. A plant which is often offered as suitable
is *Chamaecyparis lawsoniania* 'Fletcheri', and will, depending on soil
and position, be 6 to 8 feet tall in the course of ten years. Admittedly this
is in the open ground but even so no pot could contain it over such a
period of time without artificial restriction or dwarfing of growth.

Nomenclature

The real problem with dwarf conifers is that with very few exception their nomenclature is in a hopeless state of muddle. It would need a life-time's work to sort out the many forms which abound, often masquer-ading under specific and varietal names to which they have no right. These invalid names are perpetuated every day through being sold by nurserymen whose stock has been obtained from other sources labelled with names to which they have no right. The average nurseryman is not a systematic botanist, but a hard working man to whom time and labour are costly items, so he is forced to sell dwarf conifers as received regardless of whether they are true or not. This state of affairs is to some extent due to the fact that from a given form it is possible to propagate three different types of plants. When the adult stage is reached these will bear little or no relation to the form from which they were originally propagated. For example we will assume that from a plant of *Chamaecyparis lawsoniana* 'Ellwoodii', which is a semi-dwarf discovered as a chance seedling, three types of cuttings for propagating purposes are taken. One from the base, the second halfway up the plant and the last from the apex. The resultant plants after rooting will show surprising differences in both size and form. The plant from the basal cutting will retain the dwarf characteristics of the parent. The intermediate is likely to be much taller and more columnar in shape while that from the apex will form a more open and quicker growing plant, often unrecognisable when compared with the parent. Vegetative propagation from the different types of cuttings produced on a plant which often bears juvenile, intermediate and adult foliage at the same time will result in three different forms. These are sometimes given names which are rarely properly recorded, thus adding to the confusion which already exists.

Until experience is gained in dealing with these dwarf conifers reliance should be placed on those nurserymen who have made a study of these dwarf miniatures. Attendance at the shows of the Royal Horticultural Society in London or the Alpine Garden Society and Scottish Rock Garden Club will accustom one to the correct names. Amongst the members of these Societies are some of the greatest experts on dwarf conifers in this country. The specimens on show are as correctly named as is possible under present circumstances, although even these experts do not always agree. Amateurs who wish to know more about these fascinating miniatures should study Hornibrook's book on Dwarf Conifers which deals exhaustively with the subject and is to a great extent non-technical. A study of the dwarf conifers on show will be well repaid for here it is possible to get an idea of what to look for when purchasing plants.

There is an infallible test as to whether a plant is a true dwarf conifer or not and that is to pay a visit to a nursery specialising in these plants, about the last week in June or the first in July depending on the season and whether one lives in the northern or southern counties, to assess the amount of growth made in the current season. The new growth is quite distinctive both in branches and leaves. This annual rate of increase will,

with a little mental arithmetic, give the prospective purchaser a genera
guide as to whether the plant is a true dwarf or not. This assessment of
growth applies to the branches. If, for example, these grow horizontally
and the annual growth is ½ inch, the overall growth will be 1 inch in
width to ½ inch in height.

Cultivation

This does not present any great difficulty, provided one or two simple
chores are periodically carried out. The compost recommended for all
these miniatures is B made up as advised in Chapter Four, potting the
plants as directed. It will grow all varieties satisfactorily providing enough
food and humus for healthy growth and retention of their characteristic
form. At all times of the year the compost should be kept moist but not
waterlogged for dryness or excessive moisture at the roots are the two
certain methods by which these plants can be killed. Even temporary
dryness will cause disfiguration of the plant and generally shows by
pieces browning off and dying. Nothing can be done once this occurs and
the result is a plant not worth the space in a representative collection.
This lack of moisture is more to be feared in old specimens than in
younger plants. The former with their congested roots contained in pans
from which the majority of the compost has been absorbed become
almost like a ball of concrete. If these are allowed to dry out, it will be
found almost impossible for them to absorb moisture again. From April
to August a monthly plunge into a tank with enough water to reach to
the rim of the pan should be carried out in addition to the normal watering. The plants should be allowed to stay in this tank for at least one hour
so that the centre of the ball of soil is thoroughly moistened. Throughout
the growing season, April to the end of July, plenty of water can be given,
reducing the amount gradually at the end of the summer to a state where
the compost is just moist and maintaining these conditions during the
winter.

Dwarf conifers should be kept in a shaded spot from June to September
and certainly not left in the alpine house for long periods during hot
weather. The small bun forms are very susceptible to strong sunshine
and must be protected from this at all costs. They quickly show their
disapproval by the appearance of brown patches which at least spells
disfigurement if not total collapse. To sum up, the junipers and pines will
tolerate much drier conditions than the cypresses and spruce firs, which
need moist conditions with half shade to give of their best. The pans are
best turned periodically so that the specimens do not incline towards the
light thus losing their symmetrical shape, which would happen if they
were allowed to remain stationary. All dwarf conifers appreciate overhead spraying in the evenings after hot days.

In their young state the dwarf conifers are best kept growing on by

repotting every year in fresh compost. The end of August is a good time
for this task and some of the old soil should be removed, making sure that
the roots are not damaged while carrying out this operation. After the
third year bi-annual repotting is sufficient until the plant has reached the
limit of pan size. When these old specimens have reached the largest pan
capable of being housed in the alpine house or frame, they should have an
annual top-dressing, carefully removing the surface soil to the depth of
about 1 inch. This is a delicate operation. By replacing the old top soil
with fresh compost the feeding roots will tend to rise to the surface so care
must be taken not to destroy these or even disturb them more than
necessary. It is here that skilful and careful cultivators can achieve their
greatest success in keeping these aged specimens in a healthy condition.
Fresh soil is then worked in amongst the roots and, after gently firming,
the whole is well watered.

Some experts advise the removal of the plant from its pan. After carefully easing away a part of the old soil the plant is repotted in the same
container, working in fresh compost to replace that removed. This is
not to be recommended for it is an exceedingly difficult operation,
calling for great skill and care on the part of the operator. Not only is it
almost impossible to remove any appreciable amount of old soil without
causing damage to the roots but it will be found that trying to repot an
aged specimen in its old or similar sized pan, at the same time working in
fresh compost, just cannot be accomplished without further injury or
leaving air pockets which is fatal. Always remember that an old conifer
has been growing under artificial conditions in a pan, and it is comparable
to an elderly human being, and care is needed to maintain good health.
Feeding will also help to maintain good health. A recognised liquid
manure is best and should be used as directed for pot plants giving them
a bi-weekly watering during the growing season. In early spring or even
during late winter the whole collection of dwarf conifers should be given a
grooming by removing all dead foliage and branches. This is very important, particularly with the bun-shaped specimens. These, with their
compact habit, often hide dead or decaying leaves which if not removed
will induce moulds and mildew to form, attacking the healthy foliage
with dire results if prompt remedial action is not taken.

Pruning

It should not be necessary to prune these plants but sometimes the dwarf
forms will throw an abnormal shoot. A careful watch should be kept and
all such shoots removed as soon as seen. Growth can be pinched out if the
plant tends to become unbalanced. This is best carried out when the
specimen is young, so that it has a chance to build up into a good symmetrically shaped plant. A knife or secateurs must not be used, for these
will cause disfigurement.

Propagation

The only means of propagating dwarf conifers is vegetatively, that is by cuttings or layering, for with very few exceptions they will not breed true from seed, usually reverting to their normal stature as forest trees. Even the few forms which are constant and breed true, rarely oblige by setting viable seed, so they can be ignored. All, with the exception of the cedars and pines, will strike readily from cuttings, but for these two genera layering is the only way, with the exception of grafting which as stated before, is not advised. Cuttings are best taken from the base of the plant, for, as noted earlier in this chapter, if taken from other parts they are likely to result in larger and often different forms from that of the parents. By all means take basal, intermediate or apical cuttings of either juvenile, intermediate or adult foliage if there is any purpose in doing so. A record should be kept as well, for far too much haphazard propagation has been carried out over the last twenty years. It provides the main reason why nomenclature of these dwarf conifers is in such a state of chaos, with its ever-increasing list of both published and unpublished synonyms.

The Register

Starting at the end of the cutting register of which a leaf is shown on page 167, a page can be drawn up as reproduced below. The crux of this record lies in the table which gives the key to the type of cutting being propagated. Provided it is sensibly used, there is no reason why it will not materially assist in bringing order out of chaos. It is surprising how easily one forgets even after a period of a few months how or where the cuttings were taken. There are nine different ways of taking cuttings from a plant which bears the various types of foliage and each of these are recorded on the register by a single number only, this number will give the answer to the type of cutting being propagated.

Number	Type of Cutting	Foliage
1	Basal	Juvenile
2	Basal	Intermediate
3	Basal	Adult
4	Intermediate	Juvenile
5	Intermediate	Intermediate
6	Intermediate	Adult
7	Apical	Juvenile
8	Apical	Intermediate
9	Apical	Adult

For example if a plant of *Chamaecyparis lawsoniana* 'Fletcheri Nana' was being propagated and cuttings with adult foliage were being taken from the base of the plant, in the register they would be recorded as number three under the heading, *Type of Cutting*. This number is then printed on the label of the plant when potted up so that it would read as follows: *C.l.* 'F. Nana' 3. If, after growing on the cutting until it has reached a sizable plant, further cuttings are required from the new plant they should be recorded as follows. Under the heading *Plant* in the register an entry is made, *C.l.* 'F. Nana' 3, and under *Type of Cutting*, the cuttings from which (*C.l.* 'F. Nana' 3) this time for example are taken from the base

Plant	Type of Cutting	Date Taken	Date Rooted	Remarks
Chamaecyparis lawsoniana 'Fletcheri Nana'	3	26–6–54	8–9–54	Heated frame
Juniperus communis 'Echiniformis'	9	14–7–54	12–2–55	Heated frame
Chamaecyparis obtusa 'Compacta'	4	16–8–54	20–6–55	Shaded frame
Chamaecyparis obtusa 'Caespitosa'	2	16–8–54	20–6–55	Shaded frame
Chamaecyparis obtusa 'Minima'	3	16–8–54	20–6–55	Shaded frame
Chamaecyparis obtusa 'Minima'	6	16–8–54	20–6–55	Shaded frame
Chamaecyparis obtusa 'Minima'	9	16–8–54	20–6–55	Shaded frame
Cryptomeria 'Knaptonensis'	1	18–7–55	16–3–56	Heated frame
Cryptomeria 'Knaptonensis'	2	18–7–55	16–3–56	Heated frame
Cryptomeria 'Knaptonensis'	5	17–7–55	16–3–56	Heated frame
Cryptomeria 'Knaptonensis'	6	18–7–55	16–3–56	Heated frame
Cryptomeria 'Knaptonensis'	7	18–7–55	16–3–56	Heated frame

with juvenile foliage, the number 1 is recorded in the register and on the label attached to these cuttings, and also any which are potted up after rooting will bear the name *C.l.* 'F. Nana' 3, 1. Should a form which is naturally different from its parents result, either in shape, foliage or rate of growth, it will be possible to trace it back to the plant from which it originated. It may seem as if the numbering would become unwieldy but as the majority of dwarf conifers are so slow growing, it could take up to fifteen years to obtain a sizable plant in the second generation. Naturally not all dwarf conifers bear the three different types of foliage mentioned but the register must show all changes so that a true and accurate record can be made to note any variations which occur.

Cuttings

Dealing with cuttings first, there are three periods in the year when these can be taken. First, in August, when cuttings of well ripened wood with a heel of the old wood placed in a north-facing frame, should have callused by the following spring, and be well rooted by autumn. A further period until the spring of the following year should elapse and they are then potted up in compost B. Second in March, if a heated frame is available, cuttings of the previous year's growth with a heel can be taken, or green cuttings in June. By autumn a large percentage will have rooted. As an

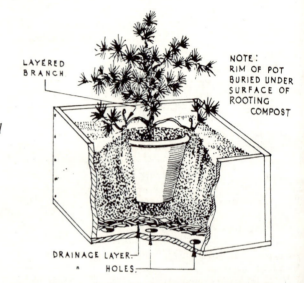

LAYERED
BRANCH

NOTE:
RIM OF POT
BURIED UNDER
SURFACE OF
ROOTING
COMPOST

26. *Layering cedars and pines*

DRAINAGE LAYER
" HOLES.

aid to striking cuttings there are hormone powders on the market which assist in the formation of roots. These are available for green, half-ripe and well-ripened wood, and the appropriate one should be used to match the type of cutting to be rooted. That they are of use has been proved over a number of years but the freshly rooted material seem to like a less rich mixture for their first potting up. This is possibly due to the large amount of root formed in a short time, in relation to the foliage. Compost A is the suggested medium for the first potting and the young plants will soon go ahead in this. Sometimes cuttings of junipers seem to be very loth to form new roots. These can be assisted if, after the cutting has callused over, it is removed and a cut with a sharp knife is made across the base, and then replaced in the propagating frame.

The genera Cedrus and Pinus present a difficulty, for they are not easy to root from cuttings and the only satisfactory method is by layering. This is often a problem, for the majority of these two genera are dwarf trees with a bole so it is not possible to layer in the normal way. If the plant to be propagated is in a small pan all that is necessary is to place it inside a large pot, deep enough so that the branches are about 1 inch below the rim. The space around the pan and pot is then filled to the rim of the larger pot with equal parts of loam, leaf-mould and sand, and this is well firmed. Before layering a slight upward cut is made at the base of each shoot where it touches the soil and each cut is carefully dusted with a rooting hormone applied with a small soft paint brush. The angle of the cut should be towards the apex of the branch. Finally the branches are pegged down. After watering carefully, small stones can be placed over the surface of the compost where the branches are pinned down, which will help to conserve moisture while they are forming roots. The pot in its container is then plunged to its rim in a plunge bed outside in a cool shady spot and kept moist until the cuttings have rooted. This can take up to two years, but no forcing should be attempted otherwise the parent plant will suffer from the too warm and close conditions. The rooted branches should be severed from their parent, then after a further period of three months potted on singly. Should the specimens to be propagated be large, the best method is to build up a wooden box to accommodate the pan and apply the same method as with the pot (Fig. 26).

Air-Layering

With the advent of polythene in varying thicknesses, air-layering is becoming more widely practised today as a means of propagating plants *in situ*. The great problem here is not rooting the cuttings, which is fairly simple, but getting the rooted cuttings to grow on after being potted up. The most successful way to date is to use an extremely poor compost for the first potting, as in a rich mixture the roots seem to stagnate and die. I think the use of hormones to induce rooting certainly throws out the balance between top growth (i.e. stem and foliage) and the amount of root formed by their use. The problem as I see it is that no plant will normally make more root than is necessary to provide sustenance to top growth. All surplus will, if the potting medium is too rich, rot and die off, thus allowing infection to spread easily over the whole of the root system, with fatal results. A poor lean compost with less available food per square inch will enable the rooted cutting to utilise its root system to the best advantage until balance is once more stabilised. The medium to try is one part loam and leaf-mould to two parts Cornish sand riddled through a $\frac{1}{16}$-inch sieve.

The procedure in air-layering is as follows. A cut is made in the wood as for ground-layering and painted with a powdered rooting hormone. Sphagnum moss is then packed round the cut extending to approximately $\frac{1}{2}$ inch on either side. The moss should first be dipped in rainwater and then squeezed out. After wrapping it round the cut it is bound with a strong thread. A small polythene tube of $\frac{1}{250}$ inch thickness is slipped over the ball of moss, allowing space on either side to help retain moisture. The ends are finally bound securely with adhesive insulating tape. Polythene has the property of allowing passage to gases like oxygen and carbon dioxide but not water-vapour. Rooting takes place more quickly than with ground-layering and an added advantage is that it is possible to see when this has taken place.

Suitable Species and Forms

All the conifers listed here are suitable for pan culture and give satisfaction over a good number of years, in fact some will certainly outlive the cultivator and yet retain their dwarf stature. In the course of years a number may outgrow the largest pan capable of holding them, but it can be a long time before it will be necessary to discard the plants. Provided care is taken, restriction of growth by delaying repotting will further extend the time that these miniatures can be retained as specimens for the alpine house and frames, although under normal conditions these plants are, owing to root restriction, necessarily slower growing when confined to a pan.

The majority of plants listed are available in commerce. All are in cultivation at the time of writing, but a diligent search will have to be made for some of the rarer forms. Many are scarce, this being due to several causes, amongst which are difficulty of increase and the extreme slowness of growth. It is always worth while to walk round some of the out of the way nurseries for one is often rewarded by the discovery of a rare form. It is over twenty-six years ago that I found a rare form of *Chamaecyparis obtusa*, the cultivar 'Compacta', which I grew in the open ground for ten years. It was then lifted and potted up and today is still only 9 inches across by 3 inches high. The cost was two shillings and a broken pot containing an aged *Juniperus communis* 'Compressa' was thrown in for luck!

There are a great number of dwarf conifers labelled under different names. Many are invalid or just synonyms, thus adding to the confusion with which these miniatures abound, and most of them are extremely rare and difficult to propagate, so they have for obvious reasons been ignored. Only those of which there is a reasonable chance of obtaining are included.

ABIES (*Pinaceae*).

A native of N.E. America, the balsam fir *A. balsamea* has produced a number of dwarf forms but only two are suitable for our purpose.

A. balsamea var. hudsonia. (E). (Syn. *A. hudsonia; Picea fraseri hudsonia*). A sterile form from the White Mountains, New Hampshire, America, at high altitudes. This has medium thin branchlets growing at an angle of 60°. The leaves are straight, at right angles to the branches, deep bright green above, the undersides have two sunken blue lines. The edges of leaf and midrib are deep dark green. Annual growth is between $\frac{1}{2}$ and 1 inch.

A. balsamea 'Nana'. (E). (Syn. *A. b.* 'Globosa'; *A. b.* 'Globosa Nana'). This is often confused with *A. b.* var. *hudsonia* and used often to be sold as such, for it has today become rare and one is more likely to get the variety *hudsonia* when asking for 'Nana'. There is a great difference between the two. In the 'Nana' form the slender branchlets grow at an angle of approximately 45°. The leaves are not straight but in the shape of an arc and bright green above. Below there are two sunken white bands divided by a raised yellow-green midrib, the whole surrounded by an edge of pale yellow. The annual growth is in the region of ½ inch.

CEDRUS (*Pinaceae*).

The cedars have produced a few forms which will help to furnish the alpine house over a number of years. All will eventually become too large although this may take twenty years depending on cultivation. Pan culture also helps considerably in restricting growth.

C. brevifolia. (E). (Syn. *C. libani* var. *brevifolia*).
This tree has now been given specific rank and is a native of Cyprus, where although slow growing it makes a tree of some height after many years. In this country however it seems to be dwarfer, its rate being less than 1 inch a year under pan culture. It forms an erect plant with a stout bole, branches almost horizontal, slightly pendulous at tip, well clothed in small linear leaves up to ½ inch in length, thick, and slightly incurved, same width along entire length but terminating in an acute sinewy tip; dark green in colour.

C. libani 'Comte de Dijon'. (E). (Syn. *C.* 'Comte de Dijon'; *C. libanitica* 'Comte de Dijon').
This is the rarest of the dwarf forms of the cedars of Lebanon and when offered by the trade *C. brevifolia* often has to do duty for this plant although it is quite distinct. It makes a very dense pyramidal bush seldom with a bole unless the plant has been grafted or suffered from starvation in its youth; branches are slightly ascending, slender, densely clothed with ½ inch fine needle-shaped dark green leaves, straight not incurved, terminating in an acute sinewy point. Annual growth is less than 1 inch in cultivation.

C. libani 'Nana'. (E). (Syn. *C. libanitica* 'Nana').
Another variety which is similar to 'Comte de Dijon', but is less upright and not so dense, forming a roundish bush. Leaves similar, dark green, longer, being about 1 inch in length, very coarse. Annual growth between 1 and 2 inches a year under normal conditions, but will be nearer 1 inch under pan culture.

C. libani 'Sargentii'. (E). (Syn. *C. libani* 'Pendula Sargentii').
Sargent's cedar is a form named after Professor Sargent of the Arnold Arboretum and if it is understood that it will outgrow a pan under normal conditions in ten to twenty years, there is no reason why it should not be included in a collection, as it is obtainable in the trade. It has a small stout bole with radiating slender branches, horizontal at first then pendulous. Leaves deep green, long, needle-shaped, up to 2 inches and densely crowded

on the close thick growth of laterals. Annual growth about 1½ inch under pan culture.

CHAMAECYPARIS (*Cupressaceae*).

For many years this genus has been lumped together with Cupressus and even today a large number of nurserymen still retain this name on their labels. Botanically the main differences between the genera Chamaecyparis, the false cypress and Cupressus, the true cypress, is that the former have flattened branches and small cones while the latter have more rounded branches and larger cones. Also included in Chamaecyparis today are the many varieties once known under the generic name of Retinospora, these being nothing more than forms of Chamaecyparis which have retained their juvenile foliage in cultivation. Of all the different genera which have produced dwarf conifers suitable for the alpine house, Chamaecyparis contains the largest number of forms and a collection could be built up with these alone to provide a display over a number of years without outgrowing their allotted space. The *obtusa* varieties are among the smallest and slowest growing of all, their annual rate of growth being almost negligible.

C. lawsoniana 'Ellwoodii'. (E). (Syn. *Cupressus l.* 'Ellwoodii').

This plant has been included because it is easily obtainable and will make a fine specimen in a pan for a few years provided it is remembered that in the open ground it will grow up to 4 feet in approximately ten years. Naturally the growth is much slower in a pan with its attendant root restriction. It originated from a seedling in Swanmore Park, Bishops Waltham, and was named after the gardener, Mr Ellwood. All plants in cultivation today are from this original plant so it can be seen that it is easy to propagate and grows rather quickly. It makes an ascending column thickening from the base to the middle of the plant, then tapering rather more abruptly, branches upright splayed, recurving; leaves grey-green, densely crowded, recurved, inner leaves very pale in colour. This plant differs from *C.l.* 'Fletcheri' which is sometimes called upon to do duty for it in that 'Fletcheri' is quicker growing, branches are upright, straight to their tips. Leaves in opposite pairs, less crowded, blue grey-green on the outside growth but dark green towards the centre of the plant.

C. lawsoniana 'Filiformis Compacta'. (E). (Syn. *C.l.* 'Filiformis Globosa'; *C.l.* 'Globosa Filiformis').

This is a form which is included for its shape and appearance but will outgrow its pan in due course. It makes a congested crowded bushlet with spreading branches, reddish-brown in colour. Leaves appressed to the drooping laterals with the exception of their tips, gives the branchlets the appearance of whipcord, small deep glaucous green. Growth 2¼ inches yearly, less under pan culture.

C. lawsoniana 'Fletcheri Nana'. (E).

The origin of this dwarf form is a mystery but it is likely to be a form which was propagated from a cutting of 'Fletcheri' taken from the base with juvenile foliage. It is intensely compact making rounded buns of congested feathery leaves, glaucous green in colour and the clue to its parentage is that the inner leaves are of a darker green. The plant is never columnar in habit, always being wider at the base than in height and retains its juvenile foliage. Annual growth is in the region of 1 inch.

C. lawsoniana 'Forsteckensis'. (E). (Syn. *C. forsteckiana*).
A dwarf conifer which has a bad name due to grafting or propagating from strong growing shoots, whereas it is a slow growing plant if increased from basal cuttings only. It forms a tight congested mass with abnormal contorted, tasselled mossy branches. Leaves glaucous green, densely crowded on the twisted 2 to 3 inch sprays. The true dwarf form has an annual growth of approximately 1 inch under pan culture.

C. lawsoniana 'Minima'. (E). (Syn. *Cupressus l.* 'Minima').
This makes a very slow growing rounded form of stiff crowded branches. The branchlets are twisted so that the sprays appear sideways, the colour of the leaves is distinctive bluish yellow-green. Annual growth 1½ inch, becoming a large plant in time.

C. lawsoniana 'Minima Aurea'. (E). (Syn. *Cupressus l.* 'Minima Aurea'; *Cupressus l.* 'Minima Aurea Rogersii').
Similar to the type this attractive conifer was raised at W. H. Roger's Red Lodge Nursery, the colour being a distinctive golden. Annual growth as for the type.

C. lawsoniana 'Pygmaea Argentea'. (E). (Syn. *C.l.* 'Pygmaea Backhouse Silver').
The holder of this name has been under a cloud for a number of years as it varies from the original plant grown in Holland but this is due to climatic conditions rather than any other reason. It makes a slow spreading half-rounded bushlet with congested semi-horizontal slender branches with sprays of dark glaucous green foliage, white tipped in their young state. Provided this plant is kept in semi-shaded conditions the white tip will persist but if retained in the alpine house, the tip will fade to a light green. Annual growth 1½ inch but this will be less under pan culture.

C. obtusa. (E). (Syn. *Cupressus obtusa*).
The species *C. obtusa* is a native of Japan, introduced into Europe in 1861 by that eminent Victorian nurseryman J. V. Veitch who was responsible for many noted plants finding their way into cultivation. There are a number of dwarf forms. In fact it is safe to say that this species has been responsible for producing more of the slow growing dwarf conifers in cultivation than any other arborescent conifer.

C. obtusa 'Caespitosa'. (E).
This is one of the three best bun forms which originated from seedlings of *C. obtusa* 'Nana Gracilis', grown in the Red Bank Nurseries of W. H. Rogers Ltd. With *C.o.* 'Juniperoides' and 'Minima' this must be considered the slowest growing of all dwarf conifers in cultivation today. It is a

rounded bun of congested tufts of small branches, the laterals so placed
that they have the appearance of doll's saucers. Leaves bright green,
crowded, minute, obtuse, appressed to the stems, giving the laterals the
appearance of whipcord. Annual growth ¼ inch.

C. obtusa 'Compacta'. (E).

A very slow growing plant and although rare in cultivation the true plant
is here as I have propagated it over the last twenty years and distributed it
amongst a number of keen growers of these miniatures. It makes a low
compact bushlet with radiating almost horizontal branches, densely clad
with dark green obtuse leaves on small fan saucer-shaped laterals. Annual
growth approximately ¼ inch. It is to all intents and purposes a miniature
form of *C.o.* 'Nana'.

C. obtusa 'Ericoides'. (E). (Syn. *Juniperus sanderi; Retinospora sanderi;*
  C. obtusa 'Sanderi').

This delightful miniature originated in Japan in the late nineties and has
never been common in this country, possibly owing to its dislike of cold
winds, but it is an admirable plant for pan culture in the alpine house,
where it receives shelter from these winds. It is a form which retains its
juvenile foliage with thick stout branches and slightly ascending stout
laterals borne at right angles to the branches. Leaves small, congested in
threes, apex obtuse not needle-shaped, flat on top, convex underneath, the
whole tightly congested, forming a rounded bush flattish on top. An
attractive plant owing to the colour of the foliage being a glossy blue-
green in spring and summer, turning to purple-red in winter. It requires
a little more sun than most *obtusa* forms and should be brought into the
alpine house in late August. Annual growth approximately ½ inch.

C. obtusa 'Flabelliformis'. (E).

A small distinct form of tight, congested, more horizontal than ascending
branches, laterals tightly packed with the minute appressed deep green
foliage, in the shape of a fan, flat not saucer-shaped like many of the *obtusa*
forms: the whole plant is wider than high. Annual growth less than 1 inch.

C. obtusa 'Juniperoides'. (E).

Another dwarf form slightly less compact than 'Ericoides', the fan shaped
branches are decurved. Leaves minute, almost needle shaped only partly
appressed, the tips being free and incurved, bright green in colour. Annual
growth ½ inch.

C. obtusa 'Juniperoides Compacta'. (E).

This is identical to the type with the exception of being smaller in all its
parts and more compact. Possibly originated either as a seedling or a basal
cutting from the type plant in Messrs Roger's nursery. Annual growth
½ inch.

C. obtusa 'Minima'. (E). (Syn. *C.o.* 'Tetragona Minima'. *C.o.* 'Pygmaea'.
  C.o. 'Minima Densa').

As its varietal name implies it is a compact tight ball of 1 inch semi-erect
branches, the minute recurved branchlets radiate in a brush-like cluster at

the top half of the branches. Leaves arranged in fours round the stem, bright glossy green, minute, oval, not obtuse but slightly pointed at apex, incurving and not appressed to stem but at a narrow angle. Annual growth about $\frac{1}{4}$ inch. The illustration between pages 488–489 of a ten year old plant from a cutting will give an idea of the rate of growth and form and it is possible to note the leaf arrangement round the branchlets.

C. obtusa 'Nana'. (E). (Syn. *C.o.* 'Nana Densa').

No dwarf conifer is more delightful than this dwarf form of the species if obtained true to name. The problem is it is a rare plant and *C.o.* 'Nana Gracilis' is often sold in its place. This is much more vigorous and will quickly attain a good size. Grafted plants too seem to grow faster than any other comparable form, so this plant should be acquired on its own roots. There is one great difference between the two forms, so that it is easy to distinguish between them. The true plant has leaves of almost dull black-green while those of 'Nana Gracilis' are bright deep green. Branches are horizontal, not so dense as in other forms but the branchlets are crowded in saucer-shaped sprays. Annual growth less than 1 inch.

C. obtusa 'Nana Aurea'. (E).

This yellow form is similar to the type but is a more vigorous and stouter plant, and will make a grand specimen for a number of years in a pan.

C. obtusa 'Nana Kosteri'. (E).

Yet another form as slow growing as *C.o.* 'Nana' and differing only on two points. The plant is more compact, and the congested appressed leaves are brownish-green. This form originated in Holland in the nurseries of M. Koster & Sons, Boskoop.

C. obtusa 'Pygmaea'. (E).

This plant must not be confused with the variety 'Pygmaea' of the trade which is a prostrate, open fan shaped form, making a large plant in spread at least, in a very short period. The true plant which is rare in cultivation is intermediate between 'Nana' and 'Nana Kosteri,' making a low bush with horizontal fan shaped branches, laterals fairly widely spaced, almost at right angles to the branch, not saucer-shaped but slightly inverted; leaves almost appressed, small obtuse and not incurved, colour shiny brown-green. There are two magnificent specimens of the true plant which can be seen in the alpine houses at Kew and Wisley. Annual growth less than 1 inch.

C. pisifera. (E). (Syn. *Cupressus pisifera; Retinospora pisifera*).

The species was introduced from Japan by J. G. Veitch in 1861 and it has produced a number of dwarf forms which are suitable for cultivation as pan plants.

C. pisifera 'Filifera Aurea'. (E).

The type plant is rather too quickly growing for pan culture but the golden form will, with its slower growing habit, be suitable over a number of years. It makes a lax open bushlet of pendulous thin branches clothed with ovate, needle tipped, loosely overlapping leaves, bright golden-yellow in colour. This plant should be given more sun than the other forms as this tends to improve the golden colour of the foliage. Annual growth approximately 1 inch.

C. pisifera 'Nana'. (E).

This is an extremely slow growing conifer, certainly one of the slowest of all the *pisifera* types, rarely exceeding ½ inch growth yearly. It makes a tight congested roundish bun-shaped specimen of fan-like branches closely clad with small branchlets and laterals, the apex of which are decurved, these being packed with the deep blue-green foliage.

C. pisifera 'Nana Aureo-Variegata'. (E). (Syn. *Retinospora pisifera* 'Nana Aureo-Variegata').

Similar to the type but more rounded and densely clothed with variegated golden-green foliage. This is in cultivation and is a desirable plant. Unfortunately it is not always the plant sent when ordered. *C.p.* 'Compacta Variegata' is often received. This is a more lax, flat-topped plant and the leaves are blotched with golden-yellow and white in place of the overall variegation of golden-yellow. Annual growth approximately 1 inch.

C. pisifera 'Plumosa Compressa'. (E). (Syn. *Cupressus pisifera* 'Plumosa Nana Compressa'; *C.p.* 'Squarrosa Nana'; *C.p.* 'Squarrosa Pygmaea'). Another very slow growing form which is still rare in cultivation, making small hummocks of tight congested ascending branches, densely clothed with laterals, bearing both juvenile and intermediate foliage, looking like a ball of moss of a rich glaucous green. Annual growth less than 1 inch.

C. pisifera 'Plumosa Nana Aurea'. (E). (Syn. *C.p.* 'Plumosa Aurea Nana').

The type plant is very desirable but unfortunately does not seem to be in cultivation here today. The light golden-yellow variety is just as good, making a compact sub-globose plant with slender branches and needle shaped rounded minute leaves, growing at right angles to the laterals. Annual growth in the region of 1 inch.

C. pisifera 'Plumosa Rogersii'. (E). (Syn. *C.p.* 'Plumosa Nana Aurea Rogersii'; *C.p.* 'Plumosa Aurea Compacta').

This makes a small broad columnar bushlet which is the main difference between the last plant and this. It is less coarse, the foliage being much finer and more at an angle of 45° than at right angles to the laterals. Colour light golden-yellow. Annual growth approximately 1 inch. Another of Messrs Rogers' fine introductions.

C. pisifera 'Squarrosa Intermedia'. (E). (Syn. *C.* 'Plumosa Pygmaea'). Both this and the next are the only two really dwarf forms of *pisifera* 'Squarrosa' which are suitable and although they are in cultivation, both are extremely rare and they are recorded here because the type plant is often sent out under the names of one or the other. *C.p.* 'S. Intermedia' is a fascinating shaped plant best described as a small cup ending in a point, bearing both juvenile and intermediate foliage, the latter being present almost exclusively on the upper part of the plant. The juvenile foliage is tightly packed on the laterals, in whorls of threes, at right angles or slightly ascending, apex incurved, small oblong, ending in an abrupt point. The intermediate foliage is about half the size, borne in opposite pairs, just as crowded as the juvenile, ascending at narrow angle, tips incurved, almost lanceolate, colour pale grass-green. Annual growth is about 1 inch under pan culture.

C. pisifera 'Squarrosa Minima'. (E).
This is a slow growing conifer, making less than 1 inch yearly with almost horizontal branches from which the ascending branchlets are tightly packed bearing leaves in whorls of three, broad, tapering to a point, glaucous green, margins dark green, midrib wide, green, this being separated by two sunken white lines, underneath two broad white lines, and a narrow keel.

CRYPTOMERIA (*Taxodiaceae*).

The type plant *C. japonica* introduced into Europe about 1884 and known as the Japanese Cedar, has produced a number of dwarf forms. As far as is known all with the exception of one, originated in Japan. These plants are very susceptible to cold and drying winds, but make admirable plants for the alpine house where protection from these can be given.

C. japonica 'Bandai-Sugi'. (E).
A fine dwarf conifer of close compact habit growing more in width than height, with irregular sized branchlets densely packed with two kinds of needle-shaped leaves, long and short, the latter thicker and more dense on the branchlets. Colour bright bluish-green, the tips turning to reddish-brown in winter. Annual growth less than 1 inch.

C. japonica 'Knaptonensis'. (E).
This is a dwarf form from the Isola Madre in Europe where it originated as a 'witches' broom'. It is a fine colour break, being almost bun-shaped with a mass of congested branchlets densely clothed with dazzling white foliage. Very slow growing, less than 1 inch a year under alpine house conditions.

C. japonica 'Vilmoriniana'. (E).
An outstanding plant which was introduced to this country in 1923 from Les Verriers, France, by Murray Hornibrook, and named after M. Philippe de Vilmorin who had introduced it from Japan about thirty-five years previously. It is absolutely essential to obtain this plant on its own roots for it to retain its dwarf habit. Grafted plants will, in the course of a year or so, throw abnormal shoots out-of-character from different parts of the plant. Unfortunately far too often *C. japonica* 'Compacta', a much taller growing form, is sold under this name. The true plant is slow growing, making less than 1 inch yearly, semi-erect with ascending branches. These are slightly incurving and well clothed with stout needle-shaped foliage of a deep green, shading to dark copper in autumn.

DACRYDIUM (*Podocarpaceae*).

This is a small genus of conifers related to the Yew from the southern hemisphere of which there is only one suitable for alpine house culture.
D. laxifolium. (E).
This dwarf conifer is a true species confined to the southern hemisphere, in fact it is endemic to New Zealand, where it is found in both the North and South Islands. It makes a charming prostrate shrublet with radiating very horizontal spreading branches. Leaves in their young state are borne at right angles to the branchlets, they are lax, linear, flat, curved, tapering to a point. When mature they are more dense, thick obtuse not pointed, but overlapping on the laterals, colour a deep glossy green. Annual growth less than 1 inch.

JUNIPERUS (*Cupressaceae*).

A large race of conifers containing a great number of semi-dwarf forms which have been given names and synonyms creating great confusion amongst these miniatures. There are really only two plants which are suitable for our purpose. Of these the Noah's Ark juniper, *J. communis* 'Compressa', known under many varietal names will in the course of time become too large for pan culture but can be used over a good number of years before reaching that state. The other, the rare and very desirable 'Hedgehog' juniper, *J.c.* 'Echiniformis' is well-named bearing a great resemblance to that animal both in appearance and touch and will never outgrow a pan in a normal average lifespan.

J. communis 'Compressa'. (E). (Syn. *J. communis* 'Hibernica Compressa'; *J. compressa*; *J. communis* 'Hispanica'; *J. hispanica*; *J. hibernica* 'Compressa').

It makes an upright perfectly symmetrical column of closely congested erect branches with acutely ascending triangular laterals, white in the juvenile state, red-brown when adult; densely clothed with the small linear foliage in whorls of three, glaucous green above with sunken narrow green midrib, below bright green and convex. Requires a sunny position to give of its best and the annual growth in a pan should not exceed 1 inch.

J. communis 'Echiniformis'. (E). (Syn. *J. oxycedrus* 'Echiniformis' *J. echiniformis*).

This is certainly one of the best of all dwarf conifers, rare and slow growing, although it is not as obtainable as it was a few years ago. I have found that it strikes quite well from cuttings of semi-ripened wood taken in August, these will root by the following spring with bottom heat. It makes a small rounded bush of slightly ascending short stout branches with small laterals densely packed with the spine-like foliage, sharp to the touch colour deep bright green. It needs protection from cold winds but is ideal for pan culture where the growth is under $\frac{1}{2}$ inch yearly.

MICROCACHRYS (*Podocarpaceae*).

This is a monotypic genus containing one species confined to the summits of the Western Range and Mount Lapeyrouse in Tasmania and is an ideal dwarf conifer for pan culture.

M. tetragona. (E).
This is a completely prostrate dwarf conifer, spreading horizontally with lax roundish red branches, laterals, alternate at regular intervals, leaves small, imbricated, appressed, not free, mid-green in colour. It is monoecious, the flowers of both sexes are borne at the apex of individual shoots. The delightful miniature cones are only ¼ inch in length, deep orange in colour and are borne in profusion on a well-established plant. The annual growth is less than 1 inch.

PICEA (*Pinaceae*).

The spruces have produced a surprising number of dwarf conifers. The Norway spruce, *P. abies*, alone having over sixty dwarf forms, although the majority will in the course of time be too large for pan culture. Also there is a great deal of confusion in their naming and care has to be exercised when buying for many are practically indistinguishable.

P. abies 'Echiniformis'. (E). (Syn. *Abies excelsa* 'Echiniformis'. *P. excelsa* 'Echiniformis').
This is a dwarf variety rare in cultivation making a low hummock more or less flat on the top. Branches light brown, horizontal, laterals slightly ascending, congested, glabrous. Leaves linear, thin rounded, long, almost 1 inch in length, sparsely set at right angles to the stem, pale yellow-green in colour. Annual growth 1 inch.

P. abies 'Gregoryana'. (E). (Syn. *Abies excelsa* 'Gregoryana'. *P. excelsa* 'Gregoryana').
A charming dwarf, making a close congested mound of individual hummocks with small densely packed branches. Laterals, thin, grey-brown, congested at a slight angle to the branches, descending at the apex. Leaves linear with abrupt tip, pale grey-green, arranged radially on all the laterals, irregularly angled, some even at right angles to the stem. Annual growth less than ½ inch. Of all the dwarf Picea, this is possibly the plant which is seldom found true, many other forms of *P. abies* doing duty for it. There are even forms of *P.a.* 'Gregoryana' but these without exception are not as slow growing or as desirable. There is one infallible test for the type plant, that is the leaves are always radially all over the plant and the emphasis is on the word 'all'.

P. abies 'Humilis'. (E). (Syn. *Abies excelsa* 'Humilis'. *P. excelsa* 'Humilis').
Another extremely slow growing plant which is still rare in cultivation, making a bushlet that is more wide than tall of crowded horizontal branches densely packed with the fine white ascending laterals. Leaves linear, rounded slightly tapering to apex, congested, radial, less than a

¼ inch, twisted or recurved, semi-right-angle to the stem pointing forward, deep glaucous green. Annual growth less than ½ inch.

P. abies 'Pygmaea'. (E). (Syn. *Abies excelsa* 'Pygmaea'; *A. parvula*; *P. excelsa* 'Pygmaea'. *P. excelsa* 'Gregoryana').

A charming dwarf with crowded irregular branches more ascending than horizontal, the glabrous white laterals also irregular in size but always semi-erect, so that the bushlet is more conical and erect then *P.a.* 'Gregoryana', which it closely resembles. Other differences are, in 'Pygmaea' the size of the laterals and branches are irregular and fasciated whereas in 'Gregoryana' they are more or less constant, leaves also much thicker, not so rounded but underneath abruptly tapering at apex, deep yellow-green not grey-green. Annual growth under ½ inch.

P. albertiana 'Conica'. (E). (Syn. *P. alba albertiana* forma 'Conica'; *P. glauca albertiana* 'Conica').

This fine plant will in time become too large for pan culture but the root restriction that growing in a pan imposes will allow a number of years to pass before this occurs. It has a distinct conical shape, tapering to a fine point and the branches are ascending, packed with fine pliable laterals of a light yellow. Leaves arranged irregularly round the stems, more on the upper surface, roundish, thin, long in relation to the laterals, width uniform, slightly incurved, terminating in an abrupt point. Colour light glaucous green. This plant should be kept away from draughty situations. Annual growth approximately 1 inch.

PINUS (*Pinaceae*).

There are over fifty species of pines, but few of these have produced dwarf forms and although a number of the species and their forms can be and are grown as specimens in pans over a period of years without becoming too large, it is as well to bear this limitation in mind if deciding to use them. I have restricted the dwarf forms to four and one of these is a true species.

P. cembra 'Pygmaea'. (E). (Syn. *P. cembra* 'Pumila'; *P. pygmaea*).

This is an extremely slow growing form, which originated from a seedling of the Arolla Pine making a small bush of close spreading pendulous branches. The leaves borne in fives are irregular, small, fine, curved, grey-green in colour and the annual growth is about 1 inch.

P. parviflora 'Brevifolia'. (E).

The species is used by the Japanese to produce the outstanding artificially dwarfed trees, an art in which they are past masters. This form which came from Japan to Europe in 1890 is a dwarf conifer requiring no artificial aid to restrict growth to retain its dwarf habit. It makes a small semi-prostrate, slightly rounded bushlet of compact crowded branches with small laterals. Leaves densely crowded in bundles of five, thick, stout, incurved, apex obtuse, bright green above, glaucous white beneath. The old leaves persist for at least two seasons. Annual growth approximately ½ inch.

P. pumila. (E).

This is the dwarfest of all pines and in its natural habitat it is quite prostrate and spreads over a very large area, rooting as it goes. Even when introduced to the lowlands in cultivation it is rarely above 1 foot in height. The plants seen in cultivation are far from typical, often being grafted, which gives them a bole and the appearance of a top-heavy tree which the first gust of a gale would tear completely from its pan. In nature and growing on its own roots in cultivation, the main stem is always prostrate or slightly ascending, never upright. It is a native of Japan and Siberia, and is considered a true species, although it has been treated as only a dwarf form of *P. cembra*, even Hornibrook calls it the Japanese and Siberian form of *P. cembra*. That there are several differences besides ultimate size is apparent by making a comparison between the two plants. The following will assist in identification.

Pinus pumila	*Pinus cembra*
Leaves 1½ inch, crowded in bundles of five. Slender curved margins serrulate right to apex, two marginal resin canals.	Leaves 2–2½ inches, crowded in bundles of five. Slender curved margins partly serrulate, never to apex, resin canal median.
Buds ovoid, obtuse, resinous scales.	Buds ovoid, acuminate, resinous scales.
Cones hairless small.	Cones slightly hairy, larger.
Habit prostrate or slightly ascending even in the lowlands.	Habit upright.

P. sylvestris 'Beauvronensis'. (E).

The Scots pine, a native of these Isles, has produced a number of dwarf forms and all are rare and difficult to obtain, but there is one in cultivation which I propose to describe as it can be occasionally found. This dwarf form of the Scots pine is believed to have originated from a witches' broom and the general appearance bears this out. It makes a dense congested mass of branches with crowded right-angled laterals packed with pairs of ½-inch leaves, slightly toothed and twisted, glaucous grey-green in colour. The annual growth is about 1 inch. Although this plant will eventually outgrow its pan it will take many years to do so.

TAXUS (*Taxaceae*).

The yews have a reputation for longevity and slowness of growth, yet strangely enough they have produced very few dwarf forms and there is only one that can be considered for our purposes.

T. baccata 'Pygmaea'. (E).

This is an extremely slow growing conifer which originally came from the Dutch nurseries of Messrs Den Ouden of Boskoop, Holland. It makes a shallow, almost oval bushlet of densely congested semi-upright branches and laterals. The small leaves are crowded, ovate, thick, recurving, dark grey-green. Annual growth is in the region of ½ inch.

THUJA (*Cupressaceae*).

The species of the Chinese Arbor-Vitae, *T. orientalis* was introduced into Europe during the eighteenth century and this has produced two dwarf forms which can be utilised for pan culture in the alpine house or frame. They should not be allowed to dry out or be placed where there is any chance of their being caught by cold winds or frosts, for their foliage is liable to be badly cut under these conditions.

T. orientalis 'Meldensis'. (E). (Syn. *Biota meldensis*; *B. orientalis* 'Meldensis').

A dwarf flat-topped, roundish, compact shrublet with numerous ascending branches, laterals and sprays crowded. Foliage needle-shaped, opposite, intermediate, glaucous green, turning to reddish-purple in winter. Annual growth less than 1 inch.

T. orientalis 'Minima Glauca'. (E). (Syn. *Biota orientalis* 'Minima Glauca').

This is smaller in all its parts than 'Meldensis' which it resembles, but it is more rounded with ascending congested branches and laterals densely clothed with fine needle-shaped juvenile glaucous green foliage, turning to yellow-brown in winter. Annual growth about ½ inch.

CHAPTER ELEVEN

GENERAL LIST
(FOR LIST OF DWARF CONIFERS SEE CHAPTER TEN)

ACANTHOLIMON (*Plumbaginaceae*).

This genus contains a number of suitable plants for the alpine house, making spiny cushions of almost indestructible foliage and everlasting flowers. They add a touch of colour in the house, especially during the winter months with their persistent cup-like bracts. All being avid sun lovers, coming as they do from Asia Minor, Persia and India, they certainly cannot be given too much sun in this country.

CULTIVATION. For alpine house culture they do well in compost A over faultless drainage and the spiny cushions should be packed tight by working in chippings from underneath. They need a normal amount of water from April to the first week in August, then the following four weeks the plants should be allowed to dry out to ripen growth; from September to April give only enough water to keep the compost from becoming arid.

PROPAGATION. Unfortunately the plants do not set viable seed in this country and also they show a reluctance to root from cuttings, and a batch will only give a small percentage of strikes. The best method is to use one of the hormone rooting powders, obtainable from horticultural sundriesmen. The grade as recommended for half-ripened cuttings should be used in conjunction with the heated propagation frame, the best period is the first two weeks of August. Another method which will give a number of rooted cuttings is to place the specimen to be propagated in a larger pan during the first week of August so that the plant is below the rim. A mixture of two parts sharp sand and one of peat is then worked into the rosettes after removing the chippings from the base of the cushion and enough is packed round until it reaches the rim of the outer pan. This compost is kept moist until the following June when, removing it carefully, it will be noticed that a number of the rosettes have rooted into it. These should be carefully detached and treated as cuttings until they are well established. Repot every other year after flowering.

A. androsaceum. (E). (Syn. *A. echinus*).

A native of Asia Minor, this makes a mound of small congested rosettes, each consisting of long thick rounded linear leaves, wider at base ending in a spine at apex, glabrous, mid-green. Flowers almost stemless, single open saucer-shaped, white, enhanced by the persisting white veined purple calyces. June. The individual leaves and rosettes are approximately one-quarter the size of *A. venustum*.

A. creticum. (E). (Syn. *A. echinus* var. *creticum*).
A much smaller and rare plant, although similar to the foregoing species with its tight congested cushion of hard 1 inch spiny rosettes and dark green hairy needle-shaped leaves, intensely painful to the touch. The flowers, two to three, nestle on the surface of the rosettes, on almost non-existent stems, white, open chalices backed by papery everlasting calyces white, striped red. June. A native of Crete.

A. echinus, see *A. androsaceum*.

A. echinus var. creticum, see *A. creticum*.

A. hohenackeri. (E).
This plant from the Eastern Caucasus, makes extremely tight, tufted cushions of linear, triangular, glaucous blue-green leaves. The flowers, up to six are borne on 2-inch arching stems, bright rose, open funnel-shaped, backed with persisting buff-coloured calyces. June.

A. libanoticum. (E).
A desirable plant from the Lebanon, this species is only a few inches high, forming hard globular spiny cushions of individual rosettes of congested thick linear leaves, dull bluey-grey in colour. Flowers, solitary on small slender stems, large, open funnel shape, white backed by persisting papery purple-veined calyces. June.

A. olivieri. (E).
Similar in appearance to *A. venustum* but with larger, more open rosettes of fleshy, linear, congested, spiny foliage, mid grey-green in colour. Flowers on graceful 3-inch arching stems, up to six bright pink, saucer-shaped, backed with everlasting light buff calyces. June. A native of Asia Minor.

A. venustum. (E).
There is no doubt that this species is the most desirable of the genus in cultivation today and a well-grown specimen is a fine sight. A native of Asia Minor, it forms open lax cushions of rosettes, made up of linear shaped foliage, wider at the base, narrowing to a spine at the apex, thick, fleshy with recurved margins, light grey-green, owing to the dense covering of minute whitish glands. Flowers in June, up to nine, on 6-inch arching stems, open saucer shaped, deep rose in colour, backed by white papery calyces which persist throughout the winter months.

Acanthophyllum spinosum, see *Dianthus noeanus*.

ACER (*Aceraceae*).
Of this large genus there is only one dwarf maple, a native of Crete, making a fine decorative shrub for pan culture in the alpine house or frame.

Above: *Chrysanthemum hosmariense* (see page 242)

Below: *Crocus candidus* 'Subflavus' (see page 250)

Above: *Crocus fleischeri* (see page 251)
Below: *Crocus kotschyanus* (see page 251)

Above: *Cypripedium speciosum* (see page 523)

Below: *Dianthus* 'Bombardier' (see page 523)

Above: *Draba mollissima* (see page 275)

Below: *Dryas octopetala* var. *minor* (see page 276)

CULTIVATION. It does well in compost B over good drainage and requires plenty of water during the spring and summer. Keep it just moist
the rest of the year.

PROPAGATION. By cuttings of well-ripened wood with a heel attached,
placed in the heated propagation frame in August. Repot every third year
in April.

A. orientale. (E). (Syn. *A. creticum*).
A small erect, much branched shrublet, almost tree-like with a short stout
bole. Branches stiff, rounded, brownish in colour, striped white. Leaves
opposite on small stalks, ovate to obovate, margins irregular, veining
reticulate, colour dull mid-green. This is a rare species and slow growing,
not likely to exceed a foot in ten years under pan culture. Flowers not
seen.

ACERAS (*Orchidaceae*).

A small genus of terrestrial orchids having one species suitable for the
alpine house or frame, where it is possible with careful cultivation to grow
it successfully for a number of years.

CULTIVATION. Compost B over faultless drainage and a few pieces of
limestone should be incorporated in the soil. Plenty of water during the
growing season, dry but not arid in winter. The tubers should be planted
in August or September 1 inch deep and made firm, plunged in a protected
frame outside and covered with dry peat. The compost should be used
damp but not wet, when no further water will be required until growth is
apparent. The plants can then be brought into the house for flowering.
Liquid manure is beneficial weekly during the growing and flowering
season. The flowering stems are best removed, after flowering.

PROPAGATION. By careful division when repotting and this should be
every third year.

A. anthropophora. (H).
The Green Man Orchid is a native of Europe, rare in Britain, with largish
tubers and lanceolate green leaves. Flowers on 8-inch spikes, greenish-
yellow and hooded green sepals. June.

ACERIPHYLLUM (*Saxifragaceae*).

A member of the saxifrage family, this is a Japanese plant which delights
in a cool spot and does well in a pan for the alpine house or frame.

CULTIVATION. Compost C is suitable with plenty of water during spring
and summer, just moist at other periods, needs a shady cool spot.

PROPAGATION. By seed in March, compost 2. Repot every other year
after flowering.

A. borisii. (E).
This makes tufts of widely lobed, almost palmate, shining green stalked
leaves with dentate margins. Flowers on 6-inch stout scapes bearing
umbels of snowy white open stars. May.

ACTINELLA (*Compositae*).

A small genus of plants related to Helenium and natives of N. America of which there is one in cultivation suitable for pan culture in the alpine house.

CULTIVATION. Compost A over faultless drainage with a normal supply of water during the growing months, dry but not arid in winter.

PROPAGATION. By seed, Compost 2 sown as soon as ripe. Repot when necessary in late April.

A. grandiflora. (H). (Syn. *Rydbergia grandiflora*).

A native of Colorado, it forms a tuft of woollen appearance, turning into much cut, pinnate segments needle-shaped, grey-green leaves. Flowers solitary on a 4-inch stout woolly stem, large sunflowers of clear orange yellow. June.

AETHIONEMA (*Cruciferae*).

A genus containing some charming species and varieties which can be used in the alpine house or frame. They are especially suitable for a beginner's collection with their ease of culture and it is mainly for that reason that they are included, although they lose nothing of their beauty grown under glass.

CULTIVATION. All do well in compost A over good drainage and they require an ample supply of water during the growing and flowering season, reducing this amount in August, to help ripen the current year's wood. Dry but not arid conditions in winter.

PROPAGATION. By seed for the species in March, compost 1 or green cuttings of the varieties in June. Repot when necessary after flowering, or if seed is required, in early April.

A. armenum. (E).

From Asia Minor comes this small compact bushlet less than 4 inches high of congested tiny pointed glaucous foliage and terminal racemes of pale pink veined flowers. June.

A. armenum 'Warley Rose'. (E).

A form which originated in the garden of Miss Willmott at Warley, which is superior to the type, making a bushlet of blue-grey leaves closely packed on erect, much divided 6-inch stems, with many terminal clusters of deep pink flowers. May–July.

A. armenum 'Warley Ruber'. (E).

This is a darker form from the same garden, otherwise similar in all respects.

A. grandiflorum. (E).

The flowers of this species from Persia are the largest of the genus, making it an attractive plant, attaining a foot in height. It forms a loose bush of undivided twigs clothed with long, narrow obtuse, glaucous foliage and loose racemes of brilliant, pale rose flowers in July.

A. kotschyi. (E).
An outstanding dwarf species from Asia Minor, forming a dense compact mound of small congested branches about 4 inches high. Leaves arranged in whorls around the stems, thick, long, narrow, tapering to a point at apex, deep bluey-green. Flowers in terminal racemes, deep pink. June.

A. oppositifolium. (E).
A native of Western Asia, this is a prostrate tufted plant of short wiry stems clothed with the opposite, obovate, fleshy, glaucous blue leaves. Flowers terminal, nestling in topmost leaves in a small cluster, four lobed, lilac-pink. May–June.

A. schistosum. (E).
Another species from Asia Minor, which is quite distinct; about 4 inches high of compact, undivided branchlets, leaves narrow linear pointed and incurved at apex, glaucous blue. Ample terminal racemes of flowers, large for the size of plant, deep rose-pink. June.

ALLIUM (*Amaryllidaceae*).

The majority of the onions are too large for alpine house or frame culture, but there are a few which can be used to provide a display after the first flush of alpine colour has passed.

CULTIVATION. Compost A is suitable and like most bulbous plants they require a dry period after flowering to ripen the bulbs for the following season. A normal supply of water while growing and flowering, dry in winter.

PROPAGATION. By seed sown in March, compost 1 or division of bulbs in spring. Repot in fresh compost as soon as growth is discernible in spring.

A. amabile. (B). (Syn. *A. yunnanense*).
From Yunnan comes this dainty species with grass like leaves, sheaths purple, and on 3-inch slender stems a small umbel of up to four up-turned, bell-shaped, deep rose flowers. July.

A. anceps, see *A. platycaule*.

A. cyaneum. (B).
This is an Asiatic species from China with small grass like channelled leaves. Flowers on 6-inch stems, a rounded umbel of clustered semi-pendant open bells, bright blue. July.

A. cyaneum var. brachystemon, see *A. kansuense*.

A. kansuense. (B). (Syn. *A. cyaneum* var. *brachystemon*).
A native of Tibet, with up to five slender linear channelled leaves and cartilaginous margins. Flowers on 3-inch scape in a small globose umbel, semi-pendant, bell-shaped, violet-blue, enhanced by the yellow anthers. August.

A. narcissiflorum. (B). (Syn. *A. pedemontanum*).
One of the best of the genus with two strap-shaped flattish green leaves and on 6-inch stems a small cluster of large semi-pendant bell-shaped bright rose flowers. August. A native of Southern Europe.

A. pedemontanum, see *A. narcissiflorum.*

A. platycaule. (B). (Syn. *A. anceps*).

A North American species, with two broad linear curved leaves tapered to base and apex and on 6-inch two-edged stems, delicate erect umbels of white veined pink flowers. June.

A. sikkimense. (B).

A delightful species from Sikkim, with rush-like foliage and on 6-inch stems pendant umbels of charming bluebell-shaped flowers. July.

A. yunnanense, see *A. amabile.*

ALSINE, see **MINUARTIA.**

ALYSSUM (*Cruciferae*).

The majority of the alyssums are too large and vigorous for the alpine house, but there are one or two which can be utilised and they certainly repay their keep with their delightful heads of golden flowers in early spring.

CULTIVATION. Easy in compost A with good drainage and an ample supply of water in spring and summer, dry but not arid conditions during the winter months.

PROPAGATION. By cuttings taken with a heel of the old wood in August. Repot only when necessary as root restriction tends to keep the plants dwarf and compact. A little liquid fertiliser is beneficial during the growing and flowering season.

A. idaeum. (E).

A native of Mount Ida, Crete, it makes a dwarf prostrate shrublet, only 1 inch or so high of slender lax branches, clothed with oblong to ovate, hairy, silvery green foliage. Flowers lemon-yellow in small terminal clusters. May.

A. montanum. (E).

A small tufted shrublet 3 inches high with prostrate grey-green branches. Leaves crowded, small, narrow, grey, hairy. Flowers in loose racemes, golden yellow with a delightful fragrance. May. A native of Europe.

A. podolicum, see *Schivereckia podolica.*

A. pyrenaicum, see *Ptilotrichum pyrenaicum.*

A. serpyllifolium. (E).

A native of S.W. Europe, this makes a delightful pan plant if cut back after flowering; although not difficult, for some unknown reason it is not often seen in these days. It forms a prostrate mat of congested branchlets densely covered with the obtuse narrow grey foliage rarely more than 2 inches high. Each lateral bears terminal racemes of bright golden-yellow flowers in June.

A. spinosum, see *Ptilotrichum spinosum.*

A. spinosum var. roseum, see *Ptilotrichum spinosum* var. *roseum.*

A. tortuosum. (E).

This makes a small shrublet only 6 inches high of tortuous stems densely clothed with the linear-lanceolate, hoary, grey-green foliage. Flowers in loose terminal racemes, bright yellow. May. A native of Hungary.

AMARACUS, see ORIGANUM.

ANACYCLUS (*Compositae*).

A small genus of plants natives of the Mediterranean region, with one species in cultivation that is suitable for pan culture, in the alpine house or frame.

CULTIVATION. It requires a well-drained soil, compost A is suitable with good protection from moisture especially round the vulnerable neck of the plant. Water is best applied by immersion in a tank and allowing this to creep so that the collar is kept dry. Dry conditions are required during the winter months.

PROPAGATION. By seed sown in March in compost 2. This plant is a gross rooter and requires repotting every year, at least, in late March.

A. depressus. (E).

A native of the Atlas Mountains, it makes prostrate, large rosettes of fine much cut, ferny light green foliage and radiating stems bearing the large, single, white daisy-like flowers with bright red backs. May.

ANCHUSA (*Boraginaceae*).

There is only one species suitable for pan culture and this has lived under a cloud for a long period, for a plant which was given an Award of Merit by the Royal Horticultural Society soon after the war, was certainly not the true species. Planted out it will grow up to three feet high, whereas the typical plant is quite dwarf and prostrate under all conditions of culture. Since the Award was given the tall species has now been identified as *A. angustissima*.

CULTIVATION. This plant should be grown in a large deep pot as it is a gross rooter and likes an open well-drained soil, compost A is suitable and a sufficiency of water during the growing season, dry but not arid in winter.

PROPAGATION. By seed sown in March, compost 2. Repotting should be carried out at least once a year after flowering as it quickly outgrows its pot.

A. caespitosa. (E).

The species is endemic to Crete, where in the White Mountains it forms quite prostrate rosettes of large, thick linear-lanceolate, bristly green foliage, margins irregular dentate, apex generally obtuse. Flowers are almost sessile, nestling in the rosettes, large rounded five lobed, deep brilliant rich blue with a central zone of white stamens.

ANCYLOSTEMON (*Gesneriaceae*).

Only one species is recorded here and that cannot be classified as easy, needing great care to maintain it in good health. It is beloved by all species of greenfly and requires constant watching to keep these at bay.

CULTIVATION. Needs a shady spot in compost C and is best accommodated under the staging during the flowering season and placed outside in a north facing frame during summer, being returned to the house for the winter. Should be kept moist at all times and a layer of sphagnum moss on the surface of the compost assists in keeping this moist; shows its aversion to draughts by the foliage turning brown and dying off.

PROPAGATION. By seed in March, compost 3, or leaf cuttings taken in June. Repot only when necessary after flowering.

A. concavus. (E).

A native of Yunnan, it makes rosettes of ramonda-like leaves, bright green, deeply serrate, apex pointed, covered with brown hairs. Flowers deep yellow; up to three are borne on 3-inch slightly ascending reddish stems, tubular five-lobed, two upper erect, the three lower larger and more spreading. May.

ANDROMEDA (*Ericaceae*).

There have been at different times a large number of plants classified under this name but there is only one true Andromeda. *A. polifolia* with pale pink flowers and having a wide distribution in the arctic and temperate regions of the N. hemisphere including N. Britain and Scotland. A number of forms have been described at different periods but only three are likely to be found in cultivation today. The true *A. polifolia compacta* is a native of N.E. Asia and bears white flowers, but is extremely rare and seldom seen in cultivation. However a form with pink flowers and labelled *compacta* has been introduced into this country from Japan and most plants under this name have originated from that country. Recently a white form named *A. polifolia compacta alba* was given an Award of Merit by the Royal Horticultural Society, whether this is the true Asian form or a white variant of the Japanese is hard to say.

CULTIVATION. Like all ericaceous plants, a soil with a high humus content is required and compost C will suit these varieties. Lime free water should be given in quantity during the growing season and the plants must be kept moist even during the winter months. They should only be brought into the alpine house while in flower and during the summer a shady place in a north facing frame is desirable. A spraying of the foliage in the evenings after hot days is also beneficial. Top-dress in early spring with similar compost.

PROPAGATION. By green cuttings taken in July. Repot when necessary after flowering.

A. caerulea, see *Phyllodoce caerulea*.

A. nana, see *Arcterica nana*.

A. polifolia. (E).

This makes a low straggling plant rarely above 6 inches high, with linear to narrow oblong entire leaves, tapering to each end, dark green above with reticulate veinings, strongly recurved, white underneath. Flowers in small terminal umbels, pendant, urn-shaped, pink. May.

A. polifolia var. compacta. (E).
A native of Japan, making an attractive evergreen shrublet up to 1 foot high. Leaves leathery, long, narrow, almost linear, tapering to both ends, margins strongly recurved, upper surface grey-green, silvery-grey beneath. Bears terminal umbels of light pink urn-shaped flowers in May.

A. polifolia var. minima. (E).
Another Japanese plant, much smaller than *compacta* never exceeding 2 inches in height and rarer in cultivation. Branches smooth, prostrate, new growth almost white, adult light brown. Leaves alternate, thick, long, narrow, tapering towards apex and base, deeply recurved, heavily veined, midrib sunken; deep shiny green above, silvery-grey beneath with pronounced midrib; stalk short almost appressed. Flowers in terminal clusters, large pendant, urn-shaped, deep rose pink. May.

ANDROSACE (*Primulaceae*).

Of all genera cultivated in pans for the alpine house possibly no others have given so much pleasure or disappointment, for without doubt well grown specimens, especially of the section Aretia, are a joy to behold and a hallmark of the successful cultivator of difficult alpines. That they can be intractable is also well known to all who aspire to grow large well-flowered cushions of *A. alpina*. These dainty cushions encrusted with dazzling white or pink stars always provide the focal point at exhibitions, at which both expert and envious beginners congregate to admire and discuss these exquisite wildlings from the vast inhospitable mountainous ranges of the world.

CULTIVATION. The aretias are not easy plants to keep in good health over a number of years although the majority do not provide any real difficulty in their youth. It is after the third season that they require skill and careful cultivation to maintain a firm roothold on life and it is here that the cultivator's skill is needed. Only a few general hints can be given as to their requirements, and the three following points are the most important. It is within my power to give a clear and concise answer to the first two, but the third and final stage can only be bought with experience, for neither the experts nor I can do more than generalise.

The first is freedom from pests. More Aretia androsaces fall victim to these than is generally realised, the tight cushions providing a safe hiding place, and a really bad infestation often takes place before becoming apparent. A constant watch must be maintained and some form of spraying or fumigation carried out at least every fortnight, and weekly if the weather is warm and moist, during the growing season. A pocket lens should be used occasionally, just opening the rosettes with a pair of forceps to see if there are pests lurking inside. Second: all dead flowers should be removed, a tedious job but one that pays dividends, for unless this is carried out there is a possibility of the decaying blooms becoming infested with fungi, and this will quickly spread to the rosette from which the flower stalk arises and in its turn adjacent rosettes soon fall an easy prey, resulting in the destruction of part of the cushion if not in total loss. Any dead rosettes must also be removed as soon as noticed, and forceps should be used to carry out this delicate operation. Gaps caused by the removal are best closed by using chippings and working these on the outer edge of the cushion until the pressure closes the gap. Some growers advocate filling by pouring sharp sand in the gap caused by the removal of the rosettes, but in my opinion this sand is liable to become damp before new rosettes can form and further rotting takes place, with disastrous consequences.

Last, watering, there is no doubt if you master this half the battle is won. Unfortunately it is impossible to give any facts about watering, for so many things have to be taken into account: time of year, weather, hot, cold, dry, windy, wet, foggy or a combination of them all! All that can be done is to give a few tips which will help, and then as experience is gained one gets an instinctive knowledge of right or wrong. During the growing and flowering season water is required in quantity, especially if the plants are growing in compost D which is an extremely rapid draining medium. The water is best applied at these periods from a can with a curved spout and start from the edge of the cushion, for if the plant has been potted on as advised in Chapter Six it will be necessary to ensure that water is reaching the compost in the original pan. If the plants are growing in any other medium, once a week at this period of the year the pan should be immersed in a tank containing enough water so that it reaches to within an inch or so of the rim of the pan and then left, until the chippings darken with the moisture, when the pan must be removed and stood to drain. A light overhead spray is beneficial late in the evenings and early mornings during hot periods, but this should cease by the beginning of September whatever the weather.

From the end of September until growth begins in early spring a dipping in a tank containing two inches of water once a month should suffice. Naturally if plunged in sand and gravel on the staging no water need be given during winter for the bulk of material will retain sufficient for the plant's purpose. Underwatering is less harmful at this time of the year and if there is any doubt as to whether it is required, withhold water, but keep a watch on the cushions as these have a tendency to become lax and open when dry. At this stage water is necessary and should be given as advised by immersion in a tank. Foggy weather provides a difficult time, but the object here should be to keep the air moving as much as possible during its presence, so that the cushions do not absorb too much moisture. Individual composts will be noted after each plant but where it is decided to use compost A in place of C two extra parts of small chippings should be added to ensure rapid drainage.

A. aizoon var. coccinea. Section Chamaejasme. (E). (Syn. *A. bulleyana*).
A native of Yunnan, this is a delightful plant which has a tendency to be
monocarpic in cultivation but can be perennial if not allowed to flower
until a number of rosettes are formed. The rosettes are large, prostrate,
grey-green in colour. Leaves leathery spatulate with hairy margins from
which on a 6-inch stem are borne the typical flowers of a glowing scarlet
with a yellow eye. June. Not a high alpine plant, it is nevertheless worthy
of a place amongst a collection of choice alpines if only for the colour of
the flowers. Compost A, and needs less water than the aretias.
PROPAGATION. By seed, compost 2 sown in February. Repot when
necessary in early April.

A. alpina. Section Aretia. (E). (Syn. *A. glacialis*).
A plant met with in all the high ranges of Europe on granite formations,
never limestone, making closely matted cushions of small rosettes. Leaves
oblong-lanceolate, grey, stellate hairy, and almost completely covered
with practically sessile pink flowers. May. Unfortunately in cultivation it
becomes more open and rarely flowers as well and certainly needs to be
grown in compost D for any reasonable chance of success.
PROPAGATION. By cuttings in June or seed in February. Compost 2.
Repot only when necessary after flowering.

A. × aretioides. (*A. alpina* × *A. obtusifolia*). (E).
A natural hybrid between *A. alpina* and *A. obtusifolia* which occurs
spontaneously wherever the two parents grow. It comes from the
Bernese Oberland and the Tyrol, but it is also found in other parts of
Europe. Rare in cultivation, it is not long-lived and makes trailing tufts
of much-branched rosettes. Leaves small oblong, ovate, blunt, curved
with stellate hairs, grey. Flowers on 1 inch scapes, several, rounded
bright pink. May. Compost D.
PROPAGATION. By cuttings in June. Repot when necessary after flowering.

A. argentea, see *A. imbricata*.

A. bulleyana, see *A. aizoon* var. *coccinea*.

A. carnea. Section Chamaejasme. (E).
This species varies more than any other Androsace and there are a number
of named forms which have been introduced into cultivation. A native of
most high alpine ranges of Europe, it is found on both limestone and
granite, where it makes close tight rosettes in tufts of narrow linear bright
green foliage, margins ciliate. Flowers on 3-inch scapes in small clustered
heads, delightful rose colour, with a pronounced yellow eye. April–May.
An easy species but requires semi-shade in summer. Compost A.
PROPAGATION. Careful division in May or seed in July will propagate the
species and its forms. Compost 2. Repot when necessary after flowering.

A. carnea var. brigantiaca. (E).
A form of the Cottian Alps with less congested rosettes, foliage broader,
apex recurving, margins dentate and ciliate. Flowers in terminal clusters
on 4-inch stems, white, sometimes pink. May.

A. carnea var. halleri. (E). (Syn. *A. halleri*).
From the Cevennes, it is very distinct with prostrate open mats of rosettes; leaves twice as large as the species, bright green with recurving apex and quite glabrous. Flowers clustered on 4-inch scapes, deep glowing pink with yellow eye. May.

A. carnea var. laggeri. (E). (Syn. *A. laggeri*).
Only found in the Pyrenees, it can be distinguished from the other forms in that it makes tight mossy hummocks, the rosettes have narrow linear leaves that are ascending, not recurved. Flowers large in small umbels on 2-inch scapes, bright pink with yellow eye. May.

A. chaixii. Section Andraspis. (Annual).
The reason for including this annual in these notes is that I originally got this plant from the late Dr Guissepi's collection under the name of *Mertensia coriacea* in a small group of pans, but there was nothing to be seen until the following spring when seedlings of *A. chaixii* appeared. These grew and flowered and each succeeding year produced an annual crop with the minimum of attention. It comes from mountains in Western France and makes single largish rosettes of glabrous, lanceolate leaves, grey-green, margins dentate. Flowers rose coloured in small umbels on 3-inch scapes. May. Compost A with plenty of water during the growing season.
PROPAGATION. By seed sown as soon as ripe in compost 2 or left in the pan where the old plants were grown and after germinating a little fresh compost sprinkled over the surface of the pan.

A. chamaejasme. Section Chamaejasme. (E).
An easy member of the section from many mountainous ranges of the world, this has naturally given rise to a good number of forms, unfortunately although desirable they are extremely rare if in cultivation at all. The typical plant is stoloniferous, making open mats of silvery, fluffy rosettes densely clothed with silky hairs. Flowers on 2-inch scapes, few in number, white with yellow eye, ageing to pink, the eye turning red. May. Compost A, requires plenty of water while growing.
PROPAGATION. By layers in July or seed sown in February, compost 2. Repot every second year after flowering.

A. charpentieri. Section Aretia. (E).
A native of Switzerland, this is a dainty but rare cushion plant from high altitudes making loose hummocks of rosettes. Leaves dull green, small, broad, apex obtuse, densely clothed with down. Flowers, solitary on 1-inch scapes are a soft shell pink, but large for size of plant. May. Best in compost D.
PROPAGATION. By seed in July, compost 2 or cuttings in June which root readily. Repot only when necessary, after flowering.

A. ciliata. Section Aretia. (E).
This delightful plant is endemic to the Pyrenees and even there it is only found on a limited number of mountain ranges. It has periods of plentifulness in cultivation. Just prior to the war it was scarce, but recently it

has become more common. Unlike the typical members of the Aretia section, the cushions are more lax, making open hummocks of large rosettes; leaves oblong-ovate glossy green, devoid of hairs except on margins. Flowers either singly or in pairs on 1-inch scapes, rich pink with yellow eye. April. Best in compost D.

PROPAGATION. By seed sown in July, compost 2. Repot only when necessary after flowering.

A. cylindrica. Section Aretia. (E).

A rare plant in nature only found at two stations in the Pyrenees but it is amenable to careful cultivation. Unfortunately it crosses too readily with *A. hirtella* and the resultant hybrid is often sent out named as the true species. It makes close compact cushions of rosettes, the leaves are congested, imbricated, short, rounded, obtuse, grey-green in colour. The large rounded milky-white flowers are borne on thread-like, 2-inch stems in April. Compost D.

PROPAGATION. By cuttings taken in June, where there is a doubt as to whether the seed will breed true, or seed sown in February, compost 2. Repot only when necessary after flowering.

A. cylindrica × A. hirtella. (E).

This is a desirable hybrid, intermediate between the two parents and bearing the almost sessile large rounded white flowers in April. Much easier than either of its parents, it responds to good cultivation in compost D.

PROPAGATION. By cuttings in June. Repot only when necessary after flowering.

A. geraniifolia. Section Pseudoprimula. (E).

An Asiatic species from the Himalayas with geranium-like foliage, covered with long hairs, shoots stoloniferous topped with long thin, up to 6-inch stems, bearing uneven clusters of deep pink buds, opening to soft pink flowers in June. Compost A over good drainage will suit this species, but it is best in half shade.

PROPAGATION. By careful division in August or if the inflorescence is bent over and allowed to come into contact with the soil it will take root. Repot every year in early April.

A. glacialis, see *A. alpina.*

A. halleri, see *A. carnea* var. *halleri.*

A. hausmannii. Section Aretia. (E).

This native of the Southern Tyrol is a difficult plant to keep in good health in cultivation, often doing well for a year or so then dying for no apparent reason. It is doubtful whether it will ever be a long-lived plant acclimatised to cultivation. The species forms tight congested hummocks, consisting of tiny rounded silver-grey leaves, completely covered with small stellate-shaped hairs. The flowers are borne on almost non-existent stems, white in bud, opening to white flushed pink. April. Small plants potted in compost D will give the best results.

PROPAGATION. By seed in compost 2 in February. Only repot when necessary after flowering.

A. × heeri. (*A. alpina* × *A. helvetica*). (E).
A natural hybrid between the two species found on the Kleinthal Alps, Switzerland. Rare in cultivation it makes less congested hummocks than *A. helvetica* although still intensely downy, but the beauty lies in the large rose coloured rounded flowers borne singly on short stems. April–May. A difficult hybrid needing careful cultivation in compost D.

PROPAGATION. By cuttings taken in July. Repot only when necessary after flowering.

A. helvetica. Section Aretia. (E).
This could be called the classic Aretian Androsace, well known to all who search for rare alpines at high altitudes in the Central European Alps. It makes huge hard domes often larger in diameter than a tea plate. The rosettes are small, densely crowded, roundish to obtuse, fat, grey-green incurving leaves, completely clothed with minute woolly hairs giving the plant the appearance of fur. Flowers solitary on almost non-existent stems, rounded, milky-white with a golden eye. May. Unfortunately not easy to flower in cultivation, often only producing a few flowers to a mature plant. It is not difficult to grow and is well suited to compost D or if A is used, at least two more parts of chippings should be added.

PROPAGATION. By cuttings taken in July or seed if set in February, compost 2. Repot only when necessary after flowering.

A. hirtella. Section Aretia. (E).
This species, a native of the Western Pyrenees, is a good alpine, which can be kept going for a number of years. The problem is, it is sometimes difficult to get the true species, for as it comes easily from seed and crosses readily with *A. cylindrica*, where these two are grown together the offspring are likely to be hybrids. The typical plant makes tight congested rounded cushions of rosettes. The leaves are narrow, small, imbricated closely on the rosettes, silvery-grey due to the intense covering of woolly hairs. Flowers solitary large rounded, white, on short stalks. April. Does well in compost D.

PROPAGATION. By seed if kept true, in February, compost 2, or cuttings taken in July. Repot only when necessary after flowering.

A. imbricata. Section Aretia. (E). (Syn. *A. argentea*).
Of all the Aretian androsaces this is the one most favoured by the majority of alpine enthusiasts. It is a native of many European Alps always growing in crevices at high elevations, where it makes tight congested cushions, generally flatter in its native habitat than in cultivation. The individual rosettes are made up of tight imbricated leaves, small, obtuse, densely covered with fine down giving the plants the appearance of silvery-white cushions. In April the whole dome will disappear under a canopy of large rounded, almost sessile, milky-white flowers. Unlike *A. helvetica* this plant

should always flower well and it does not present any great difficulty in cultivation provided the drainage is faultless. Compost D suits it and plants grown in this will live and flower well for many years.

PROPAGATION. By seed which germinates freely in February, compost 2, or cuttings taken in June. Repot only when necessary after flowering.

A. lactea. Section Chamaejasme. (E).

A native of the Jura and Tatra Mountains, this delightful easy perennial plant will give pleasure if grown as a pan plant for the alpine house or frame. It makes rosettes of shiny narrow green leaves, which increase by underground stolons and quickly fill the pan. The flowers are borne on 2-inch slender scapes up to six in number, large rounded, white, each with a yellow eye. May. This plant is best grown in compost B and requires plenty of water during the growing season; half shade is desirable during the summer months.

PROPAGATION. Easily propagated by seed sown as soon as ripe, compost 2 or division when growth starts in early spring. Repot every year after flowering.

A. laggeri, see *A. carnea* var. *laggeri*.

A. mathildae. Section Aretia. (E).

A native of the Abruzzi Mountains, Italy, this is the largest of the Aretia section. It makes a cushion of rosettes with glabrous, imbricated, linear green leaves ending in an abrupt tip. Less compact than the majority of other members of the Aretias. Flowers are single, white, on a short downy stalk. May. Does well in compost D or A if two extra parts of chippings are added.

PROPAGATION. By seed sown in February, compost 2 or rosettes detached and used as cuttings in July. Repot only when necessary after flowering.

A. muscoidea. Section Aretia. (E).

This plant is a native of the West Himalayas and is outstanding amongst the Aretian androsaces. It has come to the fore in recent years and there is no doubt that a well-grown specimen is a joy to behold as well as a source of satisfaction to its owner. It makes lax cushions on short much-branched reddish stems, bearing rosettes of narrow obtuse, silvery-grey leaves, quite devoid of hair below, but thickly covered with short grey hairs above, the margins having long white hairs. The flowers borne on short stems are single (rarely in pairs), almost star-shaped, pure white with a yellow eye. Requires careful cultivation in compost D and frequent top-dressing with chippings to prevent plant from straggling too much. May.

PROPAGATION. By cuttings taken in July. Repot only when necessary after flowering.

A. pubescens. Section Aretia. (E).

This is not often seen in cultivation although it cannot be classified as impossible to grow, for with careful cultivation it will live and flower for a number of years. A native of high European ranges, especially in the

Pyrenees, it is similar to *A. helvetica* but differs in that the leaves are more narrow and do not incurve. The flowers are borne singly on small thread-like stalks, and are large, rounded, milky-white in colour. April. Compost D will suit this species.

PROPAGATION. By seed sown in February, compost 2 or cuttings taken in July. Repot only when necessary after flowering.

A. pyrenaica. Section Aretia. (E). .

A native of the Pyrenees, this plant is normally found in any general collection of alpine plants for it is the easiest of all the high altitude aretias and is almost certain to be tried by cultivators. It makes hard rounded cushions of green rosettes, leaves hairy, narrow, rarely incurved, margined with glandular hairs. Flowers on the shortest of stems, often the buds open in between the rosettes, pure white, rounded in the best forms but often star-shaped. April. Quite easy in compost A to which two extra parts of chippings have been added, or compost D will ensure a longer life. In the latter the growth will be slower but more compact.

PROPAGATION. By seed sown in February, compost 2 which germinates readily, or cuttings in July if it is desired to propagate a good form. Repot only when necessary after flowering.

A. spinulifera. Section Chamaejasme. (E).

A plant from Yunnan, forming small rosettes of spine-tipped, closely imbricated leaves in winter, these elongating to more loose, narrow spine-tipped large leaves in spring. Flowers on 6-inch stems in umbels, rich pink. June. Compost A suits this plant which requires summer sun and dry conditions in winter.

PROPAGATION. By seed sown in August, compost 2. Repot every second year in early April.

A. villosa. Section Chamaejasme. (E).

This plant has a wide distribution and many forms abound on most mountainous ranges of Europe, Asia and N. America. The typical plant bears loose rosettes, in tufts, the leaves are narrow, crowded, densely covered with shaggy woolly silvery-grey hairs. Flowers on short slender stems in clusters, white shading to pink in the centre, fragrant. May. Compost A is suitable over faultless drainage.

PROPAGATION. By cuttings taken in July. Repot every other year after flowering.

A. villosa var. arachnoidea. (E).

A form from the Carpathians, differing from the type in that the rosettes are more congested and have larger silky hairs. Flowers on short stems in umbels of up to five, rounded white with a yellow eye. May. Same cultural requirements as for the type.

A. vitaliana, see *Douglasia vitaliana.*

A. wulfeniana. Section Aretia. (E).

A rare alpine species from the Eastern Alps, where it forms small hummocks of rosettes, leaves minute, bright green, smooth, only the margins showing traces of stellate hairs. Flowers solitary on almost non-existing stems, large, rounded, pink. May. Requires care in cultivation and seems best suited to compost D.

PROPAGATION. By seed in February, compost 2. Repot only when necessary after flowering.

ANDRYALA (*Compositae*).

A small genus of Mediterranean plants, there is one species suitable for pan culture and this is a charming sub-shrub which is very decorative throughout the year.

CULTIVATION. It is suited to compost A but a pot is better than a pan, for this plant is a gross rooter. It needs plenty of water during the growing and flowering season, in full sunshine, dry but not arid conditions in winter.

PROPAGATION. By seed in February, in compost 1. Self-sown seedlings often appear on the surface chippings. Repot every year in early April.

A. agardhii. (E).

A native of Spain, it makes woody procumbent laterals from a central rootstock with tufts of long silvery, silky, spatulate leaves which glisten in the sun. The flowers are golden daisies borne on 6-inch stems throughout the summer months. June–August.

ANEMONE (*Ranunculaceae*).

The Windflowers have a number of species and varieties which are suitable for alpine house or frame culture, but the botanists have been at work on this genus and have now placed some which were previously classified as anemones under the generic titles Hepatica and Pulsatilla. Where this has taken place a cross reference is given so that it will be easy to check the species under review. They are mostly herbaceous, tuberous or rhizomatous perennials inhabiting the temperate regions of the world, also at higher altitudes in the warmer climates, their natural distribution being the Northern part of S. America, S. Africa and Asia. Their cultural needs differ, so it will not be possible to deal with the genus as a whole but with certain chosen species.

A. alpina, see *Pulsatilla alpina*.

A. apennina. (H).

A native of S. Europe and found in England, with prostrate thick rhizomes; leaves deep green, binately pinnate, leaflets lanceolate, deeply cut. Flowers solitary, 1½ inch across on 6-inch stems, large, blue. March–April. There are also white, rose and double forms.

CULTIVATION. Compost B in half shade, plenty of water during growing season, just moist in winter.

PROPAGATION. By division in July of rhizomes or seed sown as soon as ripe, compost 2. Repot when necessary after flowering.

A. baldensis. (H). (Syn. *A. drummondii*).
A rhizome-forming species from Monte Baldo and certain other parts of Europe and N. America. Leaves biternate, leaflets many with linear lobes, curved. Flowers on 3- to 4-inch stems, 1 inch, starry white, often tinged with blue on reverse. May. *A. drummondii* is the N. American form.
CULTIVATION. Compost B with plenty of water during the growing season, just moist in winter.
PROPAGATION. By division of rhizomes in July, or seed sown as soon as ripe, compost 2. Repot when necessary after flowering.
A. blanda. (H).
A native of Eastern Europe, this makes a thick rhizome with tri-ternate green leaves, leaflets deeply cut, acute, curved inwards. Flowers on 4-inch stems deep blue, 2 inches wide. March.
CULTIVATION. Compost A, plenty of water during the growing season, less after foliage dies down.
PROPAGATION. By seed sown when ripe or division in July, compost 2. Repot when necessary after flowering.
A. blanda 'Atrocaerulea'. (H).
This is similar to the type but with dark blue large flowers. March.
A. blanda 'Rosea'. (H).
A bright pink form. March.
A. blanda var. scythinica. (H).
With pale blue flowers white inside. March. From Persia.
A. drummondii, see *A. baldensis*.
A. × fulgens. (*A. pavonina* × *A. hortensis*). (H).
This charming hybrid from Greece makes brownish tubers with slightly divided two- to five-lobed leaves. Flowers on 6-inch stems brilliant scarlet, 2 inches across with black anthers. April.
CULTIVATION. Plenty of moisture in compost A allowing the tubers to ripen after the foliage dies down.
PROPAGATION. By division of tubers in July or seed when ripe, compost 2. Repot every year after flowering.
A. halleri, see *Pulsatilla halleri*.
A. magellanica. (H).
A herbaceous species from S. America with much divided medium, green hairy leaves. Flowers on 6-inch stems, 1 inch across, deep cream with many golden stamens. May.
CULTIVATION. Compost A, plenty of water during the growing season, dryish in winter.
PROPAGATION. By seed when ripe, compost 2. Repot every year after flowering.
A. nemorosa. (H).
This is the Wood Anemone, a native of Europe including Britain, making a slender horizontal rootstock with ternate light green leaves, segments

trifid, lanceolate, deeply cut, acute. Flowers on 6-inch stems, white tinged rose on outside, 1 inch across. April.

CULTIVATION. Compost B, with plenty of water, moist during the winter months.

PROPAGATION. By division in July. Repot only when necessary after flowering. There are three varieties, all worth growing, and these are 'Allenii', lavender-blue; 'Blue Bonnet', deep blue; 'Robinsoniana', lavender-blue, greyish-white outside, and one double white, 'Alba Flora Plena'.

A. obtusiloba var. patula. (H).

An herbaceous perennial, this is the famous 'Blue Buttercup' of the Himalayas which created quite a stir twenty odd years ago. The species has a wide distribution with cream, violet and white forms but the best is *patula*, an ideal plant for the alpine house or frame. It makes basal rosettes of palmate, cordate, three-lobed hairy leaves on 3-inch stalks; leaf segments wedge shaped, deeply crenate. The flower stem is prostrate, up to 6 inches long, hairy, involucral leaf, sessile, trifid; flowers cup shaped, five recurving sepals, obovate, blue with a touch of purple, central boss of green anthers, 1½ inch across. May.

CULTIVATION. Compost B with plenty of water during the growing season, just moist at other times.

PROPAGATION. By careful division in July or seed sown while green, compost 2. Repot only when necessary after flowering.

A. potentilloides. (H).

A small species from the Himalayas, producing a prostrate basal tuft of small palmate, three-lobed green leaves on short petioles; lobes irregularly toothed. Flowers large, solitary on 3-inch erect stems, bright lilac-blue enhanced with central yellow boss; involucral leaf trifid on upper third, five narrow obovate lobes. May.

CULTIVATION. Compost B with plenty of water during the growing season, just moist in winter.

PROPAGATION. By careful division in July. Repot when necessary in July.

A. pulsatilla, see *Pulsatilla vulgaris.*

A. rupicola. (H).

A native of the Himalayas, it makes a woody rhizome; leaves rich green, trifid with short stem, leaflets deeply cut and lobed. Stem leaf sessile, bifid, similar to basal leaves; flowers on 6-inch stems, 1½ inch across, white tinged purple outside. May.

CULTIVATION. Compost B, needs water whilst in growth, just moist at other periods.

PROPAGATION. By seed sown when ripe, compost 2. Repot every other year after flowering.

A. sulphurea, see *Pulsatilla alpina* var. *sulphurea.*

A. thalictroides, see *Anemonella thalictroides.*

A. vernalis, see *Pulsatilla vernalis.*

ANEMONELLA (*Ranunculaceae*).

A genus closely related to Anemone, containing one species which makes an ideal pan plant.

CULTIVATION. Compost B requiring plenty of water while growing, moist at other times, appreciates half shade during summer.

PROPAGATION. Best by seed as this plant resents disturbance. The seed should be sown as soon as ripe, compost 2. Repot only when necessary after flowering.

A. thalictroides. (H). (Syn. *Anemone thalictroides*).

This is a tuberous-rooted perennial from N. America, with tri-ternate glabrous ferny green leaves. On a 6-inch hairy stem with its compound, glabrous, sessile stem leaf, with stalked divisions, is borne an umbel of white to pink flowers. April.

ANOMATHECA, see **LAPEIROUSIA.**

ANTHYLLIS (*Leguminosae*).

There are two suitable Kidney Vetches in cultivation for the alpine house and these, flowering as they do after the first flush of floral display is over, makes them very welcome.

CULTIVATION. Compost A over good drainage is ideal and they require normal watering during the spring and summer months, a dry warm period in August to ripen the wood, dryish but not arid in winter.

PROPAGATION. By cuttings taken with a heel in August. Repot every second year after flowering, taking care not to damage the roots during this operation.

A. erinacea, see *Erinacea anthyllis*.

A. montana. (D).

A native of S. and S.E. Europe, it makes a much-branched prostrate sub-shrub, up to 4 inches high. Leaves pinnate, consisting of eight to twelve pairs of leaflets, sessile, long narrow, acute, the upper surface covered with whitish hairs. Flowers on 4-inch hairy stems in globular heads, tightly packed typical leguminose shaped, rose-pink with a central dark stain. May.

A. montana var. rubra. (D).

From S. and S.E. Europe, is a deeper coloured form of the above and is just as suitable. May.

APHYLLANTHES (*Liliaceae*).

A native of North Africa and Spain this genus only contains one species, needing a warm position in the alpine house.

CULTIVATION. Compost B is suitable with plenty of water during the growing season, dryish in winter.

PROPAGATION. Best by seed sown as soon as ripe, compost 2, but the plant can be increased by careful division in April when it tends to out-grow its pan. After this move it may take a while for the new plants to settle down, for it is intolerant of root disturbance. Repot only when necessary in early April.

A. monspeliensis. (E).
It is a fibrous-rooted perennial with small basal, membranous leaves. Flowers on 4-inch slender green rush-like stems, and the delicate six-lobed tubular blue lilies are borne from chaffy bracts. June.

AQUILEGIA (*Ranunculaceae*).

A genus which is full of dainty species, these being scattered all over the globe, with representatives in Europe, Asia, Alaska through N. America southwards to Mexico, all have given us a quota of suitable plants for pan culture. They have one great fault, that is the majority will cross with all and sundry species and varieties; the alpines think nothing of breeding with their lowland herbaceous border cousins, so that it is difficult to keep true species unless steps are taken to stop cross-fertilisation between the different members of this genus. They are very inconsistent in their growth, even in their native habitat they vary and a number of dwarfs will produce plants ranging in height from a few inches to upwards of eighteen inches. If the aim is small compact plants they are best chosen as young adult specimens.

CULTIVATION. The majority of Columbines are sub-alpine plants, haunting open coppices or in semi-shade where the atmosphere is cool and damp, but there are some which aspire to the high open screes and here they are at their best with only a minimum of prostrate foliage topped with large single flowers. These high alpine species do well in compost A over faultless drainage, while the sub-alpine plants are best in compost B with its higher humus content. Plenty of water is needed during the growing and flowering season. The semi-woodlanders should be kept just moist in the winter, while the alpine species require dry but not arid conditions. A dryish period in August is beneficial for the alpine species, for success in keeping these plants over the winter seems to depend on the ripening of the crowns during late summer. They are not noted for longevity but can be kept going for a number of years with care.

PROPAGATION. By seed which is set freely, but care must be taken to see that the plants do not cross indiscriminately if the true species are required. July or August are the best months according to when the seed is ripe, use compost 2, and this must be sown thinly, then the seedlings can be left until the following spring before being potted on. If a large collection is grown together and it is desired to perpetuate a good form or to ensure true plants it will be necessary to increase the stock by careful division as soon as the plant begins to grow in early spring. Adult plants are best repotted only when the roots begin to appear through the drainage vent, at other times a careful removal of a little of the surface soil replacing this with fresh compost in early spring will help to maintain them in good health.

A. akitensis, see *A. flabellata* var. *pumila.*

A. akitensis var. kurilensis, see *A. flabellata* var. *nana.*

A. aurea. (H).

A native of Bulgaria, this is the only yellow European Aquilegia and unfortunately it is difficult in cultivation, for quite young plants collapse for no apparent reason. It forms basal rosettes of light green biternate foliage, sparsely covered with fine hairs, and on slightly hairy slender stems, which can be from 4 to 8 inches high, are borne the deep yellow flowers with prominent hooked spurs. May. Seems to do best in compost B but requires extremely sharp drainage round the collar of the plant, for this is the most vulnerable spot.

A. bernardii. (H).

From the island of Corsica comes this rare dainty species with basal tufts of small biternate mid-green foliage, slightly pilose. Flowers on 4-inch slender pubescent stems, large, pendant, spurs slightly curved, the whole a delightful shade of light blue. May. Compost A. This plant varies in size but the dwarf forms are ideal plants.

A. bertolonii. (H). (Syn. *A. pyrenaica* var. *bertolonii, A. reuteri*).

This plant has for many years been considered as only a geographical variant of *A. pyrenaica* from the Italian Apennine Mountains, but it has since been accorded specific rank differing as it does in many ways from that species. It forms basal tufts of slightly greyed, green biternate leaves, densely pilose underneath, petioles long and with glandular hairs. Flowers on stout stems with tufts of glandular hairs, these can be from 2 to 9 inches in height, flowers bright violet-blue, tinged green at apex of petals with curved spurs ending in a pronounced hook. May. Compost A.

A. canadensis. (H).

A Canadian species with a wide geographical distribution, which has led to many different varieties, varying height and form but all are similar to the type. Plants can sometimes be found under the name of *A. canadensis* var. *nana* but these are only dwarf editions in this very variable species. The typical species forms basal tufts of biternate, pale green, glabrous leaves, underneath covered with fine hairs. Flowers on stems which can be 6 to 12 inches high; it is best to procure this plant in flower, or when raising from seed, only keep the dwarf forms and then after the second generation the majority will generally retain their small stature. The flowers are not as large as some species being narrow but dumpy, sepals bright red, petals small, rounded pale yellow. Spurs straight, small, red in colour. May. Compost B.

A. canadensis var. alba. (H).

There is a white form of the species but as the shape of the flower is not its best point, the lack of colour does nothing to enhance its beauty. May.

A. discolor. (H). (Syn. *A. pyrenaica* var. *discolor*).
There is another species which has been entangled with *A. pyrenaica* for a long period of time and often quoted as a geographical variant. It is a native of Cantabria in Spain and makes prostrate, basal tufts of biternate mid green leaves; leaflets small, oval to ovate, stem leaves, small, three-lobed. Flowers on 4-inch, slightly glandular, pubescent stems, rarely two, erect, open, sepals blue, petals white with small incurved spurs. May. Compost A.

A. einseleana. (H).
There is another species akin to *A. pyrenaica*, but it differs in that its stamens never protrude from the petals. A native of the Bavarian alps, Austria and N. Italy. It makes basal tufts of biternate, pale green, sub-glabrous leaves, stem leaves narrow, pointed. Flower stems slender up to 6 inches high, rarely more than two flowers, pendant, rich violet-blue with small straight spur. May. Compost B.

A. elegantula. (H).
A native of Southern Colorado and parts of New Mexico, this plant is near to *A. canadensis* making dwarf basal tufts of mid-green, thin, biternate, glabrous leaves, underneath varies from glabrous to pilose. Flowers rarely more than two, on 4- to 8-inch glandular slender stems, pendant; sepals red, shading to yellow, green at tips, petals rounded, mid-yellow, spurs small straight, red. May. Compost B.

A. flabellata. (H).
A fine species from Japan, which itself is a desirable plant suitable for pan culture if the smaller forms are obtained, although it has produced four outstanding forms. The type has small tufts of biternate or even single ternate, thickish blue-grey leaves, tinged with purple, the apex of the leaflets are tridentate. Flowering stems 6 to 12 inches high, bearing up to three flowers on 2-inch hairy pedicels, sepals blue-purple, apex recurved, petals lilac shading to yellow at tip. Spurs long and hooked. May. Compost B.

A. flabellata var alba. (H).
A form with large milky-white flowers of a good substance. May. Compost B.

A. flabellata var. nana. (H). (Syn. *A. akitensis* var. *kurilensis*).
This plant was introduced and shown in this country under its synonym. It is a dwarf edition of the type barely 3 inches high with large flowers, sepals mid-blue and rounded, petals of creamy-yellow, spurs curved and hooked. May. Compost B.

A. flabellata var. nana alba. (H).
An attractive white form of the above. May. Compost B.

A. flabellata var. pumila. (H). (Syn. *A. akitensis*).
A form from the shores of the island of Rebunshiri, making a dwarf plant less than 6 inches high with large rounded, pendant flowers of a deep blue. May. Compost A.

A. jonesii. (H).
One of the gems of the race, but unfortunately not always easy to please and flower. It is a plant from almost barren screes in central Wyoming and Canada, where it forms a thick woody rootstock, from which appear a number of shoots clothed with basal ternate to biternate leaves; leaflets stout glaucous grey, congested in tight whorls and expanding in late June. The flowers are borne singly on short stems less than 2 inches high, large, erect, sepals bright blue, petals paler and short, straight spurs. June. Compost A. This is a true high alpine which is worth all the care needed to keep it happy in cultivation.

A. jonesii var. elatior. (H).
A lowland form from the Glacier National Park, it is taller, up to 6 inches high, the foliage has more green in it and the leaflets are less crowded, but with similar erect flowers. June. Compost A.

A. laramiensis. (H).
One of the rarest of American Columbines, only one locality known, in the Laramie range of S.E. Wyoming. It is the smallest species in cultivation, making tight pads of short tufted stems with small biternate, green glabrous leaves. Flowers on short scapes, small, pendant, sepals greenish-white, petals cream, spurs small hooked, white in colour. April. Compost A.

A. moorcroftiana. (H).
From the mountains of Kashmir and Tibet, this is a charming species rarely above 6 inches high, dwarfer forms less than 4 inches have been known. It makes basal tufts of biternate, long stalked, thick, glaucous-grey foliage, leaflets obovate, crowded, each in three sections. Flowers semi-pendant, sepals purple-blue, petals blue tinged with yellow at tips; spurs slightly curved, purple. May. Compost B.

A. pyrenaica. (H).
More ink has been used over this species than all the other dwarf columbines put together, for it is a very variable plant and many other species akin to it have at one time or the other been merged or cited as subspecies. The typical plant is a native of the high Pyrenees and makes tufts of basal, biternate, greenish leaves, the leaflets on short secondary petioles, are thin, glaucous beneath, sub-orbicular in shape. The flowers are borne from one to three on 4-inch stems, pendant, ranging in colour from deep lilac to violet-blue, sepals wide and spreading; spurs slender, straight. May. Compost B.

A. pyrenaica var. bertolonii, see *A. bertolonii*.

A. pyrenaica var. discolor, see *A. discolor*.

A. reuteri, see *A. bertolonii*.

A. saximontana. (H).
A native of the central Rocky Mountains, it forms a dwarf tufted plant of prostrate spreading thick stems. Foliage is thin, biternate, mid-green, glaucous below. Flowers on small stems, often nestling in the crowded foliage, semi-pendant, sepals blue, petals yellow-white shading back to

blue, hooked spurs. The whole plant rarely exceeds 4 inches. June. Compost B.

A. scopulorum. (H).

A native of central Utah and eastern Nevada, this in its dwarf form is one of the gems of the race, but unfortunately indiscriminate raising of it from seed has produced some weird forms quite unlike the typical plant. You have been warned: buy this plant in flower or if raising from seed, ruthlessly destroy all that are not dwarf compact and large flowered. It forms low, much branched, thickish stems, from which arises tufts of biternate, blue-grey foliage. The leaflets are triternate, each section having three oblong to obovate lobes, densely crowded in whorls, rounded, leathery, glabrous with more blue in the grey colouring. The leaves expand much later in the season than do those of *A. jonesii*. Flowers are borne on 3-inch stems, upright, sepals ovate-oblong with pointed apex, flax blue in colour, petals shading to white, blue or even with a tracing of red. Spurs straight, longest of the species in relation to the size of the flower, tip slightly bulbous, shading from white to blue at tip. June. Compost A.

A. scopulorum var. calcarea. (H).

This form comes from above Tropic, Garfield County, Utah, and only differs from the type in two respects. It is a dwarfer form and normally retains this smallness from seed, the other variation is that petioles are glandular-pubescent. June. Compost A.

A. thalictrifolia. (H).

A native of the Southern Tyrol and Venetian Alps, this plant varies in height even in its natural habitat from between 4 and 12 inches. In its dwarf forms it makes an ideal subject for pan culture, forming glandular pubescent stems with biternate basal leaves. Leaflets in two to three segments, cuneate-obovate, mid-green. The flowers on slender stems are semi-erect, blue-violet, sepals lanceolate, open, petals cuneate-oblong, apex obtuse, spurs slightly curved. May. Compost B.

A. triternata. (H).

A native of Arizona and Western Colorado, it is often quoted as only a form of *A. canadensis*. Ranging from 4 to 8 inches high, it makes thick prostrate, densely hairy, loosely branched stems. The basal light green leaves are triternate, glabrous above, glaucous, rarely pilose below. Leaflets coarsely cut, obovate to sub-orbicular. The flowers are semi-pendant on slender pubescent stems, sepals light red, petals yellow tinging to red at base, spurs slightly curved, light red. June. Compost B.

A. viridiflora. Semi-evergreen.

This is a charming sweet-scented species from the Altai mountains and Kansu, where it makes a plant up to 9 inches high of short branching pubescent stems with biternate basal pubescent leaves. Leaflets bright mid-green thickish coarsely cut glabrous above, glaucous-pubescent below. The flowers on upright stems are semi-pendant with obtuse, pubescent green sepals, petals brownish tinged with red-purple, spurs slightly curved. May. Compost A.

ARABIS (*Cruciferae*).

A large genus of plants containing a number of alpines which although having a good many easy showy species, have some which, with their close congested cushions, rival the androsaces in form and beauty. They are for the most part confined to the northern hemisphere although there are a few native to S. America.

CULTIVATION. None of these plants provides any difficulty, only asking for a well-drained compost. A is suitable, and the cushion types like a good packing of chippings around the collar of the plant to ensure dryness at this point. A reasonable amount of water during the growing and flowering season, dry but not arid in winter.

PROPAGATION. By green cuttings in July, except where otherwise stated. Repot only when necessary. This is normally every other year after flowering.

A. androsacea. (E).
A compact cushion plant from the Cilician Taurus, making densely tufted, silky rosettes of entire, minute, oblong-elliptic, silvery leaves. Flowers in a raceme on 1-inch stems, white. May. Seed in August. Compost 2.

A. blepharophylla. (E).
Makes basal rosettes of spatulate, rough deep green leaves, margined with bristly hairs. Flowers on 6-inch stems, open heads of glowing deep rose. April. A native of California. Seed in August. Compost 2.

A. bryoides. (E).
A native of Greece, this forms a dense cushion of congested rosettes with silky white, minute, elliptic leaves. Flowers large, white, on hairy downy 1-inch stems. April.

A. carduchorum. (E). (Syn. *Draba gigas*).
A densely tufted plant of neat green rosettes. Leaves linear, stiff, apex obtuse, margins ciliate. Flowers on 1-inch stems, white. Armenia. May.

A. 'Kellereri'. (*A. bryoides* x *A. ferdinandi-coburgi*). (E).
A hybrid raised by Sundermann, making dense congested cushions of silvery-grey, lanceolate leaves in rosette formation, hairy both sides. Flowers large white, on short hairy stems. May.

ARCTERICA (*Ericaceae*).

This is a monotypic genus, native of Japan, Kamchatka and the Bering Islands closely allied to Pieris, and has been included in that genus at different periods.

CULTIVATION. It requires a cool root run in half shade and will do well in compost C with plenty of lime-free water during the growing and flowering season, moist at other times. It should only be brought into the house for flowering, after which it is best plunged in a north facing frame for the summer, as it resents a dry atmosphere. Overhead spraying is beneficial, also top-dressing in early spring, with equal parts of leaf-mould and sharp sand which should be worked down amongst the prostrate stems.

PROPAGATION. By cuttings of half-ripened wood in June. Repot every fourth year after flowering.

A. nana. (E). (Syn. *Andromeda nana*).
It forms a dwarf prostrate mat less than 2 inches high, of wiry brownish stems, thinly covered with a white down when young. Leaves alternate, crowded small, thick oval to oblong, leathery, pointed with a minute tooth, tapering towards base, margins slightly recurved and sparsely covered with white hairs; deep glossy green. Flowers up to four pendant, urn-shape in small clusters, glistening white, fragrant. April.

ARCTOSTAPHYLOS (*Ericaceae*).

A genus composed generally of large shrubs or small trees, but there are a number of shrubs which are suitable for the rock garden and of these, three species and two varieties can be tried in the alpine house. The genus is confined to America and Mexico with the exception of two species, these being natives of arctic or alpine regions in the northern hemisphere.

CULTIVATION. All species require a moist cool root run in half shade and will do well potted up in compost C requiring damp conditions at all times, with plenty of lime-free water during the growing season. A top-dressing of equal parts loam, leaf-mould and sand well worked in amongst the prostrate branches is beneficial in early spring.

PROPAGATION. Best by green cuttings, struck in bottom heat in July, or, if available, seed in February, compost 3. Repot only when necessary after flowering.

A. alpina. (D). (Syn. *Arctous alpina*).
This plant has a wide distribution in the northern hemisphere including Scotland, where I found it while taking a party up Ben Ledi during the Alpine Garden Society's tour. It makes a dwarf prostrate plant, less than 2 inches high, spreading slowly into a wiry mat. The leaves are small, oblanceolate, tapering to base, apex obtuse, bright green, margins serrate and ciliate. Flowers in terminal clusters, up to four, urn-shaped, white with a pink flush, anthers chocolate-brown. April–May. Fruits black-purple ½ inch across. Foliage has deep autumn colouring.

A. alpina var. ruber. (D). (Syn. *Arctous a.* var. *ruber*).
This is similar in all aspects to the type with the exception of the leaves, these being lighter green, obovate, and bearing bright red drupes. A native of N. America and W. China.

A. myrtifolia, see *A. nummularia*.

A. nevadensis. (E).
A dwarf prostrate shrub only a few inches high with loose spreading

laterals, brown and smooth, slightly pilose in juvenile state. Leaves alternate, entire, oblong to obovate, apex acute and mucronate, margins slightly ciliate, bright green, lighter below, veining reticulate. Flowers in small compact racemes, urn-shaped, white flushed pink. May. Fruit globose, carmine red. A native of Oregon, U.S.A.

A. nummularia. (E). (Syn. *A. myrtifolia*).

A rare and far from easy plant to keep in good health, it seems to miss the wide open, damp peaty moors. It is up to 9 inches high with slender slightly contorted, brown hairy branches. Leaves alternate, leathery, crowded, almost entire, obovate, rounded at base, pointed at apex, bright glossy green, margined with fine hairs. Flowers in small terminal racemes, urn-shaped, white pendant, calyces deep pink. May. Fruit oblong, dark brown. *A. myrtifolia* does not seem to have any botanical standing and has been made a synonym of *A. nummularia* but I have grown a plant under that name which although similar in all other respects to the species, differs in that the flowers are pink, followed by red drupes.

ARCTOUS, see *Arctostaphylos alpina*.

ARENARIA (*Caryophyllaceae*).

The Sandworts are well-known mat-forming plants used in the rock garden and the following two representatives can be grown in pans for the alpine house. Botanically they are close to Minuartia and some species which are often listed under Arenaria are more correctly placed in Minuartia.

CULTIVATION. Easy in compost A requiring plenty of water during the growing season, dry but not arid in winter.

PROPAGATION. By seed sown in April, compost 1 or division immediately after flowering. Repot when necessary after flowering.

A. lanceolata, see *Minuartia rupestris*.

A. purpurascens. (E).

A native of the Pyrenees, this makes a loose mat of tufts only an inch or so high. Leaves ovate-lanceolate, pointed at apex, dark green. Flowers up to three on slender hairy pedicels, light purple stars. May.

A. tetraquetra. (E).

Another species from the Pyrenees, making a neat mat of grey-green. Leaves alternating on the stem giving them the appearance of being four-angled, ovate obtuse. Flowers up to three on small pedicels, starry-white. June.

ARMERIA. (*Plumbaginaceae*).

The Sea Pinks or Thrifts are mostly alpine or maritime plants of which six are suitable for pan culture in the alpine house or frame.

CULTIVATION. This is quite easy in compost A over good drainage with plenty of water while in flower, dry but not arid in winter.

PROPAGATION. By green cuttings in June. Repot only when necessary after flowering.

A. alpina, see *A. montana.*

A. caespitosa. (E).
This is a charming species forming dense rounded cushions only 2 inches high. Leaves in tufts narrow linear, three-angled, spiny, recurved, bright green. Flowers on short downy stems in dense rounded heads, pale lilac-pink and persisting. May. A native of Spain.

A. caespitosa 'Bevans Var.' (E).
This is similar to the type but the flowers are much deeper in colour. May. A native of Portugal and Spain, collected and introduced by Dr Roger Bevan, a noted grower of alpine plants.

A. halleri. (E).
From the Pyrenees, where it makes a 4-inch rounded cushion of green tufts. Leaves long linear, soft, green in colour, blunt at apex. Flowers in dense rounded clusters, bright rose, persisting. June.

A. juncea, see *A. setacea.*

A. juniperifolia. (E).
A fine compact tufted plant about 4 inches high. Leaves linear, erect, pointed at apex, rigid, deep green. Flowers in dense globular heads, deep rose. May. A native of Spain.

A. montana. (E). (Syn. *A. alpina*).
A small tufted cushion rarely above 3 inches high. Leaves linear-lanceolate, crowded, green. Flowers on 1-inch stems in dense rounded heads, deep pink. May. Native of European Alps.

A. setacea. (E). (Syn. *A. juncea*).
A native of S. Europe, making a dwarf compact cushion of almost spiny tufts. Leaves in dense erect rosettes, narrow linear, acute, grey-green. Flowers on 2-inch stems, small, in tight heads, light-rose and persisting. May.

ARNICA (*Compositae*).

A small genus of perennial herbaceous plants of the north temperate zone, containing two species that can be tried in the alpine house as pan plants.
CULTIVATION. Compost A over good drainage; dislikes lime and wet winters, otherwise quite easy.
PROPAGATION. By division in April or seed sown in February, compost 2. Repot every year after flowering.

A. montana. (H).
A native of many European mountains and well known to climbers in the Alps. It makes basal rosettes of glabrous, oblong-lanceolate, green leaves; stem leaves sessile, arranged in opposite pairs. Flowers on 6-inch stems, up to four on short stalks, large, fragrant, deep orange daisies. May.

A. nana. (H).
A native of N.W. America, this seems to be but a geographical variety of

montana differing in that the basal rosettes are tighter and leaves slightly toothed. Flowers similar. May.

ARTEMISIA (*Compositae*).

This genus has a large number of aromatic species which include shrubs, herbaceous perennials and annuals, their chief beauty lies in their gracefully cut silver or grey foliage.

CULTIVATION. Compost A over faultless drainage, the leaves should never be watered overhead as this will quickly destroy their beauty, as well as suffering from sun scorch. Dry but not arid in winter.

PROPAGATION. By green cuttings of the shrubby species in July. Repot only when necessary after flowering as slight root restriction keeps them more compact and dwarf.

A. glacialis. (E).
This is a tufted sub-shrub only a few inches high with downy shoots. Leaves bi-pinnate, segments linear, glistening silver. Flowers in terminal clusters on 2-inch stems, yellow. June. A native of Central Europe.

A. lanata. (E). (Syn. *A. pedemontana*).
A small sub-shrub only 1 inch or so high with interwoven branches. Leaves bi-pinnate, crowded, segments palmate. Colour glistening silver due to the thick covering of appressed woolly down. Flowers in small heads on almost sessile downy stems, yellow. June. A native of S. and Central Europe.

A. mutellina. (E).
Another tufted sub-shrub about 2 inches high, making basal tufts of bi-pinnate to palmate leaves with linear-filiform segments, the whole glistening silvery white on both sides. Flowers in rounded heads on 4-inch stems, pale yellow. June. A native of Central and S. Europe.

A. pedemontana, see *A. lanata*.

A. spicata. (E).
A native of the Swiss Alps, this is a tufted sub-shrub rarely above 4 inches high. Leaves tri-partite, silvery-white due to the intense covering of silky white appressed hairs. Flowers small in cylindrical spikes on 2-inch woolly stems, yellow. June.

ARTHROPODIUM (*Liliaceae*).

A small genus of plants from Australia and New Zealand, containing one which is suitable for the alpine house.

CULTIVATION. Compost B in full sun, plenty of water whilst in growth, dry but not arid in winter.

PROPAGATION. By division in April. Repot every second year in early April.

A. candidum. (H).
A tufted herbaceous perennial from New Zealand, about 6 inches high,

leaves grass like, long narrow linear, glabrous. Flowers lily-shaped on a 6-inch slender scape in a loose spike, white. June.

ASPERULA (*Rubiaceae*).

A genus which has a number of attractive species, a few of which need to be grown in the alpine house to ensure permanence.
CULTIVATION. Compost A will suit these plants and they require plenty of water in spring and summer but not over the foliage, dry conditions in winter. Close compact plants forming nice rounded cushions can be obtained if the plants are cut back after flowering.
PROPAGATION. By green cuttings taken in June and rooted in a closed frame. Repot every year after flowering.
A. arcadiensis. (E).
A native of Greece, it makes a congested cushion of soft woolly stems rarely above 3 inches high. Leaves opposite, crowded, densely woolly, silver-grey in colour. Flowers in terminal clusters up to eight, small long tubular, waxy in texture, bright rose-pink. May. This plant is best propagated by cuttings in pure sand with bottom heat. August.
A. athoa, see *A. suberosa*.
A. hirta. (E).
A native of the Pyrenees, this is an easy species which forms a soft hummock of soft twiggy stems, tightly packed with the dark green, linear, hairy leaves arranged round the stems in whorls of six. Flowers small, tubular, white ageing to pink. May.
A. nitida. (E).
This species makes a glabrous cushion of small ascending stems, leaves dark green in whorls of four, linear, incurved, apex white tipped. Flowers tubular in sessile clusters rarely above four, rose. Greece. May.
A. suberosa. (E). (Syn. *A. athoa*).
This is a well-known alpine plant from Greece, and makes a tufted, many stemmed cushion less than 3 inches high. Leaves crowded in whorls of four, narrow linear, both stem and leaves covered with silvery hairs. Flowers terminal on a 2-inch spike, long narrow tubular, pink. June. This plant should be cut back one-third after flowering to keep it neat and tidy.

ASPHODELUS (*Liliaceae*).

A small genus of plants mostly from the Mediterranean region, of which one is eminently suitable for alpine house culture.
CULTIVATION. Compost A is suitable, making sure that the drainage is faultless, as this plant is impatient of stagnant moisture. Water is best given by immersion, requires dry but not arid conditions after flowering.
PROPAGATION. By careful division in spring. Repot every second year after flowering.

A. acaulis. (E).

A native of the Atlas Mountains, it forms a basal rosette of long linear green leaves, tapering to a point, serrulate-margined, and minutely downy, these can be up to 10 inches in length. Flowers on almost non-existing scapes clustered at the centre of the rosettes, large, open star-shaped, pale rose in colour with a delightful fragrance. February-March.

ASTER (*Compositae*).

From this large range of plants only a few can be grown in the alpine house, solely because they are so easy in the rock garden that it is not necessary for them to take up room which could be utilised for choicer plants. Those dealt with under this heading will not only help to provide colour, but can be grown by beginners as a stepping stone to better specimens.

CULTIVATION. This is easy in compost A with plenty of water during the growing and flowering season, dry but not arid at other periods.

PROPAGATION. Unless stated otherwise, by division in August. Repot every year in spring.

A. alpinus. (H).

This is the typical plant found on mountains all over Europe, about 6 inches high; basal leaves, long spatulate, stem leaves lanceolate, dull green in colour. Flowers large solitary, lilac-purple with a golden eye. June-July.

A. alpinus var. albus. (H).

The white form, which is rarely found with good substantial flowers. June.

A. alpinus var. himalaicus. (H).

This is a much darker coloured form, almost red-purple and is never above 4 inches high. June.

A. alpinus var. ruber. (H).

Similar to the type but with large deep red flowers. July.

A. bellidiastrum. (H).

A native of Austria, it makes basal rosettes of obovate, green leaves, margins slightly curved. Flowers single star-shaped, white with a yellow eye on 6-inch scapes. June.

A. farreri. (H).

A native of Tibet, making tufts of lanceolate dark green leaves, margined with hairs, stem leaves small linear. Flowers singly on 6-inch scapes, deep violet with orange-red centre. June.

A. himalaicus. (H).

This is a sub-shrubby species from Sikkim, where it makes woody stems, clothed with the grey obovate to spatulate, dentate leaves, covered with fluffy down; stem leaves oblong, almost appressed. Flowers solitary on 9-inch stems, deep lavender-blue, buff on reverse of petals. May. Best propagated by green cuttings in June.

A. likiangensis. (H).
A small tufted plant of green spatulate leaves in rosette form. Flowers solitary on stems only 4 inches high, deep blue with golden eye. June. A native of Yunnan.

A. pappei, see *Felicia pappei.*

A. yunnanensis. (H).
A native of Western China, making tufts of green lanceolate-spatulate basal leaves in rosette formation, and on 9-inch stems, sparsely clothed with small linear leaves, are borne the solitary large purple flowers. June.

ASTILBE (*Saxifragaceae*).

There are a few species and varieties of this genus which owing to their late flowering habit and dwarf characteristics make them suitable for the alpine house and frame.

CULTIVATION. All do well in compost B and they require moist conditions while in growth; when dormant the soil should be kept on the dry side. Half shade is desirable in hot weather.

PROPAGATION. By division of the rootstock in April. Repot every year in early April.

A. chinensis 'Pumila'. (H).
A dwarf Chinese form rarely above 6 inches high with tufts of pinnate, pale green leaves. Flowers clustered on short stout spikes, rose-mauve in colour. July.

A. 'Crispa'. (H).
This is a hybrid of unknown parentage which originated from Japan, with basal tufts of much cut, almost feathery green leaves, quaintly crimped, the underneath bright red. Flowers on 3-inch spikes white, rose or red. July. There are a number of named forms but these only differ in the colour of the flower spikes.

A. glaberrima 'Saxatilis'. (H).
A native of Japan, this is a charming dwarf plant with tufts of ternate to biternate deep glossy green leaves, reddish beneath, margins recurved, bristly. Flowers on 3-inch red to green shaded stems in racemes of light purple with white tipped petals. July.

A. simplicifolia. (H).
This is a native of Japan, making tufts of simple ovate, much lobed glossy green foliage, often pale pink below. Flowers on small branched stems, dainty pale pink. July.

ASTRAGALUS (*Leguminosae*).

A large and mighty race of pea-shaped flowering plants, but there are not many in cultivation owing to a great extent to their difficulty in propagation. Even seed, if it ripens, is slow to germinate, and division is impossible, for all species are intolerant of root disturbance.

CULTIVATION. Compost A is suitable over good drainage; the plants need a good supply of water during the growing season, but this is best reduced in late July, so that the growth ripens well; dry but not arid in winter.

PROPAGATION. By seed if set in February, compost 2, or green cuttings, the last inch or so of the growing tip of the shoot is removed and placed in the propagating frame in August. Repot only when necessary in early April, for root restriction tends to increase the floral display. Care must be taken to disturb the roots as little as possible during this operation, for if the tap root is broken or injured it can lead to the death of the plant.

A. angustifolius. (D).
A native of Asia Minor, this is an intensely spiny congested dome-shaped, sub-shrub, less than a foot high. Leaflets up to twenty, are linear to oblong, grey-green covered with fine down. Flowers pea-shaped, few in short stalked racemes, white, violet at apex. May.

A. massiliensis, see *A. tragacantha alba*.

A. monspessulanus. (E).
A small sub-shrub only 6 inches high with small branches covered with greyish hairs, leaves in rosettes on the stems, leaflets, ten to twenty pairs, oval to oblong, green, hairy beneath. Flowers in small heads on 6-inch stalks, crowded, purple. Mediterranean region. July.

A. tragacantha. (D).
This is a dwarf slow-growing shrub rarely up to a foot in height and only attaining this stature after many years. It forms a much-branched specimen with ascending laterals, the lower parts covered with sharp spines. Leaflets in seven to eleven pairs, linear, mid-green, covered with silky down. Flowers borne in late May are the usual pea-shape in umbels up to six, pale violet-red. A native of the Mediterranean and Asia Minor regions.

A. tragacantha var. alba (D). (Syn. *A. massiliensis*).
This is similar to the type but with white flowers in May. A native of the Mediterranean region.

ASYNEUMA (*Campanulaceae*).

A small genus of plants closely related to Phyteuma and often included in that genus. There are two species both introduced recently from Turkey by Dr Peter Davis, that are saxatile high altitude alpine plants, requiring as much care as Aretian androsaces to keep them in good health.

CULTIVATION. Best in compost D, starting with small seedlings which establish best. A normal supply of water in spring and summer, reducing this to dryish conditions in winter but never arid. Care must be taken not to allow surplus moisture to remain on the cushions.

PROPAGATION. Best by seed sown in compost 2 when ripe. Repot only when necessary in late March.

A. lycium. (E).
A native from the Lycian Taurus, this has close compact tufts from a

central fleshy rootstock. Leaves minute, crowded, spatulate, entire, tapering to long stalks, green. Flowers terminal on wiry 2-inch stems, open five linear lobes, slate-blue with a protruding red stigma. May.

A. pulvinatum. (E).

From a stout fleshy rootstock are produced short branching stems, forming a close dense rounded cushion less than 1 inch high. Leaves crowded, minute, narrow lanceolate green. Flowers terminal in small racemes, open five narrow linear lobes, pale blue. May–June. A native of **Turkey**.

AZALEA included in **RHODODENDRON**.

Azalea procumbens, see *Loiseleuria procumbens.*
Azorella trifurcata, see *Bolax glebaria.*

BABIANA (*Iridaceae*).

This is a genus of South African bulbous plants which provides a number of suitable subjects for the alpine house.

CULTIVATION. About four corms should be placed in a pot, 3 inches deep in late September. Compost B, just moist, is ideal and no more water should be given until growth is discernible in spring; while in growth a good supply will be required. These corms benefit from a watering with weak liquid manure every other week as soon as the flowering spikes appear. After they have died down the pots should be stored in a dry sunny place for the corms to ripen.

PROPAGATION. Best by offsets which are removed when repotting and grown on until they reach flowering size. Seed too can be sown but requires a minimum temperature of 60°F (15°C) for satisfactory germination, April in compost 2. Repot every year in autumn, pots are preferable to pans.

B. disticha, see *B. plicata* var. *disticha.*

B. plicata. (B).

A small corm with folded lanceolate hairy leaves. Flowers tubular, 6 lobed on 6-inch scapes up to three, fragrant, pale blue. June.

B. plicata var. disticha. (B). (Syn. *B. disticha*).

This is similar to the type but smaller in all its parts. Flowers violet-blue. June.

B. stricta. (B).

Up to 12 inches high with broad lanceolate, blunt, hairy leaves. Flowers one to four tubular, three outer segments white, three inner blue, deep blotch at base. June.

B. stricta 'Rubro-Cyanea'. (B).

Only 8 inches high, leaves tapered to point, not obtuse, hairy below. Flowers large tubular, three outer segments bright blue, inner crimson. June.

B. stricta 'Sulphurea'. (B).
Similar to the type with obtuse foliage, 9 inches high, cream flowers. June.

BELLIUM (*Compositae*).

A small genus of plants which contains one suitable for the alpine house or frame.
CULTIVATION. This is easy in compost A, needs plenty of water while in growth, dry but not arid in winter.
PROPAGATION. By division in April or seed sown in February, compost 1. Repot only when necessary in early April.
B. minutum. (E).
It makes a tiny close, congested mat, rarely above an inch high with tufts of slightly hairy narrow, spatulate, minute green leaves. Flowers large for size of plant, over $\frac{1}{2}$ an inch across on 2-inch stems, white with yellow disk, petals deep red on reverse. June.

BERBERIS (*Berberidaceae*).

The Barberries are a large and widely distributed genus found in most countries of the world but absent from Australia. They are with a few exceptions, unfortunately, too large for pan culture but those enumerated below can be relied upon to remain dwarf for a good number of years under pan conditions.
CULTIVATION. Compost A will suit all species and forms but the drainage must be perfect, they require plenty of water during the growing season, dry but not arid in winter.
PROPAGATION. This is managed by taking cuttings of the current year's growth with a heel attached in July and rooting in the propagating frame. Repot only when necessary after flowering as root restriction helps to retain their dwarf habit, also when repotting care must be taken not to disturb the roots too much as they are highly intolerant of this.
B. buxifolia 'Nana'. (E).
This is a native of Chile and the type plant will reach 6 feet but the dwarf form rarely exceeds 1 foot in cultivation. It makes an erect shrub of brown hairy, spine clad branches. Leaves crowded, entire, oblong or obovate, dark green, glaucous grey beneath. Flowers solitary, pendant on short pedicels, deep yellow. May. Berries blue.
B. × darwinii 'Nana'. (E).
A seedling from *B.* × *stenophylla*, that outstanding hybrid between *B. darwinii* and *B. empetrifolia*, its form is near to the female parent *B. darwinii* while it has inherited its dwarf stature from the male. A garden hybrid, it rarely exceeds 12 inches with erect, twiggy, brown hairy shoots with sharp short spines. Leaves small oblong, bright glossy green with three teeth on each side. Flowers clustered on large racemes, orange-yellow. May. Berries very dark purple, covered with a blue bloom.

B. empetrifolia. (E).
This is a native of Chile, home of many fine Barberries and it makes a semi-prostrate shrub less than 12 inches high when mature. Branches red, glabrous, leaves entire, linear, spine tipped, margins recurved. Flowers single, golden-yellow. May. Berries dark purple with a blue bloom.

B. kumaonensis. (D).
A native of Kumaon, this is a delightful dwarf shrublet up to 12 inches high with semi-erect, yellow, glabrous branches and under alpine house conditions will retain its old foliage until early spring. Leaves crowded, obovate, dark green with up to three coarse spine tipped teeth on each side, glaucous grey beneath. Flowers solitary on short pedicels, golden-yellow. May. Berries red, no bloom.

B. osmastonii. (E).
A fairly recent introduction from Garhwal, this is a dwarf species close to *B. candidula*, only 6 inches high with glabrous, angled branches and soft spines. Leaves crowded, linear dark green, margins recurved, entire, grey-white beneath. Flowers small, solitary, deep yellow. May. Berries deep red with bloom.

B. × stenophylla. (E). (*B. darwinii × B. empetrifolia*).
This hybrid has produced a number of dwarf varieties of which three are eminently suitable for pan culture. These are all close to their parents and give a brilliant floral display in May–June.

B. × stenophylla 'Coccinea'. (E).
A good dwarf form with crimson buds opening to coral flowers. Berries purple.

B. × stenophylla 'Corallina Compacta'. (E).
Rarely above 6 inches high, has the typical foliage of its female parent, buds coral, flowers yellow, fruits purple with whitish bloom.

B. × stenophylla 'Gracilis Nana'. (E).
This is a dwarf shrub about 6 inches high with holly-shaped, spiny, mid-green yellow-flecked leaves. The young foliage is a brilliant orange-red. Flowers deep orange-yellow, berries purple.

BOLAX (*Umbelliferae*).
A small genus of plants closely related to Azorella and often confused with that genus, this includes one species suitable for pan culture in the alpine house.
CULTIVATION. Compost A over good drainage is suitable with a normal supply of water during the growing season, just moist in winter.
PROPAGATION. By cuttings in July. Repot when necessary in April.

B. glebaria. (E). (Syn. *Azorella trifurcata*).
A native of Ecuador, this is an uncommon plant making close soft cushions. Leaves tufted, thick, three-lobed, segments ovate, obtuse, glossy light apple green. Flowers minute, almost sessile in a four-flowered

umbel, golden-yellow, backed by a four-leaved involucre. June. When in flower the plant gives an impression of molten sunshine.

BOYKINIA. (*Saxifragaceae*).

A small genus of plants confined to N. America and Japan of which only one, *B. jamesii*, is suitable for the alpine house or frame.

CULTIVATION. Somehow this plant seems to have a reputation of being difficult to flower and all sorts of hints have been given on methods of achieving success with this species. My own opinion for what it is worth is that there must be two forms of the plant in cultivation, for I have never failed to flower it successfully, in fact a specimen which gained a Cultural Commendation from the R.H.S. had nineteen flowering spikes and was an eight-year-old plant which bore an increasing number of flowers each succeeding year. It does well in compost A with faultless drainage and requires plenty of moisture while making its new growth and flowers, dry but not arid conditions after growth has died away. A bi-weekly dose of liquid fertiliser works wonders in early spring and summer.

PROPAGATION. By seed in February, compost 2 or division after flowering. Repot when necessary after flowering, making sure that this is firmly done, as it seems to like a certain amount of root restriction.

B. jamesii. (H).
This is a rare American alpine from Pikes Peak, Colorado, making tufts of kidney shaped, scalloped, greeny-yellow, red margined, coarsely toothed, sticky leaves. Flowers in racemes on 4-inch stout, sticky stems, large, saxifrage like, crimson-red. May.

BRIGGSIA (*Gesneriaceae*).

A small genus of plants closely allied to Didissandra of which there are two suitable species for the alpine house; both require careful cultivation to maintain them in good health.

CULTIVATION. Although hardy, the species need protection from wind, and they quickly show their resentment of this by the edges of the leaves turning brown and they certainly require shade in some form or other. Compost B is suitable and the soil should be kept moist at all periods. They must not be retained in the alpine house during hot summer months but are best plunged in a cool, shady spot away from strong winds.

PROPAGATION. By carefully detaching offsets, which these plants form sparingly, and rooting these under a shaded bell glass in June. Leaf cuttings can also be tried but this is a long process. Seed if obtainable is also a means of increase, compost 3. February. Repot when necessary after flowering.

B. ambilis. (E).
A small creeping rhizome with ascending stems, never above 6 inches

high. Leaves towards apex in pairs, ovate, irregular, glabrous, dark green above, purplish beneath, tapering to apex, margins crenate. Flowers pendant, long, tubular, rarely in pairs on slender hairy pedicels, cream with brown markings inside. June. A native of Yunnan.

B. muscicola. (E). (Syn. *B. penlopi, Didissandra muscicola*).
A native of Bhutan, W. China, it has basal rosettes of ovate to lanceolate, bright apple-green, crinkled leaves, covered with whitish hairs, margins crenate. Flowers on 6-inch brownish stems, tubular, constricted at mouth, deep yellow with orange markings at throat. May.

B. penlopi, see *B. muscicola*.

BRODIAEA (*Amaryllidaceae*).

A genus of bulbous plants which have either been classified under Brodiaea or Triteleia and *vice-versa* at different periods. Now they have been split up into new genera causing much confusion in renaming, so here it is better to deal with them under Brodiaea and give their correct generic and specific names as well where this applies. They are natives of Western, N. and S. America and provide a number of plants suitable for the alpine house and frame.

CULTIVATION. Up to six in a pot with compost B in October, planting them just below the surface, keep them on the dry side until growth commences when water should be given freely. After the foliage dies down keep dry.

PROPAGATION. By seed in March, compost 2 or offsets which are removed when repotting the corms and grown on until flowering size is reached.

B. aurea. (B). (Syn. *Triteleia aurea*).
This is more correctly *Nothoscordum aureum* but is retained here under its well-known name. A native of Patagonia with whitish corms, leaves filiform. Flowers tubular in an umbel up to six golden-yellow with a green stripe on reverse. May.

B. coccinea, see *B. ida-maia*.

B. crocea. (B).
Correctly *Triteleia crocea*, this is a native of California with slender leaves which die down quickly. Flowers in loose umbels up to fifteen, short, tubular, star-shaped, yellow. June.

B. douglasii. (B).
This is *Triteleia grandiflora*, a native of Oregon with two light green deeply channelled leaves. Flowers in a dense umbel on a 12-inch scape, funnel-shaped, violet-blue, inner segments wavy. May.

B. elegans. (B). (Syn. *B. grandiflora*).
A native of Oregon, producing two to three linear, pointed, grooved leaves. Flowers on a firm 12-inch scape in umbels of up to eleven, short tubular, violet-purple. May.

B. grandiflora, see *B. elegans.*

B. hendersonii. (B).
More correctly *Triteleia hendersonii*, this is a native of California, making slender glabrous leaves and on 10-inch slender scapes, umbels of up to fifteen small tubular, salmon-coloured flowers, with broad purple central marking. June.

B. ida-maia. (B). (Syn. *B. coccinea*).
This should be *Dichelostemma ida-maia* and is a native of California with slender linear leaves and up to fifteen flowers in an umbel on a 12-inch stem, tubular, crimson tipped, yellowish green. June.

B. ixiodes var. splendens. (B).
About 9 inches high from Oregon, with fleshy long pointed leaves. Flowers in umbels, few, short, tubular, yellow. June. More correctly *Triteleia ixiodes* var. *splendens*.

B. lactea. (B).
This Californian should be *Triteleia hyacinthina*, making long, acute, linear leaves up to a foot high and many flowered umbels of open saucer shaped white flowers with green midribs. May.

B. stellaris. (B).
A small plant only 6 inches high of almost cylindrical leaves. Flowers in small umbels up to six, open tubular, bright purple with white centre. June. A native of California.

B. uniflora. (B). (Syn. *Triteleia uniflora*).
This is a true bulb and has been removed to a new genus, Ipheion and is now *I. uniflorum* but will be dealt with here. A native of the Argentine, sending up from six to nine long, narrow, lanceolate, bright green leaves and on 6-inch scapes, single open star-shaped flowers with a long narrow tube, pale-lilac to white over a long period. May–July.

BRUCKENTHALIA (*Ericaceae*).

This is a monotypic genus closely related to the hardy ericas, the difference between the two genera is that the stamens are attached to the corolla in Bruckenthalia and the corolla is wider at the mouth than in Erica.

CULTIVATION. Does well in compost B, requiring a cool moist root run, water is needed in plenty but this must be from a lime-free source. It is best kept in a cool shady frame during the hot summer months, and benefits from an overhead spraying during that period. Top-dress in early spring with similar compost.

PROPAGATION. By half-ripened cuttings taken in late July. Bottom heat is advised where speed of rooting is essential. Repot only when necessary after flowering.

B. spiculifolia. (E).
Less than 6 inches high, of slender erect branches, downy in juvenile state. Leaves opposite, crowded on stems, linear, apex mucronulate,

ciliate, margins recurved, mid-grey green, white beneath. Flowers crowded in terminal racemes bell shaped, rose-pink. May–June. A native of S.E. Europe and Asia Minor.

BRYANTHUS (*Ericaceae*).

This is another monotypic genus which has at one time or another been host to species now removed to other genera.

CULTIVATION. This rare and choice plant demands a cool shady spot at all times to give of its best, for it is not an easy plant, especially in the dryer atmosphere of the southern counties. Compost B is suitable, keeping it moist at all times and using lime-free water. Top-dressing with a little leaf-mould in early spring is beneficial, also spraying is required in the evening after hot days. This species is best accommodated in a cool spot, in a north facing frame and only brought into the alpine house when in flower.

PROPAGATION. By cuttings of half-ripened wood in June, or the more certain method of layering but these may take up to two years to root. They should not be disturbed after detaching from the parent plant for at least a further three or four months. Repot only when necessary after flowering.

B. aleuticus, see *Phyllodoce aleutica.*.

B. breweri, see *Phyllodoce breweri.*

B. empetriformis, see *Phyllodoce empetriformis.*

B. × erectus, see × *Phyllothamnus erectus.*

B. gmelinii. (E). (Syn. *B. musciformis*).

A native of Japan and Kamchatka, this is a slow growing prostrate shrub only a few inches high, of slender creeping branches, closely packed with small, linear, recurved leaves, margins dentate, dark green covered with fine down, white woolly beneath. Flowers in small clusters, rarely above three on thread-like stems round, flattish, four-lobed, deep rose. May.

B. glanduliflorus, see *Phyllodoce glanduliflora.*

B. musciformis, see *B. gmelinii.*

B. taxifolius, see *Phyllodoce caerulea.*

BULBOCODIUM (*Liliaceae*).

Still yet another monotypic genus from the Alps of Europe which can be used for early decoration of the alpine house or frame.

CULTIVATION. Six corms should be placed in compost B, 3 inches deep in autumn, this should be damp, not wet, and as soon as the growth appears the compost should be kept moist. After flowering and the foliage dies down, allow the corms to ripen.

PROPAGATION. By seed sown in March, compost 2, or removing offsets which are formed, when repotting. This should be carried out every year. Pots, not pans, should be used.

B. trigynum, see *Merendera trigyna.*
B. vernum. (B). (Syn. *Colchicum vernum*).
A native of the European Alps, with a small oblong black corm from which appear two to three funnel-shaped, light to deep mauve flowers, spotted white on the claw. The green leaves which appear later are broad strap shaped, concave. March.
B. vernum 'Versicolor'. (B).
Similar to the species but with flowers purple tinted white. March.

CALCEOLARIA (*Scrophulariaceae*).

A large genus mostly centred in Chile and Peru, the majority of which are not hardy in this country, but there are a few hardy species which make admirable subjects for pan culture, although some will tax the most skilful of cultivators in making them thrive. All are quaint and charming with their baggy pouch-like flowers.
CULTIVATION. Compost B is suitable but no general hints can be given except possibly for two points. All like a moist but exceedingly well drained soil, they also provide an irresistible attraction for the varied species of aphids; these attacks, unless dealt with immediately, will certainly weaken plants which are not easy, even in a healthy state.
PROPAGATION. This too differs and will be dealt with separately.
C. acutifolia. (H).
A mat-forming herbaceous perennial with slender rhizomes, leaves tufted, in pairs, ovate-oblong, hairy, pointed, green. Flowers solitary on 4-inch stems, large, golden-yellow, dotted red on lower lip. June. A native of Patagonia. Requires plenty of water while growing, moist at other periods, half shade.
PROPAGATION. By division in April. Repot every other year in early April. An easy species.
C. arachnoidea. (E).
A native of Chile, making close congested rosettes of oblong-spatulate, entire leaves, covered with white cobwebs. Flowers few on 6-inch stems, purple. June. This plant requires a dryish compost in sunshine.
PROPAGATION. By green cuttings in July. Repot every second year after flowering.
C. arachnoidea var. alba. (E).
Similar to the type but with white flowers in June.
C. biflora. (E). (Syn. *C. plantaginea*).
This makes basal rosettes of roundish, ovate, dentate green leaves, downy beneath. Flowers two, on four-inch slender stems, yellow. July. Needs a cool shady spot with plenty of moisture at all times and requires repotting every year, as it seems to exhaust the soil quickly. A native of Chile.
PROPAGATION. By seed sown in compost 2. March.
C. darwinii. (E).
A native of Patagonia, one of the gems of the race, forming basal rosettes

Above: *Dionysia michauxii* (see page 272)

Below: *Erigeron aureus* (see page 278)

Above: *Eritrichium nanum* (see page 281)

Below: *Fritillaria michailovskyi* (see page 524)

at the end of a branching rhizome, leaves pale green, oblong, margins dentate, glabrous, veins hairy. Flowers solitary on 3-inch scapes, large, rounded at back, concave at front, lower lip has wide white band with chestnut spotting at base. Needs care in cultivation with plenty of water during the growing season and benefits from a layer of live sphagnum moss on the surface of the compost, drier conditions in winter. It is best placed in a shady spot during hot summer months. Seems to do better in a large pot, not a pan, for the roots can be up to eighteen inches long and do not seem to like restriction. Repot after flowering.

PROPAGATION. By runners used as cuttings in sand, July, or if seed is set, this can be sown in March. Compost 2.

C. fothergillii. (E).
Another difficult species from Patagonia with creeping prostrate stems, leaves in rosettes, entire, spatulate, grey, covered with hairs. Flowers solitary from 4-inch branching scapes, generally a pair of stem leaves at branch, large, sulphur-yellow pouches, wider at base, red spots on lower lip. July. Needs the same careful cultivation as *C. darwinii*, must be kept moist in summer and detests winter wet.

PROPAGATION. Best by seed in February, compost 2.

C. plantaginea, see *C. biflora*.

C. polyrrhiza. (H).
A herbaceous perennial often confused with *C. acutifolia* but differs, in that this species has several flowers, not solitary, less curved lip and leaves are glandular. A native of Patagonia it makes a prostrate tufted plant, leaves in pairs, lanceolate, green. Flowers on glandular hairy scapes, up to five, yellow pouch with purple spots. June. Requires same culture as *C. acutifolia*.

C. tenella. (E).
A charming dwarf plant, quite prostrate, only an inch high with rambling, wavy reddish stems. Leaves minute, ovate, margins dentate, light green. Flowers up to three on 3-inch thread-like stems, each with two stem leaves, rounded, golden-yellow, marked with crimson spots across the lip. June. A native of Chile. This is best planted in a wide shallow pan in compost C, for it is only surface rooting. Pieces of sandstone embedded in the compost with a small face showing over which the plant can clamber are beneficial, shade is essential, sun and dry conditions are fatal. Best in a north facing frame, only being taken into the house while in flower. It quickly covers the surface of the pan and requires frequent division and repotting to maintain good health.

PROPAGATION. By division in April. Repot when necessary in early April.

CALLIANTHEMUM (*Ranunculaceae*).

A small race of plants which has representatives in both Europe and Asia, closely related to Ranunculus. There are two suited for the alpine house or frame.

CULTIVATION. Compost A is suitable and these plants require plenty of water while growing, dry but not arid after growth dies down.

PROPAGATION. By division in June. Repot only when necessary after flowering.

C. anemonoides, see *C. rutifolium*.

C. kernerianum. (H).

A dwarf prostrate plant only an inch or so high from Monte Baldo, stems reddish, leaves basal, bi-pinnate, broad, ovate, blue-grey. Flowers on 4-inch stems up to sixteen petals, pale pink, deeper on reverse. The flowers appear before the dainty foliage opens. May.

C. rutifolium. (H). (Syn. *C. anemonoides*; *Ranunculus anemonoides*).

Makes a small plant rarely above 6 inches high. Leaves grey, triangular in shape, bi-pinnate, almost fern-like with five leaflets on each pinna. Flowers on 6-inch stems, large many-petalled, pure white, or flushed pink. April. A native of Austria.

CALLUNA (*Ericaceae*).

This is a monotypic genus closely allied to Erica and differing in that Calluna has a larger coloured calyx than corolla. It is surprising the number of varieties which have sprung from the single species *C. vulgaris* and a few are useful for decoration in the alpine house.

CULTIVATION. In compost B with plenty of lime-free water while in growth, water from a chalky source will quickly prove fatal, dry but not arid in winter, likes a sunny spot.

PROPAGATION. By cuttings taken in July and kept close in the propagating frame until rooted. Repot when necessary in early April. The typical plant is a semi-erect bushy shrublet with crowded, small, linear-oblong, obtuse, sessile leaves, margins ciliate. Flowers in largish racemes generally purplish pink, with just as brightly coloured calyx.

Varieties of Calluna vulgaris:

'Alba Pumila'. (E).

Forms a very dwarf and compact bushlet only 3 inches high. Flowers white. July.

'Coccinea'. (E).

Up to 9 inches high with grey leaves and deep red flowers. August.

'Foxii Nana'. (E).

This is a very dwarf compact miniature ling, globular, bun-shaped, deep green leaves. Sparsely produced flowers of purple. August.

'Hibernica'. (E).

A miniature only 6 inches high. Compact growth and bright pink flowers in October.

'Hirsuta Compacta'. (E).

This is one of the smallest forms of ling, making an extremely tight compact cushion, the foliage densely covered with silky hairs. Sessile pink flowers in August.

'Minima'. (E).
Only 2 inches high, it forms dense mats of mid-green leaves, flowers purple. August.

'Mrs Pat'. (E).
One of the finest lings in cultivation only 6 inches high, the new growth and foliage is bright pink. Bears pink flowers in August.

'Nana Compacta'. (E).
Another small plant rarely up to 3 inches high, close compact habit with purple flowers in August.

'Tom Thumb'. (E).
A dwarf fastigiate ling after the form of the upright juniper, but never above 6 inches high and quite compact. Flowers pink. August.

CALOCHORTUS (*Liliaceae*).

A genus of bulbous plants which provides a number of charming species suitable for the alpine house. They are natives of California and Mexico, related to both tulips and Fritillaria.

CULTIVATION. Like Fritillaria, these bulbs resent being out of the soil for any length of time and deteriorate rapidly; they must be obtained from a reliable source, where fresh stock is available. Compost B is suitable over good drainage; plenty of water is needed while in growth and it must not be stopped until all sign of foliage has died down in autumn. All prefer half shade. It is essential that they be replanted while still in growth in late summer, for the roots must take hold of the fresh soil before this stops.

PROPAGATION. By offsets which are readily formed and these should be potted up in autumn. Repot every year in late summer taking care not to disturb the roots too much.

C. albus. (B).
Forms a long single shining basal leaf and on a 9-inch slender stem, solitary, rarely two, pendant, rounded, globular, fringed, dazzling white flower with reddish-brown splash at base. California.

C. amabilis. (B). (Syn. *C. pulchellus* of gardens).
A native of California, with a similar basal leaf to that of *C. albus*, and branched stem up to 12 inches high. Flowers globular, pendant, yellow. May.

C. amoenus. (B).
Basal leaf lanceolate, shining green. Flowers solitary on 6-inch stems, less globular, deep rose-pink. June. California.

C. benthamii, see *C. monophyllus.*

C. caeruleus. (B). (Syn. *C. maweanus*).
A native of the Sierra Nevada, with linear basal leaf and on a 3-inch slender flexuous stem up to five erect bell-shaped flowers, lilac lined and dotted deep blue. June.

C. howellii. (B).

A native of Oregon with a long shining leaf. Flowers on 12-inch stems, erect open bell-shaped, creamy-white. June.

C. maweanus, see *C. caeruleus*.

C. monophyllus. (B). (Syn. *C. benthamii*).

Rarely above 6 inches high with long narrow leaf and on slender 6-inch stems, up to six erect bell-shaped yellow flowers with basal brown spot. July. A native of Sierra Nevada.

C. pulchellus, see *C. amabilis*.

C. uniflorus. (B).

A native of California, making up to four linear basal leaves. Flowers on 3-inch scape, up to six on long pedicels, erect bell-shape, pale lilac. June.

CAMPANULA *(Campanulaceae)*.

A mighty race of over 250 species, of which a good number are rock garden plants, coming as they do from the alpine meadows, with outlying members studding the topmost screes with their delightful blue stars or bells. They are confined to the northern hemisphere, widely dispersed in that area but their hub seems to be in the Mediterranean region, although there are representatives in North America, Canada, Japan, Persia and the Himalayas. Without doubt this genus has furnished the rock garden with many reliable and easy plants providing an outstanding floral display after the first rush of alpine colour is over. Many of the species are not really suitable for pan culture, for these have the habit of running about the soil, to appear in fresh places and seem to seek automatically the edge of the pans in which they are growing, thus needing frequent repotting, and the centre of the pan has a tendency to become bare. Like all other large genera they have their problem children and these are mostly the high alpine species which require skill to keep them in good health; but the cultivator is amply rewarded for all the care which is lavished on these wildlings when successful.

CULTIVATION. No hard and fast rules can be laid down for this genus, as with such a wide geographical distribution at different altitudes their cultural needs must vary. Unless otherwise stated all will do well in compost A over good drainage, as this suits the large majority of campanulas grown in pans; separate cultural notes will be given for the rarer and more difficult species. Plenty of water during the growing season, dry but not arid in winter. The herbaceous species require less water once the foliage has disappeared than the evergreens.

PROPAGATION. This, too, varies with the type of plant being grown. The monocarpic species are propagated by seed which is normally set freely, sowing this in compost 2 in February. The perennials can also be raised from seed if this is sown at the same time. Unlike the great majority of plants, when seed is sown, the pans must not be covered as campanulas will not germinate readily unless exposed to natural light. Another method of increase is by detaching runners with a small piece of root attached in July and inserting these in the propagating frame until they become re-established. If runners are not formed, green cuttings can be taken where possible; this is not always an easy thing, for many of the species are so floriferous that sometimes it is difficult to find unflowering material to use. These are best taken in late July. Division also is possible and April is the best month to carry out this operation.

Most species are best repotted every year, and this is certainly advised for those that are monocarpic, for the annual repotting will build up a fine healthy specimen by the time it flowers. Repotting is best carried out as soon as the new growth is discernible, generally in April, but repotting after flowering is not advised, for being late in the season the plants which are expending all their energy in making seed, will sometimes fail to push new roots into fresh compost before winter, with dire results.

C. abietina. (H).

A native of Greece, this forms a creeping rootstock with prostrate stems rarely above a few inches high. Leaves at apex of shoots, thin ovate, margins crenate and hairy, stem leaves oblong. Flowers open funnel-shaped, starry, blue. June.

C. allionii. (H). (Syn. *C. alpestris*).

A true alpine species which in nature runs about underground in the screes, throwing up at the end of the runners tufts of linear-lanceolate, entire leaves, with a slight covering of hairs, basal leaves in a rosette, obtuse. Flowers on 1- or 2-inch stems large, solitary, bell-shaped, light purple-blue. June. West European Alps. This plant and its varieties does well in compost D in a wide pan, so that it can spread around. Top-dress every spring with equal parts of leaf-mould and sand. Repot every second year.

C. allionii var. alba. (H).

This is an outstanding white form which has become very rare. June.

C. allionii var. grandiflora. (H).

Much larger than the type plant with wider bell-shaped flowers of good substance. June.

C. alpestris, see *C. allionii.*

C. alpina. (E).

Reputed to be perennial, it is rare in cultivation and often flowers itself to death. A native of Austria and Italy, it makes a tufted plant from a single crown. Leaves crowded at base, long, narrow lanceolate, margins crenate, glabrous, sometimes woolly. Flowers on erect 6-inch branched stems, solitary, pendant, large bearded, bell-shaped, pale to dark blue. June.

C. alpina var. alba. (E).

An even rarer dwarf white form needing care to cultivate it successfully. June.

C. andrewsii. (E).

A monocarpic species which forms a basal crown with radiating flowering stems both prostrate and ascending. Leaves oval to obovate, apex acute, soft grey-green, densely clothed with hairs, margins crenate. Flowers in short racemes, both from the leaf axils and terminal; upright, long tubular, lilac-blue. June. A native of Greece.

C. argyrotricha. (H).
This is a native of the N.W. Himalayas, making a central rootstock from which radiate prostrate curved stems, clothed with ovate, dentate, grey-green leaves, covered with fine silver hairs. Flowers solitary, semi-pendant, on long thin pedicels, tubular, blue. June. Should be a perennial but often fails to reappear after flowering.

C. arvatica. (E).
A native of Spain, with a creeping rootstock and semi-prostrate stems, only an inch or so high. Leaves rounded, cordate, dentate, apex pointed, bright green, basal leaves in rosette formation. Flowers both terminal and axillary on small slender stems, sparsely clothed with linear leaves, upright open violet stars. June.

C. arvatica var. alba. (E).
Just as desirable as the type with its large, white, star-like flowers. June. Both these plants need repotting every year in April.

C. atlantis. (E).
A native of the Atlas Mountains, this is often considered as only a geographical variety of *C. malacitana*, but whatever its standing it is a charming plant. It makes large basal rosettes of long, narrow, spatulate, grey-green hairy leaves, margins minutely dentate. Flowers terminal on 6-inch prostrate radiating stems, sparsely clothed with sessile, ovate, grey-green leaves, open campanulate violet-blue, with darker veinings, white on reverse. The colour is enhanced by the prominent trifid style. June–September.

C. aucheri. (E).
This is a tufted perennial plant from the Caucasus, with upright short stems. Leaves ovate-spatulate, margins crenate, slightly downy, bright green. Flowers solitary on 3-inch stems, often with an occasional linear leaf, erect, wide, violet-blue bell, shading to white at base, covered with a fine down on outside. June.

C. barbata. (H).
A native of most European Alps on the high pastures, it is a good perennial plant if satisfied in cultivation. I collected an outstanding white form of this in the Bernese Oberland, just above Sheidegg and it persisted with me over five years, which is a fairly satisfactory period for what is often only considered a biennial, more so as the plant collected was in flower, making it at least seven years old. It forms basal rosettes of almost entire but crinkled, crowded, lanceolate, pale green hairy leaves. Flowers in a one-sided raceme, on erect stout, hirsute 9-inch stems, large bell-shaped, pale blue, pendant, bearded on margins of the reflexed lobes. June.

C. barbata var. alba. (H).
This is the glistening white form and should show no trace of colour at the base of the corolla. June.

C. betulaefolia. (H).

A native of Armenia, making tufted, fragile, leafy growths, about 4 inches high. Leaves on long stalks, subcordate, pointed, wedge-shaped, glabrous, margins dentate. Flowers on ovate leafy stalks up to 6 inches high, open tubular, varying in colour from white to pink. June–July. This is a mono-carpic species.

C. caespitosa. (H).

This is a tufted rosette forming plant from a single crown, of spatulate smooth shining leaves with irregular dentate margins. Flower stems up to 9 inches high and branching with narrow lanceolate leaves, up to three, pendant long bell-shaped five-lobed, puckered at mouth, bright violet-blue. August. A native of the Dolomites.

C. calaminthifolia. (H).

This is a monocarpic species from Asia Minor, with a basal crown and radiating prostrate stems, rosette leaves, stalked, orbicular, sharply toothed and hairy, grey-green. Flowering stems procumbent, clothed with similar but sessile foliage, flowers from leaf axils and terminal, white or pale pink upturned cups. July.

C. cashmiriana. (H).

A native of the Himalayas, it makes a central crown from which are radiated the almost horizontal slender thin brown branching stems covered with a whitish down. Leaves alternate, light green, hairy, obovate to oblong, pointed at apex, margins dentate. Flowers solitary on slender stems, broad funnel-shape, bright blue, semi-pendant. July. It requires great care in watering, especially during mild damp winters, for the crown rots easily.

C. cenisia. (H).

This is one of the glorious high alpine campanulas, in nature it runs about the cracks and crevices and granite screes at high altitudes. It forms com-pletely sessile rosettes at the end of the runners of obovate, glabrous, bright green, entire leaves, margins ciliate. Flowers solitary on a short ovate-oblong leaved stem rising from centre of rosette; erect, large, open star-shaped, slate-blue. June. It tends to retain its foliage in the alpine house. This plant is best in a wide pan in compost D and wedging pieces of slate into the compost will help the plant to retain its natural characteristics. It requires care to cultivate it successfully.

C. cenisia var alba. (H).

This is the rare white form of the species and is an outstanding plant. June.

C. dasyantha, see *C. pilosa* var. *dasyantha*.

C. elatines. (E).

A native of Piedmont, Italy, it makes a prostrate plant of horizontal branches from a central rootstock. Leaves roundish, cordate to ovate, pointed, margins dentate, stalked; either grey-green covered with down, or sometimes glabrous bright-green. Flowers on trailing stems, in loose racemes, open starry deep violet. July.

C. excisa. (H).

A difficult species to please for any period of time, a native of the Eastern Alps in high screes and crevices, it is a rampant ranger for ever seeking pastures new; this is one of the reasons why it is rarely permanent in cultivation. It makes tufts of linear, slender-pointed, entire, green leaves at the end of 3-inch slender stems. Flowers pendant, solitary, funnel-shaped, pale blue with a hole perforated at the base of each lobe. July. Compost D in a shallow pan with plenty of water while in growth; should be repotted every year in fresh compost in April. Propagation is by division when repotting.

C. formanekiana. (E).

This is one of the outstanding monocarpic species of the genus from Macedonia. It makes basal rosettes which increase with age, until with careful repotting it has a large spread about 10 inches across. Leaves long, broad, ovate, sharply dentate, crinkled, downy, hoary grey. When mature, it produces a central stout flowering stem up to 18 inches high in well-grown specimens and symmetrical laterals spreading horizontally from the base, lightly clothed with sessile, oblanceolate, toothed, grey leaves. Flowers solitary in profusion on short stems, from the main stem and laterals, large white or pale blue, deep bell-shaped with recurving lobes. May. This species increases rapidly from seed which is set freely.

C. fragilis. (E).

From a tufted perennial rootstock are borne the crowded reniform or rounded cordate, deeply lobed, green leaves on short stalks. The leaves can be either glabrous or hairy. Flowers on slender stems, open star-shaped, deep blue. July. A native of S. Italy.

C. hercegovina var. nana. (E).

The type plant is a rather sprawling species with lax wiry stems but the dwarf form is a very desirable compact variety. It makes a tight prostrate mat of tufted habit, leaves oval, green, margins serrate. Flowers erect, open bell-shaped, deep lilac. July. A native of Yugoslavia.

C. lanata. (E).

A native of Bulgaria, this is another monocarpic species forming a hard rootstock with many inbranched stems. Leaves cordate-ovate, large, grey-green covered with down, toothed and with long hairy stalks. Flowers large, solitary from leaf axils almost sessile; on stout 18-inch upright stems and also procumbent laterals at the base of the plant; up-turned semi-globular bells, cream with a fragrance of honey. The whole forms a pyramid of bloom. July. This plant should be potted on until it reaches flowering size which in a good specimen will be a 10-inch pot.

C. lasiocarpa. (E).

A native of the Rocky Mountains, it is a fine alpine house plant making tufts of smooth, long stalked, pale green, wedge-shaped leaves, coarsely toothed. Flowers solitary on 2-inch leafy stems open bell-shaped, bluish, daintily ribbed. July. This species is intolerant of winter wet.

C. mirabilis. (E).
This species from the Caucasus is monocarpic, but easily raised from seed. It makes a long fleshy rootstock with a rosette of large, ovate to obovate, leathery, coarsely-dentate, dark glossy-green leaves, margins ciliate, stalk winged. Flowers axillary on short stalks and arching 12-inch stem, sparsely clad with similar but sessile foliage, up to four, bell-shaped, rounded blooms lilac-blue in colour. August.

C. mirabilis var. alba. (E).
This is the just as desirable white form. August.

C. morettiana. (E).
One of the rare high altitude alpine campanulas from the limestone cliffs of Southern Tyrol. It is a dwarf tufted perennial, only 2 inches high, the basal rosette leaves are roundish cordate with three teeth on either side, densely hairy, stem leaves ovate, acute, the whole a soft grey. Flowers solitary on short erect small scapes, large, open funnel-shaped, violet-blue. June. This plant will do well in compost D but like so many of the high alpine plants is not long lived when brought into cultivation; it resents winter wet.

C. morettiana var. alba. (E).
This is a more charming white form which with its large single flower is even better than the type. June.

C. nitida, see *C. planiflora*.

C. orphanidea. (E).
A native of Macedonia, this is a monocarpic species forming basal rosettes of oblong, obtuse, rounded at base, grey leaves on long petioles, only slightly dentate; covered with grey downy hairs. Flowers solitary on small branch stems from main stem at the axils of elliptic sessile stem leaves, on long stalks, erect, bell-shaped, deep violet with reflexed lobes. July.

C. petrophila. (H).
A high alpine from the northern Caucasus mountains, making basal rosettes at the end of prostrate slender creeping stems. Leaves pale green, obovate to roundish with apical teeth, petioles long, slightly hairy. Flowers on slender stems clothed with obovate, sessile stem leaves, solitary terminal, pale violet-blue bells with reflexed lobes, margins bearded. July. This is a plant which seems to do better in half shade in hot dry summers, requires care in watering especially during the winter.

C. pilosa. (H).
A variable species which has created a great deal of discussion over a good number of years and even today has not been finally placed. The plant generally accepted is a dwarf perennial, 3 inches high with a creeping rootstock bearing hairy stems. Leaves green in a rosette formation, basal lanceolate, tapering to petiole, deep crenate, quite glabrous. Flowers erect up to three on 3-inch stems sparsely clothed with similar almost sessile leaves, funnel-shaped, blue, hairy on mouth, corolla lobes tapering, ciliate. June. Japan, Siberia.

234 *Collectors' Alpines*

C. pilosa var. dasyantha. (H). (Syn. *C. dasyantha*).
This is the plant which has caused quite a furore and has only added coals
to the fire, but it is considered only a geographical variant of the species,
for it originated in Japan. It is a creeping perennial, throwing runners in all
directions and at the apex of these making rosettes of bright olive-green
leaves. These are narrow ovate to obovate, margins slightly crenate,
veining and midrib depressed and pronounced, petiole small. Flowers
erect single, rarely in pairs on 2-inch stems, rounded bell-shaped, blue,
corolla lobes ovate fringed with hairs, lined white inside.

Campanula pilosa was given an Award of Merit when shown in 1935.
The variety shown as *C. dasyantha* was given a Preliminary Commendation in May 1937. I showed a similar plant under *C. pilosa* var. *dasyantha*
in April 1950; this was recommended but never ratified owing to confusion of naming. This will give some idea that the nomenclature of this
species and its variants is far from settled.

C. piperi. (H).
A native of the Olympic Mt., U.S.A., this is a small creeping perennial, inhabiting cracks and crevices, making tufted rosettes of spatulate,
thick, dark glossy green leaves, toothed and pointed at apex. Flowers
on slender stems, rarely in pairs, erect, open bell-shaped bright blue.
July. This is a difficult species and is best in compost D in which a
few embedded pieces of sandstone will help. It seems to resent too much
sun and is best in half shade. Repot only when the plant reaches the side
of its pan.

C. planiflora. (E). (Syn. *C. nitida*).
A North American species making compact basal rosettes, leaves sessile,
thick, linear-oblong, smooth dark glossy green, margins deckled and
crenulate. Flowers in racemes on a stout 9-inch scape, lower half well-
furnished with the typical foliage, upper crowded with the deep saucer-
shaped blue flowers. June.

C. planiflora var. alba. (E).
Strange as it may seem the white form is more common in cultivation
than the type which is almost rare. Just as desirable with ample spires of
large white flowers. June.

C. raineri. (H).
A native of Italy with a limited distribution. This is a charming plant
which is not common in cultivation, so care is needed in buying this plant,
for small forms of *C. carpatica* often do duty for it. It is a tufted creeping
perennial running underground and bearing at the end of the runners,
tufts of ovate to obovate, almost sessile, small ash-grey leaves, margins
dentate and ciliate. Flowers terminal solitary on 3-inch stems erect china
blue, open bell-shaped. July.

C. raineri var. alba. (H).
This is the charming white form with large flowers similar to the type.
July. Both these plants need careful cultivation in compost A over good

drainage; care in watering, full sun and dry conditions in winter are necessary for success.

C. rupestris. (E).

A native of Greece, this is another monocarpic species. From a central rootstock appear rosettes of oblong-spatulate, crenate-dentate, crimped, ash-grey leaves. Flowers on semi-procumbent radiating laterals, much branched, erect, tubular waxy lavender-blue. July.

C. saxatilis. (E).

A perennial from the island of Crete, making a stout rootstock bearing tufts of grey-green, oblong-spatulate, slightly dentate leaves tapering to base. Flower stems 4 inches high, sparsely clad with small narrow oblong leaves, flowers in loose racemes, long tubular, erect pale blue. May. Care is needed when repotting this plant for any broken root is liable to set up rotting which quickly spreads to the rest of the plant.

C. saxicola, see *Wahlenbergia saxicola*.

C. saxifraga. (H).

Forms basal rosettes almost like a large leaved mossy saxifrage of linear-lanceolate narrowing to base leaves, entire or slightly crenulate on top third, grey-green in colour. Flowers in profusion on 3-inch stems, large, semi-erect, open campanulate, violet-blue. June. Caucasus. This plant resents overhead watering which will quickly rot off the rosettes, keep dry in winter.

C. tridentata. (E).

A small tufted species from Armenia forming basal tufts. Leaves in rosette formation linear-spatulate, apex obtuse, crenate, margins ciliate. Flowers solitary on slender 4-inch stems, blue obconic bell-shaped with five spreading violet lobes. May.

C. zoysii. (E).

The last of this great genus but far from the least and unfortunately it must be accounted a difficult species to keep in good health for it tends to flower itself to death. The plant devotes its energy to making flowers and seed, but often fails to produce the new growth needed for longevity. It is a small tufted perennial with crowded basal tufts of roundish, shiny, entire green leaves, margins hairy. On 2-inch stems sparsely clad with glossy linear, entire leaves are borne up to five quaint, pendant, long tubular flowers of a pale blue constricted at throat. June. A native of Austria and Northern Italian Alps. This plant is best in compost D but in place of three parts of Cornish sand, this should be two parts sand and one part limestone chippings, although with very few exceptions I find that no pan plant demands lime, this is one of the few that need it. A long pot is better than a pan and care is needed in watering at all times.

CARMICHAELIA (*Leguminosae*).

A small genus of shrubs which are with one exception endemic to New

Zealand. There is only one small enough for our purpose, the rest ranging from 3 to 8 feet high.

CULTIVATION. It does well in compost A over good drainage and requires normal amounts of water during the growing season; dryish but not arid in winter.

PROPAGATION. This is by seed sown in February, compost 2 or cuttings with a heel in July. Repot only when necessary in early April.

C. enysii. (E).

It is a small shrub, rarely above 6 inches high with congested erect flat, light green branches. Leaves non-existent. Flowers are the usual leguminose shape, deep violet, fragrant, borne either singly or up to four in short clustered racemes. June. A native of New Zealand and quite hardy in this country.

C. enysii var. nana. (E).

This is a dwarf form of the species only an inch or so high with similar fragrant clusters of pea-shaped flowers. June.

CASSIOPE (*Ericaceae*).

This is a race of dwarf, often prostrate, acid-loving shrubs, characterised with two exceptions by the appressed foliage, giving the branches the appearance of whipcord. As a genus they are not easy to please especially in the hot dry atmosphere of the south, but many of them do well in the cooler conditions and greater atmospheric moisture in the north of England and Scotland where they will tolerate more sun than in the south. They have an alpine-arctic distribution in the northern hemisphere, climbing high in the Himalayas and down to the sea shore in Alaska.

CULTIVATION. This is best in compost C with plenty of lime-free water at all times. Top-dress in early March with equal parts of sand and flaked leaf-mould. They should only be kept in the alpine house during the flowering period; afterwards plunge in a north facing frame and spray in the evenings during hot periods. Protect from parching winds.

PROPAGATION. This is by green cuttings taken in August and rooted in a propagating frame. Seed is also a means of increase, this should be sown in February, compost 3. Repot only when necessary after flowering.

C. 'Edinburgh'. (*C. fastigiata* × *C. tetragona*). (E).

This is a fine hybrid which appeared in the Royal Botanic Gardens at Edinburgh and is certainly an improvement on its parents. It makes a close upright bushlet less than 12 inches high, only slightly branched, densely clad with bright green, closely imbricated lanceolate leaves, margined with white bristles. Flowers in terminal racemes, more at the axils of the branches, crowded, pendant, campanulate, slightly puckered at mouth, lobes recurved, white, borne on light green thin hairy stems. Calyces greenish-brown with red margins. April.

C. fastigiata. (E).

A native of the Himalayas, less than 12 inches high of four-sided branches completely clothed with the overlapping, appressed dark green, lanceolate, sessile leaves margined with white silky hairs. The pendant bell-shaped, white flowers with recurved lobes are borne from the leaf axils on slender downy stems. April.

C. hypnoides. (E). (Syn. *Harrimanella hypnoides*).
A native of the Arctic and sub-Arctic regions, this is a plant which will test the skill of the most experienced cultivator, for it is extremely difficult to grow especially in the southern counties and it has only been included here in the hope that someone will try it and succeed in growing it successfully. It is a prostrate spreading lax shrublet only a few inches high. The leaves are green, linear in shape and unlike most other species, not appressed to the stems. Flowers solitary from the leaf axils at the apex of the branches, pendant on red thread stems, bell-shaped, white with deep pink calyx. May.

C. lycopodioides. (E).
One of the easiest and in a good flowering form the best for pan culture. It makes a completely prostrate shrublet only an inch or so high of smooth branches. Leaves ovate, entire, keeled, dark glossy green, margined with a white membrane and closely appressed to the stem in four rows. Flowers solitary on smooth red thread stems from the leaf axils; white, pendant, rounded bell-shape, lobes reflexed, calyx pinkish-green. April. A native of Japan.

C. lycopodioides 'Major'. (E). (Syn. *C. rigida*).
A more robust and stouter variety of the species but I have not found this form to be as floriferous. It is a desirable plant easy to grow with bigger but less rounded pendant white bells on thread stems. April–May.

C. mertensiana. (E).
An erect species, making a slender bushlet up to 9 inches high. Leaves smooth, dark green, entire, oblong, convex, less appressed than in *C. fastigiata*. Flowers solitary, pendant, rounded bell-shaped, white, from the leaf axils on green thread stems, recurved lobes, calyx reddish. A native of N. America. April.

C. 'Muirhead'. (*C. wardii* × *C. lycopodioides*). (E).
A charming hybrid raised by Mr R. B. Cooke, Northumberland, an outstanding grower of dwarf *Ericaceae*. It is intermediate between the two parents forming a semi-erect, much branched bushlet about 6 inches high of thin wiry stems. Leaves ovate to ovate-lanceolate, appressed to the stems in rows of four, margins ciliate, partly grooved on reverse, light green. Flowers solitary on pinkish thread stems, quite hairy, white, roundish campanulate, lobes reflexed, calyx coral. April.

C. rigida, see *C. lycopodioides* 'Major'.

C. selaginoides. (E).
A dwarf compact shrublet not more than 9 inches high of tufted thickish branches. Leaves dark green, lanceolate, apex bristly, margins edged with

white membrane, closely appressed to stems in rows of four. Flowers solitary, large, on thickish downy stems, pendant open bell-shaped, white, lobes recurved, calyx green. April. A native of the Himalayas.

C. stelleriana. (E). (Syn. *Harrimanella stelleriana*).
This is a native of N.W. America, making a prostrate cushion of congested branches only a few inches high. Leaves small, mid-green, oblong-linear, obtuse at apex in rows of four at right angles to the stem, not appressed. Flowers white, pendant, deeply cut, roundish, bells on slender downy stems, calyx reddish. May. Requires more sun than the other species but must be shaded during the middle of the day.

C. tetragona. (E).
An erect or semi-erect dwarf shrublet up to 9 inches high. Leaves deep green, ovate-lanceolate, sunken midrib, closely imbricated in four rows on the branches, margins slightly ciliate. Flowers white or tinged pink on slender downy stems from the leaf axils, rounded campanulate with spreading lobes, calyx lobes pale green, tinged with carmine. This plant has a tendency to go brown at the base of the stems with age. Arctic regions. May.

C. wardii. (E).
A native of the Himalayas, it is the largest of all the cassiopes with its thick much-branching erect stems from almost prostrate branches, up to 8 inches high. Leaves dark green, lanceolate, centre grooved, margins covered with long bristly white hairs, appressed to the stems in four rows. Flowers large pendant, white flushed red inside at base, rounded bell-shaped, lobes recurved, calyx green, tipped red. Unlike other members of the genus this species often bears its flowers in small clusters from the leaf axils. April. The plant has one distinct drawback, it has a most unpleasant smell; definitely not a plant for the drawing room.

CEANOTHUS (*Rhamnaceae*).

A genus which is much favoured for its large shrubs and wall plants with blue flowers, an uncommon colour in shrubs. There is one species suitable for pan culture and as it is very slow growing will do well in a pan for a number of years.
CULTIVATION. Compost B with good drainage. It requires plenty of water and sunshine while growing; dry but not arid in winter.
PROPAGATION. By green cuttings taken with a heel and rooted in the propagating frame in August. Repot when necessary in early April.

C. prostratus. (E).
Only a few inches high but with a wide spread after many years, it makes a tangled mat of downy branches, densely clothed with the small opposite, thick, oval, large toothed, deep green leaves. Flowers bright blue, borne in terminal clusters up to twenty on the end of short leafy twigs. June. A native of California but quite hardy in the alpine house.

CELMISIA (*Compositae*).

A genus of plants confined mainly to New Zealand with one in Australia and Tasmania, containing a few which are suitable for the alpine house, where they are exceedingly decorative with their outstanding foliage covered with a white tomentum.

CULTIVATION. Compost A over good drainage will suit these species but they all have one thing in common, a dislike of too much water in winter, whereas provided the drainage is good they certainly thrive on plenty of water while in active growth.

PROPAGATION. By seeds sown in February if available, compost 2, or cuttings rooted in the closed frame in July. Repot every year after flowering.

C. argentea. (E).

A small tufted plant only a few inches high with congested, linear, silver-grey leaves, tapering to a point, white silky hairs on reverse. Flowers sessile daisy-like in small heads, white. May. A native of New Zealand.

C. coriacea. (E).

A small plant up to 9 inches high, leaves in rosettes lanceolate to ovate oblong, upper surface covered with glistening hairs, below appressed white tomentum. Flowers on woolly stems, white daisies with yellow disk. June. New Zealand.

C. hieracifolia. (E).

From a woody base this dwarf plant sends up short stems clothed with obovate to linear-oblong, thick, leaves almost glabrous above, densely covered with buff wool on underside. Flowers on 8-inch scapes large rounded, thin-rayed daisies, white with yellow centre. June. A native of New Zealand.

C. major. (E).

A small densely tufted plant only a few inches high. Leaves linear, thick, tapering gradually to a point, densely covered with white tomentum. Flowers on 8-inch stems, the usual white daisies with a yellow disk. New Zealand. June.

C. sessiliflora. (E).

A rare native of New Zealand, it forms a tight cushion of linear, tapering to a point, silver-grey leaves, covered with a fine silky down. Flowers large completely sessile white daisies with yellow disk. June. A difficult species requiring care in cultivation, no overhead watering, and beware of winter wet.

CELSIA (*Scrophulariaceae*).

A small genus of sub-shrubs and herbs closely related to Verbascum, having only one species suitable for pan culture.

CULTIVATION. Compost A in a sunny position with normal watering during the spring and summer, rather dry in winter.

PROPAGATION. By seed sown in February, compost 2. Repot every year in June.

C. acaulis. (E).

A native of Greece, it makes congested rosettes of radical, oblong, mid-green leaves, margins crenate and crinkled. Flowers on short stems, bright yellow with orange stamens, over a long period. May–August.

CENTAURIUM (*Gentianaceae*).

There is only one member of this genus which can be used for pan culture and is representative of the race which contains a good number of annual, biennial as well as perennial plants.

CULTIVATION. It is quite easy in compost A with normal watering during the growing season, dry but not arid in winter.

PROPAGATION. By seed sown as soon as ripe. Compost 2. Repot only when necessary in early April.

C. scilloides. (E). (Syn. *Erythraea diffusa*).

This is a dwarf tufted plant of semi-procumbent branches. Leaves dark green, entire, thick, concave, glabrous. Flowers on short stems, similar to *Gentiana verna*, deep pink. June. A native of Southern Europe.

Cerasus prostrata, see *Prunus prostrata*.

Chaenorrhinum origanifolium, see *Linaria origanifolia*.

CHIMAPHILA (*Pyrolaceae*).

A small genus of ever-green sub-shrubs, unfortunately at present there is only one in cultivation and this too is rare.

CULTIVATION. Compost C is needed over good drainage and a liberal amount of water should be given during the growing and flowering season, moist at other times. Top-dress in early spring with similar compost.

PROPAGATION. Take green cuttings in June and put in a closed propagating frame. Repot every other year after flowering.

C. umbellata. (E).

This is a dwarf prostrate shrublet only a few inches high. Leaves alternate, crowded, generally in whorls of up to six obovate, blunt, irregularly toothed, deep shiny green with a cream slightly raised midrib. Flowers in terminal umbels up to six open, five-lobed saucer-shaped, white flushed pink. July. A native of Japan.

CHIONODOXA (*Liliaceae*).

A small genus of bulbous plants from the Mediterranean area and Asia Minor, which provides a few early flowering species for the alpine house or frame.

CULTIVATION. They should be potted up in compost A in September. About 12 to a 6-inch pan and planted 1 inch deep. Cover with peat in

Above: *Gentiana ornata* (see page 301)

Below: *Geum reptans* (see page 304)

Above: *Haberlea rhodopensis* (see page 308)

Below: *Iris winogradowii* (see page 326)

outdoor frame until January then bring into the house. Fair amount of water January to April, normal supply April to June, then withheld.
PROPAGATION. By seed in August, compost 2, or offsets in September. Repot every year, September.
C. cretica. (B).
A native of Crete, with narrow green linear leaves and on 9-inch slender stems pale blue open star-shaped flowers. March.
C. luciliae. (B).
A small plant rarely above 4 inches high with erect, linear leaves. Flowers in loose sprays up to nine bright blue, white central zone, star-shaped. March. A native of Asia Minor.
C. luciliae 'Alba'. (B).
A form which loses nothing by being white. March.
C. luciliae 'Rosea'. (E).
A pink form, flowers not so substantial as the type. March.
C. nana. (B).
A smaller edition of *C. cretica* only a few inches high with pale lilac flowers in a loose spray, sometimes white. March. A native of Crete.
C. sardensis. (B).
A native of Asia Minor, this is only 4 inches high of linear, channelled leaves. Flowers in loose umbels, prussian-blue in colour, slightly pendant. March.
C. tmoli. (B).
From Mt. Tmolus, a later flowering species about 6 inches high with light blue ample sprays of starry flowers, shading to a white central eye. April.

CHIONOPHILA (*Scrophulariaceae*).

A monotypic genus, closely related to Penstemon from high altitudes in the Rocky mountains.
CULTIVATION. Is best in compost A with good drainage. Plenty of water during the growing season, dry but not arid in winter.
PROPAGATION. By seed in February, compost 2.
C. jamesii. (E).
A prostrate plant less than 3 inches high. Leaves entire in rosettes, leathery, spatulate, tapering to base. Flowers on short stems in dense spike, pale cream, like a dwarf Penstemon. June.

CHRYSANTHEMUM (*Compositae*).

A race of plants much beloved by the florists and cultivators of the Japanese and other exhibition varieties. It seems strange to these gardeners that there are dwarf species which can be more difficult to grow in this country than these giant varieties.
CULTIVATION. All need a well drained compost, A is suitable but the drainage must be perfect otherwise these plants will quickly rot away.

Water should be kept away from the foliage which quickly marks, otherwise normal amounts of water whilst in growth, drier conditions in winter.

PROPAGATION. By seed in March, compost 2, or division in July. Repot when necessary after flowering.

C. alpinum. (E).

A small tufted evergreen perennial only a few inches high. Leaves green, much parted, pinnate with lanceolate lobes. Flowers on 2-inch stems, white shading to yellow at centre with yellow disk. May. Not an easy plant to keep in good health. A native of the Pyrenees.

C. catananche. (E).

A native of Morocco making a small much-branched prostrate rootstock. Leaves grey, in tufts, linear with acute irregular lobes at apex. Flowers solitary on 4-inch scapes, large up to 2 inches across; buds silky, opening to show the crimson backed white daises with yellow disk, surrounded with a yellow zone. May.

C. hispanicum. (E).

A small spreading perennial up to 6 inches high. Leaves much cut, almost to base, silver-grey covered with silky hairs. Flowers large solitary white with yellow disk. May. A native of Spain.

C. hispanicum var. radicans, see *C. radicans.*

C. hispanicum var. sulphureum. (E).

This is the fine yellow flowering form with golden central disk, otherwise similar to the type.

C. hosmariense. (E). (Syn. *Leucanthemum hosmariense*).

A small woody stemmed, much-branched plant about 6 inches high with silver-grey leaves; leaflets trifid. Flowers solitary, terminal on a silver stem, large pure white daisy shape, disk golden-yellow shading to green in centre; involucre, silvery bracts, margined black. April. A native of Algeria.

C. radicans. (E). (Syn. *C. hispanicum var. radicans*).

This is a native of Spain, seems closely related to *C. hispanicum* but much smaller in all its parts, similar grey leaves and on 2-inch stems, large golden-yellow flowers tinted purple at base with golden disk. May.

CODONOPSIS (*Campanulaceae*).

A small genus of perennial herbs with charming bell flowers, the interior of the pendant flowers being exceptionally beautiful but unfortunately a number have an unpleasant odour.

CULTIVATION. Compost A is suitable with good drainage and the plants need plenty of water once they appear in spring; after growth dies down it should be withheld although the pans should not be allowed to dry out completely.

PROPAGATION. By seed sown in March, compost 2. Repot when necessary, when growth commences.

C. meleagris. (H).
A native of the Himalayas, making semi-erect stems, slender towards the top, up to 10 inches high. Leaves sessile in rosettes, at base elliptic-oblong, green margins crinkled, glaucous below, with a few soft hairs. Flowers pendant bell-shaped, greenish-blue, chequered chocolate-brown without, purple-violet inside, base green, spotted yellow. June.
C. mollis. (H).
A small tufted plant of erect stems, about 6 inches high, leaves small, ovate, grey-green due to covering of fine hairs. Flowers on slender stems pendant, tubular, wider from middle to mouth of corolla, pale blue. July. This plant is a native of Tibet and needs care in cultivation, resents overwatering and the base of the plant needs shade.
C. ovata. (H).
Possibly the best of the species, rarely above 6 inches high of branching semi-erect bluish-green stems. Leaves ovate on small stalks, light green, pointed to apex, slightly hairy on both sides, margins ciliate. Flowers solitary on slender hairy pedicels, pendant open tubular, pale blue-green, tufted, interior of flowers, black at base with pale green zone, lobes veined, red-purple. June. A native of the Himalayas.

COLCHICUM (*Liliaceae*).

A genus of bulbous plants, strictly corms, closely related to Bulbocodium and having a number of autumn flowering species. They have one drawback being large leafed, but the flowers are normally produced before the leaves appear. This is not so important when cultivated in pans for they can be placed outside after flowering so that the leaves can form and are allowed to grow naturally.
CULTIVATION. From three to six corms planted 1 inch deep in a moist but not wet compost A in July. Water is needed from the time the flower buds appear until the foliage dies down when it should be withheld and the pots given a good baking in the sun.
PROPAGATION. By seed in August, compost 2, or offsets in July. Repot every year in July.
C. agrippinum. (B).
The flowers appear in September, generally two to a spathe, tube long, white, segments mauve-white, yellow anthers, netted. Leaves in spring, long up to four semi-erect, linear-lanceolate, green, margins undulate. S. Europe.
C. autumnale var. minor. (B).
The small form produces its flowers in September, up to six to a spathe, rosy mauve, tubular, anthers yellow. Leaves in spring, coarse, up to six lanceolate, deep green. Europe including Britain.
C. autumnale var. album. (B).
Similar to the type but with white flowers and yellow anthers in September.

C. cilicicum. (B).
A native of the Taurus mountains it is a much-flowered species of white tubular, with soft pink segments, anthers golden-yellow. September. Leaves in spring, dark green, folded, broad-elliptic, long.

C. corsicum. (B).
A native of Corsica, producing in September, one flower to a sheath, lilac-rose in colour with yellow anthers. Leaves in spring, green, up to four semi-erect, linear-lanceolate.

C. fasciculare var. brachyphyllum. (B).
An autumn flowering species from the Lebanon which produces its linear-lanceolate green leaves, up to eight in number, at the same time as the flowers. Flowers three to six open tubular, pure white with pronounced blackish-brown anthers. November-December.

C. hungaricum. (B).
Normally a single flower from the sheath but sometimes more, tubular, long, pale rose or white with brownish anthers. February. Leaves, same time as the flowers, green, linear, acute. A native of Hungary.

C. libanoticum. (B).
Up to ten flowers from the sheath, with long narrow tube, open starry segments, lilac, anthers brown. Leaves up to five broad lanceolate, acute tip. March. Lebanon.

C. luteum. (B).
This species is from Nepal, bearing up to four flowers from the sheath, long, tubular, yellow tinged lilac with yellow anthers. March. Leaves at same time eventually very long linear, lanceloate, green.

C. montanum, see *Merendera montana.*

C. ritchii. (B).
A native of Palestine, with up to seven flowers from the sheath, long, tubular, segments starry, fringed at base, pale rose with brown anthers. January. Leaves up to four just after flowers, linear with undulating margins.

C. speciosum. (B).
About four flowers to a sheath, long, tubular, starry pale rose with yellow anthers. August. A native of Persia, Asia Minor.

C. speciosum var. album. (B).
A fine form much better than the type, with white flowers. September.

C. triphyllum. (B).
A native of the Atlas Mountains, with up to eight from the sheath, globular, small, tubular flowers of rose-mauve, deep orange anthers, tube white. February. Leaves, same time as the flowers, are three, plicate, deep green, linear-lanceolate.

C. variegatum. (B).
Up to three flowers from the sheath with white tube, segments deep pink, chequered, anthers brown. September. Leaves in spring, lanceolate, deep green, margins undulate. A native of Greece.

C. vernum, see *Bulbocodium vernum.*

CONANDRON (*Gesneriaceae*).

A monotypic genus from Japan, near to Streptocarpus, it is a good herbaceous perennial for alpine house culture.

CULTIVATION. It does well in compost B with good drainage in shade away from parching winds which quickly spoil the foliage. Should be brought into the house for flowering, then plunged in a shaded sheltered frame during hot months and placed under the staging in the alpine house during winter. Requires plenty of water whilst in growth, just moist at other periods.

PROPAGATION. By seed sown in February, compost 3, same treatment as for rhododendron, or by division of the tuber in early April. Repot when necessary in early April.

C. ramondioides. (H).
This is a tuberous-rooted perennial, resting over winter as a stolon, covered with an intense orange brown tomentum. Leaves basal in rosette formation, ovate-oblong, roughly dentate, crinkled, pale yellow-green. Flowers in small pendant cymes up to twelve on 4-inch pale green fleshy scapes, lilac-purple with orange centre, similar in shape to a tomato flower. June.

C. ramondioides var. leucanthemum. (H).
This is the white form of the species and is just as desirable. June.

CONVOLVULUS (*Convolvulaceae*).

A genus of plants which contains amongst its large number of species, two of the most persistent weeds that the gardener has to contend with in this country, especially on light sandy soils, namely the Greater and Lesser Bindweed. How different are the species described here, for it is an achievement to grow at least two of them and it is almost impossible to increase *C. holosericeus*. The finest specimen I know is in the collection of alpines grown by the late Mr W. T. Ingwersen. He told me that he had only managed to propagate two plants of this species by layering over a period of years, as all other means of increasing the stock had failed.

CULTIVATION. Compost A over good drainage and the plants like all available sunshine; normal water in spring and early summer, dry but not arid at other times.

PROPAGATION. By seed in March if available, compost 2, green cuttings in July, rooting them with bottom heat or layering non-flowering shoots in early June. Repot every other year in April.

C. cantabricus. (D).
A native of Spain, up to 6 inches high covered with grey hair. Leaves oblong-lanceolate to an acute point, grey with a silky down. Flowers up to three from the leaf axils, open rounded, crinkled saucers, pale pink on 6-inch stems. July.

C. cochlearis, see *C. holosericeus*.

C. cneorum. (E).

A charming dwarf shrub rarely attaining 2 feet in cultivation but can be kept dwarf by pruning. Branches slender semi-prostrate, branching, greyish green. Leaves large, congested, almost in whorls, lanceolate, tapering to base, pale grey-green, silvered with a dense covering of flat silky hairs. Flowers in terminal umbels, individually fleeting, but produced in quantity over a period; open funnel-shaped, hairy without, white striped pink on the reverse of the petals. June–July. Spain.

C. holosericeus. (E). (Sÿn. *C. cochlearis*).

This is a native of Albania, where it inhabits rocky ledges in full sunshine at high altitudes. It forms congested mats of radiating branches from a central rootstock, densely covered with linear-lanceolate, heavily veined silver leaves, with an intense covering of silky hairs. Flowers almost sessile, wide open funnel-shape, white with a glistening satiny texture. July.

C. lineatus. (D).

A native of S. Europe, this is a charming dwarf perennial of mat forming habit. Leaves on short stalks crowded, almost in whorls, apex acute, silver-grey heavily linear and covered with appressed fine silky hairs. Flowers solitary, rarely in pairs on short hairy stems, large open funnel-shaped, pale purple red. June.

C. nitidus. (D).

A native of the Spanish Sierra Nevada, it makes a cushion of prostrate radiating branches, never above 2 inches high. Leaves crowded, ovate, silver-grey, heavily veined, with a dense covering of appressed silky white hairs. Flowers almost sessile, one, sometimes two, large, open funnel-shape, glistening pink. July.

COPROSMA (*Rubiaceae*).

A genus of plants noted for their decorative fruits, not reliably hardy except in a sheltered spot outdoors; they make good specimens in pans for alpine house culture.

CULTIVATION. Compost B is suitable and the plants need plenty of water during the growing season, just moist in winter. They should be top-dressed every spring with a similar compost.

PROPAGATION. Detaching cuttings of the current year's growth with a heel of last year's wood and root in the propagating frame. June. Repot only when necessary in early April.

C. acerosa. (E).

A native of New Zealand, making a dwarf compact shrublet rarely above 9 inches in cultivation, with a mass of congested, wiry branches, densely clothed with opposite clusters of dark green linear leaves. Flowers unisexual, inconspicuous, males in small clusters, female solitary, with very attractive rounded fruits of light translucent blue. July.

C. petriei. (E).

Another New Zealand plant, quite prostrate, forming a creeping mat of intertwining twigs densely clothed with the oblong, deep green, hairy leaves. Flowers unisexual, inconspicuous solitary, followed by rich purple fruits. July.

CORALLODISCUS (*Gesneriaceae*).

A small genus of alpine house plants closely related to Didissandra and until recently included in that genus. There are two species in cultivation, but both of these are rare and require careful cultivation to give of their best.
CULTIVATION. Compost B is suitable, well drained but requiring plenty of water while growing and flowering, moist at other periods. After flowering they should be plunged in a cool shady spot for the summer, but returned to the house before frosts occur. Protection is needed against cold winds at all times.
PROPAGATION. By careful division of the plants in April or leaf cuttings in May. Repot when necessary after flowering.
C. kingianus. (E). (Syn. *Didissandra grandis*).
This species forms a dense basal rosette of large ovate lanceolate acute, thickish pronounced veined, deep green leaves, margins ciliate, light reddish brown below due to thick covering of hairs. Flowers on 6-inch light reddish brown hairy scapes, up to twelve in clustered cymes, long tubular, five unequal lobes, pale blue with deeper stripes. May. A native of China.
C. lanuginosus. (E). (Syn. *Didissandra lanuginosa*).
This is also a native of China, with rosettes of entire ovate-oblong leaves deep green, covered with reddish brown hairs, brownish below due to intense covering of hairs. Flowers on 3-inch woolly scapes in branching cymes up to twelve, semi-pendant five-lobed, tubular, deepish purple-blue. May.

CORETHROGYNE (*Compositae*).

This genus contains one species which is an outstanding dwarf shrublet for the alpine house.
CULTIVATION. Compost B with good drainage, plenty of water during the growing season, dry but not arid in winter.
PROPAGATION. By green cuttings taken in July. Repot every year in April.
C. californica. (E).
It forms a prostrate mass of semi woody branches radiating from a central rootstock. Stems slender grey-green, due to the intense covering of long woolly hairs. Leaves dentate, oval, tapered at base with obtuse apex, grey-green in colour, well clothed with fine woolly hairs, similar underneath with pronounced midrib, veining reticulate. Laterals clothed with rosettes of smaller foliage and terminal flowering stems 1 inch long with daisy-shaped, many-rayed, flesh-pink flowers, central disk, yellow. July-August. A native of California.

CORYDALIS (*Papaveraceae*).

This is a large genus of tuberous rooted plants which contains a number of charming species well suited for alpine house or frame culture.

CULTIVATION. All the species will do well in compost B and require plenty of water while in growth reducing it to just moist conditions in winter. They are better in half-shade and this should be provided during hot dry months.

PROPAGATION. Is by careful division of the plants in April, or if seed is available it is best sown as soon as ripe, compost 2. These plants resent root disturbance and should be handled carefully when repotting in April.

C. cashmeriana. (H).

This is possibly the gem of the race which is still rare in gardens and there is no doubt that it thrives much better in the cooler atmosphere of the northern counties. It makes a plant about 6 inches high of divided ternate rich green compound leaves, segments narrow oblong. The flowers in clusters up to six long narrow tubular, spurred, dazzling bright blue, lip darker. May. A native of Kashmir to Sikkim.

C. crassifolia. (H).

A native of the Himalayas, this is a rare and difficult species up to 6 inches high. Leaves reniform, thick, divided into three ovate sections, each irregularly notched, glaucous bluish-grey on small red stalks. Flowers on 6-inch stems in small clusters, pendant, tubular, spurred, purple and white. May.

C. pumila. (H).

A small tuberous perennial only a few inches high with grey-green leaves divided into three segments. Flowers on crowded 4-inch scapes, up to six long narrow, tubular, purple-red with long spur. May. Europe.

C. solida var. transylvanica. (H).

The type plant is a small tuberous root with large purple flowers, a native of Europe including Britain. The form from eastern Europe is about 4 inches high with thickish red spotted stems. Leaves ternately divided, segments ovate, sessile, bright green. Flowers on 4-inch stoutish scapes bearing a raceme of up to ten long tubular, rose-pink, flushed lavender-blue and with a long spur recurved at tip. April.

Cossonia africana, see *Raffenaldia primuloides.*

Cotyledon chrysantha, see *Rosularia pallida.*

C. pestalozzae, see *Rosularia sempervivum.*

C. sempervivum, see *Rosularia sempervivum.*

C. spinosa, see *Orostachys spinosus.*

CRASSULA (*Crassulaceae*).

This genus contains a large number of species which unfortunately are not hardy here. There are only two which can be utilised as pan plants and both these are capable of providing a first-class floral display.

Above: *Edraianthus pumilio* (see page 277)

Below: *Erigeron leiomerus* (see page 278)

Above: *Fritillaria pyrenaica* (see page 289)
Below: *Gentiana verna* (see page 302)

Above: *Geranium dalmaticum* (see page 304)

Below: *Globularia stygia* (see page 306)

Above: *Gypsophila aretioides* (see page 307)
Below: *Hebe macrantha* (see page 311)

CULTIVATION. Is easy in compost A over good drainage with a normal supply of water during the growing season, rather dry in winter.

PROPAGATION. By green cuttings taken in June. Repot every year in April.

C. sarcocaulis. (D).

A fine plant, native of S. Africa, not too hardy but will winter well in the alpine house. It makes a dwarf stunted tree-like plant with thick brown trunks, gnarled as if age old with many-branched twigs, leaves densely crowded, fleshy, linear, dull green. Flowers honey scented, in congested clusters, tubular, star-shaped, red in bud, opening to show their white interiors. August.

C. sediformis. (E).

This is a new species from S. Africa which is quite hardy here, even out of doors. It makes close compact cushions only an inch high of tight rosettes. Leaves simple, succulent, bright green, smooth, margined with a few thick glandular hairs. Flowers in profusion, almost sessile, small star-shaped, white, rose-pink on reverse. July.

CROCUS (*Iridaceae*).

This genus provides the alpine house with colour during the early months of the year and there is no doubt that they are the true harbingers of spring and the sight of a few pans of these in flower during late January seems to dispel the gloom and darkness which abounds outside in the open garden.

CULTIVATION. All are easy in a sunny position, requiring only a minimum of attention. They are best potted up in compost B, twelve to a 5-inch pan, planted about 1 inch deep. The autumn flowering species should be potted up not later than the beginning of August and the winter and spring flowering plants in September. They are best plunged into a frame and then brought into the alpine house when the buds are formed, to flower there, afterwards returning them to the frame. See that they are kept moist while the foliage is growing, reducing the water as the foliage dies away, then allow them to dry off in the pans, giving them a good baking in the sun to ripen the corms. All should be repotted each year in fresh compost. They should not be grown for more than two years in a pan. Plant the old corms in a spare bed outside for a year, then the mature corms can be lifted and repotted.

PROPAGATION. This is by offsets taken when repotting or by seed sown in February compost 2. Thin sowing is advisable, for the seedlings should not be disturbed for two seasons but allowed to grow on. When the foliage dies down after the second year, the corms can be potted up in fresh compost, where they should flower in the third season.

C. asturicus. (B).

A Spanish species about 4 inches high with violet bearded throat, segments purple with deep basal lines, leaves appear with flowers. September.

C. balansae. (B).
From Asia Minor, only 2 inches high with orange segments flushed deep brown. March.

C. biflorus. (B).
A native of S.W. Europe, 3 inches high with yellow bearded throat, segments white, outer buff with purple feathering, stigmas scarlet. February. There are many forms of this species, some of which have been named and all are worth growing.

C. boryi. (B).
From the Greek Islands, about 2 inches high with bearded orange throat, segments cream, flushed yellow at base, feathered purple. November.

C. byzantinus. (B).
A Carpathian species, only a few inches high with glabrous throat, outer segments bright purple, inner pale lilac, stigmas purple, anthers orange. October.

C. candidus. (B).
A native of Asia Minor, up to 3 inches high with smooth orange throat, segments white, outer tinged purple, stigmas orange. March.

C. candidus 'Subflavus'. (B).
Similar to the type but with yellow base colour. March.

C. carpetanus. (B).
A Spanish species, about 3 inches high with white smooth throat, segments reddish lilac with dark margins, striped blue at base outside, stigmas lilac. February.

C. chrysanthus. (B).
A native of Greece and Asia Minor, this has given rise to a number of fine seedlings which have been named. It is about 3 inches high with smooth orange-yellow throat, segments bright orange, outer feathered bronze; anthers orange, black at base. February.

C. chrysanthus 'E. A. Bowles'. (B).
A form 4 inches high with large flowers of canary yellow. January.

C. chrysanthus 'Moonlight'. (B).
This is 4 inches high with flowers of soft yellow shading to creamy primrose. January.

C. clusii. (B).
From W. Spain and Portugal, this species is about 4 inches high with bearded throat, white inside, segments light purple, deeper at base. October.

C. corsicus. (B).
A native of Corsica, up to 3 inches high, throat smooth, white, segments light purple, outer buff, feathered purple. April.

C. etruscus. (B).
An Italian species, about 3 inches high with lilac striped tube and yellow bearded throat; inner segments lilac-purple, outer pale yellow, feathered purple. March.

C. fleischeri. (B).
A native of Asia Minor, about 3 inches high with pale yellow throat not bearded, segments pure white with orange-red anthers. March.

C. hadriaticus. (B).
A native of Albania, up to 4 inches high with bearded white flushed purple throat, segments white, purple at base. October.

C. heuffelianus. (B).
A fine species from Hungary, with a 3-inch violet tube, throat white, not bearded, segments, inner pale to bright purple, deeper at apex, outer darker, variegated purple and white. March.

C. hyemalis. (B).
Less than 3 inches high with yellow unbearded throat, segments white with basal purple veining, anthers orange. A native of Palestine. December.

C. imperati. (B).
An easy and early fragrant species from S. Italy, about 3 inches high with bearded orange throat, segments bright pale purple, outer buff with purple feathering. January.

C. kotschyanus. (B).
From the Lebanon, about 3 inches high with deep yellow bearded throat, segments red-lilac veined with purple lines and orange spots at base. September.

C. laevigatus. (B).
A small fragrant species only about 2 inches high with smooth yellow throat, segments white to pale lilac, outer buff or feathered purple, anthers white. October. A native of Greece.

C. leichtlinii. (B).
A native of Asia Minor, this fragrant species is about 2 inches high, with unbearded orange throat, segments outer yellow with single grey band and yellow-blue basal spot, scarlet stigmas. February.

C. longiflorus. (B).
About 4 inches high, yellow, throat orange and bearded, segments pale lilac, changing to yellow at base, purple veining outside, scented. October. A native of Italy.

C. malyi. (B).
A native of Dalmatia, with 4-inch yellow tube and bearded orange throat, segments white stained purple at base. March.

C. medius. (B).
A native of S. France, about 2 inches high with white tube veined purple at base, within unbearded, segments deep purple with darker basal veining and bright scarlet stigmas. October.

C. minimus. (B).
Rarely up to 2 inches high, this comes from Corsica and Sardinia with unbearded white throat and rich purple segments, outer buff and feathered, deep purple. April.

C. ochroleucus. (B).
A native of Palestine, with a 3-inch buff coloured tube, orange bearded throat, pale yellowish white segments, flushed deeper yellow at base, stigmas white. October.

C. pestalozzae. (B).
Rarely above an inch in height, this native of Greece and Turkey has a white tube with yellow throat, segments white with greyish basal markings and black spotting at base of filaments. February.

C. pulchellus. (B).
This is a small species up to 3 inches high with smooth golden throat, segments lilac-lavender with dark purple veins inside, anthers white. September. A native of Greece and Asia Minor.

C. reticulatus. (B).
A native of Hungary, with yellow unbearded throat about 3 inches high, segments white flushed purple, feathered purple outside, anthers yellow. February.

C. salzmanni. (B).
Up to 4 inches high with yellow bearded throat, segments lilac, feathered purple outside. October. A native of Morocco.

C. serotinus. (B).
A native of Europe and Asia, about 2 inches high with bearded white throat, segments bright lilac, feathered with purple outside. November.

C. sieberi. (B).
A species with many geographical forms and resultant doubtful nomenclature. The plant described here is more correctly *C. sieberi* var. *versicolor* and is a native of Crete. It is about 3 inches high with glabrous orange throat, segments soft purple-blue, golden base, anthers orange, stigmas orange-scarlet. February.

C. speciosus. (B).
A native of S.E. Europe, up to 4 inches high with white throat, segments bright blue feathered with three purple veins; stigmas orange-scarlet. October.

C. 'Stellaris'. (B).
This is a fine plant of unknown origin but believed to be a garden hybrid. It makes a tube up to 2 inches high with orange throat quite smooth; segments bright orange with black lines on outside. February.

C. 'Susianus'. (B).
A native of the Crimea, up to 3 inches high with unbearded orange veined, bronze throat, segments old gold, feathered outside with dark shining brown; anthers orange. February.

C. tournefortii. (B).
A small species rarely above 2 inches high with smooth orange throat; segments bright lilac veined purple, filaments orange, anthers white. October. A native of Greece.

C. vernus. (B).

A native of many parts of Europe, producing several geographical forms. The type plant is about 3 inches high with white bearded throat, segments white, flushed purple, feathered deep purple, stigmas orange. February.

C. vernus var. albiflorus. (B).

Only 2 inches high this is a desirable white form, with orange stigmas, from the St Gothard. March.

C. versicolor. (B).

A 4-inch species with smooth throat, segments white; heavily feathered with violet outside, stigmas orange. February. A native of S. Europe.

C. vitellinus. (B).

A native of Asia Minor, about 2 inches high with pale yellow tube and throat, segments orange feathered bronze outside. Fragrant. December.

CYANANTHUS (*Campanulaceae*).

A genus of plants related to the campanulas, natives of Central and Eastern Asia, providing the cultivator with several good species for the alpine house, their late flowering display helps to provide colour when the first flush of spring and early summer is over.

CULTIVATION. They have had the reputation of being difficult but this is undeserved, provided the drainage is as it should be, for these plants require constant moisture while in growth but this must be coupled with quick drainage. Compost B is suitable and the plants need protection from sunshine in hot dry districts. Dryish conditions but not arid after the foliage dies down.

PROPAGATION. By seed sown in February, compost 2, or green cuttings taken in July. If seed is to be the means of increase a watch must be maintained so that water does not remain in the calyx, otherwise there is a chance that the seed capsule may rot. Repot when necessary in early April.

C. delavayi. (H).

A native of W. China, this species has prostrate slender much branched hairy stems. Leaves smooth, reniform, grey-green covered with bristly hairs beneath. Flowers solitary, terminal, blue bell-shaped with tufts of hairs at base of each petal lobe. August.

C. formosus. (H).

Another W. Chinese species similar to the last, about 3 inches high, of hairy purplish stems densely clothed with the greyish-green leaves, covered with silky hairs beneath. Flowers terminal, solitary, large, upturned bell-shaped, bearded at the base of petals lobes. August.

C. incanus. (H).

This makes a small tufted plant up to 4 inches high of thin straggling prostrate stems. Leaves oval, lobed, hairy margins, twisted, grey-green. Flowers solitary, terminal, open starry-shaped, powder-blue, throat bearded with silky hairs. August. A native of E. Himalayas.

C. integer, see *C. microphyllus.*

C. lobatus. (H).

About 3 inches high in radiating tufts from a stout woody rootstock. Stems trailing, slender reddish. Leaves bright green, thick sparse, deeply three to seven lobed. Flowers terminal from rounded calyx, covered with bristly black hairs, tubular, opening to five rounded violet-blue lobes, with beard of purplish hairs at throat. August. A native of the Himalayas.

C. lobatus var. albus. (H).

A less robust plant with light green leaves and large pure white flowers bearded at the throat. August.

C. lobatus var. insignis. (H).

This is a much more robust form from Yunnan and introduced under the number K.W.5949. It differs in having yellowish-green stems and much larger flowers of bright purple-blue. August.

C. microphyllus. (H). (Syn. *C. integer*). (Popular garden name).

A native of N. India and Nepal, this species produces prostrate trailing, branched reddish hairy stems from a central tufted rootstock, never above 3 inches high. Leaves entire, alternate, deep green, narrow, ovate, rounded at base, margins rolled back. Flowers solitary, terminal, upturned, violet-blue, tube rounded, lobes spreading, covered with pale blue hairs at throat. August.

C. sherriffii. (H).

A native of Bhutan and S. Tibet, it produces radiating prostrate stems from a central rootstock, when young densely covered with white wool, but elongating to less hairy branches. Leaves sessile, ovate, obtuse at apex, rarely with serrate margins, green above, but silver-grey beneath owing to covering of hairs. Flowers solitary, bell-shaped tube, with rounded lobes, bearded at throat, bright light blue shading paler to base of petals, calyx rounded covered with short bristly hairs. August.

CYATHODES (*Epacridaceae*).

This is a small genus of extremely decorative Australasian shrubs, unfortunately only two are hardy enough for alpine house culture in this country.
CULTIVATION. Compost B is suitable over good drainage. Normal watering during the growing and flowering season. A dry period in late July. Keep on the dry side but not arid in winter.
PROPAGATION. By green cuttings taken with a heel in mid-July.

C. colensoi. (E).

Makes a much branched neat erect shrublet about 12 inches high. Leaves opposite arranged in whorls along the whole of the stems; linear to oblong, tapered at base and apex, 4 inches long, $\frac{1}{16}$ inch wide, bluish silver-grey above, white beneath with three parallel blue-grey lines. Growth buds pinkish. Flowers on terminal racemes, pitcher shaped, cream in colour with a delightful fragrance. June. In late summer this bears deep pink or white berry-like drupes. A native of New Zealand.

C. empetrifolia. (E).
This species is similar to the above but differs in that it has less slender, erect stems. Leaves silver-grey linear, obtuse, margins recurved, ciliate. Flowers in May, cream, fragrant, solitary or up to four in terminal clusters. Drupe ovoid, white. New Zealand.
C. fraseri, see *Leucopogon fraseri*.

CYCLAMEN (*Primulaceae*).

There is no doubt that this genus provides a number of fine species of plants which can hardly be bettered for alpine house culture, providing, as they will, almost a complete yearly cycle of floral display. They are native of S.E. Europe, the focal point being the Mediterranean area, so that it can be seen, although a few are really hardy, the majority coming as they do from warmer climates than ours, need some sort of protection during very cold spells.

CULTIVATION. It is proposed to give only general hints here as the species vary according to their resting, growing and flowering periods. Compost B is a suitable medium and the tubers should be planted so that the top is just at the surface of the compost and one inch deep from the rim of the pan, this allows for top-dressing with large pieces of chippings. Correct watering is one of the main points in successful cultivation, for no cyclamen will tolerate stagnant conditions under any circumstances. Overhead watering should be avoided, for as most of the tubers are flat or slightly concave on their surfaces any lodgement of water here can easily set up rot and decay. If care is taken water can be given with a can having a curved spout, this being applied round the rim of the pan. Although not so easy, immersion in a tank containing two inches of water and allowing this to moisten the compost is really the best method. As these plants dislike root disturbance they are best grown in their pans for a number of years. This will necessitate the feeding of the plants during the growing season by top-dressing with a mixture of leaf-mould unsieved, to which has been added a small amount of a good general fertiliser, used dry. All species are best housed in a cold frame away from parching winds and only brought into the house for flowering, ripening the tubers where this is necessary, or during very prolonged, cold, frosty weather.

PROPAGATION. By seed which should be sown as soon as ripe in compost 2. Failure to do this will lead to retarded germination or even loss of the seed altogether. Once they have germinated they must be kept growing for as long as possible and the compost kept moist, even after the first growth has died down. They should not be potted on until the second year when they can be safely moved as soon as growth appears. Repot only when necessary.

C. africanum. (B).
This makes a rounded slightly corky tuber with concave top from which

roots appear on all parts. Leaves reniform, thick, dark green, smooth, faintly marbled, margins undulate, toothed, underneath light green. Flowers slightly scented, rose to pale pink, petals with basal splash of crimson, anthers yellow, violet lines at back. September–October. This is a native of Algeria and Morocco and is slightly tender, needing protection in hard cold spells. Needs complete drying off after the foliage dies down, in a hot dry part of the house.

C. balearicum. (B).
A native of the Balearic Isles, with a smallish fattish tuber which bears basal roots only, from the centre of the tuber. Leaves thin cordate-ovate, pointed; bluish-grey with silvery powdery markings, purple beneath. Flowers fragrant on long stems, narrow twisted white, veined lilac petals, rose-pink at base. March–April. A somewhat tender species needing protection in long cold spells. The tubers must not be allowed to dry out, they are best plunged in wet sand after the foliage has died down and not watered until growth commences.

C. cilicium. (B).
This species has a large flattish hairy tuber, rooting from the middle of the base. Leaves after the flowers, roundish cordate, deep greyish green; margins wavy, weakly toothed and spotted, underneath vinous red. Flowers light rose, pointed twisted petals with crimson markings at base, anthers yellow, slightly scented. September–October. A native of Cilicia and Asia Minor. Cultivation as for *C. balearicum*.

C. coum, see *C. orbiculatum var. coum.*

C. creticum. (B).
A rare native of Crete making a flat hairy tuber and rooting from the centre of the base. Leaves thinnish, cordate, lobed, apex of lobes mucronate, dark grey spotted silver, reddish beneath. Flowers narrow-petalled, pure white, scented. April. A tender species needing protection against prolonged frost. Cultivation as for *C. balearicum*.

C. cyprium. (B).
A native of Cyprus, it makes a flattish corky tuber rooting from side of base. Leaves olive green, margined light green, smallish obcordate, narrowly lobed, dentate, tips pale yellow, terminal lobe acute, carmine-red below. Flowers white, irregular patch of violet-red at base, petals twisted and folded at base, fragrant, anthers yellow. October. This is another tender species which will require protection from cold spells. Cultivation as for *C. africanum*.

C. europaeum. (B). (E).
This is an evergreen species coming from open woods in Central and Southern Europe. Tubers large, generally rounded, sometimes with protuberances, corky, rooting from all parts. Leaves reniform to cordate, dark green rarely with silver zone, margins crenate, underneath dark red. Flowers intensely fragrant, petals wide pointed, carmine with crimson blotch at throat. August–December. This species requires to be kept

growing and needs plenty of water from May to end of flowering season, just moist at other periods.

C. europaeum var. album. (B). (E).
This is the rare and very desirable white deliciously scented form. August-December.

C. graecum. (B).
A native of the Mediterranean area and having a wide geographical distribution throughout this region. Makes a rounded tuber covered with a vertically split corky substance, and fleshy roots from one basal spot. Leaves large, obcordate, irregular, dentate, these being reddish-brown; deep green with silver veins and markings; underneath pale green. Flowers rose-pink, carmine at base, petals not twisted, anthers crimson. September. Needs plenty of heat to ripen the tubers while resting.

C. hederaefolium, see *C. neapolitanum*.

C. hederaefolium 'Album', see *C. neapolitanum* 'Album'.

C. hiemale, see *C. orbiculatum var. hiemale*.

C. ibericum, see *C. orbiculatum*.

C. libanoticum. (B).
A native of Lebanon, this makes a very small globular corky tuber with basal tufts of roots. Leaves obcordate, bluish-green with darker patches and white zone, dentate and slightly crinkled, deep purple-red beneath. Flowers fragrant white to pale pink, deepening with age, petals large ovate, not twisted, with crimson T-shaped blotch at base. March. Requires same cultural treatment as *C. africanum*.

C. neapolitanum. (B). (Syn. *C. hederaefolium*).
This fine and easy species possibly has the widest distribution of all Cyclamen. A native of the Mediterranean area, Turkey, Corsica, Sardinia and Crete, it has also become naturalised in England. It makes large, roundish corky tubers, slightly concave on top and rooting only from the upper surface. Leaves obcordate to ivy shape on long stems with undulate lobes generally with obtuse apex, sometimes pointed, margins dentate, rarely entire, dark green to silvery grey, intensely marbled in different shapes and sizes, green beneath. Flowers light rose to deep pink with deeper basal blotch, anthers red-brown. September. A good reliable species needing same cultural conditions as for *C. balearicum*.

C. neapolitanum 'Album'. (B). (Syn. *C. hederaefolium* 'Album').
This is the fine white form of the species often found in cultivation but never recorded in nature. September.

C. orbiculatum. (B). (Syn. *C. ibericum, C. vernum*).
There has been great confusion in the naming of this species and it has been known under a variety of names but for the present these have been lumped together and covered by the single specific name of *orbiculatum*. It has a wide geographical distribution and not unnaturally the resultant variants have helped to create confusion in nomenclature; it is a native of Bulgaria, Transcaucasus, the coast line of the Black and Caspian seas,

Turkey, Syria. The tuber is globular with flattened upper surface and covered with deep brown hairs. Leaves small, entire, reniform, deep green with silver markings. Flowers carmine with deep coloured blotch at base. December-February. Cultural treatment as for *C. balearicum*.

C. orbiculatum var. coum. (B). (Syn. *C. coum*).
This has been in cultivation for many years and its origin is doubtful. It differs from the species in having small rounded reniform, dark almost black green leaves with undulate margins, red beneath. Flowers similar to the type. January.

C. orbiculatum var. hiemale. (B). (Syn. *C. hiemale*).
A form from N. Asia Minor, Turkey and Bulgaria, with dark green roundish foliage and a distinct silver zone. Flowers larger, deeper carmine and with a much earlier flowering period. November-February.

C. repandum. (B).
A native of S. France and Mediterranean Islands into Crete. It makes a thick hairy globose flattish tuber, rooting from the base. Leaves distinctive, thin cordate, open at base, pointed at apex, undulate lobed, lobes mucronate, deep green with silvery continuous pattern, red below. Flowers bright carmine red, deeper at constricted throat, petals twisted. April-May. Cultivation as for *C. balearicum*.

C. repandum var. album. (B).
This, the white form of the species, is a very desirable plant. April-May.

C. rohlfsianum. (B).
This species can only be successfully cultivated in an alpine house where frost is excluded and is recorded here because there is no doubt that although not an easy plant it is certainly worth every effort to grow it successfully. A native of Cyrenaica, N. Africa, it makes an uneven shaped, light brown corky tuber with a tendency to roundness and will produce its roots from the sides as well as the base. Leaves thin, large, reniform on reddish pink stalks, margins deeply cut irregularly dentate, almost lobed in some forms, bright green with silver markings above, red below. Flowers fragrant, rose-pink, twisted and slightly folded petals with crimson blotch at base. October-December. This plant requires a hot dry spot during the summer to ripen the tuber and care is needed in watering; once the leaves and flower buds begin to appear only very little water should be given until these begin to develop fully, when a normal amount is necessary. It will quickly show its resentment of draughts or cold drying winds.

C. vernum, see *C. orbiculatum*.
Cymbalaria aequitriloba, see *Linaria aequitriloba*.

CYPRIPEDIUM (*Orchidaceae*).
The Lady's Slipper orchids contain amongst their number some of the most delightful and charming plants for cultivation in the alpine house, provided a little care is given to cultivation. They are natives of Europe,

temperate Asia and N. America, generally in light woodland in the higher mountain regions and *C. calceolus* is a rare British native, unfortunately its rarity is due to despoliation by indiscriminate and inexperienced collectors. Imported plants are today easy to obtain from stations where it is relatively plentiful.

CULTIVATION. These terrestrial orchids are not difficult if their few essential wants are attended to. Compost B is suitable in a well-drained shallow pan, depth of soil is not important for the rhizomes should be planted just below the surface of the compost and the roots spread out horizontally. A layer of sphagnum moss over the top of the soil as a top-dressing will help to keep them cool and moist. Water in plenty is needed as soon as growth commences in spring and this is maintained until the foliage begins to die away after flowering, then the water should only be given sparingly by immersion if the compost shows any real tendency to dry out, but if the pans are plunged, no further water is necessary from the disappearance of the foliage until the following spring. Early morning sun is disliked by all these species and once all chance of late frosts are passed they do better in a shaded spot outdoors. Although hardy they seem to resent frost more in cultivation than in their natural habitat, so they are best wintered in the alpine house or frame. Top-dress every spring with a little of the potting compost after removing the sphagnum moss, working this well down amongst the dormant crowns.

PROPAGATION. By division, this is best carried out in early June, keeping the plants in a closed frame until they are re-established. Repot only when necessary after flowering.

C. acaule. (H). (Syn. *C. humile*).
Makes a plant up to 8 inches high, leaves two, broad, pale green, ribbed, slightly downy, scape slender, flowers solitary, sepals and petals twisted, greenish brown, pouch rosy-pink blotched purple. May. A native of N. America.

C. acaule var. alba. (H).
This is a rare white form which is a very desirable plant, but like so many albinos, temperamental. May.

C. arietinum. (H).
A native of N. America and Canada, producing erect, veined, twin green leaves. Flowers solitary on an 8-inch stiff scape, sepals and petals greenish brown, lip purple veined white. June.

C. calceolus. (H).
A fine species with twin, broad, deep yellowish green, ribbed, glabrous leaves. Flowers up to three on slender 8-inch stems, sepals and petals maroon, spreading and twisted; deep narrow pouch, bright yellow, lined with yellow dots. May. A native of Europe including Britain.

C. cordigerum. (H).
A native of the Himalayas, with wide lanceolate green leaves, veining pronounced margins ciliate. Flowers solitary on 6-inch stems, terminal above

twisted lanceolate leafy bracts, sepals and petals twisted creamy white flushed green, lip white, interior blotched yellow with purple-red markings. May.

C. debile. (H).
This is a native of Japan, with twin deep-green, cordate leaves and on 10-inch stems the solitary flowers with greenish petals and sepals, pouch white, veined purple. June.

C. humile, see *C. acaule*.

C. japonicum. (H).
A native of Japan, this is a charming species with twin, fan-shaped, ribbed, deep green leaves. Flowers solitary on 6-inch scapes, sepals greenish, spotted red, petals and pouch white blotched purple at lip. May.

C. macranthon. (H).
This species has twin, rich green 8-inch ribbed leaves and on 8-inch scapes are borne the solitary flowers in May, with long twisted, white streaked purple sepals and petals, pouch large wine-purple. A native of Tibet.

C. montanum. (H). (Syn. *C. occidentale*).
A native of Oregon, U.S.A., this is a charming species with twin narrow, ribbed downy green leaves about 10 inches high. Flowers up to three on 10-inch scapes, sepals and petals twisted, brownish-red, pouch white with red veins inside. May.

C. occidentale, see *C. montanum*.

C. pubescens. (H).
Bears twin, broadly lanceolate, bright green, downy, ribbed leaves and up to two flowers on a 12-inch pubescent slender stem. Petals and sepals large, twisted, greenish yellow veined purple; pouch flattened, deep yellow, mouth flecked crimson. May. A native of N. America.

C. reginae. (H). (Syn. *C. spectabile*).
A native of E. and N. America, with long wide, bright yellowish green, twin, ribbed leaves covered with a white down. Flowers up to three on 15-inch leafy stems, sepals and petals long, white flushed pink, pouch white, flushed and lined with pink. May.

C. reginae var. album. (H).
This is a charming but unfortunately rare completely albino form of the species. May.

C. spectabile, see *C. reginae*.

CYTISUS (*Leguminosae*).
A genus of sun loving plants which are extremely floriferous and useful for providing colour in the alpine house and frame in early summer, for there are a number of brooms which with the root restriction of pan culture will remain dwarf for a period of years. In fact a specimen of *C. procumbens*, a far from small plant in the open garden, although this applies to spread not height, was given the Royal Horticultural Society's Award of Merit after being grown in a 12-inch pan for ten years. They

are with few exceptions, natives of Europe especially the southern half, but there are several in N. Africa, the majority of these are taller and less hardy. Botanically the genus is near to Genista, the difference between the two being that in Cytisus the seed has a small wart like growth near its base, but is absent in Genista.

CULTIVATION. This presents no difficulty in a well-drained medium in full sun. Compost A is suitable for all the species and they require a normal supply of water during the growing and flowering season, reducing it in July so that the new wood is given a chance to ripen well. Keep dryish but not arid from October to April. Top-dress in early spring with a little of the compost to which has been added a sprinkling of bone meal, and only repot at infrequent intervals, for all Cytisus are intolerant of root disturbance.

PROPAGATION. Seed germinates freely and should be sown as soon as ripe in compost 1 but where there are a number of species grown together, vegetative means of increase is possibly safer, due to the readiness with which the species will cross with each other. Cuttings of firm wood should be inserted in the propagating frame in early August and allowed to remain until rooted the following spring. Repot only when necessary after flowering, remembering not to disturb or damage the roots.

C. albus (Hacquet), see *C. leucanthus*.

C. ardoinii. (D).
This, a native of the Maritime Alps, makes a dwarf prostrate mat-forming shrublet, rarely above 4 inches, of octagonal grooved hairy branches. Leaves narrow oblong, in threes on short stems, hairy and bright green. Flowers up to three borne on a short hairy stalk from the joint of the previous year's growth, golden-yellow, pea-shaped. May.

C. decumbens. (D). (Syn. *Genista prostrata*).
A prostrate species hugging the ground rarely above a few inches high with wiry five-angled hairy shoots. Leaves simple, oblong, pointed at apex, grey-green and hairy on both sides. Flowers in pairs, from the leaf axils of the previous year's growth, bright rich yellow, pea-shaped. May. A native of S. Europe.

C. demissus. (D). (Syn. *C. hirsutus* var. *demissus*).
One of the best for pan culture, this is a low growing species less than 3 inches high of very hairy rounded branchlets. Leaves three foliate, leaflets oval, hairy, bright green on short stems, pointed at apex. Flowers large, in pairs from the leaf axils of the previous year's growth, rich golden-yellow with brown calyx, the whole turning bronze with age. June. A native of S.E. Europe and N. Asia.

C. diffusus. (D).
A dwarf shrublet with slightly grooved erect branches, up to 9 inches high. Leaves narrow, pointed at apex, glabrous, bright green. Flowers borne along the whole length of the twigs in the leaf axils, singly or in pairs, bright rich yellow, pea-shaped. May-June. A native of S.E. Europe.

C. hirsutus var. demissus, see *C. demissus.*

C. leucanthus. (D). (Syn. *C. albus* (Hacquet)).

This species makes a low hummock of trailing, rounded hairy branches about 6 inches high. Leaves three foliate on short stems, oval, glabrous, mid-green, hairy beneath, margins ciliate. Flowers in terminal clusters from six to ten, light cream. June. A native of S.E. Europe.

C. procumbens. (D). (Syn. *Genista procumbens*).

A charming prostrate species with interwoven slender long branching stems covered with appressed hairs. Leaves simple oblong-obovate on short stalks, apex obtuse, grey-green, hairy below. Flowers in pairs from the leaf axils, brilliant yellow. May. A native of S.E. Europe including Hungary.

DABOECIA (*Ericaceae*).

A small genus of heath-like plants with two species suitable for the alpine house or frame. *D. cantabrica* has produced several good forms, which with their different colours increase the value of these dwarf shrubs.

CULTIVATION. This is easy in compost B with plenty of lime-free water during the growing and flowering season, just moist in winter. Top-dress in early spring with compost B.

PROPAGATION. The species by seed or cuttings, and the varieties from cuttings. Seed should be sown in March in compost 2 and cuttings of the side shoots are taken in June and kept in a closed frame until rooted. Repot when necessary after flowering.

D. azorica. (E).

This is a native of the Azores, making a dwarf shrub up to 9 inches high with very slender glandular, hairy stems. Leaves oblong, narrow tipped, incurved, dark green, white woolly beneath. Flowers pendant, egg-shaped with four reflexed lobes, up to ten, in erect racemes on red stems. June.

D. cantabrica. (E). (Syn. *D. polifolia*).

This is an erect bushlet which will eventually reach 18 inches with glandular slender stems. Leaves alternate, oblong-lanceolate, tipped, only slightly recurved, deep green and bristly, white tomentose below. Flowers in loose terminal racemes, pendant egg-shaped with restricted mouth and four reflexed lobes, reddish-purple. June-November. A native of S.W. Europe and W. Ireland.

D. cantabrica 'Alba'. (E).

From Connemara, W. Ireland, is similar to the type with glistening white flowers.

D. cantabrica 'Alba Globosa'. (E).

Also from Connemara, it is a dwarf form with larger more rounded, pure white flowers.

D. cantabrica 'Atropurpurea'. (E).

This is similar to the type plant but with rich wine-coloured flowers.

D. cantabrica 'Bicolor'. (E).
A unique plant with variously marked flowers of white and purple, all on the same plant.
D. cantabrica 'Nana'. (E).
This is a very dwarf form, not more than 6 inches high with the usual bright purple flowers.
D. cantabrica 'Praegerae'. (E).
An outstanding plant of recent introduction from W. Ireland about 12 inches high, similar to the type but with clear deep rose bells.
D. polifolia, see *D. cantabrica.*

DAMNACANTHUS (*Rubiaceae*).

This genus contains two known species of which only one is suitable for alpine house culture. It is only hardy in the house where it makes an interesting specimen, taking many years to reach any appreciable size.
CULTIVATION. Compost A is suitable and the plant requires plenty of water during the growing season, dryish but not arid in winter.
PROPAGATION. It is not an easy plant to propagate, the best method is by taking cuttings with a heel of the old wood in late July and placing them in the propagating frame, allowing them to remain undisturbed until the following spring. Repot only when necessary in early April.
D. indicus. (E).
A native of Japan and China, making a very slow growing erect dwarf shrub, almost tree-like, with lax, hairy, laterals ending with slender spines. Leaves opposite, oval to ovate, smooth, rounded at base, spiny at apex. Flowers from leaf axils in pairs, white, trumpet-shaped, fragrant. May. Followed by globular scarlet fruits.

DAPHNE (*Thymelaeaceae*).

A large and interesting genus, containing many dwarf shrubs suitable for alpine house and frame culture. Evergreen and deciduous species are included in the family and with one exception all are intensely fragrant and only a single plant will fill the air of the alpine house with its perfume. The genus as a whole has over a number of years built up a reputation for being difficult in cultivation but with reasonable and intelligent care they can be grown successfully.
CULTIVATION. For pan culture, compost B is suitable and room should be left in the pan for top-dressing with the same medium in early spring. A wide pan is to be preferred so the stems can be pinned down and covered with small pieces of sandstone. From personal experience I have found that *D. petraea* seems to like its neck wedged between two pieces of rock embedded in the compost. Plenty of water is required during the growing and flowering season and the plants are the better for being kept just moist in winter.

PROPAGATION. Most of the species will strike from cuttings of the previous year's wood taken in late July or early August and placed in the propagating frame until rooted. *D. arbuscula* and *D. cneorum* can be increased by layering and *D. alpina* from seed if sown as soon as ripe in compost 2. Repot only when necessary, this should not be more than once every three or four years after flowering, always bearing in mind that these plants are intolerant of root disturbance. Only the drainage material should be carefully removed and fresh compost worked in round the naked root tips, without injuring these, and then firming the compost gently.

D. alpina. (D).
A small shrublet up to 12 inches high in nature but rarely above 6 inches under pan culture, with short erect, tangled, hairy branches. Leaves long, crowded towards apex, lanceolate, covered with down on both sides, grey-green. Flowers four-lobed, tubular in terminal clusters, white and intensely fragrant. May. Found in many of the European Alps.

D. arbuscula. (E).
This is a low growing shrublet with radiating branches from a central rootstock semi-erect and reddish in the juvenile state. Leaves long, crowded towards apex, wide linear, obtuse, mid-green, downy beneath. Flowers fragrant in terminal clusters, large, four-lobed, lilac-pink. May. A native of Hungary.

D. blagayana. (E).
A charming species that is best grown in a wide shallow pan, so that its spreading laterals can be pegged down with pieces of rock, where they will root and give the best chance of a fairly satisfactory life. It makes a dwarf shrub of spreading lax branches from a central rootstock. Leaves crowded towards apex, obovate, tapering to base, sessile, smooth, mid-green. Flowers dense in large terminal clusters, creamy white, fragrant. April. A native of Styria and Carniola.

D. buxifolia, see *D. oleoides*.

D. cneorum. (E).
This is the well-known species much in demand before the last war and imported in large quantities by florists from Holland. Most of these plants were raised in almost pure peat, the whole a congested mass and it was invariably impossible to induce rooting in a normal compost, consequently they used to languish for a period and then die. Under normal conditions it makes a trailing shrub rarely above 6 inches high with hairy flexible branches. Leaves not crowded but spaced along the shoots, narrow oblong, obtuse, tapered at base, deep green glabrous grey beneath. Flowers in terminal clusters crowded, four-lobed tubular, rich deep pink and fragrant. May. A little protection from midday sun is advisable and if a wide pan is used pinning down the trailing shoots will help to retain this plant in good health. A native of Central and Southern Europe.

D. cneorum var. alba. (E).
A white form of the species slightly smaller in all its parts and far from

vigorous. Like so many albinos it has a weak constitution and is difficult in cultivation, but worth all the trouble spent when it produces its glistening white flowers. May. A native of the Jura Mountains.

D. cneorum var. eximia. (E).

A larger plant than the species up to 9 inches high, very robust, flowers larger and a deeper red-rose. May.

D. cneorum var. pygmaea. (E).

Only about 3 inches high, this is a much slower and certainly smaller edition, but extremely floriferous with its deep red-pink fragrant flowers. May.

D. cneorum var. verlotii. (E).

A distinct variety from the Bavarian Alps, smaller in size than the species, but with larger more narrow linear leaves, deep green, glaucous below. Flowers less crowded in terminal clusters narrow, tubular, deep rosy-pink with a delightful perfume. May.

D. collina. (E).

This is a native of the Mediterranean area and requires a position in the house away from cold winds. Up to 2 feet high in its native habitat, much branched, young wood downy. Leaves oblong, obtuse at apex, dark glossy green above, paler beneath, covered with fine hairs. Flowers in terminal clusters, tubular, lilac-pink, fragrant. May.

D. fioniana, see *D. × neapolitana*.

D. genkwa. (D).

The best of the deciduous dwarf daphnes but a very temperamental species in cultivation and at best must be considered a short lived plant. It should be kept going by cuttings which root easily, for the adult plants will often collapse without warning or reason. Half-shade and protection from draughts is essential. A native of China forming a slender bush up to 18 inches high, young wood silky. Leaves opposite, lanceolate, mid-green, slightly hairy below. Flowers on short stalks in clusters from the joints of the branches of the previous year's wood, tubular, four-lobed, lilac-blue. May. Unfortunately not fragrant.

D. glomerata. (E).

A rare species with an eastern Europe distribution, making a small shrub about 12 inches high of slender branches. Leaves crowded towards apex of shoots almost in whorls, oval to oblanceolate, tapered to base, apex obtuse, deep glossy green. Flowers fragrant in small racemes, long narrow tubular, four-lobed, light pink. June. Followed by roundish pink fruits.

D. × neapolitana. (E). (Syn. *D. fioniana*).

This is near to *D. oleoides* but is given by some authorities as only a natural hybrid between *D. oleoides* and *D. cneorum*, for it occurs where these two species meet in nature. It makes a good robust shrub reaching 2 feet after many years, with erect hairy branches. Leaves not congested, lanceolate, sub-acute, dark glossy green above, lighter and hairy beneath. Flowers in terminal clusters, tubular, red-purple paling with age, sweetly scented. The flowering season is from March to May and it is one of the easiest of a temperamental genus.

D. oleoides. (E). (Syn. *D. buxifolia*).

A fine dwarf shrub, tree-like in habit with an erect stoutish short trunk and much branched firm twigs, silky grey in the juvenile state. Leaves lanceolate, tapering to base, apex mucronulate, glabrous mid-green, covered with silky hairs beneath. The flowers in terminal clusters rarely above four tubular, four-lobed, white, although all colours to rose have been recorded. A plant in my possession has flowers of a dirty off-white, these are cleistogamous, flowers which never open but are self-fertilised, but it always sets a 100% crop of fruits which are extremely attractive, the colour being a rich orange red. A native of Spain and Asia. May.

D. petraea. (E). (Syn. *D. rupestris*).

The gem of the race as far as alpines go, this species rewards all the care and attention needed to bring it to perfection. All that a choice alpine should be, dwarf in habit, extremely floriferous with large flowers covering the whole plant and with a delightful perfume. A small specimen will completely fill the alpine house with its delightful fragrance. A native of the Southern Tyrol, inhabiting crevices in high perpendicular cliffs in full sun and in cultivation it requires similar conditions with unfailing moisture during the growing and flowering season and while forming the flower buds for the next year. A spreading prostrate shrub rarely above 3 inches high with slightly downy shoots. Leaves thick, crowded towards apex, sessile, oblong, tapering towards base, dark glossy green. Flowers in terminal clusters up to six large narrow, tubular, four-lobed, glistening deep pink. May-June.

D. petraea var. grandiflora. (E).

This form is generally the one met with in cultivation as *D. petraea*, it is similar to the type but with larger, more striking flowers. May-June.

D. retusa. (E).

An Asiatic species which requires, at least in the hot southern part of the country, half shade to grow it successfully. Reputed to make a shrub up to 3 feet, I cannot bear this out for although a pan plant will be expected to grow slower than one in the open rock garden, a plant obtained in 1946 was kept in a pan until 1955 and then planted out. Today in 1963 it measures 11 inches in height by 12 inches across! Many complaints that this species quickly outgrows its pan lead me to believe that *D. tangutica* is doing service for *D. retusa*. This is a stronger growing species up to 5 feet high closely allied to *D. retusa* with only minor botanical differences. In *D. tangutica* the leaves are longer and more tapered towards the apex and unlike *D. retusa* the stigma is not downy.

It makes a much-branched upright shrublet with stout erect branches. Leaves crowded towards apex of shoots, oblong-ovate, thick leathery, notched at apex, dark glossy green, paler beneath. Flowers in terminal clusters, deep purple outside, inside brilliant white tinged pink, intensely fragrant, the whole a delightful combination. May. Fruits large oval orange-red. A native of China.

D. rupestris, see *D. petraea.*

D. sericea. (E).
A native of Crete and Asia Minor, this species needs protection from cold winds. A small bushlet up to 12 inches high with smooth slender branches. Leaves lanceolate, tapering to apex, mid-green, smooth above, paler below, covered with silky hairs. Flowers in terminal clusters, up to eight, tubular, four-lobed, rose-pink, fragrant. May.

D. striata. (E).
A rare plant, rarely above 6 inches high with a loose straggling habit, branches smooth. Leaves sessile, linear, pointed and sharply tipped, tapered to base, glossy green. Flowers in largish terminal clusters, narrow, tubular, tube striped pink, lobes deep pink, heavily perfumed. May. Not an easy plant and is possibly only fit for a connoisseur's collection. European Alps.

D. striata var. alba. (E).
Similar to the species, just as temperamental, rare in gardens with glistening white flowers. May.

D. × thauma. (E).
A natural hybrid between *D. petraea* and *D. striata*, from the Cima Tombea in Italy where the two species grow. A difficult and rare plant in the garden, the best I ever saw was a plant in the scree at Kew where the colour of the flowers was white flushed pink. Only an inch or so in height of lax spreading branches. Leaves towards apex of shoots, linear-lanceolate, deep glossy green above, paler beneath, pointed at apex, tapered to base. Flowers in small terminal clusters, narrow tubular four-lobed, rose-pink. May.

DEINANTHE (*Saxifragaceae*).

A genus of two species, natives of E. Asia, they are both suitable for pan culture in the alpine house or frame, where they make attractive specimens.
CULTIVATION. A shady spot well protected from cold winds is required for these plants and they are best plunged in a shady frame during the summer. Compost B is suitable with good drainage, plenty of water is required, reducing this after the foliage dies down and then keeping the soil just moist but not wet.
PROPAGATION. By division of the rhizomes in April or seed in March, compost 2. Repot every third year in early April.

D. bifida. (H).
A native of Japan, it makes a creeping rootstock from which is produced a solitary stem topped with up to four large ovate crinkly, rough, brittle pale green glossy leaves, divided at apex. Flowers in terminal clusters, large rounded, six white oval petals with yellow stamens. July.

D. caerulea. (H).
From the creeping rootstock on a solitary stem are borne the large ovate, crinkly pale green leaves, sharply serrate, recurved at apex. Flowers in a terminal panicle, open semi-pendant, large with six oval pale lilac-blue petals with blue stamens. July. A native of China.

DIANTHUS (*Caryophyllaceae*).

A large and varied race of plants containing a great number of species and varieties suitable for the rock garden and a quota which are admirable for alpine house culture. They are mostly natives of Europe including Britain, Asia and also high ground in both Central and S. Africa.

CULTIVATION. With a few exceptions all are easy plants to cultivate requiring a light well-drained compost so that compost A is suitable with plenty of water during the growing and flowering season, dry but not arid in winter. Species demanding special treatment will be dealt with separately. Although the large majority are lime-loving plants there are notable exceptions which do not crave for this under pan culture.

PROPAGATION. By seed sown in March, compost 2, but care must be taken as some of the species hybridise readily, or green cuttings may be taken in July and kept close until rooted. Repot every other year in early spring.

D. alpinus. (E).
A native of the European Alps, making lax cushions of glabrous bright green stiff, linear leaves with blunt apex. Flowers on 2-inch leafy stems, rounded, fringed, rose-pink, central zone of white speckled crimson, throat bearded, greenish white on reverse. June. This plant will do well in compost D, retaining its dwarf habit, making a much tighter, more compact cushion and ensuring a longer life under these conditions.

D. alpinus var. albus. (E).
This is just as desirable a white form of the species. June.

D. arenarius. (E).
A small species from the Alps of N. Europe, it makes a lax cushion of grey-green linear, pointed leaves. Flowers generally solitary on a 3-inch scape, white with a green eye and red beard, fringed, fragrant. July. This species seems to like a little shade during the hot months.

D. brachyanthus. (E).
A densely tufted plant with toothed, glaucous, smooth, erect linear leaves. Flowers solitary, rounded rose-pink, lighter on reverse. July. A native of Spain.

D. callizonus. (E).
A native of S.E. Europe, making a cushion of loose tufts with glaucous linear acute leaves. Flowers solitary on 4-inch leafy scapes, pink with a white central zone dotted crimson, margins crenate. June. Does well in compost D.

D. freynii. (E).
This is a dwarf cushion forming species from Hercegovina with grey-green obtuse linear, keeled leaves. Flowers solitary on 2-inch scapes each with two pairs of leaves, rounded bright pink, bearded, margins serrate. July. Another plant which will grow well in compost D.

D. freynii var. alba. (E).
A fine white form of the species and just as desirable. July.

D. glacialis. (E).
A native of Central Europe, always found on granite formation, making a close cushion of tufted shoots, leaves linear, thick, obtuse, green. Flowers on solitary 2-inch stems, rounded, deep pink with a white central zone, greenish on reverse, fragrant, petal margins notched. June.

D. glacialis var. alba. (E).
The white form is just as good as the species and breeds true from seed. June.

D. haematocalyx. (E).
A tufted species up to 6 inches high forming close cushions of grey, linear, flat stiff leaves. Flowers up to three deep purple-red from dark red calyces, petals crenate. June. A native of Greece.

D. haematocalyx var. alpinus, see *D. pindicola.*

HYBRIDS
These are placed here under one heading as although strictly non alpine, their dwarf stature, beauty of flower and ease of culture, warrant a passing mention for they will grow well in pans for a season or two, thus brightening up the alpine house at a period when floral decoration is beginning to wane.

D. 'Ariel'. (E).
About 3 inches high, tufted green leaves and bright cherry-red flowers. July.

D. 'Boydii'. (E).
A charming close compact cushion of short bright green leaves topped by large bluish pink fringed flowers with deeper eye. July.

D. 'Elf'. (E).
Another fine plant up to 6 inches high, making a cushion of tufted silver-grey. Flowers semi-double, light crimson over a long period. July–September.

D. 'Jupiter'. (E).
A small tufted plant with flowers on 4-inch stems, double salmon-pink. June.

D. 'Little Jock'. (E).
Makes a close compact dome of tight ash-grey tufts. Flowers on 3-inch stems, double light pink. June.

D. 'Mars'. (E).
One of the best of the hybrids with its fine cushions in tufts of small

silver-grey pointed leaves. Flowers on 3-inch stems fully doubled, bright crimson. June.

These are just a few of the charming dwarf hybrids, this list could be extended greatly but space does not allow. Any good nurseryman or alpine specialist will supply others to suit one's own taste.

D. microlepis. (E).
A dwarf close compact cushion of tufted habit only 1 inch high. Leaves lax linear, obtuse, green. Flowers solitary, sessile, clear pink, margins crenate, greenish on reverse. May. A native of the Balkans.

D. neglectus. (E).
This is found in S.W. Europe, where it makes a dense mat of smooth tufts only an inch or so high. Leaves narrow, linear, flat, green. Flowers solitary on 3-inch leafy stems, bright rose with a bright green central zone, bearded, margins bi-serrate, reverse pale buff. June.

D. noeanus. (E). (Syn. *Acanthophyllum spinosum*).
A native of the Balkans, it makes a dense tufted mat a few inches high. Leaves linear-lanceolate, spiny, greyish green. Flowers up to five on a 4-inch stem in a terminal cluster, white with deeply cut petals giving the flowers a fringed effect, fragrant. June.

D. pindicola. (E). (Syn. *D. haematocalyx* var. *alpinus*).
A fine dwarf species from the Pindus range, forming a small close compact, tufted cushion. Leaves small linear, sharply pointed, silver-grey. Flowers solitary on almost non-existent wiry stems, bright reddish pink, buff on reverse, margins crenate. July.

D. simulans. (E).
This is a delightful plant for the alpine house with its slow growing tufts welded together into a tight dome. Leaves small linear, acute, blue-green. Flowers solitary, large of good roundish shape, almost sessile, deep pink, margins irregularly toothed. June. A native of Bulgaria.

DIAPENSIA (*Diapensiaceae*).

A small genus of prostrate shrubs or sub-shrubs which will tax the skill of even the hardened alpine plant cultivator to achieve a modicum of success, especially in the drier atmosphere of the southern counties.

CULTIVATION. They are best suited to compost C and demand lime-free water at all times. The ideal situation is to keep the compost cool and moist and only bring the plants into the alpine house during the flowering period. At other times they should be plunged into a shady frame and sprayed overhead in the evenings after hot days.

PROPAGATION. By careful division in April, treating each piece as a cutting until re-established. Cuttings in July from half-ripened wood. Repot only when necessary.

D. barbulata, see *Pyxidanthera barbulata*.

D. lapponica. (E).
A native of N.W. America, N. Europe and N.W. Asia, forming a prostrate

dwarf shrub of creeping habit about 3 inches high of much-branched interlaced stems. Leaves crowded, small, leathery, entire, spatulate, rounded at apex, petiolate, recurved, deep glossy green. Flowers solitary from terminal shoots on half-inch stems, campanulate with 5 rounded white lobes, shading to green inside the corolla tube. May.

D. lapponica var. obovata. (E).

This is the N.E. Asian variant from Japan and N.E. Siberia, similar to the species but the leaves are obovate with obtuse apex and just as charming white flowers. May.

DICENTRA (*Papaveraceae*).

This is a small genus of plants of which three are suitable for cultivation in the alpine house or frame and of these, one, *D. peregrina* var. *pusilla*, must be considered as one of the finest and also rarest of alpines in cultivation.

CULTIVATION. Compost B is suitable with plenty of water during the growing and flowering season, just moist as the foliage dies down. They all require a cool spot especially in the south and should only be kept in the alpine house while in flower, then plunged outside during the summer and returned to the house before frost and the cooler days return.

PROPAGATION. By division of the tuberous rootstock in July or seed sown when ripe, compost 2. Repot when necessary after flowering.

D. cucullaria. (H).

A native of N. America, rarely above 4 inches high with basal, tri-ternate, smooth, small silvery-grey leaves. Flowers in a small unbranched raceme, pearl-white, tipped yellow with straight spur. May.

D. oregana. (H).

Another N. American species, which makes stout rhizomes and tufts of silvery-grey, much cut, lacy leaves. Flowers on 4-inch stems in a loose raceme, pendant cream tipped rose, spurs small obtuse. May.

D. peregrina var. pusilla. (H).

The gem of the race from granite formations in N. Japan and Siberia, forms basal tufts with several radical ternately compound leaves from buried petioles, deeply cut into linear, acute segments, glaucous silver-grey. Flowers on slender smooth 3-inch scapes in a short cyme up to six, semi-pendant, four petalled rose-pink, the outer two reflexed at apex, inner two coherent, spurs short blunt. June.

Didissandra grandis, see *Corallodiscus kingianus*.

D. lanuginosa, see *Corallodiscus lanuginosus*.

D. muscicola, see *Briggsia muscicola*.

DIONYSIA (*Primulaceae*).

A small genus of the Primula family which has provided four species that are in cultivation today. They resemble the Aretian section of Androsace and need as much care to keep them happy. (See Appendix 1 also.)

CULTIVATION. All are best grown in compost D over faultless drainage with normal watering in spring and summer, dry but not arid in winter. Half shade is necessary during the hot summer months, and if they have to remain in the alpine house during this period a piece of white scrim suspended above the plants will provide this. There must be a constant watch for pests as this is one of the main reasons why gardeners fail with this genus, for these pests obtain a foothold in the rosettes under the foliage and the damage is done before discovery.

PROPAGATION. Best by detaching rosettes and rooting them in a close frame. July. Seed if set should be sown as soon as ripe, compost 2. Repot when necessary after flowering.

D. bryoides. (E).
A native of S.W. Persia, at high altitudes where it forms tight hummocks of dense tufts. Leaves imbricated, minute, obovate, vertical in rosette formation, bright green covered with transparent glands. Flowers stemless, long narrow tube, opening to five obovate horizontal lobes, notched at apex, rose-pink shading to white at throat. March–April.

D. curviflora. (E).
This species makes a hard cushion of hard erect minute branches. Leaves in rosette formation imbricated, minute, obovate, blunt and thick at apex, margins ciliate, light green turning reddish brown. Flowers solitary with long tube, at the apex a globular swelling, opening to five flat pink rounded petal lobes, less notched than in *D. bryoides*, with a yellow eye surrounded by a white zone. March. A native of Persia.

D. michauxii. (E).
From high altitudes in S.W. Persia, it forms a close compact cushion of short erect branches from a common rootstock. Leaves in open semi-horizontal rosette formation, minute, thick, entire, imbricated, ovate-spatulate, obtuse, covered with velvet hairs. Flowers solitary, sessile, tube long narrow, rounded swelling at base of petal lobes; five rounded ovate hairy lobes. Yellow. March.

DIOSPHAERA, see TRACHELIUM.

DODECATHEON (*Primulaceae*).

A genus of plants confined to America, closely related to Soldanella and Primula but having flowers with reflexed petals and a projecting style as with Cyclamen. There are a few which are ideal for alpine house or frame culture providing a good display of colour.

CULTIVATION. Compost B is suitable and it should be kept well-watered while the plants are in growth and flower, just moist at other periods. They are best plunged in a cold frame after the flowering season is over and left there until the following March when the pans should be brought into the house.

PROPAGATION. By seed sown as soon as ripe, compost 2, or division in August. Repot when necessary after flowering.

D. alpinum. (H).
A native of N.W. America, making thick rhizomes. Leaves in basal rosettes, upstanding, linear-oblong, apex pointed, green. Flowers up to five in umbel on an 8-inch scape, four magenta-purple reflexed lobes, tube yellow, throat white and gold rings, deep purple anthers. May.

D. hendersonii. (H).
This is about 12 inches high with thickish, irregularly dentate, oblong leaves in rosette formation. Flowers in a small umbel on a stout scape, reflexed, light violet lobes and yellow anthers. May. A native of California.

D. integrifolium. (H).
A native of British Columbia, this is a plant 10 inches high with entire spatulate leaves in a rosette. Flowers up to ten in an umbel, on a 10-inch scape, lilac-purple tinged pink. May.

DORONICUM (*Compositae*).

A small genus of plants of which there is only one in cultivation that is really suitable for pan culture, the majority being too coarse for the alpine house.

CULTIVATION. Compost A over good drainage with a normal supply of water during the growing and flowering season, dry but not arid in winter.

PROPAGATION. By division immediately after flowering. Repot every year in May.

D. cordatum. (H). (Syn. *D. cordifolium*).
From a fibrous rootstock is produced a rosette of basal cordate, dentate leaves on small stalks, central stem leaves smaller, sessile, green, covered with a few silver grey hairs, denser below. Flowers large solitary, bright yellow daisy shape with a central golden boss of stamens. April. A native of S.E. Europe.

DOUGLASIA (*Primulaceae*).

A genus of plants related to Androsace, all the species with the exception of one being natives of N. America, they are choice alpine plants which require care in cultivation to grow them successfully.

CULTIVATION. Compost A is suitable but the drainage must be perfect. Young seedlings can be tried in compost D where they make more compact and healthier specimens. Plenty of water during the growing season, dry but not arid in winter. All the species require some protection from sunshine during the hot season. Propagation is by seed sown in March, compost 2, or cuttings taken in June. Repot only when necessary after flowering.

D. dentata. (E).
A native of the Cascade Mountains, it makes a soft cushion of loose tufted

rosettes. Leaves woolly grey-green, spatulate, dentate at apex. Flowers on small scape in bracteate umbel up to six, rich purple, deep at throat, five-lobed tubular. April.

D. laevigata. (E).
This forms a lax cushion of densely tufted rosettes. Leaves stiff linear-lanceolate, glabrous green.. Flowers on a small umbel up to four on a 2-inch scape, tubular five-lobed, rose-pink with a yellow eye. April. A native of N. America.

D. montana. (E).
A native of Montana, this makes tighter domes of rosettes. Leaves linear, acute, imbricated, smooth grey-green, margins downy. Flowers on 1-inch scapes rarely above two, tubular five-lobed, bright rose-pink, lighter at base with a medium-dark streak. May.

D. vitaliana. (E). (Syn. *Androsace vitaliana*).
This is the only European representative of the genus, found in Spain and C. Europe. It makes a densely tufted plant in rosette formation. Leaves entire, linear, imbricated, grey-green, margins hairy. Flowers solitary on 1-inch scapes, narrow, tubular, five-lobed, yellow. April. This species has the reputation of being a shy flowerer, but somehow I think this has been gained through a shy-flowering form being introduced, pro-pagated and distributed, for I have always found that it flowers freely.

DRABA (*Cruciferae*).

A race of plants which somehow has just missed the bus; whether this is due to Farrer's condemnation of the genus as a whole or not is difficult to understand, for at least four species are outstanding alpine house plants and three will tax the skill of above average cultivators, to maintain them in good condition over a number of years.

CULTIVATION. All will do well in compost A over perfect drainage, requiring a normal supply of water during the growing and flowering season, dry at other periods. At no time should water be poured over the cushions. A watch should be kept for any dead or dying rosettes and these must be removed at once, otherwise there is a danger of rot spreading to the crown of the plant, resulting in total collapse. It is also best to remove all dead flowering stems, a tedious task but well worth while in the cushion species for these can also be a focal point for the entry of disease.

PROPAGATION. By seed sown in March, compost 2, or individual rosettes taken in June and struck in the propagating frame. Repot every year after flowering as these plants quickly outgrow their pans.

D. acaulis. (H).
A fine cushion plant forming a close soft mat of rosettes. Leaves entire, grey due to intense covering of white hairs, margins ciliate, the whole cushion being only an inch high. Flowers on a short scape up to three, the usual four-petalled crucifer type, golden-yellow. April. A native of the Cilician Taurus.

D. andina. (H).
This makes a close rounded cushion only 2 inches high. Leaves dense
in rosette formation, linear, rigid, pointed at apex, grey-green covered
with stellate hairs. Flowers in dense clusters on small smooth stems. Pale
yellow. April. A native of America.

D. bryoides. (H).
A native of the Caucasus Mountains, making a close compact cushion
only an inch or so high. Leaves in close rosette formation, small, stiff,
oblong, grey-green. Flowers on thread-like 1-inch stems, up to six, four-
petalled, golden-yellow. March.

D. bryoides var. imbricata. (H). (Syn. *D. imbricata*).
This form is much smaller in all its parts having the appearance of moss
with just as large four-petalled flowers of golden-yellow. March.

D. dedeana. (H).
A less compact cushion about 1 inch high but spreading to 6 inches across.
Leaves in rosette formation, crowded, linear, pointed at apex, margins
ciliate, grey-green. Flowers up to ten in a dense corymb, white, pale
violet at throat, almost stemless. April. A native of the Pyrenees.

D. dedeana var. cantabrica. (H).
This is a similar plant but with sulphur flowers. April.

D. gigas, see *Arabis carduchorum*.

D. imbricata, see *D. bryoides* var. *imbricata*.

D. mollissima. (H).
Forming a rounded close compact cushion of rosettes only 2 inches high
but up to 10 inches across in a well-grown specimen. Leaves in close rosette
formation linear to oblong, apex obtuse, grey-green covered with hairs.
Flowers in clusters on 2-inch stems, four-petalled, golden-yellow, fragrant.
April. A native of the Caucasus Mountains.

D. polytricha. (H).
A native of Turkish Armenia, forming close dense cushions only 2 inches
high. Leaves in close rosette formation, soft, oblong, entire, apex obtuse,
silver-grey due to intense covering of fine hairs. Flowers on short stems,
clustered, pale yellow. April. This species requires care in winter, the
rosettes must not absorb an excess of moisture, otherwise rotting will
take place.

D. pyrenaica, see *Petrocallis pyrenaica*.

D. rigida. (E).
A native of Armenia, this makes a tight compact cushion only an inch
or so high. Leaves stiff in rosette formation, linear to oblong-elliptic,
apex obtuse and incurved, bristly, green. Flowers on 2-inch smooth scapes
up to fifteen in a dense cluster, golden-yellow. April.

DRYAS (*Rosaceae*).
A small genus of plants of which only one, the minor form of *D. octopetala*,
is small enough for pan culture.

CULTIVATION. Compost A is suitable with good drainage, plenty of water during the growing season, just moist in winter. This plant benefits from a top-dressing of similar compost, well worked down amongst the prostrate shoots in early spring.

PROPAGATION. By seed sown when ripe, compost 2 or green cuttings in June. Repot only when necessary as root restriction helps to keep the plant both neat and tidy; this is best after flowering, taking care not to injure the roots.

D. octopetala var. minor. (E).

This is a dwarf trailing shrublet of creeping congested branches. Leaves alternate, elliptic-oblong, apex obtuse, deeply crenate, midrib hairy, dull deep green above, white below due to heavy tomentose. Flowers solitary on 1-inch hairy stalks, white, eight-petalled, followed by fluffy seed heads, strangely reminiscent of clematis. May. A native of Britain on the Arncliffe Clouder.

DRYPIS (*Caryophyllaceae*).

A monotypic genus, the one species hailing from mountainous regions of S. Europe. It is suitable for a warm spot in the alpine house, away from cold searing winds.

CULTIVATION. Compost A over faultless drainage. A normal supply of water during the growing season, dry but not arid in winter.

PROPAGATION. Seed sown in March, compost 2, the seedlings should be pricked out as soon as the first true leaves appear, taking care not to break the roots. Repot only when necessary in early April. This plant dislikes root disturbance.

D. spinosa. (E).

It forms a tufted sub-shrub of lax, dense, four-angled branches up to 4 inches high. Leaves opposite, long, narrow almost needle-shaped, very sharp, glabrous, bright shiny green. Flowers in tight congested corymbs, small five-lobed, pale pink. June.

EDRAIANTHUS (*Campanulaceae*).

A small family of plants which are closely related to the campanulas and also have a near affinity to Wahlenbergia, often being quoted under that generic title. The difference between the two genera is slight, in Edraianthus the flowers have bracts immediately below them, while in Wahlenbergia the flowers are on a long pedicel and have no bracts below.

CULTIVATION. This is satisfactory in compost A over good drainage. A good supply of water is needed during the growing season, dry but not arid in winter. All the species dislike winter wet.

PROPAGATION. By seed sown in March, compost 2, or tufts taken in late May and rooted in the propagating frame. Repot every other year in early April.

E. caudatus. (E). (Syn. *E. dalmaticus*).
This is a dwarf plant of tufted habit in rosette formation. Leaves broad, linear, entire, acute, grey-green. Flowers on 3-inch semi-prostrate stems up to eight, funnel-shaped, five petals, purple. July. Dalmatia.
E. dalmaticus, see *E. caudatus.*
E. dinaricus. (H). (Syn. *Wahlenbergia dinarica*).
A native of Dalmatia, this is a small tufted plant. Leaves linear, hairy, pointed at apex, silvery grey-green. Flowers solitary on a 3-inch stem, five-lobed funnel-shaped, violet, calyx lobes hairy on outside. June.
E. pumilio. (H). (Syn. *Wahlenbergia pumilio*).
A tight compact cushion of tufted habit similar to *E. dinaricus* but much smaller. Leaves linear, pointed at apex, hairy, silver-grey. Flowers large, stemless, upturned funnel-shaped bells of violet. May-June. Differs from *E. dinaricus* in that the calyx lobes are hairy on both sides. A native of Dalmatia.
E. serpyllifolius. (H). (Syn. *Wahlenbergia serpyllifolia*).
This forms a mat of spreading tufts. Leaves basal in rosette formation, oblanceolate, green, smooth, margins ciliate. Flowers solitary on leafy semi-prostrate stems, open bell-shaped, purple-violet, red in bud. June. A native of the Balkan Peninsula.
E. serpyllifolius 'Major'. (H).
This is a similar form from a sterile clone but with much larger flowers of rich purple-violet, constant in cultivation. June.

EPIGAEA (*Ericaceae*).

There are two species, one colour variant and a single hybrid between them in this genus; these are desirable plants but not easy of culture in the drier parts of the country where shade is essential.
CULTIVATION. Compost C is suitable in a wide shallow pan with plenty of lime-free water at all times. They should not be kept in the alpine house, only taken in during the flowering season, afterwards being plunged to their rims in a cool shady spot and sprayed both mornings and evenings during hot weather. A top-dressing in early spring with similar compost is beneficial.

Propagation is by seed sown in March, compost 3, or careful division in early September, the pieces treated as cuttings until re-established. Repot only when necessary after flowering.
E. asiatica. (E).
This is a dwarf growing creeping shrublet, making a prostrate mat of rough bristle-haired branches. Leaves coriaceous, ovate, tapering to apex, cordate at base, veining reticulated, petiole long, pinkish red, margins ciliate, dull deep green, lighter below with pronounced reddish midrib, sparsely clothed with bristly hairs. Flowers fragrant up to ten in congested racemes on a short hairy scape, globose five-lobed, white flushed pink,

reddish in bud, calyx lobes deep rose-pink, broadly lanceolate, acute. March–April. A native of Japan.

E. 'Intertexta'. (E). (Syn. *E.* 'Aurora').

A hybrid between the two parents but not so difficult to cultivate, with smaller foliage but large delightful open five-lobed flowers almost rose-red at tip of the corolla lobes. April.

E. repens. (E).

This is the Mayflower, making a prostrate creeping rooting shrublet, with bristly branches. Leaves ovate or sub-obicular, tapering to apex, cordate at base, rugose, heavily veined, dull deep green, lighter below, margins ciliate and undulate. Flowers in crowded terminal racemes up to six globose, five-lobed, fragrant, white flushed green at base, pink in bud, calyx lobes ovate, acute, pink. April. A native of N.E. America.

E. repens var. rosea. (E).

This is the extremely rare rose coloured form, in all other respects similar to the type. April.

Erica sicula, see *Pentapera sicula*.

ERIGERON (*Compositae*).

A large genus of plants containing a number which are very weedy but there are a few which can be grown in pans for the alpine house or frame.
CULTIVATION. This is easy in compost A with good drainage, normal watering during the growing season, dry but not arid in winter.
PROPAGATION. By seed sown in February, compost 2. Repot when necessary after flowering.

E. aureus. (H).

A native of N.W. America, it is about 3 inches high forming mats of basal tufts. Leaves spatulate, grey-green. Flowers solitary on violet hairy scapes, many rayed golden-yellow daisies. May–June.

E. compositus. (E). (Syn. *E. multifidus*).

A creeping prostrate, very tufted plant only an inch or so high. Leaves three-lobed, each lobe divided into three segments, ash-grey, hirsute. Flowers solitary on small hairy scapes large, lavender with greenish eye, surrounded by a golden circle. May–June. A native of N. America.

E. eriocephalus, see *E. uniflorus*.

E. leiomerus. (E).

From the Rocky Mountains, this is a small tufted plant less than 4 inches high. Leaves almost rosette formation, spatulate, grey-green. Flowers solitary on 3-inch scapes, violet-blue daisies. May.

E. multifidus, see *E. compositus*.

E. trifidus. (E).

A dwarf tufted plant only an inch or so high. Leaves three-lobed, each lobe cut into three segments, ash-grey, extremely woolly and fleshy. Flowers solitary on small hairy scapes, pale lavender-blue. June. A native of the Rocky Mountains.

E. uniflorus. (E). (Syn. *E. eriocephalus*).
A small plant up to 4 inches high of tufted habit. Leaves spatulate, grey-green, covered with white wool. Flowers solitary on 3-inch woolly stems, deep violet. May. A native of N.W. America.

ERINACEA (*Leguminosae*).

A monotypic genus with a natural distribution in France, Spain and Algeria, this is an ideal plant for pan culture in this country.
CULTIVATION. Compost A is suitable over good drainage, a normal supply of water during late spring and early summer but a good baking is essential during late July and August, for this tends to ripen the wood on which the next year's flowers are borne. Dry but not arid in winter. All available sun is essential.
PROPAGATION. By seed in March, compost 2; the ensuing seedlings should be pricked out with care for any injury to the roots is invariably fatal. Repot only when necessary after flowering, bearing in mind the family's hatred of root disturbance.
E. anthyllis. (E). (Syn. *E. pungens*; *Anthyllis erinacea*).
In its natural habitat it makes hard spiny hummocks up to 3 feet high. Cultivators with a plant 9 inches high and a foot across have a fine specimen, for it is extremely slow growing. It forms an upright hard shrub up to 1 foot high of erect, much-branched, rigid spine tipped, grey-green smooth branches. Leaves few, simple, small, linear-lanceolate, silver-grey due to intense coverings of silky hairs. Flowers carried just below the needle sharp apex of branches, up to four large leguminose, violet-blue with a red tinge. May.

ERINUS (*Scrophulariaceae*).

A small genus of plants with one species and two forms which are suitable for pan culture.
CULTIVATION. They all do well in compost A with plenty of water while growing, dry but not arid in winter.
PROPAGATION. By seed sown in March, or by division after flowering, compost 2, both the species and forms breed reasonably true. Repot when necessary.
E. alpinus. (E).
A native of Europe, it forms close congested mats of leaves in rosette formation. Leaves spatulate, deeply dentate, apex rounded and notched, hairy, deep glossy green. Flowers on 3-inch stems in small racemes, rounded, lilac-purple. May.
E. alpinus var. albus. (E).
This is the charming white form and just as desirable. May.
E. alpinus 'Dr Hanele'. (E).
A form which originated in cultivation with large flowers of carmine. May.

ERIOGONUM (*Polygonaceae*).

A large race of plants from the New World, of which there are a few suitable for the alpine house and frame.

CULTIVATION. The shrubby species require a rich medium in full sun, compost C is suitable, but the woolly species will do just as well in compost B. Good drainage is necessary but all need plenty of water while in growth, dry but not arid conditions in winter.

PROPAGATION. By seed sown when ripe, compost 2, or green cuttings taken with a heel in July. Repot only when necessary in early April for root restriction tends to increase flowering.

E. arborescens. (E).

A dwarf shrub reputed to be 3 feet in its native habitat but in cultivation rarely grows above 12 inches high, tree-like with spreading almost contorted branches, reddish-brown, striated grey. Leaves arranged in whorls at apex of stems, linear to oblong, mid-green, smooth above, white below due to intense covering of white hairs, margins recurved. Flowers clustered in terminal cymes, bright rose in bud, opening to white with green median line and pink stamens. July. A native of California.

E. microthecum. (E).

A dwarf much-branched shrublet about 9 inches high. Leaves alternate, linear to oblong, grey- green covered with white hairs. Flowers on much-forked peduncles, citron-yellow. July. A native of California.

E. ovalifolium. (E).

A small congested plant of short white hairy stems. Leaves elliptic to orbicular, tapered to base, silver-grey due to intense covering of hairs. Flowers on 4-inch stems in close umbels, white turning to pink with age, backed with bell-shaped involucres. June. N. America.

E. racemosum. (E).

A native of W. America, this is a small few-branched sub-shrub. Leaves crowded oval to orbicular, light green, pale beneath with covering of white hairs. Flowers on small branched spikes. Pink. July.

Eriogynia pectinata, see *Spiraea pectinata*.

ERITRICHIUM (*Boraginaceae*).

This genus contains a species that must be the despair of all alpine gardeners, in *E. nanum*. So easy to collect from its native habitat with all its roots intact but once introduced to gardens in the lowlands it promptly sighs for its vast wild desolate high screes and departs with a rapidity that will amaze you. It will never be an easy plant to keep going in cultivation and the most that can be expected is a maximum life of a few years.

CULTIVATION. Compost D can be tried for seedlings, making sure that there is plenty of moisture during the growing and flowering season, this must be well drained but the plant also resents dryness at the roots although the foliage has to be kept free of moisture at all times. Even during the winter the actual soil must be kept moist. Compost A is suitable for the other species which is a much easier plant to grow. Plenty of water while in growth, dry but not arid in winter.

PROPAGATION. By seed sown in January, compost 2, and exposed to frost which will assist germination. Repot when necessary after flowering; in the case of *E. nanum* it is doubtful if it will ever reach the stage for this to be put into practice.

E. nanum. (E).
A tight cushion of extremely hairy branches. Leaves crowded, linear to oblong, sessile, silver-grey owing to intense covering of long silky hairs. Flowers sessile, large rounded forget-me-nots of an intense bright blue with a yellow eye. April–May. A native of the high European Alps.

E. rupestre var. pectinatum. (H). (Syn. *E. strictum*).
This perennial herb is up to 6 inches high with upright basal linear-oblong leaves, light green, stem-leaves silver-grey covered with hairs. Flowers on 6-inch stems in long sprays of blue forget-me-nots with a yellow eye. May. A native of the Himalayas.

ERODIUM (*Geraniaceae*).

This genus will provide the alpine house or frame with a few species or varieties of plants that are suitable for pan culture, not only for their flowers but also a number have dainty foliage which is very attractive.

CULTIVATION. Compost A is suitable over good drainage and they all appreciate a warm spot. A normal supply of water is required during the growing season, dry but not arid conditions in winter.

PROPAGATION. By seed if sown when ripe in compost 2, generally in late July; green cuttings in May, or root cuttings in April. Repot every year in April.

E. chamaedryoides. (E). (Syn. *E. reichardii*).
A native of Majorca, this requires a sheltered spot in the house, where from a stout rootstock it makes dense tufts about 2 inches high. Leaves cordate, with blunt apex, crenate, dark green. Flowers solitary on a short scape, rounded saucer-shaped, white veined pink. June.

E. chamaedryoides 'Roseum'. (E).
This is the charming deep pink form which is just as desirable.

E. chrysanthum. (E).
This species is dioecious so it is necessary to grow both male and female plants, if seed is required. A native of Greece, it makes a much branched tufted plant from a thick rootstock up to 6 inches high. Leaves deeply lobed with wide blunt segments, pale grey-green. Flowers rounded, creamy yellow on short stems. June–August.

E. corsicum. (E).
A close tufted mat-forming plant. Leaves ovate, scalloped, grey-green, downy, apex obtuse. Flowers sessile, rounded clear pink with darker veinings. May–August. A native of Corsica.

E. corsicum 'Album'. (E).
This is a free flowering white form. May–August.
E. macradenum. (E).
A native of the Pyrenees, this is a tufted plant up to 6 inches high. Leaves aromatic, deeply cut, segments, lanceolate-linear, mid-green, glandular hairy. Flowers on small stems pale violet, the upper two petals blotched with deep purple at base. May–August.
E. reichardii, see *E. chamaedryoides*.
E. supracanum. (E).
This is a small tufted plant about 4 inches high. Leaves ovate to oblong, lobes deeply cut, silvery-grey due to covering of hair, green below. Flowers on 4-inch stems, white veined pink. May–August. A native of the Pyrenees.

ERYTHRAEA, see **CENTAURIUM.**

ERYTHRONIUM (*Liliaceae*).

A small genus of bulbous plants which are with the exception of one European species truly N. American. There are a number that will give a good display under alpine house or pan culture for they are plants with dainty flowers.
CULTIVATION. This is best in compost B with good drainage and the bulbs should be planted in August 1 inch deep and up to twelve in a 6-inch pan. The pans are best plunged to their rims in a cold frame in winter then brought into the house for flowering. Very little water is required while dormant but a good supply is needed during the growing season. These plants resent hot sunshine and do better in half-shade.
PROPAGATION. By offsets in August or seed sown as soon as ripe in compost 2. Repot when necessary in August.
E. albidum. (B).
A native of N. America, this has long, wide, lanceolate, slightly mottled leaves and on 6-inch stems solitary, semi-pendant, white flowers with recurved petals. April.
E. americanum. (B).
Less than 6 inches high with recurved elliptic-lanceolate, green-mottled violet and white leaves. Flowers solitary on 6-inch stems, bright yellow with blunt open spreading petals. May. A native of eastern N. America.
E. californicum. (B).
A taller growing species up to 15 inches high from California, with green, mottled brown, broad lanceolate leaves. Flowers pendant, up to four on slender scapes, cream, margins recurved with a deeper golden-yellow base. April.
E. dens-canis. (B).
This, the only non-American species, is the well-known 'Dog's Tooth'

violet and has a wide distribution throughout Europe. It has wide oval, rounded at base, tapering to apex, green leaves with white and purple-brown marks. Flowers solitary, pendant, on 6-inch stems with deeply recurved petals, purple-rose. April.

E. dens-canis var. album. (E).
This is a charming white form similar to the species with the exception of the floral colour. April.

E. grandiflorum. (B).
A native of N.W. America, this has 4-inch oblong-lanceolate plain green leaves. Flowers can be from one to four on 6-inch stems, pendant with very recurved petals, bright yellow shading to deep orange at base. May.

E. hendersonii. (B).
From the mountains of Oregon, a charming species up to 6 inches high. Leaves oblong, pale green with deep mottling of brown, base tapered and channelled. Flowers on 6-inch stems up to four, pendant with recurved petals, deep lavender and basal markings of maroon. April.

E. howellii. (B).
This is about 8 inches high with obovate-lanceolate, brown-purplish mottled green leaves. Flowers pendant, up to four on slender stems, petals less recurved, yellow, each petal having an orange spot at base. April. A native of Oregon.

E. parviflorum. (B).
A native of the Rocky Mountains, up to 8 inches high with unmarked green, oblong leaves, tapered to both base and apex. Flowers solitary, pendant, petals recurved, bright yellow with greenish tinge at base. April.

E. purpurascens. (B).
From Sierra Nevada, with large oblong to lanceolate, green tinged purple leaves, margins undulate. Flowers on 9-inch stems up to twelve in an open raceme, small pendant, petals recurved, cream flushed purple with deep orange basal markings. May.

E. revolutum. (B).
This is up to 10 inches high with lightly marked, oblong-lanceolate green leaves, the markings are white and brown. Flowers few on slender stems, pendant, petals thin much recurved, deep rose-pink. April. A native of California.

E. revolutum 'Praecox'. (B).
A form with deep cream flowers. April.

E. revolutum 'White Beauty'. (B).
This is a good white variety. April.

E. tuolumnense. (B).
A delightful species from California, with clear yellow-green, shiny, oblong-lanceolate leaves, base appressed to flowering stem. Flowers generally solitary, rarely up to four on slender 8-inch stems, pendant, petals recurved, deep yellow fading to white at base. May.

EUNOMIA (*Cruciferae*).

A genus of two species of alpine plants of which one is in cultivation and this is suitable for alpine house culture.

CULTIVATION. Compost A is ideal over good drainage and a good supply of water in spring and summer, dry but not arid in winter.

PROPAGATION. By seed sown in March, compost 2, or green cuttings in June. Repot every other year after flowering.

E. oppositifolia. (E).

A small sub-shrub with a woody base only an inch or so high but much branched. Leaves thickish, orbicular, smooth grey-green. Flowers on small stems up to twelve in terminal racemes, the usual crucifer, four-petalled, of light lavender. May. A native of Asia Minor.

EURYOPS (*Compositae*).

A race of shrubs confined to Africa and so not reliably hardy except in a cool greenhouse, but there is one species which although not common, is quite suitable for pan culture in the alpine house.

CULTIVATION. Compost A over good drainage, a fair supply of water in spring and summer, maintain dryish but not arid conditions in winter.

PROPAGATION. By green cuttings taken in July and rooted in the propagating frame. Repot every year after flowering.

E. evansii. (E).

This is a dwarf but erect shrublet rarely above 9 inches high and much branched. Leaves crowded, especially towards apex of the twigs, long narrow, grooved, recurved, top third dentate, silver-grey. Flowers solitary on short terminal stems, bright golden-yellow daisies. May. A native of the Drakensberg Mountains, S. Africa.

FELICIA (*Compositae*).

A genus of half hardy dwarf sub-shrubs or annuals closely related to the Aster which has given us one plant suitable for alpine house culture.

CULTIVATION. Compost A is suitable over good drainage and care is needed in watering, for this species will commence to flower in December, so although enough must be given, at no time must the compost be allowed to become sodden.

PROPAGATION. By green cuttings in June. Repot every year in April.

F. pappei. (E). (Syn. *Aster pappei*).

A native of S. Africa, this is a dwarf sub-shrub, much branched from a central rootstock, branches slender, lax, glandular. Leaves crowded, thick, linear, glandular, recurved, margins ciliate, light green. Flowers solitary on 9-inch glandular stems, many-rayed, petals of a china-blue with a central golden boss. January to December.

FORSYTHIA (*Oleaceae*).

A small genus of flowering shrubs which are grown extensively for their early spring beauty but much too large for the alpine house. There is a variety of *F. viridissima* which is quite suitable, rarely exceeding eight inches high even after a number of years.

CULTIVATION. Compost A is suitable with plenty of water during the growing season, dry but not arid conditions in winter.

PROPAGATION. By green cuttings in late June. Repot when necessary after flowering.

F. viridissima 'Bronxensis'. (D).
This variety originated in America and makes an erect much branched shrublet of glabrous stems about 8 inches high. Leaves after the flowers are lanceolate, entire, acute, pale green. Flowers up to three from lateral buds four-lobed, petals revolute, primrose-yellow. April.

FRANKENIA (*Frankeniaceae*).

A genus of plants mostly prostrate creeping sub-shrubs from the sea shores, hence their common name of Sea Heath, which has provided two suitable species for alpine house or frame culture.

CULTIVATION. They will do well in compost B over good drainage with a good supply of water while growing and flowering, just moist at other periods.

PROPAGATION. By careful division in April and keeping in a closed frame until re-established. Repot every other year in early April.

F. laevis. (E).
This is a prostrate sub-shrub rarely above an inch high rooting as it spreads. Leaves crowded, linear, sparsely ciliate at base, margins revolute, mid-green, changing through orange to crimson in late summer. Flowers terminal or from fork of branches, sessile, solitary, five-petalled, rose-pink. July. A native of Europe including Britain.

F. reuteri, see *F. thymifolia*.

F. thymifolia. (E). (Syn. *F. reuteri*).
A prostrate sub-shrub of crowded, close tufts of grey hairy stems about 1 inch high. Leaves congested, small, oblong, thick, covered with a fine down, grey-green in colour. Flowers fine textured, large, five-petalled, rose-red. July. A native of Spain.

FRITILLARIA (*Liliaceae*).

This is a large genus of bulbous plants with a wide distribution over the northern hemisphere, containing a number of species which are ideal for pan culture and with good cultivation increasing their floral display over the years. They have a bad name for being difficult to grow and there is no doubt a number should be placed in this category but the majority can with care be grown successfully. That they make good pan plants can be seen by the fact that a pan of *F. pyrenaica* containing three bulbs which I had grown for three years bore thirty-six flowers, and was given the R.H.S. Award of Merit.

CULTIVATION. They should be planted 3 inches deep in compost B in

September or October, but if obtained before this they must be kept in a mixture of moist peat and sharp sand until potted up, for these bulbs resent being exposed to the atmosphere for any period of time. Very little moisture is required until growth commences in the early part of the year when the soil must be kept moist. A bi-weekly dose of diluted liquid manure is beneficial when the flower buds are forming. After flowering reduce the water supply and give all available sun, but on no account should these bulbs be allowed to dry out completely. The crucial point of good cultivation is that during the dormant season the compost must contain a small degree of moisture but not enough to set up rotting. PROPAGATION. By seed sown as soon as ripe in compost 2, this should germinate the following spring and the small bulbils must not be disturbed until the foliage dies down the following year when they can be potted up in compost B. It will take these bulbs from four to six years to reach flowering size. Offsets or scales can also be used as a means of propagation, these being removed when repotting adult bulbs and then potting them up in compost B, where they will reach flowering size in three to four years. Repot when necessary in September, carefully removing some of the old compost and working in fresh.

F. acmopetala. (B).
A native of Syria, this has a stem up to 12 inches high with roughly six, long, linear, green leaves, spaced alternately up the stem. Flowers solitary, pendant, large, urn-shaped, petals recurved at mouth, olive-green streaked purple outside, inside shining yellow-green. April.

F. armena, see *F. caucasica*.

F. aurea, see *F. latifolia*.

F. biflora. (B).
Bears a stem about 6 inches high with up to six alternate, oblong-lanceolate green leaves. Flowers one to four pendant bell-shaped, dark greenish purple with a green band on each petal. April. A native of California.

F. camschatcensis. (B).
A native of Kamchatka and N.W. America, it forms a small scaly bulb from which arises a stem up to 12 inches high. Leaves borne on top half of stem are lanceolate, lower whorled, green. Flowers up to three, pendant, bell-shaped, purple-black. May.

F. caucasica. (B). (Syn. *F. armena*).
From a small bulb comes a 9-inch stem bearing up to four elliptic-lanceolate leaves on upper half. Flowers solitary, pendant, long bulbous shaped, shining dark metallic blue without, reddish brown-purple within. April. A native of Caucasus. The plant known as *F. armena* differs in having dark purple flowers.

F. cirrhosa. (B).
A native of the Himalayas it produces a stem up to 15 inches high with linear, obtuse, green leaves in twos or threes on the stem, upper leaves with tendrils at tip. Flowers pendant solitary, sometimes in pairs, long,

bell-shaped, wide at mouth, yellow tinged green, spotted brown inside, ridged on reverse. May.

F. citrina. (B).
A native of Greece, this bulb produces a stem up to 12 inches high clothed with narrow linear blue-green leaves. Flowers up to three, pendant, long open bell-shaped, pale yellow tinged green. April.

F. dasphylla. (B).
A small bulb with a stem up to 6 inches high and fleshy, oblong to lanceolate green leaves. Flowers solitary, rarely two, pendant, tubular, purple without, yellow inside. May. A native of Asia Minor.

F. drenovskii. (B).
A native of Bulgaria, this is a small bulb with a green stem up to 8 inches high. Leaves wide apart, linear, bluish green. Flowers up to three, cone-shaped, pendant, purple-brown or yellow, pale yellow, veined purple inside. April.

F. elwesii. (B).
With a stem up to 12 inches high and scattered lanceolate green leaves. Flowers solitary, pendant, bell-shaped, petals recurved green tinged purple, purple at tip. April. A native of Asia Minor.

F. glauca. (B).
A native of Oregon, U.S.A., making a small bulb and producing a stem rarely up to 6 inches high. Leaves four scattered, oblong-lanceolate, glaucous green. Flowers up to three, pendant, bell-shaped, purple suffused yellow-green. April.

F. graeca. (B).
Forms a stem up to 6 inches high with four to eight lanceolate green leaves. Flowers open bell-shaped, solitary, pendant, green, slightly chequered, margined red. A native of Greece. May.

F. karadaghensis. (B).
A native of Persia, this makes a smallish rounded bulb from which arises a 6-inch stem purple at base. Leaves green, linear-lanceolate, scattered on stem. Flowers up to three nodding or semi-erect, bell-shaped, yellow-green, marbled brown. May.

F. karelinii. (B).
A Central Asian species with 6-inch stems and linear to lanceolate grey-green leaves. Flowers from three to twelve, nodding, open, campanulate, rose-purple with green spotting outside, the centre of each petal has a slightly bulbous area. May.

F. lanceolata. (B).
A native of N.W. America, with 12-inch stems and glaucous green, wide lanceolate leaves. Flowers up to four deeply cut, pendant, open bell-shaped, dark purple, chequered greenish-yellow. May.

F. latifolia. (B). (Syn. *F. aurea*).
Has a small bulb from which arises a 6-inch, green marked brown stem. Leaves up to ten lanceolate, deep glossy green, scattered at base, in whorls

of three towards apex. Flowers solitary, pendant, squarish bell-shaped, deep purple, chequered yellowish-green. May. A native of Caucasus. *F. aurea* is only considered a form with light yellow flowers chequered red. May.

F. latifolia var. nobilis. (B).

This form is the plant which is generally sent out by nurserymen as *F. messanensis* but the true plant is quite distinct. A native of the Caucasus, rarely above 3 inches high with up to six broad lanceolate leaves, rarely scattered. Flowers large, solitary, semi-pendant open bell-shaped, deep brown-red, chequered green, very pronounced inside. May.

F. liliacea. (B).

A Californian species with a thick erect stem up to 6 inches high. Leaves green, linear to oblong-lanceolate in pairs. Flowers up to six, pendant, open campanulate, white veined green. April–May.

F. meleagris. (B).

This is a very variable species with a wide geographical distribution in Europe including Britain and is quite an easy species which does well in a pan. It is up to 9 inches high, with up to five scattered lanceolate glaucous green leaves. Flowers solitary, pendant, wine-purple chequered white with green veinings. April.

F. meleagris var. alba. (B).

This is the just as desirable white form of pendant flowers with green veinings. April–May.

F. messanensis. (B).

A native of Sicily and Crete, making a small rounded bulb with up to ten linear lanceolate, scattered leaves from centre of 10-inch stem, upper in whorl of three. Flowers solitary, pendant, long rounded bell-shaped, petals recurved, deep reddish blue, reddish brown towards mouth with broad olive-green middle band, green inside. April–May.

F. nigra. (B).

A species about 6 inches high with grass-like leaves in whorls of three at apex of stem. Flowers solitary, semi-pendant, tubular bell-shaped, deep purple-red, almost black in some lights, chequered purple-green, inside marbled green and purple. May. A native of the Mediterranean regions.

F. olivieri. (B).

A native of Persia, this makes a stem up to 15 inches high clothed with up to ten scattered leaves, basal linear, upper lanceolate. Flowers solitary, pendant, bell-shaped, margins recurved, yellow flushed red-brown, not chequered. May.

F. pluriflora. (B).

A New World species from California, with stem up to 12 inches high. Leaves basal, rarely above centre of stem, up to ten, wide, lanceolate, margins undulate. Flowers few, pendant with narrow obovate open petals, cut almost to base, deep pinkish-purple with central purple line. May.

F. pudica. (B).
Another American species from the N.W. States, with a stem approximately 6 inches high. Leaves up to six linear, scattered or in whorls of three at apex. Flowers solitary, rarely two, pendant, bell-shaped, rich yellow tinged purple at base. April.

F. pyrenaica. (B).
Possibly the best known of the European species, a native of the Pyrenees. Makes a stem up to 15 inches high with scattered, narrow lanceolate, smooth light green leaves. Flowers solitary, rarely two, pendant, roundish bell-shaped, petals recurved, brownish-purple spotted green, inside greenish-yellow. May.

F. roylei. (B).
A Himalayan species about 12 inches high. Leaves whorled in top half of stem, lanceolate. Flowers up to three, pendant, long bell-shaped, brownish-green, chequered reddish-purple inside. April.

F. sibthorpiana. (B).
A native of Greece, rarely above 6 inches high with scattered, glaucous green, linear to linear-lanceolate leaves. Flowers solitary, pendant, campanulate, yellow with red basal tinge. May.

F. tubiformis. (B).
A native of the Alpes Maritimes and S. Tyrol, this produces stems up to 6 inches high with four to six glaucous, lanceolate to linear leaves, situated half-way up the stem. Flowers solitary, semi-pendant, squat bell-shaped, velvety reddish-purple, faintly chequered reddish-yellow, chequering much more marked inside. April.

FUCHSIA (*Onagraceae*).

This genus is frowned upon by the alpine purist but there is no doubt that one species and several varieties make ideal specimens for late flowering in the alpine house.

CULTIVATION. Compost A is suitable over good drainage and these plants require a normal supply of water during the growing and flowering season. Keep dry but not arid in winter.

PROPAGATION. By cuttings taken at any time from June onwards and they root in a few weeks. Repot every year when growth commences in spring.

F. magellanica. (D).
The species from Magellan, S. America, is too large but has provided us with three suitable forms for alpine house culture.

F. magellanica 'Corallina'. (D).
This is a small shrub rarely above 3 inches high with reddish branches and deep green lanceolate-ovate, purple veined leaves. Flowers borne over a period of four months are pendant, with rich crimson sepals and purple petals. June–September. Garden origin.

F. magellanica 'Prunella'. (D).
Another delightful dwarf fuchsia less than 12 inches high with charming hanging flowers of scarlet sepals and purple petals. June–September. Garden origin.

F. magellanica 'Pumila'. (D).
A small compact shrublet only a few inches high with branches stained red. Leaves lanceolate-ovate, deep green, veined red. Flowers on slender stems, red sepals and purple petals. June–September. Garden origin.

F. procumbens. (D).
A native of New Zealand, making a dwarf prostrate shrub about 12 inches high with slender stems. Leaves alternate, almost circular, cordate at base, margins slightly dentate, deep green. Flowers solitary, erect, calyx tube yellow with green base, sepals recurved, tinged purple at apex, petals absent. July–August. Bears in September, large oblong red berries, ageing to purple.

GALANTHUS (*Amaryllidaceae*).

The Snowdrops are fine and well-known plants, flowering as they do in early spring and although best in the open ground, there are a few of the more delicate and rarer species which do well under alpine house or frame conditions.

CULTIVATION. All do well in compost B and should be planted six to a 5-inch pan in September about 1 inch deep, then placed outside in a cold frame and covered with peat until the buds are formed when they should be brought into the house for flowering. Water can be given in quantity while they are in flower, reducing this after the foliage dies down.

PROPAGATION. By seed in compost 2 sown as soon as ripe, or offsets planted up when repotting. Repot after flowering but while still in active growth, as all snowdrops move better while growing.

G. byzantinus. (B).
A native of Asia Minor, this has glaucous green leaves, margins plicate. Flowers white with inner segments marked green at tip and base. February.

G. caucasicus. (B).
A native of the Caucasus Mountains, with wide glaucous, recurved leaves. Flowers white marked green on tip of inner segments. February.

G. elwesii var. elwesii. (B).
From Asia Minor, with broad, glaucous, concave leaves. Flowers large, white, inner segments marked green at apex and from base up to midway. February.

G. elwesii 'Whittallii'. (B).
Similar to the type but with much larger flowers and inner segments sometimes almost completely tinged green. February.

G. fosteri. (B).
A native of Asia Minor, with dark green recurved leaves. Flowers large, white, inner segments green tinged up to midway and at apex. March.

G. graecus. (B).
From the Balkan Peninsula, with glaucous green, twisted, narrow lanceolate leaves. Flowers white, inner segments blotched green at apex and deep green from base. February.

G. plicatus. (B).
A native of the Crimea, with glaucous green leaves, margins folded. Flowers white, marked green at apex. March.

GAULTHERIA (*Ericaceae*).

This is an extremely interesting as well as being a very decorative genus of evergreen woodland plants having an extensive global distribution, with the exception of Europe. There are representatives in Australia, New Zealand, the Himalayas, China and America. All are floriferous and the flowers are generally succeeded by extremely decorative fruits, making the genus a very useful addition to a collection of alpine house or frame plants provided one attends to their few simple wants.

CULTIVATION. They will do well in compost C and must be kept moist at all periods, for dryness at the roots is fatal. The water used should be from a lime-free source as these plants will not tolerate lime in their compost. During the summer the pans are best plunged in a north facing frame in a cool draught-free spot and sprayed in the evenings during hot spells. Top-dress every spring with equal parts of leaf-mould, loam and sand.

PROPAGATION. By detaching small shoots of the current year's growth in August and root in the propagating frame. Seed sown in March in similar compost as advised for rhododendrons, compost 3 and subsequent treatment the same as for that genus. Repot only when the runners have reached the sides of the pan, the best time being when growth commences in spring. Care must be used not to disturb the roots unduly, as these plants are impatient of root disturbance.

G. adenothrix. (E).
A small shrublet less than 12 inches high with much branched almost contorted slender stems. Leaves alternate, thick leathery, ovate, glossy green, margins ciliate, reddish-brown, hairy beneath. Flowers solitary, on reddish-brown stems, pendant, urn-shaped, white flushed pink. June. Berries large, deep red. A native of Japan.

G. antipoda. (E).
There are a number of forms of this species, ranging from a few inches up to 18 inches in height and a choice should be made from dwarf growing specimens. Branches semi-prostrate, slender, very downy when young. Leaves alternate, ovate, coriaceous, dark green and glossy, margins serrate. Flowers solitary, pearly white on short hairy stems. June. Berries large, white and very attractive. This species should not be exposed to cold winds. New Zealand.

G. antipoda var. depressa, see *G. depressa*.

G. cumingiana. (E).
A native of Formosa, this makes a small shrub up to 12 inches high of slender red coloured branches. Leaves oval, serrate margins, apex pointed, thick, glossy dark green. Flowers globose urn-shaped, white flushed red. June. Berries reddish-brown.

G. cuneata. (E). (Syn. *G. pyroloides* var. *cuneata*).
A low compact shrublet rarely above 12 inches high with slender stems, hairy when young. Leaves narrow, ovate, leathery, dark green above, paler beneath, margins serrate. Flowers in terminal racemes, pendant, urn-shaped, white, similar to sprays of lily of the valley. June. Berries in clusters, globular, white. A native of W. China.

G. depressa. (E). (Syn. *G. antipoda* var. *depressa*).
A dwarf species botanically near to *G. antipoda* and was at one time only considered a dwarf form. It is smaller in all its parts rarely exceeding 6 inches in height with prostrate wiry stems. Leaves oval to orbicular, deep green, margins serrate and ciliate, reddish beneath. Flowers small solitary, white, pendant, urn-shaped. June. Berries large red globose. A native of New Zealand.

G. depressa 'Fructa Alba'. (E).
This is identical with the type but bearing large white globular fruits.

G. hispida. (E).
This species is a native of Australia and Tasmania, making up to 2 feet in its natural habitat but less than 12 inches in cultivation. Young wood hairy, leaves coriaceous, oval, pointed at apex, dark glossy green turning to reddish-brown, lighter below, margins serrate and bristly. Flowers in terminal panicles, urn-shaped, white. June. Berries globular, large, white.

G. humifusa. (E). (Syn. *G. myrsinites*).
This species is botanically near to *G. ovatifolia* but is smaller in all its parts. It forms a dwarf shrublet of tufted habit with erect branches up to 4 inches high, sparsely clothed with long hairs. Leaves oval, cordate at base, coriaceous, margins serrate, dark green, slightly hairy. Flowers solitary, on short stems, urn-shaped, white flushed pink. June. Berries globular scarlet. A native of British Columbia.

G. miqueliana. (E).
A native of Japan, this is a dwarf shrublet rarely above 8 inches high in its natural habitat and more likely to be less than 4 inches under pan culture. Well branched semi-prostrate wiry stems. Leaves ovate, coriaceous, margins serrate, deeply veined, glossy deep green above, paler beneath. Flowers in terminal racemes up to six white, green based or red flushed, urn-shaped. June. Fruits rounded white, well marked with depressions.

G. myrsinites, see *G. humifusa.*

G. nummularioides. (E).
A small Himalayan shrublet, only a few inches high with compact dense tufts of slender hairy stems. Leaves small, cordate, leathery, dull deep green above, paler, glossy beneath. Flowers solitary, from the underneath

of the leaf axils, white tinged pink. August. Fruits black. Needs shelter from the cold winds.

G. nummularioides var. minor, see *G. nummularioides* var. *nummularifolia*.

G. nummularioides var. minuta. (E).
A native of W. China, it is roughly a quarter of the size of the preceding species but more generous with its dainty urn-shaped solitary flowers of a curious shade of brownish-red. June. Fruits not seen.

G. nummularioides var. nummularifolia. (E). (Syn. *G.n.* var. *minor*).
Larger than the foregoing variety but even so less than 2 inches high, similar in structure but unfortunately rarely bearing its white flushed pink flowers or black roundish berries. June. A native of W. China.

G. ovatifolia. (E).
An outstanding dwarf trailing shrublet rarely above 4 inches high with semi-erect branchlets. Leaves oval, rounded at base, very coriaceous, bright dark green, heavily marked, margins serrate. Flowers solitary from the leaf axils, urn-shaped, pink. June. Berries flattish, scarlet. A native of N.W. America.

G. procumbens. (E).
A native of N. America, this is a prostrate plant of tufted habit, up to 4 inches high with slender, reddish hairy stems. Leaves borne at the apex of the branches, oval, minutely serrate, leathery, dark glossy green above, paler beneath, margins bristly, turning to shades of bronze and red in autumn. Flowers pendulous, urn-shaped, pinkish-white, are borne in the axils of the leaves at the apex of the branches. June. Berries globular, scarlet.

G. pyrolifolia. (E). (Syn. *G. pyroloides*).
A dwarf creeping plant of tufted habit, a native of the Himalayas, where it makes dense mats of slender stems rarely up to 4 inches high. Leaves at apex of shoots, oval, thick dark glossy green above, hairy beneath, margins serrate, Flowers up to six on terminal racemes, white flushed pink. May. Berries globular, black.

G. pyroloides, see *G. pyrolifolia*.

G. pyroloides var. cuneata, see *G. cuneata*.

G. rupestris. (E).
This species, a native of New Zealand, makes a prostrate dwarf shrub about 6 inches high of much-branched, bristly wiry stems. Leaves oval, thinnish, bright glossy green above, paler beneath, margins bristly, serrulate. Flowers on reddish stems, pendant, petal lobes recurved, white tinged pink. June. Berries globular, bright red. Needs shelter from cold winds.

G. sinensis. (E).
A Chinese species, up to 12 inches high with congested slender stems covered with appressed reddish hairs. Leaves oblong to ovate, dark glossy green, margins bristly, serrate. Flowers solitary from the leaf axils on short stems, white with recurved petal lobes. May. Berries globular, bright blue.

G. thymifolia. (E).
This is an outstanding dwarf shrublet from N. China, rarely above 6 inches high with prostrate reddish stems, sparsely clothed with long hairs. Leaves small, long narrow, recurved towards apex, tapered at both ends, margins serrate, glossy green above turning reddish in the adult stage, paler beneath. Flowers solitary from terminal axils, white urn-shaped. June. Fruits large roundish, lilac blue with persistent five-lobed fleshy, deep violet calyx, an attractive combination.

G. trichophylla. (E).
A good dwarf compact shrublet with lax stems up to 3 inches high. Leaves sessile, oblong to oval, deep bright green above, paler beneath, margins ciliate and slightly serrulate. Flowers solitary from the leaf axils, bell-shaped, pinkish-white. June. Berries globular, bright blue. A native of W. China.

GAYLUSSACIA *(Ericaceae)*.

A genus of plants confined to America, the Huckleberry has a close affinity to Vaccinium and has produced two species suitable for alpine house or frame culture.
CULTIVATION. Compost C is suitable with plenty of lime-free water during the growing and flowering season, just moist at other periods. The plants are best plunged into a cool north or west facing, shady plunge bed during the hot summer months and benefit from overhead spraying in the evenings.
PROPAGATION. By green cuttings in June, rooting these in the propagating frame. Seed in compost 3 when ripe.

G. brachycera. (E). (Syn. *Vaccinium brachycerum*).
A close compact shrub up to 12 inches high with erect wiry, triangular downy stems. Leaves small, crowded, oval to ovate, leathery, bright glossy green, lightly dentate, margins revolute, turning a brilliant red in autumn. Flowers erect in small dense clusters on top third of laterals, from the leaf axils, urn-shaped, white flushed pink. April–May. Fruits bluish, pear-shaped. A native of E. America.

G. dumosa. (D). (Syn. *Vaccinium hirtellum*).
The dwarf Huckleberry is a small much-branched shrub rarely 12 inches high, young wood glandular hairy. Leaves entire, obovate, pointed at apex, green covered with glandular down. Flowers campanulate, pendant in small axillary racemes, white flushed pink. May–June. Fruit globose black. A native of N.E. America.

GENISTA *(Leguminosae)*.

The Brooms have a wide distribution although almost exclusively European, but there are one or two outlying species in Asia and N. Africa. It is a large genus of flowering shrubs, generally in the wild of some hue of yellow, ranging from pale to golden and closely allied to Cytisus, there being only a slight botanical difference between the two genera.

CULTIVATION. This is simple provided their two essential needs are attended to, these being a love of sun and their dislike of root disturbance. Compost A is suitable over good drainage with plenty of water while growing and flowering, this can be reduced during late July to allow a thorough ripening of the new wood. Dry but not arid in winter.

PROPAGATION. By seed sown in March, compost 2, or cuttings with a heel taken in late July and placed in the propagating frame where they should stay until the following spring. Repot only when necessary, for root restriction will help to maintain the dwarf congested habit which is a characteristic feature of these delightful shrubs. This is best carried out in early spring. Care must be taken when repotting not to disturb the roots or break them, for they will quickly show their resentment of this treatment.

G. aspalathoides. (D). (Syn. *G. lobelli*).
A tiny prostrate shrublet rarely above 3 inches high with grooved branches, hairy when young, smooth and spiny tipped when mature. Leaves minute, linear-lanceolate, grey-green with appressed hairs. Flowers from the leaf axils, in small clusters up to four, pea-shaped, light yellow. June. A native of S.W. Europe and N. Africa.

G. dalmatica. (D). (Syn. *G. sylvestris* var. *pungens*).
This makes a delightful semi-prostrate plant up to 6 inches high with tufted habit. Branches wiry, angled, covered with hairs and terminating in sharp spines. Leaves small, linear, hirsute, light green. Flowers in upright terminal racemes, golden yellow. June. A native of Dalmatia.

G. delphinensis. (D). (Syn. *G. sagittalis* var. *minor*).
At one time only considered a dwarf form of *G. sagittalis*, it has now been given specific status. It is a very prostrate shrublet only an inch or so high, with zig-zagged winged branches. Leaves oval, light grey-green, appressed to the stems. Flowers up to three in erect, terminal clusters of a light golden-yellow. June. A native of the Pyrenees.

G. genuensis, see *G. januensis*.

G. horrida. (D).
This, a native of S.W. Europe including the mountains of Central Spain, requires as much sun as our summers will allow otherwise it is doubtful if this species will flower well. A small shrublet less than 12 inches high under pan culture with interlaced stems of grey-green terminating in a sharp spine. Leaves trifoliolate, grey-green covered with silky hairs. Flowers in small terminal clusters, bright yellow. June.

G. januensis. (D). (Syn. *G. genuensis, G. triangularis, G. scariosa, G. triquetra*).
A species with a fairly wide distribution in Central and S.E. Europe, which has given rise to the many synonyms under which it is known. It makes a small dwarf plant only 3 inches high with glabrous, three angled stems. Leaves short, narrow, ovate, dark green, smooth with

transparent margins. Flowers solitary from the terminal leaf axils on 2-inch stems, bright yellow. June.

G. lobelli, see *G. aspalathoides.*

G. patula. (D).

This is a native of S.E. Europe, where it makes a low prostrate, slow growing shrublet only a few inches high with deeply grooved and glabrous lax stems. Leaves thin, short, narrow, tipped at apex, mid-green. Flowers solitary from the leaf axils, a fine golden yellow. June.

G. pilosa. (D).

A good dwarf shrub rarely above 6 inches high in cultivation, although it is much taller in its native habitat. Stems slender, prostrate when young becoming more erect when mature. Leaves small, narrow pointed to oval, bright green above, lighter beneath due to the extensive covering of greyish-white hairs. Flowers solitary from the leaf axils, on small stems, clear yellow. June. A native of S.E. Europe including S. England.

G. procumbens, see *Cytisus procumbens.*

G. prostrata, see *Cytisus decumbens.*

G. pulchella, see *G. villarsii.*

G. sagittalis var. minor, see *G. delphinensis.*

G. scariosa, see *G. januensis.*

G. sericea. (D).

A dwarf shrublet about 9 inches high with erect, twiggy, hairy growth. Leaves simple, small, narrow, tapered at both ends, bright green, glabrous above, margins ciliate, hairy beneath. Flowers in terminal racemes clustered together, golden-yellow. June. A native of Tyrol and Dalmatia.

G. sylvestris. (D).

A species from S.E. Europe, making an erect shrub of twiggy angular stems about 12 inches high. Leaves linear, smooth, deep green. Flowers in terminal clusters, bright yellow. June.

G. sylvestris var. procumbens. (D).

This is a dwarf rock loving form of the species up to 3 inches high with angular twiggy stems. Leaves minute, linear, crowded, deep green. Flowers in terminal racemes, golden-yellow. June. A native of the Balkans.

G. sylvestris var. pungens, see *G. dalmatica.*

G. tinctoria. (D).

This species is too large for the alpine house or even the rock garden, but it has produced two dwarf forms which are suitable for our purpose.

G. tinctoria var. anxantica. (D).

A native of Italy, it forms a mass of grooved, twiggy stems only 3 inches high. Leaves narrow, pointed deep green. Flowers in erect, terminal racemes, clear yellow. June.

G. tinctoria var. humifusa. (D).

This is a prostrate shrublet up to 3 inches high with closely congested twiggy branches. Leaves minute, ovate, pointed, bright green. Flowers in terminal clusters, bright yellow. June. A native of S.E. Europe.

G. triangularis, see *G. januensis.*
G. triquetra, see *G. januensis.*
G. villarsii. (D). (Syn. *G. pulchella*).
From Dalmatia and S.E. France, this species is a charming plant only an inch or so high forming a mat of interlaced, grooved twigs. Leaves thin, minute, linear, hairy on both sides, grey. Flowers solitary from the leaf axils at the apex of the laterals, golden-yellow. June.

GENTIANA *(Gentianaceae).*

This is a large and mighty genus of both high and sub-alpine plants inhabiting a wide expanse of territory over many mountain ranges of the world, but it is the European and Asiatic species which dominate the scene in cultivation although a few from the New World are slowly arriving here. It is with impatience that we await the re-introduction of the scarlet gentians from the Andes for their first stay was but a fleeting visit, leaving us with but a memory of their flamboyant charms.

As pan plants gentians are for the most part difficult and few are really suitable for this purpose although a number will grow and flower under these conditions for a few years, rivalling all other forms of alpine plants with their intensity of colour, especially in the high alpine species.

CULTIVATION. In such a varied race only general hints can be given here and more specific directions dealt with in the notes on each species or varieties. The majority of gentians resent root disturbance once established and repotting requires care. Plenty of water is necessary during the growing season and the plants should be kept moist in winter, some of the Asiatics resent lime in any form, but this will be dealt with when they are described.

PROPAGATION. By seed sown as soon as ripe in compost 2; if left until the following spring germination will be spasmodic, the period ranging from one to four years before complete germination takes place. The seedlings should be handled with care, making sure the roots are not broken or unnecessarily disturbed, and potted on as soon as the first true leaves are formed. Division can be used with some of the species and where this applies the month will be given individually. The divided plants must be carefully watched and kept in a cool shaded frame until re-established. Repotting should only be carried out when necessary after flowering, for the early flowering plants, and in April for the autumn species.

G. acaulis. (E).
The well known *G. acaulis* is mentioned here because of its well-beloved flowers of large blue trumpets which decorate the high alpine meadows in the European Alps in early spring. The name covers a variety of plants, similar in flower in the garden, but with very little botanical standing being but a synonym covering such forms as, *angustifolia, clusii, kochiana* etc. Still for our purpose it is far better to retain the specific name *G. acaulis* and treat those described here as varieties.

G. acaulis var. alba. (E).
This is a good white form sometimes found where the type plant grows in the European Alps. It is a tufted plant of deep glossy green narrow-ovate basal leaves, pointed at apex, stem leaves smaller and ovate. Flowers solitary on 2-inch stems, wide trumpets of snow-white with green veining. April–May. Compost B over good drainage, division in June. Lime-free water.

G. acaulis var. alpina, see *G. alpina*.

G. acaulis var. angustifolia. (E).
A native of the Jura and Dauphiné, it differs from the type in having long, narrow pointed glossy green leaves and single, large, open-mouthed trumpets of deep blue on 4-inch stems. June. Compost B, good drainage, division in June.

G. acaulis var. clusii. (E).
With typical foliage in tufts, margins rough and on 3-inch stems large open trumpets of deep blue, pale in the throat, interior of tube spotted green. May. A native of the Central and Eastern Alps. Compost B, good drainage, division in June.

G. acaulis var. excisa, see *G.a.* var. *kochiana*.

G. acaulis var. kochiana. (E). (Syn. *G.a.* var. *excisa*).
Another tufted plant with basal leaves in rosette formation, lax, soft, ovate deep glossy green, stem leaves smaller. Flowers solitary on 2-inch stems, large, wide open-mouthed trumpets of azure-blue, speckled green inside. June. A native of the European Alps. Compost B, good drainage, division in July. Lime-free water.

G. alpina. (E). (Syn. *G. acaulis* var. *alpina*).
Near to the *acaulis* group, it is a native of Spain, Pyrenees and Swiss Alps, making basal tufts of broadly elliptic, thick deep glossy green leaves in rosette formation, stem leaves narrower. Flowers solitary on 2-inch stems, wide trumpets, deep blue, darker at base, spotted green inside. April–May. Compost B, good drainage, lime-free water. Division after flowering.

G. angulosa. (E). (Syn. *G. verna* var. *angulosa*).
This, a native of the Caucasus mountains is generally regarded as a geographical form of *G. verna* but has been accorded specific rank with its larger flowers and five pronounced wings on the calyx tube. It makes basal rosettes of green, oblong-lanceolate leaves, stem leaves small ovate. Flowers solitary on 3-inch stems, open saucer-shaped, rich deep blue, calyx-tube bagged and angled. April. Compost A, with good drainage and lime-free water.
PROPAGATION. By seed compost 2, sown when ripe, keeping them moving while young, resents root disturbance.

G. bavarica. (E).
A moisture-loving plant from the high alpine meadows of Europe. It makes tufts in rosette formation of basal, spatulate, thick, yellow-green

leaves, smaller at the base, stem leaves smaller and rounded. Flowers solitary on 3-inch stems, open saucer-shaped, rich deep blue, calyx-tube long, narrow angled. July. A difficult plant to keep in good health, needing compost A, with faultless drainage and lime-free water in quantities at all times while growing and flowering, just moist afterwards. Will grow well in compost D, if started off as a seedling but under these conditions too much water cannot be given. Propagation by seed in compost 2, when ripe.

G. brachyphylla. (E).

An even more difficult plant from high altitudes in the European mountains. It makes close basal tufts of thick, small, rhomboid overlapping green leaves with rough margins. Flowers solitary on 1-inch stems, open saucer-shaped, deep blue, calyx-tube long, narrow angled. June. Seedlings potted in compost D have the best chance of success with plenty of water while in growth, just moist at other times. Propagation is by seed sown when ripe, compost 2, moving them direct into compost D when large enough to handle and must be kept growing when young; any dryness at root is fatal. July.

G. cachemirica. (H).

A native of the Himalayas, this is a dwarf prostrate plant with leaves in rosette formation, basal leaves narrow ovate, upper, glaucous grey-green. Flowers solitary, or up to three on semi-procumbent 4-inch stems, tubular bell-shaped, bright blue, striped white and deeper blue with fringed plicae. July–August. Compost A, with good drainage and plenty of water while growing, keep dry but not arid after dying down. Propagation is by seed sown when ripe, compost 2.

G. farreri. (H).

An outstanding Asiatic gentian from W. China, makes a central tuft of linear-lanceolate green leaves with recurved tip. Flowering stem prostrate, slender, bearing solitary upturned narrow bell-shaped, open-mouthed flower of Cambridge blue, striped violet, greenish-blue at base, throat white. August–September. Does well in compost C and should be kept moist while growing and flowering. Propagation is by seed sown in September, compost 2, or careful division in April.

G. froelichii. (E).

A native of Austria, it makes lax rosettes of linear-oblong, thick glossy green leaves, margins revolute, stem leaves small, ovate. Flowers solitary on 2-inch stems, tubular bell-shaped, light blue, lobes erect, pointed with small pointed plicae. July. Needs careful cultivation in compost A or seedlings in compost D, plenty of water whilst in growth, just moist at other periods, resents disturbance. Propagation is by seed sown as soon as ripe in compost 2 and seedlings placed in their permanent quarters while still young.

G. georgei. (E).

A native of W. China, making basal rosettes of ovate-oblong leaves, green tinged purple, margins rough, stem-leaves oblong. Flowers solitary, sessile, tubular bell-shaped, deep purple-blue, lined green, paler and spotted throat. August–September. Needs careful cultivation in compost A with plenty of water during the growing season, keep dry but not arid in winter. Propagation is by seed in compost 2. March.

G. gilvo-striata. (E).
Forms a central crown of oblanceolate grey-green leaves from which prostrate runners with rosettes of spatulate glaucous leaves are produced. Flowers solitary on short stems, conical, pale greenish-blue with deep striping of purplish-brown outside, paler within. September. A native of Burma. Compost B will suit this species, with plenty of lime-free water while growing, keep just moist in winter. Propagation is by seed in compost 2, or cuttings of non-flowering shoots in July.

G. 'Hexa-Farreri'. (H). (*G. farreri* × *G. hexaphylla*).
A garden hybrid which is less open than *G. farreri*, making tufts of lanceolate green leaves. Flowers large, solitary, bell-shaped, deep blue, lined inside and out. August. Compost B with good drainage, plenty of water while in growth, keep dry but not arid in winter. Propagation by seed when ripe. Compost 2.

G. hexaphylla. (H).
A native of Tibet, it bears small linear, grey-green leaves in whorls of six on short stems. Flowers solitary on prostrate 3-inch stems, erect, six-lobed conical, pale blue, spotted green with dark green markings. July. Compost B with plenty of lime-free water in spring and summer, keep dry but not arid in winter. Propagation is by division in April or seed sown when ripe in compost 2.

G. 'Inverleith'. (H). (*G. farreri* × *G. veitchiorum*).
One of the best of the garden hybrids making a prostrate plant with thick, narrow linear-oblong, recurved green leaves, stem leaves shorter. Flowers solitary on 6-inch stems, long open tubular, deep Cambridge blue. September. Compost B is suitable with plenty of water during the growing season, just moist in winter. Propagation is by careful division in March.

G. kurroo. (E).
A Himalayan species, making basal rosettes of lanceolate, blunt, green leaves, stem leaves small linear. Flowers solitary on 6-inch stems, radiating from the basal rosettes, ascending at tip, narrow bell-shaped, deep blue, lighter at throat and spotted green. October. Compost B over good drainage, plenty of lime-free water, keep just moist in winter. Propagation is by seed when available, sometimes not set due to lateness in flowering. Compost 2. March.

G. lawrencei. (H).
A native of Siberia, similar to *G. farreri* but smaller, making a central rootstock with radiating 4-inch procumbent branches. Leaves linear, almost needle shaped, acute, recurved, light green, stem leaves smaller. Flowers solitary, turquoise blue, with blue bands, fading to very pale

blue at base. July. Compost C kept moist with lime-free water, keep dry but not arid in winter. Propagation is by seed sown when ripe in compost 2 or careful division in April.

G. loderi. (E).
A native of Kashmir, making a tidy close tufted rootstock from which radiates prostrate stems about 4 inches long. Leaves crowded, broad elliptic, thick, rounded, glaucous-grey with rough margins. Flowers upright, solitary, long tubular, wide open lobes, plicae upright and fringed pale blue. July. Cultivation in compost A with plenty of water while in growth, just moist in winter. Propagation is by seed in compost 2 when ripe.

G. 'Macaulayi'. (H). (*G. farreri* × *G. sino-ornata*).
A fine garden hybrid with prostrate radiating branches from a central rootstock. Leaves linear to lanceolate, tapering to point, tip recurved, light green. Flowers solitary, open funnel shaped, rich deep blue, plicae small and abrupt. September. Cultivation in compost C, plenty of lime-free water in spring and summer, just moist at other periods. Propagation is by careful division in March.

G. newberryi. (H).
A New World species from Oregon, N. America, making 2-inch tufts of basal rosettes with spatulate, green leaves, pointed at apex, stem leaves smaller. Flowers solitary, rarely two, conical, pale blue with five broad bronze bands outside, interior white, speckled green. July. Cultivation in compost B with faultless drainage, plenty of lime-free water while in growth, just moist at other periods. Propagation is by seed, compost 2.

G. ornata. (H).
One of the finest of the Asiatic species in cultivation and is not as difficult as is sometimes suggested. Makes basal rosettes with 4-inch prostrate stems ascending at apex, leaves bright glossy green, basal narrow linear, acute, stem leaves smaller. Flowers solitary at apex of stem, rounded bell-shaped, clear pale blue outside, striped purple-brown and cream, white within. A native of Nepal, it flowers in August. Does well in compost B over good drainage, plenty of lime-free water while in growth, just moist in winter. Propagation is best by careful division in March, or seed in compost 2.

G. prolata. (H).
A species from Sikkim and Bhutan, making mats of small tufts and 6-inch branched prostrate stems. Leaves narrow oblong with abrupt point, smaller towards base, bright green. Flowers solitary, terminal, erect, narrow tubular, pale blue with cream bands, corolla lobes and plicae erect. July. Cultivation in compost B with plenty of lime-free water while in growth, just moist in winter. Propagation is by seed sown in compost 2 when ripe.

G. pyrenaica. (H).
A difficult plant in cultivation but it can be grown with care, as plants

are sometimes seen at a number of alpine shows. It forms basal tufts with
3-inch stems, basal leaves crowded, linear-lanceolate with abrupt pointed
apex and rough margins. Flowers solitary, deep violet-blue, narrow
obconic, corolla lobes and plicae erect. May–June. A native of the Pyrenees
and Asia. Cultivation is best in compost C with good drainage. Plenty
of water while growing and flowering, just moist in winter. Propagation
is by seed in compost 2.

G. saxosa. (E).

A charming species from New Zealand, which has proved quite easy
in cultivation unlike the majority of alpine plants from the southern
hemisphere. It forms a central crown with tufted rosettes, from which
radiate the almost black prostrate stems, leaves of basal rosettes spatulate,
stem leaves linear-spatulate, fleshy, deep shiny green tinged brownish-
purple. Flowers in small terminal cymes, wide open star-shaped, white,
veined purple. July. Does well in compost A with plenty of water while
growing, keep dry but not arid in winter. Propagation is easy by seed,
compost 2.

G. stragulata. (E).

This is a prostrate plant from Yunnan, only an inch or so high forming
tufted shoots with 2 inch stems. Leaves basal, obovate in rosette formation,
stem leaves ovate, rounded at apex, shiny green. Flowers up to three in
terminal clusters, long tubular, restricted at throat, violet-blue, on inside
throat deeper, plicae bifid, tinged white. July. A far from easy species
requiring care in compost A with good drainage and a normal supply of
water during early spring and summer, keep dry but not arid in winter.
Propagation is by cuttings taken in July or seed if available sown in
compost 2.

G. veitchiorum. (E).

A native of W. China, it makes a basal rosette from which radiates up
to 4-inch procumbent branching stems. Basal leaves linear-oblong to
narrow spatulate, stem leaves shorter, acute, green. Flowers solitary at
apex of each stem, narrow tubular, deep royal blue, with greenish-yellow
bands, spreading lobes and wide plicae. July–August. It does well in
compost C, with good drainage and requires plenty of lime-free water
while growing, keep dry but not arid in winter. Propagation is by careful
division in March or cuttings in July.

G. verna. (E).

This is the well known Spring Gentian of high altitudes, distributed over
a very wide range of countries including Britain, Asia, the Caucasus,
Turkestan, Siberia etc. It is a loosely tufted plant of erect inbranched stems
up to 3 inches high. Leaves ovate to spatulate, stem leaves smaller, bright
green. Flowers solitary at apex of shoots, erect, open five twisted lobes,
deep azure with bifid, white tipped plicae and long tubular calyx. April–
May. This gentian requires to be grown in quantity to do well, for a
single specimen in a pan will not thrive for long. It is far better to put

up to twelve seedlings in a 6-inch pan using compost B, and firming well. With careful watering these will spread into a good sized clump. Propagation is by seed in compost 2 sown as soon as ripe.

G. verna var. alba. (E).
This is the charming but very rare albino which to my mind is less desirable than the type.

G. verna var. angulosa, see *G. angulosa.*

GERANIUM (*Geraniaceae*).

To most non-gardeners, geranium means the 'dot' plants used extensively by the bedding plant specialist, or the ever-perennial window decoration which grows longer every winter as its scarlet flowers grow less. The only right they have to the name is that they are distant cousins from a sub-tropical land attempting, one must admit with a great deal of success, to oust the rightful holders. The genus is a large one with two hundred species, inhabiting the temperate zones of the world and they provide the rock garden and the herbaceous border with a grand selection of floriferous plants, also a few which can be used for alpine house or frame culture.

CULTIVATION. The Cranesbills are not fastidious plants and will do well in compost A. A rich diet is to be avoided otherwise the plants will have a tendency to make foliage instead of flower. Give plenty of water while growing and flowering, keep dry but not arid at other times.

PROPAGATION. By seed, compost 1 in March, or division of the plants in April. Repot when necessary after flowering, generally every other year.

G. argenteum. (H).
A small tufted plant from a perennial rootstock about 3 inches high with almost all radical five parted leaves of glistening silver; lobes trifid, segments linear. Flowers large, up to two on 3-inch stems, rounded saucer-shaped, pink with darker veinings. June. A native of N. Italy.

G. argenteum var. album. (H).
This is the charming white form found by the late Mr Walter Ingwersen in the Julian Alps and well worthy of a place amongst other alpine house plants.

G. argenteum var. roseum. (H).
A form with dark cerise flowers.

G. cinereum. (H).
A native of the Pyrenees, making a tufted plant up to 5 inches high. Leaves grey-green five to seven lobed, lobes obovate with three segments. Flowers open rounded five-lobed emarginate, reddish-pink with purple veinings. June.

G. cinereum var. subcaulescens. (H). (Syn. *G. subcaulescens*).
This is the geographical form from the Balkans about 4 inches high.

Leaves similar but bright green. Flowers open rounded five-lobed of a
deep crimson with a black eye. June.

G. dalmaticum. (H).

A fine species from the Balkan Peninsula, which has come to the fore in
recent years. It makes small rhizomes with 4-inch stems. Leaves glabrous
five-fid with three obovate segments, bright green. Flowers on erect
branching stems open rounded entire, five-lobed, clear pink with coral
anthers. June.

G. farreri, see *G. napuligerum.*

G. napuligerum. (H). (Syn. *G. farreri*).

This makes short tufts from a small rhizome with fine downy slender
stems up to 3 inches high. Leaves reniform five-fid, segments obovate,
three-lobed, bright green with red margins and stalks. Flowers in pairs
on branched stems, five-lobed rounded, deckled margins, pale lavender-
pink, black anthers. May–August. A native of W. China.

G. sessiliflorum. (H).

A native of Australia and New Zealand, this is a small dwarf tap-rooted
perennial from which are produced tufts of congested, almost radical
five to seven lobed silver-grey leaves. Flowers sessile, small rounded
five-lobed, white with black anthers. May–June. Propagation is by
careful division in April.

G. subcaulescens, see *G. cinereum* var. *subcaulescens.*

GEUM (*Rosaceae*).

A small genus of plants providing but one species which is suitable for
pan culture and this is far from easy but with care can be induced to
settle down. I have grown it well in compost D using a wide shallow pan
and provided it is kept moist this species should not prove too difficult.
Propagation is by seed in compost 2 in March or lifting rooted runners
in May and kept close until re-established. Repot only when necessary.

G. reptans. (E).

This is a native of the European Alps, and no trace of this plant is seen
until one is well clear of the tree line, in fact it is on the topmost screes
at the edge of the snow line where this plant appears, threading its way
in any crack or crevice in the huge boulders that abound in these screes.
It forms a prostrate plant with a creeping rootstock producing runners.
Leaves interruptedly pinnatifid with ovate lobes, segments rounded, cut
and slightly recurved, mid-green. Flowers solitary, erect on short stems,
large rounded, golden-yellow. June. Followed by a fluffy silvery seed
head in a conical spiral.

GLAUCIDIUM (*Podophyllaceae*).

A genus containing one single species, this is an outstanding alpine house
plant which although rare is not difficult, provided its few wants are
attended to.

CULTIVATION. Is best in compost C, a cool soil with plenty of lime-free water while growing and flowering, just moist at other periods. Must be kept in a cool shady frame during the hot summer months and returned to the alpine house in the autumn.

PROPAGATION. By seed in compost 3 in March. Repot every third year after flowering.

G. palmatum. (H).

A native of Japan, it has a small tuberous rhizome from which appear unbranched 9-inch stems. Leaves two on upper third of stem, large, palmately five to seven lobed, base cordate, lobes ovate, veins pubescent, margins serrate, apex pointed, mid-green. Flowers solitary, terminal, large, four petaloid sepals of pale lavender blue. May. At the base of the flower is borne a large leafy bract, nearly orbicular, margins serrate, green.

GLOBULARIA (*Globulariaceae*).

This is a small genus of shrub-like plants forming compact cushions, for the alpine house as they do better under pan culture, there being a hint of frost tenderness after a mild winter outdoors. When well established the species are very floriferous and provide ample colour with their dainty powder puffs, generally of a pale blue shade.

CULTIVATION. This is best in compost A with good drainage, plenty of water while growing and flowering, just moist in winter.

PROPAGATION. By division in April or green cuttings in July. Repot every other year after flowering.

G. bellidifolia. (E).

A tight compact species 2 inches high, in close tufts with notched cordate leaves, deep glossy green and deeper blue powder puffs on almost sessile stems. June. A native of S. Europe.

G. cordifolia. (E).

A fine well-known rock plant making a cushion of tufted woody compact branchlets up to 3 inches high. Leaves alternate, crowded in rosettes, cordate, emarginate, bright glossy green. Flowers on erect 2-inch stems, congested into a globular head, bright mid-blue. June. A native of the Alps, Tyrol and S. Europe.

G. cordifolia var. alba. (E).

This is the charming white form of the species and very desirable. June.

G. incanescens. (E).

A dwarf cushion of interlaced branchlets up to 3 inches high. Leaves heart-shaped, congested, glaucous blue. Flowers on 2-inch erect stems, sparsely clad with small oval leaves, dainty congested balls of light blue. A native of S.E. Europe. June.

G. nana. (E).

An outstanding species though only an inch in height, making a close compact mass of interlaced laterals. Leaves minute, cordate, deep glossy

green. Flowers almost sessile, powder puffs of congested lilac-blue. June.
A native of Europe.

G. spinosa. (E).

This species is a very rare Spanish endemic, a truly saxatile plant which
although it grows in compost A will do much better in compost D with
plenty of water during the growing season. It makes a completely prostrate
mat of very congested interlaced glabrous branches. Leaves in rosettes,
minute, oblong, margins serrate, mid greenish-grey in colour. Flowers
on 1-inch stems, bright blue in a tight globular head. June.

G. stygia. (E).

Another rare species this time from Greece and needs similar cultural
treatment to that of *G. spinosa*. A dwarf cushion plant with still laxer
stems, only an inch or so in height. Leaves thick, crowded, small roundish-
ovate, wedge-shaped, smooth, bright green. Flowers on the smallest of
stems, rounded heads of black buds opening to clear bright blue. June.

G. trichosantha. (E).

A cushion of stiff crowded branches up to 3 inches high. Leaves crowded,
spatulate, toothed at apex, bright glossy green. Flowers on 6-inch stems,
clothed with linear, pointed foliage, rounded fluffy-balls of greyish-blue.
May. A native of Europe.

G. willkommii. (E).

A native of S. Europe, it makes a close congested mat only an inch high.
Leaves small, crowded, obovate to spatulate, narrowing at base, smooth,
green. Flowers on small stems, globular heads of bright blue. May.

GREVILLEA (*Proteaceae*).

A large genus of half hardy and greenhouse plants which has produced
one species that is hardy in sheltered gardens in the warmer districts,
and this plant makes an ideal specimen for the alpine house.

CULTIVATION. Compost B with lime-free water, a normal supply
during spring and summer, just moist at other periods.

PROPAGATION. By semi-ripened cuttings taken in July and rooted in the
propagating frame, repot every year in early April.

G. alpina. (E). (Syn. *G. alpestris*).

A native of S. Australia, it makes a small shrub with erect branches and
many laterals, reaching 18 inches high in time. Leaves sessile, crowded,
obtuse, downy above, hairy beneath, margins recurved, deep green. The
flowers are borne in small terminal clusters, long, narrow, tubular, base
swollen, red at throat, yellow at mouth with a curiously shaped long,
thick protruding style and stigma. This plant is rarely out of flower,
making it an attractive specimen for the alpine house. May to September.

GUNNERA (*Haloragidaceae*).

My first aquaintance with this pygmy of a race containing many giants
was in the alpine house at the Edinburgh Botanic Gardens from which I

was fortunate in obtaining a plant. It is certainly a worthwhile specimen if only to surprise most of those gardeners who see it for the first time and ask its genus.

CULTIVATION. Is best in compost C with good drainage and a good supply of water at all times, for the compost must not be allowed to dry out.

PROPAGATION. By division in spring. Repot when necessary in early April.

G. magellanica. (H).

This is a native of Magellan, S. America, making a close mat of prostrate stems from a central crown. Leaves on 2-inch petioles, radical reniform, margins crenate, green. Flowers insignificant, greenish in a globular spike. May–June.

GYPSOPHILA (*Caryophyllaceae*).

This genus has provided the alpine house with two delightful cushion plants, one a species, the other a geographical variant; neither flowers at all well but the hard cushions are in themselves attractive.

CULTIVATION. They are best in compost A, with good drainage, care in watering is needed at all times, although they require sufficient during the early spring and summer, keep dry but not arid in winter.

PROPAGATION. By detaching rosettes in April and rooting these in a closed frame. Repot only when necessary in early April.

G. aretioides. (E).

This forms a cushion of rosettes with minute, thick grey-green hairy leaves and when satisfied, stemless pearly white flowers. June. A native of Persia.

G. aretioides caucasica. (E).

A native of the Caucasus, this is smaller and even more compact, almost a scab of tight grey-green rosettes. Flowers very rarely, white, rounded, stemless. June.

HABERLEA (*Gesneriaceae*).

A genus of plants containing two species and one variety, closely related to Ramonda, they make ideal pan plants for the alpine house or frame.

CULTIVATION. Compost B is suitable, well drained and they require plenty of water while in growth and must be kept moist at other periods. After flowering they should be plunged into a cool shady spot for the summer and then returned to the house for the winter.

PROPAGATION. By division of the plants in April or leaf cuttings in May. Repot when necessary after flowering.

H. ferdinandi-coburgi. (E).

This forms tight clumps of tufted rosettes. Leaves in basal rosettes, soft hairy, ovate-oblong, margins coarsely dentate, obtuse. Flowers on short 3-inch stems, radiating from the rosettes up to four, five-lobed, tubular, the three basal lobes enlarged and swelling, pale lilac, throat white, spotted gold, hairy. May–June. A native of Bulgaria.

H. rhodopensis. (E).
Similar to *H. ferdinandi-coburgi*, but with smaller flowers, up to five on 4-inch hairy stems in pendant umbel of a deeper shade of lavender-lilac, throat white and hairy. May–June. A native of the Rhodope Mountains, Bulgaria.

H. rhodopensis var. virginalis. (E).
This is a much better plant than the species with its glistening flowers of pure white. May.

HARRIMANELLA, see CASSIOPE.

HEBE *(Scrophulariaceae).*

A large genus of shrubby plants with approximately 100 species and many hybrids and varieties. With few exceptions the genus is endemic to New Zealand and contains a good number of suitable species for pan culture. There is no doubt that with their bright evergreen habit especially during the dull winter months, the alpine house would be poorer without a representative collection of these gems. Some authorities still include the shrubby species under their old generic name of Veronica; others have placed them in Hebe, basing them on the following: their shrubby or arboreal habit, flowers in axillary racemes, local distribution in Australasia with the focal point in New Zealand, and a difference in their basic chromosome number from Veronica.

CULTIVATION. Compost A is suitable with good drainage and plenty of water during the growing season, reducing this in late August, then keeping the compost just moist in the winter months. The plants should be protected from cold drying winds which quickly defoliate the plants.
PROPAGATION. By green cuttings in July and early August. Repot when necessary in April when new growth has commenced.

H. armstrongii. (E). (Syn. *Veronica armstrongii*).
A small shrub of lax habit, much branched and up to 18 inches high. Leaves small, thick linear in vertical rows of four appressed, dull dark green. Flowers in small terminal spikes, white, June. A native of New Zealand.

H. astoni, see *H. subsimilis astoni*.
H. bidwillii, see *H. decora*.
H. buchananii. (E). (Syn. *Veronica buchananii*).
A much branched erect shrub about 12 inches high with smooth stems. Leaves crowded, opposite, oblong to orbicular, concave and slightly imbricated, glabrous light green. Flowers near the apex of the shoots in small clusters, sessile, white. June. A native of New Zealand.

H. buchananii exigua. (E). (Syn. *Veronica b. minor*).
This is the species in miniature, only an inch or so high, very desirable with

its crowded light green, rounded leaves and small stemless white flowers. June.

H. canescens. (E). (Syn. *H. lilliputiana, Veronica lilliputiana*).
An extremely minute plant, less than 1 inch high with its thread-like stems interwoven and hairy with minute, ovate, greyish leaves. Flowers solitary, large for size of plant on shortest of stems, pale blue, open saucer-shaped. June–July. This plant is now *Parahebe canescens*. A native of New Zealand.

H. carnosula. (E). (Syn. *Veronica carnosula*).
A species making a spreading bushlet in nature up to 2 feet high, but rarely above 12 inches in cultivation. Branches stout, smooth in the adult stage, hairy when young. Leaves crowded, opposite, rounded leathery, concave, glabrous dull dark green. Flowers on spikes from terminal leaf axils, congested, white. May–June. A native of New Zealand.

H. chathamica. (E). (Syn. *Veronica chathamica*).
A procumbent small shrublet, up to 12 inches high, much-branched and sparsely haired. Leaves opposite, thick, crowded, elliptic, obtuse, shiny deep green. Flowers in congested racemes from near the apex of the branches, blue. May–June. A native of New Zealand.

H. ciliolata. (E). (Syn. *H. gilliesiana, Veronica gilliesiana*).
A dwarf procumbent much branched shrublet rarely 12 inches high. Leaves arranged closely in vertical rows of four round the stems, concave, fleshy, linear, appressed, dull green, margins ciliate. Flowers in spikes near the apex of the shoots, white. June. A native of New Zealand.

H. colensoi. (E). (Syn. *Veronica colensoi*).
This is a small shrub of upright habit with smooth stout branches, up to 15 inches in time. Leaves opposite, congested at the upper half of the branches, linear-oblong, coriaceous, deep green, glaucous below with pronounced midrib. Flowers in near terminal racemes, crowded, white. June. A native of New Zealand.

H. colensoi var. hillii. (E). (Syn. *H. hillii, Veronica hillii*).
A form similar to the species roughly same in habit and height. Leaves elliptic to linear-oblong, sparsely toothed, glaucous both sides. Flowers in crowded axillary racemes, white. July.

H. decora. (E). (Syn. *H. bidwillii, Veronica bidwillii*).
A native of South Island, New Zealand, this is a prostrate much branched shrub with smooth or downy stems, less than 6 inches high, the branches rooting where they come into contact with the soil. Leaves opposite, small, not crowded, leathery, fleshy obovate, with sometimes a deep notch on either side, bright glossy green. Flowers on long slender stems from the axils of the branches, white. July. This is more correctly *Parahebe decora*.

H. decumbens. (E). (Syn. *Veronica decumbens*).
A small spreading species up to 18 inches high with reddish-black shiny branches. Leaves opposite, sparse to crowded, oblong–obovate to ovate, deep bright green, margined with red. Flowers congested in racemes near the apex of the branches, white. May–June. A native of New Zealand.

H. epacridea. (E). (Syn. *Veronica epacridea*).
A small procumbent much branched shrublet with woody contorted stems up to 6 inches high. Leaves ovate to oblong in fours in vertical rows, apex rounded, imbricated, thick fleshy, concave at front, keeled at back, dark glabrous green, margined red. Flowers crowded in terminal, oval-shaped clusters, white. July. A native of New Zealand.

H. 'Fairfieldii'. (E). (*H. hulkeans* × *H. lavaudiana*). (Syn. *Veronica* × *fairfieldii*).
This hybrid makes a small erect slender branched shrublet about 12 inches high. Leaves sparse, fleshy, ovate, apex obtuse, glabrous deep green, margins minutely crenate and reddish. Flowers in much-branched short panicles, pale lavender. July. A garden hybrid, originated in the Fairfield Nursery, New Zealand.

H. gibbsii. (E). (Syn. *Veronica gibbsii*).
A dwarf tree-like shrub with stout branches, up to 12 inches high. Leaves thick, opposite, crowded, ovate, apex obtuse, deep glabrous green, sometimes suffused with red, margined with long white hairs. Flowers congested on spikes near the apex of the branches, white. May–June. A native of New Zealand.

H. gilliesiana, see *H. ciliolata*.

H. haastii. (E). (Syn. *Veronica haastii*).
A near relative of *H. epacridea*, with similar prostrate habit and contorted branches. Foliage similar except that there is no keel at the back of the imbricated leaves. Flowers small, white, in oval terminal clusters. July. A native of New Zealand.

H. hectori. (E). (Syn. *Veronica hectori*).
A small shrublet with rounded stiff erect stems up to 12 inches high. Leaves thick, leathery, orbicular to oblong, joined at middle, appressed, apex obtuse, deep polished green. Flowers congested from the upper leaf axils, forming small terminal clusters, white. July. A native of South Island, New Zealand.

H. hillii, see *H. colensoi var. hillii*.

H. lavaudiana. (E). (Syn. *Veronica lavaudiana*).
This is a small shrublet only a few inches high with thin semi-erect stems, smooth below, downy above. Leaves opposite, dense, thick leathery, obovate, tapered to base, dentate, deep green, margins red. Flowers crowded in small spikes, arranged in a rounded corymb, rosy-pink. June–July. A native of South Island, New Zealand.

H. lilliputiana, see *H. canescens*.

H. loganioides. (E). (Syn. *Veronica loganioides*).
A dwarf procumbent sub-shrub with semi-woody, prostrate, basal branches, becoming erect and densely covered with light hairs. Leaves ovate to lanceolate, opposite pairs, crowded, thick leathery with a keel, rarely toothed on margins, dull deep green. Flowers in small terminal racemes, white. June. A native of South Island, New Zealand.

H. macrantha. (E). (Syn. *Veronica macrantha*).
This makes an upright stout, sparsely branched shrublet, up to 18 inches high. Leaves small, opposite, very thick and leathery, obovate, apex obtuse with thickened margins, coarsely toothed, bright green. Flowers fine large white in axillary racemes. June–July. A native of South Island New Zealand.

H. pagei. (E). (Syn. *Veronica pagei*; *V. pageana*).
A fine dwarf shrub less than 12 inches high with lax slender stems. Leaves crowded, obovate, glaucous. Flowers in racemes on axillary shoots, white with pronounced cherry-red stamens. June. A native of New Zealand.

H. pagei var. nana. (E).
A smaller edition of the species only a few inches high with the typical grey-green leaves and many spikes of small flowers, lighter blue with a touch of red. July.

H. propinqua. (E). (Syn. *Veronica propinqua*).
This is a dwarf species with contorted, much-branched slender stems, less than 18 inches high in cultivation. Leaves three-part, triangular, obtuse, arranged in over-lapping opposite pairs, appressed to cover the stem completely. The margins are fringed with minute hairs, dark dull green, thick and fleshy. Flowers in small terminal clusters, white. July. A native of New Zealand.

H. raoulii. (E). (Syn. *Veronica raoulii*).
A small much branched shrublet up to 9 inches high. Branches open, horizontal, spreading, covered with a fine down. Leaves opposite, spatulate, obtuse with rounded or saw-like teeth, coriaceous, yellow-green. Flowers crowded in terminal corymbs, pink. July. A native of New Zealand.

H. subsimilis astoni. (E). (Syn. *H. astoni*, *Veronica astoni*).
This forms a dwarf lax tuft of slender stems, much branched near the apex. Leaves triangular, bluntish in opposite pairs, appressed at base but apex standing clear in juvenile state; more imbricated and appressed when mature, concave, thick leathery, but not keeled, rich golden-yellow. Flowers produced in small axillary clusters near the apex of the stems, small, white, of no great value. July. A native of the Tararua Mountains, North Island, New Zealand.

H. tetragona. (E). (Syn. *Veronica tetragona*).
A good upright four-angled, much-branched shrublet up to 9 inches high. Leaves crowded in opposite pairs, erect, thick, leathery, ovate, obtuse, joined at the base, keeled bright glossy yellow-green, margins ciliate. Flowers in small terminal clusters, white. July. A native of North Island, New Zealand.

H. tetrasticha. (E). (Syn. *Veronica tetrasticha*).
A rare charming plant worthy of the necessary care needed to keep it in good health in this country. It makes a sub-erect, slender four-angled much-branched shrublet, rarely above 6 inches high, often less. Leaves

appressed to stems, congested, imbricated in four vertical lines, thick linear, wider at the base, tapered to apex, obtuse. Flowers borne on small spikes from the terminal leaf axils, white. May–June. A native of New Zealand.

HEDERA (*Araliaceae*).

The common Ivy is so well known that it needs no description here for it is found everywhere in the British Isles, giving colour during the dreary winter months even though it be of a sombre green. It has sported a number of varieties, of which there are two suitable for pan culture, retaining their dwarf stature over a number of years.

CULTIVATION. They will do well in compost B with plenty of water during the growing season, just moist at other times.

PROPAGATION. By cuttings taken with a heel and rooted in the propagating frame in August. Repot only when necessary.

H. helix 'Conglomerata'. (E).

A dwarf form very slow growing usually less than 12 inches high after many years. Leaves crowded, alternate, thick, typical ivy shaped, dark glossy green.

H. helix 'Minima'. (E).

This is the smallest of the forms with crowded leaves, three to five angular lobes of a greyish-green. Extremely slow growing.

HELICHRYSUM (*Compositae*).

This genus contains a large number of species, mostly shrubs or sub-shrubs with the majority having silvery-white foliage, densely covered with downy felt. They are ideal for culture in the alpine house with their attractive leaves acting as a foil to the other occupants, as well as their far from insignificant 'everlasting' flowers, thus providing interest in the house at a period when the floral display is at its lowest.

CULTIVATION. This is easy in compost A with good drainage and all the species require a normal amount of water during the growing and flowering season. In fact one species, *H. virgineum*, will quickly show its need during the summer months by drooping its foliage. Dry but not arid conditions are needed in winter. All dead leaves should be removed during the winter months as this not only prevents fungus infection but also keeps the specimens in a presentable condition. A sharp downward pull will bring the dead leaves away quite cleanly.

PROPAGATION. The whipcord species are best increased by cuttings pulled, not cut, from the plants, and rooted in the propagating frame. May. All others are propagated by detaching rosettes which will quickly root. June to August. Repot every year in early spring for the majority quickly outgrow their pans.

H. angustifolium. (E).

A native of the eastern Mediterranean area, it makes a sub-shrub up to

Above: *Helichrysum coralloides* (see page 313)

Below: *Helichrysum frigidum* (see page 313)

Above: *Helichrysum virgineum* (see page 314)

Below: *Heloniopsis orientalis* var. *yakusimensis* (see page 525)

Above: *Jasminum parkeri* (see page 327)

Below: *Lewisia pygmaea* (see page 338)

Above: *Linum elegans* (see page 342)
Below: *Myosotis rupicola* (see page 360)

9 inches high with erect slender branches. Leaves lanceolate, thick felted due to covering of silver-grey down. Flowers in terminal clusters on 6-inch woody stems, small, yellow, rayless. June.

H. bellidioides. (E).
A delightful and easy species only a few inches high of slender congested branches. Leaves obovate, simple, mid-green, white below owing to the covering of down. Flowers solitary in terminal clusters on slender 5-inch stems, papery white, everlasting. June. A native of New Zealand.

H. bellidioides var. prostratum. (E).
Similar to the type, this plant differs only in having almost sessile flowering stems.

H. confertum. (E).
A small dwarf compact sub-shrub rarely above 6 inches high with erect stiff branches. Leaves oblong, thick, felted, white. Flowers sessile, white with delightful golden centre. June. A native of S. Africa.

H. coralloides. (E).
This is a real treasure for the alpine house and although rare it is obtainable from several sources. A native of New Zealand, where it inhabits high cliff faces in the mountains, it forms an upright sub-shrub with erect stiff branches, densely clothed with the symmetrical appressed leaves, bright glossy dark green outside, thickly covered with white down inside. The arrangement of the leaves on the stems is such that the appearance of the plant is similar to that of coral stems. Flowers solitary at the apex of the branches, cream, lasting a long time. June.

H. frigidum. (E).
A native of Corsica, this is a semi-prostrate plant only a few inches high, of slender, much-branched stems covered with a white down. Leaves crowded, minute, linear, silver-grey, woolly. Flowers on small stems at the apex of the shoots, white with the texture of tissue paper, lasting well into the winter. May–June. The flowering shoots can be trimmed back to retain a neat compact plant.

H. marginatum, see *H. milfordiae.*

H. milfordiae. (E). (Syn. *H. marginatum*).
A native of Basutoland, this is quite hardy outdoors and also makes a fine alpine house plant. It forms a close compact cushion of soft rosettes, leaves ovate, tapered towards apex, completely covered with brilliant silky silvery hairs. Flowers solitary, quite sessile, large, crimson in bud opening to the usual white papery everlasting flowers. Through the petals which are thin in texture, the crimson colouring on the reverse can be seen, a delightful combination. June.

H. orientale. (E).
This species is up to 9 inches high, very woody at the base with loose rosettes of long obovate, extremely woolly, greyish-white leaves, pointed at apex. Flowers on slender felted 6-inch stems, in terminal clusters, buds a fine satiny light yellow opening to white. June. A native of Crete.

H. pichleri. (E).

Another fine species roughly 6 inches high with crowded rosettes. Leaves spatulate, slender at base, covered with a dense tomentum, grey-green, with a thick pronounced midrib underneath. Flowers on small felted stems in a tight corymb, yellow in bud, opening to a delightful silver-white. June. A native of S.E. Europe.

H. scutellifolium. (E).

A native of Australia, and reputed to be tender, according to the Royal Horticultural Society's *Dictionary of Gardening*, as well as being up to 5 feet high. I cannot bear this out, for plants of this species in the open rock garden here in Kent are now 6 years old, 12 inches high and have withstood 22 degrees of frost. It makes an erect shrublet with spreading laterals densely clothed with a layer of white felt. The leaves are arranged spirally round the branches, minute, rounded ball-shaped, dark glossy green, attached to the stem by microscopic petioles. Flowers in terminal clusters, creamy white. May.

H. selago. (E).

A native of New Zealand, resembling a whipcord veronica up to 8 inches high, branches stiff, erect. Leaves small, oval, deep green, appressed to the branches on white felted stems. Flowers from the apex of the stems, creamy white. July.

H. virgineum. (E).

A fine alpine house plant from the rocky cliffs on Mount Olympus in Greece. It forms a hard woody central base, bearing congested elongated rosettes of thick, fleshy, intense silver-grey long obovate leaves, tapering to a blunt point. Flowers in terminal clusters up to twelve on 6-inch woolly stems, glistening orange-pink in bud, opening to everlasting creamy white flowers. May.

HOUSTONIA (*Rubiaceae*).

A genus of plants which has two species and two varieties that can be used for pan culture and these are well known, but somehow the Bluets are not so easy to grow into large specimens for they seem to have the tendency to die away after two years or so.

CULTIVATION. Compost B suits them with good drainage and plenty of water while growing and flowering, keep moist in winter. All prefer shade and are best kept in a cool shady spot during hot summer months. PROPAGATION. By division in March, or seed sown in compost 2 when ripe, thus providing flowering plants for the following season. Repot when necessary after flowering.

H. caerulea. (E).

A close creeping mat of tufted shoots about 1 inch high. Leaves small, crowded, ovate, tapered to base, radical leaves spatulate, finely ciliate, bright green. Flowers solitary on 2-inch stems, four-petalled, rounded salver-shaped, light blue. May. A native of Virginia, U.S.A.

H. caerulea 'Alba'. (E).
Similar to the type but with pure white flowers. May.
H. caerulea 'Millards Variety'. (E).
This is the best form with large flowers of a much deeper blue. May.
H. serpyllifolia. (E).
A native of N. America, making a procumbent mat of small hairy, spatulate, bright green leaves in tufts. Flowers on 3-inch stems, each on a long terminal pedicel, four-petalled, rounded, deep violet-blue. May.

HYACINTHUS (*Liliaceae*).

This genus has provided the species from which the well-known florist Hyacinths used extensively for Christmas decorations are derived; but the true wildlings do not lose anything in comparison with the opulence of their cultivated kindred, for their dainty charm leaves nothing to be desired.

CULTIVATION. The bulbs are best planted in early September in a moist compost B to twice their depth, six to a 5-inch pan and then plunged outside in a frame covering them with a layer of peat. No other water is required until growth appears. They are brought into the house when the foliage is well above the surface and left there until after flowering. Water is required in quantity until foliage dies down, then withheld to ripen the bulbs.

PROPAGATION. By offsets in September. Seed can also be used by sowing $\frac{1}{2}$ inch deep in compost 2, September, but they require up to five years to flower by this method. Repot every year in September.

H. amethystinus. (B).
A native of Spain, this bulb produces up to eight narrow linear deeply channelled leaves and loose racemes of bright blue flowers on 6-inch stems. May.

H. amethystinus var. albus. (B).
A clear white form, flowering in early May.

H. azureus. (B). (Syn. *Muscari azureum*).
Up to five linear-lanceolate fleshy green leaves and on a 6-inch stem a dense raceme of bright blue tubular flowers. April. A native of Asia Minor.

H. fastigiatus, see *H. pouzolzii.*

H. lineatus. (B).
A native of Asia Minor, with two oblong-lanceolate, bright green leaves, tip acute. Flowers on 3-inch stems, open racemes of up to twelve tubular bell-shaped, blue. April.

H. pouzolzii. (B). (Syn. *H. fastigiatus*).
From the islands of Corsica and Sardinia, making up to six slender awl-shaped green leaves and on a 3-inch stem a small raceme of tubular bright lilac flowers. March.

H. racemosus, see *Muscari racemosum*.

To be botanically correct the following amendments should be made:

H. amethystinus is *Brimeura amethystina*.

H. pouzolzii is *Brimeura fastigiata*.

H. azureus is *Hyacinthella azurea*.

H. lineatus is *Hyacinthella lineata*.

HYPERICUM (*Guttiferae*).

A large genus of plants, the St John's Worts contain a number of species which are suitable for alpine house culture. They are for the most part easy, but one or two will test the skill of the grower to make them happy and contented in cultivation. There is a wide diversity in the size of the flowers but all are similar in shape and colour; generally five-petalled, golden-yellow with a central boss of long thin deep golden-yellow stamens.

CULTIVATION. With the exception of two species noted here, all the hypericums are of easy culture in compost A with full sun and good drainage. A normal supply of water during early spring and summer, followed by a dryish period in August, keep on the dry side in winter.

PROPAGATION. By seed sown in March, compost 2, or by division in early spring in many cases, or by green cuttings taken in July. Repot every year in April when the new growth is commencing.

H. aegypticum. (E).

A dwarf erect shrublet up to 12 inches high with much-branched stems. Leaves small ovate, pointed, grey-green. Flowers solitary on short stems, pale golden-yellow. August. A native of S. Europe.

H. buckleyi. (E).

This makes a dwarf shrub up to 12 inches high with erect, much-branched four-angled reddish stems. Leaves orbicular, bluish-green above, paler beneath, turning red in autumn. Flowers solitary rarely in threes, from the apex of the shoots, large typical golden-yellow. July. A native of America.

H. confertum. (E).

A semi-prostrate lax shrublet up to 6 inches high, with four-angled stems. Leaves crowded, small, lanceolate, obtuse at apex, grey-green, covered with small dots, margins recurved. Flowers from terminal leaf axils on short stems, rich golden-yellow. June. A native of Asia Minor.

H. coris. (E).

From the mountains of C. and S.E. Europe, this is a soft-wooded species making a mat of slender semi-erect smooth stems up to 6 inches high. Leaves in whorls up to six linear, obtuse, mid-green with a pronounced midrib below. Flowers in clusters of five on small stems from the leaf axils, bright yellow. June.

H. crenulatum. (E).

A native of S.E. Europe, where it forms a semi-prostrate shrublet of small creeping reddish branches up to 6 inches in length. Leaves oblong, leathery, mid-green with crenulate margins. Flowers in small terminal racemes, bright golden-yellow. June.

H. cuneatum. (E).
This is a very charming plant for the alpine house, less than 3 inches high, a congested mat of thin wiry red stems. Leaves small crowded, wedge-shaped, glabrous green-grey, glaucous grey below, spotted black. Flowers yellow in loose terminal clusters on short stems, buds brilliant red. July. A native of Asia Minor.

H. cuneatum var. fragile. (E).
A smaller edition of the type with dense racemes of golden-yellow flowers. This form resents cold winds and demands full sun to succeed. June.

H. empetrifolium. (E).
The type form makes a dwarf semi-erect shrublet about 12 inches high, but there is a much smaller plant only a few inches high which is very desirable. Branches slender, much angled. Leaves small, linear, in whorls of three margins recurved, grey-green. Flowers in small tiers, pale yellow. July. A native of Greece. This plant requires protection from cold winds.

H. ericoides. (E).
A difficult species, not easy to cultivate successfully, it has a distressing habit of dying back in parts for no apparent reason, seems to require a baking in late summer and faultless drainage at all times. The plant has the appearance of a dwarf heather, never more than an inch or so high with prostrate branches radiating from a central rootstock. Leaves linear, in whorls of four at apex of shoots, less crowded at base, grey-green marked with dots, margins recurved. Flowers in small loose terminal clusters at the apex of the laterals, large for size of plant, bright yellow. June to September. A native of S. Spain.

H. fragile. (E).
A native of Greece, forming a prostrate, smooth-stemmed shrublet only a few inches high from a central rootstock. Leaves linear in overlapping whorls of four, densely crowded, grey-green. Flowers in small terminal clusters, large, golden-yellow. June.

H. hyssopifolium. (E).
This is a prostrate shrublet about 6 inches high with rounded, lax, congested, red wiry stems. Leaves long, linear, grey-green, glaucous below. Flowers in long terminal racemes, deep golden-yellow. June–July. A native of N. Asia.

H. nanum. (E).
A native of the E. Mediterranean regions, this is another temperamental species, but a very desirable plant when well grown. Only an inch or so high with stiff procumbent stems well clothed with bright green orbicular leaves. Flowers in congested terminal clusters, bright golden-yellow. June–July. Needs careful watering at all times, good drainage and a

ripening period in late July and August, for this seems to be the time when it misses most its naturally hot dry habitat.

H. olympicum. (E).

This makes a small shrub up to 9 inches high with smooth slender two-edged stems. Leaves long, oblong, pointed at apex, grey-green. Flowers in terminal clusters, golden-yellow. A native of S.E. Europe, this species requires protection from cold winds. May–June.

H. repens. (H).

A native of Asia Minor, it forms a small mat of congested wiry stems less than 4 inches high. Leaves small, linear, grey-green, crowded. Flowers in loose terminal racemes, deep golden-yellow. June to August.

H. reptans. (E).

Possibly the hardiest of the dwarf hypericums, it is a native of the Himalayas, making a dwarf creeping sub-shrub only an inch or so high with self-rooting, wire-like, smooth two-edged stems. Leaves congested, small, oval, obtuse, mid-green turning red-brown in autumn. Flowers solitary at the end of the shoots, red in bud opening to golden-yellow. June–July.

H. rhodopeum. (E).

A native of S.E. Europe, it forms a prostrate tufted shrublet of crowded, congested branches up to 6 inches high, slender, wiry, covered with hairs. Leaves oval, rounded at apex, hairy, grey-green. Flowers in small clusters from leaf axils, golden-yellow. May.

IBERIS (*Cruciferae*).

The Candytufts are well-known useful plants for the rock garden, with their ease of cultivation and display of four-petalled flowers. They also provide a few which can be grown in pans for the alpine house or frame.

CULTIVATION. This is easy in compost A with good drainage. A normal supply of water during the growing and flowering season, dry but not arid in winter.

PROPAGATION. By seed using compost 1 in March or green cuttings in late June. Repot every year after flowering.

I. cappadocica, see *Ptilotrichum cappadocicum.*

I. correaefolia. (E).

A native of S. Europe, it makes a dwarf sub-shrub rarely 6 inches high of much-branched interlaced stems. Leaves alternate, crowded, entire, spatulate, glabrous bright green. Flowers in congested flattish-heads on 2-inch stems, white. May.

I. gibraltarica. (E).

A much tangled bushlet of branches up to 12 inches high. Leaves crowded, long, narrow, oval, dentate, apex rounded, glossy dark green. Flowers on 4-inch stems, often branched, flattish umbels, crowded, light lilac-blue. May–June. A native of S. Spain including Gibralter, this species requires plenty of sunshine and should be kept away from cold winds.

I. jordanii. (E).
This is a small prostrate sub-shrub less than 3 inches high. Leaves alternate, crowded, spatulate, deep green. Flowers in clustered terminal corymbs, large for size of plant, white. May. A native of Anatolia.

I. lagascana. (E).
A dwarf procumbent plant less than 6 inches high with stiff rounded branches. Leaves small, ovate, dentate, deep glossy green. Flowers in crowded terminal umbels, pure white with golden eye. May. S.E. Europe.

I. saxatilis. (E).
Makes a dwarf prostrate shrub up to 4 inches high. Leaves thick, small, crowded, oblong to linear, cylindric, margins ciliate, dull dark green. Flowers on short stems in small terminal clusters, glistening white. April–May. A native of S. Europe.

I. sempervirens 'Little Gem'. (E).
This dwarf form of the species, itself a prostrate but wide spreading plant, is only a few inches high with smooth slender branches. Leaves crowded, oblong, apex obtuse, margins ciliate, dull dark green. Flowers on 2-inch stems, large in flat terminal racemes, intense white. April.

I. taurica. (E).
A charming dwarf compact species with small semi-erect smooth branches only 2 inches high. Leaves crowded, spatulate, apex notched, grey-green covered with fine hairs. Flowers in a congested small flattish umbel, buds violet-blue opening to a glistening white. May–June. A native of Asia Minor.

I. tenoreana. (E).
This makes a small compact bushlet with erect, twisting hairy branches less than 4 inches high. Leaves oblong, linear, thick, rounded at apex, tapered towards base, margins ciliate, green. Flowers in flat terminal clusters, white, April. A native of Spain.

ILEX *(Aquifoliaceae)*.

The Hollies are represented in England by the many forms and varieties of *I. aquifolium*, the common Holly, which in one way or another provide the berried branches for the Christmas decorations. These are all too large for our purpose, but a Japanese species, *I. crenata*, has produced several varieties of which two must be considered as ideal plants for alpine house or frame culture.

CULTIVATION. Compost A is suitable with perfect drainage, requiring plenty of water during the growing season, moist in winter.

PROPAGATION. By rooting half-ripened cuttings in the propagating frame in July, but they can take a long time to become sizeable plants. Repot only when necessary in April.

I. crenata 'Bullata'. (E).
A dwarf form from Japan, very slow growing, reaching 15 inches after

many years. It makes a rounded stiff congested shrub with small twigs, densely clothed with broad oval leaves, dark glossy green. Flowers inconspicuous, dingy white followed by black fruits on minute stems.

I. crenata 'Mariesii'. (E).
This is a very slow growing form making less than an inch a year. It has short, erect, stiff branches with small twigs. Leaves crowded, broad, ovate or orbicular, dark glossy green, marked with two teeth at apex. The fruits are rounded black on minute stalks. A native of Japan, this is a very desirable pygmy, which will never become too large for a pan in an average lifetime.

INCARVILLEA (*Bignoniaceae*).

A small genus of plants which has one species that is suitable for alpine house culture and when in flower is a delightful decorative plant.
CULTIVATION. Compost B is ideal with good drainage, plenty of water while growing and flowering, keep dry but not arid in winter. This plant resents stagnant moisture at all times.
PROPAGATION. Best by seed in March, sown in compost 2. Repot every other year after flowering.

I. grandiflora. (H).
This forms a tuberous rootstock from which appears a rosette of large compound, pinnate leaves, leaflets entire, ovate, crinkled, with well-marked veining, bright dark green, margins crenate. Flowers almost sessile from centre of rosette, large up to 4 inches across, tubular five-petalled, deep cherry-red with yellow lines in tube. May–June. A native of W. China.

INULA (*Compositae*).

A genus containing a good number of species but there are only two really suitable for pan culture.
CULTIVATION. Compost A with good drainage and a sunny spot, normal supply of water while growing, dry but not arid in winter.
PROPAGATION. By seed in March, compost 1, or division in August. Repot every year after flowering.

I. acaulis. (E).
Forms prostrate, stemless tufts of oblong-spatulate, entire, light green leaves, margins bristling ciliate. Flowers solitary, sessile, large, yellow narrow-petalled daisies with purple central ring. April–May. A native of Asia Minor.

I. heterolepis. (E).
A native of S. Turkey, this is a dwarf sub-shrub less than 9 inches high with semi-procumbent woody stems. Leaves in rosette formation, large, ovate, thick stalked, covered with a dense white wool, margins minutely crenate, heavily veined below. Flowers solitary on almost prostrate leafy stems, deep yellow backed by a white woolly involucre. July–August.

Above: *Kalmiopsis leachiana* 'M. le Piniec' (see page 329)

Below: *Kelseya uniflora* (see page 330)

Above: *Paraquilegia anemonoides* (see page 381)

Below: *Phyllodoce caerulea* (see page 392)

IRIS (*Iridaceae*).

A large genus of plants with representatives in all parts of the northern hemisphere, consisting of either species with tuberous rhizomatous or bulbous rootstocks. There are a number which are eminently suitable for pan culture; all are extremely beautiful and the majority are easy to cultivate, although their needs differ in many of the species. Some are sun lovers demanding a hot dry position and a good sun baking during the summer, while others like a rich moist soil but in all cases good drainage is an essential condition for their well being.

CULTIVATION. Cultural hints will be dealt with individually, but the bulbous kinds are best potted up in compost A in September, twice the depth of the bulb and dependent on the size, from six to twelve bulbs in a 5-inch pan. The compost should be used moist, the pans placed in a cold frame, covered with peat and no further water given until growth begins. The plants are brought into the house for flowering. All species forming rhizomes must be planted with the rhizomes on the surface, and if this is not done failure is likely to occur, for it is necessary for these to ripen.

I. alata, see *I. planifolia.*

I. aucheri. (B). (Syn. *I. sindjarensis*).

A member of the Juno section from Mesopotamia, with tufts of double-channelled glossy green, narrow, lanceolate leaves, striated below. Flowers vanilla-scented on 6-inch stems, up to four violet-blue, falls with radiating dark lines, median ridge yellow. March.

CULTIVATION. Requires compost A with good drainage, normal supply of water while in growth, needs all available sun and dry conditions after foliage dies down.

PROPAGATION. By careful division in September making sure that the persistent fleshy roots are not broken. Repot only when necessary in September.

I. bakeriana. (B).

This belongs to the Xiphion group and is a native of Asia Minor. Leaves two, narrow linear, tapering to a hard point, eight angled, hollow. Flowers solitary, on 4-inch stems, standards bright purple, falls white spotted and margined-golden, crest violet, sweetly-scented. February.

PROPAGATION. By offsets in September or seed in compost 2 when ripe. Repot every year in September.

I. bloudowii. (E).

This is a bearded Iris belonging to the Pogoniris section from the Altai Mountains, E. Europe, forming a small, much-branched rhizome. Leaves in tufts 3 inches long, linear, light green. Flowers on slender 3-inch stems, solitary, rarely two, bright yellow. June.

CULTIVATION. This species must be grown in full sun and needs a sun baked soil to flower well. Water must be given sparingly at all times and a dry period is required after flowering.

PROPAGATION. By division of the rhizomes immediately after flowering. Repot when necessary in June.

I. chamaeiris. (E).

A species often confused with *I. pumila*, but differs in having a flowering stem from 1 to 6 inches high, shorter perianth tube and evergreen, retaining its foliage during the winter months. It belongs to the Pogoniris section with small rhizomes and the light green ensiform leaves in tufts. Flowers on stems varying from 1 to 6 inches, with blue standards, falls tinged yellow with purple-brown veinings and orange beard. April–May. A native of the Maritime Alps.

CULTIVATION. Compost A with good drainage, normal supply of water while growing and flowering, dry but not arid in winter, needs sun.

PROPAGATION. By careful division after flowering. Repot when necessary in late May.

I. chamaeiris var. cretica. (H).

This is the charming form from Crete, with large glowing purple flowers on 1-inch stems, falls yellow at throat, striped purple, beard golden. May.

I. cristata. (H).

A native of the S.E. United States, this belongs to the Evansia section with small rhizomes and tufts of foliage 6 inches high. Leaves up to four, small, linear, widest in the middle. Flowers on short stems, generally two, soft blue with golden-yellow crest. June.

CULTIVATION. Best in compost B with plenty of water especially during the growing season and requires half shade. Needs frequent division of the plants to flower well and is best kept dry in winter.

PROPAGATION. By division in July. Repot when necessary in July.

I. danfordiae. (B).

From the Cicilian Taurus, this belongs to the Xiphion section and flowers before the foliage has fully grown. Leaves green, four angled, hollow. Flowers solitary on 3-inch stems, bright golden-yellow, falls speckled brown. February.

CULTIVATION. Compost A with good drainage, and once the foliage appears a weekly feed of liquid manure is desirable until the leaves turn yellow, as this species seems to require feeding to help build up flowering size bulbs for the following season. These require roasting after foliage has died down.

PROPAGATION. By offsets in September. Repot when necessary in September.

I. gracilipes. (H).

A native of Japan, this belongs to the Evansia section with small fleshy rhizomes and bears thin, weak, slender sword-shaped leaves. Flowers on 9-inch slender stems, pinkish-lilac, with a wavy orange crest. June.

CULTIVATION. Requires a position in half-shade in compost C with plenty of water while growing and flowering, moist at other times.

PROPAGATION. By division in June. Repot when necessary in June.

I. histrio. (B).

A member of the Xiphion section, this is a winter-flowering species from Palestine with slender narrow, lanceolate leaves elongating to 12 inches. Flowers on short stems less than 4 inches high, standards lilac, falls pale lilac spotted violet with central yellow median line. January.

CULTIVATION. Both this, and its variety, *aintabensis*, need compost A with good drainage and a thorough roasting after flowering.

PROPAGATION. By offsets in September. Repot in September.

I. histrio var. aintabensis. (B).

A native of Aintab, similar to the species but with ground colour a light pale blue, falls have orange ridge and black spots. January.

I. histrioides. (B).

From America, this belongs to the Xiphion section which produces its flowers before the leaves and has horizontal falls and erect standards, bright blue with violet markings, the falls have a central orange ridge. Leaves wide lanceolate. January. Requires similar conditions to those given to *I. histrio*.

I. innominata. (H).

A member of the Apogon section from Oregon, making tufts of dark green, narrow lanceolate leaves. Flowers on thin wiry 3-inch stems, golden-orange with brown veinings on falls. May.

CULTIVATION. Compost B with plenty of water while growing, dry but not arid at other periods. Prefers half-shade in hot districts.

PROPAGATION. By division in July or seed in compost 2. August. Repot in July when necessary.

I. lacustris. (H).

A native of E. United States, this belongs to the Evansia section with a slender creeping rhizome and green lanceolate, channelled leaves, wide at centre. Flowers pale lilac with deep yellow crest and throat. Differs from *I. cristata* in that the standard and fall segments are wedge-shaped, not lanceolate. May–June.

CULTIVATION. Requires compost B, normal water supply while growing, dry in winter, half shade.

PROPAGATION. By division in July.

I. mellita. (H).

From the Balkans, a member of the Pogoniris section about 4 inches high with a creeping rhizome and long, narrow, deep green leaves. Flowers almost stemless, smoky reddish-brown with red-brown netting and blue spotting at margins, beard white tipped blue. May.

CULTIVATION. Requires compost A with good drainage, normal water supply in spring and early summer, but needs a good baking in August.

PROPAGATION. By division in June. Repot when necessary in June.

I. mellita var. rubromarginata. (H).

This differs from the type in having red-margined leaves. June.

I. minuta, see *I. minutoaurea*.

I. minutoaurea. (H). (Syn. *I. minuta*).

A native of Japan, belonging to the Apogon section, less than 4 inches high with green narrow, lanceolate leaves, small at flowering time, elongating afterwards. Flowers solitary on stout stems, golden-yellow tinged deep brown in the falls, and brown margins on the standards. April.

CULTIVATION. Compost B with good drainage, normal water while growing and flowering, dry at other periods.

PROPAGATION. By careful division after flowering. Repot when necessary in May.

I. persica. (B).

Included in the Juno section, it has a wide distribution from Asia Minor to S. Persia forming a basal tuft of recurved linear leaves. Flowers on 1-inch stems, pale greenish-white, rich purple-red blotch of falls. February.

CULTIVATION. Compost B with good drainage, normal supply of water in spring, dry afterwards and all available sun.

PROPAGATION. By offsets in September, taking care not to injure the persistent rootstock. Repot only when necessary in September.

I. planifolia. (B). (Syn. *I. alata*).

This species is from the Mediterranean region, belonging to the Juno section with green channelled, lanceolate, pointed leaves. Flowers on 6-inch stems, bright light blue, deep violet on the falls and golden-yellow crest at throat. November to January.

CULTIVATION. Needs careful handling as this species has persistent fleshy roots. A good baking in summer and no water during this period.

PROPAGATION. By careful division in July, or seed in compost 2 when ripe, takes three to four years to reach flowering size. Repot only when necessary in September.

I. planifolia 'Alba'. (B).

This form has pure white flowers. January.

I. planifolia 'Marginata'. (B).

A dark blue form with falls margined white. January.

I. pumila. (H).

The well-known member of the Pogoniris section about 4 inches high with a wide distribution in Europe and Asia Minor. Makes stout tufts of sword-like green leaves. Flowers solitary, almost sessile, miniature bearded irises of variable colouring, ranging from yellow to pink and purple. April.

CULTIVATION. An easy species in compost A with good drainage and a normal supply of water while growing, dry at other periods.

PROPAGATION. By division in June. Repot when necessary in June.

I. reticulata. (B).

This charming early spring flowering bulbous Iris, with its delightful scent and ease of culture is an indispensable plant for the alpine house. A member of the Xiphion section up to 6 inches high, with tufts of

four-angled, deep green, sword-shaped leaves, appearing at the same time
as the flowers. Flowers solitary on short stems, deep violet, falls violet-
purple, orange ridge, margined white. February. A native of the Caucasus.
CULTIVATION. Compost A with good drainage, normal supply of water
while in growth, dry after leaves die down.
PROPAGATION. By offsets in September. Repot when necessary in
September.
Garden varieties of *Iris reticulata:*
'Alba'. (B).
A delightful white variety, very desirable. February.
'Cantab'. (B).
This form has light blue flowers with a grey tinge and orange crest.
February.
'Krelagei'. (B).
The flowers of this form are red-purple and often come into bloom in
January.
I. ruthenica. (H).
A member of the Apogon section, it is a native of Transylvania and China,
forming tufts of narrow linear, channelled green leaves from stoutish
rhizomes. Flowers on stems up to 6 inches high, solitary, sweetly-scented
with deep violet standards and pale blue falls, netted creamy white.
May–June.
CULTIVATION. Does best in compost B requiring plenty of water while
in growth and should not be allowed to dry out at other periods.
PROPAGATION. By division immediately after flowering. Repot in late
June when necessary.
I. sindjarensis, see *I. aucheri.*
I. tenax. (H).
From Oregon, this belongs to the Apogon section, making firm linear
tough green leaves. Flowers on 10-inch stems sometimes two, bright lilac-
purple, median ridge of falls crested yellow. June.
CULTIVATION. Compost B with plenty of water while growing, dry
at other periods.
PROPAGATION. By division in July. Repot when necessary in July.
I. vartani. (B).
A member of the Xiphion section, native of Palestine, with two four-
angled slender green leaves, pointed at apex. Flowers on 6-inch stems,
pale lilac-grey, falls veined lilac, crest wavy, yellow, scented. January.
CULTIVATION. Compost A with good drainage, normal water while
growing, dry after leaves disappear and a good baking in the sun.
PROPAGATION. By offsets in September. Repot when necessary in
September.
I. verna. (H).
A native of S. United States from the Apogon section, making a tuft
of sword-like glaucous green leaves, purple at base. Flowers on a 1-inch

stem, bright lilac-blue, falls orange, tinged at base and spotted brown, no beard. May.

CULTIVATION. Requires compost B in half shade with plenty of water during the growing season, just moist at other periods.

PROPAGATION. By division in July. Repot only when necessary in July.

I. winogradowii. (B).

A native of W. Caucasus, belonging to the Xiphion section with wide lanceolate, ribbed leaves, small in the flowering state. Flowers solitary on small stems, clear pale yellow, falls marked orange on central ridge and spotted with brown dots. February.

CULTIVATION. Compost A, with good drainage, normal supply of water while in growth, dry afterwards.

PROPAGATION. By offsets in September. Repot when necessary in September.

ISOMETRUM (*Gesneriaceae*).

A small genus related to Didissandra, containing two species, of which one in suitable for alpine house culture.

CULTIVATION. Compost C will suit this species and plenty of water is necessary while growing and flowering, keep just moist at other periods. It prefers half shade and protection from cold winds, best in a shady protected spot during hot spells.

PROPAGATION. By careful division in spring, seed sown in compost 3 in March, or leaf cuttings in May. Repot when necessary in early April.

I. farreri. (E). (Syn. *Oreocharis henryana*).

A native of W. China, this forms a thick tuberous rhizome, leaves in basal rosettes, narrow ovate, thick, crinkled, margins crenate, pale green with white hairs above, brown, hairy beneath. Flowers almost tubular five-lobed, pendant in a five to seven flowered umbel on 3-inch hairy stems, salmon-pink, brownish at base. July.

ISOPYRUM (*Ranunculaceae*).

A genus of plants which has one species for pan culture in the alpine house, making a delightful subject with its dainty foliage and starry flowers.

CULTIVATION. It is best in compost C with plenty of water while growing and flowering, just moist at other times. Requires half-shade and a cool spot during hot weather.

PROPAGATION. By seed sown when ripe, compost 3. Repot when necessary after flowering.

I. grandiflorum, see *Paraquilegia anemonoides*.

I. thalictroides. (H).

This forms a creeping tuberous rootstock with much divided ferny leaves about 9 inches high, leaflets three-lobed, toothed, light green. Flowers terminal, rounded buds opening to five-petalled star-shaped, anemone-like, white, or flushed pink. March. A native of Europe.

JANKAEA (*Gesneriaceae*).

This is a monotypic genus closely related to Haberlea and Ramonda, but unlike species of these two genera, this is a difficult plant requiring care and skill to cultivate it successfully.

CULTIVATION. Compost B is suitable over faultless drainage and the collar of the plant is best wedged between small pieces of rock. It needs a normal supply of water while growing and flowering and afterwards this should be reduced until the compost is just moist. On no account must water be allowed to rest at the base of the leaves where they join the stem otherwise rotting will take place. During the winter months atmospheric moisture accumulating on the foliage can also cause damage.

PROPAGATION. By seed in compost 2, March, or leaf cuttings in June, these root faster if bottom heat can be applied. The heated frame as described in Chapter Two is suitable. Repot only when necessary.

J. heldreichii. (E). (Syn. *Ramonda heldreichii*).

From a thickened rootstock is borne small reddish-haired stems, terminating in a solitary rosette of leaves. Leaves large, entire, thick, ovate, velvety shiny silver-grey due to intense covering of downy, silky, appressed hairs, reddish-brown hairs beneath. Flowers semi-pendant on 2-inch stems, generally in pairs, open bell-shaped, four separate lobes joined at centre, bright glistening violet. May. A native of Mount Olympus, Greece.

JASMINUM (*Oleaceae*).

A large genus of climbing, trailing or slender branched, erect shrubs, containing only one species suitable for the alpine house or frame. This is a very desirable shrub giving at least nine months of pleasure with its delightfully fragrant flowers and far from inconspicuous fruits.

CULTIVATION. Compost A is ideal over good drainage and a good supply of water during late spring and summer, keeping the compost just moist at other periods.

PROPAGATION. By green cuttings in July and rooted in the propagating frame. Repot only every other year in early April as slight root restriction helps to form tight congested slow growing specimens.

J. parkeri. (E).

A dwarf contorted much-branched interlaced shrub, rarely above 6 inches high. The congested stems are smooth, grooved and well clothed with alternate five foliate, mid-green leaves. Leaflets small, oval, apex acute, tapered to base. Flowers solitary, terminal, sometimes axillary, erect five-lobed, bright yellow with a delightful fragrance. June. The globular fruit is translucent, black. A native of N.W. India.

JEFFERSONIA (*Berberidaceae*).

A genus containing two species of woodland plants which, provided their simple wants are attended to, make fine specimens for pan culture.

CULTIVATION. They do well in compost C with good drainage and require plenty of water while making growth and flowers, just moist at other periods; on no account must the soil be allowed to dry out. They should only be kept in the alpine house while in flower, afterwards plunged outside into a cool shady frame, then returned to the house in winter.

PROPAGATION. By seed sown as soon as ripe in compost 3 or careful division in late July. Repot only when necessary after flowering.

J. diphylla. (H).

A native of N.W. America, this is a tufted plant from a central rootstock. Leaves on long petioles, reniform, cut into two deep lobes, margins dentate, opening lavender-green, changing to grey-green. Flowers solitary on 9-inch stems, generally before the foliage, open bell-shaped, white; four petaloid sepals, eight small petals, yellow stamens. April.

J. dubia. (H). (Syn. *Plagiorhegma dubia*).

This is a native of Manchuria, making a small plant about 4 inches high. Leaves solitary, borne on thin reddish petioles, arising from the rootstock, roundish two-lobed, the petiole attached almost to centre of leaf, apex retuse, veins palmate, glaucous green tinged violet. Flowers solitary, open saucer-shaped on slender stems, violet-blue, stamens pale yellow. April.

KALMIA (*Ericaceae*).

A small genus of shrubs from the New World, closely allied to Rhododendron and containing a few that will make fine specimens for the alpine house or frame.

CULTIVATION. Compost C is suitable with plenty of lime-free water during the growing and flowering season, moist at other periods. The plants should only be brought into the house for flowering, afterwards plunging them into a cool shady spot and giving an overhead spraying in the evenings after hot days.

PROPAGATION. By seed in March, compost 3, or half-ripened cuttings with a heel of old wood in late July.

K. angustifolia. (E).

This is a very variable plant ranging from dwarf specimens of 6 inches to large shrubs of 3 feet. For our purpose it will be necessary to obtain the smaller types and it is best to procure these from a reputable source where such forms are grown. The type plant is a dwarf tufted-shrub of open slender, wiry downy stems. Leaves opposite, rarely in threes, oval, tapering to base, smooth, bright green, paler beneath. Flowers in congested clusters on the previous year's growth, open saucer-shaped, deep rose-red. June. A native of N. America.

K. angustifolia var. pumila. (E). (Syn. *K.a.* var. *nana*).

A named dwarf form only a few inches high with typical foliage and flowers. June.

K. angustifolia var. rubra. (E).
This is a much deeper coloured form almost ruby red and is very desirable. June.

K. angustifolia var. nana, see *K.a.* var. *pumila.*

K. carolina. (E).
A native of S. Carolina, U.S.A., this is similar to *K. angustifolia,* but is more upright, up to 12 inches high with erect, stiff branches. Leaves opposite, or in threes, oval, tapered to base, smooth bright green above, grey below due to intense covering of down. Flowers on previous year's shoots, terminal clusters of purplish-rose, saucer-shaped; lobes recurved. June.

K. glauca, see *K. polifolia.*

K. glauca var. microphylla, see *K. polifolia* var. *microphylla.*

K. polifolia. (E). (Syn. *K. glauca*).
A small erect shrub rarely above 12 inches high under pan culture. Much-branched, slender stems with two-edged twigs. Leaves opposite, rarely in threes, oblong to lanceolate, tapering to base and apex, margins recurved, deep glabrous green, greyish-white below. Flowers in terminal umbels, open saucer-shaped, rose-lilac. April–May. A native of N. America.

K. polifolia var. microphylla. (E). (Syn. *K. glauca* var. *microphylla*).
Only 6 inches high with opposite, ovate to oval, deep green leaves, grey below and terminal clusters of large, rosy-lilac, saucer-shaped flowers. May. A native of Yukon to California.

KALMIOPSIS (*Ericaceae*).

A monotypic genus which was discovered in 1930 by Mrs Leach, in the Curry Country, Oregon, after whom it has been named. It is rare in its wild state and in cultivation the stock has dwindled with neglect during the war years, although it is becoming a little easier to obtain now. Unfortunately the plant is not easy, but there is hope that a form found in S. Oregon is a much more amenable plant to cultivate. According to reports this form, named var. M. Le Piniec, presents no difficulty and flowers profusely, but whether it will prove more amenable under cultivation here remains to be seen.

CULTIVATION. Compost C with plenty of lime-free water while growing and flowering, just moist at other periods. Top-dress every spring with similar compost, adding a small sprinkling of a balanced fertiliser. After flowering the plant should be plunged in a cool shady frame and sprayed in the evenings after hot days.

PROPAGATION. By cuttings taken with a heel in July and rooted in the propagating frame. Repot only when necessary after flowering.

K. leachiana. (E).
It forms a dwarf erect tufted shrub about 9 inches high, the young wood covered with minute hairs. Leaves small, oval, leathery, dark glossy green

above, spotted with sunken yellow glands below. Flowers in loose terminal clusters on slender hairy stems, saucer-shaped, deep rose-pink. April–May.

KELSEYA (*Rosaceae*).

Another monotypic genus, related to Petrophytum, it must be considered the dwarfest of all shrubs and certainly the slowest growing, forming after many years a hard, dense cushion.

CULTIVATION. Compost A with faultless drainage and it does well with pieces of sandstone wedged under the cushion. Water with care, although sufficient should be given in late spring and summer, reducing this to dry but not arid conditions in winter.

PROPAGATION. By seed if available sown in March, compost 2, or detach rosettes and root in propagating frame in June. Repot when necessary.

K. uniflora. (E).

This forms a tight compact cushion of rosettes. Leaves minute, crowded, imbricated, entire, thick, grey-green covered with silky hairs. Flowers almost sessile, solitary, small rounded, white, or white with pink tinge. May. A native of Montana.

LAPEIROUSIA (*Iridaceae*).

A small genus of bulbous plants allied to Watsonia, and formerly known as Arnomatheca, containing only one species which is really hardy enough for the alpine house.

CULTIVATION. Compost A is suitable over good drainage, the corms, six to a 5-inch pan, should be placed 1 inch deep in March, and covered with peat until growth commences. Normal water while in growth but after foliage dies down pan should be kept dry.

PROPAGATION. By offsets when repotting. Repot every year in March.

L. cruenta, see *L. laxa*.

L. cruenta var. alba, see *L. laxa* var. *alba*.

L. laxa. (B). (Syn. *L. cruenta*).

A native of Eastern S. Africa, the corm produces narrow lanceolate leaves in a two-ranked basal tuft. Flowers on 8-inch wiry stems up to ten narrow, tubular, opening to six oblong segments, salmon-pink, blotched crimson at base of petals. August–September.

L. laxa var. alba. (B). (Syn. *L. cruenta* var. *alba*).

The charming white form is similar to the type, the base of the segments have a pale rose blotch. July–August.

LAVANDULA (*Labiatae*).

A genus of aromatic plants, the common lavender *L. spica*, has produced two dwarf forms which can be considered for pan culture and with their intensely fragrant flowers and aromatic foliage they are a 'must' for a choice collection, for merely brushing against the foliage will cause the plant to emit a delightful perfume.

CULTIVATION. Compost A is suitable with normal watering during the growing and flowering season, dry but not arid in winter. They benefit from a light clipping back after flowering.

PROPAGATION. By cuttings in August or division of the plants in April. Repot every other year in early April.

L. spica 'Alba'. (E).
This is a dwarf shrublet with erect, squarish branches about 12 inches high, grey in colour owing to covering of minute hairs. Leaves linear, apex obtuse, margins recurved, greyish-green. Flowers in whorls on crowded spikes, each flower having a pair of oval bracts at its base, white. July. A native of the Mediterranean region.

L. spica 'Nana'. (E).
A dwarf form similar to the type but less than 6 inches high with square grey downy stems and small linear pale grey downy leaves. Flowers crowded in a spike on a short stem, tubular, greyish-blue. July.

LEDUM (*Ericaceae*).

This is a genus of plants which contains a few shrubs that are ideal for culture in the alpine house or frame and with their attractive white flowers provide a foil for the more vivid and exotic occupants.

CULTIVATION. Compost C with good drainage and plenty of lime-free water in spring and summer, just moist in winter. Best kept in a cool shady frame during hot summer months and sprayed in the evenings after similar days.

PROPAGATION. By green cuttings in July, or seed sown in compost 3 in March. Repot every other year after flowering.

L. buxifolium, see *Leiophyllum buxifolium*.

L. groenlandicum. (E). (Syn. *L. latifolium*).
An erect shrub up to 2 feet high, branches clothed with rust coloured hairs. Leaves oblong to narrow oblong, tapering to base, apex obtuse, margins recurved, dull dark green above, rust-red below due to heavy tomentum. Flowers in large terminal clusters, five-petalled open, white. May. A native of Greenland and N. America.

L. groenlandicum var. compactum. (E).
A dwarf compact form rarely 12 inches high with oval to oblong typical leaves and stems covered with rust-coloured hairs. Flowers smaller, white. May.

L. hypoleucum. (E). (Syn. *L. nipponicum*).
This is a small much branched shrub about 9 inches high with rust-coloured hairy branches. Leaves rough, long, narrow, pointed, dull green, margins recurved, white below with a covering of rust-coloured wool. Flowers in small terminal clusters, open five-petalled, white. May. A native of Japan.

L. latifolium, see *L. groenlandicum*.

L. minus. (E).
This is a small form of *L. palustre* from N.E. Asia, and differs from that species in being only 1 foot high with erect branches and linear leaves. White flowers in dense clusters. May.
L. nipponicum, see *L. hypoleucum.*
L. palustre. (E).
A small thin erect shrub up to 18 inches high with stems densely covered with rust-coloured down. Leaves small, narrow oblong, wrinkled, margins recurved, dark dull green above, rust coloured beneath with heavy covering of wool. Flowers in small terminal clusters, white cup-shaped, five-petalled. May. A native of Arctic regions, Asia and America.
L. palustre var. decumbens. (E).
A more prostrate lax form less than 12 inches high with linear leaves and flowers in much looser terminal heads, white. May.

LEIOPHYLLUM (*Ericaceae*).

This is a monotypic genus related to Ledum, from the New World with two varieties, and all three plants are suitable for alpine house or frame culture.
CULTIVATION. Compost C is suitable and the plants need plenty of lime-free water during the growing and flowering season, just moist at other periods. They are best kept in a cool shady spot after flowering. Protect from cold drying winds.
PROPAGATION. By green cuttings taken in July. Repot every other year after flowering.
L. buxifolium. (E). (Syn. *Ledum buxifolium*).
The species is a dwarf shrub rarely above 12 inches high, much-branched with reddish young wood. Leaves small oblong ovate, obtuse, arranged in whorls of three or four dark glossy green, lighter beneath. Flowers in congested terminal clusters, buds pink, opening to white, five-petalled, tinged with pink. May. A native of New Jersey.
L. buxifolium var. hugeri. (E).
This variety is much dwarfer, rarely above 6 inches high, with alternate, long, narrow, deep glossy green leaves and terminal clusters of white flowers. May. A native of E. America.
L. buxifolium var. prostratum. (E). (Syn. *L. lyonii*).
This form is an even smaller prostrate shrublet, less than 6 inches high and quite compact. Leaves oblong ovate, opposite, deep glossy green, lighter beneath and small terminal clusters of white flushed pink open five-petalled flowers. May. A native of E. America.
L. lyonii, see *L.b.* var. *prostratum.*

LEONTOPODIUM (*Compositae*).

The Edelweiss is a well-known plant about which much has been written, a great deal of it false, with stories of collectors losing their lives in the

Swiss Alps, trying to gather it from almost inaccessible cliffs. Any plants found in these positions are but escapees from the meadows below. The truth is, it is not an alpine plant at all and grows quite readily in the meadows by the countless thousands; in fact it is not indigenous to Switzerland, but is a native of the Russian Tundra. The Bulgarian form is a much rarer plant and requires a great deal of skill to keep it in good health.

CULTIVATION. Compost A with good drainage and a fair supply of water while growing and flowering, keep dry but not arid after growth has died down.

PROPAGATION. Easy by seed sown in March, compost 2, or careful division in March. Repot every other year when growth commences.

L. alpinum. (H).
This forms a small tufted plant of lanceolate leaves tapering to base, grey-green in colour, due to intense covering of woolly hairs. Flowers terminal on 5-inch leafy stems, clustered and enveloped by a circle of thick white woolly bracts, like strips of white flannel. June. A native of Europe.

L. alpinum var. crassense. (H).
A much more desirable form from the Balkans, which makes tufts of thick lanceolate leaves, grey-white with intense covering of downy hairs. Flowers in clustered terminal cymes, almost insignificant but surrounded by a three-tier circle of thick white woolly bracts, the inner top tier small, the other two becoming larger, the whole forming a delightful starfish of white wool. June. This plant needs care in watering and at no time should it be applied over the leaves for this will set up crown rot very easily. Keep on the dry side in winter until new growth is discernible, then immerse the pan for a few minutes in a tank containing 2 inches of water.

LEPTOSPERMUM (*Myrtaceae*).

A genus of tender or half hardy shrubs and trees native of Australasia, but one species, *L. scoparium*, has produced two forms which are suitable for alpine house culture.

CULTIVATION. Compost B is suitable with plenty of water during the growing and flowering season, keep dryish but not arid in winter. Protect from cold drying winds.

PROPAGATION. By cuttings of ripe wood in August or seed sown in March, compost 2. Repot every year in spring.

L. scoparium 'Nanum'. (E).
The species is a tall growing plant from New Zealand, which is not hardy except in very warm sheltered gardens, but this form is more reliable as well as being less than 12 inches high. It makes a congested mat of stiff, much-branched stems, densely clothed with the small entire, glandular, narrow linear-oblong, pointed, deep green leaves. The flowers, generally solitary, are produced from the leaf axils, sessile, five-rounded petals of white flushed pink, enhanced by a large crimson eye. June.

L. scoparium 'Nichollsii Nanum'. (E).
This is an even more desirable form, rarely above 4 inches high of erect, congested, firm, sparsely haired stems. Leaves alternate, small, entire, linear, crowded, deep bronze. Flowers solitary from terminal leaf axils, bright red five-rounded petals. May.

LEUCANTHEMUM, see CHRYSANTHEMUM.

LEUCOGENES (*Compositae*).

This is a small genus containing two species of sub-shrubs endemic to New Zealand which are a 'must' for any worthwhile collection of alpine plants. *L. grandiceps* is confined to the mountains of the South Island, whereas *L. leontopodium* is native to both North and South Islands and as the specific name of the latter denotes, they are the New Zealand counterparts of the European Edelweiss, but even more decorative with their persistent sub-shrubby stems and evergreen glistening silver foliage.
CULTIVATION. Compost B is suitable with faultless drainage and a good supply of water during the growing and flowering season, dry but not arid in winter. I have found that both these species require a little protection from hot sunshine and do best in a cool half-shady spot in warm summers. Any tendency to stragglyness can be overcome by cutting back overgrown shoots, and it will be found that new growth soon appears from the base of the treated shoots.
PROPAGATION. By green cuttings taken in June and kept moist in pure sand where they quickly strike. Repot every year when growth commences.

L. grandiceps. (E).
This makes a soft woody shrublet, lax in growth but not procumbent, about 4 inches high with small rounded stems densely clothed with a fine silver woolly down. Leaves arranged in symmetrical whorls along the whole length of the branches, sessile, base appressed, small, oval, obtuse, completely covered with a fine silvery-white wool, so that the plant appears to shine. Flowers small in a congested terminal cluster, very light yellow, surrounded by a symmetrical collar of woolly, silvery, floral bracts. June.

L. leontopodium. (E).
A more upright larger edition of *L. grandiceps* with white woolly rounded stems up to 8 inches high. Leaves congested in a symmetrical pattern round the stems, oblong to ovate-lanceolate, silver-grey in colour due to covering of silky hairs. The flowers are produced on short laterals, sparsely clothed with alternate and opposite white woolly leaves, typical composite light yellow flowers surrounded by radiating silver woolly bracts. June. There is no doubt that the New Zealand plants are not easy plants to keep in good health over long periods in this country, but by

taking frequent cuttings and raising new stock it is possible always to have fine compact specimens.

LEUCOJUM (*Amaryllidaceae*).

A small genus of bulbous plants of which two species can be used for alpine house decoration, for in a quiet way they are charming and delightful subjects with their pendant flowers reminiscent of the snowdrop, although this is to be expected, for botanically they are closely related to that genus.

CULTIVATION. The Snowflakes are plants which do not like a great deal of disturbance and are best potted up 1½ inch deep in compost B, the autumn species in late July and the spring in September. When growth appears water should be given and the compost kept moist until after the foliage dies down, when it must be reduced, but the compost should not be allowed to dry out. They prefer some protection from hot sunshine and do better in a cool spot. Top-dress with similar compost when fresh growth appears and only repot with fresh compost when necessary, in July or September according to autumn or spring flowering.

PROPAGATION. By seed sown in March, compost 2, or offsets when repotting.

L. autumnale. (B).
From a small bulbous rootstock appears a slender 2-inch solitary stem, bearing up to three flowers, pendant bell-shaped, slightly restricted at mouth, white flushed pink at base. October. Leaves appear afterwards, few, rush-like slender mid-green. A native of S. Europe.

L. trichophyllum. (B).
A small bulbous plant only a few inches high with leaves appearing at the same time as the flowers. Leaves thread-like, slender, slightly hairy. Flowers pendant, generally in pairs on 4-inch slender stems, funnel-shaped, narrow petals white flushed pink at base, apex apiculate. March. A native of Morocco.

LEUCOPOGON (*Epacridaceae*).

A near relative to the heaths, this New Zealand endemic is seldom seen in Britain, although hardy, having withstood a zero temperature, it certainly deserves to be more widely grown with its fragrant flowers and edible fruits.

CULTIVATION. Compost B with plenty of lime-free water while growing, just moist at other periods, top-dress with similar compost in early spring. It is best placed in a cool shady frame during hot weather.

PROPAGATION. By detaching runners in late June, and rooting them in the propagating frame. Repot every other year after flowering.

L. fraseri. (E). (Syn. *Cyathodes fraseri*).
This forms a dense close compact mat, only a few inches high but spreading by runners. Branches wiry, semi-erect, clothed with very fine hairs.

Leaves crowded, alternate, oblong, pointed, overlapping, margins ciliate, bright deep green. Flowers solitary from leaf axils, tubular five-lobed, pinkish-white with a fine fragrance. May. Fruit edible cylindrical drupe, deep reddish-yellow.

LEUCOTHOË (*Ericaceae*).

This is a small genus of hardy shrubs from Japan and N. America but there is only one species which is dwarf enough for pan culture. Although small in stature it has the distinction of having the largest flowers of the genus.
CULTIVATION. Compost C with good drainage is needed and a large shallow pan is best so that the wide spread of the plant can be seen to advantage. Needs plenty of lime-free water during the growing season and must be kept moist at all times. Plunge in a west facing frame after flowering and spray overhead in the evenings after hot days. Top-dress with similar compost in early spring.
PROPAGATION. By half-ripened cuttings taken with a heel of old wood, early August, or seed in compost 3 in March. Repotting should only be necessary about once in four years, immediately after flowering.
L. keiskei. (E).
From a central rootstock radiate the prostrate, zig-zagged smooth shoots, red in juvenile state, not more than 6 inches high but covering an area of 12 to 18 inches. Leaves thick, alternate, large, oval to ovate, tapering to a fine point, faintly serrulate, sparsely bristly below, bright shiny red when young turning to deep glossy green when mature. Flowers in small racemes from the terminal of the shoots, pendant, cylindrical, five re-curving lobes, white. July. A native of Japan.

LEWISIA (*Portulacaceae*).

An exclusively American genus, containing species which are admirably suited for cultivation in the alpine house or frame, all of which are extremely decorative and charming. For the most part easy, they only require care in watering to form large specimens. I grew on a pan of *L. howellii* until it covered the width of a 12-inch pan and when it was twelve years old it won the premier award, the Farrer Memorial Medal for the best plant in the show, a Royal Horticultural Society's Cultural Commendation and the Sewell Medal, all in one season. It must have had at least two thousand flowers when fully out and as can be imagined it presented a charming sight.
CULTIVATION. All species do well in compost A with faultless drainage. Care is needed in watering; a normal supply should be given when new growth is evident but on no account must the compost be allowed to become sodden. The herbaceous species require less water and more sun and should be baked when the foliage dies down, while the evergreen seem much happier if given a light shading during hot summer months.

Above: *Pleione forrestii* (see page 398)

Below: *Pleione pogonioides* (see page 398)

Above: *Potentilla nitida* (see page 403)

Below: *Primula allionii* (see page 406)

Water should be reduced in August and the compost allowed to become dryish but not arid in winter.

PROPAGATION. By seed in compost 2, March, but care should be taken for the species readily cross with each other. Most species form offsets, these can be rooted by detaching in June and treated as cuttings. Leaf cuttings will also prove successful, these being taken in June. Repot immediately after flowering, making sure in the evergreen species that the collar of the plant is protected from excess moisture by using chippings for at least an inch in depth.

L. brachycalyx. (H).
A native of N.W. America, forming several rosettes at apex of a small stout stem. Leaves fleshy, spatulate, long, tapered to base, dull glaucous green. Flowers solitary, sometimes almost sessile, nestling at the base of the centre of the rosette, rounded open funnel-shape, up to ten petals, satiny white. May.

L. columbiana. (E).
This makes open rosettes of flattish linear, fleshy, dark green leaves. Flowers on slender branched sprays, small star-shaped, pink veined purple. July. A native of Columbia Rockies.

L. columbiana 'Rosea'. (E).
Similar to the type but with much darker flowers of a deep red rose. This species needs care in watering, keep just moist while growing and dryish in winter.

L. cotyledon. (E).
A native of California, this is a fine plant which will form rosettes of up to 8 inches across. Leaves in rosette formation from a short stout stem, wide obovate to spatulate, entire, not toothed, tapering slowly to base, pale green marked brown. Flowers on a number of stout scapes, in clustered panicles, salmon veined pink. June.

L. eastwoodiana. (E).
A native of Oregon, this forms a distinct trunk, rounded and stout, often branched which bears rosettes of flattish linear, dark green leaves. Flowers in tight clusters, on slender branched radiating stems, small star-shaped, deep pink veined purple. June.

L. finchii. (E).
A native of Oregon, this plant makes fine tufted symmetrical rosettes of wide stubby crinkled bright green leaves. Flowers on 6-inch stout scapes up to six open star-shaped, pale pink veined deep rose. June.

L. heckneri. (E).
From a short stout stem are borne the large rosettes of thick, fleshy, obovate to spatulate leaves with small marginal teeth, bright green. Flowers on 6-inch stems in small panicles, large, rounded, pink, striped deep rose. June. A native of California.

L. howellii. (E).
Forms large symmetrical rosettes up to 10 inches across when well grown.

Leaves large, oblong to ovate, margins deckled and toothed, bright rich green with brownish markings. Flowers large, on 6-inch stout scapes, much-branched, carrying many blooms, star-shaped, deep rose with salmon-pink markings. May. A native of Oregon.

L. howellii 'Jennifer'. (E).
A form raised by myself, much larger than the type with thick, fleshy, dark green shading to reddish-brown spatulate leaves in rosette formation, margins deckled and toothed. Flowers on 8-inch stout stems up to twenty in a racemose cyme, large, rounded, pale salmon veined red. May. Garden origin.

L. howellii 'Weald Rose'. (E).
Another outstanding form with the usual rosette of large strap-like leaves and on 6-inch stems, large cherry-pink, rounded, flowers with darker veinings. June.

L. kellogii. (H).
A native of N. California, with rosettes of thick, fleshy, linear, deep red-green, glabrous shiny leaves. Flowers on short reddish stems, red tipped in bud, opening to large, rounded, white, light yellow at base, anthers deep cream. June.

L. leeana. (E).
A native of California, this is a dwarf tufted plant with fleshy, rounded, linear, light green leaves. Flowers in panicles on 6-inch stoutish stems, small star-shaped, white, veined pink. June. This plant is very sensitive to daylight and if used for showing, is best left in the open until an hour before judging takes place, otherwise the flowers will tend to fold up.

L. nevadensis. (H).
This plant, a native of Nevada, forms a small oblong, tuberous rootstock from which is produced tufts of small, erect, linear, pointed, fleshy deep green leaves. Flowers solitary, large, almost sessile, translucent, veined, white. May. The foliage dies away quickly, after which water should be withheld until growth re-appears in early winter.

L. oppositifolia. (H).
A herbaceous species from Oregon, with tufts of large oblanceolate, obtuse, tapered to base, channelled leaves, bright shiny green above, lighter below. Flowers on 6-inch stems up to four on branching laterals, many-petalled, roundish, white. May. Requires plenty of water while growing, dry conditions after foliage dies away.

L. pygmaea. (H).
This is a dainty little plant, in a good form producing small tufted rosettes, only one-third the size of *L. brachycalyx*, leaves fleshy, oblong lanceolate, deep glossy green. Flowers nestling in the tufts, almost sessile, open star-shaped, pale pink. May–June. A native of the Rocky Mountains.

L. rediviva. (H).
A native of W. United States, this forms carrot-like fleshy roots which produce tufted rosettes of rounded, linear, obtuse, fleshy green leaves.

The outstanding flowers which appear as the foliage commences to die away are solitary on the smallest of scapes, large, rounded, pale pink veined red. June–July. Plenty of water is necessary when growth commences, normally in early December, but must be completely withheld once the plant dies down. All available sun baking is required. This is another light-sensitive plant.

L. rediviva 'Winifred Herdman'. (H).
A form from the Okanagan Valley in British Columbia, this is similar to the type but with larger more-petalled bright red-rose flowers on 2-inch slender scapes. June.

L. 'Trevosia'. (E). *L. columbiana* × *L. howellii*.
This delightful hybrid was raised by the late Dr Guiseppi and has the rosette and leaf formation of *L. columbiana*. Flowers neat smallish, roundish star-shaped, on slender stems, reddish-pink flushed magenta. June.

L. tweedyi. (E).
This is possibly the best of the genus but certainly not the easiest to grow, flower and maintain in good health. Overwatering is a sure way of killing this plant. It forms a fleshy rootstock producing tufted rosettes of large, obovate, obtuse, thick, light green leaves, margins undulate. Flowers large, of good substance, solitary on short slender yellow scapes, up to 3 inches across, rounded, apricot or flesh pink, with yellow stamens. June. A native of Washington, U.S.A.

LILIUM (*Liliaceae*).

This is a large genus of bulbous plants, mostly too large for pan culture in the alpine house or frame, but included here, for there are two species and one variety which were formerly under Nomocharis that have been tranferred to Lilium and they are ideal for our purpose.

CULTIVATION. These plants are best grown in deep pots as they require a good depth of soil. Compost B is suitable over good drainage and the bulbs should be planted about 2 inches deep. They resent exposure to air and are almost useless if obtained in a dry state. Plenty of water is required while growing and flowering, and the plants must be kept just moist after the foliage dies down and at no time must the pots be allowed to dry out. In hot districts they are best plunged amongst dwarf ericaceous plants in half-shade.

PROPAGATION. Best by seed sown in August in compost 2, this should be sown thinly and the seedlings allowed to remain undisturbed for two years in the seed pan. In April of the third year the small bulbs should be potted up separately in small pots and moved the following season into 3-inch pots, then they should flower in their fourth year. Repotting, which is carried out every other year, must be done when growth commences in late April. Do not disturb the roots when repotting as they are brittle and the loss of these can easily mean the difference between success or failure.

L. nanum. (B). (Syn. *Nomocharis nana*).
A native of Sikkim and Tibet, making a small bulb with fleshy scales. Leaves up to four, deep green about 6 inches long, slender narrow, linear, tapered to a sharp point. Flowers solitary, on 8-inch stems, pendant, bell-shaped, mid-lilac speckled reddish-purple with purple anthers. June.
L. nanum var. flavidum. (B). (Syn. *Nomocharis nana* var. *flavida*).
This form from Southern Tibet is similar to the species but has pendant bells of yellow, often with purple markings at base of petals. June.
L. oxypetalum. (B). (Syn. *Nomocharis oxypetala*).
A medium-sized bulb of loose fleshy scales from which is borne a slender stem up to 9 inches high. Leaves arranged on the stem are sessile, narrow-elliptic, deep green, lighter beneath and channelled. Flowers terminal, nestling in a whorl of leaves, semi-erect, six-petalled open bell-shaped, yellow with basal markings of purple. June.

LIMONIUM (*Plumbaginaceae*). (Syn. **STATICE**).
A large genus of plants, the Sea Lavenders were at one time listed under the generic name of Statice but these are now transferred to Limonium. They have a wide distribution but cannot be called alpine plants in the truest sense of the word for they mostly inhabit sea coasts. There are a few species which make ideal pan plants and are suitable for culture under those conditions.
CULTIVATION. Compost A is suitable over good drainage and a normal supply of water while growing, dry but not arid in winter.
PROPAGATION. By seed sown in March, compost 1. Repot every other year in early April.
L. caesium. (E).
A native of Spain, which forms small basal rosettes of obovate, obtuse leaves, grey-green owing to lime pittings. Flowers in panicles on much-branched sturdy stems, each spike bearing a solitary flower of pale pink. July–August.
L. cancellatum. (E). (Syn. *Statice cancellata*).
A native of Asia Minor, this makes basal tufts of small spatulate green leaves, from which are produced contorted branchlets, making an inter-woven net. Flowers borne at the end of these laterals are large for size of plant, five-lobed tubular, persisting calyx and more open five-lobed corolla of lavender-mauve. July.
L. cosyrense. (E).
This forms a woody base bearing tightly packed tufts of narrow, spatulate, green leaves with recurved margins. Flowers on a much-branched slender 4-inch stem and terminal spikes of up to six, five-lobed, lavender. July. A native of S. Europe.
L. gougetianum. (E).
A dwarf plant only a few inches high of spatulate, dull-green, obovate

leaves with revolute margins in rosette formation. Flowers on much-branched stems, each spike bearing up to three tubular, five-lobed, persisting calyx of white with red interior and lavender corolla. July. A native of Italy and Spain.

L. minutum. (E).
A small tufted woody species from the Mediterranean regions. Leaves obovate to spatulate, rounded at apex, margins recurved, dull green. Flowers terminal on a slender 4-inch much-branched contorted stem, one rarely two, open, violet with tubular calyx from each division. June.

LINARIA (*Scrophulariaceae*).

A genus containing a large number of species including annuals and perennials from which a few are selected as suitable for alpine house or frame culture, where they will give a fine floral display over a long period. Pan culture also has the advantage of keeping the plants within bounds, for some of the species, given the opportunity, are quite rampant.

CULTIVATION. This is easy in compost A with good drainage and plenty of sunshine; a normal supply of water while growing, keep dry but not arid in winter.

PROPAGATION. By green cuttings in June or seed in compost 1, March, but this does not always breed true as the species cross readily. Repot every year after flowering.

L. aequitriloba. (E). (Syn. *Cymbalaria aequitriloba*).
A native of Corsica, this is a prostrate plant only an inch high with small three-lobed green leaves, lobes rounded with small tip. Flowers on 1-inch stems, small snapdragons, with spur, light purple. June–September.

L. alpina. (E).
This is a close tufted plant from a central rootstock only a few inches high with thick linear, grey-green leaves in whorls of four. Flowers in small racemes, violet with long spur, lower lip orange. June–August. A native of the European Alps.

L. alpina var. alba. (E).
This is a charming white form which provides a good foil to the type. June.

L. alpina var. rosea. (E).
The best form with clear pink flowers and a golden-yellow lower lip. June.

L. faucicola. (E).
A native of Spain, with slender radiating semi-prostrate stems, basal leaves in whorls of four, upper opposite, linear, grey-green in colour. Flowers terminal on slender pedicels, small blue-violet snapdragons, hairy with long spur, lower lip lighter violet. June–August.

L. origanifolia. (E). (Syn. *Chaenorrhinum origanifolium*).
A native of the Mediterranean area, this makes a small tufted plant with erect branches up to 6 inches high. Leaves opposite, oblong to obovate,

green. Flowers in loose racemes, small, violet, spotted, lower lip lighter. June–August.

L. supina. (E).
This is a dwarf tufted plant up to 6 inches high with the linear grey leaves arranged in whorls of five near the base of the upright stems. Flowers small snapdragons, pale to deep yellow. May–August. A native of Majorca.

L. supina var. nevadensis. (E).
Similar to the type but with charming flowers of bright purple with a maroon throat. May–August.

LINUM (*Linaceae*).

A widely distributed genus of plants from the warmer temperate regions, containing annuals, perennials, herbs and shrubs, of which there are a number suitable for culture in pans.

CULTIVATION. The Flaxes prefer a light well-drained soil in full sun so compost A over good drainage will be found suitable. Give plenty of water while in growth, keep dry but not arid in winter and give a warm dryish period in late summer. These plants require protection from cold drying winds.

PROPAGATION. Easy by green cuttings taken in June and rooted in the propagating frame. Quick rooting is essential for the two shrubby species, for unless they are well established by winter, there may be difficulty in bringing them through this period. Seed sown in March, compost 2, is a ready means of increase for the herbaceous species. Repot every other year when growth is active.

L. alpinum. (H).
A small lax plant about 6 inches high, stem covered with the linear, awl-shaped, feathery grey leaves marked with semi-transparent dots. Flowers large, fleeting, in small loose corymbs, silvery pale blue. June–August. A native of S. Europe.

L. arboreum. (E).
This is a smooth compact much-branched shrub up to 12 inches high with glabrous, rounded stems. Leaves sessile, spatulate, obtuse, recurved, grey-green. Flowers in short stemmed terminal panicles, fleeting, thin textured five-petalled golden-yellow. June–September. A native of Crete.

L. elegans. (E). (Syn. *L. iberidifolium*).
A charming dwarf shrublet rarely above 6 inches high from Mount Athos in the Athos Peninsula, where it inhabits rocky meadows at high altitudes. From a central rootstock radiate procumbent, rounded, much-branched smooth stems, green in the juvenile stage, turning to brownish-green when mature and very brittle. Leaves sessile on short twigs in whorls forming a flattish pyramid, spatulate, obtuse or slightly pointed, deeply marked with a median groove, glabrous, light olive-green. Flowers large for size of plant, 1½ inch across, up to six in cymes from the apex of the

leafy pyramids on small stems, five-petalled, rounded, satiny textured, golden-yellow with lighter yellow veining. May–June. Not an easy plant in cultivation, needs care in watering and a good ripening period in late July, also protection from cold winds and severe frosts.

L. flavum. (H).
Makes basal tufts and semi-wooded stems up to 12 inches high. Leaves narrow, lanceolate, acute, green. Flowers in congested clusters on much-branched stems, fleeting, golden-yellow. June–September. A native of E. Europe.

L. iberidifolium, see *L. elegans.*

L. olympicum. (E).
A small procumbent semi-woody plant only an inch or so high. Leaves tufted, close, compact, narrow, ovate, pointed at apex, bluish-green covered with a fine down. Flowers terminal on 8-inch prostrate, sparsely leaved, light green stems, open saucer-shaped, five-lobed, rounded, lilac-pink with prominent darker veins. May. A native of Asia Minor.

L. salsoloides. (E).
A small compact plant with twiggy ascending stems from a woody base less than 6 inches high. Leaves crowded, narrow, linear, grey. Flowers large in prostrate sprays, open, rounded, pearly white, veined. June. A native of S. Europe.

L. salsoloides var. nanum. (E).
This is a more desirable form quite prostrate and compact, only an inch or so high, similar to the type with flowers just as large and outstanding. June. Needs care in watering and protection from cold winds.

L. tenuifolium. (E).
A small glabrous twiggy plant only a few inches high with much-branched thin stems. Leaves crowded, narrow, linear, grey-green. Flowers on short stems, rounded, pale pink, veined. July. A native of S. Europe.

LITHOSPERMUM (*Boraginaceae*).

This genus contains some of the best blue flowered plants, rivalling the gentians in depth of colour. Easy to cultivate provided attention is given to their few needs, although *L. diffusum* 'Heavenly Blue' has a bad reputation for suddenly collapsing without warning (who has a specimen of any great age?); there is little on record of its longevity and it is certainly a money-spinner for enterprising nurserymen.

CULTIVATION. Compost B over good drainage with plenty of lime-free water for all these plants with the exception of *L. oleifolium* which grows on limestone, just moist in winter.

PROPAGATION. By green cuttings in June. Repot every year after flowering.

L. diffusum. (E). (Syn. *L. prostratum*).
The type plant is a native of Spain and has given rise to a number of forms which are noted here. It makes a low spreading, soft wooded shrub roughly

6 inches high with long radiating lax branchlets from a central rootstock, often rooting where the shoots are in contact with the ground. Leaves alternate, sessile, arranged round the stems, base appressed, long, narrow, tapering, rounded at apex, covered with wiry hairs, margins recurved, midrib sunken, prominent below, green. Flowers sessile in small sprays from the leaf axils, short tubular, five-lobed, gentian blue. June–September.

L. diffusum 'Album'. (E).

This is similar to the type with dainty white flowers, not an improvement but a good foil to the blues of the genus. May–July.

L. diffusum 'Heavenly Blue'. (E).

The best known form with gentian blue flowers enhanced with that indescribable tinge of red. May–August.

L. diffusum 'Grace Ward'. (E).

A variety with the largest flowers of all the different forms and a very desirable plant. Unfortunately 'Heavenly Blue' often has to do duty for it. May–August.

L. 'Froebelii', see *Moltkia 'Froebelii'*.

L. graminifolium, see *Moltkia suffruticosa*.

L. 'Intermedium', see *Moltkia 'Intermedia'*.

L. oleifolium. (E).

A native of Spain, this species is found on limestone formations in nature and is a truly saxatile plant. It is one of the few plants which seems to appreciate a little old lime rubble mixed with the compost and requires faultless drainage to give of its best. A prostrate or semi-erect shrub rarely 6 inches high with rounded wiry stems covered with a greenish-white wool, ageing to brown. Leaves sessile, oval-obovate, tapered to base, arranged alternately round the twigs, forming elongated whorls, grey-green, covered with flat whitish hairs. Flowers in flattish terminal racemes five-lobed, open funnel-shaped, pinkish-blue in bud opening to a bright glistening mid-blue. May–June.

L. petraeum, see *Moltkia petraea*.

L. prostratum, see *L. diffusum*.

L. rosmarinifolium. (E).

This is a native of the mountains of Central Italy, making a compact bushy shrublet about 12 inches high with erect branches. Leaves sessile, alternate, narrow oblong, obtuse, green. Flowers in small terminal clusters, funnel-shaped, five-lobed, bright blue, lined white. February.

LLOYDIA (*Liliaceae*).

A small genus of bulbous plants of the northern hemisphere, which contains two species that can be used for pan culture in the alpine house, but these are difficult to cultivate and keep alive for any period of time.

CULTIVATION. Compost C with faultless drainage gives the best chance of success with plenty of water while in growth, just moist after the foliage dies down. Requires a cool place in the north-facing frame and must not be kept in the alpine house longer than necessary. The bulbs must not be allowed to dry out. (See Appendix 1 also.)

PROPAGATION. By seed sown in March, compost 3. Repot only when necessary while in growth.

L. serotina. (B).

This is up to 3 inches high with small semi-rounded green leaves. Flowers solitary on thin stems, rarely two, bell-shaped, semi-pendant, white tinged yellow at base outside, with three reddish stripes inside petals. June. A native of high altitudes, including the European Alps and Wales.

LOBELIA (*Campanulaceae*).

A large genus of plants with a wide distribution over both temperate and tropical regions but there are only two species which can be considered for the alpine house, neither of them alpines but useful for their late flowering habit, thus providing a display when the main flush of flowers is over.

CULTIVATION. Both these plants require a moist leafy medium in half-shade so that compost C is suitable with plenty of water during the growing season, just moist at other periods. Protect from cold drying winds. *L. syphilitica* var. *nana* requires less after the foliage has died down.

PROPAGATION. By division in early April. Repot when necessary in April.

L. linnaeoides. (E). (Syn. *Pratia linnaeoides*).

A small creeping mat-forming herb only an inch or so high. Leaves small, obicular, on thread stalks, dentate, bright shiny green. Flowers small lobelia-like, white, backs flushed light blue-violet. July–October. A native of New Zealand.

L. syphilitica var. nana. (H).

This dwarf form of the species is only a few inches high with slender stems. Leaves sessile, ovate, tapered to both ends, irregular dentate, pale green. Flowers solitary from the leaf axils, large, light blue. July. A native of E. America.

LOISELEURIA (*Ericaceae*).

A monotypic genus whose only member is commonly known as the Creeping Azalea, found on granite formations of Europe including the British Isles, always amongst low herbage in exposed positions.

CULTIVATION. This is not an easy species to flower well in cultivation, especially in the hot drier climatic conditions prevailing in the southern half of the country. Its need of sun to induce flowering must be coupled with moisture, as it will not tolerate parched conditions. Compost C is suitable with a good supply of lime-free water during the growing season and just moist at other times. It is best kept in a half-shady frame, sprayed during hot periods and only brought into the house if and when in flower.

Top-dress in early spring with a similar compost, working this well down amongst the shoots.

PROPAGATION. By layers or cuttings taken with a heel of the old wood in late July. Repot every second year in late May.

L. procumbens. (E). (Syn. *Azalea procumbens*).

It forms a mat of prostrate tangled wiry, rounded branches only an inch or so high. Leaves crowded, opposite, minute, narrow, oval, margins recurved, deep glossy green, lighter below. Flowers in small terminal clusters, open bell-shaped, five-lobed, pale pink or white. June.

LUPINUS (*Leguminosae*).

A large genus of plants, the Lupins contain a large number of annuals or herbaceous perennials well known in gardens especially so since the introduction of the Russell hybrids. There are three species which concern us here, all attractive due to their intense silver foliage and they never look so well as when protected from the weather by being grown in pans for the alpine house or frame.

CULTIVATION. This is easy in compost A over faultless drainage, these plants require normal watering while growing but dryish conditions in winter.

PROPAGATION. By seed in compost 2, March. Repot every year in early April.

L. confertus. (H).

A small plant up to 8 inches high with erect stems clothed with appressed hairs. Leaves deeply cut, six to eight segments covered with silvery-grey hairs. Flowers in a cone-shaped crowded, raceme, standard blue, centre white. June. A native of N. America.

L. lyallii. (H).

A perennial with a woody base up to 4 inches high, stems covered with silky hairs. Leaves deeply cut, leaflets six grey-green, covered with silky hairs. Flowers in a short crowded spire, short stalked, bright blue. June. A native of W.N. America.

L. ornatus. (H).

An outstanding plant rarely above 12 inches high with ascending stems from a woody base. Leaves cut into four to seven leaflets, bright silver with silky appressed hairs. Flowers in a short racemose spike, not dense, standard blue, white at centre, wings blue. June. A native of California.

Lychnis lagascae, see *Petrocoptis lagascae*.

L. pyrenaica, see *P. pyrenaica*.

LYSIONOTUS (*Gesneriaceae*).

From this small genus of dwarf shrubs there is only one species suitable for alpine house culture, for the others are not hardy and require protection in this country.

CULTIVATION. Needs care for it is a far from easy plant to grow satisfactorily. Compost C is suitable and lime-free water is essential, plenty
during the growing and flowering season, just moist when dormant.
Shade is essential during hot periods and a cool spot in a west facing frame
will be ideal, returning the pan to the alpine house in early autumn, for
the pan must not be allowed to become frost bound.
PROPAGATION. By careful division in April or if ripe seed is obtainable
this should be sown in early March, compost 3. Repot in early May when
new shoots have reached the side of the pan.
L. pauciflorus. (D).
It makes fleshy stems which run underground to the side of the pan when
satisfied before pushing up through the compost. Leaves normally in threes,
arranged round the stems on short reddish stalks, oblong, fleshy, obtuse,
evenly toothed, deep dull green above, white beneath. Flowers in small
cymes, tubular, slightly open at mouth, white flushed pink with deeper
veining inside. August–September. A native of Japan.

MAIANTHEMUM (*Liliaceae*).

A single species which is ideal for pan culture provided it is given a cool
spot and not kept in the alpine house after flowering.
CULTIVATION. Compost C is suitable with plenty of water while in
growth, just moist at other periods.
PROPAGATION. By division in April. Repot when necessary in early
April.
M. bifolium. (H).
This is a dwarf creeping herbaceous perennial with a thinnish rootstock,
from which are borne short thinnish stems, each carrying on the upper
half two cordate shiny green, acute leaves, thickly veined. Flowers on
3-inch stems in a dense raceme, up to thirty, fleshy, white. June. A native
of Europe including Britain.

MALVASTRUM (*Malvaceae*).

A genus of mostly herbs or sub-shrubs from America of which there are
two suitable for the alpine house or frame, these needing protection from
cold drying winds and prolonged frosts.
CULTIVATION. Compost A with good drainage, plenty of water while
growing and flowering, keep dry but not arid in winter.
PROPAGATION. By seed sown with bottom heat in March, compost 2,
or cuttings taken in July. Repot when necessary in late April.
M. campanulatum. (E).
This is a small sub-shrub up to 12 inches high with thin downy stems.
Leaves sessile, three to seven lobed, segments dentate, light green. Flowers
on the leafy stems in a terminal cluster, rounded five-lobed, light purple-
rose. August. A native of Chile.

M. coccineum. (E).
This is a small tufted plant about 6 inches high with light grey stems from a creeping rootstock. Leaves three to five-lobed; segments narrow, light green. Flowers on short slender stems in a terminal raceme, five-lobed, rounded, scarlet. July–September. United States.

MARGYRICARPUS (*Rosaceae*).

A small member of the mighty rose family which will make a decorative if not showy specimen for pan culture in the alpine house or frame, the attraction being the large pearl-like berries which the plant bears in profusion.
CULTIVATION. Compost A is suitable, well drained, with an ample supply of water during the growing season, keep dry but not arid in winter.
PROPAGATION. By green cuttings in May, or seed, compost 2, in February. Repot every year in late April.
M. setosus. (E).
It makes a semi-prostrate shrublet up to 6 inches high with bright yellow smooth branches covered with pinnate leaves, segments awl-shaped, reflexed, deep green. Flowers insignificant, produced from the leaf axils, followed by pearl-like white globular fruits in late August. A native of Chile.

MAZUS (*Scrophulariaceae*).

A small genus of creeping herbs, akin to Mimulus, with representatives in Asia and Australasia, from which there are three suitable species for the alpine house or frame.
CULTIVATION. Compost A with good drainage and a warm sunny position in the alpine house is required with plenty of water while growing and flowering, just moist at other periods.
PROPAGATION. By seed sown when ripe in compost 2 or division in late April. Repot every other year in April.
M. pumilio. (E).
A native of New Zealand, this forms creeping stoloniferous branches with rosettes of obovate to spatulate, blunt, green hairy leaves. Flowers small on 2-inch stems, up to six musk-like, lilac tinged violet, yellow at throat. July.
M. radicans. (E). (Syn. *Mimulus radicans*).
A dwarf prostrate mat of rooting branches and small erect laterals up to 2 inches high. Leaves crowded, obovate, obtuse, rough, bronze. Flowers small, solitary, two-lipped, five-lobed, white with violet markings. June–July. A native of New Zealand.
M. reptans. (E).
A native of the Himalayas, with prostrate, slender, much-branched stems, rooting where they touch the soil. Leaves in small tufts, narrow, spatulate,

margins dentate, green. Flowers large, up to five almost sessile, musk-like, violet-blue, white throat speckled orange. June. A quicker grower than the former species this plant needs repotting every year.

MECONOPSIS (*Papaveraceae*).

A genus of plants which have come to the fore in recent years mostly due to the introduction of the Blue Poppy, *M. betonicifolia*, from Tibet, the centre of this outstanding genus, although one species, *M. cambrica*, is a native of this country. The majority are too large for pan culture but there are three species which are suitable.

CULTIVATION. Compost C is required over good drainage and plenty of water is necessary during the growing and flowering season, just moist at other periods. Surface water is to be avoided, for any lodging in the crown of the plant will quickly set up rotting. They are best plunged in a west-facing, half-shady frame during hot spells and only brought into the house for flowering, also during the resting season in winter.

PROPAGATION. By seed sown in compost 3 for all species with the exception of *M. quintuplinervia*, which is best increased by careful division in early July. Repot only when necessary.

M. bella. (E).
A native of Nepal, this is possibly the smallest of the species being only 4 inches high. It makes a crowded tuft of bi-pinnate lobed, bright green leaves on bristly stalks. Flowers solitary on short basal stems, large rounded, four-petalled poppies of glistening pale blue, deep purple-blue filaments and yellow anthers. May. Requires careful cultivation and plenty of moisture which must have free drainage. A collar of granite chippings round the crown of the plant will help.

M. quintuplinervia. (H).
A herbaceous perennial, which when satisfied increases by underground runners, each terminating in a basal rosette of narrow-oblanceolate dull green leaves, thickly covered with creamy brown bristles. Flowers solitary on 12-inch bristly stems, pendant, rounded, bell-shaped, lavender-blue, flushed purple at base and clustered light cream stamens. June. A native of Tibet.

M. sherriffi. (E).
A recent introduction from Bhutan, this is a charming plant forming dense basal rosettes. Leaves entire, oblanceolate, pale blue-green, densely clothed with bristly golden-brown hairs. Flowers solitary, on 12-inch hairy stems, these stems bear a whorl of five lanceolate leaves about 4 inches from the base, large rounded, six-petalled, margins undulate, deep rose-red, yellow stamens, bright green stigma. May–June.

MELANDRIUM (*Caryophyllaceae*).

This genus is related to Silene, and the species listed here will mostly be found under that generic name in catalogues. They are charming plants and flowering as they do in summer after the main flush of alpine plants have gone, they provide welcome colour during that period.

CULTIVATION. Compost A is ideal over faultless drainage with plenty of water during the growing and flowering season, just moist at other periods.

PROPAGATION. By seed in compost 2 in March. Repot when necessary in early April.

M. elisabethae. (E). (Syn. *Silene elisabethae*).
This is a native of Tyrol and Italy, making basal rosettes of lanceolate, shiny green leaves, margins ciliate. Flowers on 4-inch slender stems, solitary, calyx tubular, tinged red, petals, magenta-red, deeply toothed. July–August.

M. pennsylvanicum. (E). (Syn. *Silene pennsylvanica*).
A native of N. America, this is a dwarf tufted plant with basal tufts of narrow spatulate, green leaves with a hairy stalk, stem leaves lanceolate. Flowers in small clusters on 4-inch stems, large five-petalled, irregular toothed, pink with hairy calyx. June.

M. wherryi. (E). (Syn. *Silene wherryi*).
From Ohio, this species forms basal rosettes of lanceolate green leaves. Flowers large on 6-inch stems in open terminal cymes, five-petalled bright pink, blotched rose inside at base, slightly notched, calyx long, covered with a white down. June–July.

MENZIESIA (*Ericaceae*).

A small genus of really choice shrubs of American and Japanese origin, containing a number which are suitable for pan culture in the alpine house or frame.

CULTIVATION. Compost C is ideal with plenty of lime-free water during early spring and summer, keep moist at other periods. Top-dress in early spring with similar compost and the plants should be protected against cold drying winds.

PROPAGATION. By green cuttings in June. Repot every other year after flowering.

M. ciliicalyx. (D).
This forms a small slow growing shrub, reaching only 2 feet after many years under pan culture. Branches spreading, smooth, light brown in the juvenile state, becoming greyish-brown, striated white. Leaves alternate near terminals of laterals, almost in rosettes, oval to obovate, tapered to base, midrib extending past the apex, bright light green, paler beneath, sparsely clothed with bristly hairs especially on the margins, veining reticulate. Flowers pendant, bell-shaped in small umbels from apex of previous year's growth, changing from light green at base to purple at the mouth. May. A native of Japan.

M. ciliicalyx var. lasiophylla. (D).
This is similar to the type, slow growing with larger pendant flowers,

deeper purple at apex of lobes, shading to yellowish-green at base. May. A native of Japan.

M. pilosa. (D).
A small erect shrub up to 18 inches high in cultivation, when mature. The young wood is covered with fine down, the adult smooth and hairless. Leaves alternate, borne almost in rosette formation at apex of laterals, obovate to oval, tapered to base and apex; pale greenish-yellow, margined sparsely, bristly ciliate, lighter below due to covering of down, midrib extended, veining reticulate. Flowers in small terminal clusters on previous year's wood, bell-shaped, four-lobed white flushed yellow. May. A native of N. America.

M. purpurea. (D).
Reported to be up to 8 feet in its native habitat, it rarely grows above 2 feet in cultivation, taking a number of years to reach that stature. It is a much-branched shrub, new wood reddish-brown and quite smooth. Leaves alternate, crowded near apex of laterals, oval to obovate, tapered to base, often rounded at apex, bright green, thinly covered with bristly hairs, more pronounced on margins, lighter and smooth below, veining reticulate, midrib slightly protruding. Flowers pendant in small umbels, cylindrical bell-shaped, borne on previous year's wood, four to five lobed, bright red with a tinge of purple. May. A native of Japan.

MERENDERA (*Liliaceae*).

A small genus of hardy bulbs closely related to Colchicum and sometimes listed in catalogues under that name. They are suitable subjects for pan culture and give colour in the house at a period of the year when this is at a premium.

CULTIVATION. From three to six corms planted 1 inch deep in July, in a moist but not wet compost A. Water is needed from the time the flower buds appear until the leaves die down when it should be withheld and the pots given a good baking in the sun.

PROPAGATION. By seed in August, compost 2, or offsets in July. Repot every year in July.

M. aitchisonii, see *M. robusta*.

M. bulbocodium, see *M. montana*.

M. caucasica, see *M. trigyna*.

M. montana. (B). (Syn. *M. bulbocodium*; *Colchicum montanum*).
A native of the Spanish Pyrenees, this produces a single, rarely two, flowers from a spathe, with six narrow pointed starry-shaped petals, light mauve with yellow anthers. Leaves after flowers three linear, sickle-shape, channelled, green, 3 inches long. September.

M. robusta. (B). (Syn. *M. aitchisonii*).
This is a Persian species, with up to four flowers from a spathe, each having six narrow lanceolate, sub-acute, reflexed petalled star-shaped flowers of the palest lilac, each segment flushed red at base, anthers yellow. Leaves

up to six, short at flowering time, linear, concave, deep-green with acute apex, elongating after flower dies away. February.

M. sobolifera. (B).

A species with a wide distribution over Bulgaria, Asia Minor into Persia, producing a single flower from the spathe, six-petalled, segments linear, sub-reflexed, pale lilac with a deeper flush, anthers yellowish-brown. Leaves small at the same time as the flower, narrow, lanceolate, deep green. March–April.

M. trigyna. (B). (Syn. *M. caucasica, Bulbocodium trigynum*).

A native of the Caucasus, this produces up to three flowers from a spathe. Flowers six-petalled, star-shaped, segments narrow, elliptic, sub-acute, with golden-brown anthers. Leaves after flowers, small narrow, lanceolate, apex obtuse, tapered to base, channelled, deep green. December.

MERTENSIA (*Boraginaceae*).

A medium sized genus of mostly perennial herbs with a wide distribution, containing some delightful species, the flowers of which are usually some shade of blue, and providing a few species suitable for pan culture in the alpine house or frame.

CULTIVATION. These plants are not always easy, a number having the habit of being short lived especially under pan culture. Compost B is suitable over good drainage, plenty of water is required while in growth and during the flowering period, keep dry but not arid when the foliage dies down.

PROPAGATION. By seed sown as soon as ripe, compost 2, or careful division in July. Division should not be attempted with *M. maritima* which resents disturbance and this treatment will only result in failure. Repot when necessary after flowering.

M. alpina. (H).

Forms a tufted plant with slender erect stems up to 6 inches high. Leaves alternate, oblong to spatulate, apex obtuse, smooth, blue-green. Flowers in loose terminal clusters, five-lobed, open bell-shaped, light blue. May. A native of the Rocky Mountains.

M. coriacea, see *M. viridis*.

M. coventryana. (H).

A native of the Himalayas, this produces semi-erect stems, clothed with alternate, linear, obtuse, grey-green hairy leaves. Flowers in terminal cymes, open five-lobed, star-shaped, light clear blue with protruding styles. May.

M. echioides. (H).

A native of the Himalayas, this is a tufted plant up to 6 inches high, clothed with the alternate, soft hairy, spatulate, obtuse, stalked, green leaves. Flowers in dense terminal, semi-pendant, racemes, five-lobed, funnel-shaped, deep blue, no scales in throat of corolla tube. This species requires some shade during hot months. June.

M. echioides var. elongata, see *M. elongata.*

M. elongata. (H). (Syn. *M. echioides* var. *elongata*).
Another Himalayan species, often reputed to be only a form of *M. echioides* but it differs in being smaller with oblong leaves. Flowers bright blue and small scales in throat of corolla tube. May.

M. horneri. (H).
This is a rare native of British Columbia, which forms a small irregular tuber, it produces not more than three slender 6-inch stems, clothed sparsely with the alternate, ovate, sub-acute, glaucous green leaves. Flowers terminal in crowded pendant panicles up to fifteen, long, narrow, tubular, five-lobed, open saucer-shape at mouth of tube, turquoise blue. March. This plant dies down quickly after flowering but should not be allowed to dry out.

M. lanceolata. (H).
A native of the Rocky Mountains, it makes erect slender stems up to 8 inches high. Leaves in basal tufts, spatulate, downy, margins ciliate, stem leaves few, alternate, thick, linear-oblong, downy, blue-green. Flowers terminal in an open panicle, drooping, long, narrow, tubular, more open at mouth, five-lobed, pink in bud opening to deep blue. May.

M. longiflora. (H).
A native of N. America, this is a herbaceous perennial throwing up two to three slender 6-inch stems, sparsely clad with alternate, oblong to spatulate, grey-green leaves. Flowers in terminal open panicles, up to fifteen pendant, long, narrow, tubular, five-lobed, bright blue, the last quarter of the corolla is open bell-shaped. April.

M. maritima. (H).
This is our native Oyster Plant, making prostrate branched fleshy stems clad with the thick, glaucous, ovate leaves with a blue bloom. Flowers erect in corymbose racemes at the terminal of the shoots, tubular, bell-shaped, pink in bud opening to clear blue with white throat. June.

M. nutans. (H).
Another species with slender tubers which throws up two or three, 3- to 4-inch stems. Leaves sparse, broad, lanceolate, sub-acute, glaucous green. Flowers terminal, up to ten in a loose semi-pendant panicle, narrow tubular, open at the mouth, five rounded lobes, pink in bud opening to bright blue. May. A native of N. America.

M. primuloides. (H).
This species forms a basal leafy tuft from which arises 4-inch hairy stems. Leaves small, hairy, elliptical, grey-green. Flowers terminal, in dense racemes, narrow, tubular, open at the mouth with five rounded lobes, pink in bud opening to pale violet with a golden eye. June. A native of Himalaya.

M. viridis. (H). (Syn. *M. coriacea*).
This makes close compact tufts of fleshy, wide ovate, sub-acute, glabrous light green leaves. Flowers terminal in erect clusters on short stems,

tubular, opening at the mouth to five roundish lobes, pink in bud changing to a clear blue with a white eye. May–June. A native of S.E. Wyoming.

MICROMERIA (*Labiatae*).

A genus of herbs or sub-shrubs, mostly from the Mediterranean region, of which there are three species suitable for alpine house or frame culture. CULTIVATION. This is easy in compost A with good drainage and full sun, plenty of water while in growth, keep dry but not arid in winter. All require a dry period in late summer to help to ripen the wood. PROPAGATION. By green cuttings taken with a heel in June. Repot every year in April.

M. corsica. (E).
A native of Corsica, this is a prostrate much-branched, rooting, sub-shrub, stems sparsely covered with hairs. Leaves small, entire, almost orbicular, grey-green with rough margins. Flowers large, from the leaf axils, purple. July.

M. graeca. (E).
This is a small sub-shrub up to 4 inches high with semi-erect, downy stems. Leaves thickish, ovate to obovate-oblong, narrow toward apex of stems, grey and aromatic. Flowers small in axillary few-flowered racemes, pink. July. A native of Greece.

M. piperella. (H). (Syn. *Thymus piperella*).
A species with slender thread stems up to 3 inches high. Leaves rounded to cordate, grey-green, aromatic. Flowers few in terminal clusters, small tubular, bright pink. July. A native of S.W. Europe.

MIMULUS (*Scrophulariaceae*).

A fairly large genus of mostly perennial herbs of which only two Musks are really suitable for alpine house culture.
CULTIVATION. Both require a damp soil and are well suited to compost B which if kept moist, grows these plants to perfection. Water should be reduced during winter but at no time must the soil be allowed to dry out. PROPAGATION. By seed sown in March, compost 2, division in April, or green cuttings taken in May root readily in a cool moist propagating frame.

M. cupreus. (H).
A native of Chile, this is a tufted herbaceous perennial about 6 inches high with ovate to oblong, palmately-veined leaves. Flowers on 6-inch stems, two lipped, five-lobed, copper coloured throat, yellow spotted brown. June–September. There are several forms of this plant of which the best are 'Prince Bismark', cherry-red, 'Red Emperor', crimson-scarlet, 'Whitecroft Scarlet', scarlet.

M. primuloides. (H).
A small tufted downy plant increasing by leafless thread-like runners. Leaves in rosettes, obovate, hairy, green. Flowers at end of runners,

solitary, open tubular with restricted throat, yellow spotted reddish-brown. June. Requires a cool shady spot in hot weather. A native of California.

M. radicans, see *Mazus radicans*.

MINUARTIA (*Caryophyllaceae*).

A genus of plants with a very confused nomenclature, most of which have at some time or other done duty under the generic names of Alsine or Arenaria in catalogues. Alsine is no longer a valid generic name and the species have been placed in either Arenaria or Minuartia. There are a few plants in this genus which with their cushion-forming habit make ideal subjects for pan cultivation in the alpine house or frame.

CULTIVATION. Compost A is suitable over good drainage with a normal supply of water during the growing season, keep just moist at other periods.

PROPAGATION. By seed where set, in April, compost 1, division immediately after flowering or green cuttings in July. Repot every year after flowering.

M. aretioides. (E).

A cushion-forming plant from a much-branched creeping rootstock only an inch or so high. Leaves small, ovate, thick, channelled, obtuse with short tip, glabrous green. Flowers almost sessile from terminal leaves, four-petalled, white. May. A native of European Alps.

M. rupestris. (E). (Syn. *Arenaria lanceolata*).

A native of the alps of France and Italy, this is a creeping prostrate cushion-forming, much-branched species only an inch or so high. Leaves in tufts, oblong-lanceolate, crowded, bright green, margins ciliate. Flowers up to three, terminal, rounded five-petalled, light rose on small pedicels. May.

M. saxifraga. (E).

An extremely rare species even in its natural habitat, it is confined to a few stations in the Rila mountains of Bulgaria. It forms a close rounded compact cushion an inch or so high with small narrow, linear, acute, bright green leaves in rosette formation. Flowers on 2-inch scapes up to four large, open five-petalled stars, white. May.

MITCHELLA (*Rubiaceae*).

A small genus containing two species and one variety suitable for pan culture in the alpine house or frame; these must be considered as essentially plants for the connoisseur and require that little extra care to cultivate them successfully.

CULTIVATION. Compost C over good drainage with a good supply of lime-free water during the growing season, the plants should be kept moist at other periods; top-dress with similar compost in early spring. They should not be kept in the alpine house during hot weather but placed in a north-facing frame, protected from cold winds and sprayed in the evenings after hot summer days.

PROPAGATION. By layers which often root where the stem comes in contact with the compost, these should be detached from the plant and treated as cuttings until re-established. Seed if available in compost 3, March. Repot only when necessary in late April when the roots are active.

M. repens. (E).

A prostrate, soft-wooded shrublet only an inch or so high with slender squared stems. Leaves small, opposite, almost cordate, rounded at apex, slightly notched at base, deep shiny green with white veins. Flowers in pairs, almost sessile, from terminal shoots, tubular, wide at mouth, four-lobed, white flushed purplish-red, fragrant. June. Berries oval in shape, scarlet. A native of N. America.

M. repens var. leucocarpa. (E).

Similar in all respects to the type but with large rounded white fruits.

M. undulata. (E).

This is the Japanese counterpart of *M. repens*, making a procumbent, creeping, soft wooded shrub with smooth stems. Leaves opposite, pointed, almost triangular, dark glossy green, margins undulate. Flowers in pairs from apex of shoots on shortest of stems, tubular at base, wide at mouth, four-lobed, pink flushed purple at tip, fragrant. July. Red berries.

MOLTKIA (*Boraginaceae*).

A genus of plants closely related to Lithospermum and often found under that generic name in catalogues, there being small botanical differences between the two genera. In all, three species and two hybrids are suitable for pan culture, these providing five dwarf specimens of shrubby habit with a great deal of decorative value in the alpine house or frame.

CULTIVATION. Compost A with good drainage and a normal supply of water during the growing and flowering season, followed by a dryish period in late July to ripen the current year's growth. Keep just moist in winter.

PROPAGATION. By green cuttings in July. Repot every year when new growth has commenced.

M. caerulea. (E).

A native of Asia Minor, this makes an erect shrublet about 9 inches high with hairy branches. Leaves oblong to lanceolate, pointed, grey-green owing to covering of silky hairs. Flowers in terminal spikes on 4-inch stems, long narrow tubular, five-lobed, bluish-purple. April.

M. 'Froebelii'. (E). (Syn. *Lithospermum* 'Froebelii').

A small much-branched, woody sub-shrub, stated to be a hybrid between *M. petraea* and *M. suffruticosa* about 6 inches high. Leaves long, narrow, lanceolate, covered with long appressed silky hairs, deep green. Flowers

in small branched terminal cymes, funnel-shaped, five-lobed, bright blue.
May. Garden origin.

M. 'Intermedia'. (E). (*M. petraea* × *M. suffruticosa*). (Syn. *Lithospermum* 'Intermedium').

Another garden hybrid between the two species which forms a dense bushy shrublet of erect grey-haired branches up to 15 inches high. Leaves alternate, long, narrow, grey-green due to covering of appressed silky hairs. Flowers crowded, in terminal clusters, long, tubular, five-lobed, pinkish-blue in bud opening to violet-blue. June. Garden origin.

M. petraea. (E). (Syn. *Lithospermum petraeum*).

A native of S. Albania, this is a desirable, very floriferous, dwarf shrublet up to 9 inches high with erect, stiff, rounded branches, densely clothed with greyish-green hairs. Leaves alternate, leathery, long, narrow, lanceolate, grey-green, covered with smooth grey hairs. Flowers in congested terminal clusters, opening in succession, narrow, tubular, five-lobed with protruding stamens, pinkish-blue in bud opening to a deep blue with a trace of red. June.

M. suffruticosa. (E). (Syn. *Lithospermum graminifolium*).

A more tufted and less erect shrub, up to 9 inches high with rounded twiggy stems, densely clothed with appressed soft grey hairs. Leaves alternate, long, narrow, pointed at apex, larger than in *M. petraea*, grey-green with a covering of fine hairs on both sides. Flowers from terminal shoots on 4-inch leafy stems in branched clusters, five-lobed, long, narrow, tubular, pendant, pink in bud opening to violet-blue. Stamens not protruding. June. A native of Italy.

MONESES (*Pyrolaceae*).

A monotypic genus, the one species is generally found under Pyrola, to which the genus is closely related, the main difference being that Moneses bears solitary flowers, whereas in Pyrola they are in clusters.

CULTIVATION. This is not an easy plant to grow successfully, especially in the warmer counties, for it requires a cool moist shady spot with plenty of atmospheric moisture during the growing season, not easy to obtain under pan culture. Compost C is best with plenty of lime-free water during the growing and flowering season, just moist in winter and is best plunged in a north-facing frame during summer and sprayed in hot weather.

PROPAGATION. By seed in compost 3 sown as soon as ripe or careful division in early spring. Repot only when necessary after flowering.

M. uniflora. (E). (Syn. *Pyrola uniflora*).

A small evergreen plant increasing by stolons, at the end of each, where they pierce the soil, is borne a small basal, flat, radical tuft of obovate to orbicular, thickish, bright yellow-green leaves, margins crenate. Flowers solitary, on 3-inch stoutish scapes, pendant with five slightly reflexed roundish lobes, white sometimes tinged pink, with long protruding style, fragrant. June. A native of Europe, including Britain; Japan and N. America.

MORISIA (*Cruciferae*).

This genus contains only one species which is an ideal subject for pan culture with its fine golden crucifer flowers nestling in the charming rosettes of leaves.

CULTIVATION. Compost A is suitable with good drainage and sunshine, plenty of water while growing and flowering, dry but not arid in winter.

PROPAGATION. By root cuttings taken in June or seed if set, sown when ripe in compost 2. Repot every other year after flowering.

M. monantha. (E). (Syn. *M. hypogaea*).

It makes close huddled tufts of leaves in rosette formation from a thick central rootstock, less than an inch high. Leaves thick, imparipinnate, segments up to fifteen, triangular, smaller towards base of leaf, sparsely clothed with hair, midrib channelled, deep green. Flowers solitary from the leaf axils, sessile at first then with elongating pedicel, four-lobed roundish petals of a bright golden-yellow. May. A native of Corsica.

MUSCARI (*Liliaceae*).

A genus of bulbous plants which are mostly natives of the Mediterranean area and containing a number of species that are very suitable for alpine house or frame culture.

CULTIVATION. All the Grape Hyacinths do well in compost B over good drainage, potting the bulbs 1 inch deep and 1 inch apart, up to six in a 5-inch pan, the best period is late July or August, although they can be planted later, the bulbs do not like to be out of the soil for long. After potting the pans should be plunged into a frame outside, under peat until growth commences, then a moderate supply of water given, bringing the pans into the house when the buds have formed. A bi-weekly feed of diluted liquid manure is beneficial. After the foliage dies down withhold water and give the bulbs a good baking.

PROPAGATION. By seed sown in September in compost 2 or offsets removed when repotting and potting these up as for mature bulbs. Seedlings will take from three to four years to flower. Repot every year in late July or August.

M. armeniacum. (B).

A native of N.E. Asia, this produces up to eight narrow, linear, obtuse dark green leaves, channelled underneath. Flowers in a tight raceme, dark blue, with white edged lobes, top of raceme, flowers light blue. April.

M. azureum, see *Hyacinthus azureus*.

M. botryoides. (B).

This is the Grape Hyacinth of the gardens and catalogues, which is a very easy and decorative plant. It forms semi-erect, stiff, narrow linear, channelled, glaucous green leaves. Flowers in a short dense raceme on a 6-inch scape almost globose, dark blue with minute white lobes. March. A native of the Mediterranean region.

M. botryoides var. album. (B).
Similar to the type but with rounded heads of white flowers. March.

M. latifolium. (B).
A native of Asia Minor, this bulb produces a solitary, wide lanceolate, tapered to apex, green, flat leaf. Flowers in a loose raceme on a 12-inch scape, globose, urn-shaped, pale blue at base shading to deep blue at apex. May.

M. macrocarpum, see *M. moschatum.*

M. moschatum. (B). (Syn. *M. macrocarpum*).
This is the Musk Hyacinth with long linear, concave green leaves. Flowers in a dense globular raceme on an 8-inch scape, opening purple, turning to greenish-yellow with a violet flush, fragrant. April. A native of Asia Minor.

M. moschatum var. flavum. (B).
This form has a rather loose raceme of yellowish globular flowers with purple lobes, fragrant. April.

M. neglectum. (B).
A native of France and Italy, with fleshy, narrow linear, deeply channelled green leaves. Flowers in a large dense almost globular raceme on a 6-inch scape, very deep blue, almost appearing black in some lights, fragrant. April.

M. paradoxum. (B).
A native of the Caucasus, with up to three long rounded, erect, green leaves. Flowers in a dense conical raceme on a 5-inch green scape, green tinged purple, towards apex blackish-blue, inside green, fragrant. April.

M. racemosum. (B). (Syn. *Hyacinthus racemosus*).
Produces long narrow linear, fleshy leaves. Flowers in a dense raceme on a 6-inch scape, dark blue tipped white, changing with age to purple with a scent of ripe plums. April. A native of Europe, including Britain.

MYOSOTIS (*Boraginaceae*).

A genus of plants with a wide global distribution although the majority of Forget-me-nots are generally found in Europe and Australia, containing a number of suitable species admirably suited for alpine house culture and also one or two that will tax the specialist to bring them to perfection.
CULTIVATION. Compost B is suitable over faultless drainage. A normal supply of water while growing and flowering, only just moist during the winter. Special cultural requirements for species requiring them will be given after details of the plants.
PROPAGATION. By seed sown in July, compost 2, green cuttings in late June, or division in April. Repot when necessary after flowering.

M. alpestris. (E).
A small tufted plant about 6 inches high with erect stems clothed with

appressed hairs. Leaves oblong–linear, acute. Flowers in a terminal cyme, five–rounded lobes of light blue with a yellow eye. May. A native of S.E. Europe.

M. azorica. (E).
This species is a tufted hairy–stemmed plant up to 8 inches high with oblong, obtuse, sessile, hairy green leaves. Flowers in dense racemes, violet–purple five–lobed, lighter at throat. June. A native of the Azores, this species requires protection from cold winds and overwatering in winter.

M. caespitosa. (E).
A native of Europe, including Britain, it is a small edition of the Forget-me-not, with prostrate creeping hairy stems only an inch or so high. Leaves oblong to spatulate, light green. Flowers in small terminal racemes, five–lobed, bright blue with yellow eye. June.

M. caespitosa var. rehsteineri. (E).
This is an even smaller variety from the shores of Lake Geneva, forming close congested tufts only an inch or so high with five–lobed bright blue flowers, each having a bright yellow eye. May. Requires careful winter watering, as this plant will easily damp–off if there is too much moisture present.

M. explanata. (E).
A native of South Island, New Zealand, forming a mat of prostrate hairy stems clothed with stiff white hairs. Leaves narrow spatulate, obtuse, grey–green covered with appressed, long hairs. Flowers in short racemes, almost stemless five–lobed, white with a yellow eye. July. This plant resents too much sun and is best kept in a coolish spot during hot weather. It also requires ample water while growing and flowering, dryish conditions in winter. Beware of aphids, they will quickly weaken if not kill outright a specimen, if allowed to obtain a good hold.

M. rupicola. (H).
This forms a tight compact cushion plant only up to 2 inches high in small tufts of small oblong, linear, acute, green leaves covered with appressed fine whitish hairs. Flowers almost sessile in a tight raceme, large rounded five–petalled, azure blue with a bright yellow eye. June. A native of the European Alps. This plant does well in compost D where it makes a small crowded cushion and is much longer lived under the spartan conditions provided.

Myrsine nummularia, see *Suttonia nummularia.*

MYRTUS (*Myrtaceae*).
The Myrtles are not as a rule hardy in this country but the one species which is suitable for alpine house culture will survive if not allowed to freeze.

CULTIVATION. Compost B over good drainage, with a normal supply of water while growing, just moist in winter. Top-dress every spring with similar compost. It is best kept in a west-facing, half-shady spot during hot weather.

PROPAGATION. By green cuttings taken in late June. Repot every year at the end of April.

M. nummularia. (E).

A native of the Falkland Islands and S. America, it makes a prostrate shrub of entangled wiry, smooth, roundish red stems only an inch or so high. Leaves crowded, opposite, almost orbicular, dark glossy green, margins recurved. Flowers solitary from the leaf axils on small stout stalks, small, four-lobed, white. Fruits rounded oblong, flesh-pink. June–August.

NARCISSUS (*Amaryllidaceae*).

This well known genus, embracing all the garden forms of Daffodils and Narcissi, also contains a good variety of bulbous plants, both natural species and hybrids which make ideal subjects for alpine house or frame culture. A number which bloom early in the year, including *N. bulbocodium* var. *romieuxii* which can even be in flower in late December, are never seen so well as under the sheltered conditions which the house provides during winter.

CULTIVATION. Compost B is suitable for growing these bulbs over good drainage and they should be planted at twice their depth, the minimum being 1 inch, using half pots in preference to the ordinary shallow alpine pans. August is the best month for planting; for the early flowering species this is essential, but as the bulbs are rarely dormant for any appreciable period the less time they are out of the soil the better. When potting up the bulbs the compost must be moist but not wet so that the soil is naturally firmed round the bulbs. The pans are then removed to a half-shady frame and plunged to their rims, but not covered as many of the species quickly start to grow, and it is essential that there is no top cover once they appear through the surface of the compost. They should be brought into the house or alpine frame not later than the end of November for although hardy, a few of the S. Europe species do not care for alternating periods of cold, dry and mild wet weather.

Once the foliage appears above the surface, the pans must be kept moist during the whole of the growing and flowering season, then when the foliage dies down water is withheld, so that the bulbs have a dryish period in which to ripen. I do not think that they should be allowed to dry completely out, for this often causes blindness the following season.

PROPAGATION. By seed sown thinly in compost 2 and allowed to remain two seasons in the seed pan; then after the foliage dies away they can be potted up normally and the third season should give a percentage of flowers. Division of the bulbs in August where possible is another means of increase. Repot every year in fresh compost during August.

N. asturiensis. (B). (Syn. *N. minimus*) *Pseudo-Narcissus* Section.
An early species flowering in late January, this is one of the smallest of
all dwarf narcissi rarely above 3 inches high. Leaves few, semi-erect, wide,
channelled, linear, apex obtuse. Flowers on slender stems, a weak point
in their constitution. Trumpet long, narrow at base, much wider at mouth,
often deeply dentate, golden-yellow, petal segments twisted yellow. A
native of Spain and Portugal.

N. bulbocodium. (B). *Bulbocodium* Section.
The type plant has a wide distribution over S. France and Spain and varies
from 4 to 6 inches high. Leaves up to four rounded, channelled, stem
slender, topped by long narrow funnel-shaped corona, wide at mouth,
margins crenulate, bright golden-yellow, petals erect, yellow keeled
green. March–April.
Garden and wild varieties of *Narcissus bulbocodium*:

'Conspicuus'. (B).
This is a plant up to 4 inches high with many erect green grass-like leaves.
Flowers solitary, long trumpet, slightly constricted at mouth, deep yellow,
perianth yellow tinged green on reverse. April. Garden origin.

var. citrinus. (B).
This has a few grass-like semi-prostrate leaves. Flowers solitary on 6-inch
stems, wide open trumpet, lemon-yellow, perianth light greenish-yellow.
April. A native of S. France.

var. monophyllus, see *N. cantabricus* var. *monophyllus.*

var. nivalis. (B).
A small dainty plant rarely above 3 inches high with erect rush-like foliage.
Flowers on 3-inch stems, corona small, tube inflated, longer, light orange-
yellow. A native of Spain. March.

var. rifanus. (B).
From North Africa, this rare form makes a delightful pan plant only
4 inches high with prostrate rounded deep green leaves. Flowers solitary
on 4-inch stems, long trumpet, goblet shape at mouth, pale clear yellow.
January.

var. romieuxii. (B).
A native of Morocco, this has the usual rush-like sprawling green leaves.
Flowers solitary on 4-inch stems, large open trumpets of bright pale
yellow with protruding stamens and style. December–January.

var. tananicus. (B).
A rare plant akin to *N. cantabricus* var. *monophyllus*, with small round
prostrate leaves. Flowers wide at mouth with exserted style and stamens,
glistening white. A native of North Africa. February.

var. tenuifolius. (B).
A native of Southern France and Spain, with prostrate very narrow
grass-like foliage and on 4-inch stems solitary flowers, long trumpets,
slightly constricted at mouth, segments narrow lanceolate, deep yellow.
March–April.

N. calcicola. (B). *Juncifolius* Section.
This is similar to *N. juncifolius*, but slightly taller, about 6 inches high, leaves grey-green almost round, channelled, up to four flowers on a scape with small flattish trumpet but large well-formed petals, golden-yellow. March. A native of Spain.

N. cantabricus var. monophyllus. *Bulbocodium* Section. (Syn. *N. bulbocodium* var. *monophyllus*; *N. clusii*).
A fine alpine house plant with straggly rush-like leaves. Flowers on 4-inch stems, trumpet short and wide at mouth, deckled margins with protruding stamens, perianth segments narrow, the whole a delightful glistening white. December–January. A native of the Atlas Mountains.

N. clusii, see *N. cantabricus* var. *monophyllus*.

N. cyclamineus. (B). *Cyclamineus* Section.
A native of Portugal, this is a fine dwarf Narcissus, with semi-erect, narrow linear, bright green leaves with a well-marked grooved keel. Flowers solitary on 6-inch slender rounded scape, pendant, long, narrow tubular, corona open and crenate at mouth, orange-yellow, petals strongly reflexed and twisted, lemon-yellow. February. This species likes plenty of water while in growth and prefers not to be completely dried out after foliage dies down.

N. juncifolius. (B). *Juncifolius* Section.
A native of South France, Spain and Portugal, this bulb produces up to four slender almost round, channelled, erect deep green leaves. Flowers up to four on a slender scape, each with a large, open rounded cup with crenate margins, golden-yellow, petals recurved, bright yellow, very fragrant. April.

N. marvieri, see *N. rupicola* var. *marvieri*.

N. minimus, see *N. asturiensis*.

N. minor. (B). *Pseudo-Narcissus* Section.
A native of Portugal, with upright channelled, broad rush-like, grey-green leaves. Flowers solitary on 5-inch, two-edged erect scape, semi-pendant, open funnel-shape, corona plicate at mouth, deep yellow, petals erect, twisted, pale yellow. April.

N. moschatus. (B).
From the Pyrenees, with erect grey-green, twisted, channelled leaves. Flowers on a 6-inch, two-edged scape, corona long, narrow tubular, margins slightly crenate, very pale milky white. April.

N. rupicola. (B). *Juncifolius* Section.
A native of Spain and Portugal, with up to four erect slender almost rounded, dark green leaves. Flowers solitary, on a 3-inch scape with an almost flat rounded corona and symmetrical wide petals, bright yellow. April.

N. rupicola var. marvieri. (B). (Syn. *N. marvieri*).
From Morocco, this is similar to *N. rupicola*, but it is up to 4 inches high, leaves prostrate with large solitary flowers, flat yellow corona, but the three outer, well-formed petals are white at tip. April.

N. scaberulus. (B). *Juncifolius* Section.

A native of Portugal, this bulb produces only two leaves, these being linear, obtuse, deep green, channelled twisted and almost prostrate. Flowers solitary on 4-inch, 6-ribbed scape with small flattish trumpet, deep orange and well formed petals, orange-yellow, fragrant. March.

N. serotinus. (B). *Serotinus* Section.

From Palestine, this is a rare and far from easy species, requiring care in cultivation for success. Leaves one or two, thin thread-like, prostrate, after the flowers have faded. Flowers solitary on 4-inch slender scape with deep yellow lobed corona and a well-formed perianth of creamy-white. October–November.

N. tazetta. (B). *Tazetta* Section.

This bulb, with its forms, has a wide geographical distribution from Spain eastwards. It produces up to six linear green leaves and on a 10-inch scape up to six flowers, corona cup-shaped, entire, lemon-yellow, perianth segments forming a circle, white, fragrant. January–February.

N. tazetta var. canaliculatus. (B).

This form is quite small, only 3 inches high with a citron yellow cup-shaped corona and fine petals of the palest creamy-white. January–February.

N. triandrus. (B). *Triandrus* Section.

The well-known Angel's Tears narcissus, is a native of Spain and Portugal, with up to four long slender, almost rounded channelled green leaves. Flowers on 8-inch slender scape, pendant, with rounded cup-shaped creamy-white corona, perianth segments strongly reflexed and twisted, creamy-white, stamens protruding, three. April.

N. triandrus 'Albus'. (B).

This is the form generally met with in cultivation, with white drooping flowers. April.

N. triandrus var. aurantiacus. (B).

This form is from Northern Portugal, and is a fine outstanding plant with its golden-yellow flowers. April.

N. watieri. (B). *Juncifolius* Section.

A native of Morocco, with grey-green rounded, narrow linear, erect leaves. Flowers solitary on 4-inch scapes, corona flattish, open, margins deckled, pure white, perianth segments of good wide shape, glistening white. April.

NERTERA (*Rubiaceae*).

A small genus of plants of which one species is admirably suited for alpine house culture provided it is understood that it is not really hardy and will not stand many degrees of frost, but it is worth cultivating for the exceedingly large berries which it bears.

CULTIVATION. The Bead Plant is suited to compost B with good drainage and needs plenty of water while growing, just moist at other periods.

PROPAGATION. By division in early June or by seed sown in March, compost 2. Repot when necessary in May.

N. granadensis. (E). (Syn. *N. depressa*).

A native of New Zealand and the Falkland Islands, it makes a close congested cushion of small ovate, thickish, bright green leaves. Flowers from the leaf axils, sessile, insignificant, greenish-white. June–July. Followed by roundish, large, bright orange berries in large numbers.

NIEREMBERGIA (*Solanaceae*).

This genus contains two species which will be found suitable for pan culture in the alpine house or frame and flowering as they do over a long period, do much to retain interest in the alpine house during the summer months after the first floral display is over.

CULTIVATION. Compost B is suitable over good drainage and they require plenty of water while growing and flowering, keep just moist in winter with the exception of *N. repens* which requires drier conditions after growth dies down.

PROPAGATION. By cuttings taken in late June for *N. caerulea*, and division in April for *N. repens*. Repot when necessary in April.

N. caerulea. (E). (Syn. *N. hippomanica*).

This forms an erect plant up to 8 inches high with many branched, thin stiff stems covered with white hairs. Leaves small, narrow linear, acute, sparsely hairy green. Flowers on short hairy stems in great profusion, open bell-shaped, bright violet, striped deep violet, yellow at base of petals. June–September. This plant is best cut back after flowering, for this will help it retain a more compact shape. A native of Patagonia.

N. hippomanica, see *N. caerulea*.

N. repens. (H). (Syn. *N. rivularis*).

A native of Argentina and Chile, this is a completely prostrate creeping plant of smooth slender stems which root as they come into contact with the soil. Leaves in tufts, entire, spatulate, obtuse, green. Flowers solitary on short slender stems, large open bell-shaped, white flushed yellow at base of petals. June–August.

N. rivularis, see *N. repens*.

NIGRITELLA (*Orchidaceae*).

A monotypic genus, this is the famous Vanilla Orchid, which abounds in the high alpine meadows of C. and N. Europe and scents the air with its delightful perfume of vanilla.

CULTIVATION. This is not an easy plant to grow successfully but it can be kept alive with care. Compost B is suitable over good drainage and a good supply of water is necessary while growing and flowering, but keep just moist after foliage dies down.

PROPAGATION. By careful division of the thong-like roots in early spring, retaining some of the old compost for there seems to be some bacterial association between the plant and soil. Repot only when necessary in April.

N. nigra. (H). (Syn. *N. angustifolia*).

A small plant with thong-like roots producing a small tuft of linear, acute green leaves, from the centre of which emerges a 4-inch thickish stem, topped with a congested capitate inflorescence of deep blackish-purple short spurred flowers. June. Not a beautiful plant but worth growing for its perfume alone.

NOCCAEA (*Cruciferae*).

A genus of two species with a close affinity to Thlaspi and often included under that generic name. There is one species which is suitable for pan culture and although not long-lived is a charming plant.

CULTIVATION. Compost A is suitable but if young seedlings are obtainable compost D is preferable, for not only do the plants retain their true character under these conditions, but they are longer lived. Give plenty of water while growing and flowering and keep dry but not arid in winter.

PROPAGATION. By seed sown when ripe in compost 2. Repot only when necessary after flowering.

N. stylosa. (E). (Syn. *Thlaspi stylosum*).

This is a dwarf tufted plant with crowded basal rosettes of spatulate, grey-green leaves, upper lanceolate. Flowers in a tight raceme, four-petalled, pale lilac with a prominent style. March. A native of Italy. It is best in a coolish spot during hot weather.

NOMOCHARIS (*Liliaceae*).

A genus of outstandingly beautiful bulbous plants situated botanically midway between Fritillaria and Lilium, and in fact recently at least two have been transferred from Nomocharis to Lilium. Asiatic in origin, they grow in the open alpine woodlands, often protected by dwarf rhododendrons with which they associate well, both in their natural habitat and here in cultivation.

CULTIVATION. They have a reputation for being difficult and there is no doubt that when first introduced, they were far from easy plants to cultivate, but this was due in a large measure to lack of knowledge of their requirements. There is no doubt that all the species do better in the cooler northern counties, including Scotland, but I have had no difficulty in West Kent, a far from wet district. Naturally more care is required in these drier areas. On no account must the bulbs be exposed to the air for they will rapidly deteriorate if dried, so plants must be obtained in pots or grown from seed. Compost C is suitable over faultless drainage, deep pots should be used and the bulbs like to be 3 inches below the surface if possible. They require plenty of water while growing and flowering, and prefer lime-free soil, although they have no rabid aversion to a limy

medium as far as I know. After growth dies down the compost should
be kept moist, and not allowed to dry out. A cool shady spot in a frame
among other dwarf ericaceous plants is ideal and the pots only brought
into the house for the flowering season.

PROPAGATION. Best carried out by seed, sown thinly when ripe, generally August in compost 3 and the seedlings allowed to remain undisturbed
for two years in the seed pans. In April of the third year, when growth is
beginning the small bulbils are potted up separately in small thumb pots,
moving them the following year into a larger pot at the same period.
They should make bulbs of flowering size in four to five years from seed.
Care must be taken when moving the young bulbils not to break the
extremely brittle roots as this can easily cause the death of the plant.

Species can also be increased by scales but unless a good form is required
to be perpetuated and this may be the only means, it is not advised, for
seed is set in quantity and the number of scales are limited, to say nothing
of the weakening of the plant, if this method is used to any excess. Repotting is carried out every other year in late April, when the roots have
commenced to grow, these must not be disturbed or broken and the new
compost worked in gently and firmed.

N. aperta. (B).
A native of S.W. Szechuan and Yunnan, this is a strong growing species
with a stem up to 18 inches high. Leaves on stem, solitary on lower half,
in pairs on upper, lanceolate, tapered to a point with three clear veins,
deep green, lighter below. Flowers solitary, up to six on stout almost
horizontal pedicels from the leaf axils on upper half of stem, one terminal,
semi-pendant, large, open saucer-shape, six segments, light rose-pink,
blotched all over deep crimson. Three inner segments have a deep purple
gland at base. May–June.

N. farreri. (B).
A native of Upper Burma, this bulb produces a stout erect stem up to
18 inches high. Leaves in whorls up to ten, generally less, terminal and
sub-terminal leaves solitary, narrow lanceolate, tapering to point,
recurved, three-veined, deep green, lighter below. Flowers single from
the upper solitary leaf axil, also terminal up to five on acute horizontal
pedicels, pendant, large open saucer-shape, outer three segments entire,
ovate, white with purple-red blotches, inner three wide, toothed on
upper third, white with basal spotting of deep red-purple. May–June.

N. mairei. (B).
This is possibly the best and most widely-grown of the species, but if
grown in the vicinity of other species it hybridises readily, so it is possible
that in time the true plant will tend to die out in cultivation, for the offspring are generally more robust than the parents. A native of N.E.
Yunnan, it produces a stem up to 18 inches high with the basal portion
bearing only scale-like leaves. Leaves up to five in whorls, wide lanceolate,
tapering to point, deep green, lighter beneath, three-veined. Flowers

pendant, solitary on stout horizontal pedicels from the upper half of the stem and one terminal; large wide open saucer-shape, six segments, three outer ovate, tapered to pointed apex, margins undulate, pale pink, slightly spotted purple with a deep purple blotch at base; inner segments almost orbicular heavily blotched with reddish-purple, margins fringed. May–June.

N. mairei var. candida. (B).
This is similar to the type but with white unspotted flowers, the three inner segments have a red-purple area at base. May.

N. mairei var. leucantha. (B).
This form was at one time given specific rank but is now regarded as only a variety. It differs in being a stronger growing plant with large flowers, similar in shape, but less heavily marked, the outer segments being whitish or with just a tinge of pink and the thickened top half of the filament being pale yellow, whereas in the type plant this is deep red-purple. May–June.

N. nana, see *Lilium nanum.*

N. nana var. flavida, see *Lilium n.* var. *flavidum.*

N. oxypetala, see *Lilium oxypetalum.*

N. pardanthina. (B).
A native of Yunnan, this species produces a stout stem up to 18 inches high. Leaves solitary and small on lower third of stem, in whorls of up to six on upper half, wide lanceolate tapered to apex, three-veined, deep green. Flowers solitary up to six from the upper leaf axils as well as the terminal flower, semi-pendant on horizontal pedicels, outer three segments pale rose, rarely spotted, entire and pointed, inner three segments almost orbicular, deep pink, margins fringed with deep brownish-red blotches towards base. May–June.

N. saluenensis. (B).
From Tibet and N.W. Yunnan, this is one of the species which has been in cultivation over a good number of years. It forms a stout stem up to 18 inches high, both upper and lower parts having scale-like leaves, the others being in pairs, lanceolate, tapered to base and apex, pale green, five-veined, occasionally three-veined. Flowers from upper leaf axils also terminal, solitary, large erect stiff pedicels, not so open as in other species, outer segments wide, ovate and shorter with purple blotch at base, ground colour is either white, pale pink or light yellow. May–June.

NOTOTHLASPI (*Cruciferae*).

A small genus of plants containing only two species of which one has been in cultivation. It is doubtful whether this plant is still with us today and the only reason for its inclusion is that I grew this plant over a period of two years and then lost it during an enforced absence from home. At best it is short lived, possibly only a biennial, and the problem is to bring the plants through into the second season for flowering, but whatever

its needs it must be considered a difficult plant to maintain in good health.
CULTIVATION. For any reasonable chance of success compost D should
be used and a good supply of water while growing and flowering, dry
but not arid in winter. It seems to resent hot sunshine and should be placed
in a cool half-shady frame during the hot summer months.
PROPAGATION. By seed sown as soon as ripe in compost 2 and the young
seedlings placed in their permanent position as soon as possible. No
repotting should be necessary.
N. rosulatum. (E).
A native of South Island, New Zealand, this is the Penwiper Plant,
forming an erect thickish stemmed plant from a stout tap root. Leaves
dense, basal in rosette formation, imbricated, spatulate, margins crenate,
grey-green with a covering of fine whitish hairs. Flowers on a 3-inch
fleshy stem, small petalled usual crucifer shape, in a congested conical
raceme, white and fragrant. June. The seed pods are an attraction in themselves being a flattish disk, deep brown-purple.

OMPHALODES (*Boraginaceae*).

A genus containing one species which is eminently suitable for pan
culture in the alpine house or frame, and a well grown specimen of
O. *luciliae* is indeed a perfect sight.
CULTIVATION. Compost B is ideal over faultless drainage with plenty
of water during the growing and flowering season, just moist in winter.
PROPAGATION. By careful division in June and if kept close in a shaded
frame they will soon re-establish themselves. Repot every year in early
April as although a delicate-looking plant it is a gross feeder.
O. luciliae. (E).
This is a low growing plant of basal tufts from which radiate prostrate,
glabrous grey stems only up to 3 inches high. Leaves basal, ovate to spatulate, acute, tapered to stalk, stem leaves smaller and sessile, light grey.
Flowers in loose few-flowered sprays, pink in bud, opening to rounded
saucer-shape; clear china blue. May–September. A native of Asia Minor.

OMPHALOGRAMMA (*Primulaceae*).

A small genus of plants closely related to Primula, which are not easy of
cultivation, especially in the southern drier counties, although in the more
congenial atmosphere of the northern half of the country greater success
has been achieved with these delightful wildlings.
CULTIVATION. Compost B is needed with perfect drainage and the plants
require plenty of water during the growing season and to be kept just
moist in winter. They must not be kept in the house during the hot summer
months but plunged in a cool, north-facing frame. Although delicate
looking, there is no doubt that they require feeding if they are to succeed,
and once growth has commenced a weekly feeding of a liquid manure
is not only necessary but essential.

PROPAGATION. By seed sown as soon as ripe in compost 3. Repot only when necessary after flowering.

O. delavayi. (H).

A native of Yunnan, this forms a basal tuft of a few long ovate, slender, cordate at base leaves covered with white hairs. Flowers solitary on a slender 8-inch hairy scape, open wide funnel-shape, six irregular lobes, coarsely toothed, deep purple. April.

O. elwesianum. (H).

This produces a basal tuft of stalked ovate-lanceolate, thick glabrous leaves, tapered to base. Flowers solitary on a 6-inch reddish-brown, hairy stem, funnel-shape with six open squarish dentate lobes, violet-purple. May. A native of Sikkim.

O. farreri. (H).

A native of Upper Burma, from the resting bud the solitary flowers appear before the leaves on 6-inch stoutish hairy scapes, being long, narrow, open wide at mouth, with six narrow lobes, margins serrate, deep purple. Leaves roundish to cordate, rugose, margins dentate, mid-green, slightly hairy on slender hairy stalks. May.

O. vinciflorum. (H). (Syn. *Primula vinciflora*).

This is a charming species forming a basal rosette of oblong, obtuse, sessile leaves, glandular hairy on both sides, veining prominent. Flowers solitary on sparsely hairy 6-inch scapes, tube narrow, six obovate lobes, notched at apex, violet, deeper at throat. May. A native of Yunnan.

ONOSMA (*Boraginaceae*).

A fairly large genus of plants confined to the Mediterranean area and central Asia of which there are a few that can be utilised for pan culture in the alpine house or frame, where they provide both floral beauty and charm.

CULTIVATION. Being natives of warm regions all require a well-drained light medium soil and they are suited to compost A in full sun. Care is needed in watering, and although a normal supply should be given during the growing season, the plants should be kept dry but not arid in winter; water must be kept away from the hairy foliage during this period otherwise rotting quickly takes place.

PROPAGATION. By seed sown as soon as ripe in compost 1 or green cuttings in June. Repot every year in late April.

O. albo-pilosum. (E).

A tufted sub-shrubby plant about 9 inches high, branches covered with fine stellate hairs. Leaves narrow, oblong, obtuse, tapering to base, almost sessile, rugose, grey-green. Flowers solitary in a small crooked raceme, long tubular narrowed at mouth, downy, five-lobed, pure white, flushing pink with age. May. A native of Asia Minor.

O. arenarium, see *O. echioides*.

O. cassium. (E).
This species has semi-erect stoutish stems about 10 inches high with flattish hairs. Leaves narrow, oblong, obtuse, almost sessile, green, sparsely bristled. Flowers in a pendant raceme on densely haired stems, almost sessile, five-lobed, tubular, pale cream. May. From Mount Cassia in Asia Minor.

O. decipiens, see *O. nanum.*

O. echioides. (E). (Syn. *O. arenarium*).
A native of S. Europe, this is a fine plant with much-branched ascending stems, densely covered with rough hairs. Leaves spatulate-lanceolate, sessile, covered with coarse hairs, grey-green. Flowers in small pendant racemes, large, tubular constricted at mouth, five-lobed, golden-yellow. May.

O. nanum. (E). (Syn. *O. decipiens*).
A small much tufted plant only a few inches high with erect bristly haired stems. Leaves linear, obtuse, bristly grey-green, margins revolute, midrib prominent below. Flowers in small pendant racemes, rounded, tubular, velvety white flushed pink. May–June. A native of Cilicia.

O. stellulatum. (E).
This is a dwarf sub-shrub rarely above 6 inches high with tufted, erect, stiff hairy stems. Leaves basal, linear, obtuse, acute in upper, margins revolute, grey-green, bristly haired. Flowers solitary on short stalks in small pendant racemes, long tubular, narrowed at mouth, five-lobed, yellow. June. A native of S.E. Europe.

OPHRYS (*Orchidaceae*).

A genus of terrestrial orchids of which a number can be grown successfully for a few years in pans for alpine house decoration, although it must be admitted they are more quaint than beautiful, many of them bearing a striking resemblance to insects of which the Bee and Fly Orchids are well known. A number are natives of Britain and on no account should they be dug up, for a few are both local and rare and as they can be either imported or dug up in their European habitats where they are more plentiful, their rarity here should be respected. Surprising as it may seem the depredation is generally carried out by people who rarely have the knowledge or ability to grow these delightful wildlings.

CULTIVATION. Compost B is suitable, to which should be added a few small broken pieces of chalk or limestone as this seems to be essential to their well-being. The tubers should be placed 1 inch deep and up to five in a 5-inch pan, and firm planting is essential. August to September are the best months, after which the pans are plunged into a plunge bed and only brought into the alpine house for the flowering period. Plenty of water while in growth, reducing this after the foliage dies down, then the compost should be kept dry but not arid; all available sun is essential to ripen the tubers.

PROPAGATION. By division of tubers in April. Repotting is carried out at the same time and once every three years should be sufficient.

O. apifera. (D).

A native of Europe including Britain, this is the Bee Orchid, and grows up to 6 inches producing a few broad, lanceolate, glaucous green leaves less than 3 inches long. Flowers on an erect stem, few in a widely dispersed spike, with pink sepals, veined green and a hairy brownish lip, lined yellow. May.

O. bertolinii. (D).

A native of Italy, with a few small broad, lanceolate leaves and on small stout erect stems only a few inches high, flowers with mauve pink sepals and a velvety deep crimson-brown lip with a pale blue streak. June.

O. bombyliflora. (D).

This is the Bumble Bee Orchid which is a native of S. Europe, with small oblong, lanceolate leaves and on 6-inch stems bee-like flowers, with palish green sepals and a deep chocolate-brown, almost black lip. May.

O. fusca. (D).

A small species only a few inches high from the Mediterranean region, with sparse leaves and flowers having yellow-green sepals and petals, with a velvety deeper yellow lip. May.

O. lutea. (D).

This is the Wasp Orchid, a native of S. Europe, with large narrow, oblong, green leaves. Flowers many on erect 4-inch robust stems, sepals green, incurved, petals yellowish-green, smaller, lip bright yellow and purple-brown blotch. June.

O. muscifera. (D).

A native of Britain, the Fly Orchid is a charming but far from easy species with oblong linear, green leaves and flowers on 6-inch stems, sepals and petals greenish-brown, with deep reddish-brown lip and a lighter central blotch. June.

O. speculum. (D).

The Looking-Glass Orchid is a native of S. Europe, bearing a few linear-oblong leaves and on 6-inch stems up to six flowers with greenish sepals and petals, lips large, red-brown, hirsute and bright steel-blue blotch. June.

ORCHIS (*Orchidaceae*).

This is another genus of terrestrial orchids which contains a number of species that can with care be cultivated over a number of years in pans.

CULTIVATION. Compost B over faultless drainage, but all require plenty of water while in growth, reducing this after the foliage dies down, then the plants should be kept on the dry side, but not arid. The tubers are planted up to four in a 5-inch pan, about 1 inch deep and made firm.

The best period is August to October, afterwards plunging the pans in a protected frame outside and covered with dry peat. The compost should be used damp but not wet, then no further water will be required until growth is apparent when the pans are removed from the frame and brought into the house for flowering. Liquid manure is beneficial once a week in a diluted form during the growing season and the flowering stems are best removed after the flowers fade.

PROPAGATION. By division, and is best carried out when repotting every third year in September. Yearly repotting is not advised for all species resent unnecessary disturbance.

O. foliosa, see *O. maderensis.*

O. fusca, see *O. purpurea.*

O. globosa. (D).
A native of Central and Southern Europe, a well-known species to those who travel the alpine meadows with its dense rounded heads of light lilac-pink flowers, spotted with deeper markings. June.

O. incarnata. (D).
A native of Europe including Britain, with unspotted green narrow, lanceolate leaves and on an 8-inch scape a dense spike of wine-red flowers spotted purple. June.

O. latifolia. (D).
This is the Marsh Orchid and is widely distributed over Europe, Asia and Britain with wide lanceolate green leaves, spotted deep purple. Flowers on a 10-inch scape, in a dense cluster of reddish-purple. June.

O. maculata. (D).
The Spotted Orchid is another native of Britain as well as parts of Europe, with lanceolate green leaves, spotted deep purple and on 10-inch slender scapes a dense ovoid cluster of pale lilac-rose flowers, spotted deep brownish-magenta. June.

O. maderensis. (D). (Syn. *O. foliosa*).
A native of Madeira, this species is best kept in the alpine house during really cold weather where it forms wide, obtuse, lanceolate rich green unspotted leaves and produces a slender scape up to 18 inches high, with a dense oblong spike of purple flowers with deeper markings. June.

O. mascula. (D).
This is the Early Purple Orchid which is a native of Europe including Britain, as well as N. Africa. It produces radical, lanceolate, green leaves, spotted deep purple-black and on an 8-inch scape flowers in a loose spike of a bright crimson-purple with a white spotted purple lip. April.

O. mascula var. alba. (D).
Much rarer than the type, this form has generally unspotted leaves and dainty white flowers. May.

O. militaris. (D).
The Military Orchid is a native of Europe and rare in S. England, with wide, oblong green leaves. The flowers, strangely reminiscent of helmeted

soldiers, are borne in a dense oblong spike on a 14-inch slender scape, deep rosy-pink with a lighter lip, spotted purple. May.

O. morio. (D).

Only 8 inches high, the green tinged Meadow Orchid produces a few radical unspotted bright green leaves. Flowers up to eight in a loose spike with dull purple-green veined sepals, petals greener and a lighter coloured lip, spotted deep purple. June. A native of Europe, rare in Britain.

O. morio var. alba. (D).

A delightful albino form with white petals and greenish tinged sepals. June.

O. papilionacea. (D).

This is the Italian Butterfly Orchid from S. Europe including Corsica, and requires to be kept in the alpine house during the winter. Leaves few, short linear, acute, more or less prostrate, green and unspotted. Flowers on 4-inch slender scapes, up to six bright red, lip pink spotted red, spur incurved. June.

O. purpurea. (D). (Syn. *O. fusca*).

The Brown Man Orchid produces wide, oblong, obtuse green leaves and on 10-inch scapes, large loose spikes of rose-lilac spotted purple lips and purple-brown hooded sepals. April. A rare British native but found in many parts of Europe.

O. pyramidalis. (D).

The Pyramidal Orchid is a native of Europe, Africa and also Britain with long narrow lanceolate, acute, green leaves and bearing on 12-inch slender stems a close pyramidal spike of slender spurred, pinkish-purple flowers. July.

O. sambucina. (D).

A native of the European Alps with wide oblong, obtuse green leaves and on 8-inch stems an oblong, dense, spike of purple flowers with drooping spurs and red-coloured bracts. There is also a yellow form with light green bracts otherwise similar to the type. May.

O. spectabilis. (D).

The Showy Orchid is a native of the N.W. United States with two wide oblong, obtuse shining green leaves and on a slender 6-inch stem up to six rather large flowers with hooded sepals of light purple-pink and white lip. May.

O. tridentata. (D).

A native of S. Europe with widish, acute, lanceolate leaves and on 6-inch stems a small spike of flowers with deep mauve sepals and a pink and white-crimson spotted lip. May.

O. ustulata. (D).

Widely spread in the European Alps, but much less common in this country it produces several oblong green leaves and on 6-inch stems a dense spike of flowers with purple sepals and crimson spotted white lip. May.

OREOCHARIS (*Gesneriaceae*).

A small genus of plants which provides us with three species that are suitable for the alpine house; related to the genera Ramonda and Haberlea they have a dainty charming beauty of their own.

CULTIVATION. Compost C is required over good drainage with plenty of water while growing, just moist at other periods. They need cool conditions and protection from cold winds and are best kept in a cool, protected north-facing frame during hot months and then plunged under the staging of the house during winter.

PROPAGATION. By careful division in April or leaf cuttings in May. Repot when necessary after flowering.

O. aurantiaca. (E). (Syn. *Perantha forrestii*).
A native of Yunnan, it forms basal rosettes of oblong, rugose green leaves, margins crenate, covered with silvery hairs above and light brown below. Flowers up to five on slender 5-inch red hairy stems, corolla long bulbous, two-lipped with narrow segments, bright orange, calyx red. May.

O. forrestii. (E). (Syn. *Roettlera forrestii*).
Also from Yunnan, this species has a basal rosette of ovate-oblong green leaves with prominent midrib; sparsely clad with long reddish hairs, margins sharply serrate. Flowers pendant on 4-inch slender hairy stems in a loose cyme, long tubular two-lipped, four spreading lobes, pale yellow. May.

O. henryana, see *Isometrum farreri*.

O. primuloides. (E).
This comes from Japan and forms a loose rosette of long stalked broad, ovate to orbicular, grey-green leaves covered with fine whitish hairs, margins coarsely serrate. Flowers on 4-inch slender hairy scapes in umbels of up to ten, pendant, tubular, two-lipped, four-lobed, tube white, lip mauve, throat white. May.

ORIGANUM (*Labiatae*).

A small genus of herbaceous aromatic herbs and soft-wooded plants which has produced a few suitable for alpine house or frame culture.

CULTIVATION. Compost A with faultless drainage will suit the Marjorams and a good supply of water during the growing and flowering season, give dryish but not arid conditions in winter. These plants should be kept away from cold draughty positions.

PROPAGATION. By green cuttings taken in July or careful division in March. Repot every year in early April.

O. amanum. (E).
A recently introduced plant by Peter Davis from Dildie Dag in the Amanus Mountains. This dwarf sub-shrub has thin slender stems up to 4 inches in length, with hairy sessile, grey-green ovate leaves, apex obtuse. Flowers terminal in small cymes, deep pink, labiate shape, tubular style

protruding, large purple bracts. July–August. Is best cut back after flowering which helps to retain a dwarf compact habit.

O. dictamnus. (E). (Syn. *Amaracus dictamnus*).

A native of Crete, this is a small sub-shrub up to 12 inches high. Leaves entire, thick, broad ovate, obtuse, base orbicular, grey due to intense covering of white wool on both sides. Flowers pendant in a cylindrical spike, narrow tubular, two-lipped, pink surrounded by large ruby bracts. June–July.

O. pulchrum. (E).

A native of the Levant, this is a small sub-shrub less than 6 inches high, with slender smooth procumbent stems. Leaves aromatic, oval to cordate, pointed at apex, pale green, glabrous, dotted with brown spots. Flowers terminal in small cymes, minute two-lipped, mauve, surrounded by light purple bracts. July–August.

OROSTACHYS (*Crassulaceae*).

A small genus of plants until recently included in Cotyledon and Sedum but now grouped under the generic name of Orostachys. There are two species which are suitable for alpine house culture, but they are doubtfully hardy in an alpine frame should a prolonged frosty spell occur.

CULTIVATION. Compost A over faultless drainage with care in watering at all periods, otherwise rotting will quickly take place, dry in winter.

PROPAGATION. By detaching rosettes and rooting them in sand, June, or seed sown when ripe in March, compost 1.

O. chanetii. (E). (Syn. *Sedum chanetii*).

A native of Kansu, China, with rosettes of fleshy, glaucous grey-green, convex, linear leaves, spine tipped. The flowering rosettes elongate into long spires bearing pyramids of white star-like flowers with purple anthers. September–October.

O. spinosus. (E). (Syn. *Cotyledon spinosa*; *Umbilicus spinosus*; *Sedum spinosum*).

A native of C. Asia, this makes attractive close compact symmetrical rosettes of lanceolate blue-grey, incurved, white-tipped leaves. Flowers in narrow spike, star shaped, yellow. July.

ORPHANIDESIA (*Ericaceae*).

A monotypic genus whose sole species is a most desirable plant, to be cherished if obtained; fortunately it is not so rare these days, as it has been for many years. A far from easy plant to cultivate, especially in the southern half of the country, for it detests hot dry positions. I have a plant which has never looked so well as when growing in a peat bed in almost full shade.

CULTIVATION. Compost C is ideal with good drainage and a liberal supply of lime-free water, in fact the plant must be kept moist at all times. It should not be retained in the house except during the flowering period; at other times it is best accommodated in a shady, north-facing frame and

Above: *Narcissus bulbocodium* var. *romieuxii* (see page 362)

Below: *Narcissus triandrus* 'Albus' (see page 364)

Above left: *Nomocharis mairei* (see page 367)   Above centre: *Oxalis enneaphylla* (see page 379)
Below: *Paeonia cambessedesii* (see page 380)

Above right: *Phyteuma comosum* (see page 394)

Below: *Phlox nana* var. *ensifolia* (see page 391)

Above: *Primula marginata* 'Caerulea' (see page 411)
Below: *Primula marginata* 'Linda Pope' (see page 411)

sprayed in the evenings during hot weather. Avoid cold drying winds.
PROPAGATION. By seed, compost 3 in March, or by rooted layers which
must not be disturbed until well established. Repot only when necessary
in late April.

O. gaultherioides. (E).

A native of the Lazic Pontus in the Black Sea region, where in wooded
glades it forms a semi-procumbent dwarf shrub rarely above a foot high
with reddish-brown stems covered with brownish hair. Leaves alternate,
large, up to 3 inches, ovate to oblong, pointed with a short spine, heavily
reticulate veinings, covered with rough bristles, margins ciliate, dull
mid-green. Flowers from terminal leaf axils, generally in pairs, calyx
five-pointed lobes, green flushed crimson, corolla large, entire, open
funnel-shape, with undulating margins, rose-pink. April.

OTHONNOPSIS (*Compositae*).

A small genus of sub-shrubs related to Senecio, of which one is suitable
and hardy enough for the alpine house.
CULTIVATION. Compost A over good drainage is required with a fair
supply of water during the growing season, dry but not arid in winter.
This plant is best kept in the alpine house in winter as it detests cold winds
and prolonged bouts of frost.
PROPAGATION. By green cuttings taken in late June. Repot every year
in late April.

O. cheirifolia. (E).

This is a small spreading sub-shrub less than 12 inches high with tufts
of thickish lanceolate to spatulate, glaucous grey sessile leaves, rounded
at apex. Flowers solitary on sparsely leaved 8-inch scapes, large daisy-like,
orange-yellow. June. A native of Algeria.

OURISIA (*Scrophulariaceae*).

This genus is confined to the Andes, New Zealand and Tasmania, and
contains numerous species which are suitable for pan culture (see below and
Appendix 1).
CULTIVATION. Compost B is ideal with faultless drainage and plenty
of water while growing, keep on the dry side in winter. They are best
in half-shade during the hot summer months.
PROPAGATION. By division in April or seed sown when ripe in compost 2.
Repot when necessary in April.

O. alpina. (E).

This is a native of the Andes, forming a loose rosette of hairy stalked
ovate green leaves, cordate at base, margins crenate. Flowers on 6-inch
hairy stems in an open raceme, semi-pendant, tubular, two-lipped, upper
two-lobed; lower three-lobed, tube pink flushed red; upper lobes pink,
lower white tinged rose with red dots in throat. June.

O. coccinea. (E).
Leaves in basal tufts, oval-oblong, stalked, green, margins coarsely
dentate. Flowers on 6-inch scapes in small pendant clusters, tubular
two-lipped, upper two-lobed, lower three-lobed, scarlet with protruding
cream anthers. June–July. A native of the Andes.

OXALIS (*Oxalidaceae*).

A large and mighty genus of herbaceous and bulbous plants mostly
found in tropical and sub-tropical regions, but a number appear in temperate regions and this genus contains at least two that have become
troublesome weeds in rock gardens and where introduced are impossible
to eradicate. Two such pests are O. *corniculata* with its forms, and
O. *repens*; both should be avoided like the plague.

CULTIVATION. This does not present any great difficulty and both the
bulbous and herbaceous species will do well in compost B over good
drainage; all require a normal supply of water while growing and flowering, reducing this after the foliage dies down, keep dry but not arid in
winter. The bulbous species should be potted $\frac{1}{2}$ inch deep and $\frac{1}{2}$ inch apart
in 6-inch pans, the spring flowering plants in January, the summer in
March, the autumn in August. All these should be repotted annually.
The herbaceous species are best repotted in April.

PROPAGATION. By division when repotting or offsets of the bulbous
species.

O. adenophylla. (B).
A native of Chile, this has a bulbous rootstock producing a basal rosette
of long stalked crinkled leaves, rounded fan-shaped, up to twelve obcordate leaflets, glaucous silver green. Flowers on 3-inch stems up to
three goblet-shaped, five-lobed, lilac-pink with a deeper veining and
crimson eye. May–June.

O. brasiliensis. (B).
A small bulbous plant only 3 inches high with a basal rosette of long slender
stalked leaves, leaflets three obcordate, green. Flowers solitary on slender
stems, five-lobed, purple-red with yellow throat. May. A native of
Brazil.

O. chrysantha. (H).
A prostrate stem-rooting species native of Brazil, from the nodes of which
are produced basal rosettes of trifoliate leaves, the leaflets being triangular-
obcordate pale green, with whitish hairs. Flowers solitary on 2-inch stems,
open bell-shaped, five-lobed, golden-yellow. June. The pan should not
be allowed to freeze during the winter.

O. deppei. (B).
From a black roundish bulb is produced a stemless rosette of up to six long
stalked leaves. Leaflets four ovate to orbicular, green, emarginate with
purple, glabrous and minutely dentate. Flowers in small umbels on 6-inch

stems, up to twelve open bell-shaped, five-lobed, brownish-red. May–June. A native of Mexico.

O. enneaphylla. (B).

A native of the Falkland Islands, this is a bulbous rooted plant with long stalked leaves, leaflets from nine to twenty obcordate, hirsute, silvery grey, emarginate red-brown. Flowers on 3-inch stems, open goblet-shaped, white, five-lobed, fragrant, throat pale yellowish-green. May–June. Requires protection from very cold weather.

O. enneaphylla var. rosea. (B).

This is an outstanding form similar to the type but with dainty pink-flushed flowers. May–June.

O. hirta. (B).

Another bulbous species from S. Africa, producing slender stems up to 9 inches long clothed with alternate, sessile leaves; leaflets trifoliate, linear, hirsute, green. Flowers solitary from the upper leaf axils, tubular, tube yellow, petals five-lobed, bright magenta. November. Should not be allowed to freeze in winter and no water should be given until the the end of July or the beginning of August for it to produce flowers.

O. laciniata. (H). (Syn. *O. squamosa-radicosa*).

A recent introduction from Patagonia with fleshy rhizomes, producing palmate, grey-green leaves on thin stalks, margins pinkish-mauve. Leaves in seven to nine segments folded in middle, margins undulate, petioles pinkish. Flowers on 1-inch stems, solitary, five-lobed, open goblet-shape, deep lavender-blue, veined purple, fragrant. June–August. This plant is very variable in colour ranging from blue through violet to light purple.

O. lactea, see *O. magellanica*.

O. lobata. (B).

A small bulbous species about 3 inches high with a basal rosette of long, hairy stalked leaves; leaflets obcordate in threes, bright green, often marked with black spots. Flowers solitary on 3-inch stems, open bell-shaped, five-lobed, golden-yellow. September. A native of Chile.

O. magellanica. (H). (Syn. *O. lactea*).

A dwarf creeping rooting perennial only an inch or so high, forming a mat with tufts of basal leaves on long hairy stalks; leaflets three, obcordate, two-lobed, bronze-green. Flowers solitary, open five-lobed, large chalices, white. May. A native of S. America.

O. oregana. (H).

This is a rhizome-forming plant with basal rosettes of long stalked leaves; leaflets three, obcordate, green, glabrous above, slightly hairy below. Flowers solitary on 3-inch slender stems, open bell-shaped, five-lobed, rose-red with yellow throat. May. A native of Oregon, N. America.

O. purpurea. (B).

A native of S. Africa, this is a bulbous plant with up to eight leaves in a basal rosette, leaflets three, orbicular, two-lobed, green, purple below, margins ciliate. Flowers on 2-inch stems, open tubular, tube yellow, petals five-lobed, purple. May.

O. squamosa-radicosa, see *O. laciniata.*

O. valdiviensis. (B).

This bulbous plant forms dense tufts of long stalked leaves; leaflets three, obcordate, green. Flowers on 6-inch stems, up to six tubular bell-shaped, five-lobed, bright yellow. August. A native of Chile.

OXYCOCCUS, see **VACCINIUM.**

Paederota bonarota, see *Veronica bonarota.*

PAEONIA (*Ranunculaceae*).

A genus of plants containing both herbaceous and shrubby members, natives of Europe, temperate Asia, N.W. America and China, but there is only one species that is suitable as a pan plant in the alpine house or frame, for they are for the most part too large for pan culture.

CULTIVATION. Compost B is suitable but a pot should be used in preference to a pan as a long root run is necessary. Once growth commences plenty of water is needed and should be maintained until after flowering, when it can be reduced, maintain dry but not arid conditions in winter. Half-shade during hot summer months.

PROPAGATION. By seed, sown as soon as ripe in compost 2. The seeds being large are best sown singly in small thumb pots and then potted on as required with not too much root disturbance, a state which this plant resents. Repot every third year in early autumn.

P. cambessedesii. (H).

A native of the Balearic Isles, with a tuberous rootstock. Leaves ternately pinnatisect, leaflets entire, ovate, lanceolate, acute, deep bronze-red, the underneath reddish-green with red veins. Flowers solitary on 12-inch stems, large open saucer-shape, up to eight ovate petals, deep rose, and large central boss of deep golden anthers on red filaments, carpels red-purple. May. These are followed in October by the three-winged seed pods which open to display the decorative rows of black and red globular seeds.

Parahebe canescens, see *Hebe canescens.*

P. decora, see *Hebe decora.*

PARAQUILEGIA (*Ranunculaceae*).

A small genus of very rare desirable plants of which there is at present only one in cultivation and even this is slow to increase owing to the fact that seed, the only method of propagation, is not often set.

CULTIVATION. Compost A over faultless drainage, but great care is needed with watering, enough must be given while the plant is in growth, but at no time must the compost become waterlogged; dry conditions when the foliage dies away, but not arid in winter.

PROPAGATION. By seed sown as soon as ripe in compost 2. Repot only when necessary after flowering.

P. anemonoides. (H). (Syn. *P. grandiflora*; *Isopyrum grandiflorum*).
It forms close dense tufts from a thick rootstock with stout bristles. Leaves radical two to four ternatisect, segments two to three lobed, obovate, grey-green. Flowers large, solitary on 3-inch slender stems, goblet-shape, five rounded, concave petals, white to deep lavender-blue, enhanced by the central boss of golden stamens. May. A native of China.

PAROCHETUS *(Leguminosae).*

A genus containing one species, the Shamrock Pea, which although a fast growing plant, is included here because of its habit of flowering during the winter months, the dainty floral display starting in October and going through to February while the weather is open.
CULTIVATION. Compost A is suitable with plenty of water during the growing season, keep just moist at other periods. Protect from hard freezing conditions.
PROPAGATION. By cuttings taken in July. Repot when necessary in April.
P. communis. (E).
A native of the Himalayas, with prostrate, spreading, rooting, thin stems. Leaves on 2-inch stalks, three foliolate, leaflets truncate, dentate, bright green. Flowers solitary from the leaf axils almost sessile, pea-shaped, bright blue shading to pink. October to February.

PARONYCHIA *(Caryophyllaceae).*

A genus of plants which although not florally showy, has three species which are delightful with their decorative white bracts.
CULTIVATION. Compost A is suitable over good drainage, with a normal supply of water during the growing season, keep dry but not arid in winter.
PROPAGATION. By division in early April. Repot when necessary in early April.
P. argentea. (E).
A small prostrate plant rarely above 2 inches high, forming a mat of lanceolate to elliptic, acute, silvery grey leaves with wide stipules. Flowers minute in dense axillary and terminal heads with conspicuous shiny white bracts. July. A native of S. Europe.
P. capitata. (E). (Syn. *P. nivea*).
Similar in habit and formation to *P. argentea* but with green, oblong-lanceolate leaves and inconspicuous white flowers with silvery bracts. July. A native of S. Europe.
P. kapela. (E).
A native of the Mediterranean regions, this species makes a close compact

mat of prostrate 3-inch stems. Leaves lanceolate to oblanceolate, obtuse, blue-green with large membranous silvery stipules. Flowers in a dense clustered head, inconspicuous but with large decorative silvery bracts. July.
P. nivea, see *P. capitata.*

PASSERINA (*Thymelaeaceae*).

There is one species of this genus which is suitable for pan culture and this is a delightful free-flowering shrublet of easy culture for the alpine house or frame.
CULTIVATION. Compost B with plenty of water during the growing period, just moist in winter, top-dress in early spring with similar compost.
PROPAGATION. By cuttings of half-ripened wood taken in late July. Repot every other year after flowering.
P. nivalis. (E). (Syn. *Thymelaea nivalis*).
A native of the Pyrenees, it makes a small sub-shrub with slender hairy stems rarely up to 6 inches high. Leaves fleshy, linear, sessile, pointed, crowded on shoot in whorls of three, margins sparsely ciliate, dull grey-green. Flowers solitary, sessile from the leaf axils, tubular four-lobed, bright yellow. March.

PENSTEMON (*Scrophulariaceae*).

A genus of plants, the Beard Tongues, are with one exception wholly American and they make an outstanding contribution to the number of available specimens which are late flowering subjects for the alpine house or frame. They have one great fault, the majority are short lived, but this is offset to a certain extent by their ease of propagation.
CULTIVATION. These plants require a richer diet than the majority of alpines for any attempt to starve them will not only weaken their constitution with a resultant dearth of flowers, but they are more likely to suffer from the scourge which attacks this genus, the dying back of whole branches. Compost B is suitable over good drainage, plenty of water while growing and flowering, followed by a dryish period in late August, which they seem to relish. Keep dry but not arid in winter. A bi-weekly dose of weak liquid manure fertiliser is beneficial when the buds commence to form.
PROPAGATION. By green cuttings in August rooted in the propagating frame. Repot every year in April.
P. albertinus. (E).
A dwarf compact sub-shrub only a few inches high. Leaves opposite, linear, mid-green. Flowers in small terminal clusters, rich lavender-blue. May–June. A native of N.W. America.
P. ambiguus. (E).
A rounded neat shrub less than 12 inches high with congested hairy

branches. Leaves thick linear, acute, toothed, mid-green. Flowers in terminal racemes, tubular five-rounded petals, rose, paler inside. June–July. A native of W. America.

P. barrettae. (D).
From N.W. America, this is an erect shrub up to 12 inches high. Leaves crowded, oval to oblanceolate, deep green, margins often coloured red. Flowers in small erect clusters, bright purple. May.

P. corymbosis. (D).
This is a much branched erect shrublet reaching a foot in height. Leaves opposite, oblong, dentate, tapered to base, pointed at apex, deep glossy green. Flowers on hairy stems in small clusters, tubular, two-lipped, bright crimson with a touch of orange. July. A native of California.

P. davidsonii. (E).
A small sub-shrub with creeping running stems from which are borne the 2-inch erect branches. Leaves small obovate, entire, smooth glaucous grey. Flowers large, ruby-red. June–July. California.

P. davidsonii var. alba. (E).
The white form is a much rarer plant with pale green obovate to oval leaves and flowers of pure ivory-white. June–July. California.

P. erianthera. (E).
A native of N. America, this is a charming dwarf sub-shrub about 4 inches high, with congested semi-prostrate, hairy, glandular branches. Leaves oblong, coriaceous, deep green. Flowers in dense clusters, tubular, bright lavender-rose. June.

P. fruticosus var. cardwellii. (E).
A small open lax shrub less than 12 inches high. Leaves long, narrow, tapering to apex, and base, thick, margins dentate, deep glossy green. Flowers in small terminal clusters, tubular, bright blue with a splash of red. July. A native of N. America.

P. lyallii. (E). (Syn. *P. menziesii* var. *lyallii*).
An erect sub-shrub up to 12 inches high. Leaves lanceolate, opposite, tapering to apex, dull mid-green. Flowers in terminal clusters, large, purple. May–June. A native of Western North America.

P. menziesii. (E).
From N.W. America, making a small shrublet variable in height but generally less than 9 inches, much-branched semi-prostrate, slender stems, covered with hair. Leaves thick, opposite, obovate, short stalked, tapering to base, rounded at apex, dentate, bright glossy green. Flowers in clusters, up to six from terminal stems, tubular, two-lipped, deep blue with a touch of red. June.

P. menziesii var. lyallii, see *P. lyallii*.
P.m. var. scouleri, see *P. scouleri*.

P. newberryi. (E).
A native of N.W. America, this is a dwarf sub-shrub with erect slender stems up to 12 inches high. Leaves opposite, roundish, leathery, dentate,

grey-green. Flowers in terminal clusters on short stalked sprays, two-lipped, tubular, brilliant red. June.

P. pinifolius. (E).

A fine dwarf shrublet only 3 inches high with radiating light brown smooth lax branches. Leaves crowded, linear, thick, bright glossy green, arranged in small clusters like pine needles. Flowers on 4-inch stems, sparsely furnished with similar foliage, the top half bearing up to six long, tubular, two-lipped, mandarin red blooms, the basal lip divided into three narrow segments, upper slightly notched. June. A native of Arizona and New Mexico.

P. roezlii. (E).

This is a native of California, making a small shrublet of slender wiry branches, less than 9 inches high. Leaves opposite, linear, sessile, rounded at apex, deep green. Flowers on loose stems, tubular, two-lipped, dark blue with a dash of violet. July.

P. rupicola. (E).

A native of W. America, this is one of the best of the genus and is often offered in catalogues as *P. roezlii*. It is a prostrate sub-shrub only a few inches high of crowded, hairy, glandular stems. Leaves alternate, oval to orbicular, basal half dentate, veins hairy, grey-green. Flowers on short stems, large, tubular, two-lipped, brilliant crimson. June. In full bloom the flowers will completely obscure the foliage.

P. scouleri. (E). (Syn. *P. menziesii* var. *scouleri*).

This is a small compact shrub up to 18 inches high with lax slender, downy stems. Leaves opposite, almost sessile, long narrow, tapered to base, pointed at apex with small terminal serrations. Flowers in small terminal racemes, two-lipped, tubular, blue shaded red. June. A native of W. America.

P. 'Six Hills Hybrid'. (*P. davidsonii* × *P. cristatus*). (E).

This is a garden hybrid which originated in the famous Six Hills Nursery and is one of the best dwarf penstemons. Only 6 inches high it is a dwarf sub-shrub with slender branches. Leaves ovate, opposite, grey-green, margins slightly dentate. Flowers in small terminal racemes, tubular, two-lipped, pale mauve. June.

PENTACHONDRA (*Epacridaceae*).

A small genus of New Zealand shrubs of which there is only one in cultivation today suitable for pan culture, and this can be grown successfully provided it can be sheltered from prolonged frosts.

CULTIVATION. Compost B is ideal over good drainage and a normal supply of water is required while growing and flowering. The plants should be kept just moist at other periods. Needs protection from hot sunshine in the south and cold searching winds.

PROPAGATION. By green cuttings in June and rooting them in the propagating frame. Repot only when necessary in early spring when new growth commences.

P. pumila. (E).

It makes a dwarf congested shrub, rarely above 6 inches high with thick prostrate branches and erect twigs covered with fine hairs. Leaves small, congested, narrow oblong, blunt, concave, bright glossy-green, margined with fine hairs. Flowers solitary at apex of twigs, almost sessile, cylindrical, white. May. Followed by large bright red berries.

PENTAPERA (*Ericaceae*).

This small genus, closely related to the heathers, contains one species and one geographical variant, suitable for pan culture in the alpine house or frame. Unlike the great majority of *Ericaceae* both these plants are found on limestone formations in their natural habitat, but they are best grown in a neutral medium.

CULTIVATION. Compost B with good drainage and a fair supply of water during the growing season, dry but not arid in winter.

PROPAGATION. By seed in March, compost 2, or green cuttings taken in July.

P. sicula. (E). (Syn. *Erica sicula*).

Forms a small prostrate straggling shrub up to 6 inches high with slender wiry, slightly hairy stems. Leaves crowded in whorls of four, linear, deep green, grooved below. Flowers in terminal clusters up to four large erica-shape, lobes five reflexed, pale pink with deep brown anthers. May–June. A rare endemic found on Mount Cofano, Sicily.

P. sicula var. libanotica. (E).

This is a more erect and much less spreading form with upright branches, reaching 18 inches when mature. Leaves crowded in whorls of four, linear, dull dark green tinged white at apex. Flowers terminal in small clusters on short stems, pitcher-shaped, pendant, five slightly reflexed lobes, white flushed pink. May. A native of Cyprus and the Lebanon.

Perantha forrestii, see *Oreocharis aurantiaca.*

PERNETTYA (*Ericaceae*).

A genus of mostly dwarf shrubs which contain a number of species and varieties that are suitable for culture in pans. Botanically they are near to Gaultheria, there being only slight differences between the two genera. One is that the fleshy calyx present in Gaultheria is much reduced or absent in Pernettya.

CULTIVATION. Compost C will be found suitable and all the plants require moist conditions, with plenty of lime-free water during the spring and summer, just moist in winter. During the warm summer months they are best accommodated in a west- or north-facing shady frame and overhead spraying is beneficial in the evenings. Top-dress with similar compost in early spring.

PROPAGATION. By green cuttings taken in August and rooted in the propagating frame, or seed sown in March, compost 3. Repot only when necessary in early April.

P. empetrifolia, see *P. pumila.*

P. leucocarpa. (E).

A native of Chile, this is a prostrate sub-shrub up to 12 inches high, spreading by underground runners; branches congested, wiry, slender. Leaves alternate, oblong on short stalks, margins slightly dentate, deep glossy green, hairy when young. Flowers on short stems from the leaf axils, urn-shaped, white flushed pink. May. Fruits rounded, white or flushed pink.

P. leucocarpa var. linearis. (E).

A smaller form rarely up to 9 inches high, branches crowded, leaves dense, linear, pointed at apex. Flowers and fruit similar to the species. May.

P. magellanica, see *P. pumila.*

P. mucronata 'Nana'. (E).

This is the dwarf form of the well-known species, a plant which rarely exceeds 6 inches in height, with stiff, wiry, pinkish-green stems, sparsely covered with bristly hairs. Leaves alternate, arranged spirally round the stems, long oval, rounded at base, apex terminating in a sharp spine; two to four teeth on each side of leaf, dark glossy green, deep irregular veining, light grey-green below. Flowers produced form the leaf axils, solitary on short stems, urn-shaped, white flushed pink. May. Fruit roundish, reddish-blue. Origin unknown, possibly from a dwarf seedling of *P. mucronata.*

P. mucronata var. rupicola. (E).

A native of Chile, this form is about 6 inches high with semi-prostrate lax, wiry stems, covered with fine down. Leaves alternate, congested, narrow oval, pointed at apex, toothed towards base, dark glossy-green. Flowers solitary from leaf axils, pendant, urn-shaped, white, five-lobed. May. Fruit globose, pink to red.

P. nana. (E).

A native of South Island, New Zealand, this is a dwarf wiry plant of erect 3-inch stems. Leaves small oval, coriaceous, glandular, serrulate-bristly, green. Flowers solitary from the leaf axils, semi-pendant, campanulate, five-lobed, white. May. Fruit rounded depressed, red streaked white with a persisting swollen calyx.

P. nigra, see *P. prostrata.*

P. pentlandii, see *P. prostrata* var. *pentlandii.*

P. prostrata. (E). (Syn. *P. nigra*).

From S. America comes this delightful dwarf congested, prostrate shrub rarely up to 6 inches high, branches woolly with occasional stiff hairs. Leaves on small stalks, oval, pointed tapered to base, slightly dentate, margins ciliate, deep bright green, paler beneath. Flowers solitary on short stems, pendant, urn-shaped, white. June. Fruit rounded, violet.

P. prostrata var. pentlandii. (E). (Syn. *P. pentlandii*).
This is similar to the species but with more erect branches up to 12 inches high. Flowers solitary, pendant, white. June. Fruit deep violet. A native of Chile.

P. pumila. (E). (Syn. *P. empetrifolia*; *P. magellanica*).
A native of the Falkland Islands, this increases by underground runners and is rarely above 4 inches high, stem stiff, wiry, lightish grey-green in juvenile state, reddish-brown when mature. Leaves alternate, arranged closely round the stems, giving them a spiral appearance; thick obtuse, rounded at base, dark glossy green. Flowers from leaf axils, pendant, bell-shaped, five-lobed, white. May. Fruit globose, white or pink.

P. tasmanica. (E).
This is a prostrate sub-shrub of crowded, thin wiry lax branches, reddish-brown and glabrous, increasing by underground runners. Leaves thick, alternate, almost in whorls, minute, long, narrow, tapered to base, apex acute, margins serrulate, glossy green. Flowers solitary on short stems from leaf axils, five-lobed, white, urn-shaped. May. Fruits borne in abundance, globose red with a persisting swollen calyx. A native of Tasmania.

PETROCALLIS (*Cruciferae*).

A genus containing one suitable species for alpine house or frame culture closely related to Draba and often included in that genus.
CULTIVATION. Compost A over faultless drainage or compost D gives better results, for in this medium the species is much more compact and longer lived. A normal supply of water is necessary during the growing and flowering season, dry but not arid in winter.
PROPAGATION. By cuttings taken in August and kept in a close frame until rooted. Repot only when necessary after flowering.

P. pyrenaica. (E). (Syn. *Draba pyrenaica*).
A native of the Pyrenees and Hungary, this forms a tight densely tufted cushion of small downy stems only an inch or so high. Leaves minute in tufts, wedge-shaped, apex toothed, green. Flowers in small clusters on 1-inch stems, cruciform, pale lilac, fragrant. May.

PETROCOPTIS (*Caryophyllaceae*).

A small genus in which are included two species and one variety for pan culture, both closely related to Lychnis and often referred to by this genus in catalogues.
CULTIVATION. Compost A is suitable over good drainage and a normal supply of water during the growing and flowering season, dry but not arid in winter.
PROPAGATION. By seed sown in March, compost 2. Repot every other year in early April.

P. lagascae. (E). (Syn. *Lychnis lagascae*).
A small tufted mat only a few inches high with small, thick, obovate to oblong grey-green leaves in rosette formation. Flowers on 4-inch stems in profusion, star-like, carmine rose with white centre. June. A native of the Pyrenees.

P. pyrenaica. (E). (Syn. *Lychnis pyrenaica*).
A small tufted plant only a few inches high. Basal leaves spatulate, apical cordate, grey-green. Flowers star-like on long stems, pale pink. June. A native of the Pyrenees.

P. pyrenaica var. grandiflora rosea. (E).
This is a similar plant but with much larger flowers of a bright rose-pink. June.

PETROCOSMEA (*Gesneriaceae*).

A small genus of herbs which has one species in cultivation for alpine house culture, and although doubts have been cast upon its hardiness, it will survive so long as the soil is not allowed to freeze for any appreciable period.

CULTIVATION. Compost B over good drainage with plenty of water during the growing and flowering period; requires protection from hot sunshine and cold winds.

PROPAGATION. By careful division in early April or leaf cuttings in May. Repot when necessary in April.

P. kerrii. (E).
A native of Siam, it forms a small thickish rhizome from which are borne the rosettes of fleshy, elliptic-ovate, deep green leaves on short hairy petioles; margins dentate and ciliate, underneath of leaves light with white silk hairs. Flowers on 2-inch scapes in a smallish umbel, open two-lipped, upper two-fid, white with yellow basal markings, lower three-fid white. July–August.

PETROPHYTUM (*Rosaceae*).

A small genus of plants closely related to Spiraea and they have often been placed in that genus by some authorities. They differ in that the inflorescence of Spiraea is generally a panicle or corymb, in Petrophytum the flowers are borne in a crowded raceme.

CULTIVATION. They do well in compost A over good drainage with plenty of water during the growing and flowering season, keep dry but not arid in winter.

PROPAGATION. By green cuttings taken in June and rooted in the propagating frame. Repot only when necessary in April.

P. caespitosum. (E). (Syn. *Spiraea caespitosa*).
This, a native of N. America, is a true alpine shrub and with the possible exception of the rare *Kelseya uniflora*, also of the *Rosaceae* family, must

be considered the dwarfest of all shrubs. It makes a tight congested mass of procumbent stiff branches from a central rootstock, less than an inch high. Leaves in tight rosettes, spatulate, entire with an acute point, grey-green in colour owing to covering of fine silky hairs. Flowers in terminal racemes, very numerous, small densely packed, white. July.

P. hendersonii. (E). (Syn. *Spiraea hendersonii*).
A dwarf prostrate shrub endemic to the Olympic Mountains of N. America and near to *P. caespitosum*. It forms a tight congested mat of prostrate branches only an inch high densely clothed with alternate, oblanceolate, thick, grey-green leaves. Flowers on 2-inch stems, crowded globular racemes of small fluffy, creamy white. June.

PHACELIA (*Hydrophyllaceae*).

A genus of mostly annual plants which include the delightful *P. campanularia*, well known for its gentian blue flowers in the summer border; there is one perennial species that is suitable for pan culture in the alpine house or frame.

CULTIVATION. Compost A is suitable over good drainage; this plant requires a normal supply of water while growing and flowering but must have dryish conditions after the growth has died down.

PROPAGATION. By seed, compost 2 in March. Repot every year in April when growth commences.

P. sericea. (H).
A native of Idaho, N.W. America, this is a small perennial herb with erect stems up to 8 inches high covered with silky hairs. Leaves basal, stalked, deeply lobed, segments lanceolate, upper, entire sessile, silvery-grey owing to intense covering of silky hairs. Flowers terminal on 8-inch scape in dense raceme, five-lobed, bell-shaped, bright blue. May–June.

PHILESIA (*Liliaceae*).

A genus containing one shrub eminently suitable for pan culture, provided its few needs are attended to.

CULTIVATION. Compost B is suitable with plenty of lime-free water during the growing and flowering season, keep just moist at other periods. It requires a cool semi-shady spot in summer, protection from drying winds and drought; spraying with lime-free water in the evenings after hot days is also beneficial.

PROPAGATION. By green cuttings, or suckers treated as cuttings, taken in July and rooted in the shady propagating frame. Repot only when necessary in early April.

P. magellanica. (E). (Syn. *P. buxifolia*).
A native of S. Chile, this makes a small semi-prostrate shrub less than 12 inches high, with stiff congested smooth branches. Leaves alternate, densely clustered at apex of stems, tough, lanceolate, margins recurved,

bright glossy deep green above, greyish-green below. Flowers solitary at terminal of shoot, large pendant, tubular, three-petalled, deep rosy-red. June–July.

PHLOX (*Polemoniaceae*).

A typical American genus of plants, there has been, as in the case of Penstemon, a great deal of confusion in the nomenclature of the species and even today it is still in a state of flux and the names of today are liable to be the synonyms of tomorrow. They do not as a rule take kindly to pan culture but one or two can only be grown under these conditions for any reasonable chance of successful cultivation.

CULTIVATION. Unless otherwise stated all require a light well-drained medium and compost A is suitable. A normal supply of water is necessary during the growing and flowering season, dry but not arid in winter.

PROPAGATION. Best by green cuttings taken in May for a general run of increase but where special requirements are needed they will be dealt with individually. Repot every year after flowering.

P. adsurgens. (E).
A native of California and Oregon, it forms semi-prostrate glabrous stems about 6 inches high. Leaves tufted, ovate, acute, shiny green. Flowers in loose corymbs, large, open, rich salmon-pink with central deeper pink stripe to each lobe. May–June. Needs a cool spot during hot summer months, best propagated by cuttings in July.

P. alyssifolia. (E).
A small sub-shrubby plant only a few inches high, shoots prostrate covered with white hairs. Leaves small oblong-linear, thickish, greenish with white margins and ciliate. Flowers large, rounded, up to three on short stems, white often flushed pink. June. A native of the Rockies, N. America.

P. bryoides. (E). (Syn. *P. caespitosa* var. *bryoides*).
A rare species not often seen in cultivation, although it can be grown with care, it rivals the Aretia androsaces with its hard silvery cushions and is a 'must' for any truly representative collection. It forms a close tufted cushion from a woody base and rootstock. Leaves minute linear to lanceolate, stiff, apex pointed, imbricated in columnar form, silvery owing to intense covering of hair. Flowers solitary, tubular, opening to five wedge-shaped entire lobes, the whole a dazzling white. May–June. A native of Colorado and Wyoming. This plant does well in compost D and requires careful watering especially in winter. Propagation by seed sown in March, compost 2.

P. caespitosa. (E).
A species from N.W. America, with semi-prostrate mats of leafy branches, up to 6 inches high. Leaves lanceolate, stiff, acute with rigid narrow silvery membrane, light green. Flowers solitary, almost sessile, long tubed with

five pale lilac, entire lobes. May–June. Requires care in watering. Propagation by seed in March, compost 2.

P. caespitosa var. bryoides, see *P. bryoides.*

P. caespitosa var. condensata. (E). (Syn. *P. condensata*).
Similar to the species but more congested with crowded lanceolate rigid hairy green leaves. Flowers long-tubed, five-lobed, white. May–June. A native of Oregon.

P. condensata, see *P. caespitosa* var. *condensata.*

P. douglasii. (E).
A small prostrate species rarely above 3 inches high with densely glandular stems. Leaves crowded, small lanceolate, wider at base, acute, green. Flowers almost sessile, open five-lobed, bright pink. May–June. A native of Nevada.

P. douglasii var. alba. (E).
A desirable white form with large rounded pure white flowers. May–June.

P. mesoleuca, see *P. nana* var. *ensifolia.*

P. nana var. ensifolia. (D). (Syn. *P. mesoleuca*).
This must be considered the best of the dwarf phlox in cultivation and no other has created such a stir in recent years as this prostrate sub-shrub, for a well established plant is a glorious sight with its numerous large, glowing deep rose flowers. A native of Mexico it forms a low somewhat straggly mass of wiry brittle stems, radiating from a central woody rootstock about 3 inches high, much-branched, often tortuous and glabrous. Leaves in small tufts, linear to lanceolate, thick, recurving, acute, pale green covered with glandular hairs. Flowers terminal up to four on 1-inch stems, large, five oval lobes, deep rose with a white eye. May–June. Root cuttings were thought to be the only method of increase, a task not lightly undertaken in breaking up a specimen plant for this purpose. I have rooted cuttings by taking off the small tufts of foliage in May and without trimming and using the heated propagating frame as described in an earlier chapter; they rooted in a matter of six weeks.

PHYLLODOCE (*Ericaceae*).

A genus of plants which are confined to the northern hemisphere but widely distributed over this area, from America through Alaska, Japan over North Asia, Scotland, Greenland and completing the circle in Northern Canada. There are a number which are very suitable for alpine house and frame culture, proving delightful subjects for this purpose, provided their few needs are attended to.

CULTIVATION. They are suited to compost C with plenty of lime-free water at all periods. The ideal state is for the soil to be kept in a moist condition but not waterlogged. The plants should only be brought into the house for the flowering period, at other times they are best plunged in a shady frame. During the summer a spray with cool water is beneficial after the sun has set. Top-dress in early spring with the same type of compost.

PROPAGATION. By green cuttings taken in June and rooted in the propagating frame. Repot every other year after flowering, taking care not to disturb the roots too much.

P. aleutica. (E). (Syn. *Bryanthus aleuticus*; *Phyllodoce pallasiana*).
This is a dwarf semi-procumbent shrublet up to 8 inches high, the wiry stems completely clothed with leaves arranged round the stems. Leaves small, linear, deeply recurved, margins minutely dentate, apex blunt, tapering towards base, deep green above, yellowish below with a median white line. Flowers in clusters from terminal shoots, each on a short glandular stalk, pendant, globular, urn-shaped, pale yellow. May. A native of the Aleutian Islands, Alaska, Japan and Kamchatka.

P. alpina. (E).
A native of Japan, this is a semi-prostrate shrub up to 3 inches high. Leaves congested, small, linear, minute marginal serrations, obtuse. Flowers in small terminal clusters, urn-shaped, reddish-blue. May.

P. amabilis, see *P. nipponica* var. *amabilis*.

P. breweri. (E). (Syn. *Bryanthus breweri*).
A small spreading semi-prostrate shrublet, erect in the juvenile state with stiff branches up to 9 inches high. Leaves crowded, arranged symmetrically round the stems, sessile, linear, blunt, tapered towards base, margins recurved, dark glossy green. Flowers in long terminal racemes, each on short glandular stems, open bell-shaped, reddish-blue. May. A native of the Cascade Mountains and Sierra Nevada.

P. caerulea. (E). (Syn. *Andromeda caerulea*; *Bryanthus taxifolius*).
A semi-procumbent, much-branched shrublet less than 6 inches high with both erect and horizontal wiry stems. Leaves congested, linear, apex obtuse, minute marginal serrations, dark glossy green. Flowers in terminal clusters up to six pendant, pitcher-shaped on short glandular stems, light reddish-blue. April–May. A native of Europe, Asia, N. America, and Ben Lawers, among other Perthshire Hills.

P. empetriformis. (E). (Syn. *Bryanthus empetriformis*).
One of the finest of the phyllodoces and by far the easiest species of the genus to grow. It makes a low tufted semi-procumbent shrublet rarely above 6 inches high, stems erect in juvenile state. Leaves crowded, small, linear, obtuse, tapering to base with minute marginal serrations; recurved, deep glossy green. Flowers in terminal clusters up to six from the leaf axils, each on a small glandular stem, urn-shaped, pendant, bright red with a touch of blue. April–May. A native of N. America.

P. erecta, see × *Phyllothamnus* 'Erectus'.

P. glanduliflora. (E). (Syn. *Bryanthus glanduliflorus*).
A fine dwarf shrublet up to 6 inches high of tufted habit with erect branches. Leaves congested, linear, obtuse, tapered to base, deeply recurved margins, slightly dentate, dark green with a median white line

beneath. Flowers in terminal clusters, each on a slender wiry, glandular stalk, urn-shaped, pendant, five-lobed, yellow. May. A native of Western N. America and Alaska.

P. × intermedia. (E). *P. empetriformis* × *P. glanduliflora.*
This is a natural hybrid found where the two species meet in British Columbia. It is similar in shape to the latter species with congested, blunt, linear leaves, margins recurved, dark glossy green. Flowers in small terminal clusters are borne on short glandular stems, pendant five-lobed, pointed, urn-shaped, rose-pink. May.

P. nipponica. (E).
There is no doubt that this species is the finest of the genus when well grown, as all can testify who saw the magnificent pan of it exhibited by Major Walmsley, which received a First Class Certificate and the Farrer Memorial for the best plant in the show at a combined Royal Horticultural and Alpine Garden Society's Show in London a few years ago. It is a dwarf, compact, erect shrublet rarely above 6 inches high. Leaves crowded, linear, rounded at apex, recurved with minute marginal serrations, dark glossy green above, white with an intense covering of down below. Flowers produced from the upper half of the stems in clusters, up to seven from the leaf axils on slender glandular stems, bell-shaped, glistening white, sepals green. April–May. A native of Japan.

P. nipponica var. amabilis. (E). (Syn. *P. amabilis*).
Similar to the type with the exception of having red sepals and rose tipped white flowers. April.

P. pallasiana, see *P. aleutica.*

P. tsugifolia. (E).
This is a dwarf erect much-branched shrub with wiry stems about 12 inches high. Leaves crowded, alternate, linear, tapered to apex and base, margins recurved with minute serrations, deep bright green above, glaucous below. Flowers in stiff terminal clusters, five part reddish sepals, corolla pitcher-shaped, five white recurved lobes, flushed pink, each on a slender reddish erect stem. April. A native of Japan.

× PHYLLOTHAMNUS (*Ericaceae*).

This is possibly the only bigeneric hybrid suitable for pan culture in the alpine house or frame and is the result of a cross between *Phyllodoce empetriformis* and *Rhodothamnus chamaecistus,* raised over a hundred years ago in the nursery of Messrs. Cunningham and Fraser of Edinburgh.

CULTIVATION. Compost C is suitable with good drainage and plenty of lime-free water while growing and flowering, keep just moist at other periods. Needs to be plunged into a cool shady frame during the hot summer months and it benefits from a light spraying in the evenings after similar days.

PROPAGATION. By cuttings taken in July and rooted in the shady propagating frame. Repot every other year after flowering.

× **P. 'Erectus'.** (E). (Syn. *Bryanthus* × *erectus*; *Phyllodoce erecta*).
This forms a dwarf much-branched erect shrub up to 12 inches high.
Leaves alternate, crowded, linear, pointed, margins recurved and slightly
dentate, dark glossy green. Flowers solitary on slender glandular stems
at apex of shoots in clusters, from six to ten campanulate five-lobed,
rose-pink. May.

PHYTEUMA (*Campanulaceae*).

This genus is a well-known one to all who have trod the alpine meadows
of Europe where they take up the flowering season after the first flush
of alpine flowers has passed in the lush alpine meadows. There are a few
which make ideal pan plants and one at least, *P. comosum*, which can be
truly classified as a real alpine and is always an object of much admiration
when shown.
CULTIVATION. Compost A is suitable over good drainage and a fair
supply of water when growth commences in spring, reducing this after
flowering; dry conditions required in winter.
PROPAGATION. By seed sown in March, compost 2, and in the case of
P. comosum by crushing the whole of the dead flower and sowing the chaff.
Repot only when necessary in spring when growth has started.
P. comosum. (H).
This forms a tufted plant from a stout rootstock about 3 inches high.
Leaves, basal in rosette formation, ovate, cordate, long stalked, coarsely
toothed; stem leaves ovate-lanceolate, acute, petiole short, blue-grey.
Flowers on short scapes in loose roundish umbels, tubular, inflated at
base, club-like, five linear lobes, lilac deepening to purple at base. June.
A native of Dalmatia, S. Tyrol. This plant does well wedged between
pieces of limestone.
P. comosum var. album. (H).
This is a very desirable but unfortunately rare white form of the species.
June.
P. hemisphaericum. (H).
Produces small tufts from a perennial fleshy rootstock. Leaves in erect
tufts, entire, narrow linear, acute, almost grass-like, green. Flowers on
3-inch stems in a ring of short bracts, up to ten typical bright blue in an
almost complete sphere. June. A native of the European Alps.
P. pauciflorum. (H).
This species has tufts of leaves in rosette formation from a fleshy rootstock.
Leaves short, spatulate, tapered to base, green. Flowers typical on 2-inch
scapes in dense spikes up to seven, dark blue shading to violet-blue at
apex. June. A native of the European Alps.

PIMELEA (*Thymelaeaceae*).

A small genus of shrubby plants, the New Zealand Daphnes are not
considered too hardy, but the two noted here will endure many degrees

of frost without any harm. They are quite suitable for pan culture making delightful specimens with their sweetly scented flowers and glistening white berries.

CULTIVATION. Compost B is suitable over good drainage and a normal supply of water while growing and flowering, keep dry but not arid in winter. Keep the plants away from cold draughty winds which are detrimental.

PROPAGATION. By half-ripened cuttings taken with a heel in July or seed sown in March, compost 2. Repot when necessary after flowering.

P. coarctata, see *P. prostrata* var. *coarctata*.

P. prostrata. (E).

A small prostrate shrublet only an inch or so high with glabrous black crowded branches and laterals. Leaves minute, ovate to obovate, obtuse, tapered to base, recurved, sessile, grey-green. Flowers up to ten in an axillary terminal cluster, white, silky daphne-like with a delightful perfume. May. These are followed by oval white berries. A native of New Zealand.

P. prostrata var. coarctata. (E). (Syn. *P. coarctata*).

A form of *P. prostrata* which has for many years been grown under the name of *P. coarctata*, even at Wisley a plant is still labelled with this name, but its origin is a mystery for I can find no record of this plant and no flora on New Zealand plants mentions it, but whatever its botanical standing it is a delightful plant. It makes a prostrate dwarf shrublet an inch or so high with congested interlaced stiff, wiry, greyish-green, not black, branches and twigs. Leaves minute, opposite, ovate, sessile, grey-green. Flowers in small axillary terminal clusters, four-lobed daphne-like, covered with silky hairs, white, scented. May. Followed by glistening white berries.

PINGUICULA *(Lentibulariaceae)*.

A small genus of perennial herbs, the Butterworts are well known for their insectivorous habits, found in boggy regions mostly in the northern hemisphere and attracting small insects to their sticky glandular leaves, on which they are trapped and their digestible portions turned into nitrogenous food, which is absorbed by the leaves.

CULTIVATION. They require a slightly different compost from any of those normally advocated for the culture of alpine plants in pans. To compost A should be added half the quantity of sphagnum moss and at least one-third of the pan should consist of drainage material, this being broken brick. During the growing season the pan is best used with a saucer and this kept full of rain water; after growth has died away, the saucer can be removed and the compost kept just moist throughout the winter months. If grown in the alpine house these plants benefit from a weekly watering with a diluted liquid manure.

PROPAGATION. By division in early spring or leaf cuttings taken in May. Repot only when necessary, when growth commences in April.

P. alpina. (H).

A small species about 2 inches high forming a basal rosette of elliptic leaves, fleshy, light green, margins incurved, slightly hairy, glandular. Flowers solitary on fleshy stems, gloxinia-shaped, unequal lips, white with golden throat, spur short conical. May–June. A native of Arctic Europe including Britain.

P. grandiflora. (H).

A native of W. Europe including S.W. Ireland, this forms basal rosettes of oval, obtuse, succulent light green glandular leaves, margins incurved. Flowers on 6-inch scapes, open five-lobed, violet-blue, lower lip white, purple at base, short conical spur. June–July.

P. vulgaris. (H).

A native of Europe including Britain, this has a ground-hugging basal rosette of thick fleshy, oblong, obtuse leaves, light green, sticky glandular with incurved margins. Flowers on 4-inch stems, open tubular, five-lobed, violet, lower lip broader; spur short, conical. May.

PLAGIORHEGMA, see JEFFERSONIA.

PLANTAGO (*Plantaginaceae*).

A genus of plants which include a number of species which are a curse to all who aspire to cultivate a lovely green lawn and difficult to eradicate but as with so many genera containing these pests there is generally at least one species which is not only a rarity but also far from easy to keep in good health.

CULTIVATION. Compost A with faultless drainage in full sun, a normal supply of water during the growing season but care must be taken to see that water does not lodge in the centre of the rosettes, otherwise rotting will soon set up, dry conditions in winter.

PROPAGATION. By seed sown as soon as ripe, compost 1. Repot when necessary in late April.

P. nivalis. (E).

A native of Spain, this forms a basal rosette of oblong-lanceolate, sessile, entire, pointed leaves, silver-grey in colour, owing to intense covering of silky silver hairs. Flowers valueless, being of the usual plantain type, but these are necessary to provide seed for increase. The beauty lies in the shimmering silver colour of the rosettes.

PLEIONE (*Orchidaceae*).

This genus of outstanding plants has come to the fore during recent years owing in no small measure to the ease in which a number of the species, especially *P. pricei* and *P. formosana* can be cultivated and kept through the winter with only cold frame or alpine house protection.

There are now a number of different species available and provided their few needs are attended to they prove quite satisfactory plants for alpine house or frame culture.

CULTIVATION. Pleiones are surface rooting and only a shallow pan is required, deep pans are of no use for the plants cannot take advantage of it and there is a great likelihood of the compost souring, owing to the excess of water which cannot be absorbed by the roots. I have found compost B ideal over good drainage and the psuedo-bulbs, these being nothing more than annually renewed thickened stems, are placed on the surface of the compost. A small amount of compost is added so that the thickest part is just covered, and these are then well firmed. When completed there should be at least one inch of the pan left above the surface of the soil. It will be necessary to find a supply of moss to cover the whole of the soil's surface; this is absolutely essential, for the roots that are produced all practically live on the surface of the soil and must be protected at all times from drying out. Sphagnum moss can be used but it does not always take readily to the dryish atmospheric conditions of the alpine house and has to be replaced frequently. The best time to pot up pleiones is in late March when growth is due to start if fresh psuedo-bulbs are used, but the moving of established plants is best carried out as soon as the flowers fade, at the same time doing any repotting that is required. For March-planted bulbs the compost should be moist but not wet, and once planted no further water is required until growth is apparent; then a small supply is necessary until the flowers appear; plenty is required during the active stage of the plants; and then as the foliage dies away, water is withheld and no further supply given until the following season. All these plants are best plunged into a shady frame and only brought into the alpine house for flowering and during the winter; an overhead spray with cool water is also appreciated during hot spells.

PROPAGATION. Simple, for most plants produce up to three new psuedo-bulbs from each mature plant and these can be used for fresh stock, potting them up as required, as soon as the flowers fade from the adult bulb.

P. formosana. (B).

A native of Formosa, this is one of the finest, easiest and most seen of the pleiones. It forms a pseudo-bulb, roundish in outline, flattish on top, bright green, tinged pale violet. The leaves, which begin to appear as the flowering stem lengthens, are bright green, widely-lanceolate and ribbed. Flowers solitary on stout 2-inch stems with an apical bract, open funnel shaped, pale mauve, labellum fringed, spotted brown and light reddish-brown, lamellae four, deep cream; two petals and three sepals, bright mauve. April–May.

Since these notes were written Mr P. Francis Hunt of Kew has examined living material of plants imported from Formosa and has reached the conclusion that *P. formosana* and *P. pricei* are conspecific, and although tend to vary in colour of pseudo-bulbs and flowers (especially the number of lamellae), these variations are not constant. As *P. formosana* has priority the name pricei is invalid and descriptions under this name must be regarded as forms of *P. formosana*.

P. formosana var. alba. (B).

This is the beautiful and very desirable form with glistening white flowers on 2-inch stems and fringed labellum of pale yellow. April–May.

P. forrestii. (B).

A rare yellow flowered species with rather large conical light green pseudo-bulbs with vertical ridges. Flowers before the leaves, solitary on a 3-inch stem, open funnel-shaped, labellum fringed, light orange-yellow, spotted mid-brown, lamellae seven; petals and sepals of a darker colour. April–May. Leaves wide lanceolate, green, ribbed. A native of W. China.

P. henryi, see *P. pogonioides*.

P. hookeriana. (B).

A native of the Himalayas, this makes a small smooth deep green pseudo-bulb. Leaves bright green, lanceolate, only lightly ribbed. Flowers solitary on a 2-inch stem, wide open, funnel-shaped, white, with labellum blotched orange; petals and sepals light rose tinged deep mauve at base, petals veined bright mauve, lamellae five rows of cream-coloured hairs. May.

P. humilis. (B).

A native of Nepal, this species forms small flask-like deep green pseudo-bulbs. Flowers before the leaves on 2-inch stems semi-pendant, pale rose-white, lip blotched deep mauve or reddish-brown, petals and sepals pale mauve, lamellae six, purple-blue. April. Leaves wide lanceolate, dull purple-green, ribbed.

P. limprichtii. (B).

A native of W. China, with smallish roundish pseudo-bulbs of deep green. Leaves deep green, faintly ribbed, lanceolate. Flowers on 2-inch pinkish stems with a terminal rose bract, deep red-purple, wide funnel-shape, labellum spotted crimson-purple, fringed, throat white with two lamellae, petals and sepals reddish-purple. April–May.

P. maculata. (B).

From Khasia, Assam, this forms irregular, depressed, roundish pseudo-bulbs, light green marked with mauve-brown. Leaves in pairs, wide lanceolate, ribbed, light yellowish-green. Flowers solitary on 2-inch stems, open tubular, white streaked purple, labellum entire, white, blotched crimson-purple, lamellae five fringed, interspaced with deep mauve; petals and sepals white. April–May.

P. maculata var. virginea. (B).

This is a pure white, with throat of labellum a light yellow. April–May.

P. pogonioides. (B). (Syn. *P. henryi*).

A native of China, this makes a narrow oval bright green pseudo-bulb.

Leaves same time as flower, solitary, wide lanceolate with apical notch, bright green ribbed. Flowers solitary on 2-inch stems, open tubular, light purple; petals and sepals light purple, deeper at base, labellum pale mauve spotted deep purple, lamellae four fringed. April–May.

P. praecox. (B).
From Burma and N. India, these produce large flattish pseudo-bulbs, slightly conical in centre, mottled green and deep brown, with small wart-like protuberances. Leaves large up to three lanceolate, green, plicate. Flowers solitary on 2-inch stems, large open rose, labellum pale rose, fringed; lamellae five ridges, fringed, petals and sepals rose-purple. April.

P. praecox var. alba. (B).
This form has white flowers with rim of labellum tinged deep yellow. April.

P. pricei. (B).
A native of Formosa, this forms a smallish slightly flattened pseudo-bulb of deep green flushed purple. Leaves mature after flowers, lanceolate, ribbed, green. Flowers on 2-inch stems, large open tubular, white flushed rose, labellum white, rose on the small fringe; lamellae, two irregular keels with reddish-brown spots and lines. Petals and sepals reddish light mauve, deeper at base. April. This is now conspecific with *P. formosana*.

P. yunnanensis. (B).
A native of W. China, it makes small slightly flattish, light olive-green pseudo-bulbs. Leaves long, narrow, lanceolate, ribbed, green. Flowers on 3-inch stems, wide funnel-shaped, rose-purple, deeply fringed, labellum blotched deep purplish-brown; lamellae three ridges, whitish. Petals and sepals bright red-purple. April–May.

POLEMONIUM (*Polemoniaceae*).

A small genus of plants natives of N. and C. America, also Europe and Asia, of which a few species can be utilised for pan culture in the alpine house or frame.

CULTIVATION. Compost B is suitable over good drainage with a normal supply of water during the growing season, keep dry but not arid in winter; best in a cool spot during hot dry weather in summer.

PROPAGATION. By division in early September. Repot when necessary after flowering.

P. confertum. (H).
A native of Wyoming, making a thick woody rhizome. Leaves narrow, pinnately dissected, leaflets up to forty in whorls of four to six roundish ovate, twisted, grey-green. Flowers on 6-inch stems in a dense terminal cluster, open tubular, lobes five oval, rotate, blue. June.

P. mellitum. (H).
This species from the Rocky Mountains is similar, but leaflets more numerous in whorls of four roundish to linear, grey-green. Flowers

dainty in a dense terminal cluster on 6-inch stems, five-lobed, open tubular, creamy white. May.

P. viscosum. (H).

A native of Idaho, has a thick woody rhizome and narrow pinnately dissected leaves, leaflets up to forty in whorls of four to six roundish, grey-green, slightly sticky. Flowers on 4-inch stems, terminal clusters of small tubular, five-lobed violet-blue. May.

POLYGALA *(Polygalaceae).*

A genus of plants with a wide distribution containing a number that can be used for pan culture. All plants noted here with the exception of *P. paucifolia*, an American species, are natives of Europe.

CULTIVATION. Compost B is suitable over good drainage and plenty of water during the growing and flowering season, keep the plants just moist at other periods. Top-dress with similar compost in early spring, working this well down amongst the shoots.

PROPAGATION. By detaching runners with roots where possible, treating these as cuttings in late June, or green cuttings in June. Repot every other year immediately after flowering.

P. calcarea. (E).

A native of Europe including Britain, this makes mats of creeping, rooting prostrate stems only an inch or so high. Leaves in basal rosettes, spatulate, tapered to base, reflexed, bright green. Flowers in short terminal racemes up to twelve bright blue, keel fringed with paler blue crest. May.

P. chamaebuxus. (E).

A native of C. Europe, this is a dwarf shrub rarely above 6 inches high and increasing by suckers when established. Stems slender and erect. Leaves alternate, small, oblong, pointed, smooth, dull mid green. Flowers are borne on short stems from the leaf axils of the terminal shoots, reminiscent of pea flowers, sepals five and three petals forming a keel, white, mouth of keel bright yellow, fragrant. May.

P. chamaebuxus var. grandiflora, see *P. chamaebuxus* var. *purpurea.*

P. chamaebuxus var. purpurea. (E). (Syn. *P.c.* var. *grandiflora*).

This variety is identical with the species in form and habit but has attractive flowers of purple-red charmingly set off by the yellow mouth of the keel. April

P. paucifolia. (E).

A native of N. America, this is a small prostrate shrublet rarely above an inch or so high but spreading and increasing by underground stolons. Leaves congested, ovate, slightly decurved, tapered to apex and base, pale green, deep purple beneath. Flowers on short stems of a light rich carmine, wing petals plain but the keel fringed with bristly hairs. May. The R.H.S. *Dictionary of Gardening* quotes this as a herbaceous perennial but it is definitely shrubby and evergreen.

Above: *Primula rubra* (see page 527)

Below: *Primula pubescens* 'The General' (see page 527)

Above: *Primula bracteosa* (see page 415)

Below: *Pulsatilla occidentalis* (see page 527)

P. vayredae. (E).
A native of Spain, this is confined to a small area of the E. Pyrenees, making a creeping prostrate shrublet only an inch or so high with wiry glabrous stems. Leaves alternate, linear, thick, pointed, margins ciliate when young, absent in the adult stage, dull mid green. Flowers up to three in terminal leaf axils on the previous year's wood, wing petals purple, keel purplish at base shading to yellow at mouth. May.

POLYGONUM (*Polygonaceae*).

A genus of plants containing a number of species which are more or less garden weeds but there are two species that are suitable for pan culture in the alpine house or frame.
CULTIVATION. Compost A over good drainage with a normal supply of water during the growing season, dry but not arid in winter.
PROPAGATION. By division in March for the herbaceous species and cuttings with a heel in June for the evergreen. Repot every year in late March as these plants soon outgrow their pans.
P. tenuicaule. (H).
A fairly recent introduction from Japan, with a prostrate rambling rhizome. Leaves in tufts from a brownish sheathing stipule, ovate to elliptic, base cuneate, stalk winged, light green, purple on reverse. Flowers which appear before the leaves are on 3-inch scapes in a cylindrical raceme, small white bell-shaped with five lobes and exserted stamens, fragrant. April. Requires semi-shade during hot weather.
P. vacciniifolium. (E).
A native of the Himalayas, this is a late flowering procumbent species less than 6 inches high, with mat-forming woody, well-branched stems. Leaves small, ovate, tapering to base and apex, glossy bright green tinged red, lighter below. Flowers on 2-inch leafy scapes in crowded, almost sessile racemes, small, bell-shaped, five-lobed, rose-pink with exserted stamens. August–September. Requires plenty of sunshine.

POTENTILLA (*Rosaceae*).

A large genus of plants mostly herbaceous but with a few shrubs or sub-shrubs, natives of the northern hemisphere. There are a number of the Cinquefoils which make fine alpine house or frame plants and of these the shrubby species or varieties help to extend the flowering season into late summer.
CULTIVATION. All require a light compost, and A is suitable over good drainage with a normal supply of water while growing and flowering, keep dry but not arid in winter.
PROPAGATION. By seed sown in February, compost 2, division in April, cuttings or offsets in late July rooted in the propagating frame. Repot every year in April.

P. alba. (H).

A native of C. Europe, this is a low spreading plant with basal tufts of stalked palmate leaves, leaflets three to five lanceolate, apex dentate, silvery-green, white below. Flowers on 2-inch stems up to five in loose terminal clusters, five-lobed roundish petals, white. April–June.

P. alpestris, see *P. crantzii*.

P. aurea. (H).

A native of the European Alps including the Pyrenees, this is a few-stalked semi-woody perennial about 4 inches high, stems covered with appressed hairs. Leaves palmate, stalked, segments five oblong, with three to five teeth at apex, smooth, dull green, silvery hairy below. Flowers on slender 3-inch scapes in a loose cluster, five-lobed, bright yellow with deeper basal colouring. May–June.

P. aurea var. compacta. (H).

This is a much smaller edition of the type only an inch or so high but with just as large golden-yellow flowers. May–June.

P. crantzii. (H). (Syn. *P. alpestris*).

This has a wide distribution over the northern hemisphere, forming a much-stemmed erect plant. Leaves palmate, stalked, leaflets five obovate, coarsely dentate at apex, hirsute, dull green. Flowers on 4-inch stems in a loose cluster, five rounded lobes, golden-yellow with a deeper basal colouring. June–July.

P. curviseta. (E).

A native of the Himalayas, this is a charming mat-forming plant only a few inches high. Leaves small, crowded, trifid, dentate, bright green. Flowers solitary on short stems, rounded golden-yellow. May–June.

P. 'Davurica'. (*P. glabra* × *P. parvifolia*). (D).

This hybrid is a small much-branched very slow growing shrub, less than 12 inches high with pendant stems. Leaves palmate, sessile, leaflets five long oval, obtuse, glabrous, mid-green; three central joined at base. Flowers solitary on small hairy stems, five roundish petals, white with green bracts. June–August.

P. fruticosa. (D).

The species is a shrubby plant which varies considerably in height from 1 to 4 feet but there are several named dwarf forms and these under pan culture will retain their dwarf habit over a good number of years. The type plant is a compact roundish shrub with erect branches and twiggy brown stems. Leaves sessile, palmate with three, five or seven leaflets, linear to lanceolate, overlapping, acute, the three central united at base, glabrous mid-green, minutely hairy below, margins recurved. Flowers generally on short hairy stems, five-lobed, deep yellow petals alternating with five greenish-yellow bracts. July–September. Native of England, Ireland, Europe and America.

P. fruticosa var. beesii. (D). (Syn. *P.f.* var. *nana argentea*).

A dwarf form less than 12 inches high from China, with the typical palmate leaves. Leaflets three to five silver-grey and large, five-lobed open goblets, golden-yellow flowers. July.

P. fruticosa var. mandschurica. (D).
This is a dwarf shrublet less than 12 inches high with erect purplish stems and five-foliate leaves of silver-grey, the three terminal leaflets joined at base. Flowers on short terminal stalks, large five rounded lobes, bright cream. July. A native of Manchuria.

P. fruticosa var. nana argentea, see *P.f.* var. *beesii.*

P. fruticosa var. pyrenaica. (D).
A dwarf mountain variety from the Pyrenees, less than 12 inches high very compact and bushy. Leaves palmate three to five small lanceolate, acute, leaflets. Flowers five-lobed shining yellow. July.

P. nevadensis. (E).
This makes a semi-prostrate tufted plant only 4 inches high. Basal leaves palmate, stalked, leaflets five obovate-lanceolate, coarsely crenate, glabrous green, silky haired below. Flowers on three-foliate leaved stems in small clusters on hairy pedicels, five-lobed, brilliant yellow. June–July. A native of the Sierra Nevada, Spain.

P. nevadensis var. condensata. (E).
A much rarer and more compact tufted plant, differing from the type in having leaves of silver-grey due to the intense covering of silvery hairs on both sides of the leaves. Flowers similar to the species. July.

P. nitida. (E).
This plant can be the despair of cultivators, often proving for no known reason to be shy-flowering in cultivation. It seems to resent overfeeding and often does better when slightly pot bound. It is a small tufted plant forming a close mat of semi-erect stems only a few inches high. Leaves three-foliate, leaflets obovate to spatulate, sometimes three dentate, grey-green, silky hairs on both sides. Flowers solitary, rarely in pairs, five-lobed, petals rose-pink, open saucer-shaped, sepals purplish. June–July. A native of European Alps.

P. nitida var. alba. (E).
This is the very desirable white form which is a rare plant and even if obtainable proves just as shy-flowering. June–July.

P. verna. (H).
A small carpet-forming plant with semi-erect bristly hairy stems about 6 inches high. Leaves palmate, stalked, leaflets five to seven obovate, obtuse, dentate at apex, green covered with silky down on both sides. Flowers rounded five-lobed golden-yellow in a small cyme. April–August. A native of Europe including Britain.

P. verna var. nana. (H).
A dwarf edition of the type from C. Europe, forming a mat only an inch high with five-partite green leaves, leaflets wedge-shaped, toothed at apex. Flowers in a small cyme, five-lobed, golden-yellow. April–August.

P. villosa. (H).
A native of Siberia, this is a semi-prostrate plant with ascending stems up to 4 inches high. Leaves palmate, stalked, leaflets three obovate, wedge-shaped, dentate, fawn-coloured, covered on both sides with a silky down. Flowers on 4-inch stems in a small cluster, large, golden-yellow, five-lobed, rounded petals. May–June.

PRATIA (*Campanulaceae*).

A small genus of plants chiefly from the southern hemisphere, related to the Lobelia family; there is one variety which is suitable for pan culture and which has delightful berries.
CULTIVATION. Compost B over good drainage and plenty of water during the growing season, keep just moist in winter.
PROPAGATION. By seed, compost 2, in March or green cuttings taken in June. Repot when necessary in late April.
P. angulata var. treadwellii. (E).
This New Zealander is a prostrate mat-forming plant only an inch or so high of creeping, slightly hairy stems. Leaves thickish, alternate, small, sub-orbicular, cordate at base, coarsely dentate, bronzy-green. Flowers typical lobelia-shaped, white, lined light mauve. June–July. Followed by large globose purple red berries.
P. linnaeoides, see *Lobelia linnaeoides*.

PRIMULA (*Primulaceae*).

A large and mighty genus of plants embracing both sun and shade-lovers from most parts of the world and inhabiting many differing aspects, from the lowland meadows and woodlands of our own native land, where the Primrose *P. vulgaris*, the Cowslip *P. officinalis*, and the Oxlip *P. elatior*, abound delighting us in early spring; then through the high altitude rock-loving Europeans including the enchanting *P. allionii*, *P. glutinosa* and *P. minima* to that mighty awe-inspiring race of Asiatics which has given us the ultimate in rare, beautiful and difficult species.

The New World is poorly represented, there being but a few species in cultivation today, but over the last thirty years the number of Asiatics which have been introduced is enormous, and there are plenty more waiting. Many of these are considered difficult or even intractable in our climate but by careful cultivation a good number are proving reliable and more amenable to cultivation, this is truer in the north where climatic conditions are better, but even in the south with careful culture many species are settling down. Naturally as a larger amount of material becomes available so experimentation can be carried out, to find the best conditions for these exquisite wildlings.

General Cultivation

After growing the Asiatics over a number of years in the dry climate of the south east and then seeing their counterparts in the cooler more moisture-laden atmosphere of the northern counties and Scotland where they grow robust and healthy—*P. sonchifolia* comes up for all the world like a cos lettuce under these conditions—there can be no doubt that in the south they must remain to a certain extent problem children, requiring more attention and nursing than their robust Scottish-grown cousins.

The Europeans present a different problem, here the tables are turned and they are certainly more at home in the southern regions, for unlike the Asiatics a drier atmosphere and more sun is necessary for their well-being and with few exceptions all are easy to grow, given the less moist conditions. Most of them are rock dwellers in their native habitat and require a much sparser fare than the Asiatics so that they will retain their desirable dwarf compact habit. It can be safely said that all primulas resent water in their foliage, the Europeans mainly because of the danger of spoiling the wonderful farina with which a large number are covered. This is where cultivation under alpine house or frame conditions allows it to be seen to its best advantage and the foliage should never be handled, for this will leave unsightly marks where touched; also some species, especially those with sticky foliage like *P. allionii* and *P. glutinosa*, will soon rot away if water is allowed to settle at the base of the rosettes.

The Asiatics are very susceptible to water on their leaves which will quickly set up rot, spreading from the foliage to the crown which soon becomes infected and the loss of the plant will occur in a short space of time. A number of the Asiatic species are also covered with farina which in nature acts as a shield against excessive moisture during their resting state which is generally a crown bud. There is generally in nature a protective covering of snow to keep them safe and dry. This may seem illogical in the light of what has been written before, that they grow better in the northern counties in a moisture laden atmosphere, but the operative word is 'grow' and a high humidity is required and is even a necessity while these plants are making their growth and flowers. Also during the winter the climate changes are not so great as in the northern counties there being more prolonged spells of cold extending often into early spring which prohibits growth until these have passed. How different down south where early spring is often heralded with fine warm weather only to be followed by cold frosty spells which soon nip any precarious growth to say nothing of the loss of the flowers owing to frosted buds.

As the European and Asiatic species and varieties are not only geographically miles apart but also their requirements in cultivation are likewise, I propose to deal with them separately, thus specific cultivation hints can be given to each group and any requiring individual attention will be noted under the heading of the plant being described. A point to bear in mind is that all primulas like to be potted hard, that is, real pressure should be applied when repotting so that the compost is really firm and the plant secure, for they seem to resent a loose soil.

EUROPEAN PRIMULAS

CULTIVATION. All these primulas like a light porous soil and compost A will suit them admirably making sure that the drainage is perfect. Water in quantity is needed while the plants are in active growth and during the flowering period, reducing this after new growth is completed. Dryish but not arid conditions are required during the winter. Water is best applied through a small can with a curved spout as it is necessary to see that none is poured over the foliage.

PROPAGATION. This can be from seed, cuttings or division, depending on the species; in the case of the hybrids, cuttings or division are the only methods of reproduction, for even if they ripen seed in this country they will certainly not breed true. As the time and method varies with different species each will be dealt with separately.

P. allionii. (E). Section Auricula.

I think it can be safely said that this species and its many forms are more common in cultivation today than in its native habitat where it is a rare plant confined to a few stations in the Maritime Alps. It makes tight congested rosettes building themselves up into a bun of obovate, sticky glandular, grey-green leaves. The flowers are large, in some forms up to $1\frac{1}{2}$ inches across, in umbels from two to seven on a short scape which rarely rises above the rosette, giving the plant an appearance of a dome of colour. The flowers of the type-plant vary from rose-pink to deep rose-red. March–April.

CULTIVATION. This is an easy plant to grow under alpine house or frame conditions if the following cultural hints are attended to. No overhead watering at any time and what is more important is the removal of all dead foliage and flowering scapes, for these if left are the focal point for the entry of fungi that will quickly set up rot, doing untold damage in a very short period.

PROPAGATION. By seed in compost 2 for the species, sown as soon as ripe, or green cuttings taken in July for both species and colour forms. Repotting is best carried out immediately after flowering is over or if seed is required as soon as this is ripe. Firm potting is necessary and if the plants are not repotted yearly a weekly dose of weak liquid fertiliser should be given as soon as the buds form.

Varieties of *Primula allionii*:

var. alba. (E).

The pure white form is extremely delightful but should be chosen when in flower for so many albas have a touch of pink, generally at the base of the petals which mars the effect. April.

'Apple Blossom'. (E).

A delightful seedling raised by the late Frank Barker, who used to exhibit the most wonderful pans of the species and its forms at the Royal Horticultural Society's Shows. It has light mauve-pink flowers with wavy-edged petals. April.

'Crowsley var'. (E).
This form was collected by Dr Roger Bevan in the Maritime Alps and has large deep bright crimson flowers. March–April.
'Praecox'. (E).
An extremely early flowering variety which in a mild spell will produce its rose-pink flowers in December.
'Viscountess Byng'. (E).
From a seedling raised by Frank Barker, with large rose-pink, white-eyed flowers. The petals are large and rounded, thus forming a complete rounded flower. March.
P. auricula. (E). Section Auricula.
The type plant is well known and has a wide distribution in nature with many geographic forms and variants. The margins of the leaves are heavily covered with farina in a number of the forms and the flowers, tubular bell-shaped, yellow are borne in an umbel on stout scapes. All are easy to grow and a number are fragrant making a good display in early spring. Propagation is by division in July. Repot every other year after flowering.
P. auricula var. albo-cincta. (E).
A fine form with large broad obovate, serrated yellow-green leaves, densely margined with silver. Flowers in one sided umbels on 3-inch scapes, long, tubular, yellow with white eye; very fragrant. April–May.
P. auricula var. ciliata. (E).
A small neat edition of the type from the Tyrol, leaves obovate, light green, smooth, no farina. Flowers rich golden-yellow, in small umbels on slender scapes, very fragrant. May.
P. × berninae. (*P. rubra* × *P. viscosa*). (E).
This is a natural hybrid from stations where the two species grow in the Engadine and above Bernina, making a small compact plant similar to its parents about 3 inches high. Flowers open large in one-sided umbels of a blue-mauve. May.
PROPAGATION. By offsets in late June. Repot every second year after flowering.
P. × berninae 'Windrush' (E).
A compact form with wide open, large, bright pink flushed mauve flowers and is just as desirable. Raised from seed in the early twenties by the late Paul Rosenheim.
P. × biflora. (*P. minima* × *P. glutinosa*). (E).
A really charming hybrid, forming small humps of tight rosettes of rounded glossy green foliage with a notch at the apex. The flowers are borne on slender 2-inch scapes in pairs; open large rosy-purple, the petals being notched. May.
PROPAGATION. By offsets in July. Repot every second year after flowering.
P. × bilekii. (*P. minima* × *P. rubra*). (E).
Another fine plant near to *minima* but with wide obovate, deeply notched,

sticky deep green leaves and large purple flowers on short scapes. May.

PROPAGATION. By offsets in July. Repot every other year after flowering.

P. carniolica. (E). Section Auricula.

An outstanding species from the Maritime and Julian Alps, rare in nature but locally abundant where found. It does well in cultivation but is best grown in compost B for it appreciates a soil with a moister and richer humus content in shade than most other European species. It makes a few rosettes of long ovate-lanceolate, obtuse, deep glossy green leathery leaves with a winged stalk. Flowers in a one-sided umbel on a slender 4-inch scape, narrow tubular, wide at mouth, crinkly, soft rose flowers with a white eye. It is very fragrant. May. This plant is devoid of any farina and should be plunged outside in a shady frame after flowering.

PROPAGATION. By seed, compost 2, or careful division after flowering, these being treated as cuttings. Repot every second year after flowering.

P. carniolica var. alba. (E).

The rare white form was in cultivation before the war but whether it is today is rather problematical. If obtainable it is to be cherished, for a more outstanding plant would be hard to find. May.

P. clusiana. (H). Section Auricula.

A charming easy good-tempered plant requiring sun to make it flower freely. It forms prostrate rosettes of ovate bright glossy green leaves with tough margins. Flowers in umbels of up to six on short scapes rarely above 3 inches high, carmine in colour with a white eye, the petals are deeply cut. A native of Austria. May.

PROPAGATION. By division after flowering. Repot every June as this plant is a quick grower and soon exhausts the soil.

P. cottia. (H). Section Auricula.

A native of the Cottian Alps, but still rare in cultivation due to difficulty in establishing it successfully. It makes small rosettes of long obovate hairy woolly leaves, margins reddish-brown in the juvenile state due to intense covering of soft hairs. Flowers in small umbels on 3-inch scapes, long tubular, rose-pink in colour. May.

PROPAGATION. By seed sown as soon as ripe if available in compost 2 otherwise careful division after flowering. Repot only when necessary after flowering, as this plant seems to resent disturbance.

P. deorum. (E). Section Auricula.

This plant is sometimes seen in a collection of alpines today, but not to the extent it was a generation ago. A native of Bulgaria, it makes rosettes of narrow, ovate acute leaves, quite thick and tough. Flowers up to ten in an umbel on a 4-inch scape, open tubular, deep purple, petal-segments notched. May. This plant needs ample water especially during the growing and flowering season.

PROPAGATION. By division after flowering. Repot every other year in June.

P. farinosa. (H). Section Farinosae.

A native of most European Alps, including Britain, it is a charming plant for pan culture where its intensely powdered foliage and scape is never seen to better advantage. The success of growing this primula well is to imitate its natural tendency in nature, that is, it should always be grown in clumps, never as a single specimen.

From rosettes of ovate, crinkly, light green leaves spring the 2-inch slender scapes bearing the umbels of up to eight flowers, the colour ranging from pink to light purple, each with a distinctive yellow eye. April. This species needs light shade and plenty of water at all times, even in winter the soil must not be allowed to dry out.

PROPAGATION. It is short-lived but can be easily raised from seed, the best plan is to sow this as soon as ripe, very thinly in compost 2 in a 5-inch pan and remove all unwanted seedlings to avoid overcrowding, allowing those left to form mature plants.

P. farinosa var. alba. (H).

The white form is sometimes met with but as the species is short lived, the white form keeps appearing and disappearing. It is noted here because the glistening white flowers with their golden-yellow eye are outstanding and desirable. April.

P. × floerkeana. (*P. minima* × *P. glutinosa*). (E).

A charming hybrid with small rosettes of short wedge-shaped crenulate leaves and on almost minute scapes, large deeply cut, petalled flowers of a bright purple. May. Needs care in cultivating, requiring good drainage.

PROPAGATION. By careful division after flowering. Repot every second year.

P. × forsteri. (*P. minima* × *P. rubra*). (E.)

Large, glossy deep green obovate, dentate leaves in rosettes; short stems topped with the large deeply-cut petalled flowers of bright rose. The flowers are sometimes borne in pairs and are often larger than the individual rosettes. May. Requires cool conditions.

PROPAGATION. By division after flowering. Repot every other year after flowering.

P. frondosa. (H). Section Farinosae.

A native of the Balkans, it is in appearance a larger edition of *P. farinosa* and like this, densely covered with farina especially on the underside of the leaves. The foliage is large, spatulate, light green with fine crinkled margins. Flowers in rounded umbels on 4-inch scapes, bright rose with a yellow eye. April. Requires same conditions as *P. farinosa* but is more permanent and good forms can be increased by division after flowering. Repot only when necessary after flowering.

P. glutinosa. (E). Section Auricula.

One of the finest but unfortunately not the easiest of the European primulas from the southern and eastern Alps. It makes rosettes of dull green intensely sticky, oblong leaves and when satisfied bears on 3-inch stems violet-blue delightfully scented flowers up to six on slender scapes. June. I found a large deep rich purple-blue form above Vent in the Tyrol, which when brought back lived for three years but never flowered again. The best chance of success is to plant this species in compost B and give plenty of water during the flowering season.

PROPAGATION. By careful division in July. Repot only when necessary after flowering.

P. halleri, see *P. longiflora*.

P. × heerii. (*P. rubra* × *P. integrifolia*). (E).
A natural hybrid sometimes found on the Swiss Alps where its parents grow, making rosettes of narrow, entire, glaucous green leaves from which, on short scapes, are borne the rich rose-red flowers, rarely above four. May–June.

PROPAGATION. By careful division after flowering. Repot only when necessary in early April.

P. helvetica var. alba, see *P. pubescens* '*Alba*'.

P. kitaibeliana. (E). Section Auricula.
A native of Croatian Alps, this is a rare plant in gardens today, very often some forms of *P. viscosa* or *P. integrifolia*, a less charming species, doing duty for it. The true plant makes rosettes of thin oblong-lanceolate, light green glutinous leaves, distinguished by a faint repellant odour. The flowers are borne on 2-inch scapes, singly, rarely in pairs, large rose-lilac with a white eye, petals notched. June.

PROPAGATION. By division or seed if obtainable in compost 2 when ripe. Repot every second year after flowering.

P. longiflora. (H). Section Farinosae. (Syn. *P. halleri*).
A plant which is akin to *P. farinosa* from the eastern Alps of Europe, making rosettes of long narrow, lanceolate, whitish-green serrated leaves the undersides being covered with farina. Scape long, up to 4 inches high, bearing in small umbels deep purple-pink flowers with a golden eye. The corolla-tube being long for the size of the flower is one of the distinguishing features of this plant. June. Needs similar cultivation to *P. farinosa* and should be planted several in a pan.

PROPAGATION. By seed sown as soon as ripe, compost 2. Do not repot unless the pan becomes overcrowded, a most unlikely occurrence in cultivation; this should be carried out after flowering.

P. marginata. (E). Section Auricula.
This species and its many forms will be found where any representative collection of alpines is grown for all are easy and possess fine foliage, outstanding flowers and a delightful perfume. It is confined in nature to a few stations in the Maritime and Cottian Alps. The type plant has rosettes of large, serrated, oblong foliage with silver margins due to the intense edging of farina. These are topped with umbels of up to twenty

open funnel-shaped, deeply farinose, lavender flowers on a slender scape, very fragrant. May.

PROPAGATION. Is easy by cuttings which root readily if taken after the plant has flowered. Repot every year in early April.

P. marginata 'Caerulea'. (E).

A delightful almost true light blue form. April.

P. marginata 'Hyacintha'. (E).

Is considered a form of *P. marginata* raised by the late G. H. Berry. Leaves in rosette formation long, ovate, margins serrate, light green, covered with farina. Flowers on a 4-inch upright stout scape in an umbel, up to six large, rounded, deep violet-blue with cream eye. May. This is one of the best forms with the large flowers and their delightful perfume.

P. marginata 'Linda Pope'. (E).

Possibly the best of the marginata forms but not always the easiest to flower well. Makes mid-green rosettes of jagged edged leaves, very farinose and outstanding large perfectly symmetrical, fragrant flowers of a rich lavender-blue with a white eye. May. This plant flowers best when young so that propagation, which is by cuttings taken after flowering, should be carried out frequently to keep a supply of strong young specimens.

P. marginata 'Prichards var.' (E).

Near to 'Linda Pope' and although not so large in flower these are produced in profusion, bright lavender-blue, fragrant. May.

P. 'Marven'. (*P. marginata* × *P. × venusta*). (E).

A garden hybrid with the typical auricula foliage edged with golden farina and stout scapes, up to 4 inches high, bearing umbels of eight to twelve deep purple-blue flowers with a white eye. May.

PROPAGATION. By cuttings in June. Repot every year after flowering.

P. minima. (H). Section Auricula.

From the eastern Alps, this is the smallest of all the European species, but fortunately the flower is one of the largest in a good form, although this species is not noted for its free-flowering. It is a dwarf plant of small woody stems with rosettes of little, bright shiny green, wedge-shaped, dentate, apex obtuse leaves. Flowers singly, rarely in pairs, on minute scapes, rounded, deeply cut, bright rose-pink in colour. May.

PROPAGATION. By offsets in June. Repot every other year in June.

P. minima var. alba. (H).

This is a delightful albino, sometimes found in the wild growing with the type plant and is greatly to be desired. May.

CULTIVATION. As for *P. minima*.

P. × pubescens. (*P. auricula* × *P. rubra*). (E).

Of all the hybrids this is subject to more variations than any other; even in the stations in which it is found growing wild there is a great diversity amongst the seedlings and this is multiplied a hundredfold in cultivation. It is considered to be a natural hybrid between *P. auricula* and *P. rubra*, but to classify a type form would be an almost impossible task and all that can be said is that it makes a stout woody trunk with clusters of rosettes the leaves being oval, tapered to the apex and often with dentate margins. The flower scape is about 4 inches high with umbels of flowers ranging through pink, violet and crimson with a white eye. May–June.

PROPAGATION. By division in July for the good forms or by seed sown as soon as ripe, compost 2, if new material is required. Repot every year after flowering. There are several good named forms and the following are worth growing.

P. pubescens 'Alba'. (E). (Syn. *P. helvetica* var. *alba*).
A good white form with a robust constitution. May.

P. pubescens 'Faldonside'. (E).
With deep crimson flowers, needs care in cultivation as the stock is getting weak due to intensive propagation by vegetative means. Best in compost B and a weekly feed of liquid fertiliser when buds are forming. May.

P. pubescens 'Mrs J. H. Wilson'. (E).
A good form with scapes up to 6 inches and crowded umbels of very fragrant bright lilac flowers with a cream eye. May.

P. pubescens 'The Cardinal'. (E).
This is another form with a poor constitution which is best grown in compost B and fed with fertiliser once buds are formed. Flowers a rich velvety red. May.

P. scotica. (H). Section Farinosae.
This is a miniature edition of *P. farinosa*, which amongst other localities is found in the northern counties of Scotland. It makes small rosettes of narrow crinkly, ovate leaves, densely powdered with farina and 1-inch scapes carrying umbels of small light purple flowers with a yellow eye. April.

PROPAGATION. Is best by seed sown in July, compost 2, in pans where they are to flower. It dislikes root-disturbance and for any chance of real success, this species should not be grown singly, but in groups. As these plants are short-lived no repotting is necessary, but after the first year a weekly watering of very diluted liquid manure, a quarter strength is sufficient, will help to maintain health during the growing and flowering season.

P. tyrolensis. (E). Section Auricula.
A native of the Austrian Tyrol where in a few places it inhabits clefts in rock faces or in the screes at the base of rock formations. It makes a small stout woody stem with rosettes of obovate, sticky, dull green leaves, margins slightly incurved and dentate, apex terminating in a blunt point. The flowers are large deep red purple with a white eye, borne either singly or in pairs on a short scape. June.

PROPAGATION. By cuttings in July. Repot every other year after flowering.

P. villosa. (E). Section Auricula.

This plant comes from the eastern Alps, found always in rocky screes. In cultivation it makes almost prostrate rosettes of sticky, ovate leaves, broad at the apex, margins dentate for last third, ending in a blunt point. The leaf surface bears minute glandular reddish-brown hairs. The flowers are in tight umbels on a 4-inch scape, rose-red in colour with a white eye. May.

PROPAGATION. By division in June or cuttings in July. Repot every other year, in June.

ASIATIC PRIMULAS

It is doubtful whether any other genus, with the possible exception of Rhododendron, has seen so many new introductions or re-introductions over the last decade or so as the Asiatic primulas and it is not surprising that a number are proving amenable to cultivation with the increase of material, especially in the cooler and moister northern counties and Scotland. That they will never really be easy plants to cultivate in the drier parts of the country is evident but with careful cultivation a number can be grown satisfactorily. Many of these Asiatics are rare in cultivation but all listed here are being grown in this country, although a diligent search will be necessary to obtain some of the rarer species.

CULTIVATION. These plants require an open but moist compost well enriched with humus, water stagnation must be prevented at all costs especially during the winter season, a period when in their natural habitat they are invariably kept dry by a covering of snow. This does not mean that the plants when grown in pans should be allowed to dry out at this time of the year, for nothing can prove more fatal, the soil should be kept so that it is just moist to the touch. With the majority, if a frame can be spared facing north, they will do better here than in the alpine house while resting and making their new growth, all that is necessary is to plunge them to their rims after flowering in a bed of coarse sand which has been previously well moistened and also given a good dusting of HCH powder. This should ensure freedom from pests. As the foliage dies back it should be removed to prevent moulds and no more water should be necessary until growth begins in early spring. Air should be given at all times except during periods of frosty weather when the frame should be closed and protected from really severe and prolonged cold spells with a covering of frost mats. These must be removed immediately the frost goes and the frame opened, wiping the inside of the lights should there be any condensation on them. It is absolutely essential, especially in the southern counties, that these plants should not be kept in the alpine house during hot summer months. Another point to bear in mind is, a sharp watch must be kept for pests, especially red spider and root aphis which can be extremely destructive if not fatal. Compost B over good drainage will suit the majority of the Asiatics and all require plenty of water while growing and flowering.

P. amabilis. (H). Section Nivales.

A native of S.W. China, this dwarf rarely exceeds 3 inches in height, making rosettes of ovate, pale green leaves, densely covered with farina and bearing on a small powdered scape erect large flowers which range from pink to blue in colour. April. A difficult plant to keep in cultivation, it resents winter moisture at all times.

PROPAGATION. By seed which should be sown very thinly in compost 2 as soon as ripe and not disturbed during the first winter of its life. Repot only when necessary after flowering.

P. atrodentata. (H). Section Denticulata.

A charming species from the eastern Himalayas, it forms small rosettes of long obovate, mid-green leaves, margins finely dentate, the whole covered with rough short hairs. Flowers in a small head on variable sized scapes, not so globose as *P. denticulata*, lobes deeply cut at apex, pale lilac with white eye. The whole delightfully fragrant. April–May. This species likes a cool spot to give of its best.

PROPAGATION. By division after flowering. Repot every second year after flowering.

P. aureata. (E). Section Petiolares.

This plant turned up as a stray seedling in the Royal Botanic Gardens, Edinburgh, and its country of origin is a mystery. It forms delightful rosettes of spatulate foliage densely coated with white farina, margins irregular, dentate, midrib deep red. Flowers large, rounded, borne in umbels of up to ten on an almost non-existent scape, orange merging to yellow. March.

PROPAGATION. By division after flowering or green seed, compost 2. Repot every year after flowering.

P. aureata var. forma. (E).

This form is similar to the species but with cream flowers and a dark yellow uneven eye, the colour spreading over the petals. March. A great deal of confusion exists over this form and it has been named by Dr Fletcher of Edinburgh although he is not convinced that this naming is correct and may have to be changed.

P. bella. (H). Section Minutissimae.

A really difficult species this, from Yunnan, which requires skill in cultivation, making prostrate straggling rhizomes terminating in rosettes of obovate leaves, margins dentate. Flowers solitary, large open saucer-shaped, on small slender scapes, ranging from pink to violet in colour. April–May.

PROPAGATION. By seed, compost 2, but unfortunately seed is rarely set in our climate, although fertilisation with the aid of a small camel hair brush will sometimes help. Repot only when necessary after flowering but a little top-dressing in early spring is beneficial.

P. bellidifolia. (H). Section Muscarioides.

This delightful primula is from Tibet, and quite easy to grow although it often tends to be monocarpic. It makes spreading rosettes of lax, dull green, rounded leaves, with no trace of farina and on 4-inch scapes are borne a spire of nodding red-blue bells. April–May.

PROPAGATION. By seed, which is freely set, either as soon as ripe in compost 2 when the seedlings will need alpine house protection during the winter, or the following March. Repotting is only necessary if the plants can be induced to become perennial.

P. bhutanica. (H). Section Petiolares.

A native of Assam and Bhutan, this is one of the best of the section, making large rosettes of spatulate leaves with deeply dentate margins. In their early state covered with farina which tends to disappear after flowering, exposing the characteristic deep red midrib. Flowers large, rounded clear ice-blue to deep blue with white eye, petals tridentate at apex, borne in small umbels on short pedicels which elongate after flowering. March–April.

From the botanist's point of view this species is now considered to be conspecific with *P. whitei*, the latter name having priority. Both have been retained here because for garden purposes they differ in several respects.

PROPAGATION. By seed sown green, compost 2, or division after flowering. Repot every year in May.

P. boothii. (E). Section Petiolares.

A native of Bhutan, it makes rosettes of obovate to almost spatulate dark green foliage with dentate margins and red midrib. Flowers on slender 1-inch scapes, petals notched at apex, purple-pink; throat has a zonal ring of white. February–March. A difficult species to grow, this certainly needs the alpine house during the winter months as it is doubtful whether it is really hardy. The best chance of success in propagation is to sow the seed while still green, compost 2. Repot every year after flowering.

P. bracteosa. (E). Section Petiolares.

This is a delightful and quite easy Primula from Bhutan, which has settled down in cultivation. It makes rosettes of long obovate, bright green leaves with a dusting of farina on both sides. The flowers, borne on a short scape are rounded, lilac-pink with a yellow eye, surrounded by a white zone. March. After flowering the scape elongates and produces vegetative buds at the apex, these should be pegged down and in a few weeks will have taken root. The young plantlets are then severed from the parent and after a lapse of three weeks should be potted up.

P. 'Bractworth'. (E). (*P. bracteosa* × *edgeworthii*).

This hybrid was raised by Mrs C. B. Saunders of Farnborough, Kent, and is certainly an improvement on either of its parents. It makes rosettes of obovate to spatulate leaves, densely covered with white farina, margins coarsely dentate. Flowers large on small scapes, rounded petals notched at apex, deep violet mauve with orange eye. March.

PROPAGATION. By division after flowering or by pegging down the vegetative bud, which is formed at the apex of the flowering scape. Repot every year after flowering.

P. calderiana. (H). Section Petiolares.

A native of Sikkim, this plant makes fairly large rosettes of light green 9-inch leaves with small denticulate margins, devoid of farina on the top surface but has traces underneath. Flowers in small umbels on 9-inch scapes, rounded, deep purple with yellow eye. April.

PROPAGATION. By seed sown green, or division after flowering. Repot every year after flowering. Compost 2.

P. cardiophylla, see *P. rotundifolia*.

P. chamaethauma. (H). Section Petiolares.

A rare plant from Tibet, and not too easy in cultivation, making small rosettes of narrow, spatulate, dark green leaves, lighter near the margins which are crinkled and dentate. Flowers large, rounded, borne on single farinose stalks, red-violet with yellow eye. April.

PROPAGATION. By careful division after flowering. Repot every year after flowering.

P. clarkei. (H). Section Farinosae.

From Kashmir, comes this delightful dwarf Primula making in cultivation loose rosettes of rounded, mid-green foliage with no trace of farina and on short scapes, dainty bright pink flowers with a yellow eye, enhanced by an outer zone of white. The corolla lobes have a deep notch at apex. March–April. This species requires very moist conditions while growing and flowering.

PROPAGATION. By division after flowering. Repot only when necessary, as this plant likes to grow in a mass.

P. eburnea. (H). Section Soldanelloideae.

A native of Bhutan and S.E. Tibet, this forms basal rosettes of elliptic to ovate, obtuse, pale green, glandular, silky haired leaves, margins dentate. Fragrant white flowers on an 8-inch farinose slender scape up to twelve semi-pendant, funnel-shaped, in a rounded cluster; calyx and corolla lobes white, farinose on back. April–May.

PROPAGATION. By seed in March, compost 2. Care is needed in watering, especially during the winter months when no moisture must be allowed in the dormant crown. Repot only when necessary after flowering.

P. edgeworthii. (E). Section Petiolares. (Syn. *P. winteri*).

This is possibly the best known of all the Asiatic primulas for the alpine house and certainly one of the most charming. It is a native of the N.W. Himalayas and makes large rosettes of obovate foliage, densely covered with white farina, margins dentate and crinkled. Flowers on short scapes, pale mauve with yellow throat and white eye; the corolla lobes are irregularly notched and the plant has a delightful fragrance. February–March. One of the easiest of the Asiatics to grow, only requiring that the crown of the plant is kept dry.

Above: *Pulsatilla vernalis* (see page 426)

Below: *Pulsatilla vulgaris* 'Rubra' (see page 528)

Above: *Ranunculus parnassifolius* (see page 431)

Below: *Rhododendron myrtilloides* (see page 441)

PROPAGATION. By seed sown green, compost 2, or division after flowering. Repot every year after flowering.

P. edgeworthii var. alba. (E).
This is the white form which although charming loses a great deal against the similar coloured background of the leaves. February–March. Culture and propagation as for the species.

P. forrestii. (H). Section Bullatae.
A really saxatile member of the Asiatics, from crevices at high altitudes in Yunnan, making hard woody trunks topped with open rosettes of wrinkled ovate to obovate leaves, margins widely dentate, covered with glandular hairs. Flowers large on a stout scape in small umbels of rounded, yellow with orange eye, scented. June. This plant requires drier and more sunny conditions than the majority of the Asiatics and should be planted in compost A. It does better if the woody trunk is wedged between pieces of rock in the pan so that the rosettes lie sideways; it resents overhead watering.

PROPAGATION. By seed sown in March, compost 2. Repot only when necessary after flowering.

P. gambeliana. (H). Section Rotundifolia.
From Sikkim, making small tufts of orbicular, glabrous leaves with long stalks, base cordate, margins serrate. Flowers in small umbels on a firm short scape, large, rounded corolla lobes, each with a rounded notch at apex, light purple with a yellow throat. April. Not an easy plant but worth the care needed to cultivate it successfully, requires plenty of moisture during the growing season, dryish conditions during the winter, the danger point being the tip of the resting bud which is extremely susceptible to winter wet.

PROPAGATION. By seed sown as soon as ripe, when obtainable, compost 2. Care must be taken when potting up this plant as the roots are brittle; it requires a large deep pot not a pan. Repot only when necessary after flowering.

P. geraniifolia. (H). Section Cortusoides.
A native of Sikkim, this is a far from easy plant to grow although it is more amenable under alpine house culture, where it forms small tufts of crinkly, hairy geranium-like foliage with dentate margins. Flowers on 6-inch scapes in a loose umbel, deep red-rose. July. This plant requires to be grown in the shade and needs more than one specimen in a pan as it seems to like the association of other plants.

PROPAGATION. By seed sown in March, compost 2. Repot only when necessary in early April.

P. gracilipes. (E). Section Petiolares.
A very hardy species widely distributed in nature including Nepal, Sikkim and Tibet. In cultivation it makes compact rosettes of oblong-ovate to elliptic leaves, margins irregular dentate, rarely farinose. The scented flowers are borne singly on small stalks, from an almost non-existent

scape and range in colour from pink-blue to mauve with a yellow eye, outlined with a white zone. April.

PROPAGATION. By careful division, seed sown green, compost 2, or leaf cuttings. Repot every year after flowering.

P. hyacinthina. (H). Section Muscardioides.

A rare and difficult species from Tibet, making an open rosette of long oblanceolate, hairy leaves, apex obtuse, margins dentate and dusted with white farina. Flowers are borne on a 10-inch powdered scape in a loose umbel of tubular, pendant, violet bells with a delicious scent of wild hyacinths. May. Needs care in watering, especially during the resting period.

PROPAGATION. By seed when ripe, compost 2. Repot every year after flowering.

P. jaffreyana. (H). Section Farinosae.

This is a native of Tibet, making small rosettes of long narrow, obovate foliage, margins dentate, densely clothed with farina, especially on the underneath. Flowers on 6-inch scapes in small umbels, pale lilac with a greenish-yellow eye, covered with farina. May. Requires careful cultivation in a moist soil and is easily propagated by seed when ripe, compost 2. Repot only when necessary after flowering.

P. modesta. (H). Section Farinosae.

A native of Japan, making small rosettes of intensely farinose spatulate-shaped leaves with crinkled, crenulated margins, the undersides of the leaves are covered with a yellow farina. Flowers on 4-inch slender scapes in umbels, light purple. April.

PROPAGATION. By seed sown in March, compost 2. Repot when necessary after flowering.

P. nutans. (H). Section Soldanelloideae.

A shade loving species from Yunnan, it is unfortunately very short-lived, almost monocarpic in cultivation, although it has been known to flower two seasons running, which seems to belie this. It makes lax rosettes of oblong, hairy grey-green leaves, tapering to a short winged stalk, slightly pointed at apex. The flowers are borne on slender 10-inch scapes, a rounded cluster of pendant open bells of lavender-blue and delightfully scented. June. Requires good moisture during the growing season but the resting bud must be kept dry during winter.

PROPAGATION. By seed sown in March, compost 2. Repot only when and if necessary after flowering.

P. 'Pandora'. (*P. edgeworthii* × *P. scapigera*). (E).

Another charming hybrid raised by Mrs Saunders of Farnborough, Kent. It is midway between the two parents, the foliage is dark green, non-farinose, long, obovate, margins dentate. Flowers on a short scape, large, mauve in colour with a yellow eye. April.

PROPAGATION. By division after flowering. Repot every year after flowering.

P. pusilla. (H). Section Minutissimae.

A dainty Primula from Bhutan, Sikkim and Nepal but rarely seen in cultivation owing to its apparent inability to set seed. It forms prostrate rosettes of small sub-orbicular leaves with deeply cut margins, the undersides covered with yellow farina. Flowers are borne on slender scapes, either singly or in pairs, petals deeply winged, pale blue-violet and a characteristic cluster of white hairs in the throat. April. Not an easy plant but it can with care and good cultivation be grown and produce flowers.
PROPAGATION. Imported seed seems to be the only method of increase, this germinates readily in compost 2. Repot only when necessary.

P. ramzanae. (H). Section Rotundifolia.

A recent introduction from W. Nepal from material sent home by the Polunin, Sykes and Williams expedition to that country. It winters as a resting bud of scales tinged dark purple. In early spring both the leaves and flowering scapes with buds commence to grow together. Mature leaves ovate orbicular, apex rounded, base cordate, margins coarsely dentate, deep green, glabrous, covered with a white farinose below, petiole tinged purple. Flowers fragrant on 3-inch purple tinged scape, opening to five deeply cut, rounded lobes, bright purple with a yellow eye, surrounded by a white zone. April.
PROPAGATION. By seed sown when ripe, compost 2. Repot when necessary after flowering.

P. reidii. (H). Section Soldanelloideae.

A native of the Himalayas, growing in wet screes; this is a far from easy plant to keep happy in cultivation needing plenty of water during the growing and flowering season; the compost should be wet at this period. Keep dry but not arid in winter. It makes oblong to wide lanceolate rosettes of soft green leaves with rounded apex, margins decurved and dentate. The leaves are non-farinose but covered with hairs, dense on the undersides. The slender farinose scape bears an umbel of up to eight semi-pendant, ivory-white, campanulate bells, enhanced by a covering of glistening farina and a delicious perfume. May.
PROPAGATION. By seed sown in March, compost 2. Repot only when necessary after flowering.

P. reidii var. williamsii. (H). Section Soldanelloideae.

A form that was collected by Polunin, Sykes and Williams from W. Nepal in 1952 and seems more amenable to cultivation than the type. The plant is similar but bears larger campanulate lilac-blue flowers shading to white covered with silvered farina. May. Cultivation and propagation as for *P. reidii*.

P. reinii. (H). Section Reinii.

Coming as it does from high woodlands in Japan, this species needs shade in cultivation but it is not difficult to grow. It forms tufts of reniform to cordate, hairy, soft textured bright green leaves with dentate margins on 2 to 3-inch stalks. Flowers are borne on 4-inch scapes in open umbels of up to four lilac-pink in colour with a yellow eye. The petals are deeply cleft, giving the flowers the appearance of stars. April–May. It is best kept in a shady frame during hot months.

PROPAGATION. By seed sown when ripe, compost 2. Repot only when necessary after flowering.

P. reptans. (H). Section Minutissimae.

A native of N.W. Himalayas, where it runs about rooting as it goes, forming mats of minute, cordate, almost palmate dark green leaves. Flowers large, on small scapes, solitary, petals rounded, deeply incised, of pure violet with a white eye. May. Requires careful cultivation in compost A with plenty of moisture during the growing season.

PROPAGATION. By rooting stolons in June. Repot only when necessary after flowering.

P. rockii. (H). Section Bullatae.

This plant which is similar to *P. forrestii*, comes from China, and differs in that it is smaller in all its parts but has distinctive red stalks to its leaves, absent in *P. forrestii*. The flowers are golden-yellow with a deeper eye and fringed petals, emitting a delightful perfume. June. Needs same treatment as *P. forrestii*.

P. rotundifolia. (H). Section Rotundifolia. (Syn. *P. cardiophylla*).

A native of Nepal, this Primula has proved fairly amenable to alpine house culture but requires to be kept dry during its resting period. It makes tufts of stalked, thick cordate, reniform leaves with dentate margins, the undersides of the leaves are densely coated with yellow farina. Flowers on 6-inch slender scapes in one, sometimes two, tiers of fine rounded petalled blooms, mauve-pink with a golden eye. May.

PROPAGATION. Is by seed in March, compost 2. Repot every year after flowering.

P. scapigera. (E). Section Petiolares.

A plant from the Himalayas, similar to *P. edgeworthii* but differing in that there is no trace of meal. It makes large rosettes of pale green elliptic leaves with very coarsely cut margins and bears on short scapes, purplish-pink rounded flowers with a yellow eye, surrounded with a zone of white. March.

PROPAGATION. By division after flowering, seed sown green, compost 2, or leaf cuttings. Repot every year after flowering.

P. scapigera var. alba. (E).

A rare desirable form which appeared in cultivation a few years ago with large rounded flowers of a fine texture standing out well against the foliage. March. As the flowers of the type plant vary even from division, white forms are liable to occur.

P. sessilis. (E). Section Petiolares.

Another plant which has been mistaken for *P. edgeworthii*, it comes from the Himalayas and makes large rosettes of oblong-obovate pale green leaves with deep red midrib and veins; margins dentate, apex obtuse.

Flowers from an almost non-existent scape on small pedicels, pale mauve, rounded with a yellow throat, surrounded by a white zone. April.

PROPAGATION. By seed sown green or division in May. Repot every year after flowering.

P. sessilis var. alba. (E).

The white form in cultivation has flowers of poor texture but there should be in time with careful selection, better plants with flowers nearer to the type. March.

P. sherriffae. (H). Section Soldanelloideae.

A native of S.E. Bhutan, where it was discovered by Captain Sherriff after whom it was named. It is a delightful Primula, making rosettes of oblanceolate, almost entire leaves covered with soft hairs and fringed at margins, apex rounded, tapering to winged stalks. On a 4-inch scape is carried up to six horizontally set funnel-shaped flowers, the tube is as long as the flower is wide, but is narrow in width from the throat of the corolla to the calyx. They are pale violet with a white margin and daintily flecked with farina. May. This plant is not hardy, except in very mild localities and is definitely an alpine house primula, requiring cool conditions, plenty of water in the growing season, and keeping dryish during winter.

PROPAGATION. Is by seed sown in March, compost 2. Repot only when necessary after flowering.

P. sino-plantaginea. (E). Section Nivales.

A Primula from Yunnan, which has been in cultivation a number of years but is still far from common. It makes tufts of long, narrow almost lanceolate leaves with recurved margins, tapering to a blunt apex, densely coated with yellow farina on the undersides. On a 6-inch stout farinose scape is borne an almost globular head of violet-purple scented flowers. April.

PROPAGATION. Is by seed in March, compost 2. Repot when necessary after flowering.

P. sonchifolia. (H). Section Petiolares.

This plant is a native of W. Yunnan, and in its resting state has all the appearance of a bulb. The leaves grow at the same time as the flowers on their short scape appear, afterwards forming a basal rosette, spatulate with deeply dentate margins but unlike its near relative, *P. bhutanica*, the midrib is pale green not red. The scape which elongates at approximately the same rate as the foliage bears umbels of from four to twelve lavender to pinkish-blue, yellow-eyed flowers. March. An easy plant to grow but it never seems to be at its best in the southern parts of the country, unlike the northern where it is almost cabbage like.

PROPAGATION. Is by seed sown green, compost 2. Repot every year after flowering.

P. tayloriana. (H). Section Farinosae.

A native of S.E. Tibet and a new species introduced as recently as 1947 by Ludlow and Sherriff. It forms basal rosettes of small pale green, ovate leaves with dentate margins, underneath farinose. Flowers on slender 4-inch scapes in umbels, violet-mauve with a white eye. March. Like *P. farinosa* this plant should not be grown as a single specimen but a number together in a pan.

PROPAGATION. It is short lived but easily raised from seed in March, compost 2. Should not need repotting during the lifetime of the plant.

P. tenella. (H). Section Minutissimae.

This Primula is a difficult plant and is likely to remain so, although it has been in and out of cultivation for over eighty years. A native of Bhutan, it consists of small tufts of obovate to spatulate leaves, apex rounded and margins dentate; covered with white farina on both sides but more dense on the lower. Flowers singly, rarely in pairs on a short scape, rounded, funnel-shaped, violet-blue with white eye. May. It requires plenty of water during the growing season but the drainage must be faultless. Compost A is advised, and the plant should be kept dry but not arid during the winter months.

PROPAGATION. Is by seed in March, compost 2. Repot only when necessary after flowering.

P. umbratilis. (H). Section Soldanelloideae.

A native of the Bhutan, this is another high alpine Primula which is not easy to keep in good health for long. It makes open rosettes of oblong leaves narrowing to a blunt point at apex and more abrupt to winged stalk; margins coarsely dentate, leaves covered with hairs on both surfaces. Flowers on 4-inch hairy scapes in small umbels of up to six pendant, funnel-shaped, blue fragrant flowers with just a touch of purple. April–May. Needs care in watering, requiring ample during the growing season and only just enough to keep the compost from drying out in winter.

PROPAGATION. By seed in March, compost 2. Repot when necessary after flowering.

P. umbratilis var. alba. (H).

This is the desirable milky white form requiring similar conditions to the type but it seems to have become extremely rare in cultivation today. April.

P. vinciflora, see *Omphalogramma vinciflorum.*

P. waddellii. (H). Section Minutissimae.

I first saw this charming Primula in a frame in Windsor Great Park during a tour I led of delegates to the 2nd International Rock Garden Conference 1951 where it had been raised from Ludlow and Sherriff seed collected in Bhutan. It makes small rosettes only 1 inch across of spatulate, thickish light green leaves, dentate margins near apex, slightly farinose. Flowers single lavender-blue on a minute scape with a white eye. May. Not easy as it tends to die off during the winter months but worth every care.

PROPAGATION. Is by seed in March, compost 2. It is doubtful whether it will live long enough to need repotting.

P. wattii. (H). Section Soldanelloideae.
Another charming but difficult Primula from Sikkim, which barely retains a foothold in cultivation. It makes tufts of oblanceolate leaves, apex
obtuse, narrowing to a short winged stalk, margins dentate to coarsely
crenulate and both sides of leaves covered with long hairs. Flowers on
4-inch scape almost in a rounded cluster, rich violet bells with a white eye,
the petal margins almost fringed. April–May. Although a good perennial
in nature, it is difficult to keep after flowering in cultivation.
PROPAGATION. Is by seed in March when obtainable, compost 2. Repotting unnecessary.

P. whitei. (H). Section Petiolares.
This is a native of Bhutan, making rosettes of mid-green ovate leaves,
tapering to apex, margins dentate, leaves covered with a small amount of
farina. Flowers on almost non-existent scapes are pale blue with brownish-
orange eye and covered with farina. April. It responds well to good
cultivation requiring plenty of moisture during the growing season, keep
dry but not arid when the bud is dormant.
PROPAGATION. Is by seed sown green, compost 2, or division after
flowering. Repot every year in May.

P. wigramiana. (H). Section Soldanelloideae.
Another charming but difficult Primula from Nepal where it makes
rosettes of broad ovate crinkled leaves, margins slightly dentate and hairy
on both sides. Flowers on a 6-inch scape up to four in a close umbel,
pendulous, open bell-shaped, white, covered with farina. April.
PROPAGATION. Is by seed sown in March, compost 2, the difficulty is to
get the young plants through the first winter safely. Repot only when
necessary after flowering.

P. winteri, see *P. edgeworthii*.

P. wollastoni. (H). Section Soldanelloideae.
A native of Tibet, it has been in cultivation for nearly thirty years and is
one of the easiest of the difficult section. It makes basal rosettes of ovate
hairy almost entire or slightly serrated leaves, powdered with farina on the
undersides. The flowers are borne on a 3-inch hairy scape, up to twelve
pendulous tubular bells of a bright powder-blue, dotted with farina.
April.
PROPAGATION. Rarely sets seed but it can be propagated by root cuttings
or from buds which often appear from the surface roots. Repot every
second year after flowering.

PRUNUS (*Rosaceae*).

A large and mighty genus containing plums, apricots, cherries, peaches
and cherry laurels; all either edible or ornamental which do a great deal
to brighten our gardens in early spring, as well as having a utilitarian
purpose. There is unfortunately only one species suitable for pan culture
in the alpine house or frame and this, though a very desirable plant, is far

from common in cultivation and is not often offered in nurserymen's catalogues.

CULTIVATION. Compost A over faultless drainage with an ample supply of water during the growing season, it seems to appreciate a dryish period during the last two weeks in July to ripen the wood. Failure to do this is often the cause of its getting a reputation as a poor flowerer. It should be kept dry but not arid after the foliage has fallen, and it requires plenty of sunshine.

PROPAGATION. By cuttings of half-ripened wood with a heel, placed in the propagating frame in July. Bottom heat is beneficial in striking this plant. Repot only when necessary in early April, for root restriction seems to produce more flowers.

P. prostrata. (D). (Syn. *Cerasus prostrata*).

The Mountain Cherry, a native of the Levant, is rarely up to 18 inches high with slender lax branchlets covered with a greyish-black down. Leaves ovate, pointed, sharply serrate, minute, hairy beneath, mid-green. Flowers borne in leaf clusters, solitary, rarely in pairs on small stalks, five-petalled, saucer-shaped, light rose. May; followed by almost stemless reddish cherries.

PTEROCEPHALUS (*Dipsaceae*).

A small genus of plants, natives of the Mediterranean region, allied to Scabious, of which there is one suitable for pan culture.

CULTIVATION. Compost B over good drainage, requiring plenty of water during growth, keep dry but not arid in winter; needs plenty of sunshine.

PROPAGATION. By division in late April. Repot when necessary at the same time.

P. parnassi. (E).

This is a dwarf prostrate plant with a mat of woody stems only about 4 inches high. Leaves simple, elliptic, grey-green, margins crenate. Flowers on 2-inch stout stems, large scabious-like heads of purple-pink. July–August. A native of Greece.

PTILOTRICHUM (*Cruciferae*).

A small genus of plants closely allied to Alyssum and often listed under that heading in catalogues and books. There are a few dwarf shrubby species which are suitable for alpine house or frame culture.

CULTIVATION. They will do well in compost A over faultless drainage and water should be given sparingly. Keep dry but not arid in winter; all appreciate sunshine.

PROPAGATION. By seed in compost 1, March, or green cuttings taken in June. Repot every year after flowering.

P. cappadocicum. (E). (Syn. *Iberis cappadocica*).

A native of Armenia, Cappadocica, this is a small tufted starry downed sub-shrub less than 3 inches high. Leaves entire, crowded, minute, elliptic, silver-grey. Flowers in a congested corymb, four-petalled, white. May.

P. pyrenaicum. (E). (Syn. *Alyssum pyrenaicum*).
This is a small shrub rarely above 9 inches high with obovate, thick, silver leaves, covered with fine hairs. Flowers in dense spikes, the usual four-petalled, crucifer type, white with deep brown anthers. June. A native of the Eastern Pyrenees.

P. reverchonii. (E).
A rare dwarf shrub of pleasing and charming habit. It makes a small bush up to 9 inches high with erect stems. Leaves crowded in rosette formation, spatulate, sometimes bluntly pointed, light greyish-green. Flowers in dense globular terminal heads of four large rounded petals, white with a green eye, fragrant. April. A native of the Sierra Carjora, Spain, its only known station, from where it was introduced into cultivation by Messrs. Heywood and Davis in 1948.

P. spinosum. (E). (Syn. *Alyssum spinosum*).
This makes a 9-inch bushlet of erect branches and congested laterals with silver-grey lanceolate leaves, the adult wood becomes intensely spiny. Flowers in large corymbs, white, borne in great profusion, completely hiding the foliage. June. Young plants have the hoary appearance of old age. A native of Spain.

P. spinosum var. roseum. (E). (Syn. *Alyssum spinosum* var. *roseum*).
This is the rare pink form of the type flowering in June.

PULSATILLA (*Ranunculaceae*).

A small genus of plants closely related to Anemone and until recently included in that genus, the difference between the two being only botanically slight.
CULTIVATION. A light open compost is needed and all will do well in compost A over good drainage with a normal supply of water during the growing season, keep dry but not arid in winter.
PROPAGATION. Best by seed sown as soon as ripe in compost 2. Repot when necessary after flowering.

P. alpina. (H). (Syn. *Anemone alpina*).
A fine species variable in height from 4 to 12 inches with bi-ternate leaves, leaflets pinnate, deeply serrated, green with hairy margins; involucre similar. Flowers on variable slender stems, blue in bud opening to a large six-sepalled open chalice of pure white inside with yellow central boss of stamens. May–June. A native of European Alps.

P. alpina var. sulphurea. (H). (Syn. *Anemone sulphurea*).
This form is similar to the type in growth and foliage but with large open cup-shaped flowers of sulphur-yellow. May. A native of the European Alps.

P. halleri. (H). (Syn. *Anemone halleri*).

A native of Switzerland and Austria, with bi-pinnate leaves, leaflets deeply cut, narrow linear, covered with silky hairs. Flowers on 10-inch slender stems, open cup-shaped with six sepals of deep violet. April–May.

P. vernalis. (E). (Syn. *Anemone vernalis*).

This is the finest of all the Windflowers, aptly named the Lady of the Snows and found on the topmost limit of alpine meadows in Europe. It retains its foliage throughout the winter months, producing this in small tufts of up to three leaves. Leaves pinnate, leaflets many partite, wide linear, coarsely cut, bronzy-green. Flowers on 2-inch silky haired stoutish stems, furry bronze violet bud opening to a six-lobed chalice of glistening white backed with violet and gold and a large central boss of yellow stamens. April.

P. vulgaris. (H). (Syn. *Anemone pulsatilla*).

The Pasque Flower is well known and loved, making a fibrous rooted plant about 6 inches high. Leaves pinnate, leaflets many-partite, linear, green. Flowers on 6-inch shaggy stems, involucre, linear, covered with silky fur; buds also shaggy, opening to a six-lobed chalice of rich purple with central boss of golden-yellow stamens. April. A native of Europe, including Britain. There are many good colour forms of this species ranging from white to a deep crimson scarlet and to increase these it is necessary to take root cuttings in July.

PUSCHKINIA (*Liliaceae*).

A genus containing two species of bulbous plants closely related to Chionodoxa of which one is in cultivation and is suitable for pot culture in the alpine house or frame.

CULTIVATION. The bulbs should be planted in September, 2 inches deep using pots, not pans, in compost B about six to a five-inch pot. They should be plunged under the staging and protected during the winter, then as growth commences the protective material is removed and the plants placed on the staging. Give plenty of water while growing and flowering, reducing this as the foliage dies down, then the pots must be given a good baking.

PROPAGATION. By seed sown in August, compost 2, or offsets removed when repotting, this should be every year in September.

P. libanotica, see *P. scilloides*.

P. scilloides. (B). (Syn. *P. libanotica*).

The Striped Squill produces a few lanceolate, concave dark green leaves. Flowers on 6-inch stems up to six pendant, bluish-white, bell-shaped tube with five spreading segments, each perianth segment having a median porcelain-blue stripe. March. A native of Asia.

P. scilloides var. compacta. (B).

This is similar to the type but more compact and with a larger spike of pendant flowers. March. Asia.

PYGMEA (*Scrophulariaceae*).

A genus containing a few species all endemic to New Zealand, formerly included in Veronica and nearly always found under that name in English catalogues. There are two species in cultivation at present and we hope for the time when more are available for experienced plantsmen to grow them to perfection, a far from easy task (see below and Appendix 1).

CULTIVATION. This is best in compost D with a normal supply of water during the growing and flowering season, and kept dry but not arid in winter. A constant watch must be maintained against pests for if these are allowed to obtain a hold the resultant damage could be fatal.

PROPAGATION. By green cuttings in June keeping these close until rooted. Repot only when necessary as root restriction seems to keep the plant compact and healthy.

P. pulvinaris. (E). (Syn. *Veronica pulvinaris*).

A native of New Zealand, this is a plant to tax the most skilful of cultivators, for, as a small specimen, it is not difficult to grow provided it is not overwatered, but the problem is how to flower and cultivate a large specimen. It forms a tight cushion less than 1 inch high from a stout woody rootstock with woody rooting stems and small rosettes of linear-spatulate to small lanceolate, imbricated, grey-green leaves densely clothed with fine hairs. Flowers stemless, five-lobed, very pale blue, almost white, open saucer-shaped with blue anthers. June.

PYROLA (*Pyrolaceae*).

This genus contains a number of species but only a few of the Wintergreens are suitable for pan culture and these are not easy to grow, for damage to their long stolons often results in the death of the plant.

CULTIVATION. Compost C is suitable over good drainage and they seem to prefer a wide shallow pan, so that they can range just below the surface. Plenty of lime-free water is required while growing and flowering, just moist at other periods. They require to be placed in a north-facing frame and only brought into the house during the flowering period. If collected from their native habitat, a small amount of the soil in which they are growing should be taken as well. Under these conditions they re-establish themselves much easier, due no doubt to a mycorrhiza; that is an association between the root cells and a fungus mycelium growing in the soil, both being of benefit to each other.

PROPAGATION. Best by seed sown when ripe in compost 3 or careful division when growth commences, taking care that the compost ball is not broken round the divided portions. Repot only when necessary in early April.

P. media. (E).

A stoloniferous perennial about 4 inches high with roundish, ovate, dull green leaves. Flowers on a slender scape in a raceme, semi-pendant, five-lobed globular cup-shaped, white tinged red. June. A native of Europe including Britain.

P. minor. (E).

A small creeping plant with roundish, ovate, dull green leaves and long stalk. Flowers on a slender 8-inch scape, semi-pendant, five-lobed, globular, white flushed red. June. A native of Europe, Britain and N. America.

P. rotundifolia. (E).

A prostrate stoloniferous plant only a few inches high with almost orbicular dull green long stalked leaves. Flowers on 9-inch scapes up to twelve semi-pendant five-lobed, open cup-shape, white with a delightful fragrance. May. A native of Europe, Britain and N. America. I collected this species just above Grindelwald by the side of a rivulet in light coniferous woodlands in 1947, bringing with it some of the peaty silt in which it was growing. It did well for four years in a pan, then after moving it was planted in a small raised peat bed containing choice ericaceous plants and promptly took possession, coming up over the whole of the shady side, even through the joints of the peat wall, each stoloniferous runner erupting in a growing bud.

P. uniflora, see *Moneses uniflora*.

PYXIDANTHERA (*Diapensiaceae*).

This is a monotypic genus and a desirable, rare shrublet, and one that will tax the skill of the specialist, for it is a difficult plant to cultivate successfully in this country.

CULTIVATION. Compost C with plenty of lime-free water in early spring and summer over faultless drainage, keep just moist at other periods. This plant must not be kept in the alpine house except when in flower during the summer months, but plunged in a north-facing shady frame and sprayed overhead in the evenings. Protect from cold drying winds at all times.

PROPAGATION. By careful division of the plants in April, treating each piece as a cutting, placing them in a closed cool north-facing frame until they have become re-established. Repot only when necessary in April.

P. barbulata. (E). (Syn. *Diapensia barbulata*).

This is an extremely dwarf shrublet from the pine barrens of New Jersey, where it hugs the ground, never above an inch or so high with close congested branches. Leaves small, crowded, linear to lanceolate, incurved, coriaceous, deep bronze-green often turning to a reddish-brown. Flowers solitary from rounded buds, opening to five-petalled stars of a bright pale pink. May.

RAFFENALDIA (*Cruciferae*).

A small genus containing one species which is suitable for alpine house culture, where it will be in flower almost continually throughout the year with its peak display in winter.

CULTIVATION. Compost A over good drainage and care is needed in watering at all times, not allowing the compost to become waterlogged otherwise the thick fleshy rootstock will soon rot.

PROPAGATION. By seed sown in May, compost 2. Repot only when necessary in late April.

R. primuloides. (E). (Syn. *Cossonia africana*).

A native of N. Africa, this forms a very thick rounded rootstock from which radiates short stout leaves. Leaves pinnatipartite in rosette formation with large obovate, terminal lobe, green. Flowers axillary on small scapes, four-petalled, yellow veined lilac. January–December.

RAMONDA (*Gesneriaceae*).

A small genus of only three species closely related to Haberlea and requiring similar treatment, they make ideal plants for the alpine house or frame.

CULTIVATION. Compost B is suitable over good drainage, requiring plenty of water while in growth, keep just moist in winter. After flowering they are best plunged in a cool shady spot for the summer and can be kept in a frame during the winter, or in a plunge bed under the staging.

PROPAGATION. By seed in March, compost 2, division in April, or leaf cuttings in May. Repot when necessary after flowering.

R. heldreichii, see *Jankaea heldreichii*.

R. myconi. (E). (Syn. *R. pyrenaica*).

A native of the Pyrenees, this species produces a rosette of large ovate green leaves, softly rugose, margins deeply toothed covered with long reddish hairs. Flowers three to five on a 4-inch scape, large roundish, open five-lobed, lavender-blue with a yellow centre and long style. May–June.

R. myconi var. alba. (E).

A form similar to the type but with bright glistening white flowers. May–June.

R. myconi var. rosea. (E).

This form is outstanding in a deep pink shade but is very variable and there are some wishy-washy shades, definitely a plant to obtain in flower. May–June.

R. nathaliae. (E).

A native of Bulgaria and Serbia, this makes basal rosettes of ovate, rugose, bright green leaves with darker marginal hairs. Flowers on 4-inch scapes up to six, four open-petalled, lavender-blue with deep orange throat. May–June.

R. nathaliae var. alba. (E).

There is a good white form, but in a pure white it is a scarce plant, to be treasured once obtained. May–June.

R. pyrenaica, see *R. myconi*.

R. serbica. (E).

A native of the Balkans, this makes a basal rosette of obovate, deeply toothed, rugose, green leaves margined with long reddish-brown hairs. Flowers on a 4-inch stoutish scape, five-petalled up to six not so open, more cup-shaped, lilac-blue, style short. May–June.

RANUNCULUS (*Ranunculaceae*).

A large genus of plants, the Buttercups are distributed over the whole world but mostly found in the northern hemisphere, where some are persistent agricultural weeds. There are a number which are suitable for pan culture, many of them being extremely decorative.

CULTIVATION. They will do well in compost B and all need a normal supply of water while growing and flowering. The herbaceous perennials should have dry but not arid conditions in winter, while the evergreen species require slightly moister conditions.

PROPAGATION. By seed sown in March, compost 2, or division in August or September. Where special requirements are needed, these will be noted after the description of the species. Repot when necessary after flowering.

R. alpestris. (H).

A native of the European Alps, it makes a small tufted plant about 4 inches high. Leaves orbicular to cordate, three-lobed, deep glossy green, veined, apex obtuse and deeply crenate. Flowers solitary on 4-inch stem, five-petalled roundish, white with golden stamens. May–June. Propagate by seed, compost 2. March.

R. alpestris var. traunfellneri. (H).

This variety from the eastern European Alps is smaller in all its parts with more finely cut dull green leaves and large solitary five-lobed white flowers. May–June.

R. anemonoides, see *Callianthemum rutifolium*.

R. calandrinioides. (H).

An outstanding species but unfortunately there are many poor, narrow petalled forms in cultivation and it is certainly a plant to be chosen in flower. It makes a tufted plant from a thickish roundish rootstock. Leaves up to six, long, narrow lanceolate to ovate-lanceolate, glaucous green, deckled margins. Flowers on stout 6-inch stems up to three, large, five wide petals, white flushed pink with yellow anthers. December to March. A native of Morocco.

CULTIVATION. When the foliage dies down in June, water should be withheld and the plant placed where it can get all available sun. At the end of October the old compost is carefully shaken away and the brittle crown complete with the shrivelled roots repotted (a pot is better than a pan) in fresh compost, resting the top of the crown just below the surface of the soil. Top-dress with 1 inch of limestone chippings and plunge the pot into 3 inches of water until the compost darkens on the surface and within a week the growing tip will appear.

PROPAGATION. Best by seed sown in June, compost 2, or division of the crowns which will divide and fall apart when repotting.

R. crenatus. (E).
A charming dainty species from Hungary and Macedonia, only a few inches high. The leaves are prostrate, orbicular to cordate, apex crenate, mid-green. Flowers on 2-inch stems, five-lobed, roundish, buttercup shape, pure white with a golden eye. May.
PROPAGATION. By division in August. Repot in early April when necessary.

R. glacialis. (H).
A native of European Mountains and Arctic regions, this is indeed the glory of the high alpine 'Buttercups'. Never met with until one has climbed high enough to reach the edge of the eternal snows, there will be found this beauty, always on granite formations in loose wet screes, so easy to collect, but let us admit, difficult to keep in cultivation for any length of time. Compost D is required and plenty of lime-free water while the plant is growing and flowering, just moist at other periods. Propagation is best by seed sown when ripe, compost 2. Do not disturb this plant more than is necessary. It makes a thick rootstock and thick radical palmate leaves, three-partite, segments obtuse, three-fid grey-green. Flowers on 3-inch stems, large, rounded, five petals, glistening white, changing through pink to red after fertilisation. June.

R. parnassifolius. (H).
A native of the Alps and Pyrenees, this has radical, cordate, stalked, dark glossy green leaves. Stem leaves sessile, ovate-lanceolate, margins ciliate and reddish. Flowers large on 6-inch stems with overlapping, roundish petals, white, margins tinged pink. May–June. Propagate from seed, compost 2. March.

R. sequieri. (H).
This is the limestone species akin to *R. glacialis* and only differs from it in that the sepals are hairy, whereas in *R. glacialis* they are glabrous. Requires similar cultural needs and is just as difficult to maintain in cultivation. June. European Alps.

RAOULIA (*Compositae*).

A small genus of plants related to Helichrysum and native of New Zealand and Australia. Some of them are easy but there are at least two high alpine species which will tax the most skilful of growers to cultivate them successfully.
CULTIVATION. With the exception of the two difficult species these plants do well in compost A over faultless drainage; a normal supply of water while growing, keep dry but not arid in winter. All require sunshine.
PROPAGATION. By division in August for the easy species. Repot when necessary in April.

R. australis. (E).

A native of New Zealand, it makes a flat carpet of grey tomentose leaves only an inch high. Flowers sessile, small tubular, pale yellow giving the plant the appearance of molten gold in July.

R. eximia. (E).

This is the Vegetable Sheep from high altitudes in New Zealand and when removed from there, its one desire is to return, for it is a rare and difficult plant to cultivate successfully. My only success was growing it in compost D with care in watering at all times, and it was kept on the dry side in winter. Propagation is by detaching individual rosettes in June and striking these in pure sand. If this plant ever requires repotting, an unlikely event, it is best not disturbed but placed in a double pan as advised in the chapter on repotting, in compost D. The species forms individual rosettes of minute grey-green leaves but so covered with a white wool-like substance as to appear just $\frac{1}{4}$-inch pads of soft greyish-white silk, forming into a roundish cushion. The only method of telling the living plant is that the rosettes seem to give off an indescribable bluey-grey iridescent sheen. A dead plant will remain whole as an 'everlasting' for a long period. No record exists of its ever flowering in cultivation.

R. glabra. (E).

Another mat-forming species only an inch or so high made up of tufts in rosette formation of minute glabrous green leaves. Flowers minute, tubular almost sessile, white. June–July. A native of New Zealand.

R. grandiflora. (E).

A native of Australia, this is another far from easy plant to keep in good health and it has the same cultural needs as *R. eximia*. It makes a low cushion only an inch high of needle-shaped metallic silver leaves in rosette formation, increasing by small stoloniferous runners. Flowers on short stems, small daisy-like, white petals numerous, thin, slightly reflexed. June. Requires a sunny position to give of its best.

R. lutescens. (E).

The smallest of the species, just forming a scab of extremely minute, grey leaves, covered on both sides with hairs. Flowers microscopic, lemon yellow. June–July. This plant is extremely attractive when in flower, appearing as a splash of yellow across the pan. A native of New Zealand.

R. subsericea. (E).

This makes a close carpet of minute green leaves, glabrous above, hairy below and small white heads of almost sessile flowers in June. A native of New Zealand.

RHODODENDRON. (*Ericaceae*).

This genus is one of the largest if one takes into account the number of species, hybrids and varieties, providing plants for all tastes, with the proviso that these can be given lime-free soil. In the alpine house lime-free soil can be provided without difficulty, and the frame may have its quota.

There are very few real dwarfs, but all enumerated here can be grown under pan culture for a good number of years before becoming too large and unwieldy. The root restriction due to pan culture will in itself restrain growth, while a little judicious pinching back of vigorous shoots will maintain the dwarf stature of the plant as well as giving it uniformity. One sees at early alpine shows, specimen plants of R. *leucaspis* which are quite a few years old, yet well contained within the confines of a large pan. This same species will grow over a yard across in a matter of five years or so, in the open garden; this is but one example of the adaptability of the genus.

So vast and diverse are the different forms and colours, that there are plants to cater for all tastes. All hues with the exception of the true blue are possible and even this elusive colour is almost true in good forms of R. 'Blue Diamond' (R. *intrifast* × R. *augustinii*), an outstanding hybrid which can be grown in a pan for a period. The colours range from glistening whites through shell pinks, light rose, scarlet to flaming crimson, pale cream, yellows, brilliant orange back to pale blue, on to violets and startling magentas, all are fully represented. The shapes and different constructions of the flowers too are extremely varied, so much so that it is possible that botanists may in time have to divide the genus Rhododendron into new genera.

These shapes range from wide saucer-like flowers, borne singly on short stems through daphne-shaped terminal clusters to heads of open campanulate and long tubular bells. Now also included in the genus are species and varieties of Azalea, but where these are listed the generic name has been retained as a synonym, for in many nurserymen's catalogues this name will still be retained. Even after flowering the foliage is an attraction in itself, the diversity of shape and colour has to be seen to be believed and the beauty of their leaves is enhanced by the invariably contrasting hue of their lower surfaces. A large number of the species are intensely aromatic when touched, giving the alpine house an indescribable atmosphere of high alpine open copses, so beloved by those plant enthusiasts who visit them in their natural habitats.

The genus has its main centre in the Asiatic zone, embracing parts of India, Burma, Tibet, and China, with the Himalayas as the hub. Here the number of species is prolific, with the tree and large shrub members dominating the foothills and the middle distances, and on the higher alpine ranges the dwarf mat-forming types taking the place of heather as found on open Scottish moors. Several species are also native of Japan while America has its quota, but unfortunately the genus is not well represented in Europe; only two dwarf species of any note are found there, R. *ferrugineum* and R. *hirsutum*. These are the beloved Alpenrose of the Swiss tourist guides and picture postcards. The latter is of doubtful specific rank and is often quoted as only a geographical form with hairy leaves, indigenous to limestone formations.

CULTIVATION. The culture of the dwarf species and varieties for pan culture is easy, provided their few requirements are attended to. It is essential for them to have an open moist lime-free compost which contains plenty of humus, in fact a compost just on the acid side is ideal. The compost recommended for all these plants is C, as described in Chapter Four. Peat is not essential for it tends to sour if left in a pot for any length of time as well as to a great extent only acting as a mechanical agent, for the food value is practically nil, whereas leaf-mould supplies needed nourishment. The high leaf-mould content of the compost provides the abundance of humus which these plants love, and also this medium does not pack readily, thus facilitating quick drainage. At the same time it absorbs enough moisture for their requirements, this being released as needed.

A pot large enough to contain the plant and roots quite comfortably should be used as overpotting is not detrimental to rhododendrons, in fact a buffer of soil between the pot and the roots helps to maintain cool conditions which these plants like. Enough room should be left at the top of the pot, $1\frac{1}{2}$ inch is about right, to allow periodic top-dressing to be carried out. This is best applied in early spring when growth begins, for it will be found that the roots will quickly grow into this top layer. Repotting should only be necessary every other year. Unless required for increasing the stock none of these plants should be allowed to set seed. All flower heads should be removed as soon as they fade, a tedious operation but well worth while, for unless this is done they are prone to set a great deal of seed. The strength of the plant goes into achieving this effort and the likelihood of buds for the following season being formed on laterals bearing seed is very remote.

It is most essential that lime-free water is used, for unlike outdoor cultivation on acid soils where mains water from a chalk source would not affect acidity to any great extent, its use on pan plants, over a period, would have disastrous results. Even the mains supply from a lime-free source which undergoes periodic chlorination to maintain freshness can cause chlorosis with its attendant ill effects. I think that this is where one must be dogmatic and state definitely, that to maintain healthy rhododendrons in pans, and this also applies to all calcifuge plants, rain water only should be used. It should not be too difficult for rain water to be collected either in a water butt or some other container during wet seasons, even if a storage tank is not attached to the alpine house or where the plants are grown in frames, and then to save this, only using it for plants which require lime-free water. All water which is stored is best kept free from algae, which will quickly form if allowed to stagnate, by adding a small amount of permanganate of potash, just enough to turn the water a light pink. No rhododendron likes the warm dry atmosphere of an alpine house during hot summer months so all are best plunged in a north- or west-facing frame and kept cool. When a hot spell is experienced a light spraying of the foliage twice a day, once in the early morning and again last thing in the evening after the sun has set will help to maintain the plants in good health. At normal times during the summer months the evening spray should be sufficient.

PRUNING. In time the majority of pot grown rhododendrons will out-grow the largest available pot suitable for the alpine house or frame, but this will not be for many years. During this period they can be kept in good shape by judicious pruning. It is possible to cut back well into the old wood, for rhododendrons will readily break from this part of the plant. This operation is best carried out immediately after flowering. A number of species have a tendency to throw abnormally long straggling shoots from plants which would otherwise be of a good shape; here too these can be pinched back to retain uniformity.

PROPAGATION. There are two normal methods by which the majority of rhododendrons can be increased, these are by seed and cuttings. Seed is a ready but slow means of increase as most of the species set a large amount of viable seed, but where a large collection is grown in close proximity to each other, this may not breed true, although there is a chance of raising a new hybrid of value when this method is adopted. Seed is best sown in February as advised in Chapter Five, in compost 3. Cuttings are taken in July, using short laterals of the current year's growth, with a heel of old wood, and rooting them in a closed propagating frame.

The following is a fairly representative list of dwarf species, including one hybrid, which are suitable for alpine house or frame culture in pots. Only those which are in commerce have been listed, but there should be enough to satisfy all but the specialist, to whom it is essential to grow all and every one. Where practical, classification is in accordance with the Royal Horticultural Society's *Rhododendron Handbook*, which is the most up to date authority on rhododendrons in print for gardeners today. Following the specific or varietal name is the series or sub-series abbreviated to *s* or *s.s.*, to which the plant under review belongs. To avoid repetition it should be noted that all rhododendrons have short stalked, alternate, entire leaves.

R. anthopogon. (*s.* Anthopogon). (E).
A native of Kashmir, from an altitude of up to 16,000 feet. It forms a compact extremely aromatic shrublet with erect branches, densely clothed with rough brown wool, less than 2 feet in height. Leaves oval, pointed at apex, glossy green covered with brown scales beneath. Flowers in compact terminal clusters, five-lobed, open tubular, light pink. April.

R. anthopogon. var. haemonium. (E).
Similar to the type but with dainty light yellow flowers. April.

R. aperantum. (*s.* Neriiflorum. *s.s.* Sanguineum). (E).
This is a slow growing mat-forming, spreading species from altitudes of between 12,000 and 14,000 feet in Burma. Branches numerous with

scale-covered stems up to 9 inches high. Leaves oval, tapered to apex, dark green, glaucous beneath. Flowers in terminal clusters up to six, tubular bell-shaped and ranging in colour from white to rose or yellow. May–June.

R. 'Blue Diamond'. (*R. intrifast* × *R. augustinii*). (E).
This grand hybrid produces the nearest to a true blue that has so far been raised or discovered. It is best obtained when in flower, for there are a good number of inferior colour forms which are far from what the ideal type can be. It makes an erect, slow growing compact bush reaching 18 inches after many years in a pan. Leaves oval to ovate, bright green. Flowers in terminal clusters, large, open saucer-shape, rich blue in colour with just a dash of red in the pigment. April.

R. brachyanthum. (*s.* and *s.s.* Glaucum). (E).
A native of Yunnan, China, making a dwarf stiff bushlet, with decumbent branches of bright reddish-brown, sparsely clad with scales. Leaves oval, apex recurved, dark bright green, glaucous beneath, terminating in a minute acuminate tooth with a pronounced reddish midrib; scales on both sides. Flowers up to eight in terminal clusters, bell-shaped, yellow tinged green. June.

R. brachyanthum var. hypolepidotum. (E). (Syn. *R. charitostreptum*).
A more erect form, sometimes given specific rank, with much-branched, slender brownish-green stems. Leaves oval to obovate, dark mid-green and heavily netted with veins above, light grey-green, scaly beneath. Flowers in small terminal clusters, bell-shaped, yellow. May. A native of China and Tibet.

R. calciphilum (*s.* Saluenense). (E).
This, a native of Burma, at high elevations on limestone formations, makes a compact prostrate bush of tight congested branches and bears singly or in pairs, open saucer-shaped, rosy purple flowers in May.

R. calostrotum. (*s.* Saluenense). (E).
A fine dwarf shrub rarely above 12 inches high from Upper Burma. Stems slender, light brown, leaves oval to lanceolate, thin, mid-green above, glaucous beneath, short stalks, margined with bristles, underneath turning reddish-brown in the adult stage, due to the dense covering of fine scales. Flowers terminal on small pedicels, rounded, open, flat, pink to purple with deeper spots. May.

R. campylogynum. (*s.* Campylogynum). (E).
From Yunnan, China, where it makes a dwarf free flowering shrub, eventually reaching 2 feet. Branches congested, leaves oval to orbicular with a minute acuminate tooth at apex, dark green, paler beneath, margins recurved. Flowers wide bell-shape on long stalks, rose-purple to almost black-purple, style protruding bent downwards. May.

R. camtschaticum. (*s.* Camtschaticum). (D). (Syn. *Therorhodion cam-tschaticum*).
This is a native of Kamtschatka and other parts of N.E. Asia, and is not

easy in the warm drier south but does well in the cooler and more humid northern climate. The finest plant I have ever seen of this species is growing in the Royal Botanic Gardens, Edinburgh, home of many delightful dwarf rhododendrons in cultivation. It requires sunshine in the north and midlands but needs a cool shady site in the south. It makes a 4-inch high tuft of congested stems. Leaves oval, nearly sessile, thin with pronounced veining, quite glaucous. Flowers on 1-inch stems, well clear of the foliage, solitary, rarely in pairs, terminal on young wood, open rounded, rosy-crimson, upper petals spotted purple. May.

R. cantabile, see *R. russatum.*

R. charitostreptum, see *R. brachyanthum* var. *hypolepidotum.*

R. cephalanthum. (*s.* Anthopogon). (E).
From W. Szechwan at an altitude of 10,000 feet, this dwarf shrub is up to 2 feet high with lax, thin, bristly, scaly branchlets, leaves oval, obtuse, dark glossy green, light brown beneath, covered with thin scales, margins decurved, apex terminating in a small acuminate tooth. Flowers in crowded terminal clusters tubular, opening to five extending lobes, white. May.

R. cephalanthum var. crebreflorum. (E). (Syn. *R. crebreflorum*).
This is similar to the species but smaller, rarely above 9 inches high with clustered, terminal heads of tubular rosy-pink flowers. An outstanding plant but requires care in the south of England. May.

R. chameunum. (*s.* Saluenense). (E).
From Tibet, this is a dwarf prostrate shrub rarely above 6 inches high, of semi-erect congested hairy branches, leaves oval, glabrous, scaly below, mid-green. Flowers terminal, up to three on short pedicels, deep purple-rose with crimson markings.

R. charitopes. (*s.* and *s.s.* Glaucum). (E).
A native of Upper Burma, making a bushlet up to a foot high with erect light brown slender twigs. Leaves crowded at apex of shoots ovate to obovate, deep glossy green, glaucous below, scaly on both sides, underneath scales yellow, terminating in an acuminate tooth. Flowers on short slender stalks up to three in a terminal cluster, open bell-shape, pinkish-mauve, spotted with crimson on upper petals. May.

R. chrysanthum. (*s.* Ponticum *s.s.* Caucasicum). (E).
A rare and difficult species from Japan and N. Asia, only a few inches high and slowly spreading with stiff horizontal branches. Leaves tufted, narrow, ovate, glabrous, dull mid-green, lighter below, margins recurved. Flowers up to five in an erect terminal cluster, open bell-shape, yellow. May. Needs careful cultivation in half shade but requires sun to ripen current year's growth. It has a distressing habit of dying off in parts.

R. chryseum. (*s.* Lapponicum). (E).
From W. China, this makes a small shrub up to 2 feet high with much-branched reddish scaly stems. Leaves oblong with a dense covering of scales on both sides, margins recurved, dull olive-green, brownish-white

beneath. Flowers in terminal clusters up to six, slightly funnel-shaped, deep yellow. April–May.

R. cosmetum. (*s*. Saluenense). (E).
This is a fine dwarf shrub only a few inches high making a mass of twiggy branches. Leaves dark green, oval to ovate, turning to bronze in winter. Flowers terminal on short stems, open saucer-shape, rosy-purple. May. A native of N.W. Yunnan.

R. crebreflorum, see *R. cephalanthum* var. *crebreflorum*.

R. dasypetalum. (*s*. Lapponicum). (E).
A native of Yunnan, this forms a bush of dwarf erect, stiff branches about 12 inches high with grey-green oval scaly leaves, brownish-grey beneath. Flowers terminal, short, funnel-shaped, purple-rose. April.

R. didymum. (*s*. Neriiflorum. *s.s.* Sanguineum). (E).
This is a low shrub up to 2 feet high with much-branched bristly twigs. Leaves obovate, dark glossy green, covered with a grey-white down beneath. Flowers in terminal clusters up to six bell-shaped, dark crimson almost black, with red stamens. July. A native of S.E. Tibet on high limestone formations.

R. fastigiatum. (*s*. Lapponicum). (E).
An erect shrublet from 12 to 18 inches high, branches thin, twiggy, covered with brownish scales. Leaves clustered at apex of stems, oval to obovate, dark olive green, grey beneath, scales on both sides, prominent on midrib and short reddish stalk. Flowers in small terminal clusters, small funnel-shaped, light purple. April. A native of Yunnan, this shrub will often give a second crop of flowers in September.

R. ferrugineum. (*s*. Ferrugineum). (E).
This is the beloved Alpenrose of Switzerland, sheeting high open meadows with its dainty flowers, gaining more in spread than in height, for even in cultivation it rarely exceeds 2 feet and only obtains this stature after many years. It makes a compact bushlet of procumbent stems, the young shoots covered with rust-coloured scales. Leaves oval, tapering to apex and base, deep glossy green, golden-brown beneath due to intense covering of rust coloured scales. Flowers small, up to twelve in terminal clusters, deep rosy crimson. June.

R. ferrugineum var. album. (E).
This is the very choice white form of the species which is worth searching for. June.

R. flavidum. (*s*. Lapponicum). (E).
A native of W. Szechwan, China, it makes a dense congested rounded shrub rarely above 15 inches high with very scaly branches and laterals. Leaves oval, oblong, leathery, deep green, lighter beneath, scales on both sides. Flowers small, funnel-shaped in terminal clusters up to six, a fine primrose-yellow. March–April.

R. forrestii. (*s*. Neriiflorum. *s.s.* Forrestii). (E).
From N.W. Yunnan and S.E. Tibet, one of the finest of all dwarf

rhododendrons if it can be induced to flower well. This is its weakness, however, and it will only produce a sparse crop in most seasons. It makes a prostrate shrub of stout creeping stems only a few inches high. Leaves oval to orbicular, dark glossy green, thick textured, purple beneath, veins conspicuously grooved. Flowers on short stems, terminal, solitary, rarely in pairs, long narrow, bell-shaped, waxy in texture, extremely large for size of plant, deep rich crimson. May. This plant requires plenty of moisture at all times but drainage must be perfect, for any stagnation in the compost is fatal. Pieces of sandstone should be spread over the surface roots in the pan and the plant should be given more sunshine than is normal for rhododendrons, thus allowing the current year's growth to ripen, essential if flower buds are to be set.

R. forrestii var. repens. (E). (Syn. *R. repens*).
R. repens which used to be a separate species is now included in *R. forrestii*, and differs only slightly botanically, the leaves of *R. forrestii* being purple underneath, whereas those of *R. forrestii* var. *repens* are light green.

R. hanceanum 'Nanum'. (*s.* Triflorum. *s.s.* Hanceanum). (E).
A native of W. China, this is the dwarf form of *R. hanceanum* which is constant in cultivation, rarely above 6 inches high with erect, stiff, light brown, glossy stems. Leaves crowded, obovate to lanceolate, deep glossy green, lighter beneath. Veining heavy and reticulated on both sides, scaling is only slight. Flowers open tubular in terminal clusters, pale yellow. April. Reputed to be shy-flowering, I think that is only a question of obtaining a free-flowering form, for I have never had any difficulty in that respect, so it is best to buy this form in bud.

R. hirsutum. (*s.* Ferrugineum). (E).
A native of Europe, this is the hairy counterpart of *R. ferrugineum* and unlike that species is found on limestone formations but requires acid conditions in cultivation. It is similar in size but differs for garden purposes in being less scaly and very bristly. The leaves are bright green above, slightly scaly beneath. Flowers borne in close terminal clusters, small, tubular, deep pink to almost rich crimson. May–June.

R. hirsutum var. albiflorum. (E).
This is a rare white form which is a very desirable plant if obtainable. June.

R. impeditum. (*s.* Lapponicum). (E).
From W. China, it makes a close prostrate mat of horizontal greenish-brown wiry stems. Leaves oval to ovate, dark dull green, glaucous beneath, densely clothed on both sides with scales, margins slightly recurved. Flowers in terminal clusters up to three open, tubular, pale purple with a slight fragrance. April.

R. imperator. (*s.* Uniflorum). (E).
A native of Upper Burma, this is a small prostrate shrublet only a few inches high, branches horizontal, lax, scaly. Leaves lanceolate, short acuminate tooth at apex, tapered towards base, margins recurved, dark

glossy green, silver-grey beneath. Flowers solitary, rarely in pairs, terminal on red pedicels, open funnel-shaped, deep rose-purple. May.

R. intricatum. (*s.* Lapponicum). (E).
A neat rounded shrublet up to 12 inches high with reddish-brown scaly branches. Leaves oval to orbicular, dark green, paler below, both sides covered with glistening scales. Flowers small, tubular in terminal clusters, mauve. April. A good plant for pan culture as it will flower from one year old rooted cuttings. A native of Szechwan, W. China.

R. keiskei. (*s.* and *s.s.* Triflorum). (E).
This Japanese species is a prostrate compact shrublet with brownish scaly branches. Leaves oval to oblong, acute, deep green, both sides covered with scales, denser below. Flowers in clusters of four, open bell-shaped, lemon-yellow. April.

R. keleticum. (*s.* Saluenense). (E).
A native of Tibet, making a small shrublet of much-branched slender light brown scaly stems. Leaves thin, oblong to obovate, glossy green, light brownish-green below, sparsely scaled beneath, margins ciliate and slightly decurved. Flowers on slender hairy stems, open saucer-shape, purplish-crimson spotted with deeper markings. May.

R. lapponicum. (*s.* Lapponicum). (E).
This is the typical species of the series, unfortunately not easy in cultivation, requiring care and similar conditions to *R. camtschaticum*. It is a native of Europe, Asia and N. America, making an upright shrub rarely above 12 inches high with scaly stems. Leaves oval to obovate, dark green, yellowish below. Flowers in terminal clusters up to six small, tubular, bright purple but often tending to blue in a good form. February.

R. ledoides, see *R. trichostomum* var. *ledoides*.

R. lepidotum. (*s.* and *s.s.* Lepidotum). (E).
A native of high altitudes in Nepal and Sikkim, up to 18 inches high of erect slender stems, the young wood, leaves and flower stalks densely clothed with minute scales. Leaves oblong, deep green, paler beneath. Flowers on short stems up to three, open saucer-shaped, in colours which range from pink to purple. May–June.

R. leucaspis. (*s.* Boothii. *s.s.* Megeratum). (E).
This species is one of the best for alpine house culture and can always be relied upon to produce flowers for the first spring show of the Alpine Garden Society in London. It makes a low shrub up to 12 inches high. There are two forms of this plant, one quite dwarf, while the other will grow to 4 feet with spreading semi-erect, stout bristly mid-brown hairy stems. Leaves terminal, bristly, large for size of plant, oval to obovate, dark olive-green, glaucous below, scaly upper surface, midrib and margins covered with fine hairs. Flowers over 2 inches across in small terminal clusters, open saucer-shaped, pure satiny white, enhanced by the dark brown, protruding anthers and bent style. February-March. A native of Tibet, this plant will flower from seed or cuttings in two years.

Above: *Primula* 'Pandora' (see page 418)

Below: *Ranunculus calandrinioides* (see page 430)

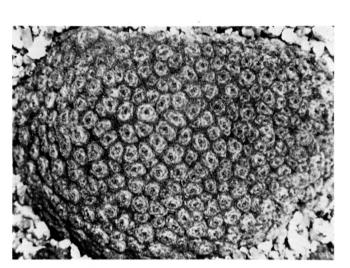

Above left: *Raoulia eximia* (see page 432)   Above centre: *Raoulia grandiflora* (see page 432)

Below: *Rhododendron leucaspis* (see page 440)

Above: *Rhodohypoxis* 'Ruth' (see page 445)

Below: *Sanguinaria canadensis* 'Flora Plena' (see page 451)

Above: *Saxifraga florulenta* (see page 463)
Below: *Saxifraga* 'Petraschii' (see page 470)

R. 'Linearifolium'. (*s.* Azalea, *s.s.* Obtusum). (E). (Syn. *Azalea lineari-folia*).

A Japanese garden form of *R. linearifolium* var. *macrosepalum*, it is a flattish bush up to 2 feet after many years of spreading rather than grow-ing, with erect, stiff much-branched stems. Leaves long, linear, mid-green, tapering, hairy. Flowers in terminal clusters up to three consist of long narrow lobes, similar to the foliage, bright lilac. May. The plant both in and out of flower has a very shaggy appearance.

R. lowndesii. (*s.* Lepidotum). (D).

A recently collected plant from Nepal, this is a new and rare species and unlike the majority of dwarf rhododendrons it is deciduous after making a small but fine display of coloured foliage in autumn. Less than 6 inches high of prostrate wiry twigs, clothed with the oblanceolate, pale green leaves, apex rounded with acuminate tooth, glabrous or rarely hairy beneath. Flowers terminal up to three on large slender hairy stems, open, campanulate, pale yellow, upper lobes spotted or streaked with deeper yellow. May.

R. ludlowii. (*s.* Lepidotum). (E).

A native of Tibet, this is another new and rare species making a small shrublet rarely above 9 inches high, thin, semi-erect branches. Leaves obovate, thick, leathery, green. Flowers terminal, solitary, rarely in pairs, open, tubular, primrose-yellow with deeper yellow markings. May.

R. megeratum. (*s.* Boothii. *s.s.* Megeratum). (E).

A near relative to *R. leucaspis*, it makes a low semi-erect shrub about 9 inches high with much-branched, very twiggy laterals, growing at all angles, light reddish-brown covered with bristles. Flowers in terminal clusters up to three open saucer-shaped, bright yellow with protruding chocolate-brown anthers and bent style. April. A native of N.W. Yunnan.

R. microleucum. (*s.* Lapponicum). (E).

A native of Asia and N. America, this is a choice rare shrub about 1 foot high of erect twiggy branches, covered with scales. Leaves crowded, narrow almost linear, pale green covered with buff scales. Flowers in small terminal clusters, short funnel-shaped, glistening white. May.

R. myrtilloides. (*s.* Campylogynum). (E).

About 6 inches in height of erect stout, reddish-brown branches. Leaves obovate, arranged round the stems, minutely toothed, dark glossy green above, glaucous below, sparsely dotted with scales on both sides. Flowers solitary on slender stems, bell-shaped, deep plum. May. A native of N.E. Burma. More correctly *R. campylogynum* var. *myrtilloides*.

R. nitens. (*s.* Saluenense). (E).

This is a late flowering species from N.E. Burma, making a compact prostrate shrub up to 6 inches high. Branches slender, brownish-green, scaly. Leaves long, narrow oval, rounded or blunt at apex, tapered to base, margins ciliate, bright glossy green with light scales, greyish below. Flowers on short pedicels, open saucer-shaped, bright magenta. July.

R. nivale. (*s.* Lapponicum). (E).
A small dwarf shrublet less than 6 inches high with stiff open branchlets. Leaves oval, small, deep olive-green, margins ciliate, light rust-brown and scaly below. Terminal clusters of bright magenta, small funnel-shaped flowers in May. A native of Burma.

R. obtusum var. amoenum. (*s.* Azalea. *s.s.* Obtusum). (E).
This makes a tight bushy shrub rarely above 2 feet but slow growing. Leaves oval, very deep shiny green with bristles on both sides. Flowers in terminal clusters, small, rosy purple. May. A native of Japan.

R. obtusum var. japonicum. (E).
Similar to *amoenum* but smaller in all its parts, with the exception of the rosy purple flowers which makes this a superior plant. May. A native of Japan.

R. pemakoense. (*s.* Uniflorum). (E).
This is an upright dwarf shrub rarely above 12 inches high, spreading by underground runners, a rare occurrence in this genus. Stems light green, leaves on longish stalks, narrowly obovate, dark glossy green above, intensely aromatic. Flowers single, rarely in pairs, open, tubular, light pinkish-purple. April. A native of the province of Pemako, E. Tibet.

R. prostratum. (*s.* Saluenense). (E).
A native of China, from high elevations, in fact it is generally the last shrub found before the snow line is reached. It forms a low mass of tangled hairy branches and laterals. Leaves small, oblong, bright glossy green above, scaly below. Flowers solitary, sometimes in pairs, open saucer-shape, on small hairy pedicels, light violet spotted red. April.

R. pumilum. (*s.* Uniflorum). (E).
A native of Burma and Assam, this is a delightful dwarf species, rarely above 6 inches high, leaves oval, dark glossy green, lighter beneath. Flowers on short stems up to three terminal, bell-shaped, rose-pink. April–May.

R. racemosum. (*s.* Virgatum). (E).
This will eventually become too large for pan culture but flowering as it does from one year old cuttings and considering the ease with which it is possible to trim it into shape it makes an ideal plant for pan culture over a number of years. It forms a much-branched, semi-prostrate shrublet with short wiry stems, light brown and scaly. Leaves oval, apex recurved, tapering to base, dull green above, glaucous beneath, covered with minute scales. Flowers open bell-shaped, up to six in terminal and axillary clusters. April. The colour ranges from white through pale pink to deep pink. The best form of this species is that which was introduced from Forrest's 1921–22 expedition in N.W. Yunnan, under number 19,404.

R. radicans. (*s.* Saluenense). (E).
Possibly the smallest of all the rhododendron species, less than 1 inch in height, with quite prostrate and compact wiry, brownish-red branches. Leaves minute, lanceolate, clustered at the end of the thin wiry twigs,

deep glossy green above, light brownish-green below, scaly. Flowers solitary on 1-inch bristly stems, open campanulate with crinkled margins, up to 1½ inches across, varying in colour from light mauve to deep purple. May. A native of S.E. Tibet.

R. radinum, see *R. trichostomum* var. *radinum*.

R. repens, see *R. forrestii* var. *repens*.

R. riparium. (*s*. Saluenense). (E).
A native of Tibet, rarely above 9 inches high of congested branches, densely crowded with dull green, oval to oblong leaves, lighter beneath. Flowers terminal on short stems, open saucer-shaped, purple with darker spotting. May.

R. rupicola. (*s*. Lapponicum). (E).
This is a delightful dwarf compact shrub which will eventually reach 18 inches. The branches are densely covered with glabrous dull deep green, oval to oblong leaves, light rust beneath, apex terminating in a short acuminate tooth. Flowers up to five in terminal clusters, tubular, rich purple. May. A native of Yunnan, China.

R. russatum. (*s*. Lapponicum). (E). (Syn. *R. cantabile*).
R. cantabile has until recently been considered a distinct species, but it is now regarded as a dwarf form of *R. russatum*. From personal experience it is to be preferred, for its small compact habit. The dwarf form is a shrub which will reach 2 feet after many years, making very leafy, congested yellowish-brown branches with oval to ovate dull green leaves, rounded at apex, the lower surface rusty yellow in colour. Branches, laterals and leaves are densely covered with brown scales. Flowers in terminal clusters up to ten open campanulate with a short tube, blue-purplish with a white throat and extending red style. April. A native of Yunnan.

R. saluenense. (*s*. Saluenense). (E).
The type plant of the series varies in height but there are dwarf forms which rarely exceed 12 inches and only that, after many years. It is a compact shrub with slender bristly branches, erect, light brown, covered with scales. Leaves rough, oval to obovate, terminating in a minute acuminate tooth, dark green above, light greenish-brown beneath, with pronounced reddish midrib and scaly. Flowers terminal in pairs on short bristly shoots, open saucer-shape, deep purple with darker spottings. May. A native of Yunnan.

R. sargentianum. (*s*. Anthopogon). (E).
In its best form this is a 'must', as a specimen for pan culture, but there are many forms which are far from desirable, having either a reluctance to flower or being poor and wishy-washy. Definitely a plant to obtain in flower. It makes a dwarf, compact, very aromatic shrub with downy stiff, scaly branches up to 1 foot high under pan culture, densely clothed with minute oval, deep green glossy leaves, paler, woolly below. Flowers in terminal clusters up to twelve on short stalks, open tubular, bright pale yellow. May. A native of Szechwan, China.

R. scintillans. (*s.* Lapponicum). (E).
A native of Yunnan, this is another species which should be chosen in
flower, for at its best it is almost a royal blue, but there are far too many
poor lavender-blue forms about. It makes an open shrublet less than 2 feet
high of thin scaly shoots. Leaves lanceolate, apex acute, tapered towards
base, dark green, grey beneath. Flowers in terminal clusters, up to six open
bell-shaped with small tube. April.

R. setosum. (*s.* Lapponicum). (E).
A native of the Himalayas, it is a rare plant in cultivation in this country at
present, but worth every attention, if and when obtainable. Reuthe of
Keston used to list this species and it was growing well at the Royal
Botanic Gardens, Edinburgh. It makes a small prostrate shrub up to 6
inches high, very compact and bushy with very bristly stems. Leaves
oblong, dark green, lighter beneath, scaly, margins bristly. Flowers in terminal clusters up to eight funnel-shaped, bright pinkish-purple. April–May.

R. sphaeranthum, see *R. trichostomum.*

R. tapetiforme. (*s.* Lapponicum). (E).
This is the smallest of the series only a few inches high, with prostrate
stiff branches. Leaves oval to ovate, dull green, paler beneath, densely
clothed with scales. Flowers up to six in terminal clusters, small tubular,
pinky-mauve. April. A native of Tibet.

R. trichostomum. (*s.* Anthopogon). (E). (Syn. *R. sphaeranthum*; *R.*
  ledoides; *R. radinum*).
Until recently the three synonyms were regarded as distinct species, but
now *R. sphaeranthum* is *R. trichostomum, R. ledoides* is *R.t.* var. *ledoides,* and
R. radinum is *R.t.* var. *radinum.* The type plant is a much-branched shrub
eventually reaching 3 feet in the open ground, but less than 18 inches under
pan culture, with upright slender stems, densely covered with scales, deep
brown in colour with white striations. Leaves long, narrow, oblong, very
deep dull brownish-green above, light brownish-green beneath, completely covered with brown scales on both sides, margins slightly recurved
and edged with scales, also an occasional hair or so. Flowers in rounded
terminal clusters up to twenty daphne-like, fine rose-pink, corolla scaly
outside. April. This plant is intensely aromatic and on a warm day one is
aware of its presence when entering the alpine house. A native of W.
Szechwan. *R.t.* var. *ledoides* and *R. radinum* have only slight botanical
differences, the corolla of the former is glabrous while that of the latter is
densely scaly outside.

R. uniflorum. (*s.* Uniflorum). (E).
The type plant of the series is a small prostrate shrub only a few inches
high with dark green, oblong to oval leaves, lighter beneath. Flowers
singly, rarely in pairs on short stems, open saucer-shape, purple. April. A
native of Tibet.

R. williamsianum. (*s.* Thomsonii. *s.s.* Souliei). (E).
This will eventually make a large shrub more spreading than tall, but it

can be grown for a number of years in a pan. Branches thin, wiry, glossy reddish-brown. Leaves terminal, orbicular to rounded, smooth, dull mid-green above, light grey-green below, deeply reticulated veining, margins slightly recurved, apex terminating in a blunt acuminate tooth, petiole long, smooth, reddish-blue. The young foliage is a delightful shade of bronze. Flowers in terminal pairs, large, bell-shaped, wax-like in substance, a beautiful shell-pink. April. A native of China.

RHODOHYPOXIS (*Hypoxidaceae*).

A monotypic genus closely related to Hypoxis, and although there is only one species there are many coloured forms, all of which are outstanding plants for pan culture.

CULTIVATION. Compost B is suitable over faultless drainage; the plants require plenty of lime-free water during the growing season, after growth dies down no further supply is necessary until it re-appears the following spring.

PROPAGATION. Best by division, essential for good forms. This must be carried out while the plants are actually in growth, for they will not transplant well while dormant. Seed is also a means of increase, sowing this in March in compost 2. The resulting seedlings are liable to produce a number of different forms, some with thin narrow petals and these should be weeded out. Repot when necessary in late April.

R. baurei. (H).

This forms ovoid, short rhizomes from which is produced a tuft of erect, lanceolate, deeply channelled tapering green leaves, sparsely covered with silky hairs on both sides. Flowers solitary, from leaf axils on a stiff 3-inch stem, perianth in two layers of three petals, rose-red, lighter on reverse. May–September. A native of the Drakensburg Mountains, S. Africa.

R. baurei var. platypetala. (H).

This is the white form of the species which has today been superseded by selected seedlings, for example R. 'Ruth' is a large white form with wide petals of good substance. May–September.

Other good named forms are 'Eva', deep red; 'Margaret Rose', bright pink; 'The Major', glowing deep pink.

RHODOTHAMNUS (*Ericaceae*).

A monotypic genus, this species is very suitable for alpine house or frame culture, being one of the outstanding plants in that great *Ericaceae* family.

CULTIVATION. Compost C over good drainage is ideal and plenty of lime-free water is required during spring and summer, but a dry period, not arid, to ripen the current year's wood seems to be necessary in late July. Keep moist in winter and top-dress with similar compost in early spring.

PROPAGATION. By seed sown in August, compost 3, or very careful division in spring. Each piece should have a few roots attached and be treated as a cutting until re-established. Repot only when necessary, for this plant seems to dislike root disturbance.

R. chamaecistus. (E).

A native of the Tyrol and E. Siberia, this makes a dwarf shrub up to 9 inches high of branching semi-erect stems, young wood glandular, hairy. Leaves oval to ovate, small, shiny bright green, margined with stiff hairs. Flowers borne in small terminal clusters, rounded, up to four open, flat, five-petalled, bright rose. April.

RICOTIA (*Cruciferae*).

A small genus of plants of which there is one suitable for alpine house culture. It is a new introduction by Peter Davis from Tahtali Dagh in Western Anatolia and is not proving an easy plant in cultivation, for it seems to want to flower itself to death.

CULTIVATION. Compost A over faultless drainage; care is needed in watering at all times, for an excess will quickly rot the thick succulent-like stems, dry but not arid in winter.

PROPAGATION. By seed when ripe, compost 2. Repot only when necessary in early April.

R. davisiae. (E).

This has a woody rootstock from which fleshy brittle stems up to 3 inches high are borne. Leaves thick, trifoliate, segments ovate, two notches at apex, stalks long, rounded, thick. Flowers on 3-inch fleshy stems in a small umbel, four-lobed, rounded petals notched at apex, pink. April–September.

Roettlera forrestii, see *Oreocharis forrestii*.

ROMULEA (*Iridaceae*).

A genus of small bulbous-like corms of which a number are hardy and suitable for alpine house culture in pans. Mostly natives of W. Europe and Mediterranean region, also S. Africa; allied to the Crocus.

CULTIVATION. Compost B over good drainage, planting the corms in September about 2 inches deep. They require a normal amount of water while in growth, dry conditions after foliage dies down.

PROPAGATION. By offsets taken when repotting, this should be carried out every year in September.

R. bulbocodium. (B).

A native of the Mediterranean region, up to 6 inches high with semi-erect linear green channelled leaves. Flowers solitary, open, tubular, light violet, segments yellow at base. March.

R. columnae. (B).

This is a small species about 4 inches high with semi-erect linear, green leaves, channelled on upper surface. Flowers on small stems up to three bluish-violet, yellow at base. March. A native of the Mediterranean and Britain.

R. requienii. (B).
A native of Corsica, this has prostrate, rounded, green, linear leaves. Flowers on 4-inch stems up to three open segments with short tube, violet with yellow anthers. March.

ROSA (*Rosaceae*).

There is no doubt that roses are synonymous with English gardens and their colour and variety are legion but, and this is a big but, they are not usually associated with alpines, looking too formal amongst the true wildlings. Still there are a few forms which are quite suitable for pan culture, providing colour over a long period in the alpine house or frame.
CULTIVATION. Compost B is suitable with good drainage. A fair supply of water is necessary during the growing and flowering season, keep just moist at other periods.
PROPAGATION. By green cuttings taken in June and rooted in the propagating frame.
R. chinensis 'Minima'. (D). (Syn. *R. lawranceana*; *R. roulettii*).
This is a dwarf China Rose, less than 12 inches high with almost smooth branches. Leaflets three to five ovate, obtuse, reddish-purple in colour. Flowers double rose-red. June.
R. gallica 'Pumila'. (D).
A small prostrate rose only 6 inches high. Leaflets three to five thick, roundish, ovate, deep green. Flowers single, red. May.
R. lawranceana, see *R. chinensis* 'Minima'.
R. 'Peon'. (D).
A dwarf bush of unknown parentage up to 6 inches high with clusters of small crimson rambler-type flowers. May.
R. roulettii, see *R. chinensis* 'Minima'.

ROSCOEA (*Zingiberaceae*).

A small genus of plants, natives of the Himalayas and China, of which there are two species that can be used for pan culture in the alpine house. These plants are late risers and usually appear only towards the end of spring.
CULTIVATION. Compost B is suitable and pots should be used instead of pans, for the rhizomatous roots need to be planted deeply. All require plenty of water while in growth, just moist after growth dies down; best in half shade.
PROPAGATION. By seed sown in March, compost 2, or careful division of the roots in spring. Repot when necessary after flowering.
R. alpina. (H).
A native of the Himalayas, this sends up in late spring tufts of light green lanceolate, slender pointed leaves, incurved in the shape of a hood. Flowers on short 2-inch stems up to four with long tubular calyx, three corolla lobes, dorsal erect, lateral two spreading, rose-pink. July.

R. purpurea var. procera. (H).
From Sikkim, this form is not as large as the type with the exception of the flowers, it produces two sheathing, sessile, lanceolate, slender pointed, light green leaves. Flowers on short stems, nestling in the incurved foliage, up to four calyx tubular, three corolla lobes, dorsal arching, lateral smaller spreading, lip large bi-fid, deep purple-blue. July.

ROSULARIA (*Crassulaceae*).

A variable genus of which the species have at one time or another been included in Cotyledon, Sedum or Umbilicus. They make good alpine house plants for few can be considered hardy outdoors.
CULTIVATION. Compost A over faultless drainage, they require only a small amount of water, for an excess will soon cause the plants to rot, keep dry in winter.
PROPAGATION. By division of the plants after flowering. Repot only when necessary after flowering, as root restriction will keep these plants compact.
R. pallida. (E). (Syn. *Cotyledon chrysantha*; *Umbilicus chrysanthus*).
A native of Asia Minor, this makes rosettes of small pale green, narrow ovate, acute leaves covered with a soft down, margins ciliate. Flowers on 4-inch slender, leafy stems in a terminal cluster, semi-pendant, five-lobed, star-shaped, pale yellow. May.
R. sempervivum. (E). (Syn. *Cotyledon sempervivum*; *C. pestalozzae*; *Umbilicus sempervivum*).
A variable species from the Caucasus and Asia Minor, it makes rosettes of pale grey-green spatulate, hairy, glandular leaves, turning pale bronze. Flowers on slender 3-inch glandular stems, five-lobed, starry, light pink. June.

RYDBERGIA, see ACTINELLA

SAGINA (*Caryophyllaceae*).

A small genus containing a number of species which are weeds or little more, but there is one which will tax the most skilful of growers, to bring to any size and maintain it in good health. It is an extremely rare British native, discovered and named after the late Dr W. B. Boyd, who introduced so many fine alpine plants into cultivation.
CULTIVATION. I have found that it does well in compost D and is to be recommended, although provided care is taken in watering, compost A will also be suitable. Needs a normal supply of water during the growing season, keep dry but not arid in winter.
PROPAGATION. By detaching tufts in June, placing these round the edge of a pot filled with silver sand and plunging into the propagating frame. Repot only when necessary in late April as this plant is an extremely slow grower.

S. boydii. (E).
This makes a close compact cushion from an underground much-branched stem. Leaves in tufts awl-shaped, stiff, fleshy, mucronate, extremely glossy, dark green. Flowers insignificant, minute, sessile, five grey-white sepals. May. A native of Scotland.

SALIX (*Salicaceae*).

The Willows are a large genus of plants, embracing over 300 species, ranging from tall trees through upright shrubs to creeping prostrate rock-hugging shrublets, inhabiting exposed positions at high altitudes in the northern hemisphere. These dwarfs in company with the creeping Azalea, *Loiseleuria procumbens*, are the last of the hard-wooded plants to be found almost up to the line of the eternal snows. With few exceptions all the species are dioecious, that is, male and female flowers are borne on different plants. The catkins of the male plants have generally a greater decorative value than the female species and are to be preferred for this reason.
CULTIVATION. All do well in compost B with plenty of water during the growing season, keep just moist in winter. Top-dress with similar compost in early spring.
PROPAGATION. Easy, by well ripened cuttings taken in November and placed in individual small pots, plunged into a cold frame and kept moist until rooted. Repot only when necessary, bearing in mind that all willows are intolerant of root disturbance.

S. apoda. (Male form). (D).
This is a charming and attractive dwarf shrublet, rarely exceeding an inch or so in height, making a procumbent mat of creeping bronze-green branches. Leaves small, tufted, ovate, tapering to base, margins minutely serrate, texture thin, veining not pronounced, bright apple-green in colour. Catkins large, long, narrow, oval; emerging dark grey, turning rose-pink, afterwards changing to orange, owing to colour of pollen; bracts black-tipped. April. A native of the Caucasus.

S. arbuscula var. humilis. (D).
A native of Europe including Scotland, this is a dwarf edition of the type, rarely up to 6 inches high, making a much-branched congested mat of smooth stems. Leaves alternate, generally entire, oval to oblong, tapered at apex and base, glabrous, dark green above, grey beneath. Catkins produced at apex of small leafy stems. May. Female larger than the male.

S. × boydii. (D). (*S. reticulata* × *S. lapponum*).
One of the finest if not the best of all the willows in cultivation today. It is still a rare plant, although discovered over sixty years ago, due no doubt to its slow growth. It is a natural hybrid found by the late Dr William Boyd, while plant hunting in Forfarshire, and is considered to be a cross between *S. reticulata* and *S. lapponum*. The original plant, still in the garden of Miss Boyd at Melrose, is only 3 feet in height after all these years. It makes a small erect, stiff, dwarf tree with a distinct bole, rounded and

gnarled, giving the appearance of extreme old age. Leaves entire, alternate, wide obovate to cordate, blunt, deeply veined, grey-white due to covering of fine down on both sides. Catkins erect, oval, silky pale yellow. May.

S. herbacea. (D).
A prostrate shrublet with radiating round smooth stems, rarely 2 inches high. Leaves sparse, rarely above four on branches, alternate, oval, cordate at base with an indentation at apex, margins minutely dentate, veining reticulate, dark glossy green. Catkins on short pedicels, oblong, yellow. May. A native of Great Britain and Ireland.

S. myrsinites. (D).
A native of Europe including Scotland and Ireland, this is a semi-erect shrub of slender hairy stems up to 12 inches high, brown, shiny in adult state. Leaves alternate, oval, pointed at apex, tapered to base, margins minutely dentate, veining pronounced, light green. Catkins upright on small leafy stems, long, oval, reddish-yellow. May.

S. myrsinites var. jacquiniana. (D).
This is a geographical form from the Tyrol, differing from the type in having entire leaves and deep orange-red catkins. May.

S. myrtilloides. (D).
It is essential to get a dwarf form of this species, for it is very variable, ranging in size from 3 inches to over 3 feet. A much-branched twiggy shrublet with smooth stems. Leaves alternate, entire, oblong, pointed at apex, rounded at base, margins incurved, mid-olive green above, reddish-blue below. Catkins on small leafy stems, almost sessile, long, narrow, rounded at apex. April. A native of high altitudes in N. Europe.

S. myrtilloides var. pedicellaris. (D). (Syn. *S. pedicellaris*).
This is a geographical form from N. America, differing from the type in having long, narrow leaves, rounded at apex and not pointed.

S. pedicellaris, see *S. myrtilloides* var. *pedicellaris*.

S. polaris. (D).
A true arctic species from the Polar regions. It is near to *S. herbacea*, quite prostrate, adhering to the contours of rock formations. The leaves are smaller and entire.

S. reticulata. (D).
One of the best species of the genus, making a dwarf rock-hugging shrublet rarely above an inch or so high of congested, angled, smooth, brownish branches. Leaves alternate on short stalks, up to four on stem, sparse, oval to rounded; margins irregular, occasionally tapered at apex, crinkled, green above, greyish-white with deep reticulated veins beneath. Catkins on lax stalks at apex of twigs, oval to globular, yellow. May. A native of Europe including Scotland.

S. retusa. (D).
A much-branched procumbent shrublet only an inch or so high, with greenish-brown smooth stems. Leaves alternate, entire, long, oval,

roundish or blunt, tapered to base, smooth, dark glossy green, downy beneath. Catkins on small leafy stalks, oval, yellow. May. A native of C. and E. Europe.

S. serpyllifolia. (D).

A pygmy edition of *S. retusa* and often quoted as a dwarf form of that species. Quite prostrate, making a dense congested mat of smooth wiry stems. Leaves small, oval to orbicular, tapered or acute apex, margins slightly indentate, dark glossy green. Catkins on short leafy stalks, cylindrical, yellow. May. A native of Europe, often found in exposed positions at high altitudes as a tiny mass of congested twigs, almost scab like, the whole plant only an inch or so across but when introduced into cultivation it invariably reverts to type.

SANGUINARIA *(Papaveraceae).*

A monotypic genus, native of N. America, in cool woodlands where it displays its fleeting but delightful pure white flowers to great advantage. CULTIVATION. Compost C over good drainage, needs plenty of water during the growing season, keep just moist in winter; it requires shade and is best placed in a north-facing frame after flowering.
PROPAGATION. By careful division in March. Care should be taken not to break the thick fleshy roots at other periods, for the break will exude a red sap and this will weaken the plant. Repot carefully when necessary in April.

S. canadensis. (H).

The Bloodroot forms a thick, tuberous creeping horizontal rootstock and from each bud is produced a single large reniform, scalloped, pale bluey-grey leaf. Flowers solitary, before the leaves are fully expanded, on 4-inch stems, large, open chalices of up to twelve petals, pure white. April.

S. canadensis 'Flora Plena'. (H).

This is the rare double form with a rounded head of glistening white, comprised of up to fifty petals.

SANTOLINA *(Compositae).*

A small genus of shrubs which add interest to the alpine house with their dainty sometimes silvery foliage and heads of yellow flowers. All are intensely aromatic thus adding to their charm and usefulness.
CULTIVATION. Compost A will be found suitable with good drainage, plenty of water during the growing and flowering season, reducing this in late August when they benefit from a dry period at this time; keep dry but not arid in winter.
PROPAGATION. By green cuttings taken with a heel in June. Repot every year in April.

S. chamaecyparissus. (E).

This is a much-branched bushy shrublet up to 18 inches high, commonly known as Lavender Cotton, with erect stems covered with a thick white

wool. Leaves pinnatisect, dense on short twigs, alternate, long narrow, dentate, grey-green, covered with a thick white wool. Flowers in great profusion, solitary on long slender stems, rounded mop-heads, without ray florets, golden-yellow. June–July. A native of the Mediterranean area.
S. chamaecyparissus 'Nana'. (E).
A much smaller and more desirable variety with intensely silvered foliage, less than 8 inches high. Flowers on short slender stems, golden, half-suns. July. Garden origin.
S. leucantha, see *S. pinnata*.
S. pinnata. (E). (Syn. *S. leucantha*).
Not so showy as the other species, it makes an upright shrub about 18 inches high with slender bushy twigs, quite devoid of wool. Leaves on short stalks, crowded, pinnate, segments small, long, narrow, in rows of four glabrous, mid-green. Flowers on erect stems up to three on short stalks, rounded, creamy white. July. A native of Italy.

SAPONARIA (*Caryophyllaceae*).

The Soapworts are a genus of plants which have an affinity to Dianthus and Gypsophila, and the majority of them are suitable for the rock garden, but there are a few plants which are ideal for pan culture in the alpine house or frame, and at least one of them will tax the skill of the cultivator.
CULTIVATION. Compost A over good drainage, a normal supply of water during the growing season, keep dry but not arid in winter.
PROPAGATION. By cuttings with a heel of the old wood in July. Repot only when necessary.
S. caespitosa. (E).
A native of the Pyrenees, this makes a tight compact cushion only an inch or so high. Leaves in tufts, radical, linear, acute, glabrous, minutely dentate. Flowers in small umbels, open star-shaped with notched, narrow petals. Pink. May–June.
S. cypria. (E).
A native of Cyprus, making a mat of leaves in tufts. Basal leaves spatulate, obtuse, grey, stem leaves smaller, oblong-linear. Flowers in small cymes on 2-inch stems, starry, rose-pink. May–June.
S. pumila. (E). (Syn. *Silene pumila*; *S. pumilio*).
A rare and difficult species from the European Alps, forming a dense compact cushion from a central branching rootstock. Leaves in rosettes, thick, narrow, linear, light green, glabrous. Flowers solitary, on short two-leaved stems, large for size of plant, open five-lobed petals, rose with inflated calyx. May–June. This plant is more permanent if grown in compost D taking care that it does not become waterlogged.

SAXIFRAGA (*Saxifragaceae*).

A large and varied genus of plants, the Rockfoils have provided the alpine gardener with a great number of species, hybrids and varieties, which are quite rightly stated to be the backbone of a collection of alpine house plants. Strange as it may seem, taking into consideration the dwarf, compact habit possessed by these cushion-like plants of this genus, today they do not find the support amongst the newer generation of alpine gardeners. Is it because for the most part, they are too easy? Somehow the 12-inch pans that used to be a feature of the alpine shows, prior to the last war, seem strangely lacking now.

There is no doubt that for cultivators who are just beginning to grow a collection of alpines in pans, saxifrages will provide both the easy and not so easy plants with which to test their ability and skill, and dare one say, even a genus in which to specialise, for there is a need for a dedicated cultivator to grow a really representative collection of the many species and hybrids in which this large race abounds. That the species, hybrids and varieties listed here are not complete would soon be apparent to a specialist, but space forbids a fully comprehensive survey as the number of named hybrids alone is too numerous. What is attempted is a general overall picture of worthwhile plants, fully realising that one man's meat is another man's poison! There are enough enumerated to whet the appetite of the average collector, adding as titbits a few difficult plants that have not only given me great fun in growing but have also been the instigators of many arguments amongst friends at shows.

In nature they have a wide distribution in the north and south temperate and arctic zones, Asia and spasmodically in South America, but are entirely absent from Australia and South Africa. Covering as they do such large areas of the world's mountain ranges, it is apparent that they will have diverse shapes and sizes suitable to their environment in their natural habitats. These variations have enabled botanists to divide them into fifteen sections, and this alone will give some idea of their different formations. It is not proposed to give a complete account of their botanical differences, but by enumerating these singly, and adding cultural notes as well as only dealing with the sections that apply to plants suitable for alpine house or frame culture, much repetition when dealing with the plants will be avoided. All are evergreen except where noted.

HIRCULUS Section.
Mat forming, rarely in rosette formation, oval undivided leaves, deciduous. Flowers yellow to orange on leafy stems.
CULTIVATION. These species are best in compost D with a constant supply of water at all times, especially when in growth. They do not mind sun as long as there is plenty of water present.
PROPAGATION. By seed sown in February, compost 2. Repot only when necessary after flowering.

DACTYLOIDES Section.
Contains the so-called Mossy saxifrages which make cushions of soft

rosettes with cleft leaves either hairy or glabrous. Flowers ranging from white, pink to deep red.

CULTIVATION. All require plenty of water in the growing season, keep dryish but not arid in winter, compost A will suit and the cushions should be top-dressed in spring to prevent the centres from drying off. Shade is essential in summer. Repot every year after flowering.

PROPAGATION. By careful division in spring; green cuttings in June or seed sown in February, compost 1.

TRACHYPHYLLUM Section.

Small mat-forming species, leaves narrow not divided, margins bristly, apex pointed. Flowers large white, yellow to deep yellow on few-branched stems.

CULTIVATION. Requires lime-free conditions in compost A with plenty of water during the growing season, just moist at other periods; half-shade in summer. Repot every second year.

PROPAGATION. By seed sown in February, compost 2.

XANTHIZOON Section.

Contains all the many forms of *S. aizoides*, making loose mats of stems, leaves linear, oblong, dentate or bristly margins, rarely or only in loose rosettes. Flowers pale to deep yellow, sometimes purple or deep red, solitary or in loose cymes.

CULTIVATION. Compost A with plenty of water, moist only from September to April. Half-shade in summer. Repot only when necessary after flowering.

PROPAGATION. By cuttings in June.

EUAIZOONIA Section.

This contains all the silver saxifrages with their bold outstanding rosettes of broad or narrow strap-like leaves, normally heavily encrusted with lime pits. Most rosettes form offsets, the flowering one dying. Flowers in large branching panicles, often spotted, white, pink, red, rarely yellow.

CULTIVATION. Compost A will suit all species, hybrids and varieties and a small amount of lime rubble can be added if required, although my own experience is that they do just as well without it. Water in plenty is needed during the growing and flowering season, keep dry but not arid in winter. All appreciate some shade in summer when grown in pans. Repot when necessary after flowering.

PROPAGATION. By division in spring or taking rosettes, as cuttings in June.

KABSCHIA Section.

Forming tight mounds of either tufted linear leaved, or broader obtuse, or rounded rosettes. Flowers on short, sometimes almost sessile stems, singly or a few on branched stems, large, clear coloured white, yellow, pink, lilac or red.

CULTIVATION. These plants will do well in compost A over faultless drainage, requiring to be kept moist during the growing and flowering season, keep dryish but not arid in winter. They appreciate top-dressing immediately after flowering with the same compost. Shading is necessary for all members of this section, especially during hot weather, for they burn quickly if neglected during this period. Repot only when necessary after flowering as root restriction helps to maintain close compact cushions. With old-established plants which would be difficult to move safely, a bi-weekly watering with liquid manure will be appreciated during the growing and flowering season.

PROPAGATION. Best accomplished by detaching rosettes in late May and rooting these in a closed frame. Seed is not really satisfactory for the Kabschias readily cross with each other, but if seedlings are required, it is best sown in February, compost 2.

ENGLERIA Section. (More correctly sub-section Mediae, Kabschia group.)

This section contains plants with flatter more rounded rosettes, generally of silver-grey, very symmetrical in formation. Flowers on leafy, glandular coloured stems, flowers normally rather small but enhanced by the large, baggy highly-coloured glandular calyces around them.

CULTIVATION. Similar to Kabschia section, but they can be repotted more frequently if required after flowering.

PROPAGATION. By cuttings in May or seed will breed true if the flowering plants are isolated, this is best sown in February, compost 2.

PORPHYRION Section.

Prostrate rambling mat-forming plants only showing signs of rosette formation at end of stems, leaves opposite, spreading or recurved, apex often ciliate. Flowers either singly or a few on short, or almost sessile stems, red-purple or rarely white forms.

CULTIVATION. Requires an open medium, compost A, with plenty of moisture during the growing and flowering season, keep just moist at other periods. Top-dressing is essential to keep them in good health, this is best carried out in early spring. They are best in a cool spot after flowering and detest alpine house conditions in the summer. Repot only when necessary after flowering.

PROPAGATION. Division after flowering or cuttings in late May.

S. 'Ada' (Kabschia). (*S. tombeanensis* × *S. burseriana* 'Crenata').
Garden origin, compact, close silvery-grey hummocks. Flowers two or three on stiff 2-inch stems, rounded, white. April.

S. adenodes. (Dactyloides).
A native of the Andes, forming tight mossy cushions, foliage oblong-lanceolate, obtuse, covered with sticky glandular hairs. Flowers rounded, white on short stems. May.

S. 'Affinis'. (Kabschia). (Parentage unknown).
A fine hybrid raised by Suedermann, compact small rosettes of grey-green leaves. Flowers on small stems, white. April.

S. aizoides var. atrorubens (Xanthizoon).
This form has bright green, thin, oblong, linear leaves, the rosettes in a loose mat bearing sprays of blood red flowers on 3-inch stems. May.

S. aizoides var. autumnalis.
More compact than the type, forming close cushions of green, linear foliage and orange flowers on 2-inch stems. June.

S. aizoon var. baldensis, see *S. aizoon* var. *minutifolia.*

S. aizoon var. hirsuta. (Euaizoonia). (Syn. *S.a.* var. *tyrrhenica*).
A native of Corsica, with compact grey-green rosettes covered with tiny hairs. Flowers on 6-inch hairy stems, creamy with a few red spots. June.

S. aizoon var. hirtella. (Syn. *S.a.* var. *tyrrhenica hirtella*).
Similar to *S.a.* var. *hirsuta* but smaller in all its parts. June.

S. aizoon var. minor.
This is a small form from middle Europe, with close compact rosettes of grey-green, spatulate leaves and on 3-inch stems, creamy white flowers. June.

S. aizoon var. minutifolia (Syn. *S.a.* var. *baldensis*).
A native of Mount Baldi, Lombardy, it makes prostrate congested rosettes of minute, thick, ash-grey, broadly spatulate red leaves below, topped with sprays of creamy white flowers on 2-inch stems. June.

S. aizoon var. rosea.
This Bulgarian form makes rosettes of deep green, strap-shaped leaves, heavily margined with silver, pointed at apex, reddish towards base and bears 9-inch sprays of deep pink flowers in June.

S. aizoon var. tyrrhenica, see *S. aizoon* var. *hirsuta.*

S. aizoon var. tyrrhenica hirtella, see *S. aizoon* var. *hirtella.*

S. aizoon var. venetia.
Another small form from the Venetian Alps, with close congested rosettes of small dull green spatulate leaves heavily encrusted with silver, underneath a deep brown-red. Flowers on 3-inch stems on ample sprays, white. June.

S. 'Allenii'. (Kabschia).
A garden hybrid, reputed to have as one parent *S. burseriana* 'Crenata', the other unknown, making hummocks of congested spiny grey rosettes and creamy flowers with crinkled margins. April.

S. 'Amitie'. (Kabschia). (*S. lilacina* × *S. dalmatica*).
This hybrid makes compact silvery green cushions and lilac flowers on 2-inch stems, fading to white. March.

S. amoena. (Dactyloides).
A miniature mossy, of bright green soft cushions with pink flowers on short stems. A native of Europe, requires a cool spot in summer. May.

S. andersonii. (Kabschia).
A native of Sikkim, where it makes loose cushions of rosettes, crowded,

tiny, spatulate, imbricated, recurved, grey-green leaves. Flowers on 2-inch stems, up to four pink. April.

S. 'Arco Valleyi'. (Kabschia). (*S. lilacina* × *S. burseriana 'Minor'*).
Makes a humped cushion of silver-grey rosettes, topped with soft rose flowers on 2-inch stems. March.

S. aretioides. (Kabschia).
A native of the Pyrenees, with tight hard grey-green uneven hummocks of small rosettes. Flowers in a few-flowered corymb on 2-inch stems, yellow with baggy calyces. April.

S. aretioides var. primulina, see *S. diapensioides* var. *lutea*.

S. 'Assimilis'. (Kabschia).
A hybrid of unknown parentage making dense silver-grey cushions topped with rounded white flowers on 1-inch stems. March.

S. aspera. (Trachyphyllum).
This is a charming European species making open mats of mossy rosettes, leaves bright green, margined with bristles. Flowers in small heads which are borne on elongated shoots from the rosettes, straw coloured with orange dots. June.

S. aspera var. bryoides.
A miniature edition, of closer compact habit, flowers often single on un-branched stems, yellow with red dots. June.

S. 'Bellisant'. (Kabschia).
A fine hybrid, parentage uncertain, with hard spiny hummocks of grey-green foliage. Flowers on 2-inch stems, large, rounded, light rose. March.

S. 'Bertolonii'. (*S. stribrnyi* × *S. porophylla thessalica*).
An Engleria hybrid, with tight rosettes of spiny silver-grey leaves and on glandular stems often stained with purple in a raceme, flowers of purple-red. April.

S. 'Biasolettii'. (*S. porophylla thessalica* × *S. grisebachii*).
Another charming Engleria hybrid with medium-sized rosettes of over-lapping silvered leaves which elongate into glandular stems bearing a spike of pendant red flowers and crimson-haired bracts. April.

S. 'Bilekii'. (*S. ferdinandi-coburgii* × *S. tombeanensis*).
A Kabschia hybrid with iron-hard hummocks of small, grey-green, linear, acute, incurved leaves in rosettes. Flowers few, pale yellow, on short glandular stems. April.

S. blepharophylla. (Porphyrion).
This is a rare plant from the Central Alps of Europe with rosettes of dark green obtuse leaves, margins hairy. Flowers almost stemless, starry red-purple. April. Requires care in cultivation, should never be allowed to dry out and needs frequent top-dressing with a mixture of leaf-mould and coarse sand.

S. 'Boekleri'. (*S. ferdinandi-coburgii* × *S. stribrnyi*).
This is a Kabschia-Engleria hybrid with small congested flattish light green rosettes. Flowers on 3-inch glandular stems, orange flushed red. April.

S. 'Borisii'. (*S. ferdinandi-coburgii* × *S. marginata*).
This Kabschia hybrid makes close cushions of neat rosettes with bluish-grey leaves. Flowers, fine rounded lemon-yellow, up to four on 2-inch red stems. April.

S. boryi. (Kabschia).
A native of the Grecian Alps, this species is akin to *S. marginata* with close grey-green rosettes, topped on 2-inch stems with up to five large well-formed flowers of a glistening white. April.

S. 'Boydii'. (*S. aretioides* × *S. marginata* var. *rocheliana*).
A charming Kabschia hybrid, raised by that great plantsman the late Dr Boyd at Kelso, Scotland. It forms close compact rosettes of blue-grey, from which spring the red-tinged flower stems, bearing the large, rounded, lemon-yellow flowers. April. This hybrid is now becoming rare, owing to great care being needed in its cultivation, for all the true plants are from that original cross, as further crosses have failed to produce plants with the large flowers of good substance.

S. 'Boydii Alba'. (*S. burseriana* × *S. marginata* var. *rocheliana*).
Another Kabschia hybrid from the late Dr Boyd's garden, forming compact rosettes of light grey leaves and up to three large white flowers of a good form on 2-inch stems. April.

S. burseriana. (Kabschia).
The typical plant is well-known and is widely distributed over the eastern European Alps, where it makes congested hard hummocks of spiny silver-grey to grey-green leaves and on 2-inch red stems, bearing up to three red buds, opening to sparkling white flowers. April.
Garden and wild varieties of *Saxifraga burseriana:*

'Crenata'.
A smaller form with crimped and notched flowers on 2-inch stems. April.

'Gloria'.
Another outstanding form with brilliant red stems and large white flowers. April.

'His Majesty'.
Possibly wrongly named, reputed to be a hybrid, but it must be included for its charm and beauty with silver-grey rosettes and large rounded pink flushed white flowers. April.

'Magna', see *S.b.* 'Major'.

'Major'. (Syn. *S.b.* 'Magna').
Similar to the type with the exception of the flower stem which is green not red and the large white flowers are solitary. April.

var. minor.
A really small edition of the type with glistening white flowers. April. A native of the Karawankens.

'Sulphurea'.
Here again this form may be a hybrid of unknown parentage with its

greeny-grey spiny rosettes, red stems and large crenulated flowers of a pale yellow. March.

var. tridentata, see *S.b.* var. *tridentina.*

var. tridentina. (Syn. *S.b.* var. *tridentata*).
This is a huge flowered form from Italy and with its ample glistening white flowers on red stems is a 'must'.

S. 'Buttercup'. (*S.* 'Haagii' × *S.* 'Faldonside').
A hybrid which itself has two hybrid parents, producing iron-tight cushions of dark green needle leaves and on 2-inch stems, bright yellow flowers of good substance and form. April.

S. caesia. (Kabschia).
Forms tight compact low spreading cushions of small congested rosettes with tiny grey-green leaves, well furnished with lime pits. Flowers rounded, pure white on branching 2-inch stems. May. A native of the Pyrenees and Eastern Alps.

S. caesia var. baldensis.
From the Trentino Alps, this is similar to the type but with more flowers on glandular stems. May.

S. caesia var. subacaulis.
Even smaller than the type with the white flowers borne on solitary stems. May.

S. callosa. (Euaizoonia). (Syn. *S. lingulata*).
The finest of the encrusted silver saxifrages with outstanding symmetrical rosettes, gracefulness of flowering stem and purity of flower. It makes humped rosettes of many long, narrow outstanding blue-grey leaves, thickening to recurved acute tips and densely silvered margins. Flowers on 12-inch arching glabrous red stems, one sided panicles of pure white. June. A native of the Maritime Alps it requires shade in cultivation.

S. callosa var. bellardii.
A form from the S.W. Alps and Appennines with mat-like habit and no regular rosettes; leaves long, narrow, blue-grey with silver margins. Flowers on arching stems in panicles, white. June.

S. callosa var. catalaunica. (Syn. *S. catalaunica*).
With large rosettes, leaves not so numerous as in the type, dark green, wide, thick, slightly grooved, apex pointed, enmarginated with silver beads. Flowering-stem stiff, more erect, reddish, viscid, up to 12 inches high, flowers white in a large panicle. June. A native of N.E. Spain.

S. callosa var. lantoscana. (Syn. *S. lantoscana*).
A smaller edition of the type, the rosette leaves are shorter, broader, more recurved with swollen tips, dark green with a touch of grey, margins heavily encrusted with lime. Flowers on 8-inch arching stems, one sided, very dense, pure white. June. Requires more shade than the others.

S. cartilaginea. (Euaizoonia).
The typical species is a native of the Caucasus, where it forms fine 2-inch rosettes of stout, leathery, green, silver encrusted leaves, pointed at apex,

margins crenulate. Flowers on stiff, upright, much-branched, 6-inch stems, in oval panicles, starry white. June.

S. cartilaginea var. kolenatiana, see *S. kolenatiana.*

S. cartilaginea 'Major'.
A larger form, rosettes up to 3 inches across with open branched stems up to 12 inches high and red flowers in a panicle. June.

S. cartilaginea 'Minor'.
Similar to the major but smaller in all its parts with the flowering stem not exceeding 4 inches. June.

S. catalaunica, see *S. callosa catalaunica.*

S. cebenensis. (Dactyloides). (Syn. *S. prostiana*).
A rare species from the Alps of central France, where it makes close compact mounds of dark green rosettes, leaves glandular, sticky, emit a delightful fragrance of lemon. In May on 1-inch thread stems are borne the substantial rounded, glistening white flowers. Not difficult to grow, provided it is kept on the dry side in winter and given half-shade after flowering.

S. 'Cecil Davis'. (*S. longifolia* × *S. aizoon*).
This is one of the best Euaizoonia hybrids with its outstanding symmetrical, flattish rosettes of leathery, blue-grey, broadly spatulate foliage, heavily encrusted and pitted with lime, abruptly pointed at apex. Flowers of white on 6-inch reddish stems in panicles. June.

S. 'Cerise Queen'. (Syn. *S.* 'Christine').
This is a Kabschia hybrid of unknown parentage with hard compact cushions of grey-green leaves and on 1-inch stems flowers of bright cerise-red. April.

S. 'Cherry Trees'. (*S. aretioides* × *S. marginata* var. *rocheliana*).
Another of the Kabschia hybrids raised by the late Dr Boyd, it is now becoming enfeebled with age and needs careful cultivation. Forms hard hummocks of grey-green leaves and on 1-inch stems fine golden-yellow, rounded flowers. April.

S. 'Christine'. see *S.* 'Cerise Queen'.

S. chrysantha. (Hirculus).
One of the rare American saxifrages from the Rocky Mountains, where it makes small clumps of little rosettes with green thyme-like leaves. Flowers borne on dainty thread-like 1-inch stems, golden-yellow. May. A difficult plant to grow successfully, requires plenty of moisture in the growing season and must be kept moist in the winter. One part finely chopped sphagnum moss mixed with compost D helps to maintain good health. Needs shade in summer.

S. × churchillii. (*S. hostii* × *aizoon*).
This is a natural hybrid found in the eastern Alps, where it makes large rosettes of long, narrow, very stiff, grey-green leaves, margins heavily silvered. Flowers on 9-inch, slightly pubescent stems, large, white. May.

S. 'Clarkei'. (*S. vandellii* × *S. media*).
A Suendermann–Kabschia hybrid, with small congested rosettes of grey-green leaves and rose-red flowers borne on 2-inch stems. March.

S. cochlearis. (Euaizoonia).
The species typical is a plant of strong lime-encrusted rosettes in dense congested hummocks from the Maritime Alps and bearing glistening white flowers on one sided branching red stems. May.

S. cochlearis var. major.
This is a much larger plant but just as desirable with fine white flowers on red stems. May.

S. cochlearis var. minor. (Syn. *S. probynii*).
On the other hand this form is as small as *S.c.* var. *major* is large, and a good pan plant. Leaves more glaucous than the type plant. This plant often does duty for *S. valdensis*, but one difference is that in *S. cochlearis* the leaves of the rosettes are always distinct and apart, with apex rounded, whereas in *S. valdensis* they are tightly pressed together and with thickened pointed apex.

S. corymbosa. (Engleria).
A native of Bulgaria and Asia Minor, this species makes rosettes of grey-green narrow leaves, broadly tipped at apex and margins pitted with lime. Flowers yellow on 3 inch glandular stems from green glandular baggy calyces. May.

S. corymbosa var. luteo-viridis. (Syn. *S.* × *luteo-viridis*).
A form from the Carpathians and Transylvania, similar to the type but the leaves are narrower and acutely pointed at tip with yellow flowers and green calyces on 6-inch stems. May.

S. cotyledon. (Euaizoonia).
This species has a wide distribution in nature over Western Europe and north into Norway and Iceland, thus giving rise to several good forms, all of which are extremely decorative in the alpine house where, if the foliage is kept dry, they repay by showing off their jewel-encrusted leaves. The typical plant makes large, flattish rosettes of broad, obtuse, or rounded, silver-grey finely toothed leaves, heavily encrusted with lime pits. Flowers on curved reddish stems, up to 2 feet tall in good forms, in grand panicles, glistening white with greenish tinged centres. June.

S. cotyledon var. caterhamensis.
This is a large form from Norway, just as fine rosettes with broader leaves but having the white flowers very heavily spotted with red, on stout stems. June.

S. cotyledon var. icelandica.
If confined to one rosette, by removing offsets for propagating purposes and not allowing the plant to flower for at least two seasons, it will make a specimen which will gain envious glances from fellow enthusiasts with the large blue-grey rosette and a flower spike which will reach up to 3 feet of pure white flowers. June. Place of origin is unknown, but it is doubtful whether it came from Iceland.

S. cotyledon var. norvegica.
A form from Norway, which makes large broad leaf rosettes of silver-grey, pointed tipped leaves and on red stems up to 18 inches, white spotted red flowers in quantity. June.

S. cotyledon var. pauciflora.
A native of high mountains in Sweden and the Pyrenees, this is the smallest of the cotyledons, but in cultivation it certainly has a tendency to grow larger than in its native habitat. Similar to the type but with small rosettes and proportionately-sized stem and white flowers. Rarely exceeds 12 inches. June.

S. cotyledon var. pyramidalis.
An outstanding form from the Pyrenees, which makes large broad leaf blue-grey rosettes topped by panicles of large glistening white flowers in pyramidical form. The rosettes turn to mahogany-red in winter when kept on the dry side. June.

S. 'Cranborne'.
A Kabschia of unknown parentage, raised by Messrs Pritchard of Christchurch, making hard domed cushions of grey-green rosettes and on 1-inch stems outstanding well-rounded deep pink flowers. March.

S. 'Delia'. (*S.* × *godroniana* × *S. lilacina*).
This hybrid Kabschia makes close congested hummocks of tiny obtuse leaves in rosette formation and on 1-inch stems, white lilac tinged flowers. April.

S. diapensioides. (Kabschia).
One of the best species, from the S.W. European Alps, extremely slow growing, making prostrate scabs of iron-hard rosettes of blue-grey obtuse leaves and on 1-inch stems are one, sometimes two, large well formed milk-white flowers. May–June. Be careful of winter wet for this species, as it will quickly show its dislike by dying off.

S. diapensioides var. lutea (Syn. *S. aretioides* var. *primulina*).
The yellow form of *S. diapensioides* is the one more commonly met with in collections but its actual origin is unknown, for there is no record of where it came from. It is similar to the species but with large yellow flowers. May–June. Needs same cultural care.

S. 'Doerfleri'. (*S. grisebachii* × *S. stribrnyi*).
An Engleria hybrid with medium-sized symmetrical rosettes of grey, obtuse leaves with marginal lime-pits and on 3-inch glandular stems fine red-purple flowers from deeper baggy calyces. April.

S. 'Dr Ramsey'. (*S. longifolia* × *S. cochlearis*).
This is an outstanding Euaizoonia hybrid, making large, extremely symmetrical silver-grey rosettes, encrusted and margined with lime. Flowers are borne in sprays on arching 12-inch stems, large, pure white. June.

S. 'Edithae'. (*S. marginata* × *S. stribrnyi*).
This is an Engleria, Kabschia hybrid, raised by Suendermann, making close

hummocks of grey-green rosettes and nice rounded pink flowers on 2-inch stems. April.

S. × 'Elysium'. (*S. × godroniana × S. lilacina*).
Another Kabschia hybrid, which is a very minute plant, making tiny silver-grey iron-hard domes and on 1-inch stems rose-pink flowers. March.

S. × engleri. (*S. hostii × S. crustata*).
This is a natural Euaizoonia hybrid from the Carinthian and Venetian Alps, with medium-sized rosettes of strap-like silver-grey leaves and white flowers on much-branched 12-inch stems. June.

S. erioblasta, see *S. globulifera* var. *erioblasta.*

S. 'Esther'. (*S. cochlearis × S. aizoon lutea*).
A charming Euaizoonia hybrid with fine rosettes of slender leaves of silver-grey, heavily encrusted with lime and bearing on 6-inch slender arching stems, sprays of light yellow flowers. May.

S. 'Etheline'. (*S. tombeanensis × S. burseriana minor*).
This Kabschia hybrid has tight congested minute rosettes of silver-grey with white flowers, pink in bud stage, on thin, 1-inch thread-like stems. April.

S. 'Eudoxiana'. (*S. ferdinandi-coburgii × S. sancta*).
Another charming Kabschia hybrid, making rounded domes of spiny rosettes. Leaves silver-grey. Flowers light yellow on 2-inch stems. April.

S. exarata. (Dactyloides).
This scarce mossy, a native of the Pyrenees, Abruzzi and Balkan Mountains is a charming plant for alpine house culture, requiring a little skill to grow it successfully. It makes close neat cushions of rosettes with tripartite green leaves covered with sticky glandular hairs, the two side lobes are two-lobed, slightly aromatic and on 2-inch stems are borne several rounded white or cream flowers. May.

S. 'Faldonside'. (*S. aretioides × S. marginata rocheliana*).
Raised by Dr Boyd at Faldonside, Scotland, it is the finest of the yellow Kabschia hybrids, it forms tight iron-hard cushions of silver-grey spiny leaves and on 2-inch red stems, large, well formed, lemon-yellow flowers with wavy margins. March.

S. ferdinandi-coburgii. (Kabschia).
This Balkan species from the Rhodope Mountains has been used extensively in producing outstanding hybrids, but is itself a charming plant, making close cushions of spiny silver-grey leaves, followed by red buds on 2-inch stems which open to bright yellow flowers. March.

S. 'Fleischeri'. (*S. grisebachii × S. corymbosa* var. *luteo-viridis*).
An attractive Engleria hybrid with symmetrical rosettes of silver-grey and on 3-inch stems, spikes of bright orange-red flowers. April.

S. florulenta. (Euaizoonia).
An extremely rare monocarpic species from the Maritime Alps, where it

makes large symmetrical rosettes up to 4 inches across of overlapping, dark green, entire, upturned spine-tipped leaves. Flowers on much-branched, stiff pubescent stems, rosy-purple in a dense viscid spray, enclosed in baggy woolly calyces. May. It rarely flowers in cultivation, but seed is the only method of increase, the rosettes just becoming larger and larger. It is a difficult plant and requires very careful cultivation in shade, and dry conditions in winter, for any trace of moisture lodging in the centre of the rosettes is fatal.

S. × forsteri. (*S. caesia* × *S. mutata*).
A natural Kabschia from N. Tyrol, where it makes congested mounds of grey-green tiny rosettes. Flowers on frail stems up to three rounded, light golden-yellow. May. Rare in cultivation, needs care in a semi-shaded cool spot.

S. 'Fovant'. (*S. valdensis* × *S. longifolia* 'Tumbling Waters').
An outstanding silver-encrusted Euaizoonia hybrid saxifrage with flat congested rosettes nearly double the size of *S. valdensis*. Leaves spatulate, blue-grey, apex recurved and pointed, densely encrusted with lime pits. Flowers white, up to three on pubescent stems in a loose small spray. June.

S. 'Francis Cade'. (*S. cochlearis* × *S. callosa*).
A charming Euaizoonia hybrid with symmetrical radiating rosettes, leaves large, narrow, blue-grey, pointed at apex, well encrusted with silver. Flowers in one-sided sprays, pure white on 9-inch reddish stems. June.

S. × gaudinii. (*S. aizoon* × *S. cotyledon* var. *pyramidalis*).
A natural Euaizoonia hybrid from the Pyrenees and Central Alps, the rosettes resemble *S. cotyledon*, leaves leathery, strap-shape, widening towards apex, dentate. Flowers on 12-inch branching red pubescent stems, white with red spots. June.

S. 'Gem'. (*S. burseriana* 'Gloria' × *S.* 'Irvingii').
A fine Kabschia hybrid with close congested, spiny, grey rosettes and on 2-inch stems, flowers of pale pink with deeper eye. March.

S. globulifera var. erioblasta. (Dactyloides). (Syn. *S. erioblasta*).
A fine mat-making form of the species from Spain, with obovoid gem buds, densely clothed in silver-grey fur, opening into rosettes of bright green, slightly three-lobed leaves, turning red in winter. Flowers white on 1-inch thread stems. June.

S. globulifera var. oranensis. (Syn. *S. oranensis*).
A fine form from Oran, Algiers, this 'Mossy' saxifrage makes compact domes of oblong gem buds, glabrous outside, opening to rosettes of bright green palmate three cleft leaves. Flowers on 2-inch stems, clothed with few entire leaves and up to four rounded white flowers. June. Both these two forms require careful cultivation and seem to like a dry period after flowering when the rosettes shrink into gem buds. During the winter they must not be allowed to dry out.

S. 'Gloriosa'.
A hybrid Kabschia of unknown parentage but a very attractive plant. Makes tight, close cushions of silver-grey leaves and on 1-inch stems, rich red flowers, fading to pink with age. March.

S. × godroniana. (*S. aretioides* × *S. media*).
This natural hybrid from the Haute Garonne in the Pyrenees is a Kabschia-Engleria cross, with the rosettes in fine symmetrical formation, silver-grey and regular marginal lime-pits. Flowers on 3-inch glandular stems, yellow deepening to orange at base. April.

S. grisebachii. (Engleria).
A native of Macedonia, Greece and Albania, it is the finest of all the Englerias and makes an outstanding plant for alpine house or frame. The rosettes are large, up to 3 inches across, very symmetrical, silver-grey. Leaves spatulate, cartilaginous and heavily encrusted. The flowering rosette becomes crimson at the centre, then elongates into large leafy arching stems at the apex of which are carried the large baggy calyces and small rose flowers. All parts of the flowering stem, stem leaves and calyces are completely covered with crimson-red, glandular hairs. March.

S. grisebachii 'Wisley var.'
A form cultivated in the R.H.S. Gardens at Wisley for many years but it has been found wild in Albania. Much larger, with more intense colour and flowers not so hidden as in the type plant. March.

S. Gusmussii. (*S. porophylla* var. *thessalica* × *S. corymbosa* var. *luteoviridis*).
An Engleria hybrid raised by Suendermann with rosettes of narrow sharply pointed silver-grey leaves in a tight cluster. Flowers on 4-inch stems with small spatulate leaves, hairy, reddish-orange in colour. March. This plant is now becoming rare with age and requires careful cultivation and guarding against winter wet.

S. Hofmannii. (*S. burseriana* 'Major' × *S. porophylla* var. *thessalica*).
This is a Kabschia-Engleria hybrid, another of Suendermann's raising with congested rosettes of silver-grey leaves, narrow, spiny. Flowers on 4-inch stems, red-purple in colour. March.

S. hostii. (Euaizoonia).
A native of the Eastern and Southern Alps, forming large flattened rosettes. Leaves deep greyish-green, thick, narrow, apex obtuse, crimson at base in winter, margins beaded with incrustations. Flowers in corymbs on thickish 12-inch stems, white, rarely spotted pink. June.

S. hostii var. altissima.
A much larger form than the type, more upstanding, leaves long, recurving with freely branched 18-inch reddish stems and dense spires of cream spotted red flowers. June.

S. hostii var. rhaetica.
A geographical variant with narrower leaves, apex acute. Flowers similar to the type. June.

S. imbricata. (Kabschia).
From the Himalayas, a rare species similar to an Aretian Androsace with its tight congested cushions of small rosettes, leaves minute, imbricated, grey-green. Flowers almost sessile, rounded, white. April. Needs same care as an Aretian Androsace and is best in compost D.

S. 'Iris Prichard'. (*S.* × *godroniana* × *S. lilacina*).
A Kabschia hybrid with Engleria blood in the seed parent, making neat congested domes of grey tufts and flowers of apricot-rose on 3-inch reddish stems. April.

S. 'Irvingii'. (*S. burseriana* × *S. lilacina*).
This Kabschia hybrid is one of the first to flower in early spring, these often appearing in February. It makes rosettes in close tufts, leaves spiny blue-grey. Flowers on 1-inch stems, opening from bright pink buds to lilac-pink blossoms with a deeper eye.

S. 'Jenkinsae'. (*S. burseriana* × *S. lilacina*).
Similar to *S.* 'Irvingii', but slightly larger rosettes of grey-green and more prodigious in flowering. February.

S. juniperifolia. (Kabschia).
A Caucasian species, very variable in nature with rosettes of dark green needle-like leaves and bearing on 2-inch stems, small clusters of yellow flowers. May. The true plant, whatever its form always emits an aroma of the juniper berry when crushed.

S. 'Kathleen Pincent'.
Parentage unknown but it is almost certainly an Euaizoonia hybrid of *S. callosa* blood. It makes large, many leaved symmetrical rosettes of glossy, blue-green. Leaves spatulate with slightly recurving abrupt apex, margins lime-encrusted. Flowers on 12-inch reddish-brown stems, rose-pink. June.

S. 'kellereri'. (*S. burseriana* × *S. stribrnyi*).
This is a Kabschia-Engleria hybrid which has large silvery rosettes and on 4-inch stems, sprays of soft pink flowers. February.

S. 'kewensis'. (*S. burseriana* 'Macrantha' × *S. porophylla*).
Another Kabschia-Engleria cross, making tight rosettes of long wide grey leaves. Flowers on 3-inch stems, pale pink. February.

S. kolenatiana. (Euaizoonia). (Syn. *S. cartilaginea* var. *kolenatiana*).
A native of the Caucasus, closely related to *S. cartilaginea* but more lax, with large rosettes of long, broad, pale green acuminate leaves, red at apex. Flowers on 6-inch red stems, clothed with few lance-shaped leaves, bright rose. June.

S. kolenatiana var. atropurpurea.
This is a really rare form collected by the late Mr W. E. Th. Ingwersen in Daghestan, it is similar to the type but bears dark blood-red flowers. June. This plant requires care in cultivation and should be kept dry but not arid in winter.

S. kolenatiana. var. major. (Syn. *S. sendtneri*).
A larger edition of the type, flowers on 9-inch stems, red. June.

S. 'Lady Beatrix Stanley'. (*S.* × *godroniana* × *S. lilacina*).
A Kabschia hybrid with Engleria blood from the seed parent with fine dark green rosettes of neat overlapping leaves and large deep pink flowers on 1-inch stems. March.

S. 'Landaueri'.
The parentage of this obvious Engleria hybrid is unknown but it has fine symmetrical silver-grey rosettes, long spatulate, obtuse leaves. Flowers on 3-inch stems, white flushed pink. April.

S. lantoscana, see *S. callosa* var. *lantoscana*.

S. 'Laurent Ward'. (*S.* × *frederici-augustii* × *S. lilacina*).
An Engleria-Kabschia hybrid which makes flattish cushions of silver-grey rosettes and dark red flowers on 2-inch stems. March.

S. 'Leyboldii'. (*S. marginata* var. *rocheliana* × *S. vandellii*).
An extremely slow growing Kabschia hybrid, making compact iron-hard, hummocks of close imbricated rosettes, the leaves blue-grey. Flowers fine, rounded, white, on 2-inch stems. March.

S. lilacina. (Kabschia).
A charming native of the Western Himalayas, always creating interest when a well grown specimen is shown. It makes small, tight, mat-forming rosettes with minute, green leaves and almost sessile, clear lavender-blue flowers with a deeper eye. March. One of the more fastidious plants, demanding a lime-free medium and half-shade for its successful cultivation.

S. lingulata, see *S. callosa*.

S. longifolia. (Euaizoonia).
The most outstanding species of this section and only surpassed in the rosette formation by the rare and difficult *S. florulenta*. A native of the Pyrenees and Spain it is monocarpic, never forming offsets, so that seed is the only method of increase and it is absolutely necessary to take precautions that the plant does not hybridise with other silver saxifrages, for this it will do with the greatest of ease and the resultant plants will be anything but true *longifolia*. The symmetrical rosettes are large, up to 12 inches across by flowering time, this may be from five to seven years. Leaves long, linear or linear-lingulate, glabrous, blue-green, reflexed margins entire or slightly crenate to abrupt tip. Flowers on erect, stout, densely leafy pubescent stems, up to 2 feet high, white. The flowering panicle commences right from the base of the stem where it joins the rosette. June.

S. longifolia 'Walpole var'.
Known as Mt. Usher variety, this is a fine seedling possibly crossed with *S. callosa*, differing from the species in that it produces offsets but the flowering spike is smaller. June.

S. × **luteo-viridis,** see *S. corymbosa* var. *luteo-viridis*.

S. marginata. (Kabschia).
The type plant has a wide geographical distribution from Italy to the Balkans, tending to produce smaller forms as they go eastwards. The

Italian plant which does duty for the species typical, makes flat cushions of densely packed rosettes, leaves green, fleshy, obtuse, marginal bands of lime encrustations. Flowers on 2-inch leafy stems up to four large, pure white. April.

S. marginata. var. coriophylla.

This form, from the Carpathians to E. Greece, is smaller than the type, rosettes and leaves more congested, grey-green. Flowers on 2-inch leafy stems, rarely above two, pure white. April.

S. marginata var. karadzicensis.

A rare form from N. Albania, about the same size as *S. caesia* but can be distinguished from that species by the typical leafy 1-inch flowering stem which bears up to three glistening white flowers. May.

S. marginata var. rocheliana.

A native of Dalmatia, Albania and Greece, an even closer compact cushion with more obtuse leaves, shorter stems and smaller white flowers. May.

S. marginata var. rocheliana purpurea.

A small form, but with purple calyces and red buds opening to white rounded flowers. May.

S. marginata var. rocheliana lutea.

This is similar but with pale yellow flowers. May.

S. media (Engleria).

A native of the Pyrenees, making symmetrical rosettes of silver-grey 1-inch leaves and encrusted lime margins. Flowers, pink on 4-inch leafy stems, enclosed in deep red, woolly calyces. April.

S. 'Megasaeflora'.

This is a Kabschia hybrid of unknown parentage but the tight spiny grey-green rosettes are similar to *S. burseriana*. Flowers on 2-inch stems, petals thin but large, pink deepening towards their base. April.

S. montenegrina, see *S. porophylla* var. *montenegrina*.

S. 'Myra'. (*S. scardica* × *S. lilacina*).

A Kabschia hybrid with one of the deepest colours, the flowers being a bright cherry-red on 1-inch stems over compact rosettes of dense, grey-green leaves. March.

S. 'Obristii'. (*S. burseriana* × *S. marginata*).

A Kabschia hybrid making larger, more outstanding rosettes of grey-green leaves than *S. burseriana* and on 2-inch stems, up to four red-flushed buds opening to large, glistening white, well-rounded flowers. April.

S. oppositifolia. (Porphyrion).

This species has a wide and variable distribution over Europe including the British Isles, Northern Asia and America and with such a large geographical spread it is not surprising that there are a great number of forms. The type plant, if there can be but one, makes close congested mats of creeping stems densely clothed with the blunt to rounded keeled leaves, margins hairy. Flowers on almost non-existing stems, purple in great profusion.

April. All the forms do well in compost A with plenty of water during the growing and flowering season, just moist at other times. It needs top-dressing in early spring with the same compost, working this well down amongst the leaves.

Wild and garden varieties of *S. oppositifolia:*

var. alba.

The white form but unfortunately has only small starry flowers, sparsely produced. April.

blepharophylla.

A native of the central Alps with large oval to rounded concave leaves, marginal hairs incurving. Flowers large but of poor form, purple red. April.

var. latina.

A fine plant from Italy, with outstanding silver-green leaves and on 1-inch stems, large rose-pink flowers.

var. rudolphiana.

A rare and difficult form from high altitudes in the Gross Glockner range, making tight congested mats of upright shoots densely covered with over-lapping, rounded leaves and sessile cup-like, deep rose-purple flowers. April. Needs care in cultivation and is best in compost D which should be kept wet during the growing and flowering season, moist at other periods.

var. speciosa.

This is a good form from the southern Alps, making rather loose mats of opposite rounded green leaves and rich red rose flowers. April.

var. vaccariana.

An easy variety whose habitat is in the Graian Alps, making rambling mats of congested dark green leaves and completely covered with the deep red-purple cup-like stemless flowers in April.

'W.A. Clark'.

From the old nurseries of Backhouse of York, this is a close compact form with bright crimson rose flowers in April.

'Wetterhorn var'.

As the varietal name implies this originated from the Wetterhorn in the Bernese Oberland, with the typical foliage but densely covered with medium-sized outstanding rich crimson flowers. April.

S. oranensis, see *S. globulifera* var. *oranensis.*

S. pasumensis. (Hirculus).

A native of the Himalayas, this is a small rosette-forming species. Leaves oval to obovate, overlapping, margins ciliate, greyish-green. Flowers on a much-branched leafy stem, large star-shaped, bright yellow. May.

S. × patens. (*S. caesia* × *S. aizoides*).

This is a natural sectional hybrid of Kabschia and Xanthizoon and occurs where the two species meet in the Bavarian, Austrian and Dauphiné Alps. It makes loose rosettes of small flattish grey-green leaves and on 3-inch branching stems, flowers of a deep yellow. May.

S. × pectinata. (*S. aizoon × S. incrustata*).

This encrusted Euaizoonia hybrid makes rather ragged rosettes of flat, long narrow leathery, glossy dark blue-green leaves with serrated margins, acute, tip pointed. Flowers smallish on 6-inch brownish-red stems, creamy white. June. A natural hybrid from Carniola.

S. pentadactylis. (Dactyloides).

A 'Mossy' from the Spanish Pyrenees, which forms close low mats of aromatic viscid green leaves, quite devoid of hairs, these being three cleft and the two outer segments two cleft. Flowers on branching 2-inch stems, varying in number from three to thirty, white tinged yellow at base of petals. June. Requires compost D with plenty of water during the growing season, followed by a dryish period in August. This treatment helps to maintain a compact slow-growing plant.

S. 'Petraschii'. (*S. tombeanensis × S. marginata* var. *rocheliana*).

A Kabschia hybrid making tight dense hummocks of grey-green foliage and bearing on 2-inch stems, large rounded, white, crinkle-edged flowers. April.

S. porophylla. (Engleria).

An Italian species, which has several geographical forms, all good plants for the alpine house. The species makes fine symmetrical flattish rosettes of spatulate glaucous leaves. Flowering stem up to 6 inches high, two-thirds clothed with narrow spatulate glandular hairy leaves. Flowers on upper third, pink, enclosed in baggy purple calyces. April.

S. porophylla var. montenegrina. (Syn. *S. montenegrina*).

A native of Montenegro and Albania, this is similar to *S. grisebachii*, but smaller in all its parts. Making fine rosettes, rounded, of broad silver-grey leaves, rounded apex with tip margins lime encrusted. Flowers similar to the species. April.

S. porophylla var. sibthorpiana.

From the southern Balkans, rosette leaves spatulate, wide, acute, glaucous. Flowers on 6-inch heavy glandular stems, dark purple calyces covering pale purple flowers. April.

S. porophylla var. thessalica.

A native of Montenegro and Greece, this makes close rosettes in hummocks, silver-grey, with 6-inch flowering stems, partly clothed with narrow glandular hairy foliage. Flowers rose-pink, enclosed in baggy, purple calyces. April.

S. porophylla var. thessalica alpina.

This is a form from Montenegro, which is less than half the size of *S.p. thessalica* but otherwise similar. April.

S. × 'Portae'. (*S. crustata × S. aizoon*).

This encrusted Euaizoon hybrid makes close set rosettes of narrow sage-green leaves with acute teeth, widening towards apex, less incurved. Flowers on 6-inch reddish hairy stems are in open creamy spikes. June.

S. pravislavia. (Kabschia).
A native of Macedonia, where it forms hard hummocks of deep green rosettes of spiny leaves. Flowers rounded, deep yellow on 2-inch stems. April.

S. probynii, see *S. cochlearis* var. *minor.*

S. 'Prosenii'.
An Engleria hybrid of unknown parentage making small imbricated rosettes of grey-green. Flowers on 2-inch branching stems, bright orange, produced over a long period. April–May.

S. prostiana, see *S. cebenensis.*

S. retusa. (Porphyrion).
A densely tufted woody mat of prostrate stems, leaves oval to oblong, lanceolate, overlapping. Flowers on 2-inch branching stems, small clusters, ruby-red, starry. April. A native of the Pyrenees.

S. 'Riverslea'. (*S. lilacina* × *S. porophylla*).
This is a grand Kabschia-Engleria hybrid which makes iron-hard domes of silver-grey leaves. Flowers on 1-inch stems, large, deep purple-rose. March.

S. scardica. (Kabschia).
A native of Greece and Macedonia, it forms hard dome-like mounds of columnar rosettes, leaves spiny, blue-grey, margins lime-pitted. Flowers on 3-inch sparsely leafed stems, in small flattish umbels, pure white. May.

S. scardica obtusa.
A smaller form differing from the type in having less spiny foliage and the rosettes are more spreading and mat-like. Flowers white. May.

S. 'Schottii'. (*S. corymbosa* var. *luteo-viridis* × *S. stribrnyi*).
This is an Engleria hybrid making small tufted rosettes of narrow, broadly-pointed grey-green leaves. Flowers on 3-inch branching glandular stems covered with red hairs, yellow. April.

S. scleropoda. (Kabschia).
From the W. Caucasus, this species makes tufted rosettes of long imbricated acute green leaves, erect in juvenile state, recurved in adult. Flowers on 2-inch stems in a small cluster, yellow. Petals and sepals equal length with projecting anthers. April.

S. sendtneri, see *S. kolenatiana* var. *major.*

S. 'Splendida'. (*S. cotyledon* × *S. longifolia*).
An Euaizoonia hybrid of large fine symmetrical rosettes, leaves thick, long, narrow, broader at apex, acutely pointed, smooth, blue-green, deeply lime-pitted, reflexed, margins entire. Flowers on 6-inch stout pubescent stems in a loose spray, white. June.

S. spruneri. (Kabschia).
Makes crowded cushions of grey-green rosettes, leaves thick, obtuse at apex, margins covered with glandular hairs. Flowers on 2-inch stems in flattish head, white. May. A native from the Thessalian Olympus and Bulgaria.

S. squarrosa. (Kabschia).

A really minute plant, certainly the smallest of the Kabschias, with its tiny flattish rosettes of grey leaves. Flowers on 2-inch glandular branching stems, white. June. A native of the Tyrol, it is not an easy plant in cultivation and requires similar conditions to the Aretian androsaces, so is best planted in compost D where it will amaze with its slowness of growth.

S. stribrnyi. (Engleria).

This species from the Rhodope Mountains, Bulgaria, makes fine rounded rosettes of silver-grey broad leaves. Flowers pink on 3-inch, branched glandular stems, enclosed in shaggy purple calyces. April.

S. stribrnyi var. zollikoferi. (Syn. *S. zollikoferi*).

This form from Bulgaria is similar to the type, but the branching flower stems are covered with purple glandular hairs and the pink flowers enclosed in the large glandular calyces are more prominent. May.

S. × tiroliensis. (*S. caesia* × *S. squarrosa*). (Syn. *S. × tyrolensis*).

This is a natural Kabschia hybrid from the Julian and S.E. Alps, where it makes fine small rosettes of grey leaves and on 2-inch stems, pure white, rounded flowers. May.

S. tombeanensis. (Kabschia).

Has a fairly wide distribution in the southern Alps, making hard congested rosettes of silver-grey, thick leaves, often flushed red. Flowers on 2-inch glandular stems up to five large, rounded, pure white. May.

S. 'Tumbling Waters'. (*S. callosa* × *S. longifolia*).

An outstanding Euaizoonia hybrid close to *S. longifolia* with its symmetrical silvered rosettes of strap-like leaves and huge panicles of white stars, up to 2 feet. Differs only from that species in having the ability to make offsets, which enables this hybrid to become a permanent feature. June.

S. × tyrolensis, see *S. × tiroliensis*.

S. valdensis. (Euaizoonia).

The smallest of the silver saxifrages with tight congested slow-growing rosettes of imbricated leaves. Leaves dark grey-green, spatulate, recurved with thickened acute tip, encrusted with very large but few lime pits. Flowers glistening white, up to ten in a congested truss on stout reddish densely glandular stems. May–June. French Alps.

S. × zimmeteri. (*S. aizoon* × *S. cuneifolia*).

A natural Euaizoonia-Robertsonia hybrid from Austria, making compact rosettes of thick glossy green leaves, margined with grey. Flowers on 4-inch branching stems, starry white with orange anthers. June.

S. zollikoferi, see *S. stribrnyi* var. *zollikoferi*.

SCHIVERECKIA (*Cruciferae*).

A genus of two species, both being suitable for alpine house or frame culture, they are closely related to Alyssum and are often included in that genus.

CULTIVATION. Compost A over faultless drainage, a normal supply of water while growing and flowering, keep dry but not arid in winter.

PROPAGATION. By cuttings with a heel of the old wood in August. Repot only when necessary after flowering.

S. doerfleri. (E).

A native of Asia Minor and the Balkans, this is a dwarf cushion-forming plant about 2 inches high. Leaves lanceolate in rosette formation, clothed with long stellate hairs, silver grey. Flowers in small clusters, four-petalled, white. May.

S. podolica. (E). (Syn. *Alyssum podolicum*).

From E. Europe, this is a larger species up to 5 inches high with leaves in rosette formation, lanceolate, silver-grey, margins two toothed. Flowers on 3-inch leafy stems in a terminal corymb, four-petalled, white. April.

SCHIZOCODON (*Diapensiaceae*).

This is a monotypic genus but there are four varieties of the single species, all of which are first class plants for pan culture, where they supply an outstanding floral display as well as autumn foliage colouration.

CULTIVATION. Compost C is a suitable medium with a good supply of lime-free water during the growing and flowering season and the plants should be kept moist at other periods. They are best kept in a half-shady plunge bed and only brought into the alpine house for flowering, for they detest hot dry conditions. All benefit from overhead spraying in the evenings during hot dry weather. Top-dress in early spring with similar compost, working this well down amongst the tufted shoots.

PROPAGATION. By careful division with roots attached and placing these in a cool shady frame until established, or seed sown in compost 3, March. Repot only when necessary after flowering.

S. macrophyllus, see *S. soldanelloides* var. *magnus*.

S. soldanelloides. (E).

This is a small procumbent tufted sub-shrub rarely above 2 inches high with thin wiry stems. Leaves coriaceous, crowded in tufts, orbicular to cordate, unevenly dentate, bright green above, paler beneath, turning to red and bronze in autumn. Flowers up to four in racemes on short stems from upright stalks, almost erect, open campanulate, margins deeply fringed, rich rose. April–May. A native of Japan.

S. soldanelloides var. alpinus. (E).

A smaller form, rarely above 1 inch high and with proportionate stems and leaves. Flowers large, almost pendant in terminal clusters, campanulate open fringed-bells, deep rose. May. A native of Japan.

S. soldanelloides var. ilicifolius. (E).

This is a rare Japanese form, making a dwarf prostrate mat only an inch or so high with short slender stems. Leaves crowded, cordate, deeply cut irregular teeth, dark glossy green above, paler beneath. Flowers congested on a 4-inch scape, pendant campanulate, fringed, deep pink in colour. May.

S. soldanelloides var. ilicifolius albus. (E).

A rare but extremely dainty white form which is worthy of every attention if obtainable. May. Japan.

S. soldanelloides var. magnus (E). (Syn. *S. macrophyllus*).

This is a prostrate sub-shrub which until recently had specific rank but is now only regarded as a large form. It is up to 2 inches high with thin wiry stems, increasing by runners when satisfied. Leaves in tufts, large, cordate, unevenly serrated, dark glossy green above, paler beneath, veining pronounced, reticulate. The leaves turn to delightful shades of red and bronze with exposure. Flowers congested on 1-inch erect stems, pendant, campanulate, deeply fringed, rich pink. April. Japan.

SCILLA (*Liliaceae*).

A large genus of bulbous plants, natives of Europe, Asia and Africa, the Squill is a well-known early spring-flowering bulb and there are a few species and varieties which make ideal pan plants for the alpine house or frame.

CULTIVATION. Compost B is suitable and the bulbs can be potted up from August to September, 1 inch apart, 1 inch deep. The pans should be plunged in a frame and covered with peat or ashes until growth commences, then brought into the house for flowering. Normal supply of water until growth dies away then dry; feed bi-weekly with liquid manure.

PROPAGATION. By offsets removed when repotting, or seed sown in compost 2, September; they will take three to four years to flower from seed. Repot every year in fresh compost. August–September.

S. adlamii. (B).

A native of E. Natal, this has a single fleshy linear leaf. Flowers on a slender 3-inch stem in a short raceme, six-lobed, mauve-purple. April. This species is best kept in the alpine house as a prolonged frost will kill it.

S. bifolia. (B).

From the Mediterranean region, this produces two narrow reddish-green, linear leaves, hooded at apex. Flowers in a small raceme three to eight open star-shaped, six-lobed, gentian blue. February–March.

S. bifolia var. alba. (B).

Similar to the type but with creamy white flowers. February–March.

S. bifolia var. rosea. (B).

Another variety with charming deep rose flowers. February–March.

S. chinensis. (B).

A native of China, this plant requires alpine house protection in winter. It has from two to three stiff, acute, linear, channelled green leaves. Flowers in a dense raceme up to fifty on a 9-inch scape, open star-shape, six-lobed, rose-pink. June.

S. pratensis. (B).

A native of Jugoslavia, with up to six ribbon-shaped, smooth green leaves, tapering to base and apex. Flowers on 9-inch scapes in a dense raceme, bell-shaped, violet-blue with dark purple stamens. May.

S. siberica. (B).
A native of E. Russia, Siberia, this has from two to four narrow strap-shaped, semi-erect, channelled green leaves. Flowers on fleshy 4-inch stems, up to three, semi-pendant, open saucer-shaped, six-lobed, bright blue. March.

S. siberica var. alba. (B).
This is the just as charming white form. March.

S. siberica var. atrocoerulea. (B).
A larger flowered form with deep blue flowers. March.

S. siberica var. taurica. (B).
This is an early flowering form often in flower at the beginning of February with charming light blue flowers.

S. tubergeniana. (B).
A native of Persia, with two to four narrow strap-shaped flat leaves. Flowers up to three alternate, from upper third of 6-inch scape, open six-lobed, blue with darker median stripe on segments. March.

S. verna. (B).
This species is a native of Europe including Britain, with narrow linear, obtuse, recurved, concave green leaves. Flowers on 6-inch scape, sub-corymbose up to twelve, six-lobed star-shaped, bright light blue. April.

SEDUM (*Crassulaceae*).

This is a large and mighty race of plants, containing many species and forms which are suitable for culture in the alpine house or frame. Not only do they provide a first-class floral display, but they have the added attraction of foliage colouration in many of the species. I have never had any great feeling for the Stonecrops ever since, in the early days, I made the mistake of planting *S. album* in my first rock garden and then spent many weary hours, unsuccessfully I must add, in trying to eradicate what had become a pernicious weed. Not content with colonising every available bare patch, it also took root in the middle of cushion plants; the fleshy leaves, possibly dropped by birds, are only too ready to start afresh to the detriment of its host. They have a wide distribution in nature, there being a good quota from Europe including Britain, Asia Minor, Africa, also new species from the Himalayas, China and Tibet, while the hardy, near hardy, to downright tender Mexican species are legion.

CULTIVATION. This is quite simple, they are all with few exceptions sun lovers and will do well in compost A over faultless drainage. Water can be given normally during the growing season, but they seem to like a dry arid period in August to ripen the growth, keep dry but not arid in winter. Large specimens in pans benefit from a bi-weekly dose of a diluted liquid manure, half normal strength is ideal, during May and June. This seems to keep the plants in good health as well as increasing foliage colouration.

PROPAGATION. There is no difficulty in increasing the stock of the species, for every fleshy leaf that is allowed to come into contact with the soil will invariably root quite easily at all times of the year with the exception of winter. Seed too is a means of propagation, this being sown in March, in compost 1. Repot when necessary after flowering.

S. adenotrichum. (E).
A native of the Himalayas, up to 3 inches high making open mats of hairy stems. Leaves in rosette formation, narrow, linear, fleshy, obtuse, glabrous. Flowers on 3-inch stems in glandular hairy panicles up to twelve white stars. April.

S. anglicum var. minus. (E).
This dwarf form is a mat-forming plant with slender rooting stems. Leaves crowded, elliptic, fleshy, grey-green, tinged red. Flowers in cymes on short two-branched stems, rose-tinted stars. June. A native of Europe.

S. bourgaei. (E).
A sub-shrubby species from C. Mexico, with erect glabrous branching red stems less than 12 inches high. Leaves alternate, linear, obtuse, fleshy, flattened, green. Flowers on terminal of branches in a loose cyme, white tinged red. August–October. Best in the alpine house, requires protection in a very cold prolonged spell.

S. brevifolium. (E).
A prostrate creeping plant with thread-like stems an inch or so long. Leaves dense, ovoid in four rows, green covered with a blue-grey farina, flushed red. Flowers, few in a cyme on 1-inch stems, white star-shaped, with purple anthers. June. A native of the W. Mediterranean.

S. brevifolium var. quinquefolium. (E).
Similar to the type but with thicker stems and the leaves in five rows almost spirally arranged. July.

S. cauticola. (H).
A native of Japan, this forms trailing mats of procumbent stems clothed with orbicular-spatulate, opposite, short-stalked leaves, the colour being glaucous green, margined red. Flowers in terminal and axillary flattish cymes of a deep purple red. September.

S. chanetii, see *Orostachys chanetii*.

S. corsicum, see *S. dasyphyllum* var. *glanduliferum*.

S. dasyphyllum. (E).
This is a native of S. Europe and N. Africa, and forms a low-growing mat of tufted much-branched stems. Leaves dense, opposite, ovate, succulent, pinkish-grey. Flowers on short 1-inch, two-branched cymes, white with pink midrib. June.

S. dasyphyllum var. glanduliferum. (E). (Syn. *S. corsicum*).
A native of Sicily and Corsica, this form differs from the species in that both the leaves and stems are covered with small glandular hairs. June.

S. ellacombianum. (H).

A native of Japan, this produces many unbranched arching stems up to 6 inches high. Leaves opposite, obovate, glabrous green, margins dentate. Flowers terminal in a flat leafy cluster, yellow star-shaped. June.

S. ewersii. (H).

A variable plant having a wide distribution from the Himalayas to Mongolia, it makes many rambling, semi-erect, rounded, forked branches. Leaves almost orbicular, clasping, minutely toothed, glaucous green. Flowers terminal at end of laterals and branches in a dense cyme, varying from pale pink to an almost deep red in a good form. August–September.

S. hobsonii. (H). (Syn. *S. praegerianum*).

A native of S. Tibet, this forms a stalked basal rosette of entire, fleshy flat, green leaves from a thick perennial rootstock, producing prostrate leafy stems, about 4 inches long; stem leaves linear-oblong, obtuse, reflexed, green tipped red. Flowers in lax terminal cymes, few, ovoid, bell-shaped, rose-pink. July. This plant is best increased by seed, sown in March, compost 1.

S. humifusum. (E).

This is a Mexican species, making a prostrate mat of small shoots and producing erect stems less than an inch high. Leaves in small elongated rosettes, obovate, thick, overlapping, ciliate, grey-green often tinged red. Flowers solitary on short reddish stems, yellow stars. May–June. Needs alpine house protection in winter.

S. lydium. (E).

A native of W. Asia Minor, this makes a prostrate mat of small rooting stems only an inch or so high. Leaves linear, cylindrical, minute raised blotches at apex, green, turning red on exposure. Flowers in a corymbose cyme on 2-inch stems, star-like, white, pink tipped and purple anthers. June.

S. multiceps. (D).

This is a shrubby species from Algeria, making a small erect, much-branched plant up to 6 inches high with woody brown stems. Leaves alternate, arranged in six to seven spiral rows, towards the ends of the laterals, linear-oblong, flat on upper surface, thick fleshy, bright green. Flowers on 2 inch leafy shoots in small cymes, bright yellow, largish stars. August.

S. oaxacanum. (E).

A charming Mexican species from the Oaxaca district, making a prostrate mat of much-branched reddish-purple, pimpled stems only an inch or so high. Leaves dense, sessile, alternate, obovate, obtuse, flat on upper surface, spurred, grey-green. Flowers up to three at apex of branches, bright yellow stars, unfortunately not free flowering. June.

S. pilosum. (E).

A monocarpic species from Asia Minor, which is a charming plant for the alpine house, forming dense rosettes. Leaves linear-spatulate, obtuse, incurved, covered with fine hairs, dark green. Flowers on 3-inch leafy stems, stem leaves oblong-obovate, in a crowded much-branched panicled cyme, deep pink, open goblet shape. May–June.

S. populifolium. (E).
This originates from Siberia, making an erect shrubby plant up to 12 inches high with smooth reddish-brown branches in the adult stage. Leaves alternate, crowded at the terminal of the lateral, ovate, deep irregularly dentate, acute, base cordate, borne on slender stalks. Flowers in terminal much-branched corymbose cymes, star-like, white flushed pink with purple anthers and a delightful scent of hawthorn. July.

S. praegerianum, see *S. hobsonii.*

S. primuloides. (D).
A native of Yunnan, this is a dwarf sub-shrub only 3 inches high with stout, congested, smooth stems and branches. Leaves fleshy narrow, ovate, arranged in dense rosettes, deep green, at terminal of laterals, petiole flat and wider at base, reddish. Flowers up to three on short leafy stems, heather-like, closed at mouth, white backed green. August.

S. sempervivoides. (E).
Another monocarpic species related to *S. pilosum,* but larger, it forms a flat rosette of grey-green spatulate hairy leaves, tinged reddish-brown towards apex. The centre of the rosette elongates into a 6-inch stem, clad with thick bronzy coloured leaves, topped with a loose panicle of erect bell-shaped flowers of a dazzling crimson, stamens yellow. A native of Asia Minor.
PROPAGATION. From seed which is freely set. Compost 1.

S. spathulifolium. (E).
This makes a close hummock of many-branched stems, increasing by basal runners. Leaves on small shoots in terminal flattish rosettes, spatulate, abrupt pointed, recurving apex, glaucous grey, turning red on exposure. Flowers on short stems from axillary rosettes in dense cymes, starry-yellow. June. A native of western America.

S. spathulifolium 'Cassa Blanca'. (E).
This variant comes from S. California and is smaller than the type, covered with a dense opaque farina that hides the normal colour of the foliage. Flowers yellow. June.

S. spathulifolium var. purpureum. (E).
A form from N.W. America, larger than the type but with juvenile leaves of glaucous white changing to deep purple in the adult state. Flowers bright orange. June.

S. spinosum, see *Orostachys spinosus.*

S. stahlii. (E).
Another Mexican species, best in the alpine house where it forms a dense, slender stemmed, downy, reddish plant about 6 inches high. Leaves opposite, egg-shaped, obtuse, shiny green turning to reddish-brown. Flowers in terminal cymes, yellow star-like. July. Falling leaves if left will root quite easily.

S. winkleri. (E).
A native of Gibraltar, making a mat of prostrate runners, often underground, from which are produced tufts of both flowering and non-flowering small hairy stems. Leaves in rosette formation at terminal of shoots, spatulate-oblong, pale green and pubescent. Flowers on short hairy stems in a broad corymb, large, white, star-like, veined green with purple anthers. July.

SELAGO (*Scrophulariaceae*).

A large genus of dwarf or under shrubs from S. and Tropical Africa, but there are only two that can be considered hardy and suitable for pan culture in the alpine house, where they make charming pan plants.
CULTIVATION. Compost A with a normal supply of water during the growing and flowering season. Keep dry but not arid from December to late April.
PROPAGATION. By cuttings with a heel in July. Repot when necessary in late April.
S. galpinii. (E).
This is a dwarf bushy shrublet less than 9 inches high with semi-procumbent much-branched downy stems. Leaves crowded, linear, greenish-grey in the juvenile state due to covering of hairs, deeper green and glabrous when adult. The flowers are small, borne in congested terminal panicles, corolla tubular with five roundish narrow lobes, deep lilac. September–November. A native of high altitudes in Basutoland.
S. sandersonii. (E).
A native of Hanglip Mountains, S. Africa, this makes a dwarf much-branched shrublet, less than 12 inches high, stems wiry. Leaves crowded, linear, acute, grey-green, covered with fine hairs in the juvenile state. Flowers in long terminal panicles, open five-lobed, lilac. October.

SEMPERVIVELLA (*Crassulaceae*).

A small genus from the Himalayas, containing one species in cultivation suitable for pan culture in the alpine house or frame.
CULTIVATION. Compost A over good drainage with a normal supply of water while growing, keep dry but not arid in winter.
PROPAGATION. By division of the rosettes in late August. Repot when necessary.
S. alba. (E). (Syn. *Sempervivum album*).
This makes a close mat of glandular rosettes. Leaves broad-oblong, obtuse, flat on upper surface, incurved, pale green flushed rose underneath. Flowers on procumbent 3-inch stems in cymes, up to eight flat star-shaped, white, red tipped in bud stage. August. A native of the Himalayas.

SEMPERVIVUM (*Crassulaceae*).

The Houseleek with its many species and varieties must surely be some of the first plants potted up for the alpine house or frame by beginners of this fascinating hobby. Easy of culture and requiring but a minimum of attention they will thrive and delight their cultivators, not only in winter when the alpine house and frame have a drab dreary look but more so in spring when the leaf colouration is at its height.

They have one great drawback, their willingness to cross with all and sundry, and this has given the genus a bad name with cultivators who like to know that the specimen being grown is indeed that stated on the label. Far too often first, second and even triple hybrids are dispatched under invalid names. Don't, let me hasten to implore you, blame the nurseryman, for when even the botanist has found difficulty in naming, the poor vendor cannot be held responsible for what is often a chaotic state of affairs. There are two firms in this country that I know of, there are no doubt others, who have made a study of these plants and who can be relied upon to send out species and varieties true to name. First, that old-established firm of alpine plant growers, Messrs. Ingwersen; both father and son have helped greatly in bringing order out of chaos. The other, a newcomer in years but with the advantage of youth and enthusiasm, is Alan Smith, who is making an exhaustive study of these plants and has built up a large collection over the last ten years or so, weeding out those of unreliable parentage and doubtful species.

CULTIVATION. It can safely be said that no other genus of alpine plants is more suitable for pan culture than the Houseleeks. Hardy, compact, almost indestructible, thriving on neglect, no other plants would stand up to this treatment. A normal sandy soil with care in watering is their only essential requirement to maintain them in good health and character. Overfeeding produces rank open rosettes from which the foliage colouration seems to be bleached out and this, coupled with any tendency to overwater, will quickly set up stem rot. Large specimens in pans which have possibly exhausted their compost will benefit from small doses of liquid manure every other week in spring.

Some of the species are too prone to set flowers and although a number bear charming heads of blooms, the attending scape is normally quite out of character, completely throwing out of balance any form between the rosettes and their flowering stems, these being in the main but large, thick, elongated rosettes. The individual flowering rosettes are monocarpic, thus a disfiguring gap is left in what is normally a compact hummock of congested rosettes. If the main object is to maintain uniformity it is better to remove carefully all rosettes which are likely to flower before the flowering stem has begun to grow to any extent. It is quite easy to distinguish between a flowering and a non-flowering rosette, for the centre of the rosette starts to elongate at an early stage. With few exceptions all sempervivums increase by offsets, which are normally produced freely, too freely in a large number of species, and these should be carefully worked into position in the pan or removed if there is any chance of overcrowding, for the main object is to build up a pan of close even rosettes without too much congestion.

Compost A is suitable over good drainage. Water should only be given when necessary but this must be thorough, making sure that the compost is completely moistened. The succulent leaves have a great capacity for water storage and once a specimen pan is built up it should only be necessary to water once a week during the growing period and only once a month or even less, depending on the weather, in winter.

PROPAGATION. This is best by offsets which will root at practically any period of the year. Those species which increase by the rosette-dividing are best propagated by division in July. Seed is not considered reliable, for if a collection of these plants is grown, they will intercross only too readily. This has added to the confusion in naming, for far too many inferior hybrids are in cultivation, doing duty for species and their varieties. Repot only when necessary in April, the object being only to move the plants when the rosettes have spread to the rim of the pan, thus keeping the plant close and compact.

S. album, see *Sempervivella alba.*

S. allionii, see *S. hirsutum.*

S. altum. (E).
A native of the Caucasus Alps, it has largish open rosettes of hairy light green leaves which turn bright red in early summer. Flowers red, yellow anthers.

S. andreanum. (E).
A fine distinctive plant from N. Spain, making a medium rosette of few leaves and the centre forming a tight congested cone. Leaves bright green, brown tipped, turning dull green in winter. Flowers pink, quickly makes large symmetrical hummocks.

S. arachnoideum. (E).
This is the well-known Cobweb Houseleek, easy to grow and one of the most decorative for pan culture, never looking so well when grown outside, as our winter's wet tends to destroy the network of hairs. It forms tight congested rosettes of leaves which can be green, brownish-green or even reddish, then the whole plant is covered with white thread-like hairs from leaf to leaf. Flowers on 2-inch stems are quite charming, unlike the majority of species, for with their wider petals of deep rose they are in better proportion. Summer. A native of the European Alps.

S. arachnoideum var. fasciatum (E).
This differs from the type only in the formation of the rosettes, these are abnormal, growing like coxcombs.

S. arachnoideum var. tomentosum. (E).
Bigger rosettes of green leaves with deep red apex and well covered with long hairs.

S. arenarium. (E).
One of the smallest species, from the eastern European Alps, making semi-compact rosettes of congested fine smooth green leaves, tipped with red. Flowers, yellow on a less stout scape than the majority of the species. Summer. A fine pan plant.

S. armenum. (E).
A native of Turkish Armenia, making nice rosettes of open smooth green leaves tipped with purple-red. Flowers yellow. Summer. A much slower growing species.

S. ballsii. (E).
This makes medium rosettes, only semi-compact but densely crowded with smooth green leaves and a few marginal hairs. Flowers poor, pink. Summer. A slow growing species, with few offsets. Native of Greece.

S. cantabricum. (E).
A native of N. Spain, with medium-sized open rosettes of thinnish, deep green leaves, apex dark brown, the whole extremely pilose. Flowers a good pink, striped green. Summer.

S. caucasicum. (E).
A medium-sized rosette, leaves not so crowded, slightly hairy, bright green, apex deep brown, spine tipped. Flowers red. Summer. Offsets on long stolons. A native of the eastern Alps.

S. ciliosum. (E).
A native of Bulgaria, this is a charming species making globular rosettes of imbricated, incurved, translucent-haired grey-green leaves, margined with long hairs. Flowers yellow. Summer. Offsets in plenty, on long stolons.

S. ciliosum var. borisii. (E).
A geographical form from one station in Bulgaria, with smaller rosettes, similar to the type but with much greater density of long white hairs, giving the plant the appearance of a white hummock. I raced against time and traffic across London to the 1954 Chelsea Flower Show to get an Award of Merit for this form with twenty-three flowering stems, arriving just as the Rock Garden Committee were starting to sit.

S. ciliosum var. ali botusch. (E).
Similar to the type but with the leaves having a red tinge and shorter hairs. Southern Bulgaria.

S. ciliosum var. mali hat. (E).
A native of the Mali Mountain in W. Macedonia, this is a distinctive form with smaller, tighter, globular rosettes than the type, deep purple-red and short woolly hairs.

S. dolomiticum. (E).
One of the less easy species to grow, this plant resents winter dampness in any form. It is a native of the eastern Alps and makes smallish flattish rosettes of bright green upright leaves, turning scarlet with age, covered with hairs in centre of rosettes, large on the margins, adult leaves puberulus. Flowers bright carmine. Summer.

S. erythraeum. (E).
A fine Bulgarian species on limestone formations. Forms symmetrical medium-sized rosettes of greeny-plum, a difficult colour to match but always easy to identify by the presence of the extremely minute dense indumentum on the leaves which gives the effect of a bloom. Flowers bright pink. Summer.

S. erythraeum pirin form. (E).
This is the Pirin Mountain form on granite and differs from the type in having small rosettes, these being green in colour.

S. giuseppii. (E).
Collected by the late Dr Giuseppi in N. Spain in 1934 and named after him. This forms tight congested hummocks of medium-sized rosettes, bright green leaves, darker at the apex, often brownish-green. Leaves in centre of rosettes become extremely hairy, giving it the appearance of white wool. Flowers rose-red. Summer.

S. globiferum. (E).
A Caucasian species with large lax rosettes, light yellowish-green leaves, covered with fine downy hairs on both sides, margins ciliate. Flowers, yellow tinged green, light purple at base. Summer.

S. grandiflorum. (E).
Medium to large open rosettes of dull green leaves, densely covered with a sticky glandular indumentum and having a brown flush at tip. Flowers yellow, purple at base of petals. Summer. A native of the Swiss Alps.

S. heuffelii. (E).
An unmistakable Houseleek with its peculiar habit of increasing by the individual rosettes dividing. It makes a tight congested clump of medium-sized rosettes with broad, apple-green leaves, slightly hairy, flattish on face, convex on back, margins and apex stained a dull red also ciliate, intensely pointed almost spiny. Flowers yellow. Summer. A native of Bulgaria.

S. hirsutum. (E). (Syn. *S. allionii*).
This is a native of the Maritime Alps and makes globular rosettes of light yellow-green, tightly packed pubescent leaves, tipped red when adult, increases rapidly by offsets on thin stems. Flowers yellow with thin petals. It rarely flowers in cultivation but this is no loss.

S. ingwersenii. (E).
A new sempervivum of fairly recent introduction and named after that grand plantsman of alpine fame, the late W. E. Th. Ingwersen, who discovered it in the 1935 Caucasian expedition. It makes medium-sized flattish rosettes of bright green leaves, tapered to base, covered with a fine down, margins ciliate, apex reddish-brown. Flowers on stout scapes, red margined white. Summer. Offsets numerous on long deep red stolons.

S. kindingeri. (E).
A native of the Balkans, with large flattish, open, few-leaved rosettes. Leaves apple-green, intensely hairy, margins ciliate, apex red. Flowers on

hairy scapes with large ovate leaves, yellow striped red at base of petals. Summer. Offsets few on short stolons.

S. kosaninii. (E).
This species makes large flattish rosettes of crowded fleshy leaves, these being a dull deep green, stained brown at apex, the whole clothed with fine hairs. Flowers on thick heavy stems, red with green on reverse. Summer. Offsets on long leafy stolons. A native of Montenegro.

S. leucanthum. (E).
A native of the Bulgarian Rila Mountains, where it makes semi-open rosettes, medium sized, light green almost lanceolate leaves, the centre rosette leaves incurved, margins ciliate, both sides covered with hairs, apex deep brown. Flowers on slender scapes, yellow, in summer. Offsets on large thickish hairy stolons.

S. macedonicum. (E).
This forms hard flattish rosettes, small to medium in size, in loose mats. Leaves deepish green, tightly incurved outside, covered with a fine down, margins ciliate, tinged brown on exposure. Flowers on short scape, red. Summer. Offsets numerous on long leafy stolons. A native of Macedonia.

S. minus. (E).
A fine rare species from Anatolia, making very small, few leaved, globular rosettes. Leaves olive-green, covered with a fine down, margins sparsely ciliate, purple at base, apex obtuse, outside bronze. Flowers on slender stems, light yellow-green. Summer.

S. minus var. glabrum. (E).
With larger more open rosettes, leaves glabrous, thinner, light green, base purple, the whole turning reddish-brown in summer. A native of Anatolia.

S. nevadense. (E).
This species makes a compact dense clump of medium sized rosettes. Leaves smooth, green, incurved in centre of rosette, more open towards outer leaves, backs turning bright red in summer. Flowers rose-red on leafy scapes. Summer. Offsets numerous on thin stolons. A native of Spain.

S. octopodes. (E).
From N. Macedonia comes this charming Sempervivum of small rounded rosettes with thick, green obtuse leaves, covered with fine hairs, margins ciliate, apex tinged dark brown. Flowers on slender leafy stems, bright yellow with a basal red blotch. Summer. Offsets in quantity on long slender stolons.

S. ossetiense. (E).
Another Caucasian species of medium-sized rosettes of few upright, narrow, lanceolate, thick green leaves, covered with fine down, margins ciliate, apex tinged brown. Flowers on a small scape, white, tinged purple at base, striped purple. Summer.

S. pittonii. (E).
Makes small flattish rosettes with dull greyish-green very hairy leaves, apex

tinged purple. Flowers on slender leafy scapes, yellow. Summer. Offsets on long slender stolons. A native of Styria.

S. pumilum. (E).
A native of the Caucasus, this makes a dense compact clump of small globular rosettes with bright green, smooth leaves, apex light red. Flowers purple-mauve in summer. Offsets on stout stolons.

S. reginae-amaliae. (E).
From the mountains of Greece, where it forms medium to large rosettes in a compact form. Leaves dull green covered with fine hairs, margins ciliate, the whole becoming tinged with purple on exposure to sunshine. Flowers on tapering erect stems, red. Summer. Offsets few.

S. tectorum var. calcareum 'Monstrosum'. (E).
The type plant is the easiest of all the Houseleeks to grow and has very large open flattish rosettes of green smooth leaves with a reddish-brown apex, crimson at base, margins ciliate. This curious form makes upright rounded rosettes of very thick fleshy leaves as deep as they are wide, almost circular with incurving pointed tip, light apple-green, apex reddish-brown. It is nothing more than an abnormal form, but retains it under cultivation.

S. thompsonianum. (E).
A native of Austria, with rounded small half-opened rosettes, leaves incurved, apple green, densely clad with fine hairs, margins ciliate, apex acute, stained red on exposure. Flowers in summer, compact, yellow with white margins. Offsets numerous on slender stolons.

S. wulfenii. (E).
A native of the Swiss and Austrian Alps, it is a slow-growing species of symmetrical largish rosettes with central leaves incurved and slightly elongated, leaves glaucous grey-green, smooth, tinged purple at apex. Flowers yellow, lined crimson at base of petals. Summer. Offsets few.

S. zelebori. (E).
This makes large few leaved open rosettes, with large dull green leaves, shading to dark brown at apex, the whole having a decided pale purple sheen, due to intense covering of velvet hairs. Flowers on tapering leafy scapes, yellow flushed crimson at base in summer. A native of Serbia and N. Bulgaria.

SENECIO (*Compositae*).

One of the largest genera in the world with a wide distribution, there are a great number of weeds or plants of poor merit and only a few are suitable for our purpose.

CULTIVATION. Compost A over good drainage with a normal supply of water during the growing season, keep dry but not arid in winter.

PROPAGATION. By green cuttings in May or seed sown when ripe, compost 2. Repot every other year after flowering.

S. incanus. (E).

A native of the eastern Alps, forming tufts up to 4 inches high. Basal leaves obovate, with incised lobes, upper oblong, segments linear, bright silvery grey covered with white hairs. Flowers in small corymbs, small daisy-like, yellow. May.

S. tyroliensis. (E).

This is the best of the dwarf shrubby senecios and may be a dwarf geographical form of *S. abrotanifolius* from high altitudes in the Tyrol. It makes a ground-hugging shrublet with radiating light green, glabrous, rounded branches, less than an inch high. Leaves alternate, arranged in whorls on the last few inches of the branches, five-part, segments dentate, thick fleshy, apex acute, margins recurved, deep glossy green. Flowers on 6-inch stems, large, orange-red discs, surrounded by ragged florets of a similar colour. June.

S. uniflorus. (E).

A native of the southern Alps, it forms a dense tuft with silvery white leaves almost in rosette formation. Basal leaves oblong, coarsely cut and stalked, upper entire, linear, sessile, margins undulate. Flowers on 2-inch stems, solitary, large, orange-yellow. May.

SHORTIA (*Diapensiaceae*).

A small genus of sub-shrubs closely related to Schizocodon and having much in common, but whereas the latter is confined to Japan, Shortia has one species there, and another native to N. Carolina.

CULTIVATION. This is best in compost C with good drainage. Plenty of lime-free water is needed in the growing and flowering season and the compost must be kept moist at other periods. Shade is essential and the plants should only be brought into the alpine house for flowering, during other seasons they are best plunged in a cool shady frame and sprayed in the evenings after hot days. Top-dress in early spring with similar compost, working this well down amongst the tufts.

PROPAGATION. By careful division in late March, planting the divisions in a cool shady frame until re-established. Seed if available in March, in compost 3. Repot only when necessary, every third year should be sufficient, and is best carried out immediately after flowering.

S. galacifolia. (E).

A native of N. Carolina, this makes a congested mat of wiry slender stems, rarely above 4 inches high. Leaves tufted on short stems, rounded to cordate, dentate, heavily veined, wavy, deep shiny green above, lighter beneath turning to shades of crimson in late autumn. Flowers solitary on 3-inch stems, broad tubular, five to six-lobed, joined near base, margins deeply crenate, white. April.

S. uniflora. (E).

A native of Japan, this is a prostrate plant, rarely above an inch high in tight widely spaced congested tufts. Leaves rounded on long smooth stalks, with facing groove; margined with irregular blunt serrations, more pronounced at apex, recurved at base, veins reticulated and outstanding; bright glossy green above, paler beneath, both stem and leaf turning to brilliant red in autumn. Flowers solitary on short scapes, large open campanulate five to six-lobes, joined at base, margins deeply serrated, bright pink, stamens white. April.

S. uniflora var. grandiflora. (E).
This is an outstanding form which is much larger in all its parts, more tufted and compact with typical foliage and flowers in proportion. April. A native of Japan.

S. uniflora var. rosea. (E).
Another fine form with similar habit but deep rose-pink flowers in early spring. This plant is often in flower at the end of February in sheltered gardens and alpine houses. A native of Japan.

SILENE (*Caryophyllaceae*).

A large genus of plants widely distributed over most parts of the northern hemisphere and S. Africa, and having a number which make ideal specimens for the alpine house or frame, ranging from compact cushion-plants to those more open but with just as attractive floral decoration. They are closely allied to Melandrium and are sometimes quoted under that generic name.

CULTIVATION. Compost A is suitable over faultless drainage with a normal supply of water during the growing season, keep dry but not arid in winter. The herbaceous perennials require less moisture at this period than the evergreen species.

PROPAGATION. By seed sown when ripe, compost 2, division in early April, or green cuttings in late June. Repot when necessary after flowering.

S. acaulis. (E).
A native of a large area in the northern hemisphere including Britain, this makes a dense tufted cushion about 2 inches high. Leaves crowded, small, linear, obtuse, glossy green, hairy at base, keeled on reverse. Flowers solitary, almost sessile with reddish-purple, rounded calyx and five-lobed open, notched pink petals. May–June. The species is, unfortunately, not free flowering in cultivation although some of its forms are more generous than others. Propagation is best by division in April.

S. acaulis var. alba. (E).
This is the white form which is just as diffident in producing its similar flowers. May–June.

S. acaulis var. elongata, see *S. elongata*.

S. acaulis var. exscapa. (E). (Syn. *S. exscapa*).
A much freer flowering form from the Pyrenees, with small erect, bright green, linear-acute leaves in tight congested tufts and many sessile typical flowers of light pink. May.

S. cretica. (E).
This is a dwarf shrubby species from the Mediterranean area, which makes
a charming specimen. From a central hard woody rootstock radiate the
prostrate, thick, brittle, grey striated white stems, less than 6 inches high.
Each node produces a brownish-white wiry persistent hair up to 1½ inch
long. Leaves in terminal rosettes, arranged symmetrically round the stem,
apex decurved, ending in a soft spine; glossy olive-green above, paler
below, midrib pronounced. Flowers on a much-branched erect leafy
stem, narrow tubular calyx with five-petalled, deeply notched corolla,
pink. June. Best propagated by seed which is freely set, compost 2.
March.
S. elisabethae, see *Melandrium elisabethae.*
S. elongata. (E). (Syn. *S. acaulis* var. *elongata*).
A native of the W. Graian Alps, this makes rounded cushions of acute
small, linear, green leaves in tufts, not so crowded as in *S. acaulis.* Flowers
solitary on 2-inch stems, large, bell-shaped, reddish calyx and five-lobed
corolla, petals deeply notched, bright pink. May–June. Best propagated
by division in April.
S. exscapa, see *S. acaulis* var. *exscapa.*
S. hookeri. (H).
This is a fleshy rooted perennial from California, with radiating prostrate
stems from a central crown. Leaves basal in rosette formation, elliptic-
spatulate, tapered to base, petiole long, apex acute, downy, grey-green.
Flowers axillary on 2-inch slender, leafy stems, calyx inflated, bell-shaped,
five petals, each lobe deeply cut into four segments and two erect white
scales, salmon-pink with white basal rays. June–July. Propagation is by
seed sown as soon as ripe, compost 2; hand-pollination will ensure a better
set. Care is needed in watering, especially during the winter months and
the seedlings should be potted on as soon as possible, taking care, for the
fleshy roots resent undue disturbance.
S. ingramii. (H).
Another native of California with a fleshy creeping rootstock from a
central crown. Leaves basal in rosettes, elliptic-lanceolate, acute, tapering
to long petiole, green. Flowers large, axillary on leafy slender 2-inch
stems, calyx long, globular, petals five-lobed, each lobe with four deep
coarsely-cut segments, deep rose-pink with two erect white scales at base.
June–July. A smaller plant than *S. hookeri* but larger flowers. Needs similar cultural treatment.
S. keiskei. (H).
A charming species from Japan, making a tufted mat of slender, downy,
reddish-green stems. Leaves small, arranged in alternate opposite pairs,
narrow, elliptic, margins minutely dentate, ciliate, light green. Flowers
solitary on 2-inch stems, calyx long tubular, covered with a mauve down,
corolla five-lobed, each lobe notched, deep pale purple. July–August.
Best propagated by seed, compost 2, March.

Above: *Trachelium asperuloides* (see page 503)
Below: *Tulipa aucheriana* (see page 506)

Above: *Tulipa pulchella* (see page 509)

Below: *Tulipa tarda* (see page 509)

Above: *Chamaecyparis obtusa* 'Minima' (see page 174)

Below: *Chamaecyparis obtusa* 'Minima', a ten-year-old plant raised from a cutting and still less than 1½ inches tall (see page 175)

Above: *Juniperus communis* 'Echiniformis' (see page 178)
Below: *Microcachrys tetragona* (see page 179)

S. keiskei var. minor. (H).
This form is smaller in all its parts, rarely above 2 inches high, more compact and with similar flowers. July–August.
S. pennsylvanica, see *Melandrium pennsylvanicum.*
S. pumila, see *Saponaria pumila.*
S. pumilio, see *Saponaria pumila.*
S. wherryi, see *Melandrium wherryi.*

SISYRINCHIUM (*Iridaceae*).
A genus of slender tuberous rooted perennials, of which *S. angustifolium* and *S. striatum* can become almost weeds in the rock garden with their ease of increase by seeding indiscriminately, often in the centre of a choice plant. The Satin Flowers are native of N. and S. America, and there are at least two species which require careful cultivation to become perennial inhabitants of the alpine house or frame.
CULTIVATION. Compost B is suitable over good drainage and a normal supply of water is required during the growing and flowering season, keep dry but not arid in winter.
PROPAGATION. By division or seed, compost 2, but this will be dealt with separately for each species. Repot only when necessary after flowering.
S. bellum. (E).
A small tufted plant about 6 inches high with green, short, wide linear leaves. Flowers in small terminal clusters, open funnel-shaped, deep violet-purple with yellow throat. June–September. An easy species from California, best divided in late March or early April. Seed when ripe.
S. douglasii. (H). (Syn. *S. grandiflorum*).
An early flowering and far from easy species, from British Columbia, with a creeping rootstock, producing 8-inch unbranched leafy stems. Leaves erect, linear, rounded, striated, deep green. Flowers large, terminal, semi-pendant, narrow, bell-shaped, deep purple with white veinings. February. Care is needed in watering this species, the compost must not be allowed to become sodden, best in half-shade. Propagation is best by careful division in early June.
S. douglasii var. album. (H). (Syn. *S. grandiflorum* var. *album*).
This is the very desirable white form with large semi-pendant pure white flowers of good texture, but it can be just as temperamental as the type. February.
S. filifolium. (H).
A native of the Falkland Islands, up to 8 inches high with thin rush-like deep green leaves. Flowers from terminal off-shoots, erect, open bell-shaped, white, striated pink, purple at base. May. Requires similar conditions and propagation to those for *S. douglasii.*
S. grandiflorum, see *S. douglasii.*
S. grandiflorum var. album, see *S. douglasii* var. *album.*

SOLDANELLA (*Primulaceae*).

A small genus of truly alpine plants, often found pushing their flowers through the melting snows in early spring on high alpine meadows in their native habitat.

CULTIVATION. Compost B over good drainage suits them with plenty of water while growing and flowering, keep dry but not arid in winter. In the southern counties, they do best in a light shady spot after flowering, for although light is essential the species also require a cool moist atmosphere to give of their best. Care should be taken that the flower buds, which are formed early, do not damp-off in the mild moist spells often experienced during our winters. Also, although hardy, the buds can be destroyed by exposure to excessive cold spells, for it must be remembered that in their native habitat these plants are protected by a covering of snow during such periods.

PROPAGATION. By seed sown as soon as ripe in compost 2, for like so many genera of the family *Primulaceae* the seed has a low viability, or careful division may be used immediately after flowering. Repot when necessary at the same time.

S. alpina. (E).

A native of the Pyrenees and eastern Alps, this has a fleshy rootstock, producing tufts of reniform to orbicular thick green leaves, cordate at base. Flowers on 3-inch slender stems, up to three pendant, open bell-shaped, five-lobed, lavender-blue with bright red streakings on inside; corolla-lobes are deeply frilled. April.

S. × ganderi. (E). *S. alpina × S. minima.*

A natural hybrid found when its parents meet in the Alps, it is near to *S. minima* but a more robust edition of this species. It forms tufts of entire, orbicular, leathery, bright glossy green leaves. Flowers up to three on slender 3-inch stems, five-lobed, pendant, open bell-shaped, pale lilac with deeper lines of colour inside, lobes fringed, not so deeply cut as in *S. alpina.* March.

S. minima. (E).

A native of the southern Alps, with a fleshy rootstock and tufts of small entire, orbicular, glossy green leaves on long stalks. Flowers solitary on slender 2-inch stems, pendant, tubular bell-shaped, five-lobed, pale blue with violet streakings on inside, lobes fringed. April.

S. minima var. alba. (E).

A charming white form often found in company with the coloured, growing side by side in their natural habitat. April.

S. montana. (E).

A widely distributed species over the European Alps, forming a close tuft of large orbicular dark green leaves, deeply cordate at base, margins undulate, petiole long, glandular, hairy. Flowers on 5-inch stout stems, up to ten large five-lobed, open bell-shaped, margins deeply and unevenly fringed, segments recurved, lavender-blue. April.

S. pindicola. (E).
A native of the Balkans, Mount Pindus, Albania, this produces tufts of large cordate, reniform, dull green, long stalked leaves, glaucous blue below. Flowers on 3-inch stems up to three pendant, open funnel-shaped, five lobes, deeply cut, lavender-lilac. April.

S. pusilla. (E).
A widely distributed species over the European Alps, with tufts of stalked, reniform to orbicular, thick deep glossy green leaves. Flowers solitary on slender 3-inch stems, pendant, narrow, tubular five-lobed, lobes fringed, pale lavender-blue. March.

SORBUS (*Rosaceae*).

A genus of trees and shrubs allied to Pyrus, with a wide distribution over Europe, N. America and N. Asia, of which there is one species in cultivation that is suitable for pan culture in the alpine house or frame and this is of recent introduction.

CULTIVATION. Compost B over good drainage with a normal supply of water during the growing season, keep dry but not arid when the leaves fall.

PROPAGATION. By detaching the rooted runners which the plant makes and potting them up in early June, keeping them close until re-established. Repot when necessary in April.

S. reducta. (D).
A native of W. China and N. Burma, this is a dwarf slow-growing shrub up to 12 inches high in time, with smooth reddish-grey, stout, semi-erect branches, laterals having a few bristles. Leaves alternate, pinnate, leaflets sessile nine to thirteen narrow ovate, tapered to apex, coarsely serrate, serrations ending in a mucronate tip, deep glossy green above with a few appressed white hairs, veining reticulate. Flowers in terminal clusters, small five-petalled white, slightly downy on inner surface. April–May. Berries globose, crimson. Foliage has a good autumn colouring.

SPIRAEA (*Rosaceae*).

A large and varied genus of plants containing tall herbaceous perennials and shrubs of which there are a few that make good pan plants for alpine house or frame culture.

CULTIVATION. All do well in compost A with good drainage. A good supply of water is necessary while growing and flowering, keep dry but not arid when dormant.

PROPAGATION. By division in March, suckers which can be removed with roots attached, or by rooting detached rosettes in early June in the propagating frame. Repot only when necessary in March.

S. bullata. (D). (Syn. *S. crispifolia*).
A tight congested ball of erect stiff branches rarely up to 12 inches high, stems reddish-brown, due to intense covering of down. Leaves crowded,

wide ovate, almost rounded, dentate, margins recurved, dull dark green. Flowers in profusion, wide flattish congested corymbs from the apex of the current year's shoots, rose. July. A native of Japan, this is an ideal plant for the alpine house, providing colour after the first flush of the spring display is over.

S. caespitosa, see *Petrophytum caespitosum.*

S. crispifolia, see *S. bullata.*

S. decumbens. (D). (Syn. *S. procumbens*).

A native of the Austrian Tyrol, it makes a small prostrate shrublet with slender branches, open and lax, rarely above 6 inches high. Leaves oval, tapering with serrations towards apex, dull mid-green. Flowers small in tight corymbs on erect wiry stems. White. June–July.

S. decumbens var. tomentosa, see *S. hacquetii.*

S. hacquetii. (D). (Syn. *S. decumbens* var. *tomentosa*).

A dwarf species only a few inches high with slender downy branches. Leaves almost oblanceolate, tapering with small teeth near apex, covered with fine down, dull mid-green. Flowers in tight corymbs on thin wiry stems, white. June. A native of N. Italy and the Austrian Tyrol.

S. hendersonii, see *Petrophytum hendersonii.*

S. pectinata. (E). (Syn. *Eriogynia pectinata*).

This is the only dwarf evergreen species; seems to prefer half-shade in cultivation and is best plunged in a west-facing frame after flowering. It forms a small dwarf shrub, throwing up tufts from underground runners with smooth rounded branches. Leaves deeply cut three-lobed, each lobe cut into three narrow lanceolate segments, bright shining green, leaf stalk winged. Flowers on erect stems, clothed with small leaves in racemes of up to twenty, white. June. A native of Alaska.

S. procumbens, see *S. decumbens.*

STACHYS (*Labiatae*).

This genus has one species which is a useful addition to the alpine house, a small spiny shrub which arrived in cultivation from a recent expedition by Peter Davis, who sent the seed home from Karpathos in the Aegean; it is also found in Crete.

CULTIVATION. Compost A is suitable with good drainage, a fair supply of water during the growing and flowering season, keep dry but not arid in winter. It requires protection from cold winds and prolonged frost.

PROPAGATION. From seed sown in February, compost 2. Repot when necessary after flowering.

S. spinosa. (E).

It forms a congested mass of tortuous branches, quite prostrate, ending in long soft spines, silver-grey and very hairy. Leaves in short spiny pairs, crossing at right angles to each other, crowded at base, smaller and fewer towards apex, grey covered with fine hairs. Flowers stemless from the leaf

axils, two-lipped, five-lobed, white flushed pink with brownish streakings.
June.

STATICE, see LIMONIUM.

STERNBERGIA (*Amaryllidaceae*).

A small genus of bulbous plants, natives of S. Europe, Caucasus and
Persia, which has provided us with two species that make ideal pan plants
for the alpine house.

CULTIVATION. Compost A is suitable over good drainage; bulbs should
be planted 1 inch deep in July, the soil should be just moist, then no further water is required until growth is discernible, when a normal supply is
given; this is reduced after foliage dies down, then keep on dry side. These
bulbs benefit from a mild liquid manure, applied weekly during the
growing and flowering season.

PROPAGATION. By division of the bulbs in July and repotting is carried
out at the same time. Do not repot more than necessary as these plants
seem to resent root disturbance; this is evident by their reluctance to
flower for a period after repotting.

S. fischeriana. (B).
Produces its leaves at the same time as the flowers, these being up to eight
linear, obtuse, green. Flowers generally solitary from a white spathe with
funnel-shaped tube and crocus-like perianth of bright yellow. February.
A native of the Caucasus.

S. lutea. (B).
This species produces its flowers before the leaves, generally solitary on a
3-inch scape, tube small funnel-shaped, perianth campanulate, segments
concave, golden-yellow. Leaves linear, channelled, obtuse up to six. A
native of S. Europe.

S. lutea var. sicula. (B).
A native of Sicily, this has large flowers of clear yellow, similar to the
type but with narrower perianth segments. September.

STYLIDIUM (*Stylidiaceae*).

A genus of plants mostly natives of Australia, containing two species which
are sometimes cultivated in alpine houses, but even there they will not
tolerate long spells of freezing weather without harm. They are included
more for the curious habit of the long protruding bent style which if
touched contracts violently, like a trigger of a pistol across the face of the
flower and stamens, thus ensuring fertilisation, then returning to its
normal position after a short period.

CULTIVATION. Compost A is suitable over good drainage, requiring a
normal supply of water applied carefully to prevent rotting, dry in
winter. Full sunshine and protection from cold searing winds are needed.

PROPAGATION. By rooting detached rosettes in June. Repot only when
necessary in late April.

S. caespitosum. (E).

A native of W. Australia, this is a prostrate plant forming close compact cushions. Leaves small, 1 inch long in rosette formation, crowded, linear, tapered to pointed apex, bright green tipped red. Flowers on 8-inch branching stems in a loose panicle, open five-lobed, in two ascending pairs and a lower lip, white blotched red at base, style long, bent, green. June.

S. graminifolium. (E).

This species is also a native of W. Australia, forming a whorled tuft of rigid, flattish linear, slightly serrated, grey-green pointed leaves on a short stem. Flowers in a loose raceme from the centre of the tuft, on a stem varying in height from 6 to 18 inches, five-lobed, the basal lobe longer, varying in colour from a light pink to a magenta. June.

SUTTONIA (*Myrsinaceae*).

A small genus of trees and shrubs but there is only one dwarf species suitable and hardy enough for pan culture in the alpine house.

CULTIVATION. Compost B with plenty of water during the growing season, keeping the plant just moist at other periods. Protect from cold parching winds and place outside in a west-facing frame during hot periods. Top-dress with similar compost in early spring.

PROPAGATION. By green cuttings in late June. Repot every other year after flowering.

S. nummularia. (E). (Syn. *Myrsine nummularia*).

It forms a prostrate shrublet less than 3 inches high with trailing, wiry, reddish, sparsely-haired branchlets. Leaves alternate, thick, orbicular with a slight indentation at apex, smooth, glossy dark green. Flowers in pairs, rarely threes, insignificant on the smallest of stems, four-petalled, creamy-white, followed by orbicular blue-purple berries. June. A native of New Zealand.

SYMPHYANDRA (*Campanulaceae*).

A small genus of plants closely related to Campanula, of which there are two species that are suitable for pan culture in the alpine house or frame. Neither can be considered very hardy but they will survive all but the hardest of winters without frost protection.

CULTIVATION. Compost A is suitable over good drainage with a normal supply of water while in growth, keep dry but not arid in winter.

PROPAGATION. By seed sown in April, compost 2, or green cuttings in April. Repot when necessary in early spring.

S. cretica. (E).

A native of Crete, it is a close tufted plant of spreading foliage. Leaves large, glabrous, ovate, apex acute, base cordate, petiole long, light green. Flowers up to four on slender, wiry, sparsely leaved 18-inch stems,

pendant, tubular, bell-shaped, recurved lobes, pale lilac-blue. August.
S. wanneri. (E).
A really outstanding plant which unfortunately can only be considered as
monocarpic, but if kept on the move by repotting will fill a 12-inch pan
before flowering and this is a wonderful sight. It is about 6 inches high
in rosette formation. Leaves crowded, lanceolate, tapered to a winged
stalk, margins serrate, deep green covered with fine hairs, lighter below.
Flowers, on 9-inch erect, branching rounded striped hairy stems, are large
pendant tubular bell-shaped, blue, lighter at base. May. A native of the
E. Alps of Europe.

SYNTHYRIS (*Scrophulariaceae*).
A small genus of plants related to Veronica and natives of N.W. America,
which has produced two species and varieties that make ideal alpine house
or frame plants.
CULTIVATION. Compost C over good drainage, these plants require
plenty of water, especially during the summer months, keep just moist in
winter. They are best kept in a cool shady spot in summer.
PROPAGATION. By careful division in late May, or seed in compost 3
when ripe. Repot when necessary in May.
S. lanuginosa var. pinnatifida. (E).
A native of the Olympic Mountains, this is a true high alpine with basal
rosettes. Leaves pinnate, segments wide, short, lanceolate, thick, silver-
grey due to thick covering of felt, petioles long. Flowers on 2-inch thick-
felted stems, upper third having two whorls of trifid, sessile, narrow, ovate
leaves, in a dense raceme, small, four-lobed, deep green woolly calyx,
corolla four-lobed purple, stamens protruding. March. This plant is best
grown in compost B and requires plenty of water in summer but it should
be kept on the dry side in winter.
S. reniformis. (E). (Syn. *S. rotundifolia*).
This forms a tufted plant about 4 inches high with large kidney-shaped
greeny bronze leaves, bluntly crenate, hairy. Flowers on 4-inch stems in a
small raceme, small open, tubular, four-lobed, pendant, lavender-blue
with orange stamens. March. A native of California.
S. reniformis var. cordata. (E). (Syn. *S. rotundifolia* var. *sweetzeri*).
This is similar to the type but differs in having cordate bronze leaves and
red stems, margins widely crenate and darker blue flowers. February.
A native of California.
S. rotundifolia, see *S. reniformis.*
S. rotundifolia var. sweetzeri, see *S. reniformis* var. *cordata.*
S. stellata. (E).
A native of Oregon, this is a small tufted plant with cordate to orbicular,
slightly lobed and coarsely dentate, glabrous green leaves. Flowers small,
in a dense raceme, on 4-inch erect stems, •semi-pendant, four-lobed,

violet-blue with protruding stamens enhanced by the sharply toothed bracts. March.

SYRINGA (*Oleaceae*).

It is with great diffidence that I have included the following two species as suitable for pan culture in the alpine house or frame, for both Lilacs will in course of time outgrow their pans, although in their favour it must be stated that it will take a number of years before that state of affairs is apparent, for pan culture tends to restrict growth. There are two reasons why these plants have been noted here. First, the species are seen every year on the show benches as specimens in the dwarf shrub classes. Secondly both are extremely floriferous, and flowering in six months from a rooted cutting is not unknown; a shapely plant can be built up within two years. Much confusion seems to have arisen over the naming of these two plants and as a non-botanist I offer the descriptions below in the hope that it will be possible to differentiate between them.

CULTIVATION. Compost A is suitable over good drainage with a normal supply of water while in growth, just moist in winter.

PROPAGATION. By green cuttings in June which root quite easily. Repot only when necessary, this should not be more than once every three years.

S. microphylla. (D).

A small shrub with slender downy greenish shoots reaching up to five feet in time. Leaves ovate to orbicular $\frac{1}{2}$ to $1\frac{1}{2}$ inch in length, $\frac{1}{3}$ to $\frac{3}{4}$ inch wide, dark green above, greyish-green below with a slight covering of down on both sides, margins ciliate. Flowers in 3-inch panicles, narrow, tubular with four wide open rounded lobes, bright lilac, fragrant. May. A native of N. and W. China.

S. palibiniana. (D).

This is an erect much-branched shrub, eventually reaching 10 feet with smooth, rarely downy, shoots, reddish-purple in the young state. Leaves oval to lanceolate, $1\frac{1}{2}$ to 2 inches long, $\frac{1}{2}$ to $\frac{3}{4}$ inch wide, pointed, tapered to base, dull dark green, glabrous, lighter and downy below. Flowers in pairs in terminal panicles, up to 4 inches long, sparsely set with tubular, very narrow four roundish lobes, deep lilac outside, white within, fragrant. May. A native of Korea.

TALINUM (*Portulacaceae*).

A small genus of plants, natives of America, S. Africa and W. Indies and for the most part suitable only for the warm greenhouse, but there are two species which are quite hardy, making ideal pan plants with their quaint but not unattractive flowers.

CULTIVATION. Compost A over good drainage with a normal supply of water during the growing season, keep dry but not arid in winter.

PROPAGATION. By seed, compost 2, when ripe. Repot when necessary in late April.

Above: *Rhododendron forrestii* (see page 438)

Below: *Rhododendron forrestii* var. *repens* (see page 439)

Above: *Rhododendron nakaharai* (see page 529)

Below: *Sempervivum arachnoideum* (see page 481)

T. okanoganense. (D).
A native of N.W. America with prostrate creeping stems only an inch or so high and small grey-green linear fleshy leaves. Flowers open goblets on very small slender stems, white with crowded yellow stamens. June.
T. spinescens. (D).
A small sub-shrub with a few stout branches up to 4 inches high. Leaves terminal in rosette formation, semi-cylindrical, fleshy, midrib persisting after leaf dies. Flowers small cup-shaped on wiry branching stems, violet with boss of yellow stamens. July–August. A native of N.W. America.

TANAKAEA (*Saxifragaceae*).
A monotypic genus which makes a good alpine house or frame plant and is extremely decorative when in flower.
CULTIVATION. Compost C is a suitable medium and this plant requires plenty of lime-free water during the growing season and is best kept moist in winter. It needs a cool shady spot to give of its best and should be plunged in a shady frame during the hot summer months. Top-dress with similar compost in early spring.
PROPAGATION. By division of the rhizome in April. Repot as necessary during the same month.
T. radicans. (E).
This makes an oblique rhizome with creeping and stoloniferous runners, quite procumbent. Leaves in tufts, fleshy ovate-lanceolate, acute, sub-cordate at base, petiole long, margins thick cartilaginous, widely serrulate, serrulations spine tipped, dull deep green, very pale below. Flowers small on a slender 4-inch scape, in a dense paniculate cyme, the inflorescence is similar to that of a small Astilbe. April. A native of Japan.

TECOPHILAEA (*Tecophilaceae*).
A genus of plants containing two species of which only one, and two varieties, is generally met with in cultivation. These corms are not the easiest of plants to cultivate successfully but they are certainly worth every effort, for a flowering plant is indeed an outstanding sight, always attracting attention in a collection of alpine plants.
CULTIVATION. The Chilean Crocus are best planted up to three in a 5-inch pot, placing the two corms 2 inches deep, compost B is suitable and the corms should be potted up in late August. Pots should be covered with ashes or coarse fibre until growth commences. A normal supply of water during the growing season, this should be withheld once the foliage dies down and the pot exposed to all possible sun. A weekly feed of weak liquid manure is beneficial once growth is well formed.
PROPAGATION. By offsets in August. Repot only when necessary at the same period.
T. cyanocrocus (B).
From a fibrous-coated corm are produced two to three radical, narrow,

linear-lanceolate bright glossy green leaves, margins undulate. Flowers one to three on 3-inch scapes, open trumpets of a glorious gentian blue with a white throat, fragrant. March. A native of the Chilean Andes.

T. cyanocrocus 'Leichtlinii'. (B).
This form is more easily obtained and differs from the species in that the foliage is narrow-linear and the solitary flowers are open campanulate, six-lobed, white in throat, upper third gentian blue, the whole striped sky-blue, fragrant. March.

T. cyanocrocus 'Violacea'. (B).
This is the rarest form of all with intense violet-blue flowers but not an improvement on the type plant. March.

TEUCRIUM (*Labiatae*).

A large genus of plants which contains a number of species that are suitable for pan culture and although not showy they have a quiet charm of their own, plus the fact that flowering in late summer, they will help to prolong the floral display in the alpine house and frame.

CULTIVATION. Compost A is suitable over good drainage with a normal supply of water while growing and flowering, keep dry but not arid in winter.

PROPAGATION. By green cuttings in July. Repot every year at end of April.

T. chamaedrys. (E).
A small semi-prostrate sub-shrub up to 9 inches high with slender stems, densely covered with down. Leaves opposite, oval to ovate, deeply toothed, stalk winged, light mid-green, covered with fine hairs. Flowers in whorls from leaf axils up to six long tubular two-lipped, five-lobed; calyx purplish-red, lips bright rose. July–August. A native of S. Europe.

T. montanum. (E).
This forms a small tufted procumbent sub-shrub rarely above 2 inches high with hairy semi-erect, thin slender branches. Leaves opposite, crowded on stem, linear, tapered to base and apex, mid-green, slightly downy, silver-grey below due to the thick downy covering. Flowers in congested terminal clusters, tubular two-lipped, five-lobed calyx, yellow, upper lip has reddish streaks. July–August. A native of S. Europe.

T. polium. (E).
A small shrublet rarely above 6 inches high with both prostrate and semi-erect crowded branches. Leaves crowded, linear, grey-green, obtuse, margins slightly crenate. Flowers in small loose terminal globular heads, two-lipped citron-yellow. July. A native of Europe.

T. pyrenaicum. (E).
This is a small semi-prostrate shrublet with slender, wiry, hairy branches. Leaves crowded, opposite, small, long narrow rounded, scalloped, covered with hairs on both sides, bright green above, lighter beneath. Flowers

crowded in terminal clusters, tubular two-lipped, cream-coloured, calyx five-lobed and soft lilac. July–August. A native of S.E. Europe.

T. sandrasicum. (E).
A native of S. Turkey, this makes a densely branched dwarf sub-shrub about 9 inches high. Leaves entire, small, linear, grey-green above, white beneath, densely covered with soft hairs. Flowers in small cymes from the leaf axils, lavender blue. June.

T. subspinosum. (E).
A small woody shrublet with congested branches up to 1 foot high, very twiggy, often ending in a silver-grey spine. Leaves congested, fleshy, opposite, small, linear, rounded at base, tapering to apex, dark glossy green above, silvery-grey beneath, margins decurved. The whole sparsely furnished with bristly hairs, twice the length of the foliage. Flowers in terminal clusters two-lipped, pale lilac, five narrow calyx lobes of a deeper hue. July–August. A native of S. Europe.

THALICTRUM (*Ranunculaceae*).

The Meadow Rues are a large genus of herbaceous perennials of which there are but three that can be cultivated in the alpine house or frame, where they make attractive pan plants.

CULTIVATION. Compost B is suitable over good drainage and they require plenty of water in growth, this being reduced after the foliage dies away, when the soil should be kept just moist.

PROPAGATION. By division of the tuberous roots in late March. Repot only when necessary in March as these plants resent too much disturbance.

T. alpinum. (H).
A native of the northern hemisphere including the Arctic regions and Britain, with a stoloniferous root system and producing its leaves in tufts. Leaves ternate, division three-pinnate, segments three- or five-lobed at apex, obtuse, green, glaucous below. Flowers on 4-inch slender stems in a small raceme up to six, sepals narrow, greenish-yellow with a tassel of bright yellow anthers on purplish filaments. June.

T. kiusianum. (H).
A native of Japan, forming tuberous roots where the stoloniferous runners touch the soil. Leaves small, two-ternate, leaflets three-to five-lobed, pale green. Flowers on 4-inch wiry stems in a few-flowered open corymb, sepals narrow, rose-purple with a tassel of pink anthers on thread-like filaments. June.

T. kiusianum var. album. (H).
This is the just as desirable form with tasselled flowers of white. June.

T. orientale. (H).
A charming species, native of Asia Minor and Greece with sprawling procumbent stems. Leaves two-ternate with three-lobed segments, margins crenate, purple-grey. Flowers large in a loose cluster, white flushed pink with yellow anthers. April.

THERORHODION, see *Rhododendron camtschaticum.*

THLASPI (*Cruciferae*).

A genus of plants which are mostly dwarf growing perennial herbs with a large global distribution, containing one species from the high alpine screes of Europe that, although not too difficult, will tax the grower to keep in good health for any appreciable period, for it seems to miss the loose debris among which it likes to wander, as anybody who has tried to collect the plant in its entirety will testify.

CULTIVATION. Compost A will grow this species for a period, but if young plants are obtainable I would recommend compost D, for in this medium it is permanent and happier. Give a normal supply of water while in growth, reducing this to a dry but not arid state in winter, especially in the open compost.

PROPAGATION. By green cuttings in May, or seed in compost 2 when ripe. Repot only when necessary, immediately after flowering.

T. rotundifolium (E).

A creeping prostrate plant with stoloniferous runners up to 2 inches high, from which are borne tufts of basal, almost orbicular, fleshy, grey-green leaves, minutely toothed with a long petiole. Stem leaves entire, ovate, sessile. Flowers in terminal clusters, four-petalled, rose-lilac with yellow anthers and delightfully perfumed. May. A native of the European Alps.

T. stylosum, see *Noccaea stylosa.*

Thymelaea nivalis, see *Passerina nivalis.*

THYMUS (*Labiatae*).

This is a genus of aromatic shrubs including a number of species which are well suited for alpine house or frame culture, in fact some of them will not thrive in the open rock garden and must be grown in pans for any chance of success.

CULTIVATION. Compost A is suitable for the Thymes over faultless drainage. Watering should be carried out with care and all species appreciate a dry period in late July, give dryish but not arid conditions in winter and protection from cold drying winds at all times.

PROPAGATION. By detaching rooted runners or green cuttings in early June. Repot every year in early April.

T. billardieri, see *T. integer.*

T. caespititius. (E).

This forms a prostrate mat of interwoven, lax, woody stems less than 2 inches high. Leaves opposite, crowded in tufts, linear, margins covered with grey hairs, grey-green. Flowers on 1-inch erect hairy stems from the leaf axils, light lilac-blue. July. A native of S.E. Europe.

T. carnosus. (E).

A native of Portugal, this is an erect small shrub up to 6 inches high with firm hairy, almost parallel branches. Leaves in tiers, clustered at the nodes, small, thick, elliptic, sessile, sparsely covered with hairs. Flowers in hemispherical heads of pink. June.

T. cilicicus. (E).

A recently introduced species from Asia Minor, making a close upright, much-branched shrub about 4 inches high of erect hairy branches. Leaves sessile, linear, hard, bristly, veined grey-green, margins ciliate, downy below. Flowers in globular heads, surrounded by small hairy green bracts, pale mauve. June.

T. comosus. (E). (Syn. *T. transsilvanicus*).

This species forms a procumbent straggly shrublet up to 4 inches high of hairy branches with a strong smell of turpentine. Leaves wide, ovate, obtuse, base orbicular on long petiole, grey-green, hairy with thick marginal vein. Flowers in open globular heads with roundish bracts and light purple flowers. June. A native of E. Europe.

T. herba-barona. (E).

A dwarf often procumbent, woody sub-shrub only a few inches high, very aromatic, reminiscent of caraway seed. Stems sprawling, thick, clothed with fine hairs. Leaves small lanceolate, mid-green, glabrous above, hairy beneath, narrow, ciliate. Flowers in loose globular heads, deep pink. June. A native of Corsica.

T. integer. (E). (Syn. *T. billardieri*).

This is a rare prostrate sub-shrub, only an inch or so high with rambling, congested and contorted, square, light brown, downy branches, often rooting where they come in contact with the compost. An extremely aromatic species and certainly one of the gems of the race. Leaves in tufted whorls at intervals along the branches, small crowded, linear, bright green and downy below. Flowers on 1-inch stems with long white hairs at apex of the branches, small clusters of long narrow tubular, lilac-pink. May–June. A native of Crete. This plant requires good cultivation with special attention to watering for it to succeed.

T. longiflorus. (E). (Syn. *T. moroderi*).

A fine small rare Thyme, recently brought into cultivation from Spain. It is aromatic with erect, crowded twiggy, woody, finely-downy branches up to 9 inches high. Leaves borne near the apex of the branches and laterals, small, opposite, linear, tapered to apex, mid-green, greyish-green beneath, covered with a fine down, margins revolute. Flowers in terminal clusters; from purple bracts appear the tubular labiate flowers, lilac-purple with a white lip. July. Requires care in watering and a good ripening period during late summer.

T. membranaceus. (E).

An upright rounded aromatic bushlet, rarely above 8 inches high with erect, wiry branches, very twiggy, brown, glabrous. Leaves crowded, small, stiff, linear, rounded at base, tapered to apex, obtuse, greyish-green, lighter below, margins recurved. Flowers on short leafy stems in terminal clusters, white, narrow two-lipped, arising from large pink flushed papery bracts. June. A native of Spain. Sunshine is essential for this plant to produce a good crop of flowers.

T. membranaceus var. murcicus. (E). (Syn. *T. murcicus*).
This is a small compact aromatic, much-branched shrublet up to 9 inches high. Leaves crowded, rhomboid-ovate, pointed, light grey-green. Flowers, long, narrow, tubular, white, from large white papery bracts which are more attractive than the actual flowers. July. A native of Spain. Requires same conditions as the species.

T. moroderi, see *T. longiflorus*.

T. murcicus, see *T. membranaceus* var. *murcicus*.

T. nitidus. (E).
A small shrublet with lax, wiry stems up to 6 inches high and ascending hairy laterals. Leaves thick, small, ovate, rhomboid, deep glossy green, lighter below, margins ciliate. Flowers in loose terminal clusters, two-lipped, lower broad, three roundish lobes, lilac-pink in colour. June–July. A native of Marettimo.

T. piperella, see *Micromeria piperella*.

T. transsilvanicus, see *T. comosus*.

T. villosus. (E).
This forms a small conical shrublet with upright branches about 4 inches high, densely clothed with minute hairs. Leaves clustered at internodes formed along the shoots, linear, sessile, grey-green, margins revolute covered with long white hairs. Flowers in globular heads, deep rose emerging from green bracts. July. A native of Portugal.

TOWNSENDIA (*Compositae*).

A small genus of plants confined to the western half of N. America, of which there are two in cultivation today, both being suitable for pan culture.

CULTIVATION. Compost A over good drainage with a normal supply of water during the growing and flowering season, keep dry but not arid in winter, but care is needed at this period that moisture does not collect around the neck of the plants.

PROPAGATION. By seed sown as soon as ripe in compost 2. Repot in late March or early April when necessary.

T. exscapa. (E). (Syn. *T. sericea, T. wilcoxiana*).
A native of W. America, this makes tight rosettes of linear, spatulate leaves of grey-green, slightly downy, margins serrate. Flowers almost sessile, solitary, nestling in the leaf rosette, large, deep lavender-blue with very large golden eye. May. The colour varies from white to a light purple, which led to the splitting of this species into different species, but they have now all been brought under the one specific name.

T. grandiflora. (E).
A native of the Rocky Mountains, this forms basal rosettes of narrow

spatulate, grey-green leaves from which on a few 6-inch stems are borne the large violet, daisy-like flowers, enhanced with a central boss of gold. June.

T. sericea, see *T. exscapa.*

T. wilcoxiana, see *T. exscapa.*

TRACHELIUM (*Campanulaceae*).

A small genus of plants which have a confused nomenclature, they have been classified under Diosphaera, Campanula and Tracheliopsis at different periods and even today this genus is still far from settled. They make good alpine house plants and are worth all the necessary care to maintain them in good condition.

CULTIVATION. Compost A over good drainage with a normal supply of water during the growing season but never allow the compost to become waterlogged, keep dry but not arid in winter. These plants should be lightly clipped over after flowering, this will help to maintain close compact plants as well as keeping the plants healthy.

PROPAGATION. By green cuttings taken in June and kept close until rooted. Repot every other year in March, top-dress with a little fine compost in early March.

T. asperuloides. (E). (Syn. *Diosphaera asperuloides*).
A native of Greece, this forms a soft rounded cushion of leaves in rosette formation only an inch or so high. Leaves imbricated, small, entire, obovate-orbicular, sessile, soft glossy green. Flowers at apex of small shoots up to five divided into five narrow linear lobes, light blue. July.

T. lanceolatum. (E).
A rare species endemic to Sicily, it makes an upright woody dwarf shrublet about 6 inches high. Leaves more or less basal, thinnish, narrow, lanceolate, slightly recurved, glabrous light green, margins dentate. Flowers in a flattish panicle, long, narrow, tubular and short open lobes, violet-blue with protruding style. July–September.

T. rumelianum. (E). (Syn. *Diosphaera dubia*).
A native of Bulgaria and Greece, this differs from *T. asperuloides* in having a woody rootstock from which radiate prostrate leafy 8-inch stems. Leaves sessile, narrow, ovate, or oblong, serrated, green. Flowers in dense terminal clusters, tubular with five open, narrow linear lobes, pale lilac-blue. July.

TRIFOLIUM (*Leguminosae*).

A large genus of plants widely distributed over the world with the greater majority in the northern hemisphere, including the Clover and Shamrock in this vast genus. One species and a variety are suitable for alpine house or frame culture and these are delightfully charming plants.

CULTIVATION. Compost B over good drainage with plenty of water during the growing and flowering season, keep just moist in winter.
PROPAGATION. By seed in compost 2 when ripe. Repot when necessary in late March.

T. uniflorum. (E).
This is a creeping tufted plant less than 2 inches high, with trifoliate leaves, segments ovate, dentate, green tinged red. Flowers from centre of tufts on short stems, solitary pea-shaped, standards blue-purple, keel and wings crimson. June. A native of Asia Minor.

T. uniflorum var. sternbergianum. (E).
Just as dwarf, with charming foliage, standards white, wings crimson, making a good foil to the species. June.

TRILLIUM (*Liliaceae*).

Wood Lilies are rarely grown in pans in the alpine house but twelve members of this genus will do well so grown (see below and Appendix 1).
CULTIVATION. Compost C is a suitable medium over good drainage and they require plenty of water, lime-free seems to suit them best, in the growing season. Keep just moist in winter. They need shade to give of their best and should only be brought into the house for flowering, afterwards returned to a cool shady frame. Top-dress in early March with similar compost.
PROPAGATION. By careful division of the roots in late August but this family detests root disturbance and it should not be carried out more than is necessary. Seed sown in compost 3 when ripe is also a means of increase. Repot only when necessary after flowering, taking care not to disturb the roots too much.

T. nivale. (H).
This forms a short thick erect rhizome from which is produced a 6-inch stout stem, at the apex is a whorl of three oval, five-nerved obtuse leaves, blunt at base with a short petiole; bright shining green blotched purple. Flowers solitary, large, erect, on a 1-inch stem, three slightly wavy oblong petals backed by three lanceolate sepals, white. April. A native of S.E. United States.

T. undulatum. (E).
A native of eastern N. America, this has a thick fleshy rootstock and bears slender 6-inch erect stems, generally in pairs, apex of which is a whorl of three broad ovate leaves, pointed at apex, rounded at base, margins undulate on a short petiole, bright green. Flowers solitary on 2-inch slender stems, three oblong petals with wavy margins, 3 smaller sepals, lanceolate, white with purple markings at base. May.

TRIPTILION (*Compositae*).

A small genus of plants from Chile, of which there is one species suitable for pan culture in the alpine house.

CULTIVATION. Compost A over good drainage with a fair supply of water during the spring and summer, keep dry but not arid in winter.
PROPAGATION. By seed sown in April, compost 2, or division in August. Repot when necessary in April.

T. spinosum. (E).
This forms basal rosettes of pinnately-lobed leaves of bright green, the apex of the lobes ending in a spine. Flowers on 6-inch wiry, leafy stems in a terminal corymb of blue daisies. June. A native of Chile.

TRITELEIA, see **BRODIAEA.**

TROCHOCARPA (*Epacridaceae*).
This member of a small Australasian genus makes a good pan plant for the alpine house, as it is doubtfully hardy outside except in the milder countries.
CULTIVATION. Compost B is suitable with plenty of water during the flowering season, keep just moist at other times. This plant should be protected from cold winds and prolonged frost.
PROPAGATION. By cuttings taken with a heel in late June. Repot only when necessary in late April.

T. thymifolia. (E).
It is a small erect shrub reaching 2 feet after many years. Branches thick, rounded, deep brown: wiry slender twigs in a congested mass are borne at the apex. Leaves alternate, entire, oblong, pointed, tapered to base, dull mid-green, petiole large for size of leaf, appressed, reddish-brown. Flowers terminal, small, in congested pendant spires, rich rosy-red, followed by pale reddish-blue berries. May–June. A native of Tasmania.

TSUSIOPHYLLUM (*Ericaceae*).
A rare dwarf monotypic shrublet from Japan, the country of many beautiful plants, it is unfortunately not too easy of culture in this country, requiring skilful care to grow it successfully.
CULTIVATION. It needs compost C over good drainage and plenty of lime-free water during the growing season, keeping it moist at other times. The plant should be kept in a cool shady frame at all times and only brought into the house during cold winter spells and when in flower. It benefits from a spray in the evenings after hot days. Top-dress with similar compost in early spring.
PROPAGATION. By cuttings of half-ripened wood in July. Repot only when necessary in early April.

T. tanakae. (E).
It forms a semi-upright shrublet, much-branched, about 12 inches high, the juvenile wood covered with appressed hairs. Leaves alternate, small oval to oblanceolate, covered with fine flat hairs, grey-green, margins

slightly recurved. Flowers, small in pairs, rarely threes, below a terminal rosette of leaves, tubular, five rounded, open-lobes, ivory-white. June.

TULIPA (*Liliaceae*).

A large genus of bulbous plants from western and central Europe, with outliers in N. Africa, the Tulip species have given us a number which with their diversity of forms and colouring, make ideal pan plants for decoration in the alpine house or frame. They are easy to grow and provide a splash of colour in early spring.

CULTIVATION. The bulbs should be planted in pots using compost B, the deeper depth being required for the tulip species, as deep as the pots will allow, up to four in a 5-inch pot. Planting can be carried out between September and November, and the bulbs should be well firmed. After plunging the pots, cover them with dried fibre in a cold frame, bringing them into the alpine house when growth is well formed. A normal supply of water is required as soon as growth appears and maintained when the buds show, and a weekly dose of liquid manure is beneficial. After the foliage dies down water is withheld and the pots placed in a sunny spot to ripen the bulbs.

PROPAGATION. By seed sown in compost 2, March, or offsets when repotting. Repot every year. September to November.

T. auchcriana. (B).
A native of Persia, this species has up to five long, tapering linear, green leaves with undulated margins. Flowers up to three on 3-inch stems, open star-shaped, pale rose with a light bronze basal blotch, outer segments have olive-green stripes on reverse, inner two green veins. April.

T. australis. (B).
A native of the Mediterranean region with up to five wide lanceolate, channelled, glabrous, green leaves. Flowers on 6-inch stems, pendant urn-shaped in bud, open star-shaped, yellow, red flushed on reverse, segments reflexed at apex, fragrant. April.

T. batalinii. (B).
A native of Bukhara, this has a basal rosette of linear, green leaves. Flowers on 6-inch stems, open narrow star-shaped, segments soft creamy-yellow with a deeper greenish-yellow blotch at base. April.

T. biflora. (B).
A native of the Caucasus regions, with glaucous green, linear leaves. Flowers up to three on 5-inch stems, open star-like, white stained yellow at base, outer segments green and red on reverse, inner has central green line. April.

T. celsiana. (B). (Syn. *T. persica*).
A native of Persia, Spain and N. Africa with up to five narrow strap-shaped, glaucous green leaves. Flowers up to three on 6-inch stems, open flattish star-shaped, yellow, reverse has bronze flushings. May.

T. chrysantha, see *T. stellata* var. *chrysantha*.

T. clusiana. (B).
A central Asian species with long linear, glaucous green folded leaves. Flowers solitary on 10-inch stems, white narrow pointed buds with red bands; open star-shaped, white with basal red blotch inside. April.

T. dasystemon, see *T. tarda.*

T. eichleri. (B).
A native of Asia Minor, with up to five wide, glaucous green leaves. Flowers solitary on stiff 8-inch hairy stems, open, wide bell-shaped, bright scarlet with basal black blotch, surrounded by a golden band, outside of segments striped silver-grey. April.

T. fosteriana. (B).
A native of Asia Minor, with three wide, tapering glaucous green leaves. Flowers solitary, large on 8-inch stems, wide, open, scarlet with basal black blotch surrounded by a band of gold, outside of segments paler. April.

T. greigii. (B).
This species is a native of Turkistan, with up to four glaucous green leaves with reddish-brown stripes. Flowers solitary, open campanulate with recurved margins on 8-inch downy stems, bright orange-scarlet with black central blotch at base of segments. April.

T. hageri. (B).
This is a native of Greece and Asia Minor, with up to five wide lanceolate, dark green smooth leaves. Flowers one to four on 8-inch stems, open bell-shaped, deep coppery-red with greenish-yellow basal blotch, surrounded by a yellow band, outside of segments have a green central stripe. April.

T. hoogiana. (B).
This is a central Asian species, with up to eight wide lanceolate, glaucous green, channelled leaves. Flowers solitary on slender 12-inch stems, open bell-shaped, deep scarlet with basal greenish-black markings, surrounded by a golden ring. April.

T. humilis. (B).
From N.W. Persia, this species bears up to four linear, faintly glaucous, deep green leaves. Flowers solitary, rarely in pairs on 4-inch slender stems, buds pointed, pale rose to purple with yellow basal markings, inner segments striped crimson on reverse. April.

T. ingens. (B).
Another Central Asian species, with up to five long lanceolate green leaves. Flowers solitary on 9-inch reddish stems, open bell-shaped, bright scarlet with black basal blotch, segments yellow-brown on reverse. April.

T. kaufmanniana. (B).
This, the Water Lily Tulip, has been taken in hand by breeders and there are many selected forms, some outstanding, but to me they all lack the gracefulness of the wild species. A native of Turkistan, this bears up to five wide grey-green leaves. Flowers solitary on 6-inch stems, open star-shaped, light creamy-yellow, deeper at base of petals, outer segments striped and flushed rose on reverse. February.

T. kolpakowskiana. (B).
Another species from Turkistan, with up to four wide lanceolate, glaucous green leaves. Flowers solitary, rarely in pairs, on a 6-inch stem, star-shaped, expanding and segments reflexing, clear bright yellow, reverse yellow-green and flushed red. April.

T. kolpakowskiana var. coccinea, see *T. ostrowskiana.*

T. kuschkensis. (B).
From Turkistan, this species has up to four wide linear, glaucous green leaves. Flowers solitary · on 8-inch stems, bell-shaped, flattish when mature, margins recurved, vinous red, black basal blotch at base, surrounded with yellow band. April.

T. linifolia. (B).
A central Asian species with linear, deckle-edged, green leaves in rosette formation. Flowers solitary on 6-inch stems, open cup-shaped, bright scarlet with basal bluish-black blotch. April.

T. lownei. (B).
From the Lebanon, with two wide linear, slightly folded, glabrous green leaves. Flowers solitary, rather globular on 3-inch stems, pale pink with basal yellow blotch, outer segments flushed green and red on reverse. April.

T. micheliana. (B).
A native of Persia, with four glaucous green, wide linear leaves. Flowers solitary on 9-inch stems, open bell-shaped, light scarlet with black basal margined pale yellow blotch. April.

T. montana. (B). (Syn. *T. wilsoniana*).
A Persian species with up to four lanceolate, green leaves. Flowers solitary, open star-shaped on 5-inch stems, brilliant scarlet with small black basal blotch. April.

T. orphanidea. (B).
A native of Turkey and Greece, with up to four lanceolate, channelled, bright green leaves, glaucous inside. Flowers solitary, open star-shaped, brownish-red, reverse of outer segments flushed green and purple, yellow zone at centre of inner segments. April.

T. ostrowskiana. (B). (Syn. *T. kolpakowskiana* var. *coccinea*).
From Turkistan, this species bears up to four erect, lanceolate, green leaves. Flowers solitary on 8-inch stems, open bell-shaped, segments reflexed, brilliant scarlet with deep yellowish-green basal blotch. April.

T. persica, see *T. celsiana.*

T. polychroma. (B).
A Persian species with up to four wide lanceolate, erect, glaucous green leaves. Flowers few on 6-inch stems, open cup-shaped, white flushed pink, yellowish towards base, reverse of outer segments flushed bluish-grey. February.

T. praecox. (B).
An Italian species with up to five wide lanceolate, glaucous green, erect leaves. Flowers solitary on 10-inch stems, open flattish, segments reflexed,

scarlet with yellow margined blackish basal blotch, outer segments orange stained green on reverse. March.

T. praestans. (B).
From Algeria, this species bears a number of wide lanceolate, grey-green, channelled leaves. Flowers up to four on 8-inch downy, slightly reddish stems, open bell-shaped, bright red. March.

T. pulchella. (B).
A native of Asia Minor, with up to three lightly channelled, linear, smooth green leaves. Flowers up to three open bell-shaped, flattish on 4-inch stems, bright crimson with bluish-black blotch and white surround, reverse of outer segments, grey-green. March.

T. sprengeri. (B).
An Asia Minor species with up to six wide lanceolate, shiny green leaves. Flowers solitary on 12-inch slender stems, open star-shaped with reflexed segments, dull scarlet, lighter on reverse. May.

T. stellata. (B).
A Himalayan species with up to five basal grey-green lanceolate leaves, margins undulate. Flowers solitary, flat star-shaped with recurving petals, white with pale yellow basal blotch, outer segments have red flush on reverse. April.

T. stellata var. chrysantha. (B). (Syn. *T. chrysantha*).
This variety has segments of a bright yellow, flushed red on reverse. April.

T. tarda. (B). (Syn. *T. dasystemon*).
A native of Turkistan, with up to seven wide lanceolate, smooth green recurving leaves in rosette formation. Flowers up to six on 4-inch stems, open stars, bright yellow, margins of segments flushed white, inner segments have two red-purple and one olive-green line on reverse, outer segments flushed red and green. May.

T. turkestanica. (B).
Another Turkistan species, generally with three long linear, reflexed green leaves. Flowers several on 8-inch stems, narrow, pointed, star-shape, yellowish-white with light orange basal blotch, outer segments orange-brown on reverse. March.

T. urumiensis. (B).
A species from Asia Minor, with up to four narrow tapering, channelled, smooth, dull green leaves. Flowers solitary or rarely in pairs on 2-inch stems, narrow bell-shape, bright yellow, outer segments flushed red and green, inner three greenish veins. April. Not easy in cultivation, requires care in watering and a good roasting of the bulbs after the foliage dies away.

T. violacea. (B).
From Persia comes this species, with up to five lanceolate, slightly glaucous, green leaves. Flowers solitary on 4-inch stems, wide, open stars, purplish-blue with a yellow margined bluish-green basal blotch, outer segments violet on reverse. April.

T. violacea var. pallida. (B).
Similar to the type but with light violet flowers and deeper basal flush.
April.
T. wilsoniana, see *T. montana.*
T. whittallii. (B).
A native of Smyrna, with up to four narrow strap-shaped, smooth, folded
green leaves. Flowers solitary on 12-inch stems, open bell-shaped, bright
orange with deep olive basal blotch, outer segments flushed brownish-
yellow and green. April.

Umbilicus chrysanthus, see *Rosularia pallida.*
Umbilicus sempervivum, see *Rosularia sempervivum.*
Umbilicus spinosus, see *Orostachys spinosus.*

UVULARIA (*Liliaceae*).

A small genus of hardy rhizomatous plants of which there is one species
and a variety that make charming alpine house plants.
CULTIVATION. Compost B over good drainage with a normal supply of
lime-free water during the growing season, keep just on the moist side
when foliage dies away. Requires a shady spot and is best kept in a cool
frame when out of flower.
PROPAGATION. By careful division after flowering. Repot every other
year after flowering.
U. grandiflora. (H).
This plant produces long stems up to 12 inches high and on the upper third
is borne the oblong, perfoliate, glabrous veined, green leaves, lighter below. Flowers up to three on small pendant stems from the leaf axils with
long narrow, acute segments, yellow. May. A native of Quebec.
U. grandiflora var. pallida. (H).
Similar to the type but with sulphur-yellow flowers. May.

VACCINIUM (*Ericaceae*).

A large genus of shrubs covering most parts of the northern hemisphere,
including Britain, but more prominent in the New World where there is
abundant material to choose from. Some of these species are suitable for
pan culture either in the alpine house or frame providing a quiet but
attractive display of flowers in early spring, followed later by beautiful
fruits and in many cases a glorious display of autumn tints.
CULTIVATION. The Cranberries do well in compost C over good drainage and plenty of lime-free water during the growing and flowering
season, keep just moist in winter. During July and August they are best
plunged in a west-facing frame and sprayed in the evenings after hot days.
Top-dress in early spring with similar compost.
PROPAGATION. By seed in compost 3, March, or half-ripened cuttings

taken in July. Repot only when necessary, for root restriction seems to improve flowering and helps the plants to keep a dwarf compact habit.

V. brachycerum, see *Gaylussacia brachycera*.

V. caespitosum. (D).
This, a native of N. America, is a small shrublet making tufts rarely above 6 inches high with smooth, rounded, sometimes hairy branches. Leaves alternate, obovate, tapered to base, bright glossy green, margins dentate. Flowers solitary from the leaf axils on slender decurved stalks, urn-shaped, five semi-pointed lobes, pale rose-pink. May. Berries black with a silvery-blue bloom.

V. caespitosum var. major. (D).
This form is similar to the type but more erect, up to 12 inches high with larger flowers and fruits. May.

V. canadense, see *V. myrtilloides*.

V. delavayi. (E).
A shrub up to 2 feet in time but taking many years to reach that size. It forms a close compact, semi-erect plant increasing by suckers, branches slim, sturdy, brown with a thin covering of hairs. Leaves alternate, thick, crowded, oval to ovate, slightly tapering to base with a small petiole, notched at apex, bright glossy green, paler below, margins decurved. Flowers in terminal and axillary racemes on bristly stems, five pointed lobes, urn-shaped, white flushed pale pink. May. Berries rounded black with a grey bloom. A well-flowered specimen of this was given an Award of Merit at Chelsea in 1951, after I had received a Cultural Commendation the previous year. A native of Yunnan, China.

V. deliciosum. (D).
A dwarf tufted shrublet about 9 inches high with rounded glabrous stems. Leaves opposite, thick, obovate, pointed at apex, tapered to base, slightly crenate, bright green, glaucous below. Flowers pendant from the leaf axils, solitary, roundish urn-shaped, five-lobed, pink. May. Berries black with a grey bloom. A native of the Olympic Mountains, N.W. America.

V. fragile. (E). (Syn. *V. setosum*).
This makes a small shrub less than 18 inches under pan culture with rounded branches, densely clothed with reddish-brown bristles. Leaves alternate, oval to ovate, tapering, margins serrulate, glabrous, bright green, covered with down below. Flowers in crowded pubescent racemes from the terminal leaf axils, urn-shaped, five pointed reflexed lobes, rose-pink. May. Berries globular, black. A native of W. China.

V. hirtellum, see *Gaylussacia dumosa*.

V. macrocarpon. (E). (Syn. *Oxycoccus macrocarpus*).
A procumbent creeping shrublet only a few inches high with slender wiry stems. Leaves alternate, small, oval to oblong, almost sessile, dark glossy green, whitish below with recurved margins. Flowers in small terminal clusters, pendant on short stems, four long, narrow, pink reflexed petals, strangely reminiscent of a cyclamen with a close bunch of eight extending

stamens. May–June. The fruits are red globose berries, crowded on well-established plants. A native of eastern N. America.

V. modestum. (E).

A native of W. Yunnan, this is a dwarf shrublet less than 6 inches high with slender procumbent stems and ascending laterals. Leaves at apex of shoots, ovate to obovate, tapered to base, smooth glossy green, glaucous below. Flowers solitary from terminal leaf axils, flattish, roundish, five reflexed lobes, deep rose. Fruit globose, glaucous violet. May.

V. moupinense. (E).

A small compact shrublet, eventually reaching a height of 18 inches with congested, woolly, grooved branches. Leaves crowded, alternate, entire, obovate to oval, apex obtuse, tapered to base, deep glossy green. Flowers in terminal axillary racemes, crowded, pendulous on bright reddish stems, urn-shaped five narrow tooth-like lobes, reddish-brown. May. Berries globular, deep purple. A native of W. Szechwan, China.

V. myrsinites. (E). (Syn. *V. nitidum*).

A small prostrate plant spreading by suckers, rarely above 12 inches high with slender, angled, hairy branches. Leaves alternate, oval, pointed at apex, tapered to base, margins minutely dentate, smooth, dark green, paler beneath with deeply marked veins, bristly. Flowers in small terminal clusters, pitcher-shaped, five tooth-like lobes, white flushed pink. May. Berries globular, black with a grey bloom. A native of S.E. United States.

V. myrtilloides. (D). (Syn. *V. canadense*).

This forms a procumbent, twiggy, bristly shrublet up to 12 inches high. Leaves alternate, entire, long, oval, tapered to base and apex, mid-green covered with fine hairs on both sides. Flowers in small crowded axillary clusters, five-lobed, bell-shaped, white tinged rose. May. Berries deep bluish-black. A native of eastern N. America.

V. nitidum, see *V. myrsinites*.

V. nummularia. (E).

An outstanding dwarf shrub which needs protection from cold winds and prolonged frosts. It makes a compact much-branched plant, spreading by runners, less than 18 inches high when mature. Branches stout, erect, reddish-brown, densely clothed with stiff brown bristles. Leaves alternate, thick, leathery, orbicular with pronounced net-veining on upper surface, margins ciliate, petiole short, dull, mid-green, glaucous below. Flowers in terminal and axillary crowded racemes, narrow pitcher-shaped, five-lobed, pinkish. May. Fruit a round berry, black. A native of N. India.

V. oxycoccus. (E). (Syn. *Oxycoccus palustris*, *O. quadripetalus*).

This is our native Cranberry, locally abundant on the acid moist peat beds of the high ground in the northern counties and Scottish moors. My specimens are from cuttings taken from a plant on Ben Ledi in Perthshire. It forms long prostrate thread-like, wiry, brownish runners. Leaves sparse, alternate, minute, ovate, pointed at apex, rounded at base, petiole short, red, margins decurved, deep glossy green above, bluish beneath. Flowers

Above: *Soldanella pusilla* (see page 491)

Below: *Tulipa kaufmanniana* (see page 507)

Above: *Viola cenisia* (see page 516)

Below: *Viola dubyana* (see page 531)

in small terminal clusters on short stems, four reflexed pink lobes with crowded protruding stamens. June. Berries globose, red, smaller than in *V. macrocarpon*, but still attractive.

V. praestans. (D).

A small procumbent shrublet, less than 4 inches high, with solitary stems from a creeping rootstock. Leaves alternate, obovate, rounded with a small spine, tapered to base, minutely serrulate, glabrous mid-green, slightly hairy below. Brilliant autumn colouration of the foliage. Flowers solitary, or rarely a small cluster on short stems, each having two narrow leaf-bracts, bell-shaped, five erect lobes, white flushed pink. June. Berries globular, bright red. A native of Japan.

V. retusum. (E).

A small dwarf shrub rarely above 9 inches high with semi-erect downy shoots. Leaves obovate, obtuse, notched at apex, tapered to base, thick, entire, glabrous bright green, margins recurved. Flowers generally solitary from the terminal shoots, rounded urn-shaped, five-lobed, white striped red. May. Fruits not seen. A rare and far from easy plant which so far does not tend to flower freely even under protected conditions. A native of the Himalayas.

V. setosum, see *V. fragile.*

V. vitis-idaea. (E).

A small shrub about 9 inches high with procumbent wiry stems, clothed with minute, black hairs. Leaves alternate, small, ovate, notched at apex, deep bright green above, paler beneath with a few black dots. Flowers in dense terminal racemes, bell-shaped, well marked, four-lobed, white flushed pink. May. Berries rounded, deep red. A native of America, Asia and Britain.

V. vitis-idaea var. minus. (E).

This is a much smaller edition of the species, only a few inches high, but with just as large clusters of pink flowers and globose deep red berries. May.

VALERIANA (*Valerianaceae*).

A large genus of plants with a wide distribution and although a number are suitable for the rock garden, there is only one, and this is a charming species, that can be considered as suitable for pan culture.

CULTIVATION. Compost A over good drainage, a normal supply of water while growing and flowering, keep dry but not arid in winter.

PROPAGATION. By division after flowering. Repot every other year after flowering.

V. supina. (E).

A native of the mountains of central Europe, this is a mat-forming plant in close tufts. Leaves small, entire, oval to orbicular, dark shining green, margins ciliate. Flowers on the shortest of stems in loose corymbs, small, tubular, five-lobed, white tinged pink, fragrant. June.

VERBASCUM (*Scrophulariaceae*).

A genus containing a large number of species, most of which are too large for pan culture but these enumerated here are ideal for that purpose, giving a fine display of flowers in their season.

CULTIVATION. Compost A with good drainage is suitable and they require a normal supply of water during the growing and flowering season, keep dry but not arid in winter.

PROPAGATION. By seed, compost 2 in February, root cuttings, April, or cuttings taken with a heel in late May. Repot every year in late April.

V. dumulosum. (E).

This small sub-shrubby species is a recent introduction from S.W. Anatolia, discovered and introduced by Peter Davis during his recent plant hunting expedition in that area. It makes an erect plant up to 12 inches high, with stout woolly stems, densely covered with whorls of leaves, arranged along their entire length. Leaves ovate, tapering to a thick appressed petiole, greyish-white in colour due to the intense covering of wool. Flowers in small terminal racemes of up to twelve open saucer-shaped, bright yellow with deep basal crimson blotch, stamens completely surrounded with violet wool. May–June.

V. pestalozzae. (E).

A much dwarfer and more compact species about 9 inches high with densely woolly stems. Leaves crowded in whorls, ovate to narrow oval, tapered to base on short petiole, not so appressed as in *V. dumulosum*; apex obtuse, sometimes pointed, coarse irregular, minute marginal serrations, greyish-white due to intense covering of white wool; midrib pronounced on underside, veining reticulate. Flowers in small terminal racemes on woolly 9-inch stems, sparsely clad with the typical foliage, open saucer-shaped, clear yellow, stamens covered with orange wool. May. This is a choice and desirable plant introduced by Peter Davis from Lycia in Asia Minor and promises to be a useful addition to a representative collection of fine alpine house plants.

V. spinosum. (E).

This forms a compact globular mass of congested branches and spines, silver-grey in colour, up to 12 inches high. Leaves oblong, lobed, with grey tomentum. Flowers solitary from the leaf axils in great profusion, small, saucer-shaped, yellow with orange filaments. August. Endemic to Crete.

VERONICA (*Scrophulariaceae*).

A genus of plants containing a number of species suitable for pan culture, in fact the Speedwells never look so happy when grown outdoors, as many come from a warmer climate than ours, usually the Middle East. Some authorities have placed the shrubby members of the genus under Hebe, and these should be referred to under that heading.

CULTIVATION. Compost A is suitable for all the species with good drainage and plenty of water during the growing season, reducing this in late August, then keeping the compost just moist in the winter months. PROPAGATION. By green cuttings in July and early August. Repot every year in April when growth has commenced.

V. armena. (E).
A small procumbent plant only 2 inches high with radiating branched stems. Leaves opposite, pinnate, segments linear, green. Flowers in small loose sprays, bright gentian blue. June–July. A native of Armenia.

V. bombycina. (E).
A fine and delicate plant making tufts of lax stems clothed with white wool, less than 6 inches high. Leaves ovate to spatulate, sessile, white due to intense covering of white wool. Flowers in small terminal racemes, four-lobed, open bell-shaped, pale milky blue. June. A native of Lebanon. This plant has a reputation for being difficult and hard to keep in character, but the answer is simple, take a pair of scissors to it after flowering and cut it close back, and it will then remain both neat and tidy. This brought its reward with a Cultural Commendation for a 10-inch pan of it from the Royal Horticultural Society.

V. bonarota. (H). (Syn. *Paederota bonarota*).
A small tufted plant about 4 inches high with downy stems. Leaves, basal orbicular, upper lanceolate, dentate, deep glossy green. Flowers in close terminal spikes of open bell-shape, opal-blue. May–June. A native of S. Europe.

V. caespitosa. (E).
A native of Asia Minor, this is a fine pan plant only 2 inches high of tufted shoots. Leaves small, spatulate, obtuse, green covered with minute greyish hairs, margins reddish. Flowers generally solitary, almost sessile on the tufts, large, pink. May–June.

V. cinerea. (E).
A small tufted plant about 6 inches high of erect woody stems. Leaves thin, lanceolate to linear, sessile, ash-grey due to intense covering of white hairs, margins incurved. Flowers on thin stems in spikes of up to twenty, pale blue, four-lobed, saucer-shaped. June–July. A native of Greece.

V. pulvinaris, see *Pygmea pulvinaris*.

V. telephilifolia. (H).
A native of Armenia, this is a delightful tufted plant with slender branches only a few inches high. Leaves in rosette formation, fleshy, obovate to spatulate, pearly grey. Flowers in short axillary racemes, four-lobed, clear blue. July. Not an easy plant to keep in good health, resents too much water at any time.

VIOLA (*Violaceae*).

A large genus of plants widely distributed over the north and south temperate zones and having both easy and difficult species, of which there are a few which make good alpine house plants, although as a rule they do not thrive too well under pan culture.

CULTIVATION. All seem to require a more or less cool root run and they will do well in compost B over good drainage, and require plenty of water while growing and flowering, keep just moist at other times.

PROPAGATION. By seed when ripe compost 2, division in April or August, or green cuttings in July but these will be dealt with individually for each species. Repotting is best carried out every other year after flowering.

V. biflora. (H).
A native of the European Alps, it makes a slender semi-prostrate plant with erect smooth stems, only a few inches high. Leaves reniform, minutely crenate, slightly hairy, bright green. Flowers in pairs, small bright yellow, veined black, spur short, blunt. April. Requires half-shade. Divide in early April.

V. blanda. (H).
A native of N. America, this is a dwarf species only a few inches high with shining green, stalked, ovate leaves, cordate at base and margins slightly crenate, upper surface has few small hairs. Flowers on short stems, white veined purple with a short blunt spur, fragrant. April. Does best in half-shade, divide in April.

V. calcarata. (E).
This native of the central European Alps has a slender creeping branched rhizome. Leaves long stalked, lanceolate to narrow oval, base wedge-shaped, margins crenate, undulate, slightly ciliate, green. Flowers large, deep violet blue, or yellow with long slender spur. May. Best in half-shade in hot weather. Propagate by green cuttings in July.

V. cazorlensis. (H).
This is a rare prostrate sub-shrub up to 6 inches high, with erect wiry stems. Leaves narrow-oblanceolate, grey-green. Flowers on wiry stems, rose-lilac, lower petal deeply cut, spur long and curving. June. A native of S. Spain. Requires careful cultivation in compost A and water should be given sparingly with extra care in winter. Propagation is by green cuttings in July.

V. cenisia. (H).
A typical high alpine viola, with a thin taproot from which radiates prostrate slender laterals. Leaves entire, small narrow ovate on short petioles, obtuse, base cuneate, green. Flowers on slender stems, light violet-blue with broad petals and slender spur. June. Water with care, especially in winter. European Alps. Propagation by seed sown when ripe.

V. delphinantha. (H).
Another dwarf sub-shrub allied to *V. cazorlensis* and requiring similar treatment. It forms a compact plant with erect twiggy laterals about 3 inches high. Leaves linear, with free stipules, grey-green. Flowers on slender wiry stems, rose-lilac, lower petal rarely notched, with long slender curved spur. June. A native of Greece and Bulgaria.

V. eizanensis. (H).
A native of Japan, this is a charming plant with a stout rhizome and underground stems. Leaves trifid, segments sub-divided, lobes linear lanceolate, long stalked, green. Flowers largish, sessile, rose-pink, short spur, fragrant. April. Requires half-shade. Propagate by seed sown as soon as ripe.

V. flettii. (H).
A native of western N. America, this has a slender creeping rhizome up to 4 inches high and wiry leafy stems. Leaves stalked, reniform to broad ovate, obtuse, cordate at base, margins slightly crenate, green with purple veins, purple below. Flowers lavender, fading to yellow in throat, veined violet, spur short, blunt, yellow. May. Propagation by seed when ripe.

V. grisebachiana. (E).
A native of the Balkan Peninsula, with a slender branching rhizome and stems less than 3 inches high. Leaves congested, ovate to spatulate, cuneate at base, glabrous, margins slightly crenate. Flowers large, lavender-blue with notched petals and a long slender pointed spur. April. Needs similar cultivation and propagation to that for *V. cenisia*, but is a difficult plant to cultivate successfully.

V. hederacea. (E).
A charming species from Australia that makes delightful pan plants, and which is hardy in the alpine house. From a small vertical rhizome are produced long wiry underground stolons and stemless tufts of reniform, bright green leaves, cordate at base and margins slightly crenate. Flowers on thread-like 1-inch stems, violet flushed white at tips of petals, lateral petals twisted, minute spur. May. Propagation is by seed sown in April.

V. pedata. (H).
This is the Bird's Foot Violet from North America with a short erect rhizome. Leaves in tufts, stemless, palmate, segments narrow obovate, tapered to apex, coarsely crenate on upper third, green, margins ciliate. Flowers large, upper two petals deep lilac, lower three pale with darker veins, golden-yellow in throat with whitish zone on basal petals, spur short. May–June. Requires careful cultivation in compost D with plenty of water while growing and flowering, keep just moist at other periods. Propagation is by careful division in August.

V. yakusimana. (E).
A native of S. Japan, this has a small compact rhizome with prostrate stems less than an inch high. Leaves crowded in a mat, reniform, obtuse, cordate at base, minutely crenate, glabrous deep green. Flowers small, almost stemless, upper four petals white, basal veined lavender-blue. May–June. Requires a cool spot in hot weather with plenty of water during the growing season. Propagation is by seed sown when ripe.

WAHLENBERGIA (*Campanulaceae*).

A large genus of plants closely related to both Campanula and Edraianthus and often included in the latter, there being only a slight botanical difference between the two genera; see Edraianthus. The genus has a wide global distribution including one British native but they are mostly S. African, Asiatic and Australian plants.

CULTIVATION. Compost A over good drainage is suitable and they require a normal supply of water during the growing season, keep dry but not arid in winter.

PROPAGATION. Best by seed sown when ripe in compost 2. Repot when necessary in April.

W. dinarica, see *Edraianthus dinaricus*.

W. mathewsii. (H).
A small herbaceous perennial from New Zealand, with small wiry stoloniferous stems from a woody rootstock, about 4 inches high. Leaves in basal tufts, linear. Flowers on thin wiry stems, erect bell-shaped, corolla lobes open, pale lilac with white median stripe. July–August.

W. pumilio, see *Edraianthus pumilio*.

W. saxicola. (E). (Syn. *Campanula saxicola*).
A dwarf slowly spreading plant up to 4 inches high. Leaves tufted, narrow, spatulate to oblanceolate, glabrous, sometimes minutely crenate. Flowers solitary, open bell-shaped, pale grey-blue. May. A native of Tasmania.

W. serpyllifolia, see *Edraianthus serpyllifolius*.

WELDENIA (*Commelinaceae*).

A monotypic genus, this plant always created a stir when shown at the Alpine shows about fifteen years ago and a possesser of a plant was looked upon with envy, for the only then known method of increase was by root cuttings, until it was discovered the plant was capable of producing viable seed.

CULTIVATION. It will do well in compost A over faultless drainage and prefers a pot to a pan, for the extra depth is required for the long fleshy thong-like roots it produces. No water should be given during the resting season, but as soon as growth commences in early April a normal supply is necessary until the foliage dies away, when it should be withheld. It is necessary to keep this plant from freezing in winter or the result will be a total loss.

PROPAGATION. By seed sown in March, compost 2 or root cuttings in April. Repot every year in April.

W. candida. (H).
A native of Mexico and Guatemala, this forms a thick branching tuberous rootstock from which is produced a stout short stem. Leaves up to eight in rosette formation, large, wide strap-shaped, tapering to apex, folding at base, margins undulate, pale green, curiously marked in a few places with tufts of small white hairs. Flowers solitary, sessile, but the long narrow tube lifts them well above the foliage, open cup-shape, corolla pure satiny white, in rapid succession during May to June.

WULFENIA (*Scrophulariaceae*).

A small genus of plants which contains two species that are suitable for culture in the alpine house or frame, unfortunately these plants are still rare in cultivation as well as in their native habitat, although known since the last century.

CULTIVATION. Compost B over good drainage with a normal supply of water while growing and flowering, keep dryish but not arid in winter.

PROPAGATION. By seed sown when ripe, compost 2. Repot when necessary in April.

W. baldaccii. (E).

A native of Albania, this has a thick rhizome from which is produced basal rosettes of narrow obovate, tapering to a medium stalk, light green leaves, margins deeply crenate, covered with a few hairs. Flowers in a loose spike on 4-inch slender scapes, narrow, tubular, four roundish lobes, lilac-blue. May.

W. orientalis. (E).

This is a native of the Taurus Mountains and produces a thickish creeping rhizome. Leaves fleshy in rosette formation, narrow obovate to spatulate, tapering to a short stalk, glabrous bright green, margins red, irregularly dentate, almost lobed. Flowers on 6-inch slender scapes in a loose spike, long, narrow tubular with four reflexed, notched lobes, bright lilac-blue, deeper at base of tube and enhanced by the brownish-purple calyx. April.

APPENDIX 1

Additions to General Plant List

ANDROSACE *(Primulaceae)*

A. sarmentosa var. watkinsii. Section Chamaejasme. (E).
The species, a native of Yunnan, is an easy well-tempered rock plant but the variety is a much smaller edition suitable for pan culture. It is a creeping, brownish, stolon-forming plant only an inch or so high with congested rosettes of small ovate-lanceolate silvery-haired entire foliage. Flowers in umbels, rose-pink, on 1-inch stems. May. (Other androsaces are described on pages 191 to 199.)

AQUILEGIA *(Ranunculaceae).*

A. nivalis. (II).
A rare species from Kashmir which can be from 2 to 6 inches in height with bi-ternate basal leaves on short to long petioles, leaflets obvate, three-part, glabrous green above, glaucous below. Flowers solitary, generally erect, deep, bright blue sepals, petals deep purple-blue, spurs short and curved. May. (Other aquilegias are described on pages 203 to 208).

ARTEMISIA *(Compositae).*

A. granatensis. (E).
Only a few inches high, this species forms a dense, congested shrub with many prostrate laterals covered with fine silky down. Leaves alternate palmate, minute, petiole flat, lobes linear, covered with a silvery appressed down. Flowers in semi-globular heads up to four on 2-inch, downy, slender scapes, very pale yellow. July–August. A native of Spain. (Other artemisias are described on page 212.)

CALANTHE *(Orchidaceae)*

A genus of plants including over 40 species of which few are considered suitable for pan cultivation in the alpine house. Those which are suitable have increased in numbers slowly over a period and so must be included as worthwhile plants.
CULTIVATION. Compost C with a little chopped sphagnum moss added is ideal. Repot every second year.

PROPAGATION. By careful division of the pseudo-bulbs in early spring.
C. discolor. (D).
A native of Japan, it produces a tuft of oblong, deep green, ribbed leaves about 9 inches long. Flowers on a 12-inch scape in a many-flowered raceme; sepals and petals claret, tip white. June. There is also a form with paler foliage and pale green sepals and petals which is very attractive.
C. tricarinata. (D).
A native of Nepal, this species forms a tuft of oval to oval-oblong, deep green, ribbed leaves about 9 inches long. Flowers on a 12-inch scape in a loose raceme; sepals greenish, petals basal white, lip rose-purple edged white, disk keeled. June.

CARDUNCELLUS (*Compositae*).

A small genus of plants mostly confined to the Mediterranean region of which there are three that are suitable for pan culture.
CULTIVATION. Compost A over good drainage. An ample supply of water while growing is ideal. Dislikes winter damp.
PROPAGATION. This is by root division in early spring.
C. mitissimus. (E).
A native of S. France and Spain, this is a plant up to 7 inches high with flat rosettes of pinnatifid, spiny-tipped leaves. Flowers in a thistle-like head, sessile, tubular, blue. May–June.
C. pinnatus. (E).
From N. Africa, making a rosette of pinnatipartite grey-green leaves about 5 inches across with spiny tips. Flowers sessile in a thistle-like head, blue. June.
C. rhaponticoides. (E).
A native of the Atlas Mountains, it makes large rosettes about 9 inches across of thick, obvate-lanceolate, crenate, deep green leaves, tapered to a long, flat petiole which is flushed red-purple, extending to a point into the blade of the leaf; margins fringed with long, wiry hairs. Flowers in a single congested head, ray florets lavender-violet, disk florets violet-blue. May–June.

CELMISIA (*Compositae*).

C. du-rietzii. (E).
This is a robust sub-shrub about 7 inches high with leaves in a semi-erect rosette formation. Leaves narrow spatulate, apex sub-acute to obtuse, mucronate; three parallel grooves on upper surface, glabrous, dull green margins with scattered mucronate teeth. Lower surface covered with appressed woolly, silvery hair. Sheath translucent, glabrous. Flowers on a stoutish 7-inch scape, ray-florets white, narrow-obovate; disk-florets narrow triangular, yellow. June. New Zealand.
C. gracilenta. (E).
This is a tufted plant up to 9 inches high. The stem is false being composed

of a congested thin, pale, only slightly hairy sheath about 2 inches high. Leaves thickish, semi-ascending, linear, tapering to an apiculate apex, entire, margins almost completely recurved, upper surface covered with long, satiny white hairs, beneath white, woolly tomentose. Flowers solitary on a 9-inch, slender scape covered with appressed white wool, ray-florets slender, long oblong, toothed at apex, white with yellow disk. June. A native of New Zealand.

C. hectori. (E).
This is a tufted plant, much branched from a central rootstock up to 5 inches high with woody stems and stiff leaves in erect rosette formation. Leaves silvery, spatulate to oblong, narrowed to imbricated leaf sheaths, densely clothed in appressed white tomentum, margins entire above, white tomentose below. Flowers on 4-inch stout scape clothed with appressed silky white hairs, ray-florets not so numerous, long, narrow three-toothed. June. New Zealand.

C. hieracifolia. (E).
A small tufted plant forming a pseudo-stem about 2 inches long of crowded, glabrous sheaths. Leaves thick oblong to elliptic-oblong, obtuse, margins crenate, narrowed to short petiole, glabrous on upper surface, pale green, densely covered with a light buff tomentum below. Flowers solitary on a stout 9-inch dense glandular hairy scape; ray-florets narrow, linear, disk yellow. A native of New Zealand.

C. hookeri. (E).
This makes a tufted specimen from a stout rootstock and stiff leaves in rosette formation up to 8 inches high. Leaves oblong to spatulate-oblong, thick, ribbed, upper surface thinly floccose, sage-green, densely clothed with appressed, soft, white, woolly tomentum below, margined with woolly hairs. Flowers white, solitary on a stout 8-inch scape up to 3 inches across, long narrow-rayed daisies with a large central golden-yellow disk. June. New Zealand. (Other celmisias are described on page 239.)

CLAYTONIA (*Portulaceae*).
A small genus of dwarf plants with a global distribution of which one is suitable for cultivation in pans.
CULTIVATION. Compost B over good drainage with plenty of moisture during the growing season; dry but not arid in winter.
PROPAGATION. This is by seed, Compost 2 in April, or division in the same month.

C. nivalis. (E).
A native of the United States of America, this is a tufted mat-forming plant only about 2 inches high. Leaves in rosette formation, sessile, thick, fleshy, strap-shaped. Flowers in small, slender, terminal cymes, borne horizontally to the rosettes, bright rich pink. May.

CROCUS (*Iridaceae*).
C. scardicus. (B).
Only a few inches high, this species has only recently been introduced to cultivation from Macedonia. It flowers before the leaves appear, these flowers being deep golden-yellow with a white throat and tube and with the base of each tepal feathered with purple. March–April. (Other crocuses are described on pages 249 to 253.)

CYPRIPEDIUM (*Orchidaceae*).
C. speciosum. (H).
A native of Japan, about 12 inches high with ribbed, light green, downy leaves. Flowers large, solitary, sepals and petals light pink, lip white flushed rose-pink. May. (Other cypripediums are described on pages 258 to 260.)

DIANTHUS (*Caryophyllaceae*).
D. 'Atkinsonii'. (E).
A plant of poor constitution, but it cannot be omitted because of its large, crimson-red flowers on 8-inch stems. June to August.
D. 'Audrey Prichard'. (E).
A compact plant about 6 inches across and the same in height with deep rose-red, double flowers and a fragrance reminiscent of cloves. July–August.
D. 'Blairside Crimson'. (E).
Of close tufted habit, 6 inches high with large, rounded, deep rose flowers with dark crimson centres. June–July.
D. 'Bombardier'. (E).
This is a small, congested plant about 4 inches high with bright carnation-like flowers of crimson-scarlet. June–July.
D. 'Elizabeth'. (E).
Up to 4 inches high with tufted foliage and large, double, highly perfumed flowers; bright pink and with a brownish central zone. June.
D. 'Ernest Ballard'. (E).
A close, compact plant with rigid silver-grey leaves borne in tufts and large, double, dark crimson, fragrant flowers. June to August.
D. 'Forsteri'. (E).
Another mat-forming plant about 6 inches high with clustered flowers on 6-inch stems; brilliant magenta-crimson with a blue central zone. June–July.
D. 'Fusilier'. (E).
Another fine hybrid about 6 inches high. Foliage tufted, grey-green, flowers single, rich scarlet-crimson. June–July.
D. 'Grenadier'. (E).
Only 4 inches high with erect, stiff, grey foliage in tufts. Flowers on stout scapes, large, double, scarlet-maroon. June–July.

D. 'Highland Fraser'. (E).
This is a rather larger plant than the others, being up to 12 inches high in a good form, but it is included for its unusual flowers. These are large, rounded and of a velvety dark red with deep crimson markings set off by white flashes. May–June.

D. 'Holmsted'. (E).
A tufted form up to 8 inches high with very large, rounded flowers of a light rose-pink, the margins of the petals being fringed. June–July.

D. 'Jordans'. (E).
A good flowering form less than 6 inches high with cherry-red flowers enhanced by a green central zone. May to August.

D. 'La Bourbille'. (E).
A *gratianopolitanus* hybrid, it makes a tufted mat of silver-grey, soft leaves only 1 inch or so high. Flowers on short stems, rich pink with fringed petals. June–July. (Other dianthuses are described on pages 268 to 270.)

DIONYSIA (*Primulaceae*).

D. aretioides 'Paul Furse'. (E).
This clone is a much more compact plant than the species and bears larger five-petalled flowers of a rich, bright yellow. April.

D. freitagii. (E).
A native of N. Afghanistan, it forms a lax, tufted cushion of largish leaves with raised veins covered with farina. Flowers solitary, sessile, with a long tube, violet, deeper at the base, white throated. April. (Other dionysias are described on pages 271 and 272.)

ERIGERON (*Compositae*).

E. simplex. (E).
A native of N.W. America, this is a tufted plant about 4 inches high. Leaves radical, lanceolate, grey-green. Flowers on 4-inch scapes, large, black in bud opening to many-rayed violet flowers. May–June. (Other erigerons are described on pages 278 and 279.)

FRITILLARIA (*Liliaceae*).

F. michailovskyi. (B).
A native of eastern Armenia, this species is up to 3 inches tall with the stem normally bearing up to three scattered half-twisted, wide, lanceolate leaves. Flowers solitary, semi-pendant, wide, bell-shaped, exterior reddish-brown with golden-yellow recurved tips; inside reddish-purple, slightly chequered, golden-yellow at tip. April.

F. pyrenaica var. lutea. (B).
This variety is sometimes found in the Pyrenees where the species grows, but, unlike *F. pyrenaica*, it has unmarked, clear pale lemon flowers. May. (Other fritillarias are described on pages 285 to 289.)

GENTIANA (*Gentianaceae*).

G. septemfida. (H).

An easy-going species up to 8 inches high and with a similar spread; semi-erect leafy stems. Leaves ovate, acute, glossy green. Flowers in small terminal and axillary clusters, narrow bell-shaped, bright blue with lighter spots on interior, plicea long, much cut. August–September. S.W. Asia. (Other gentians are described on pages 297 to 303.)

HELONIOPSIS (*Liliaceae*).

These plants are natives of Japan and Formosa. Three of the four in cultivation today make good pan plants.

CULTIVATION. Compost B, with plenty of water during the growing season; moist but not arid in winter.

PROPAGATION. This is by division in the autumn.

H. orientalis var. breviscapa. (E).

It has a small, thick rhizome producing a basal rosette of spatulate, tapered, bright green leaves. Flowers lily-like on a 6-inch scape, semi-pendant in a cluster, much cut; segments obovate, bluish-white, striped, stamens reddish-blue. May. A native of Japan.

H. orientalis var. japonica. (E).

This produces a basal rosette from a stout horizontal rhizome. Leaves oblanceolate, large, shiny green, tinged brown at the apex. Flowers on a 6-inch scape in a pendant raceme of up to 12 on long pedicels, segments narrow obovate, pale pink with exserted reddish-blue stamens and purple stigma. May. A native of Japan.

H. orientalis var. yakusimensis. (E).

The best of the species in cultivation, this makes a dainty plant only 2 inches in height when in flower. It forms tight basal rosettes of wide lanceolate, bright green leaves, narrowing towards a sheathing base, tapered to a sharp, soft apex, margins irregularly crenate. Flowers on stout, thick 2-inch scapes, stem leaves narrow lanceolate, sheathing; flowers pendant, open bell-shaped, lobes spreading, white shaded to deep violet at base, anthers deep violet. Has a delightful perfume of almond blossom. April. Japan.

IRIS (*Iridaceae*).

I. tenuis. (E).

A native of N.W. Oregon and a member of the Evansia section, this forms slender rhizomes from which arise tufts of pale green ensiform leaves in threes, rarely above 6 inches high. Flowers on slender but strong 6-inch stems, large, pure white faintly veined with yellow. June–July. Not an easy species to flower but worth every attempt to do so.

CULTIVATION. Compost C over good drainage; keep moist at all times.

PROPAGATION. Careful division in June or July. (Other irises are described on pages 321 to 326.)

LLOYDIA (*Liliaceae*).

L. longiscapa. (B).
A native of the Himalayas and a difficult plant to cultivate, this makes tufts of roundish linear, bright glossy green leaves. Flowers up to two on a 4-inch scape, pendant bell-shaped, six widish golden-yellow petals with greenish median stripe on outside. June. (Another lloydia is described on pages 344 and 345.)

MYOSOTIS (*Boraginaceae*).

M. macrantha. (E).
A choice creeping, prostrate plant with radiating, semi-erect laterals emerging from rosettes about 4 inches high. Leaves in rosettes, obovate to lanceolate-spatulate, to acute tip, tapered to base, petiole long, pale green, covered with tapering appressed hairs. Laterals few-leaved, lower oblong, upper lanceolate, base abrupt, apex sub-acute, with appressed hairs. Flowers in a simple ebracteate cyme in a large cluster, small, narrow funnel-shaped, five roundish lobes, brownish-orange. June. New Zealand.

A distinct colour break in this genus and a very charming plant for pan culture. (Other myosotises are described on pages 359 and 360.)

OURISIA (*Scrophulariaceae*).

O. caespitosa. (E).
A prostrate, much-branched plant rooting at the nodes; less than 1 inch in height. Leaves crowded, thick, narrow spatulate to oblong with up to three notches on either side of the revolute margins, glabrous light green. Flowers on 3-inch peduncles with thread-like pedicels, two-lipped, open tubular, white. June. New Zealand.

O. caespitosa var. gracilis. (E).
This differs from the species in having oval, entire, yellow-green leaves; flowers solitary from a single bract on a thread-like pedicel, white. June. New Zealand.

O. macrocarpa. (E).
A prostrate plant which roots where the nodes touch the soil and terminates in a tuft of erect leaves. Leaves thick, broad-ovate, crenate-dentate, glabrous, petiolate, margins ciliate, green above, purple below. Flowers on a 12-inch peduncle with stem leaves below floral bracts, open two-lipped, upper bi-lobed, lower tri-lobed, lobes broad, white, pedicels slender. June–July. New Zealand.

O. macrophylla. (E).
This is a decumbent plant with rooting stems and tufts of erect leaves. Leaves broad to narrow ovate, narrow dentate-crenate, petiolate, glabrous. Flowers on a 12-inch leafy peduncle, bracts in whorls with up to eight flowers on each tier of bracts; open two-lipped, upper two-lobed, lower three-lobed, white, yellow in throat. June–July. New Zealand.

O. microphylla. (E).
A mat-forming plant only about 2 inches high of tufted stems with appressed, bright green, oval leaves. Flowers from axil of leaves on slender scapes, large for size of plant, tubular, open, five-lobed, deep pink, white-throated flowers. May–June. A native of the Andes, South America.

O. sessilifolia. (E).
This is a prostrate plant with short stems, each terminating in a rosette of leaves. Leaves thickish, spatulate to sub-orbicular, margins finely crenate, upper surface and margins clothed in long, tapering hairs, glabrous below, pale green, petiole broad. Flowers on a 5-inch scape, generally naked, floral bracts in pairs, up to six, tubular on thin pedicels, white on exterior, purple interior, margined white. June–July. New Zealand. (Other ourisias are described on pages 377 and 378.)

OXALIS (*Oxalidaceae*).

O. obtusa. (H).
This is a native of Australia but it seems to be quite hardy in the alpine house. It forms small tufts of five obovate leaves; rosettes less than $\frac{1}{2}$ inch high and up to 2 inches across, pale green in colour. Flowers up to $1\frac{1}{2}$ inches in size, solitary on a small, reddish-green, slender, pubescent stem, bright pink with deeper veinings and a clear orange-yellow eye. May to July. (Other oxalises are described on pages 378 to 380.)

PRIMULA (*Primulaceae*).

P. 'Beatrice Wooster'. (*P. allionii* × 'Linda Pope'). (E).
A hybrid with foliage similar to that of *P. allionii* but less sticky. It bears well-formed rose-pink flowers in early spring on 2-inch farinose scapes.

P. pubescens 'The General'. (E).
Another outstanding form with bright terra-cotta red flowers. Unfortunately, it also has a poor constitution and culture as recommended for *P. pubescens* 'The Cardinal' (which see, page 412) is the best.

P. rubra. Section Auricula. (E). (Syn. *P. hirsuta*).
A prostrate plant only an inch or so high with 1- to 2-inch oval to obovate, green, glandular leaves, coarsely toothed on upper half. Flowers on a 2-inch stem, up to three, petal lobes notched, deep pink to lilac. March. A native of the Central Alps, Europe. (Other primulas are described on pages 404 to 423.)

PULSATILLA (*Ranunculaceae*).

P. occidentalis. (H). (Syn. *Anemeone occidentalis*).
A species from N.W. America of about 9 inches in height with much-cut, pinnate foliage that appears just after the buds unfold. Flowers on thickly soft-white-haired scapes above woolly pinnate involucre, large, creamy-white, often blue on reverse. May.

P. vulgaris 'Coccinea'. (E).
A good break from a colour which can often be disappointing in this species; rich red-purple with a large central boss of orange stamens. April.

P. vulgaris 'Rubra'. (E).
An outstanding colour form with large ruby-red flowers. May. (Other pulsatillas are described on pages 425 and 426.)

PYGMEA (*Scrophulaciaceae*).

P. thomsonii. (E).
This makes a close cushion with spreading, rooting, woody stems, similar to *P. pulvinaris*; branches slender, erect. Leaves closely imbricated, tightly appressed, only tips visible, more or less rhomboid ovate, sub-acute, inner surface covered with dense fine hairs, margins finely ciliate with an apical tuft of hairs, greyish-yellow-green. Flowers sessile with five ovate obtuse lobes, white. June. (*P. pulvinaris* is described on page 427.)

RANUNCULUS (*Ranunculaceae*).

R. insignis. (H).
A native of New Zealand, this is a tufted plant up to 9 inches high and about the same across. Radical leaves, thick, cordate to reniform, margins crenate, deep green, covered with shaggy hairs below, petioles stout; stem leaves smaller, similar, lobed, lobes linear-oblong. Flowers on stout scapes, petals obovate from five to ten, emarginate, golden-yellow. April.
PROPAGATION. By seed sown when ripe, Compost 2.

R. lobulatus. (H).
A slender-branched plant up to 9 inches high with sparsely haired stems. Leaves radical, bright green, reniform, margins two- to three-lobed, lobes crenate, sometimes again lobed, base ovate-cordate, nerves sunken and prominent; white-haired below, petioles stout, channelled, brownish; stem leaves tri-lobed, petioles shorter. Flowers on 8-inch, slightly pilose scapes, up to twelve; sepals ovate-oblong, reflexed, petals five or six, obovate, bright yellow. May. New Zealand. (Other ranunculuses are described on pages 430 and 431.)

RAOULIA (*Compositae*).

R. buchananii. (E).
This is the Blue Vegetable Sheep, and, like *R. eximia*, it makes close, congested sea-green rosettes with a dark central zone arising from a woody stock. Leaves densely imbricate, broadly wedge-shaped with a slender point. I have not seen it in flower, but the colour should be dark crimson. New Zealand.

Like *R. eximia*, this is a difficult plant to cultivate and it is best in Compost D. Do not allow it to dry out in winter.
PROPAGATION. By individual rosettes, striking these in pure sand in June. (Other raoulias are described on pages 431 and 432.)

RHODODENDRON (*Ericaceae*).

R. nakaharai. (*s. Azalea s.s. Obtusum*). (E).
A native of Formosa, this species makes a prostrate small shrub with clinging, hairy stems and small lanceolate leaves which are persistent. Flowers in terminal clusters, funnel-shaped, deep brownish-red. June. (Other rhododendrons are described on pages 432 to 445.)

SAPONARIA (*Caryophyllaceae*).

S. 'Bressingham Hybrid'. (E).
This is a first-class hybrid raised at Blooms Nurseries, Bressingham, Norfolk from a cross between *S. ocymoides* 'Rubra Compacta' and *S.* × *olivana*. It forms a prostrate mass of reddish stems covered with hairs only an inch or so high and with a spread of 6 inches. Leaves in pairs, congested, linear-lanceolate, sparsely downy, midrib sunken. Flowers terminal in small clusters at apex of shoots with a pair of small linear leaves; petals wedge-shaped, rounded, deep pink with a central zone of white hairs at throat, calyx red, inflated, covered with a woolly down. May. (Other saponarias are described on page 452.)

SEDUM (*Crassulaceae*).

S. tartarinowii. (H).
This is a small, prostrate plant with dwarf, glabrous stems up to 4 inches high and 6 inches across. Leaves thickish, alternate, linear-lanceolate, flat on upper surface, convex below, grey-green, irregularly dentate. Flowers terminal in a corymb, star-like, pink. July–August. North China. (Other sedums are described on pages 475 to 479.)

SILENE (*Caryophyllaceae*).

S. californica. (H).
This is an erect perennial herb about 6 inches high with many elliptic-ovate, glandular-downy, abruptly pointed leaves. Flowers deeply four-cleft, five-petalled, brilliant crimson. May. A native of California. (Other silenes are described on pages 487 to 489.)

TRILLIUM (*Liliaceae*).

T. cernuum. (H).
This species produces up to three stems about 9 inches high, at the apex of which are borne three wide, rhomboidal, acute, sessile, light green leaves. Flowers pendant on short peduncles, three oblong-ovate, recurving white petals, sepals lanceolate, margins undulate. April. Eastern North America.
T. choropetalum. (H).
A native of western America, this is up to 8 inches high with large, roundish, deep green, mottled leaves. Flowers sessile with long, narrow petals, white shading to yellow at base. June.

T. erectum. (H).

A plant up to 12 inches high producing a single, erect stem. Leaves at apex of stem, three rhomboid, sessile, deep green, tapered to apex, acute at base. Flowers on 2- to 4-inch peduncles curving at apex, three oval reddish-purple petals, sepals smaller, lanceolate, brownish. May. Eastern North America. This is not a plant for confined quarters as it has an unpleasant scent.

T. erectum 'Album'. (H).

Similar to the type but with petals of a greensih creamy-white. May.

T. erectum 'Ochroleucum'. (H).

A form with flowers of a pale yellowish-white. May.

T. grandiflorum. (H).

Produces a glabrous, unbranched stem up to 12 inches high, bearing at the apex three sessile, wide rhomboid-ovate, pale green, shiny leaves, acuminate, tapered to base. Flowers solitary on 1- to 3-inch peduncles, petals erect, obovate, obtuse, sepals lanceolate, heavily nerved, pure white ageing to a flushed pink, anthers yellow. May. N. America.

T. grandiflorum 'Fl. Pl.' (H).

This very rare mutation is worth every attention with its fully double white flowers that fade to pink with age. May.

T. grandiflorum 'Roseum'. (H).

A form with pale pink flowers. May.

T. grandiflorum 'Rubrum'. (H).

Another form with flowers of a deep rose which age to an even deeper colour. May.

T. rivale. (H).

A native of California and Oregon, this species has slender stems which can be from 2 to 8 inches high with three leaves, ovate cordate at the base. Flowers three part, ovate acute at apex, undulating margins, white, purple dots in throat. April.

CULTIVATION. Compost C with one extra part of sharp sand. (Other trilliums are described on page 504.)

VERBASCUM (*Scrophulariaceae*).

V. 'Letitia'. (E).

A hybrid between *V. dumulosum* and *V. spinosum*, making a crowded, woody sub-shrub about 8 inches high. Leaves in rosettes, lanceolate with small lobes narrowed to a small petiole, blue-grey covered with a fine woolly down. Flowers in large racemes at apex of stems, open saucer-shaped, bright yellow, brown at base, anthers orange. May to July. Originated at The Royal Horticultural Society's Wisley Garden in Surrey. (Other verbascums are described on page 514.)

VIOLA (*Violaceae*).

V. dubyana. (H).
A native of the Italian Alps, this makes tufts of short, hairy stems. Leaves basal, small, rounded, upper narrow-lanceolate, stipules divided at base, linear segments. Flowers deep violet, yellow spot on basal petal, spur slender, semi-pendant. June. (Other violas are described on pages 515 to 517.)

WAHLENBERGIA (*Campanulaceae*).

W. albomarginata. (H).
A dwarf, rambling plant which arises from a slender rhizome producing rosettes at the apex of small stems about 4 inches high. Leaves in rosettes, thickish, elliptic to lanceolate, almost sessile with whitish, firm, tough, yet flexible margins, sparsely hairy. Flowers large, erect, solitary on 3-inch peduncles, bell-shaped, five-lobed, pale blue with deeper veinings. June. A native of New Zealand, this plant proves to be short-lived and must be kept going by seed.

W. albomarginata var. pygmaea, see *W. pygmaea*.

W. pygmaea. (H). (Syn. *W. albomarginata var. pygmaea*).
This is a tufted plant only about 1 inch high. Leaves radical, crowded in whorls of three, linear-spatulate, obtuse tapered to base, margins with two small, crenulate teeth on either side, pale shining green. Flowers solitary, pendant, corolla five-lobed, triangular, sub-acute, pale blue. June–July. New Zealand. (Other wahlenbergias are described on pages 517 and 518.)

APPENDIX 2

Nomenclature changes

Since this work was first published in 1964 there have been numerous botanical name changes and the following is a revised list. Those on the left are as in the body of the text; those on the right are the currently valid names:

Juniperus communis 'Echiniformis' = *Juniperus chinensis* 'Echiniformis'
Acer orientale = *Acer sempervirens*
Aceras anthropophora = *Aceras anthropophorum*
Aceriphyllum borisii = *Mukdenia rossii*
Androsace imbricata = *Androsace vandellii*
Armeria caespitosa = *Armeria juniperifolia*
Artemisia lanata = *Artemisia pedemontana*
Artemisia mutellina = *Artemisia umbelliformis*
Astragalus tragacantha = *Astragalis massiliensis*
Astragalus tragacantha var. *alba* = *Astragalis massiliensis alba*
Boykinia jamesii = *Telesonix jamesii*
Brodiaea uniflora = *Ipheion uniflorum*
Campanula abietina = *Campanula patula* sub.sp. *abietina*
Campanula allionii = *Campanula alpestris*
Campanula caespitosa = *Campanula cespitosa*
Celsia = *Verbascum*
Chrysanthemum hosmariense = *Leucanthemum hosmariense*
Crocus asturicas = *Crocus serotinus* sub.sp. *clusii*
Crocus byzantinus = *Crocus banaticus*
Crocus candidus = *Crocus vernus* sub.sp. *vernus*
Crocus clusii = *Crocus scrotinus* sub.sp. *clusii*
Crocus heuffelianus = *Crocus vernus* sub.sp. *vernus*
Crocus pestalozzae = *Crocus biflorus*
Crocus 'Suisianus' = *Crocus angustifolius*
Cyclamen europaeum = *Cyclamen purpurascens*
Cyclamen ibericum = *Cyclamen coum*
Cyclamen neapolitanum = *Cyclamen hedaraefolium*
Cyclamen orbiculatum = *Cyclamen coum*
Cyclamen orbiculatum var. *hiemale* = *Cyclamen coum*
Cytisus demissus = *Chamaecytisus hirsutus*
Cytisus diffusus = *Cytisus pseudoprocumbens*
Cytisus leucanthus = *Chamaecytisus albus*

Daphne collina = Daphne sericea (form)
Dianthus neglectus = Dianthus pavonius
Dianthus pindicola = Dianthus haematocalyx var. *pindicola*
Dicentra peregrina var. *pusilla = Dicentra peregrina*
Douglasia vitaliana = Vitaliana primuliflora
Edraianthus caudatus = Edraianthus dinaricus
Erodium chamaedryoides = Erodium reichardii
Erodium macradenum = Erodium petraeum sub.sp. *glandulosum*
Erodium supracanum = Erodium rupestre
Euryops evansii = Euryops acraeus
Fritillaria citrina = Fritillaria bithynica
Fritillaria dasyphylla = Fritillaria bithynica var. *dasyphylla*
Fritillaria nigra = Fritillaria pyrenaica
Fritillaria sibthorpiana = Fritillaria euboeica
Genista dalmatica = Genista sylvestris (local form)
Genista delphinensis = Chamaespartium delphinensis
Genista horrida = Echinospartum horridum
Genista patula = Genista tinctoria (local form)
Genista villarsii = Genista pulchella
Gentiana acaulis var. *angustifolia = Gentiana angustifolia*
Gentiana acaulis var. *clusii = Gentiana clusii*
Globularia bellidifolia = Globularia meridionalis
Globularia nana = Globularia repens
Globularia willkommii = Globularia punctata
Hebe pagei = Hebe pinquifolia 'Pagei'
Helichrysum pichleri = Helichrysum orientale
Helichrysum virgineum = Helichrysum sibthorpii
Hyacinthus amethystinus = Brimeura amethystina
Hyacinthus pouzolzii = Brimeura fastigiata
Hypericum repens = Hypericum linarioides
Hypericum rhodopeum = Hypericum cerastoides
Iberis jordanii = Iberis pruitii
Iberis taurica = Iberis simplex
Incarvillea grandiflora = Incarvillea mairei
Inula heterolepis = Inula verbascifolia sub.sp. *heterolepis*
Iris chamaeiris = Iris lutescens sub.sp. *lutescens*
Iris chamaeiris var. *cretica = Iris cretensis*
Iris mellita = Iris sauveolens
Iris mellita var. *rubromarginata = Iris sauveolens*
Jeffersonia (Berberidaceae) = *Jeffersonia* (Podophyllaceae)
Lewisia finchii = Lewisia cotyledon var. *finchii*
Lewisia heckneri = Lewisia cotyledon var. *heckneri*
Lewisia howellii = Lewisia cotyledon var. *howellii*
Linaria aequitriloba = Cymbalaria aequitriloba
Linaria origanifolia = Chaenorhinum origanifolium
Linum alpinum = Linum perenne var. *alpinum*
Linum salsoloides = Linum suffruticosum var. *salsoloides*
Linum saloloides nanum = Linum suffruticosum var. *salsoloides nanum*
Lithospermum = Lithodora
Lithospermum diffusum = Lithodora diffusa
Lithospermum oleifolium = Lithodora oleifolia

Lithospermum rosmarinifolium = Lithospermum rosmarinifolia
Merendera montana = Merendera pyrenaica
Micromeria piperella = Micromeria marginata
Minuartia aretioides = Minuartia cherlerioides
Muscari racemosum = Muscari neglectum
Myosotis caespitosa = Myosotis laxa var. *caespitosa*
Myosotis caespitosa var. *rehsteineri = Myosotis rehsteineri*
Myosotis rupicola = Myosotis alpestris (dwarf form)
Narcissus juncifolius = Narcissus requienii
Narcissus moschatus = Narcissus pseudonarcissus sub.sp. *moschatus*
Noccaea = Thlaspi
Noccaea stylosa = Thlaspi stylosum
Onosma stellulatum = Onosma stellutata
Ophrys muscifera = Ophrys insectifera
Orchis globosa = Traunsteinera globosa
Orchis incarnata = Dactylorhiza incarnata.
Orchis pyramidalis = Anacamptis pyramidalis
Orchis latifolia = Dactylorhiza majalis
Orchis maculata = Dactylorhiza maculata
Orchis sambucina = Dactylorhiza sambucina
Origanum pulchrum = Origanum scabrum var. *pulchrum*
Orphanidesia = Epigaea
Orphanidesia gaultherioides = Epigaea gaultherioides
Othonnopsis cheirifolia = Hertia cheirifolia
Paraquilegia anemonoides = Paraquilegia grandiflora
Passerina = Thymelaea
Passerina nivalis = Thymelaea nivalis
Phlox nana var. *ensifolia = Phlox triovulata*
Phyteuma comosum = Physoplexis comosa
Phyteuma pauciflorum = Phyteuma globulariifolium
Pleione formosana = Pleione bulbocodioides
Pleione limprichtii = Pleione bulbocodioides
Pleione pogonioides = Pleione bulbocodioides
Pleione pricei = Pleione bulbocodioides
Potentilla verna = Potentilla taberaemontani
Primula cottia = Primula villosa form
Primula longiflora = Primula halleri
Pterocephalus parnassi = Pterocephalus perennis sub.sp. *parnassi*
Raoulia australis = Raoulia hookeri
Raoulia lutescens = Raoulia australis
Rhododendron cosmetum = Rhododendron chameunum
Rhododendron myrtilloides = Rhododendron campylogynum var. *myrtilloides*
Santolina chamaecyparissus 'Nana' = *Santolina chamaecyparissus* var. *corsica*
Santolina pinnata = Santolina chamaecyparissus sub.sp. *tomentosa*
Saxifraga burseriana = Saxifraga burserana
Schizocodon = Shortia
Schizocodon soldanelloides = Shortia soldanelloides
Scilla pratensis = Scilla litardierei
Sedum spathulifolium 'Cassa Blanca' = *Sedum spathulifolium* 'Capa Blanca'
Sedum winkleri = Sedum hirsutum var. *baeticum*
Sempervivum heuffelii = Jovibarba heuffelii
Sempervivum hirsutum = Jovibarba allionii

Sempervivum tectorum var. *calcareum* 'Monstrosum' = *Sempervivum calcareum* 'Monstrosum'

Senecio tyrolienis = *Senecio abrotanifolus* sub.sp. *tirolienis*

Senecio uniflorus = *Senecio halleri*

Spiraea hacquetii = *Spiraea decumbens* var. *tomentosa*

Syringa palibiniana = *Syringa velutina*

Trachelium lanceolatum = *Trachelium caeruleum* sub.sp. *lanceolatum*

Trachelium rumelianum = *Trachelium jacquinii* sub.sp. *rumelianum*

Tsusiophyllum tanakae = *Rhododendron tanakae*

Tulipa australis = *Tulipa sylvestris* sub.sp. *australis*

Tulipa celsiana = *Tulipa sylvestris* sub.sp. *australis* (form)

Tulipa hageri = *Tulipa orphanidea*

APPENDIX 3

Plastic Pots. Leaving aside the home-made square pans, I referred only to clay pots on pages 57 and 58, not the plastic pots which are in such wide use nowadays. The latter have the merit, in general usage, of being available in a comprehensive range, of being light to handle and cheap to buy, in comparison with clay pots. My own experience with plastic pots is limited, but I am of the opinion that, with few exceptions, they are not suitable for growing rare alpines in.

APPENDIX 4

Metric/Imperial Conversion Scale

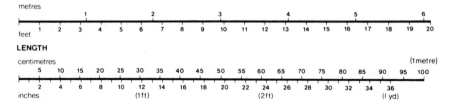

BIBLIOGRAPHY

The English Rock Garden. Reginald Farrer.
The Present Day Rock Garden. Dr Sampson Clay.
The R.H.S. Dictionary of Gardening.
The New Zealand Flora. Professor Allan.
The Manual of the New Zealand Flora. T. F. Cheesman.
Trees and Shrubs Hardy in the British Isles. W. J. Bean.
The Species of Rhododendron. R.H.S.
Dwarf and Slow-growing Conifers. M. Hornibrook.
Manual of Cultivated Trees and Shrubs. A. Rehder.
Hardy Bulbs. C. H. Grey.
A Handbook of Crocus and Colchicum. E. A. Bowles.
Alpines under Glass. R. E. Heath.
Shrubs for the Rock Garden and Alpine House. R. E. Heath.
Miniature Rock Gardens. R. E. Heath.
The Kew Hand List of Conifers.
The Kew Hand List of Rock Plants.
The Quarterly Bulletins of the Alpine Garden Society. Vols. 1 to 48.
The Bulletins of the Scottish Rock Garden Club. Vols. 1 to 17.
The New Flora and Silva. Vols. 1 to 11.
Alpines in Colour and Cultivation. T. C. Mansfield.
Shrubs in Colour and Cultivation. T. C. Mansfield.
Flowering Plants and Ferns. J. C. Willis.
The Rock Garden Conference Report. R.H.S.
Alpine Flowers of Japan. H. Takeda.
Alpen Flora. Professor C. Schroter.
Campanulas. H. Clifford Crook.
Primulas in the Garden. K. C. Corsar.
Flora Europaea. Vols. 1 to 5.

INDEX

As the lists of plants on pp. 170–531 are in alphabetical order they have not
been included in this index. The figures in parenthesis refer to the line drawings.

Aerosols, 127
Air-layering, 169–170
Alpenrose, *see Rhododendron ferrugineum*,
    438
Alpine, definition of, 153–154
  frames, *see* Frames
  Garden Society, 16, 163
  houses, aluminium, 20
    atmosphere, buoyant, 33
      damp, 31
    base, 20
    cleanliness, 19–20, 110–113
    concrete, 20
    condensation, 20
    construction of, 21, (22), 23, (24),
      (26), 25–28, (27), (29), 30–36,
      (35), (36), (37), 38
    damping down, 102
    estimating cubic capacity, 128
    foundations of, 25
    framework, 26–27, (26), (29)
    fumigation, 128
      aerosols, 127
      equipment, care of, 129
    galvanised iron, 20
    glass, 27–28
      substitutes, 27–28
    heating of, 31–34
      cost of, 33
      electrically, 33–34
      methods, 34
      oil lamps, 34
      humidity, avoiding, 31–32

Alpine houses (*contd.*)—
  maintenance of, 31
  painting, 31
  shading, 34–36, (35), (36), (37), 38,
    108–110
    blinds for, 35–36, (35), 109
    racks, (37), 38, 108
    repairs to, 112
    scrim or muslin, 35, 109
    washes for, 35–36, 109
  site, 19, 21, (22), 25
  size of, 20
  spraying plants, 101–102
  staging, 28, (29), 30
  table, 30
  temperature of, 20–21
  types of, 19, 20
  ventilation, 105–108, (106)
    autumn and winter, 107–108
    in fog, 107–108
    spring and summer, 105–106
  ventilators, 20
  water tank, (22), 23, (24), 25, 56–57
  watering plants, 99–104
    autumn and winter, 104
    during holidays, 102–103
    spring–summer, 100–103
  wood, 20
  woodwork, preserving, 31
  pans, 57
Ants, 133
Aphids, 134–135, (134)
Appendices, 520

Bacteria, 66
  effect of sterilisation on, 68
Barberries, *see* Berberis, 218–219
Bead Plant, *see* Nertera, 364–365
Beard Tongues, *see* Penstemon, 382
Bee Orchid, *see* Ophrys apifera, 372
Benomyl, 132, 142
Birds, 140, (141)
Bird's Foot Violet, *see Viola pedata*, 517
Blackfly, *see* Aphids
Blinds, for alpine house, 35, (35)
  roller, 109
Blue Poppy, *see* Meconopsis, 349
Borax, 131
Botanical terms, 157–160, (156), (157)
Bouisol, 132
Bricks, rendering of, 25–26
Broom, *see* Genista, 294–297; *see* Cytisus, 260–262
Brown Man Orchid, *see Orchis purpurea*, 374
Brush, camel hair, 55
Bumble Bee Orchid, *see Ophrys bombyliflora*, 372
Buttercups, *see* Ranunculus, 430–431
Butterwort, *see* Pinguicula, 395–396

Cabinet, wooden, 56
Candytuft, *see* Iberis, 318–319
Capsid bugs, 135, (135)
Carbaryl, 131, 135, 140
Card index, (122), 123–124
Caterpillars, 135, (135)
Cedar, *see* Cedrus, 171
Cedars, layering, 168, (168)
Cedarwood, oiling, 31
Chilean Crocus, *see* Tecophilaea, 497–498
Chinese Arbor-Vitae, *see* Thuja, 182
Chippings, 64–65
  applying, 119
Cinquefoil, *see* Potentilla, 401–404
Classification, 146–147
Clover, *see* Trifolium, 503–504
Columbine, *see* Aquilegia, 203–208
Common names, use, 155–156

Composts, 62–63, 65–66, 69–70
  firmer for, 76, (76)
  John Innes, 65
  preparation of, 66
  sterilisation, 66–69
    biological effect of, 68
    chemical, 66–67
    heat, 67–69
      electric cooker for, 68
      temperature, 67–69
    storage after, 69
Condensation, 20, 47
Conifers, dwarf, 161–182
  cultivation, repotting, 165
    summer treatment, 164
    young plants, 164–165
  feeding, 165
  forms, *see* Alphabetical list, 170–182
  growth, rate of, 162
  hybrids, *see* Alphabetical list, 170–182
  nomenclature, 162–164
  propagation, 166
    air-layering, 169–170
    cuttings, 166, 168–169
      register, 166–167
    grafting, 166
    layering, 166, (168)
    witches' brooms, 162
  pruning, 165
  purchasing, 161–162
  species, *see* Alphabetical list, 170–182, also 520–531
  varieties and forms, *see* Alphabetical list, 170–182, also 520–531
Constructing alpine house, *see* Alpine houses
Copper compound, 132
Cowslip, *see* Primula, 404
Cranberry, *see* Vaccinium, 510–513
Cranesbills, *see* Geranium, 303
Creeping Azalea, *see* Loiseleuria, 345–346
Creosote, 50–51
Cultivation, Alpines, *see* Alpine houses; Conifers, dwarf, *see* Conifers
Cuprinol, 48, 50, 75

Cuprinol (*contd.*) —
  Green, 31
  for blinds, 36
  for frame wood, 41
  for shade racks, 38
Cuttings, *see* Propagation, Conifers

Daffodils, *see* Narcissus, 361–364
Damping down, 102
Damping-off disease, 141
Derris, 131
Dibber, 54, (55)
Dicotyledons, 79, (79)
Dimethoate, 131
Diseases, 140–142
  fungus, prevalence, 127
  and pests, 125–142
Division, 71, 81–82
Drainage, 59–60, 118
  materials, 59–60

Early Purple Orchid, *see* Orchis mascula,
  373
Earthworms, 66, 68, 75, 140
Edelweiss, *see* Leontopodium, 332–333
Eelworms, 66
Electric heaters, 33–34
Electricity for propagating frames, 93–94
Ericaceous plants, sowing, 77
Everlasting flowers, *see* Helichrysum,
  312–314
Exhibiting, 143–150
  choice of plant, 149
  grooming containers, 148
    plants, 148
  judge's decision, 150
  labelling, 149
  preparation for, 147–150
  schedules, 144–147
  shrubs, pruning before, 148–149
  top-dressing, replacing, 149
  watering, 149

False Cypress, *see* Chamaecyparis, 172

Feeding, 113–116
  fertilisers, balanced, 115
    liquid, 116
  for rooted cuttings, 97
Fish-netting over ventilators, 140, (141)
Flax, *see* Linum, 342–343
Flowers, arrangement of, (157)
Fly Orchid, *see* Ophrys muscifera, 372
Fogs, 107–108
Foliage, types of, (156)
Forceps, 55
Forget-me-nots, *see* Myosotis, 359–360
Formaldehyde, 67
Formalin, 67
Frames, cleanliness, 83, 110–113
  construction of, (40), 41, (42), (46),
    47–51, (48), (50)
  base, 41
  lights for, (42), 43, 51
  materials for, (40), 41, 42, (42), (46),
    (48), (50)
  propagating, (22), 47–51, (48), (50)
  screws, 41
  shade laths, (37), 43–44, 45, (46), 47
    racks, (37), 43–44, 45, (46), 47
  sizes, 47
  ventilators, 45, (46)
  propagation, construction, (22), 47–51,
    (48), (50)
  base, fixing to, 48
  disinfecting after, 48
  drainage, 47, (48)
    material, 49
  heating, 49–50, (50), 51
  shading, 108–110
    repairs to, 112
  uses of, 39
  watering, *see* Alpine houses; Pro-
    pagation
Frost, 32
Fuel, hard, heating, 34
Fumigation, 128–129
Fungi, spores, 66, 75
  sterilisation, effect on, 68
Fungus diseases, prevalence, 127

Gas, heating by, 34
Glass, 27–28
  care of, 19–20
  substitutes, 27–28
Grafting, 71, 82
Granite chippings, 64–65
Grape Hyacinths, *see* Muscari, 358–359
Greenfly, *see* Aphids

HCH, 49, 89, 90, 91, 112, 126, 128, 131, 133, 134, 135, 136, 138, 139, 413
Heating, *see* Alpine houses; Frames, propagation
Holly, *see* Ilex, 319–320
Houseleek, *see* Sempervivum, 480–485
Huckleberry, *see* Gaylussacia, 294
Humidity, avoiding, 31–32
Hyacinths, *see* Hyacinthus, 315–316
Hybrids, *see* Dwarf Conifers, 170–182; General list, 183–519

Inflorescences, types of, (157)
International Code of Botanical Nomenclature, 156
Italian Butterfly Orchid, *see* Orchis papilionacea, 374
Ivy, *see* Hedera, 312

Japanese Cedar, *see* Cryptomeria, 177
Jasmine, *see* Jasminum, 327
John Innes Composts, 65
Juniper, *see* Juniperus, 178

Kidney Vetches, *see* Anthyllis, 202

Labels, 60–61
  types of, 59–60, 96
Labelling, cuttings, 95–96
Lady of the Snows, *see* Pulsatilla vernalis, 426
Lady's Slipper Orchid, *see* Cypripedium, 258–260
Lavender, *see* Lavandula, 330–331

Layering, 71, 166, (168)
Leaf-mould, 64
Lens, 55
Lichens, 75, 97, 111
Lilac, *see* Syringa, 496
Lime, 63
Limestone chipping, 64–65
Lindane, 131
Liverwort, 78, 97, 111
Loam, 63
'Long Tom,' 58
Looking-glass Orchid, *see* Ophrys speculum, 372
Lupins, *see* Lupinus, 346

Malathion, 131, 135, 136, 137, 138, 139
Maple, *see* Acer, 184–185
Marjorams, *see* Origanum, 375–376
Marsh Orchid, *see* Orchis latifolia, 373
Meadow Orchid, *see* Orchis morio, 374
  Rues, *see* Thalictrum, 499
Mealy bugs, 135–136, (136)
Metaldehyde, 131
Methiocarb, 132
Mildews, 142
Military Orchid, *see* Orchis militaris, 373
Millipedes, 136, (136)
Monocotyledons, 79, (79)
Moss, 97
Musk Hyacinth, *see* Muscari moschatum, 359
Musks, *see* Mimulus, 354–355
Myrtles, *see* Myrtus, 360

Nematodes, 59
New Zealand Daphnes, *see* Pimelea, 394–395
Nicotine, 131
Noah's Ark Juniper, *see* Juniperus communis 'Compressa', 178
Nomenclature, 154–157
  changes, 532
  conifers, dwarf, 162–164
Nozzles for watering cans, 54

Oil Lamps, 34
Orchids, sowing, 77
Overpotting, 116–117
 dangers of, 80
Oxlip, *see* Primula, 404
Oyster Plant, *see Mertensia maritima*, 353

Painting, woodwork, 31
Pans, 57–59, (58)
 construction of, 57–58, (58)
 disinfecting, 59
 drainage, 59–60
 for seed, 58–59, 75–76
 sizes of, 57
 soaking, 59
Pasque flower, *see Pulsatilla vulgaris*, 426
Peat, 64
Penwiper Plants, *see Notothlaspi rosulatum*, 369
Permanganate of potash, 48, 57, 59, 75,
 88, 89, 91, 93, 97, 111
Permethrin, 132
Pests, 66, 125–140
 and diseases, 125–142
 effect of soil sterilisation on, 68
Pine, *see* Pinus, 180–181
 layering, 168, (168)
Pirimicarb, 132
Pirimophos-methyl, 132
Plunge beds, (22), 44
 construction of, 44
 use of, 44
Potassium permanganate, 59, 140
Pot brush, 55
Pots, clay, 57, 58
 plastic, 535
Potting-on, 78–81
 compost for, 80
  storing, 53
 seed pans for, 80
 treatment after, 80–81
Potting shed, construction, 51–53, (52)
 cost, 52
 size, 51
Primrose, *see* Primula, 404

Primula root aphid, 134
Propagation, 71–98
 Conifers, *see* Conifers
 cuttings, 82–98
  advantages of, 83
  fertilisers for, 97
  frames for, cleanliness, 88
   heated, 93–94
   management of, 94–98
   north facing, 87–88
    preparation of, 88–91, 93
   south facing, 91–93
    preparation of, 91–92
    shading, 92
    watering, 92, (92)
  green, 83–84, (83)
  half-ripened, 84–85, (84)
  hardwood, 84–85, (85)
  in frames, 89, 90–91
   compost for, 90, 91
    watering with permanganate,
     91
   drainage, 90–91
  in pots in frames, 89–90
   compost for, 89, 90
   pests and diseases, 89
   size of pots, 89
   watering, 90
  inserting, 94–95
  labelling, 95–96
  leaf, 86–87, (86)
  records of, 96–97
  root, 85–86, (85)
  rooted, potting on, 78–81
   compost for, 80, 97–98
  rooting, 87
  rot, avoiding, 95
  watering, in frames, 92, (92), 97
 division, 71, 81–82
 grafting, 71, 82
 layering, 71
  dwarf conifers, 166, (168)
 seed, 72–81
  composts for, 73–75
  germination of, 72–73

Seed (*contd.*) —
  pans, 58–59, 75–76
Purchasing alpine houses, 20
  plants, 117
Pyramidal Orchid, *see Orchis pyramidalis*, 374

Records of cutting, 96–97
Red spider mite, 136–137, (136)
Repotting, 81, 113–121
  bulbs, 121
  chippings, applying, 119
  compost D, (121)
  method, 118–119
  pans, choice of, 118
    drainage, 118
  roots, damage to, 118
  treatment of plants, 120–121
  watering after, 119
Resmithrin, 132
Rhododendrons, sowing, 77
Rockfoils, *see Saxifraga*, 452–472
Root aphis, 117
Rust, 127, 142

St. John's Wort, *see Hypericum*, 316–318
Sand, 64
  sharp silver, for cuttings, 95
Sandwort, *see Arenaria*, 210
Satin Flowers, *see Sisyrinchium*, 489
Scale insects, 137, (137)
Scissors, 55
Scottish Rock Garden Club, 16, 145, 163
Sea Heath, *see Frankenia*, 285
  Lavender, *see Limonium*, 340–341
  Pinks, *see Armeria*, 210–211
Seed, 71, 72–81
  boxes, 75
  composts for, 73–75
  germination of, 72–73
  pans, 75–76
    drainage of, 75
    firmer for, 76, (76)
    sterilising, 75
  sowing, 76–78
    diseases, 78

Seed, sowing (*contd.*)—
  drainage, 77
  pans for, 58–59
  in plastic containers, 77–78
  in sphagnum moss, 77
  treatment after, 78
  viable, 71
Seedlings, potting-on, 78–81
Shade racks, (37), 38, 45–47, (46), 108, 109
Shading, 34–36, (35), (36), (37), 38, 108–110
  blinds, 35–36, (35), (36), 109
  repairs to, 112
  scrim or muslin, 35, 109
Shading, shade wash, 35, 109
  washes for, 35–36
Shamrock, *see Trifolium*, 503–504
  Pea, *see Parochetus*, 381
Showy Orchid, *see Orchis spectabilis*, 374
Sieves, 56
Site, alpine house, 19
Slugs, 59, 75, 137, (137)
Small duster, 130
Smoke generators, 128, 130
Smoke generators, 131
Snails, 137, (137)
Snowdrops, *see Galanthus*, 290–291
Snowflake, *see Leucojum*, 335
Soapworts, *see Saponaria*, 452
Sowing seed, *see Seed Sowing*
Species, *see* General List, 183–519; Dwarf Conifers, 170–182
Speedwells, *see Veronica*, 514–515
Spotted Orchid, *see Orchis maculata*, 373
Spraying equipment, 54
  care of, 129
  nozzles for, 54
  pneumatic pump, 130
  types of, 130
  utensils, 127
  vapouriser, 128
Spring Gentian, *see Gentiana verna*, 302
Springtails, 138, (138)

Spruce, *see* Picea, 179–180
Squill, *see* Scilla, 474–475
Sterilisation, 66–69
  chemical, 66–67
  heat, 67–69
Stonecrops, *see* Sedum, 475–479
Striped Squill, *see Puschkinia scilloides*, 426
Sulphur, 133
Systemic insecticide, 129

Tecnazene, 133
Thermometers, 56
Thiophanate-methyl, 133
Thiram, 133
Thrifts, *see* Armeria, 210–211
Thrips, 138, (138)
Thyme, *see* Thymus, 500–502
Tool cabinet, 56
Tools, 54–56
  care of, 57
Top-dressing, 112, 114, 121–123
Tulips, *see* Tulipa, 506–510
Types of alpine houses, 19–20

Vanilla Orchid, *see* Nigritella, 365
Varieties, *see* General List, 183–519; Dwarf Conifers, 170–182
Vegetable Sheep, *see Raoulia eximia*, 432

Ventilation, alpine houses, 105–108, (106)
  cold frames containing seedlings, 80
Ventilators, 20
Vermiculite for cuttings in frames, 91–92
Vine weevil, 66
  grubs, 138, (138)
Violet, *see* Viola, 515–517
Virus diseases and aphids, 134

Wasp Orchid, *see Ophrys lutea*, 372
Water, chlorination of, 23
  tank, (22), 23, (24), 25, 56–57
Watering, *see* Propagation; Alpine houses
Weed seeds, 66
  sterilisation, effect of, 68
White fly, 139
Willows, *see* Salix, 449–451
Windflower, *see* Anemone, 199–201
Windflowers, *see* Pulsatilla, 425–426
Wintergreens, *see* Pyrola, 427–428
Wireworms, 139
Witches' brooms, 162
Woodlice, 59, 75, 139–140, (140)
Wood Lilies, *see* Trillium, 504
Wood preservative, *see* Cuprinol
Worms, 75, 111

Yews, *see* Taxus, 181–182